TOYS A to Z

A Guide and Dictionary for Collectors, Antique Dealers and Enthusiasts

Mark Rich

© 2001 by Mark Rich

Published by

krause publications

700 E. State Street • Iola, WI 54990-0001
Telephone: 715/445-2214

Please call or write for our free catalog.
Our toll-free number to place an order or obtain a free catalog is 800-258-0929
or please use our regular business telephone 715-445-2214
for editorial comment and further information.

Library of Congress Catalog Number: 2001-086364
ISBN: 0-87349-240-4

Printed in the United States of America

INTRODUCTION: DICTIONARY OF TOYS

If you are a collector, nostalgia buff, or historian, you will find Toys A to Z a unique research tool. Not restricted to any particular category or type of plaything, it embraces a full range of topics, having entries on Colonial childhood games and 19th century toy manufacturers alongside entries on bubble blowers, electrical toys, and "Little Orphan Annie." If you are curious about Disneyana, children's furniture, early childhood and toddler toys, children's books, popular dolls, Christmas items, play houses, balls, play equipment, toy cars, toy household items, radio and TV related toys, cartoon characters, wagons, sleds, rubber toys, wood toys, plastic toys, metal toys, games, velocipedes, and even bicycles, you will find information here you cannot find anywhere else, presented in a compact and useful form. The entries include companies, individual toy makers, historical notes, and individual toys of importance. Hundreds of trade names appear with cross-listings to manufacturers, making it possible to identify many otherwise anonymously produced items.

The book places emphasis on American toy manufacturers and their products, especially of the 20th century. While I cannot claim it to be exhaustively complete, I do believe it to be the most extensive and useful such reference ever published.

The entries are arranged alphabetically. While this may sound straightforward, you would do well to keep in mind a few practices I followed in arranging listings. You may find, for instance, that some company names elude discovery. Many were named after their founders, or had identical names as their founders. These company names I consequently alphabetized as though the founder's last name came first. Despite the risk that this may pose obstacles for researchers, I have chosen to do this not only for its intrinsic logic but because it was the practice followed by the toy industry itself. Thus, the N.N. Hill Brass Co. appears under the letter H, for Hill, and not under the letter N, which you might think would be the case, at first glance. This practice solved for me the difficulty that I could not tell, in several instances, if the name I had in hand was the name of an individual or a company named after an individual. For a few of the more confusing instances, I have provided cross-references.

The names of fictional, stage or comic characters are listed in quotation marks, to indicate they are to be taken as a whole. They are alphabetized from the beginning of the name. Few would think, for instance, to look under "Drummond" if seeking information on "Ace Drummond," or under "Gordon" if seeking "Flash Gordon." The practice is extended to the names of media personalities whose names or stage names became, in a sense, trade names, such as "Shirley Temple" or "Roy Rogers."

Thus, because of the above practices, "Buck Jones" appears under the letter B, while manufacturer Howard B. Jones appears under the letter J.

Within entries, the terms "prewar" and "postwar" refer to World War II, with "Boomer" used roughly synonymously for the latter term. Due to exigencies of available time and space, and to my desire to cover the earlier years as thoroughly as possible, the entries include minimal reference to the last decades of the 20th century.

Writing a reference work is an exacting and exhausting task. I can only hope, in this case, that the exhaustion did not compromise the exactness. I also sincerely hope you will enjoy using this book as the tool it is, and be forgiving of the inevitable flaws. If you are interested in toys and their history, or are a collector of any sort, then you know first-hand what it is to be engaged in a labor of love, with all its limitations – and all its rewards.

Mark Rich

▲
The 19-1/2 inch "Spirit of Columbia" was made by the American Flyer Mfg. Co. in the late 1920s.

In the 1920s, Arcade released the "Andy Gump" auto cast –iron toy. ▶

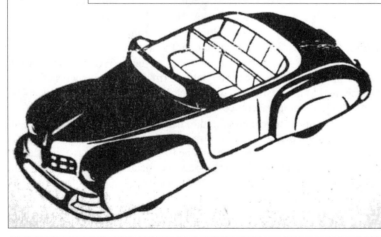

Auburn Rubber Co. made this toy car in the 1940s-50s.

Aa

A.&B. Wig Co., Inc. Organized in the late 1930s, A. & B. Wig Co., based on East 17th Street, New York City, specialized in doll wigs.

A.&E. Tool and Gage see *Midgetoy.*

A.&H. Doll Mfg. Corp. The plastic "Marcie," "Donna," "Gigi," and "Gigi's Li'l Sister" were made by this postwar doll company, based in Woodside, Long Island, N.Y. The dolls measured from 6 to 26 inches tall.

A.&J. Kitchen Tool Co. A prewar company, A. & J. Kitchen Tool Co. of Chicago produced toy kitchen utensils.

A.&L. Mfg. Co., Inc. Based in Brooklyn, N.Y., this firm made postwar games for adults.

A.&L. Novelty Co, Inc. Postwar dancing dolls, stuffed dolls, and boudoir dolls were made by this Brooklyn, N.Y., firm.

A&W Root Beer This soft-drink company took a foray into toy territory in 1975, when it issued two sizes of a plush "Great Root Bear," a vaguely "Yogi Bear" looking stuffed animal with the A&W logo on his shirt. In 1976, A&W issued a hand-puppet of the same bear.

"A.B.C." card game or lotto see *Ed-U-Cards Mfg. Co.*

"ABC Family" looms see *The Brothers Mfg. Co.*

A.B.C. Products, Inc. Based in West Los Angeles, Calif., in the late 1930s, A.B.C. made miniature engines and mechanical construction sets.

"A.B.C." Stencils and paints, late prewar, see *Parker Bros.* "ABC" toy-filled Christmas stockings, see *Royal Crest Products Co.*

A.B.C. Toys, Inc. This Broadway, New York City, firm was a postwar manufacturer of dolls and novelties.

A-J Aircraft Co. This Portland, Ore., company made postwar flying airplanes and gliders, and model boat kits.

"A1" Asakusa Toy Ltd., Japan.

"A-1" see *Ay-Won Toy & Novelty Corp.*

"AHI," or "AHI Brand" Aoshin, Japan.

"AK" Japanese tinplate toy-maker, circa 1920s.

A.M.F. Cycle Co. This Little Rock, Ark., company made postwar bicycles.

"AMF" wheel goods, see *American Machine & Foundry Co.*

AMT Corp. AMT Corp. specialized in scale-model cars in the 1950s and '60s, expanding its line in the 1960s and '70s to include a variety of model kits based on popular and TV-related characters. Early issues include models of "Dracula" and the "Munsters" dragster in 1965; the "Man from U.N.C.L.E." car in 1966; and the "USS Enterprise" in 1966 and '67. Issues in the 1970s include "Mr. Spock" in 1973; the "Girl from U.N.C.L.E." car in 1974; "Big Foot" in 1978; the "Flintstones Rock Crusher" and "Flintstones Sports Car" in 1974; and the "KISS Custom Chevy Van" in 1977.

"A.P.L." stuffed animals, prewar see *Knickerbocker Toy Co.*

"A.R." This French manufacturer of toy vehicles began in the '20s, producing toys in tin plate, cast iron, lead, and zinc alloy. The company specialized in Peugeot miniatures.

"A.S." In Nuremberg, Germany, a man named Adolf Schumann produced tin-litho toy cars from the 1910 through the mid-'30s. The "A.S." trademark appears on the car door.

"A.S.C." Aoshin, Japan.

"A.S.G.W." Gunthermann, German.

"A.T.C." Asahi Toy Co., Japan.

"A.T.F." Toys see *American Toy & Furniture Co., Inc.*

Abba International Products Co. Based in New Hartford, N.Y., Abba International Products made prewar toys including boomerangs, skates, and "Wit's Whoopee Whip Top."

Abbott Mfg. Co., Inc. Abbot Manufacturing made prewar games and mechanical toys. It was based on Broadway in New York City in the mid-1930s.

Academy Die-Casting & Plating Co. Based in the Fifth Avenue Building, Academy made Western-style cap pistols in the Boomer years.

Accurate Model Aircraft Co. A Chicago company, Accurate Model Aircraft Co. produced gliders, toy airplanes, and novelties in the mid-1930s.

Accurate Products Co. Based in Chicago, Accurate made toy airplanes, gliders, kits, and novelties in the late 1930s.

"Ace Agates" see *Akro Agate Co.*

"Ace Auto" see *Murray-Ohio Mfg. Co.*

"Ace Airplane" see *Western Aircraft Mfg. Co.*

"Ace Drummond" This hero of a 13-episode 1936 Universal serial was featured on a pin-back button marked "Junior Pilots Club."

"Ace Gun" see *The Dent Hardware Co.*

Ace Leather Goods Co. A prewar manufacturer, Ace Leather Goods Co. released, in 1930, the "American Football Game."

Ace Mfg. Co. Ace Mfg. Co. produced moving picture projectors and reels for 16mm film, which were used for prewar children's films, as well as Christmas tree holders. The prewar company was based in Milwaukee, Wis.

Ace Products A Pasadena, Calif., firm, Ace made model car kits in the 1950s-'60s.

Ace Toy Mfg. Co. Based on Broadway, New York City, Ace Toy made stuffed fur and plush toy animals and dolls in the Boomer years.

Ace Toy Mold Co. Based in Toledo, Ohio, Ace Toy Mold Co. was best known for its prewar "Kast-A-Toy" metal casting sets, which enabled children to cast their own toys from metal. The "Kast-A-Toy" sets were available in both non-electric and electric forms, the latter introduced in 1934. The company also issued "Ace Metal Toy Lacquer."

"Aces High" The "Aces High" name was used several times, including by Durable Toy & Novelty Corp. and Parker Bros. in the mid-1930s. The latter was a beanbag game.

"Ack-Ack" gun see *Maco Toys.*

Ack-Ack, Inc. This East Detroit, Mich., firm made rapid-fire, multiple-ball shooting guns in the early 1960s.

Ackermann, F.B. Based on Union Square in New York City, F.B. Ackermann imported dolls and decorative items before the war.

Ackley, Edith Flack Edith Flack Ackley was one of several doll designers whose patterns for rag dolls appeared in popular magazines including Woman's Home Companion in the 1920s and '30s. Her 1938 book *Dolls to Make for Fun and Profit,* remains of considerable interest to rag-doll enthusiasts.

Acme Can Co. A prewar Philadelphia company, Acme Can Co. produced toy ice cream freezers and decorated drums.

Acme Leather Products Co. In prewar times, makers of youth sports goods had not split off into a separate sports-equipment industry, and considered themselves part of the toy-making world. Acme Leather Products, based on Broadway in New York City, manufactured prewar sporting equipment, including footballs, basketballs, and soccer balls.

Acme Pistol Cap, Inc. This Columbus, Ohio, firm made repeating toy cap pistols and paper caps in the late 1930s.

Acme Plastic Toys, Inc. Perhaps the best known of the postwar toy companies bearing the "Acme" name, this Manhattan, N.Y., firm produced hard-plastic toy cars, motorcycles, baby strollers, and aircraft in the postwar years up to 1950. It produced many toys identical to Thomas Toy vehicles, the difference being the Acme imprint. Owner Ben Shapiro was also a financial partner in Thomas Toys, and relied upon Islyn Thomas for many, if not all, of the Acme toy designs. Thomas bought out Acme in 1950. The toys carried only the Thomas name thereafter.

Acme Toy Mfg. Co. Acme Toy Mfg. Co., established in 1910, emphasized its line of "Acme Dolls" through the 1920s and '30s. Located on West 19th Street, New York City, in the '20s, it moved to West 21st Street after the Great Depression, and continued in operation through the prewar years.

Acme Toy & Novelty Co. A prewar manufacturer based in Bridgeport, Conn., Acme Toy & Novelty produced pull toys, sand toys, Easter toys, and play sets using plywood pieces in the early 1930s. By the end of the decade it was making "Comical Pig and Kitten" swings, rockers for dolls, infant table and chair sets, a juvenile drawing table, and garage and gas station toys of plywood.

Acme Toy Works A Chicago company owned by Jacob Lauth, this 1903 to 1907 firm produced two metal toy vehicles, the curved-dash Oldsmobile roadster and a delivery truck, both clockwork. Lauth subsequently produced real autos under the Lauth-Jergens Co. name.

Acme Toys, Inc. Acme Toys of Cleveland, Ohio, was an early manufacturer of toys that became commonplace in the dime stores and convenience stores after the war: parachute toys. It produced items in the mid to late 1930s including "Parachute Shooter,"

"Magic Parachute," the "Cellophane Airplane Kite" of the early 1930s, and shooting games. The "Parachute Shooter" continued to be a popular item into the 1960s.

Acorn Industries Based in Plainview, N.Y., Acorn issued "Ben Hur" toys in the early 1960s, including games, paint sets, sword, helmet, and armor.

acrylic see *"thermoplastics."*

action figure Some very ancient toys appear to be action figures, having doll-size bodies and jointed limbs. Even so, toy collectors usually date the beginning of the action figure to 1963, when Don Levine, director of development for Hasbro, was considering ideas for a toy based on the TV series, "The Lieutenant." Executives at Hasbro thought boys would never play with dolls. Their concern gave rise to the term, "action figures." The original boxes for the G.I. Joe figures were marked "Action Soldier," "Action Sailor," "Action Pilot," and "Action Marine."

The word "action" was used directly in the names of several other action figures from other companies, as in Ideal Toy Company's "Captain Action," released in 1966, or Mego's "Action Jackson," in 1974. All this helped reinforce the public perception that action figures are not dolls.

Some of the ambiguity of the distinction can be seen in the fact that some action-figure collectors include in their collections Mattel's "Ken," the male counterpart to "Barbie." Although this is less the case in recent years, historically, action figures have been predominantly male figures. Ironically, the consequently few female figures are among the most highly valued.

"Action Jackson" In 1974, Mego issued its 8-inch action figure, "Action Jackson," and his female counterpart, "Dinah-Mite." "Action Jackson" was provided with numerous outfits, to provide him with a variety of vocations, from "Air Force Pilot," "Navy Sailor," or "Aussie Marine" to fisherman, hockey player, or football player. The figures are of moderate value to action-figure collectors, with the scarcer black versions being the most sought-after. Accessories included two play sets, the "Jungle House" and the "Lost Continent," and a variety of vehicles, including the "Dune Buggy," "Campmobile," "Mustang," "Safari Jeep," "Rescue Helicopter," and "Scramble Cycle," all issued in 1974.

"Action" miniature automobiles
see *Argo Industries Corp.*

Action Toy Co., Inc. Based in Denver, Colo., in the mid-Boomer years, Action Toy made plastic airplanes, rocket satellites, space stations, and novelties.

Action Tri-Play Toys This Chicago firm made the "Wreckmobile" come-apart friction auto in 1960, and premium toy items.

Active Doll Corp. Based in Brooklyn, N.Y., Active manufactured dolls, doll clothes, and doll packages in the postwar years.

activity boxes Activity boxes were assortments of playthings contained in kits or outfits, often produced by manufacturers with publishing interests. A typical selection were produced by Colorforms in the 1950s and '60s. The company divided its sets into its trademark "Colorforms 'Stick-On' Toys," games, Christmas items, coloring sets, craft sets, and jigsaw puzzles. Companies in the Boomer period, when activity boxes were especially common, included Eberhard Faber Toy & Game Co., Samuel Gabriel Sons & Co., Grosset & Dunlap, Harrett Gilmar, Fred Kroll Associates, the Platt & Munk Co., Rennoc Games & Toys, Rosebud Art Co., the Saalfield Publishing Co., and Venus Pen & Pencil Corp.

Adams & Co. Adams & Co. produced 19th century games, including "Squails," issued in the 1870s. In the 20th century, based in Bethlehem, Penn., it continued to have some involvement in toys, producing prewar children's field glasses.

Adams, Emma Emma Adams won a Diploma of Merit for her rag dolls at the Chicago World Columbian Exposition in 1893. This encouraged her to sell her dolls, which she had been making since 1891, as "Columbian Dolls." They were sold by Marshall Fields and better toyshops. Her sister and partner in the business, Marietta Adams Ruttan, continued the business after Emma's death. See also *Columbian Doll.*

George F. Adams & Co. Indoor croquet sets, ring toss, ten pins, and wooden tops were among the postwar products of this Moscow, Vt., firm.

Josiah Adams, Josiah Adams published the "Game of Kings" card game in 1845.

The Leonard Adams Studio This Buffalo, N.Y., firm was established in the late 1930s to produce games including musical games and card games. During the Boomer years, Adams emphasized the combination: musical card games.

S.S. Adams Co. Based in Asbury Park, N.J., S.S. Adams was an important producer of prewar and postwar jokers' novelties, magic accessories, puzzles, noisemakers, and party favors.

Adams Plastic Products This Boomer-years manufacturer issued vacuum-plated bell telephones and TV stools. It was based in Cincinnati, Ohio.

Adanta Novelties Corp. The "Yasmin Doll" line of the 1950s was issued by this West 26th Street, New York City, firm. The line included plastic, latex, and walking dolls, as well as stuffed animals. The firm moved to West 37th Street by the 1960s.

"Adco" dolls see *Arcadia Doll Co. Inc.*

"The Addams Family" The "Addams" family first appeared on paper from the pen of cartoonist Charles Addams, in 1938. His were perhaps the only New Yorker cartoons to turn into a pop-culture phenomenon. "The Addams Family" ABC TV show made its debut in 1964, lasting two seasons. It inspired playthings including coloring books by the Saalfield Publishing Co.; dolls by Remco Industries; games by Ideal Toy Corp. and Milton Bradley Co.; model kits by Aurora Plastics; play sets by Colorforms; and puppets by Ideal.

Addaword, Inc. The "Addaword" tile word game of the 1950s and '60s was made by this Seattle, Wash., firm.

adding machines Toy adding machines were common Boomer toys, made by manufacturers including Sterling Plastics Co. and Wolverine Supply & Mfg. Co.

"Adele" dolls see *Cameo Doll Co.*

Adler Favor & Novelty Co. In the 1920s, this St. Louis, Mo., firm issued "Floppidolls," "Loppipets," "Ragdolls," infant dolls, and "Bunny Dolls" in its "Adler Doll" line. Its "Doodle Dear" tumble clown of the late 1920s featured a washable face and soft body. In the post-Great Depression years, Adler produced noisemakers, paper hats, and novelty cloth dolls, among other party-related items of the 1930s. By the end of the decade, it had obtained a license to issue Walt Disney character candy novelties and party favors. Adler continued its novelty orientation in the Boomer years, issuing party favors, nut cups, centerpieces, paper hats, and bride and groom figures.

Admiar Rubber Co. Unlike many other prewar companies specializing in rubber toys, Admiar Rubber Co. was based in Brooklyn, N.Y., in the earlier 1930s, moving to Long Island, by the end of the decade. It specialized in jointed, all-rubber dolls, which were sold by Ideal Novelty & Toy Co. under the "Admiar" trade name.

"Admiral Byrd's Game" see *Parker Bros., Inc.*

"Admiration" see *Northeastern Plastics.*

Admiration Dolls, Inc. Based on Broadway, New York City, Admiration made novelty dressed plastic and vinyl dolls in the postwar years.

Admiration Toy Co., Inc. A specialist in postwar plastic miniature costume dolls, Admiration Toy was based on West 147th Street, New York City.

"Adora" dolls see *Dolls of Hollywood.*

"ADTCO" see *Atlas Doll & Toy Co.*

Adrena Doll Co. Based on West 17th Street, New York City, Adrena was established in the late 1930s to manufacture dolls and novelties.

Advance Crayon & Color Corp. Based in Brooklyn, N.Y., Advance issued crayons, paints, modeling clay, chalk finger paints, and metal paint boxes in the postwar years.

Adult Games, Inc. A Gary, Ind., firm, Adult Games was founded in the late 1930s to issue the "Poker-Golf" game, dice, dice cups, and game boards.

The Advance Doll & Toy Co. In the mid-1950s, this firm issued doll and carriage sets that combined a folding stroller with a 20- or 24-inch doll. The doll snapped onto the carriage, and appeared to walk alongside it. Advance's walking dolls were named "Wanda" and "Winnie." "Tama" was a walking, talking, and singing doll. The firm was based in West Haven, Conn.

Advance Manufacturing Co. Advance Manufacturing was a manufacturer of games and ashtrays, located in Minneapolis, Minn., in the early 1930s.

Advance Games Advance issued the games "Bengalee," "Looping the Loop," and "Three Point Landing" in the 1940s.

Advanced Products Advanced made die-cast farm toys in the 1:16 scale in the '50s.

"The Adventures of Robin Hood" see *"Robin Hood."*

"Aerco Plane" see *A.E. Rittenhouse Co.*

"Aerial Catapult Airplanes" The "Aerial Catapult" airplanes were toys issued in the mid-1930s by Milton Bradley Co. An "Aero" catapult airplane was issued at the same time by American Junior Aircraft Co.

aerial toys In the toy industry, "aerial toys" included toys ranging from gliders and flying airplanes to aerial disks. The single manufacturer to produce aerial toys from the earlier years of the 20th century through the Boomer period was Acme Toys. Toy models

A

of airplanes, zeppelins, and spaceships were also listed as "aerial toys" by some manufacturers. Construction kits and shelf models, however, were not.

The two most important forms of aerial toys were spinners and propeller airplanes. In the Boomer years, for instance, Action Toy Co. released its "Satellites," which were vertically rising propellers capable of reaching 30 feet, and its "Plastic Magic Planes," with rubber-band engines.

Manufacturers in the earlier 20th century included American Junior Aircraft Co., Captive Flight Devices, the Hi-Flier Mfg. Co., Indian Archery & Toy Corp., Kirchhof Patent Co., McCreary Mfg. Co., Mystoplane Co., Sail-Me Co., Samour Mfg. Co., Ferdinand Strauss Toys, and Woerner Mfg., Works. By the late prewar years, companies included Arcade Mfg. Co., E.C. Bangert Co., the Flying Toy Co., Heaney Laboratory, Indian Archery & Toy Corp., Paul Jones, Newton Mfg. Co., A.M. Samour Mfg. Co., Special Products Co., and Woerner's Mfg. Works.

Postwar manufacturers included Action Toy Co., Aurora Plastics, Broadfield Air-Models, Colonial Moulded Plastics Co., Dowst Mfg. Co., Enterprise Model Aircraft & Supply Co., Gladen Enterprises, Hale-Nass Corp., Hammat & Sons, Irwin Corp., Kaye Novelty Co., Lamalco Toys, North Pacific Products Co., Park Plastics Co., Pinwheel Products Co., Scientific Products Co., Victor Stanzel & Co., and Transogram Co.

The "Metalcraft Flying Field" took off in the 1920s.

"Aero Flyer" and "Aero-Flyer" see *Auto-Wheel Coaster Co., Inc.*

Aero Mfg. Co. Aero Manufacturing Co., based in Philadelphia, Penn., produced prewar juvenile vehicles.

Aero Model Builders Guild Located in Hempstead, N.Y., Aero Model Builders Guild produced prewar model airplane and ship construction kits.

Aero Model Co. The "Silver Ace" model planes, construction sets and supplies of the 1920s were made by this Chicago company.

The "Silver Ace Monoplane" was made by Aero Model Co. in the 1920s.

"Aero Racer" see *Sheboygan Coaster & Wagon Works.*

"Aero Speeder" and "Aero Zeps" see *Buffalo Toy & Tool Works.*

"Aerocycle" The "Aerocycle" was a 1930s streamline bicycle by Arnold, Schwinn & Co.

"Aeroflite" late 1930s; see *Garton Toy Co.*

Aerolux Light Corp. Based on Eleventh Avenue, New York City, Aerolux issued children's lamps featuring Popeye and other cartoon characters. It was founded in the later 1930s.

"Aeromite" see *Wen-Mac Corp.*

"Aeroplane Constructor" see *Meccano.*

"Aerotrol" kits see *Berkeley Models.*

Aetna Novelty Co. Founded in 1897, Aetna manufactured doll apparel through the 1920s, when it was located at West 17th Street, New York City, and through the prewar years, when it was located on Fifth Avenue. It specialized in doll coats, rain sets, and novelty apparel.

"Agates" Agates are marbles made from semiprecious stones, such as carnelian, bloodstone, rose quartz, or tiger's eye. The word also became a generic name for marbles, at least as far as manufacturers were concerned. Two of the largest makers of early machine marbles used the word in their names: Akro Agates and the Christensen Agate Co.

"Aggies" see *"Agates."*

Aid's, Inc. This Anaheim, Calif., company made Boomer-period toy guns.

"Aim Toothpaste" In 1974, Lever Brothers Co., which produced Aim Toothpaste, offered vinyl, jointed Looney Tunes figures by R. Dakin & Co. of "Tweety," "Bugs Bunny," "Road Runner," "Wile E. Coyote," and "Sylvester the Cat." In 1976, a similar promotion featured a Dakin vinyl figure of "Smokey Bear."

Ainslie Knitting Machine Co., Inc.
Ainslie issued the "Knit-Master" knitting machine from the late 1930s through the postwar years. It was based in Brooklyn, N.Y.

"Air Cruiser" Late 1930s, see *Garton Toy Co.*

Air Flite Toy Luggage Based in Nashua, N.H., Air Flite specialized in toy luggage in the Boomer years. The firm produced the highly sought 1965 vinyl lunch box "The Beatles."

"Air King" Late 1930s, see *Hamilton Steel Products Co.*

Air-King Model Co. Located in Portland, Ore., Air-King issued "Falcon Fleet" model airplanes, miniature gasoline engines, gliders, model airplane accessories, and model cement in the late 1930s.

"Air King" skates see *Schmid Bros.*

"Air Kraft" see *The Boy Toymaker Co.*

"Air-Liner" folding bicycle see *Compax Mfg. Co.*

"Air-Plane Control" marionettes see *Hazelle's Marionettes.*

"Aircrafted" The "Aircrafted" bicycles were produced by Huffman Mfg. Co. in the 1930s.

Airfix A British company based in London, Airfix began producing plastic soldiers in the early 1960s. Its line included Western, World War II, Medieval, and space figures. In the '60s through '80s, the company issued a number of model kits, particularly the 1967 "Monkeemobile" and the 1965 "James Bond Aston Martin." Many of its models depict historical figures.

"Airflow" The "Airflow" automobile, often called a Lincoln Airflow or a Doodlebug, was produced in the 1930s by manufacturers including Hubley Mfg. Co., Corcoran Mfg. Co., and Kingsbury Mfg. Co.

Skippy Racers' sharp-looking "Airflow DeSoto" from 1934.

"Airking" flying airplane 1930s, see *American Junior Aircraft Co.*

"Airline" "Airline" was a trademark used by the A. Schoenhut Co. for its construction trains in the 1930s.

"Airline Racer" The "Airline Racer" was a mid-1930s streamline sled by S.L. Allen & Co. "Airline Eagle" was used in the late 1930s.

Airline Textile Mfg. Co. Based in Des Moines, Iowa, Airline made postwar miniature airline flight bags and toy bag novelties.

Airlite Aluminum Corp. In the 1950s and '60s, Airlite made juvenile folding aluminum furniture.

airplane construction kits and models The making of airplane construction kits and models was an important part of the prewar toy manufacturing world, becoming a separate category in the post-Great Depression years. Manufacturers in the 1930s included Accurate Model Aircraft Co., Aero Model Builders Guild, Allied Industries, American Balsa Wood Co., American Junior Aircraft Co., American Model Aircraft Co., American Wunder Mfg. Co., Bay State Model Airplane Co., Broadfield Glider Co., Cleveland Model & Supply Co., Comet Model Airplane & Supply Co., Construct-A-Plane Co., Crescent Model Aircraft Co., E.W. Davies Aircraft Co., A.W. Drake Mfg. Co., Falcon Model Airplane Co., the Fleischmann Transportation Co., Golden Aircrafts Corp., Paul K. Guillow, Heathe Model Airplane Co., Ideal Aeroplane & Supply Co., Irwin Novelty Co., J. and J. Mfg. Co., Paul Jones, K. & B. Novelty & Mfg. Co., Kingsbury Mfg. Co., Megow's Model Airplane Shop, Northwestern Model Supply Co., the Peerless Model Airplane Co., Roland P. Place Co., Robert Pollock Co., A.E. Rittenhouse Co., Royal Toy & Novelty Co., Sail-Me Co., A.M. Samour Mfg. Co., Scientific Model Airplane Co., Selchow & Righter Co., Selley Mfg. Co., the Straits Corp., Thornecrafter, Tropical Model Airplane Co., United Electric Mfg. Co., Universal Sales Corp., United Model Airplane & Supply Co., Universal Model Airplanes, Viking Aircraft Co., George D. Wanner & Co., Western Aircrat Mfg. Co., Whitfield Paper Works, Wurtzer Mfg. Co., and Youngstown Tool & Mfg. Co. Their number was reduced by the late prewar years.

airplane glue see *airplane cement.*

airplane pedal vehicles The toy industry used such interesting terms as "aeroplane auto" in trying to describe the airplane vehicle toys, which were essentially pedal cars. The various pedal car manufacturers issued them, with 1930s examples including "Air Mail" by Garton Toy Co. and "Air Pilot" from American National Co.

airplane toys Airplane toys became an important part of the toy manufacturing industry as experimental and commercial airplanes gained greater fame in the 1920s. Earlier manufacturers included the Aero Model Co., American Flyer Mfg. Co., Arcade Mfg. Co., the Brown Industries, Cawood Mfg. Co., Clinton Toy Co., the Dan-D Mfg. Co., M. Carlton Dank, Dowae Toys, Flying Toy Co., Hubley Mfg. Co., Ideal Aeroplane & Supply Co., Marks Bros Co., Mt. Carmel Mfg. Co., Sail-Me Co., the A. Schoenhut Co., Selley Mfg. Co., U.S. Model Aircraft Corp., and Louis Wolf & Co. The airplane pull-toy became an important item in the 1930s. Manufacturers included All Metal Products Co., Arcade Mfg. Co., Dowst Mfg. Co., Hubley Mfg. Co., Keystone Mfg. Co., Murray-Ohio Mfg. Co., the John C. Turner Corp. A few manufacturers, including Dale Radioplane Co., the Lionel Corp., and Loynes Specialty Products, were making electric airplanes by late in the decade. Most airplane engines, however, were fuel engines, often used in conjunction with construction kits. Engine manufacturers included Air-King Model Co., American Junior Aircraft Co., E.W. Davies Aircraft Co., G.H.Q. Motors, Manufactured Specialties Co., Scientific Model Airplane Co., and Syncro Devices.

The most common airplane toys were gliders, however. Prewar manufacturers included Accurate Products Co., Air-King Model Co., American Junior Aircraft Co., the Comet Model Airplane & Supply Co., Dale Radioplane Co., E.W. Davies Aircraft Co., Emmert-Hammes & Co., Paul K. Guillow, the Hi-Flier Mfg. Co., Loynes Specialty Products, Selley Mfg. Co., and Western Aircraft Mfg. Co. See also under *aerial toys*, for other glider and propeller airplane toy manufacturers. Postwar glider manufacturers, many of whom used plastic rather than the previously used balsa wood, included Aurora Plastics, Broadfield Air-Models, Enterprise Model Aircraft & Supply Co., Gladen Enterprises, and North Pacific Products.

While some postwar firms made die-cast toy airplanes, including Hubley, Midgetoy, and Dowst Mfg. Co., most smaller toy airplanes of the Boomer years were plastic. Manufacturers included Action Toy Co., Argo Industry Corp., Payton Products, Plasticraft Mfg.

A

Co., Renwal Toy Corp., Thomas Mfg. Corp., and Wen-Mac Corp. Pinwheel airplanes were made by Kaye Novelty Co. and Pinwheel Products Co.

The Hubley Mfg. Co. made the "No. 430-S Airplane" in the 1960s.

airplane cement In the later prewar years and through the Boomer years, the smell of airplane cement became one of the commonplaces of childhood. Manufacturers included Comet Model Hobbycraft, Leech Products Co., Pactra Chemical Co., Victor Stanzel & Co., and the Testor Corp.

Airway Model Plane Co. This Brooklyn, N.Y., firm made model airplanes in the late 1930s.

Ajax Hardware Mfg. Co. A prewar company based in Tonawanda, N.Y., Ajax Hardware produced the "Little Giant Model Maker" set, a construction toy.

Ajax Plastic Corp. Founded in 1949 by Harry Sternberg, Ajax started its soft-plastic toy line with copies of "Beton" Western figures and Barclay soldiers. The company, which seems to have survived into the late 1960s, may never have originated any toy designs itself. It also produced horses, football players, dinosaurs, and a few space people. See also *Royal Desserts*.

"Akana," trade name see *Dowst Mfg. Co.*

The Akro Agate Co. An early manufacturer of machine-made glass marbles, Akro Agate is noted for having produced "corkscrew" marbles, especially "Popeyes." "Popeyes" were made with a combination of clear, white, and two opaque-colored types of glass. The company, based in Clarksburg,

W.Va., used the slogan, "Shoot Straight as a Kro Flies." The company also produced some games, such as "Kings" and "Clicks," toy tea sets, and glass novelties in the 1930s. The "Play-Time Glass Dishes" and "The Little American Maid Tea Sets" were issued in either topaz or green.

Aktoy Mfg. Co. Aktoy, based in San Francisco, Calif., made Boomer-years latex molded animal toys for young children.

"Akwa-Kar" see *Irwin Corp.*

"Al-Velvet" see *W.R. Woodard Co.*

The Alabama Indestructible Doll Ella Louise Smith of Roanoke, Ala., began making dolls just before the dawn of the 1900s. By 1904, she was displaying her "Alabama babies" at the St. Louis Exposition. She also exhibited in the 1907 Jamestown Exposition. Many of her dolls were made with fabric-covered plaster for the heads. Production continued through 1925.

Alabama Machine Co. Based in Eufaula, Ala., the Alabama Machine Co. produced prewar playground devices and equipment, as well as mechanical devices for window displays.

Alabe Crafts, Inc. This Cincinnati, Ohio, firm issued fortune-telling games, costume sets, and novelties in the Boomer years. Alabe Crafts' most famous novelty toy was the "Magic '8' Ball," introduced in 1946.

Aladdin Plastics, Inc. This late 1940s and early '50s Los Angeles, Calif., company made plastic infants' toys, including a "Talking Humpty Dumpty" roly-poly.

Aladdin Toy Mfg. Corp. Aladdin was an important postwar manufacturer of spring-wound and mechanical toys, spring motors, and metal stampings. Based in Brooklyn, N.Y., it did assembly work for other manufacturers and manufactured "tearing doll assemblies" for crying vinyl dolls.

"Aladdin" transformers see *The Lionel Corp.*

"The Alamo" This popular American historical site arrived in the homes of countless children in the form of play sets from Louis

Marx & Co. in the 1950s and '60s. The play set came in at least 11 versions, including a number of "Davy Crockett at the Alamo" variations.

Alamos Distributing Corp. Based in St. Louis, Mo., Alamos issued the "Mexican Jumping Beans" popular in the postwar years.

Alan-Jay Plastics, Inc. Infants' toys, squeeze toys, roly-polys, and nightlights were specialties of this postwar Webster Avenue, New York City, firm.

"Alaska" toy refrigerator 1930s, see *The Hubley Mfg. Co.*

Alberhill Coal & Clay Co. Located in South Pasadena, Calif., the prewar Alberhill Coal & Clay Co. produced "Clay Make" modeling clay.

Alberts Productions Established in the late 1930s, this Chicago firm manufactured toy tunnels, forts, trench systems, and roly-poly dolls.

J.E. Albright Co. J.E. Albright sold boxes of marbles that had been manufactured by Christensen Agate. It used the "Albright Brand" imprint. The company was based in Ravenna, Ohio, in the 1920s and '30s.

Alcott, Louisa May Born in 1832 in Germantown, Penn., Louisa May Alcott became one of America's most famous writers by the late 1800s, her reputation due in large part to her books for children. Her first book, *Flower Fables*, 1854, consisted of tales she wrote to entertain the daughter of Ralph Waldo Emerson. In 1867, she became editor of the children's magazine *Merry's Museum.* Her famous novel, *Little Women,* published in two volumes in 1868-69, won her a lasting following. It was followed by *Little Men* in 1871 and *Jo's Boys* in 1886. She died in 1888.

Aldon Industries, Inc. This Rego Park, N.Y., firm issued postwar plastic skill games and three-dimensional plastic cutouts.

Alelyunas & Co. The "Freight Run" combination board game and construction

toy of the 1950s-'60s was issued by this Haddonfield, N.J., firm.

Alexander Doll Co. Located on West 22nd Street in New York City, the Alexander Doll Co. ranked among the premiere doll manufacturers in the 1920s and '30s. The "Alexander Dolls" soon included the "Madame Alexander" line, which would become famous for its character dolls in the 1930s and later. The company obtained license in the late 1930s to issue Walt Disney character dolls.

Alexander, Beatrice Behrman see *Alexander Doll Co.*

"Alfred E. Neuman" *MAD Magazine,* founded in 1955, revived an old advertising character from the late 1800s, whom the MAD staff renamed "Alfred E. Neuman," employing illustrator Norman Mingo to create the definitive image. The most famous "Alfred E. Neuman" toy is the pirated one, an unlicensed doll produced by Baby Barry Toy Co. in 1961. Also desirable is the model kit made by Aurora Plastics in 1965.

"Alfred Hitchcock" Two postwar games took advantage of Alfred Hitchcock's popularity: the "Alfred Hitchcock Presents Game" issued in 1958 and the "Alfred Hitchcock's Why Mystery Game" in 1965, both by Milton Bradley Co.

"Algonquin" toboggans see *Withington.*

"Algy" stuffed toys postwar, see *Ideal Novelty & Toy Corp.*

"Alice" crayons 1930s see *The Ullman Mfg. Co.*

"Alice in Wonderland" Whatever people may think, *Alice in Wonderland* was not a Disney creation, although the Disney animated version has certainly provided a popular set of images that come to many people's minds at mention of the title. Even the basic visual natures of the characters are not Disney's, since they are closely based on the original illustrations by the fabulous illustrator Sir John Tenniel. At least one game, moreover, did appear before Disney's appro-

A

priation of the story, issued in 1923 by Stoll & Edwards.

Some dolls and toys seem to have appeared in the wake of the 1933 live-action film of *Alice in Wonderland* directed by Norman McLeod. An unknown manufacturer released an enameled metal premium ring in 1933, to coincide with the animated movie release. Around the same time, Parker Brothers issued an "Alice in Wonderland" board game. Other 1930s toys included cutouts from Milton Bradley Co.; doll dresses from Molly-'Es Doll Outfitters; a board game by Milton Bradley Co.; a domino game and paint book from Stoll & Einson Games; and tea sets from the Richardson Co. Madame Alexander issued an "Alice in Wonderland" doll in the 1930s, as part of the company's series of literary character dolls.

The doll remained part of the Alexander Doll Co. line through the Boomer years. "Mad Hatter" and "March Hare" soft dolls were made by Carb Mfg. Corp. The Walt Disney version, successful neither critically nor popularly at its first release in 1951, was followed by a set of "Alice in Wonderland" plastic figures from Louis Marx Co. The HO-scale figures were part of Louis Marx & Co.'s "Disneykins" series in the '60s. Six-inch "Alice in Wonderland" figures also appeared from the Evan K. Shaw Co. in the '50s. Late in the decade, Nancy Ann Storybook Dolls issued "Alice Thru the Looking Glass" dolls.

Besides the many editions of the original story, activity books included a Whitman paint book and punch-out-book, both in the '50s. The Hanna-Barbera *The New Alice in Wonderland* show appeared in 1966.

"Alice Teen" dolls see *Sayco Doll Corp.*

"All-American" The "All-American" wide-gauge train was a 1930s product of the American Flyer Mfg. Co. The "All American" or "All-American" trademark was also used on various unrelated games from F.D. Peters Co., Parker Bros., and Ozan Products Co. in the prewar years. The trade name tends to be more confusing than helpful in tracking down manufacturers in the postwar years as well, with "All-American" items

appearing from companies including Effanbee Doll Co., Elka Toys, Cadaco-Ellis, Pet Toy of New Hampshire, and Superior Toy & Mfg. Co.

All American Toy Company This West-coast company operated between 1948 and 1955 in Salem, Ore., under founder Clay Steinke. It produced about a dozen toy trucks and construction vehicles, the most popular being the "Timber Toter," a log truck measuring 38 inches. As would also happen with Smith-Miller, a collector bought the defunct company's molds and parts, and created a new line emphasizing limited editions and replacement parts.

All-Fair Toys In the 1920s, the Alderman-Fairchild Company of Rochester, N.Y., was a manufacturer of paper boxes and games. It made games as early as 1921. When it decided to separate its game-making division from its main operations, the company formed All-Fair Toys, which was moved to Churchville, N.Y., under the direction of H.G. Fisher.

All-Fair produced at least 50 games from the '20s through the early '40s. Card games in the '20s included "Fortune Telling" and an "Old Maid" set featuring characters from famous nursery rhymes. Board games included "X-Plor-US" in 1922; "Tutoom, Journey to the Treasures of Pharaoh" in 1923; "Auto Race Jr." and "Toonin Radio Game" in 1925; "Animal & Bird Lotto," "Match 'Em," and "Witzi-Wits" in 1926; "Game of the World Flyers" in 1926; "The Way to the White House" in 1927; "Caption Hop Across Junior," "Hi-Way Henry," and "Stop and Go" in 1928; and "The Capital Cities Air Derby" and "Speedem Junior Auto Race Game." The activity games "Tip the Bellboy" and "Bingo" also appeared in 1929.

The 1930s saw the appearance of such activity games as "Our Gang Tipple Topple Game" in 1930; "Bean-Em," "Busto," "Flap Jacks," and "Jav-Lin" in 1931; and "Bow-O-Winks," "Dim Those Lights," "Jaunty Butler," and "Simba" in 1932. The card games "Buck Rogers in the 25th Century" and "Skippy" appeared in 1936; "Frank Buck's Bring 'Em Back Alive Game" in 1937; and

A

"Patch Word" in 1938. Board games of the 1930s included "Stop and Shop" in 1930; "Battle of the Ballots," "Glydor," "Sky Hawks," and "Watch on De Rind" in 1931; "Cities" in 1932; and "WPA: Work, Progress, Action" in 1935.

A variety of board games appeared in 1940, including "Add-Too," "Ko-Ko the Clown," "Monkey Shines," and "Treasure Hunt. "Cargo for Victory" and "Game of International Spy" appeared in 1943. Other 1940s games also included "General Headquarters" and "Original Game of Zoom."

Aside from the quality paper-litho games and puzzles the company issued, the company is remembered among toy historians for having Herman Guy Fisher as its president from 1926 to 1930. With a group of investors, Fisher made an attempt to buy All-Fair in 1930. Disappointed in that effort, he went on to help form Fisher-Price Toys. For an apparently nominal sum, Fisher-Price bought All-Fair's logo, "Our Work Is Child's Play." Fisher's departure apparently did not rob the company of its entire creative force. The company's major character games generally came about after he left. See also *E.E. Fairchild Corp.*, which issued picture puzzles and games under the "All-Fair" name through the Boomer years.

All-Metal Products Co. Based in

Wyandotte, Mich., the All-Metal Products Co. was prominent from its founding in 1921 through the prewar years, making a name for itself with toy pop-guns, pistols, steel toys, and leather holster sets. By the late 1930s, it was also producing snow shovels, mechanical toys, lithographed toys, and such target games as "Spin 'Em Target Game." Its most important toys were toy vehicles, made of pressed steel. Its line included stake trucks, streamlined cars, ambulances, toy garages, service stations, and racecars. Notable toys included the "Rocket Racer" of the mid-'30s and the small "Roitan Cigars" advertising car of the late '30s.

During wartime, All-Metal made holster sets, toy guns, airplanes, armored trucks, die-cut boxed sets, and construction sets, all of cardboard, wood, and other non-critical materials. The firm resumed metal toy production after the war, and added some plastic toys to its line. It bought Hafner Mfg. Co. in 1950.

The company continued to thrive in the earlier Boomer years. In the early 1950s, its line included the "Double Barrel Pop Gun" and the "Double Holster Set" with leather holsters and die-cast repeating cap pistols; the "Hafner Trains" line of mechanical trains, which were attractively lithographed; and the "Rider Fire Truck," a heavy-gauge riding toy, 32 1/2 inches long, with a bicycle-type seat on top, red flashing light on the cab roof, and a siren. The line of toy trucks included the "Auto Service Truck," which came with a variety of tools, including a working jack; "Auto Transport," with plastic cars; "Deluxe Van Truck," with "Wyandotte Van Lines" on the side; and "Dump Truck with Shovel," which featured a crank-lifting dumping bed and a 12-inch steel shovel for filling it. The line was diminished by the mid-1950s and came to an end in 1956.

All-Nu Barclay sculptor Frank Krupp founded the All-Nu toy company in the late 1930s, incorporating in 1938 in Yonkers, N.Y., and moving in 1941 to Manhattan, N.Y. All-Nu produced toy soldiers and novelties. Most desirable are the rare slush-mold soldiers. Some of the figures show extremely careful sculpting. The "Newsreel" cameraman, which shows a soldier in his helmet kneeling behind a two-reel camera, is possibly the single-most valuable toy soldier of American make.

In lead, the company also made majorettes, football players, western horseback figures, and polo players. All-Nu made Barclay-style slush-mold military vehicles, now extremely rare, which were marked only "Made in USA," and the 1941 sulky "Trotter." Hampered by the government's impounding of all lead shipments in December, 1941, Krupp designed cardboard soldiers, which All-Nu produced in 1942-43. These are moderately valued by collectors. Krupp went into bankruptcy in the mid-'40s.

"All Purpose" doll 1930s, see *Kashner Novelty Corp.*

A

"All Time Hit Parade Dolls" 1950s and '60s, see *Nancy Ann Dressed Dolls, Inc.*

All Western Plastics, Inc. This mid-'40s company is known for its "Roundup King Top," a plastic yo-yo featuring Roy Rogers and Trigger on the obverse and an announcement of the contest to find "the King and Queen of 'Roundup King' Top Spinners," who would get to meet Roy. Although an attractive item, a warehouse find keeps this from being a valuable one.

All Work Mfg. Co. The "Tumble Tub" all-steel outdoor playthings of the mid-Boomer years were produced by this Oakland, Calif., firm.

Allbright Electric Corp. Located on West 21st Street in New York City, Allbright Electric Corp. manufactured flashlights, penlights, advertising novelties, and dry batteries for the prewar toy trade.

Allen, Jimmy, see *Jimmy Allen Flying Club.*

S.L. Allen & Co. A Philadelphia, Penn., company that started as a manufacturer of agricultural equipment in the 1800s, S.L. Allen & Co. manufactured the "Flexible Flyer" and "Firefly" lines of coaster sleds. Other products used related names: "Flexy Racers," "Flexy Whirls," and "Flexy Quoit" kits. In the late 1930s, the company produced the "Yankee Clipper" and Mickey Mouse and Donald Duck sleds. The "Flexible Flyer" and "Yankee Clipper" sleds remained famous through the Boomer years, as did the "Flexy Racer" coasters.

Allied Cabinet Corp. The "U.S. Traveler" line of all-wood wheel goods was issued during wartime by this Chicago company. The "U.S. Traveler," "Patrol," and "Chief" three-wheel carts were hand-carts, with the drive anchored to the rear wheel. The wagon in the line had four wheels. All the wheels were wood, of necessity.

Allied-Grand Doll Mfg. Co. A Brooklyn, N.Y., company, Allied-Grand Doll Manufacturing produced prewar composition character dolls through the 1930s. In the postwar years, the firm shifted to making vinyl, latex, and plastic dolls.

Allied Industries Based in Chicago, Allied Industries produced prewar airplane and hangar construction sets.

Allied Manfacturers of America Based on Broadway, New York City, Allied Manufactures produced wheel goods, shoo-flies, play yards, bicycles, playground equipment, kindergarten items, and juvenile furniture. It was established in the late 1930s.

Allied Manufacturing Co. Allied Manufacturing Co. specialized in camera and film-related toys. Based in Chicago, it produced prewar toy items including the "Foto-Reel Camera," "Film Funnies," and "Komic Kamera."

Allied Molding Corp. Active in the early '50s, Allied Molding of Flushing, N.Y., made plastic vehicle toys—especially trucks and construction vehicles—and dollhouse accessories.

"Allied Quality Doll" see *Allied-Grand Doll Mfg. Co.*

Allison's This Brooklyn, N.Y., company specialized in toy-filled Christmas stockings, candy and toy prize boxes, and children's games in the Boomer period.

Allison Studios, Inc. Circus sets, barn sets, Noah's arks, pull toys, and wooden animals and figures were postwar products of this Wilmington, Ill., company.

K.&B. Allyn Co. In addition to model airplanes and engines, Allyn made plastic boats and model outboard engines in the 1950s and '60s. The firm was based in Los Angeles, Calif.

Almore Plastics see *Archer Plastics.*

Alox Mfg. Co., The Alox Manufacturing produced jump ropes, lassos, play ropes, ring toss, braids, whips, walking canes, spinning ropes, jigsaw puzzles, and wood whistles in the years after the Great Depression. By the late 1930s, it had added spinning ropes, elastic cord exercisers, sirens, bubble pipes, and tops. Based in St. Louis, Mo., Alox continued to thrive in the Boomer years, when it produced kites, sirens, marbles, and checkers, as well as its earlier product line.

"Alphacolor," also "Alphasite," see *Weber-Costello Co.*

Alpha Toys
Based in London, England, J.K. Farnell and Co. made cloth dolls under the "Alpha Toys" name from 1915 through the '30s. Alpha Toys issued various character dolls created by artist Chloe Preston in the '20s, including "Little Britain," "Little Miss Cracker," and "Pal Peter." The '20s also saw the appearances of comic characters and James Riddell storybook characters "Augustus," "Annabelle," and "Ambrose." Farnell further sold souvenir sailor dolls similar to the more famous ones produced by Norah Wellings. The U.S. distributor was Louis Wolf.

alphabet blocks see *blocks,* also *Charles M. Crandall.*

alphabet sets
Having physical letters to play with would help children learn their alphabet, thought manufacturers of educational toys. Letter-shaped toys became common in the prewar years from manufacturers including the A.I. Root Co. and National Playthings, and, in the postwar years, from Bar Zim Toy Mfg. Co., Henry Katz, and A.M. Shephard Co.

Alphabet Soup Co., Inc.
The "Goomicus Alphabet Soup" word game of the 1950s and '60s was issued by this Brooklyn, N.Y., company.

The Alphadice Co.
Located on West 52nd Street in New York City, this manufacturer was responsible for the prewar "Alphadice" game.

"Alphonse and Gaston"
These early comic characters were represented in several vehicle toys, including the "Alphonse and Gaston Automobile" by the Kenton Hardware Co., with animated movement, and the "Alphonse in Cart" cast-iron knodder, made by Hubley Mfg. Co. in several versions in the early 1900s. The automobile, which is of the early horseless-carriage variety with a driver in front and the two comic characters facing each other within the open carriage, has sold at auction for prices over $10,000. Fred Opper's original strips were collected in 1903 under the title *Alphonse & Gaston & Leon* and published by Hearst's New York American & Journal.

Alps Shoji Co.
This Japanese company, founded in 1948 in Tokyo, produced battery-operated and wind-up tinplate toys. Many are marked simply "Alps." Imprints included "Rock Valley Toy."

Althof, Bergmann
The company of Althof, Bergmann flourished from 1867 into the 1870s in New York City, making several horse-drawn tin toys, bell toys, toy furniture, banks, and clockwork toys.

aluminum
While we tend to think of aluminum as a fairly recent material for toys, it does well to remember such items as the "Mickey Mouse Aluminum Play Set" and the "Mickey Mouse Aluminum Baking Set," made in the 1930s by the Aluminum Specialty Company. Perhaps even more chastening to our notion of that up-to-date metal are the "Domestic Science" aluminum pots and pans set from 1919. Aluminum toy dishes became commonplace in the 1920s, from companies including Transogram Co. Some toy lines are noted for using aluminum, such as Lansing Slik Toys, which made farm and construction vehicles. Many prized premium rings, such as the Kellogg's baseball rings, were made of the metal. Major prewar manufacturers using aluminum include Dent Hardware Co., Faith Mfg. Co., and Metal Goods Corp. See also *cooking utensils, tea sets.*

This 18-piece aluminum tea set debuted in the 1920s.

Aluminum Goods Mfg. Co. Based in Manitowoc, Wis., Aluminum Goods Mfg. Co. produced prewar aluminum play sets for children, including cooking, baking, tea, kitchen, and sand sets, and play electric stoves. In the late 1930s, it issued the "Mirro Cinderella" line of aluminum play sets. The company also obtained license to issue Walt Disney character-related dishes and cooking utensils.

Aluminum Hardwares, Inc. The "Freez-Fun" portable backyard ice-skating rinks of the Boomer years were made by this Forest Park, Ill., firm.

Aluminum Specialty Co. Like Aluminum Goods Mfg. Co., Aluminum Specialty Co. was based in Manitowoc, Wis. It produced prewar children's aluminum cooking and tea sets, and enjoyed substantial success in the postwar years. Its line included "Kiddykook" and "Wonderland" children's aluminum and plastic cooking, baking, coffee, and tea sets, as well as baseball training games, rope swings, and stainless aluminum Christmas trees. In the Boomer years, after curtailing toy production, the firm's "Kiddykook Chilton Ware" miniature utensils enjoyed widespread acceptance. Although still called Aluminum Specialty, it also made polyethylene tea sets, baking sets, and percolator sets, as well as action games.

Aluminum Specialty Co. made the "Kiddykook Cake Cover and Tray" in the 1950s.

Alvimar Mfg. Co., Inc. Alvimar manufactured plastic inflatable toys in the 1950s and '60s, using characters including "Casper the Friendly Ghost," "Lassie," and "Sad Sack." Its extensive line included beach and play balls, swim rings, floats, pools, oats, mats, roly-polys, novelty toys, tub toys, and infant toys. Alvimar was based on Park Avenue, New York City.

"Alvin & the Chipmunks" see *"The Chipmunks."*

Alvin Industries, Inc. This postwar juvenile furniture manufacturer was based in Chicago.

"Always Did Despise a Mule" Two important early banks bore this name. The first, issued in 1879, featured a black jockey on a mule. The second, in 1897, showed the jockey on a bench facing the kicking mule.

"Always On Top" This early motto of the Cracker Jack Co. is found on some of the confection's toys in between 1910 and the '30s.

Alwill Projecto Corp. A firm based on West 60th Street, New York City, in the late 1930s, Alwill produced the "Projecto" game.

The "New York World's Fair Twins" were inflatable toys made by Alvimar Mfg. Co., in 1964.

"Amaco" see *American Art Clay Co.*

The Aman & Sandman Box & Lumber Co. Manufacturer of the 1930s "Sketch-A-Scope" drawing device, Aman & Sandman Box & Lumber was located in Cincinnati, Ohio.

Amberg Dolls Based on Broadway, New York City, Amberg Dolls enjoyed success in the late 1920s with the "It" doll, which was described as "the doll with a 'Body Twist' all its own!" An all-composition doll, "It" could twist at the waist into different poses. The doll retailed at $3. Amberg's other dolls included the "Vanta Baby" line, "Amfelt Art Dolls," "Little Amby," "Twinkle Twins," and the "Teenie Weenies." It used the "Every Known Kind of Doll and Toy Animal" slogan.

"Ambrite" see the *American Crayon Co.*

"Amco" "Amco" wooden toys were made through the 1930s by Anchor Mfg. Co. The "Amco" name was also used in the late '30s by Comet Model Airplane & Supply Co. for airplane kits and by Ammidon & Co. for Christmas stockings.

"Amer Tots" dolls see *Alexander Doll Co.*

"America" toy airplane 1930s, see the *Hubley Mfg. Co.*

America, Inc. This Chicago firm produced the 1930s "America" card game.

"American Ace" The "American Ace" name was used on 1930s and '40s coaster wagons and sleds by American National Co. The name was also used on postwar pistol caps by J. Halpern Co.

American Acme Co. Located in Emigsville, Pa., American Acme Co. produced prewar and postwar sleds, shooflies, children's furniture, and playground equipment.

American Advertising & Research Corp. Based in Chicago, Ill., American Advertising & Research issued late 1930s displays, posters, paper cutouts, and juvenile giveaways featuring the cartoon characters coming into national prominence before the war.

American Alloy American Alloy, American Lead Toy & Novelty Co., and Toy Creations may have been the same company, or a series of related toy-soldier companies operating from 1939 into the late '40s. Louis Picco, president of American Alloy, was involved in all three concerns.

American Art Clay Co. An Indianapolis, Ind., company, American Art Clay manufactured "Permoplast" modeling play outfits, "Amaco Modeling Clay Sets," and "Rainbow-Wax" toy sets, chalk, and crayon sets. It continued the "Permoplast" and "Amaco" lines through the Boomer years, adding

"Plasti-i-Clay," as well as finger paint and water color sets.

"American Art Dolls" "American Art Dolls" were a lower-end, made-in-America version of the popular "Kathy Kruse" cloth dolls made in Germany in the 1910s. The dolls were given such names as "Buddy" for the country boy, "Ulrich" for the boy in the fez, and "Liesel" for the Germanic high-country girl. The uniformed boy doll, however, was simply the "Boy Scout." They were sold by the distributors Strobel and Wilken Co. of New York City.

American Artists' Color Works, Inc. The "Sargent" colors and crafts outfits, modeling clay, chalks, inks, and crayons of the postwar years were produced by this Fifth Avenue, New York City, firm.

American Automatic Electric Sales. Co. Based in Chicago, the American Automatic Electric Sales produced the 1930s "Real-Phone" electric talking telephones, consisting of pairs of desk telephones strung together by wire. "They look and handle just like real telephones," the company's ads promised, "And they 'talk up'—crisp and clear." The company also made the "Official Boy Scout Field Set," which was a field telegraph unit with telephone handset.

American Ball Co. Manufacturer of the prewar "Bull's Eye" steel air rifle shot, American Ball Co. also made the "Copprotect" air rifle shot for Daisy Mfg. Co. It was located in Minneapolis, Minn.

American Balsa Wood Co. Located in Los Angeles, American Balsa Wood Co. produced gliders, kites, model airplanes, and advertising novelties in the 1930s.

"American Beauty" The "American Beauty" coaster wagon of the 1930s and '40s was made by Radio Steel & Mfg. Co.

American Boomerang Co. This prewar boomerang manufacturer was located in Closter, N.J.

"American Boy" play gun 1930s, see *J.C. Mfg. Co.*

"American Bricks" see *Halsam Products Co.*

American Bubble Pipe Co. This Rockaway, N.Y., firm's line of bubble blowers in the 1920s included the "Gem Bubbler," which produced bubbles on top and bottom of the bowl, and the "Wonder Bubbler," for blowing giant bubbles, chain bubbles, and bubbles within bubbles. In the 1930s and '40s, the firm was based in Long Island, N.Y.

"American Buddy" American National Co. made the 1930s and '40s "American Buddy" and "American Chief" coaster wagons.

American Ceramic Co. This Sebring, Ohio, company was formed in the late 1930s to produce American-made China toy tea sets.

American Character Doll Co. This East 17th Street, New York City, manufacturer enjoyed success with several lines in the pre-Great Depression years, especially with its assortment of "Campbell Kids" dolls. Its "Petite Doll" line included "Puggy," described as a "mischievous little rascal," and the baby dolls "Happy Tot" and "Toddle Tot."

After the Depression, American Character Doll Co. was issuing the dolls "Toodles," "Sally," and "Sally-Joy." The "Toddletot," "Botteltot," "Marvel Tot," "Puggy," and "Paratex" dolls were made into the '40s.

The "Toddletot" doll, new in 1934, introduced the innovation of "side sleeping" eyes. The doll's eyes would remain open in the standing position, and when lying on her back or left side. Her eyes would finally close if turned on her right side. The doll had a wig of real human hair.

American Character Dolls was among the earlier doll companies to take advantage of the medium of TV for advertising. It advertised its lead dolls on "Miss Frances' Ding Dong School" and "The Pinkie Lee Show" by the mid-1950s. The dolls included the "Sweet Sue" dolls, which could bend their knees, sit, kneel, walk, and stand without support; the "Lifesize Sweet Sue" doll was 31 inches tall,

and had arms jointed at the elbows. Others were "Toodles," a baby doll; "Ricky Jr.," based on the famous TV baby of the "I Love Lucy Show;" "Pretty Baby," a crying doll with sleep eyes; and "Tiny Tears," a doll similar to the dolls by Sun Rubber that drank, wet, cried, and blew bubbles. Other postwar dolls included "Toni" and "Betsy McCall."

The "Tiny Tears" doll by American Character Doll Co. drank, wet, cried and blew bubbles.

"American Chief" see *"American Buddy."*

American Colortype Co. Based in Chicago, American Colortype Co. produced paper doll cutouts and toy books in the mid-1930s, in addition to Christmas tags and seals. By the end of the decade, it was specializing in holiday cards, tags, seals, and postcards. The line continued through the war years.

American Crafts-Products Co. American Crafts-Products was founded in Washington, D.C., in the late 1930s to produce stuffed animal toys, gourd-headed dolls, and sand toys.

American Crayon Co. American Crayon Co. as established in 1835 in Sandusky, Ohio. In the 1920s, it made toy watercolor and crayon outfits under the "Old Faithful" trade name. In the '30s, it expanded its products to include painting, coloring, stenciling, tracing, and modeling sets. The firm's postwar line continued along similar lines, adding chalks, toys, juvenile books, and preschool toys.

"American Dart" air rifle see *Upton Machine Co.*

American Doll & Novelty Co. Based on West 20th Street in New York City, American Doll & Novelty Co. manufactured flapper dolls, boudoir novelties, and stuffed animals in the mid-1930s.

"American Eagle" see *The Alox Mfg. Co.*

American Eagle Defenders A comic-book club, the American Eagle Defenders had two premiums—a pin-back button featuring a masked figure in front of a coin-style eagle, and a membership card.

American Electric Toy Co. Based in Chicago, American Electric Toy issued the "Real Phones" of 1934, working communications toys that rang and allowed conversation over long distances. They retailed at $6.

American Electric Toy & Novelty Co. This Brooklyn, N.Y., firm produced prewar electrical and mechanical toys. By the late 1930s it was manufacturing toy steam engines, electric motors, and games.

American Electrical Products Co. Based in Mansfield, Ohio, American Electrical was founded in the late 1930s to produce toy steam engines, games, and electric motors.

American Fixture & Show Case Mfg. Co. American Fixture of St. Louis, Mo., made juvenile tables and chairs of tubular chrome in the late 1930s.

American Flag Co. In addition to flags, pennants, and banners, the American Flag Co. produced prewar leather holsters, Indian and cowboy suits, masquerade costumes, and various decorative goods. It was located on Mercer Street, New York City.

"American Flyer" bicycle late 1930s, see *D.P. Harris Hardware & Mfg. Co.*

American Flyer Mfg. Co. American Flyer, one of the famous names in American toy trains, is one of several owing its existence to the creative energies of William F. Hafner. Hafner had invented a reliable clockwork motor around the turn of the century and immediately saw its potential for toy making. He founded the Toy Auto Co. in 1901, changing its name in 1902 to the William F. Hafner Co. This company made toy cars and trucks. In 1905, he adapted his motor to a cast-iron train engine.

Needing financial backing to produce the train toys in large quantities, in 1907 Hafner joined the Edmonds-Metzel Manufacturing Co. The trains were immediate successes. Edmonds-Metzel, under W.O. Coleman, Sr., had been a manufacturer of farmer's hardware. It now turned its resources entirely to the production of toy trains. In 1910 it changed its name to the American Flyer Manufacturing Co. Apparently because of financial or other disagreements, Hafner left the company in 1914.

By the end of the 1920s, American Flyer's leading wide-gauge trains included No. 1495, "Old Ironsides" steam-type freight train, and No. 1497 "The Warrior," and No. 1488 "The Minute Man" steam-type passenger trains. These sets retailed at $50 to $75 in 1929.

The company was also an important manufacturer of toy airplanes, with its line including the monoplanes "Spirit of America," "Spirit of Columbia," and "The Lone Eagle," and the biplane "The Sky King." Made of heavy gauge steel, the airplanes included belt-driven propellers. "The Lone Eagle" and "Spirit of Columbia" were clockwork toys, with brakes to start and stop them. "Spirit of America" and "The Sky King" were pull-toys. These toys measured from 18 to 21 inches long.

In the 1920s, the company also entered into a mutually beneficial arrangement of distributing Structo toys.

By the mid-1930s, based on South Halsted Street in Chicago, American Flyer was producing a characteristic variety of products, including wind-up and electric trains, transformers, miniature railway equipment, buildings, and accessories. American Flyer introduced a toy typewriter, capable of both capital and small letters, which met with success. The firm also distributed Structo Mfg. Co. vehicle toys and Empire express wind-up trains.

American Flyer was purchased in 1937 by A.C. Gilbert. In the first years, Gilbert marketed a successful 3/16-scale line. Both American Flyer and its competitor Lionel were largely forced out of the toy business by World War II. American Flyer returned in 1946 with the two-rail system, for realism, for the S-gauge toys. In the '50s, American flyer was ranked second only to Lionel. The company, purchased in the early '60s by Jack Wrather, suffered a decline through that decade. In 1966, Lionel purchased the remnants of the company, and halted production of American Flyer trains. See *Hafner, William F.,* and *A.C. Gilbert.*

This engine was made in the 1920s by the American Flyer Mfg. Co.

American Foam Latex Corp. This Pittsburgh, Penn., firm made stuffed dolls and animals in the Boomer period.

American Football Co. American Football issued the game "Fobaga" in 1942.

American Game Co. Based in Revere, Mass., American Game made the "Scoop-Ball" game of the 1950s and '60s.

American Games Co. The Game of Baffle Ball was a leading 1930s item of manufacture from the American Games Co., of Chicago.

"American Girl" The "American Girl" trademark was used on prewar toy sewing machines by National Sewing Machine Co. In the late 1930s, Royal Doll Mfg. Co. made an "American Girl" doll.

American Girl's Book Appearing in the early 1800s, this magazine may have included the first published directions for making rag dolls in America.

The American Import Co. A prewar importer and jobber based in San Francisco, American Import Co. imported toys, novelties, carnival goods, and sports equipment.

American Indian dolls American Indian dolls began receiving attention from the American and European collecting community by the early 1900s, being exhibited in the International Doll Exhibition in Liege, Belgium. More than 50 were exhibited, as a demonstration of the bone-needle sewing, weaving, and leather-making skills of the American Indian children.

American Indian games see *lacrosse, football, snow snake, bows and arrows.*

American Indian toys see *tops.*

American Junior Aircraft Co. Based in Portland, Ore., American Junior Aircraft Co. produced prewar "ready to fly" toy airplanes and gliders, as well as assembly kits.

"The American Lady and Her Children" This title was commonly used by late 1800s publishers of paper dolls, including Kimmel & Forster.

American Lead Toy & Novelty Co. see *American Alloy.*

"American Logs" see *Halsam Products Co.*

American Machine & Foundry Co. Based on Madison Avenue, New York City, American Machine & Foundry issued the "AMF Roadmaster" bicycles of the Boomer years, "AMF" cars, tractors, and wagons, and "AMF Junior" trikes and bikes.

The "Deluxe Roadmaster" was produced by American Machine and Foundry Co.

American Made Products, Inc. This Bloomington, Ill., company made wooden toy building blocks in the late 1930s.

American Made Toy Co. Based on Union Square, New York City, with a factory in Brooklyn, American Made Toy Co. issued toy animals in the 1920s, with characters including "Howie," "Happie," "Herbie," "Snoopie," "Gloomy Gil," and "Aunty Bimbo." American Made Toy produced stuffed novelties, teddy bears, Easter rabbits, and Halloween toys into the mid-1930s.

American Maid Artcraft Studios A

manufacturer of board games, anagrams, puzzles, toy boats, and novelties, American Maid Artcraft Studios was located in Schenectady, N.Y., in the mid-1930s.

American Manufacturing Concern

This Falconer, N.Y., company was issuing a full line of wooden toys in the 1920s, including a "Children's Playtown" with miniature wood buildings, a wooden train set, tool kits, and bags of toy blocks. American Mfg. Concern's "Falcon" toys also included building lumber, construction blocks, upright and baby grand toy pianos, work benches, the "Buddy" snow skates, desk blackboards, and auto cribs.

In the '30s, when it adopted the "Falcon Toys That Last" slogan, its line consisted of building blocks, wagon blocks, bags of blocks, tool chests, workbenches, wall and easel blackboards, "Buddy" snow skates, and educational toys.

In wartime and the following Boomer years, American Mfg. Concern emphasized slate and composition blackboards and wallboards, wood blocks, sand toys, desk sets, chalkboards, slates, doll cradles, doll furniture, rocking horses, shooflies, peg tables, and wood toys.

"Falcon Building Lumber" by the American Manufacturing Concern, 1920s.

The American Mask Mfg. Co. In

addition to masks, the American Mask Mfg.

Co. of Findlay, Ohio, produced other prewar costume items, including papier-mache heads and noses, "luloups," wigs, beards, and moustaches. The company also made dominoes.

American Merchandise Co. Based on

West 23rd Street in New York City, American Merchandise Co. produced prewar mechanical toys, stuffed toys, whistles, toy guns, microscopes, and rubber toys.

American Merri-Lei Corp. A manufac-

turer of Halloween, Easter, and Christmas goods, American Merri-Lei was located on West 23rd Street, New York City, in the mid-1930s, and on Sixth Avenue by late in the decade. In the Boomer period, located in Brooklyn, N.Y., Merri-Lei continued to issue a similar line of holiday goods, as well as Hawaiian leis.

American Metal Box Co. Doll trunks,

roller skate cases, toy chests, and toy luggage were specialties of this Newark, N.J., firm in the postwar years.

American Metal Specialties Corp.

The "Amsco" toys, "Doll-E-toys," and "Kidd-E-Toys" of the 1950s and '60s were made by this Hatboro, Penn., company. Its lead items included the "Campbell Kids Chuck Wagon Set," "Doll-E-Nurser," "Doll-E-Layette," and "Doll-E-Shopper" shopping cart, of the mid-1950s. The line also included doll highchairs, cribs, and beds.

American Metal Specialties Corp. made the "Doll-E-Crib" in the 1950s.

American Metal Toys Royce Reyff and

Raymond ("Roy") Pierson founded American Metal Toys in 1937, manufacturing metal toy soldiers and spring cannons in its factory located on North Racine Avenue, Chicago. The company lasted until 1942, when wartime metal restrictions forced the company to stop operations. The molds, including work by noted toy soldier sculptor Harry Kassdowski, were sold to Lincoln Logs.

American Mill & Mfg. Co. This Dallas firm produced prewar playground equipment.

American Miniatures, Inc. Founded in the late 1930s on West 31st Street, New York City, American Miniatures produced cardboard miniature houses.

American Mint Corp. In the late '30s into the early '40s, American Mint sold its candies in cardboard containers bearing the likeness of soldiers from around the world. About 2 1/2 inches tall, the containers are sought by both candy-wrapper collectors and some toy soldier collectors.

American Mirror Works This postwar Lincoln Avenue, New York City, firm made mirror-action toys featuring Walt Disney characters.

American Model Aircraft Co. This maker of model airplane construction kits was based in Brooklyn, N.Y.

The American-National Co. Based in Toledo, Ohio, American-National produced pedal cars and pressed-steel trucks in the '20s and '30s. "The Line Beautiful" of the 1920s included juvenile autos, velocipedes, coaster and express wagons, hand-cars, pedal bikes, scooters, baby walkers, park cycles, doll carriages, baby carriages, invalid chairs, and play-yard equipment. Through the 1930s, its line continued the focus on sidewalk toys, with "Skippy Racers," nursery equipment, and playground equipment added.

Founded by the brothers William, Walter, and Harry Diemer in 1894, the company produced toys from as early as 1918. American-National used the "Raise the Kids on Wheels" slogan, and the "Giant" trade name. The company's name often appeared with "American National" not hyphenated.

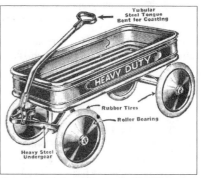

American-National Co. made this "Heavy Duty Wagon" in the 1920s.

American Novelty Co. Despite its name, this Petersburg, Va., company produced prewar children's furniture and shooflies.

American Novelty Works Based in Herndon, Penn., American Novelty Works produced toy wood blocks and game boards in the mid-1930s, including one called "Jump."

American Original Toys, Inc. This Bend, Ore., company made the "Build-Over" and "Fun Gun" of the 1920s.

American Paper Specialty Co. This postwar publisher of Valentines and Christmas cards was based in Chicago.

American Party Favor Co. Noisemakers including crickets, metal horns, cowbells, and tambourines were made by this Boomer period manufacturer, located in Pittston, Penn. The firm also made favors, leis, and hats.

"American Plastic Bricks" see *Halsam Products Co.*

American Play Co. Space toys were the specialty of this 1950s to 1960s firm, based in the Fifth Avenue Building, New York City.

American Playground Device Co. Based in Anderson, Ind., American Playground Device made prewar and postwar children's lawn and playground equipment, as well as swimming pool equipment.

American Proca Corp. Based in the Fifth Avenue Building in the late 1930s, American Proca made electric phonographs and combination phonographs and projectors, including items for the juvenile market.

American Publishing
American Publishing issued the game "Rambles" in 1881.

American Publishing Corp.
A postwar maker of games, this company issued such titles as "Ski Gammon," a 1962 game.

American Rice Food and Manufacturing Company
Makers of Cook's Flaked Rice and Cook's Malto Rice around the turn of the century, American Rice Food issued several promotional cloth toys and dolls. They include the "Cooks Teddy Bear," patented 1907, and two versions of "Miss Flaked Rice" in 1899 and 1901. The "Miss Malto-Rice" cloth doll probably dates from a similar time.

"American Skyline"
see *Elgo Plastics, Inc.* and *Halsam Products Co.*

"American" sleds
Both Hedlund Mfg. Co. and Metal Industries made sleds under the "American" name in the 1950s and '60s.

American Slate Works
This Slatington, Penn., company made blackboards in the late 1930s.

American Soldier Co.
Formed in 1898 by Charles W. Bieser in Brooklyn, N.Y., the American Soldier Co. also went under the business name of Eureka Mfg. Co., or Eureka Metal Co. The "Eureka" name was dropped in 1903.

Although the company produced Britains-like hollow cast 52mm soldiers, it apparently was most noted for its toy display trays. Bieser invented and patented a tray that would both protect and display the toy figures. He worked a deal with Britains that allowed him to use their soldiers in his trays, while Britains used his trays for their soldiers.

The company produced "Rough Riders" in 1904, and in the 1920s, "American Heroes and Young Americans" (Boy Scouts). After 1906, the figures were solid cast. The company ventured into celluloid toys in its target-shooting sets, which included birds and mammals made of the early plastic. The company faded away by the Depression. In 1930, its assets were purchased by Selchow and Richter.

American Stuffed Novelty Co.
Based on West 20th Street, New York City, this 1920s manufacturer made art and flapper dolls with silk and mohair wigs.

American Thermoplastics Products Corp.
This Union, N.J., firm made the "Atco" vinyl plastic jump ropes and "Swing-A-Ring" hoops of the 1950s and '60s.

American Tissue Mills
Based in Holyoke, Mass., American Tissue Mills produced prewar paper toys, novelties and decorations, especially related to Christmas. The "Perkins" trade name was adopted by the late 1930s for novelties including noisemakers, snapping mottoes, and hats.

American Tool Works
A Chicago, Ill., firm, American Tool Works made the "Sterling" air gun in 1890.

American Toy & Furniture Co., Inc.
During World War II, this firm combined product lines of companies including Home Foundry Mfg. Co., American Craft, and Rapaport Bros., although the latter reestablished itself separately again in the postwar years. The wartime line included craft sets, doll furniture, and dollhouses. Tool sets, wood-burning sets, and metal tapping sets were specialties of this Chicago company in the postwar years. It issued the "A.T.F." preschool toys and pounding board toys, sand boxes, and the "Toy Lawn-Mobile" of the 1950s and '60s. Some of its activity sets were character related, such as the "Superman" wood-burning set of 1979.

One of American Toy & Furniture Co.'s specialties was "The Bang-Out Bench" in the 1950s.

American Toy Airship Co. A prewar manufacturer of toy steam engines, games, electric motors, and toy dirigible balloons, American Toy Airship was based in Mansfield, Ohio.

American Toy & Mfg. Corp. Based in Abilene, Kan., American Toy & Mfg. Corp. produced prewar toy wheelbarrows and action toys.

American Toy & Novelty Mfg. Co. This prewar Philadelphia, Penn., company produced stuffed dolls and animal toys, using a variety of materials.

American Toy Co. From 1868 to 1972, the J. & E. Stevens Co. and George W. Brown Co. issued a combined catalog under the American Toy Co. name.

American Toy Co. American Toy Co. was a company founded in 1927 that briefly combined the production efforts of Kilgore Mfg. Co., Andes Foundry Co., and Federal Toy Co.

American Toy Corp. American Toy Corp. of Baltimore, Md., founded in the late 1930s, manufactured plush saddle horses, wagons, and Easter carts.

American Toy Products Wood toys including sailboats, pop-up peg benches, and wood and upholstered rocking chairs were specialties of this postwar Beverly, Mass., firm. The firm also made table tennis sets and the aluminum "Dollie-Baths" in the 1950s and '60s.

American Toy Works Located on Chatham Square, New York City, in the 1920s, American Toy Works issued "Surprise Packages—We Specialize in Them," which retailed at 25 and 50 cents. Although the company was issuing games as early as 1925, with such titles as "Flip It" and "Checkers & Avion," it released its most notable titles in the 1930s, including the "Walt Disney's Ski Jump Target Game." Other games in that decade included "An Exciting Motor Boat Race" in 1930; "The Lid's Off" in 1937; "Pinocchio Target Game" and "Snow White and the Seven Dwarfs" in 1938; and "Let's

Play Golf" in 1939. The company's "Library of Games" appeared in 1938.

During the '30s, when it was based in Long Island, N.Y., American Toy Works also made paint sets including the 1932 "Reg'lar Fellers" set. By the end of the decade, it listed among its products "Every Day Play Sets," embroidery outfits, crepe paper doll outfits, educational toy money, mosaic sets, "Knitting Dolly" spool sets, Santa Claus surprise packages, "Shadow Stencil Craft and Crayon," "A Million Funny Faces," bingo, and clay sets.

In 1940, the company issued the "Superman Action Game," as well as "Aero-Chute," "Let's Play Polo," and "Opportunity Hour." During wartime, the firm's "Atwo" line continued with craft and art sets, games, hammer and peg tables, wooden toys, and kindergarten toys.

American Toyland Creators A toy company active in Brooklyn, N.Y., in the 1910s, American Toyland Creators made mechanical toys, including a working submarine toy.

American Toys, Inc. American Toys of Baltimore, Md., produced prewar plush saddle horses, wagons, rabbit toys, and Easter carts.

"American Toys," late 1920s see *Andes Foundry Co., Kilgore Mfg. Co., Inc.*

American Toy Works Doing business from the New York City's Fifth Avenue Building, American Toy Works produced paint sets, embroidery outfits, crepe paper doll outfits, educational toys, toy money, and miscellaneous other prewar games and activity toys.

"American Trotter" see *velocipede.*

"American" velocipedes postwar see *Hettrick Mfg. Co.*

American Visual Aids This postwar Brooklyn, N.Y., manufacturer of blackboards also made checkerboards and magnetic boards.

A

American Wading Pool This Pittsburgh, Penn., firm issued wading pools in the 1920s, including the "Puddle Duck Pool."

"American West" In 1973, Mego issued the American West Series of 8-inch action figures. All of interest to action-figure and Western collectors, the series included "Buffalo Bill Cody," "Cochise," "Davy Crockett," "Sitting Bull," "Wild Bill Hickock," and "Wyatt Earp." The series also featured one horse, "Shadow," and the desirable "Dodge City" play set in vinyl. The figures appeared in both boxed and carded forms.

American Wunder Mfg. Co. Based in Rock Island, Ill., American Wunder produced prewar lumber building sets, toy ironing boards, and wood airplanes and boats. By the end of the 1930s, it appeared to have narrowed its focus to its "Wunder Lumber" construction sets.

"America's Premier Line," stuffed animals see *Knickerbocker Toy Co.*

Amerline One of many companies in the '50s and '60s specializing in plastic toys, Amerline manufactured toy telephones, swimming animals, plastic coin changers, and boats. It was located in Chicago.

Ames Bag & Packing Corp. Based in Selma, Ala., Ames made postwar cotton novelty toys.

Ames Products Co. This Holyoke, Mass., firm made postwar children's laundry sets and related toys.

"Amico" see *Ammidon & Co.*

The Amloid Co. The Amloid Co. was established in the late 1930s in Lodi, N.J., to make celluloid infants' toys. As Amloid Co., it manufactured plastic toys in the 1950s and '60s at its new location in Rochelle Park, N.J.

Ammidon & Co. Founded in 1886, Ammidon made a specialty of its "Amico" Christmas stockings and novelties. Retailing in the 10 cent to $1 range by the 1920s, the stockings were "filled with toys of real play value." In the 1930s, in addition to Stockings, Ammidon also manufactured "tin putty and bean blowers," among other playthings.

"Amos an' Andy" Amos and Andy were the creations of Freeman Gosden and Charles Correll. After creating the characters "Sam" and "Henry" for Chicago station WGN in the '20s, they created Amos and Andy for new the network NBC. The show first aired on Aug. 19, 1929. The sponsor, Pepsodent, issued the majority of known "Amos and Andy" premiums in the early years of the show's popularity. The most valuable are the 1931 jigsaw puzzle and the cardboard stand-up figures, issued in two sizes in 1930 and 1931. In the '30s Louis Marx & Co. also issued tin wind-up figures, as well as the tin wind-up "Amos an' Andy Fresh Air Taxi Cab."

"Amsco" see *American Metal Specialties Corp.*

Amsdan & Co. An early manufacturer, Amsdan & Co. released the "Three Merry Men" game in 1865.

Amtac Industries The "Skeeter" scooter assembly kit of the Boomer years was made by this Chicago, Ill., firm.

anagram An anagram is a sort of word game, played by rearranging the letters of a word or phrase to form another one. "Mage" is an anagram for "game," for instance. As a pastime, it was invented by a Salem, Mass., school teacher around 1850. At least one early game company, the Peter G. Thompson Co., formally issued an "Anagrams" game, in 1885. Prewar manufacturers of the game included Milton Bradley Co., the Embossing Co., the Fox Toy Co., Parker Bros., the A.I. Root Co., Selchow & Righter Co., and Transogram Co.

Anchor Buggy & Carriage Co. This Cincinnati, Ohio, firm made scale-model hobby kits of horse-drawn vehicles, as well as assembled models, in the 1950s and '60s.

"Anchor Brand," late 1930s see *North & Judd Mfg. Co.*

Anchor Mfg. Co. Based in Springfield, Mo., Anchor Mfg. Co. made "Amco" wooden toys, rocking horses, stick horses, wheelbarrows, table and chair sets, and pull toys, in the late 1930s.

Anchor Post Fence Co. Based in Baltimore, Md., Anchor Post Fence made merry-go-rounds and metal sand boxes in the mid-1930s.

"Anchor Stone Building Sets" see *Richter, A.C. Gilbert, Block House., Inc.*

Anchor Toy Corp. Based in New York's Fifth Avenue Building, New York City, Anchor Toy Corp. issued the prewar "Roleasy" wooden toys in the mid-1930s. It also advertised hand-decorated Easter toys, pull toys, toy furniture, all of wood, and the "famous" "Tak-A-Peg." Interestingly, the company shared a president, Charles S. Raizen, with Transogram Co.

"Anco" see *Arrow Novelty Co.*

Andersen's Fairy Tales The famous tales of Hans Christian Andersen were first put into book form in 1835.

Anderson Mfg. Co. This Norway, Mich., firm made parlor games and baseball games in the late 1930s.

Anderson Rubber Co. A producer of rubber toy balloons, novelties, and leather sports equipment, Anderson Rubber Co. was based in Akron, Ohio, in the 1930s to the '60s.

Anderson Steam Vulcanizer Co. Based in Indianapolis, Ind., this manufacturer issued the prewar games "Spin-A-Rim" and "Parachute."

Andes Foundry Co. Eugene Andes founded this foundry in Lancaster, Penn., in 1919. The company first made cast-iron parts and paper caps for Kilgore Mfg. Co., with whom, along with Feder Mfg. Co., it merged in 1927, becoming a part of the "American Toys" line before being dissolved a few years later. Andes Foundry toys included the "Arctic" ice cream wagon, toy airplanes, and toy stake and dump trucks.

"Andover" see *F.W. Woolnough Corp.*

Herbert Andrews, A manufacturer of prewar wooden toys, Herbert Andrews made doll furniture, toy windmills, and other painted wooden toys.

O.B. Andrews Co. Based in Chattanooga, Tenn., O.B. Andrews received an early license through Kay Kamen to produce Disney playhouses. The line included the "Mickey Mouse Playhouse," nearly 4 feet high, and the "Mickey Mouse Miniature Playhouse," at doll size. Andrews also introduced the boxed play set "Uncle Remus and His Critters," which contained stories by Joel Chandler Harris, a cardboard cabin, and cardboard "Uncle Remus" characters, in 1934. The firm's games included "Min-U-Var," a checkers game played with military ships and airplanes, and "Mid-Way Ring-Over," a ring-toss game with clown targets in a miniature booth.

"The Mickey Mouse Playhouse" was an early licensed product by O.B. Andrews Co.

"Andy Gard" see *General Molds & Plastics Corp.*

"Andy Gump" see *"The Gumps."*

"Andy Panda" This Walter Lantz character, while little known today, was popular enough in its time to inspire several toys and banks, including the "Andy Panda Tin Book Bank," which was a tin-litho bank, 5 inches tall, in the shape of a book. A composition bank also exists. Andy Panda first appeared in *Crackajack Funnies* in 1941.

"Angel" vinyl dolls see *M.&S. Doll Co.*

Angelus Marshmallows At one time, Angelus Marshmallows were the second most famous product of the Cracker Jack Company. The figure of Angelus herself, a young girl never seen without a box of marshmallows, provided an ideal companion figure to Sailor Jack. The two appeared

A

together on at least one toy, the colorful and valuable "Two Toppers" wood and metal top, from the 1930s. The Angelus logo also appeared on promotional toys including a tin horse-drawn wagon and the "Jack, Jane and Jerry" cutout paper dolls. A variety of toy-size books were also issued. In the '20s, a series of storybooks appeared with such titles as "In Candy Land" and "Play Time," while in the '30s the "Stories of the Presidents" series appeared.

Angelus Press Based in Los Angeles, Angelus published the prewar "Words" card game.

Anglo American Apparently a small company, Anglo American released the game "The Cake Walk" in the 1900s.

animal-drawn toy vehicles Collectors and decorators interested in the truly antique feel a natural attraction for horse-drawn vehicles, which were made in toy versions by such companies as Arcade Mfg. Co., Bliss, Carpenter Mfg. Co., James Fallows, George Brown, Gibbs Mfg. Co., Harris, Hubley Mfg. Co., the Ives Corporation, Kenton Hardware, Pratt & Letchworth, and Wilkins. The majority of the early toys were made of cast iron or tin.

Animal Kingdom Toy Co. Best on West 21st Street, New York City, this firm specialized in stuffed fur and plush animals in the Boomer years.

animal toys see *stuffed toy animals.*

Animal Mfg. Corp. This Carbondale, Ill., company produced the mid-1930s "Play Pony."

"Animaland" figures see *Multiple Products Corp.*

Animate Toy Co. This New York City firm was established in the toy business as early as 1915, when it released its game, "Bugville Games." The company is best known as a manufacturer of tin wind-ups, with the most famous being its climbing tractors, starting with the "Baby Tractor" patented in 1916. It moved by the '30s to East Orange, N.J. Animate's 1930s "lifelike moving toys" included toy versions of insects and small mammals. It also made toy road building and logging sets.

"Animate" toys see *Woodhaven Metal Stamping Co.*

Anita Novelty Co., see *European Doll Mfg. Co.*

Ankerum Mfg. Co. Ankerum, founded in the late 1930s in Philadelphia, Penn., made train track ballast, as well as "green grass cloth Christmas mats."

"Ann Drock" juvenile kitchen sets 1930s, see *The Washburn Co.*

Annalee Mobilitee Dolls, Inc. Annalee Davis Thorndike sold her first dolls through the New Hampshire League of Arts and Crafts in the 1930s. She started Annalee Mobilitee Dolls Inc. in 1954, after the failure of the family chicken farm. The dolls incorporated a wire armature designed by her husband, Charles "Chip" Thorndike. The majority of the early dolls were skiers, which were used as tourist curio dolls. All Annalee dolls are handmade. Labels were not used until the 1950s. From 1935 to 1959, all had yarn hair. Synthetic hair was increasingly used subsequently.

E.M. Annelots Co. This Pelham, N.Y., firm manufactured stuffed animals before the war.

"Annette" dolls prewar see *Perfect Novelties Mfg. Co.*

"Annette" toys prewar see *Fulton Specialty Co.*

"Annette Funicello" This star of "The Mickey Mouse Club" inspired a wealth of paper toys and associational items, including paper dolls and coloring books in the 1950s and '60s by Whitman Publishing Co. Parker Bros. also issued the 1958 game, "Annette's Secret Passage."

"Annie" see *"Little Orphan Annie."*

"Annie Oakley" Annie Oakley entered Western folklore through her talents with the gun, and subsequently entered pop culture through the heady Boomer phenomenon of television. "Annie Oakley" items included books by Whitman Publishing Co., cowgirl suits by Herman Iskin & Co., games by Milton Bradley Co., squeeze toys by Alan-Jay Plastics, and "3-D" color film cards by Tru-Vue Co. The popular heroine also figured in play sets by Louis Marx & Co., plastic figures by Hartland Plastics, and a 1955 Aladdin lunch box. The official properties were licensed by Mitchell J. Hamilburg Agency.

"Annie Roonie" "Annie Roonie" dolls were issued in the 1930s by George Borgfeldt Corp. Annie Roonie figures were issued in wood, composition and bisque. The composition figure, 4 inches tall, was issued in the 1940s.

Annin & Co. New York City-based Annin & Co. made rag dolls in the 1920s, including a large doll made to commemorate the Sesquicentennial. Apparently the same company, based on New York's Fifth Avenue, specialized in flags, banners, and decorations in the Boomer years.

ant houses The ant house toys of the 1950s and '60s were wonders of comic book pages. The "Uncle Milton's Ant Farm" was a product of E. Joseph Cossman & Co., while the "Ant Paradise" ant house was made by Butterfly Art Jewelry.

C.&R. Anthony, Inc. "Barber's Big league Baseball" game of the 1950s and '60s was published by this Fourth Avenue, New York City, firm.

Anti-Monopoly, Inc. This early-1970s company was apparently dedicated to the single game, naturally called "Anti-Monopoly."

antimony A pliable metal used for small toys, which were usually less than an inch in length. Many of these were small "antique" cars or horse-drawn vehicles, made in postwar Japan. Due to the brittleness of the material, these were usually packaged in small cardboard boxes with simple labels. The modest quality of the detail and modeling tends to be reflected in modest collector values.

Antioch Bookplate Co. This Yellow Springs, Ohio, publisher issued postwar children's card games.

Aoshin A Tokyo-based company, Aoshin produced tinplate toys in the '50s and '60s, including several notable space toys. The company also produced small die-cast cars, presumably to compete with Matchbox. More crude than the British-manufactured toys, the car, antique automobile, and military truck series have limited collector appeal. The company made some solid-cast 30mm metal soldiers in the '50s and early '60s. As was the case with the vehicle toys, the figures were apparently not original to the company. Toys marked with "ASC" or "AHI" markings were made by Aoshin.

Apex Mfg. Co. Based in Norristown, Penn., this company made the "Apex" darts of the 1920s. The company survived the Great Depression to issue darts and related games through the prewar years. By the late 1930s, the company was issuing dart baseball, spin-arrow games, dart wheels, and bull's-eye dart targets. In the Boomer years, Apex's line of dart games grew to include spin-arrow games and dart golf.

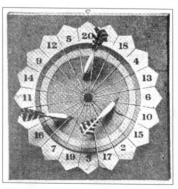

"Apex Darts Game" of the 1920s.

Apex Mfg. Co. Apex Mfg. Co. of San Francisco, Calif., manufactured the "Funny Face" toy of the mid-1930s.

Apex Tire & Rubber Co. This Pawtucket, R.I., company made multicolored rubber sand pails, shovels, rakes, and boats in the Boomer years.

"Apollo," trademark prewar see *Delta Electric Co.*

A

Apollo Knitting Co. Based in Philadelphia, Penn., Apollo Knitting specialized in prewar dolls' "mercerized" rayon silk socks and stockings.

Apollometal Artcraft Based on Broadway, New York City, Apollometal Artcraft produced a prewar metal construction set, which included tools, instructions, and sheet metal.

Richard Appel's Jo King Corp. Based on Spring Street, New York City, this Boomer-era firm made magic and joke novelties, and puzzles.

Applause Originally the gift division of Knickerbocker, Applause has specialized in licensed items that have largely been marketed through Hallmark. Knickerbocker was purchased in 1983 by Hasbro. Applause is known for its PVC "California Raisin" figures and the "Raggedy Ann and Andy" dolls, which have borne the Applause label since 1981.

Apon Novelty Co. Based in Philadelphia, Penn., Apon issued "Snow White & Seven Dwarfs" Halloween masks in the late 1930s.

Appleton Toy & Furniture Co. The "Appleton Line" of the 1920s included chairs, rockers, table sets, and shooflies, adding bassinets and cribs late in the decade. One of its biggest sellers at the end of the decade was the "Cal's Colt" exerciser, consisting of a wood base supporting a flexible metal strip, on the top of which a riding-horse seat was affixed, on which the child rode. "Cal's Colt" was patented in 1928.

Despite its popularity, or perhaps because of it, it was apparently sold to Kiddie Gym, which issued the toy after the Great Depression. Based in Appleton, Wis., this manufacturer produced children's table sets, shooflies, doll high chairs, "Gee Gee" horses, nursery chairs, and highchairs through the prewar years. In the Boomer years, as Appleton Juvenile Furniture Co., a division of Playskool Mfg. Co., its line included musical rockers, hammer-nail and peg desks, and doll furniture.

The Appleton Toy and Furniture Co. made toy chairs, rockers table sets and bassinets.

Applicator Enterprises, Inc. The "Poly-Foam" tub toys of the 1950s and '60s were made by this Inwood, Long Island, N.Y., company.

"Aquaman" A DC Comics superhero who first appeared in 1941, Aquaman appeared in the "Captain Action" series in two versions, in 1966 and '67, in the "Official World's Greatest Super Heroes" series from Mego Corp. in the '70s, and the Kenner Products Co. "Super Powers" series, 1984-86.

"Aquamite" see *Wen-Mac Corp.*

Arandell Products Co. Jump ropes and lariats were among the specialties of this Boomer-era Philadelphia, Penn., firm.

Arbuckle Brothers Coffee Best known among collectors for their trade cards, this venerable coffee company offered two pairs of cloth dolls in 1931. One pair depicted "Jack" and "Jill," and the other, "Mary" with her lamb and "Tom the Piper's Son."

Arbur Products A small English manufacturer operating in the late 1940s to early '50s, Arbur produced die-cast toy vehicles, usually in 1:50 scale, derivative of Dinky models.

Arby's The world exploded with toys in the 1980s, when fast-food restaurants wholeheartedly embraced the idea of premium toys to go with their child-sized meals. Arby's released "Little Miss" and "Mr. Men" figures early in the decade, and upped the ante at the end of the decade with several series of "Looney Toons" figures. In the '90s the restaurant issued several series of distinctive "Babar" toys.

Arcade Mfg. Co. Arcade Manufacturing Co. of Freeport, Ill., made cast-iron toys from the late 1800s into the early 1940s. Its first toys included miniature coffee mills and presumably penny toys, made as early as 1884. It manufactured toys of miscellaneous materials during World War II, and closed in 1946.

As a foundry under the "Arcade" name, the company had operated since 1885, under founders E.H. and Charles Morgan. Previously, from 1868 to 1885, it had been known as Novelty Iron Works. Arcade's earliest toys included novelties, small stoves, banks, and floor trains. By the 1910, Arcade was producing horse-drawn vehicles, which were a major part of its toy line into the '30s. Notable is the "Tom Mix Big Six Circus Wagon," partly of wood, of 1936. In 1920, it adopted the trade slogan, "They Look Real."

In 1922, the company made the move that would ensure the fame of its toy-making name. The toy proved popular and went through several versions. It introduced a Yellow Cab toy through an exclusive, mutually profitable arrangement with the Yellow Cab Company. Arcade also made Austins, Buicks, Chevrolets, and Fords, as well as Allis-Chalmers, Avery, Fordson, McCormick-Deering, and Oliver farm equipment.

The slogan "They Look Real" was used on the "Arcade Cast Iron Toys" line of the 1920s, when the Freeport, Ill., manufacturer was making toy bedroom, bathroom, kitchen, dining room, living room, and laundry sets; McCormick-Deering Thresher and other International Harvester implements; Mack fire and dump trucks; Hotpoint stoves; the "Yellow Cab" and other "Yellow" truck and coach miniatures; and household hardware including coffee mills and mop sticks.

Among the best-selling items for the company in the years before the Great Depression were the Ford Weaver Wrecker, Ford Dump Truck, Ford Coupe with rumble seat, Ford Tudor Sedan, Show Boat, Mack Dump Truck, McCormick-Deering Spreader, Wagon and Logs, McCormick-Deering Wagon, Fordson Tractor and Plow, Fordson

Tractor and Trailer, jack sets, lawn mowers, windmills, bowling alley game, and its miniature room sets.

Besides the Yellow Cab, its most famous toy is the Greyhound Lines "A Century of Progress" bus, which it made in several versions in 1933 in conjunction with the Chicago Worlds Fair of that year. The exclusive arrangement to produce the bus replicas saved the company from near-bankruptcy in the aftermath of the Great Depression. The company also made souvenir toys for the Great Lakes Exposition of 1936 and the New York Worlds Fair of 1939.

In the 1930s, the company was advertising a wide variety of cast-iron and wood toys, including "Pullman Railplanes, Chevrolet, DeSoto, Plymouth and Ford cars and truck models. Doll house furniture, including kitchen sets, bathroom sets, stoves, refrigerators and radio banks, jackstones and jack sets, bowling alleys, marble, baseball and shooting games, coin banks, toy lawn mowers, and garden sets." Its line included more than 300 toy items. In the late 1930s it introduced "Aracade Model Makers," which were issued with and without motors, and woodworking equipment.

Arcade is considered among the most important manufacturers of cast-iron toys, having produced more than 250 different models.

Arcade Mfg. Co. specialized in cast-iron toys like this truck from 1934.

Arcadia Doll Co., Inc. This Bronx, N.Y., firm made Boomer-era plastic, rubber-skin, vinyl, and baby dolls.

Arcadia Hosiery Co. Based in Lansdale, Pa., this prewar company made doll stockings and tubings.

"Arcadian" see *Binney & Smith.*

A

Archer Plastics, Inc. Archer, a subsidiary of Almor Plastics, is one of the important names in vintage space toys, and perhaps the most important manufacturer of hard-plastic space toys. It gained quick renown in 1953 with its 95mm "Space People," which may have been the first such toys made. The figures were issued in bronze, green, silver, and maroon-purple metallic colors. The company reputedly sold 10 million in the first year of production. These figures have recently been reproduced.

Archer also made notable futuristic vehicles in hard plastic, some scaled to match the space people, and SF-theme play sets. Archer produced some plastic "Action Soldiers" and a "Junior Corral Set" of western figures, the latter apparently based upon "Beton" toys. The company also ventured into semi-educational toys with its "Child Guidance Toys," and made puzzles and novelties. It was based in the Bronx, N.Y., in the 1950s and '60s.

Archer Toy Co. Archer Toy Company made games in the 1930s, including a 1930 "Air Mail" game.

"Arco" see *Auburn Rubber Co.*

Arco Tubular Skate Corp. Established in the late 1930s in Endicott, N.Y., Arco made roller and ice skates. The firm became Arco Skates in the Boomer years, moving production to Marathon, N.Y. It produced ice skates, double runner ice skates, sled ice skates, ice skate and shoe outfits, and roller skates.

Arcy Toy Mfg. Co. Arcy, a manufacturer of Mama dolls in the 1920s, was based on Wooster Street, New York City, moving to Broadway in the '30s. By the late 1930s it changed its name to Arcy Doll & Toy Co., Inc.

The Ardee Co. This Brooklyn, N.Y., firm made the "Dollie Dainties" doll clothing of the Boomer years.

Ardee Plastics Co., Inc. Based in Long Island City, N.Y., this company produced simple plastic toys including floor train sets with molded-in, stationary wheels, in the 1950s.

Arenstein, Seymour and Effrem

The Arenstein brothers, Seymour and Effrem, born 1916 and 1920, respectively, founded Lido Toy Co. in October 1947, with the purchase of Elite Toy Co., which had also used the Lido name. In the '40s, before his involvement with Lido, Seymour Arenstein had worked for his uncle William Shaland, then the country's largest importer of toys. Nearly a decade after the demise of Lido, he returned to toy-making in 1973, forming the company Joy Toy.

Argo Industries Corp. Argo specialized in "real" food-mix sets, miniature autos, juvenile furniture, water bicycles, and water toys from the 1950s into the '60s. It was located in Woodside, Long Island, N.Y. Its "Action Fleet" was a set of small lithographed steel cars in a variety of styles but in a Hudson-like shape, first issued in the earlier 1950s. Many of Argo's toys were made of plastic.

The "Junior Chef Poppity Popper" was just one of Argo Industries' "real food" toys.

"Arista" see *Rosebud Art Co.*

Aristo-Craft Distinctive Miniatures

Aristo-Craft, based in Newark, N.J., made "H.O." scale trains, kits, and accessories; wood ship models; and battery motors in the 1950s and '60s. The company was a division of Polk's Model Craft Hobbies.

"Arist-O-Kratt" harmonicas see *William Kratt Co.*

"Aristocrat" stuffed toys see *Master Industries.*

ark see *Noah's ark.*

A

Ark Toy Makers A Toledo, Ohio, company, Ark Toy produced prewar hardwood building block sets, which it issued in bags, boxes, and wagons, in both plain and printed forms. It moved its offices to the Fifth Avenue Building in New York City, by the late 1930s.

"Arkitoy Play Lumber" see *G.B. Lewis Co.*

W.H. Arkley Established in Street Johnsbury, Vt., in the late 1930s, W.H. Arkley made wooden construction kits for toy trains, steam shovels, and trucks.

Arlane Mfg. Co. Magic sets, disguise kits, premium novelties, tricks, jokes, and rubber masks were specialties of this Boomer-era Philadelphia, Penn., company.

Arlington Hat Co., Inc. This postwar Broadway, New York City, firm made Western felt and straw hats, and novelty hats, using the "Arlin" trade name.

Arlington Paint & Varnish Co. This Wooster, Ohio, company made paint sets in the late 1930s.

armature 1. Toy soldier collectors, or even military action-figure collectors, may use this word in its older sense, as referring to arms and armor. Among doll collectors in general, the term usually refers to the internal skeleton or structural support in a doll, usually a cloth doll. This sense of the word probably descends from its architectural use, as when it describes the structural iron or steel skeleton within a building.

2. The rotating part of an electric motor, as in the motors of electric trains.

Armor Industries, Inc. The "Slik-Toy" farm toys, cars and trucks of the 1950s and '60s were made by this Lansing, Iowa, firm.

"Armstrong" bicycle, see *Chain Bike Corp.*

"Armstrong of the S.B.I." see *Jack Armstrong.*

Arnart Imports In the '60s, Arnart Imports sold a series of "Wizard of Oz" banks, now of high interest to Oz collectors.

Arney Amusement Devices A prewar company based in Green Bay, Wis., Arney produced children's vehicles, playground devices, circus toys, and indoor "Pocket Carom."

"Arnold" educational toys see *Chaspec Mfg. Co.*

Arnold Printworks Based in North Adams, Mass., Arnold Printworks offered prints and dress goods in the late 19th and early 20th centuries. The company also sold "doll sheets," which featured a wide variety of cut-and-sew dolls based on the designs of Charity and Celia Smith, including a character named "Arnold Cat."

Arnold Printworks offered a set of Palmer Cox "Brownies" in 1882. The set of twelve included "Brownies" representing several nationalities and occupations, including the "Dude," the Canadian, "John Bull," the policeman, and "Uncle Sam." The fabric company also issued sheets for character dolls "Pickaninny," later known as "Blossom," "Little Red Ridinghood," "Pitti Sing," and the "Our Little Soldier Boys" series. The 15-inch "Columbian Sailor" appeared the next year, in conjunction with the Columbian Exposition. In 1912, the company issued a "Gibson Girl" doll based on Edward Gibson's illustrations. Arnold made several notable contributions to the world of advertising dolls, starting in 1905 with "Sunny Jim," for Force cereal. It issued "Aunt Jemima Pancake Flour" dolls in 1910 and 1940, and "Rastus the Cream of Wheat Chef" in 1921 and later years. "Buster Brown" and his dog "Tige" were also issued.

Arnold, Schwinn & Co. Based on N. Kildare Avenue, Chicago, this prewar company produced bicycles. In the postwar years it employed the "Schwinn-built" slogan.

Arranbee Doll Co. Established on Broadway, New York City, in the 1920s, Arranbee rose to prominence in the years before the Great Depression. By the late 1930s, it moved offices to the New YorkCity's Fifth Avenue Building. In the postwar years, as a division of Vogue Dolls, Arranbee made doll clothing, trunks and suitcases, and the "Littlest Angel," "Sweet Pea," "Angel Face," and "Nancy" doll lines.

A

Arranjay Wig Co. This postwar West 20th Street, New York City, manufacturer of doll and costume wigs included Santa wig and beard sets in its line. It was a division of Meyer Jacoby & Son.

Arrco Playing Card Co. Chicago-based Arrco began issuing board and cloth games in the late 1930s. The company continued producing games into the Boomer years, with 1950s titles including "Go Go Go," "Skeeter," and "Trail Drive."

"Arrow" coaster wagon prewar see *Lullabye Furniture Co.*

Arrow Craft Co. Based in Detroit, Mich., Arrow Craft made archery sets in the late 1930s.

Arrow Fur Co., Inc. Fur and plush stuffed toys were the specialty of this West 24th Street, New York City, firm, from the late 1930s through the Boomer years.

Arrow Leather Goods Mfg. Co. This Chicago firm made postwar leather handicraft kits.

Arrow Mfg. Co. Based in Cleveland, Ohio, in the mid-1930s, this company produced heavy gauge steel toys, including trucks, cars, and "grab buckets," as well as some games and "Toyville" florist greenhouses.

Arrow Novelty Co. A producer of holster and pistol sets and Indian-design silver jewelry, Arrow Novelty Co., based on West 14th Street, New York City, also produced the original prewar "Skookum" Indian dolls and "burnt leather novelties."

"Arrow" pistol prewar see *The Elastic Tip Co.*

"Arrow" roller skates prewar see *Hustler Corp.*

Arrow Rubber & Plastics Corp. Vinyl toys were the specialty of this East Paterson, N.J., firm in the 1950s and '60s.

Arrow Sales Co., Inc. Arrow was a manufacturer of gun and holster sets in the Boomer years. It was based in Boston, Mass.

Arrow Specialty Co. Based in Norwalk, Conn., Arrow Specialty produced prewar celluloid novelties and table tennis balls. By the late 1930s it was specializing in table tennis and badminton equipment.

The Art Award Co., Inc. This Brooklyn, N.Y., firm made numbered oil paint sets, pencil sets, and mosaic craft sets in the Boomer years.

The Art Crayon Co. A prewar producer of wax crayons and water coloring accessories, Art Crayon was based in Brooklyn, N.Y. It moved offices to New York's Fifth Avenue Building in the postwar years, and added chalk crayons and modeling clay to its line.

Art Deco As a movement in design, Art Deco influenced nearly every aspect of daily life in this and other countries. Even children grew up as Art Deco children, with teethers and rattles reflecting the stylized, geometrical forms favored by the moment, and with toys up through the early '50s reflecting some of the movement's thoughts about streamlining and geometric simplifying of design elements. That the movement had this kind of influence would have been unsurprising to its founders, since they advocated the philosophy of bringing art into the everyday.

Art Doll Accessories Corp. Established on Broadway, New York City, in the late 1930s, Art Doll Accessories made doll shoes, stockings, rubber pants, and knitted novelties.

Art Fabric Mills Art Fabric Mills, based in New Haven, Conn., began its doll-making days with the cloth, "30-inch Life Sized Doll" in 1900. Despite its name, the doll was available in sizes as small as 6 inches tall. Other early cloth dolls include a "Punch and Judy" set and the advertising figure "Miss Flaked Rice" for Cook's Flaked Rice. In 1903, the company made cloth dolls of the Carl Schultze character "Foxy Grampa," in 11- and 20-inch sizes. Other early dolls included "Uncle Billy" and the *New York Herald's* "Buster Brown." Later cloth dolls include a "Dolly Dingle" doll and such characters as "Merrie Marie," "Belly Good Cook," and the "Newly Wed Kid."

A

The Art Metal Works The "Ronson Toys" of the 1920s was made by this Newark, N.J., firm. Items included a machine gun, revolver, "Talk-O-Phone," "Pussy Cat," "Santa Claus," "Archie," "Magic Pinwheel," "Magic Sparkler," repeater, rifle, "Firefly," and "Starlight."

Art Model Based in Pesaro, Italy, Art Model produces licensed 1:43 scale versions of Ferraris.

Art Neckwear Co. This Philadelphia, Penn., company issued Edgar Bergen character-related neckwear in the late 1930s.

Art Nouveau Although this artistic movement probably had little impact on the world of toys, it did greatly influence the design of related childhood items, especially the more fancy rattles and teethers of ivory and silver made in the late 1800s. For probably much longer than in other areas of our cultural life, the Art Nouveau movement heavily influenced children's book illustrations.

Art Novelty Dolls' Shoes Co. As its name indicates, this prewar company, based on Greene Street, New York City, made doll shoes.

Artascope A 1920s optical toy made with pressed steel and mirrors.

"Artco" see *Standard Crayon Mfg. Co.*

"Artcraft" cards see *The Saalfield Publishing Co.*

"Artcraft" loom see *Structo Mfg. Co.*

Artex Mfg. Co. A Boomer-era manufacturer of washable cloth books, Artex was located in Kansas City, Mo.

"Arthur Godfrey" ukeleles see *Emenee Industries.*

articulated In farm toys, "articulated" designates a piece of machinery designed to bend in the middle for the purpose of steering.

articulated train A streamlined toy train having cars that are connected by vestibules or vestibule-like attachments, with the trucks being located under the couplers, instead of beneath the cars.

artificial flowers While not generally considered a toy item, prewar artificial plants and flowers were often made by companies associated with the toy trade.

artificial snow The manufacturing industry surrounding the Christmas holiday grew to such a point that the production of artificial snow was an important source of revenue for a number of companies between the Great Depression and World War II. Prewar manufacturers, all having ties to the toy industry, included the Hy-Sil Mfg. Co., Metal Goods Corp., National Tinsel Mfg. Co., the Ohio Art Co., and Z-Ro-Art Snow Co. It was sometimes made of asbestos, by companies such as Douglas Mfg. Co. of Louisville, Ky.

"Artista" see *Binney & Smith.*

"Artistamp" see *Fulton Specialty Co.*

Artistic Doll Corp. Based on Greene Street, New York City, this company manufactured composition dolls and doll heads, arms, and legs from the post-Great Depression years through the Boomer years. In the 1950s and '60s it produced plastic and vinyl dolls, doll parts, and novelties.

Artistic Toy Co. Established in Philadelphia, Penn., in the late 1930s, Artistic Toy issued soft toys, dolls, and novelties through the Boomer years.

Arts & Crafts Studio Based on West 35th Street, New York City, this prewar company specialized in "soft," or stuffed, dolls and animals. In the late 1930s, Arts & Crafts Studio boasted of having an "exclusive line."

Artwood Toy Manufacturing Co. This 1930s company made wooden construction toys, including the "Building Boats with Blocks" kit of mid-decade, a building-block set. Based on West 22nd Street, New York City, it also made infant beaded dolls and wooden novelty games. By the late 1930s, Artwood was also issuing soldier sets, pastry sets, quoits, educational games, boat sets, bubble pipes, jump ropes, spools, ten pins, and wagons.

A

Asahi Toy Co. A toy and novelty company, Asahi was founded in 1950 in Tokyo. It began with high-quality tinplate toys, and expanded in 1960 into the 1:43 scale die-cast market with the "Model Pet" line of toy cars based largely upon Japanese automobiles. These toy cars were apparently marketed in Great Britain but not the U.S.

Asakusa Toy Ltd. This tinplate toy company was founded in 1950 in Tokyo. The mark "A1" appears on Asakusa toys.

Asbury Mills Infants' dolls and toys were postwar specialties of this Broadway, New York City, firm.

Ashland Rubber Products Co. This Ashland, Ohio, firm was a postwar balloon manufacturer.

Ashton Models A New England company, Ashton Models produced hand-built models of firefighting equipment in 1:43 scale.

"Ask the Boy Who Owns One" 1920s slogan, see *Keystone Mfg. Co.*

Associated Hobby Mfrs., Inc. This Meadowbrook, Penn., company made plastic scale models of autos, boats, and wild game in the 1950s and '60s.

Associated Mfrs. Co. Based in San Francisco, this company produced Christmas ornaments and lights in the mid-1930s. It also imported toys.

Associated Syndicate A Des Moines, Iowa, firm, Associated Syndicate was established in the late 1930s with a specialty in producing wooden tap-dancing dolls with the names "Dancin-Dan," "Dancin-Dina," "Dancin-Dan, Jr.," and "Dizzy." The company also made "Checkerola," a Chinese peg game, the "Takeoff" airplane game, and the "static trick" toy "Go-Stik."

associations and organizations, toy industry Various organizations formed as the toy industry matured in the prewar years. They included Toy Manufacturers of the U.S.A., Inc., American Toy Managers' Association, Associated Doll Manufacturers of New York, Inc., Cycle Traces of America, Inc., Stuffed Toy Manufacturers Association, The Toy Knights, and Toy Wholesalers Division of the Wholesale Stationers of the U.S.A., Inc. All except Cycle Trades of America and the Toy Wholesalers Division maintained offices in New York City's Fifth Avenue Building. Contrary to the impression its name might give, Associated Toy & Doll Factories, based on Fifth Avenue in the late 1930s, were manufacturers representatives, not a manufacturing association.

Astor Doll & Toy Mfg. Corp. This Brooklyn, N.Y., firm made vinyl, latex, and plastic dolls, including walking dolls, in the Boomer years. It also made stuffed plush animals and novelties.

Astra Pharos A British company, Astra Pharos produced realistic military toys in the early '40s.

"Astro Modelers" see *American Play Co.*

Astrolite A 1960s construction toy maker, Astrolite provided the materials for building a futuristic city, including working lights.

Asturias A San Francisco-based toy soldier company in business in the '40s, Asturias may have sold toys made in Mexico.

"At Play Toys" see the *Rushton Co.*

"At-Play Toys" see *Atlanta Playthings Co.*

"Atco," see *American Thermoplastics Products Corp.*

Athearn This Los Angeles firm made scale model railroad equipment in the postwar years.

"Athlete" bicycles late 1930s, see *D.P. Harris Hardware & Mfg. Co.*

The Athol Comb Co. Children's "Athoware" dresser sets, plastic banks and novelties, doll accessories, and boy's military brush sets were specialties of this Fifth Avenue, New York City, firm in the 1950s and '60s.

Atlanta Novelty Mfg. Corp. Dolls and toys were postwar specialties of this Park Avenue, New York City, firm.

Atlanta Playthings Co. Based in Atlanta, Ga., this company made stuffed dolls, and mohair and plush toy animals from the 1930s through the Boomer years. The firm was affiliated with the Rushton Co.

Atlantic Chair Co. Based in Gardner, Mass., this company made prewar children's chairs and rockers.

Atlantic Toy Mfg. Co., Inc. Based on Wooster Street, New York City, Atlantic made mama and baby dolls in the 1920s and earlier '30s.

"Atlas" The "Atlas" air rifle was first made in 1890, in Ilion, N.Y., by a company of the same name. Atlas also made the "Victory" of 1899, commemorating Dewey's victory at Manila Bay.

"Atlas" crayon see *Standard Crayon Mfg. Co.*

Atlas Doll & Toy Co. Based in Baltimore, Md., Atlas made moving-eye mama dolls in the 1920s. It manufactured coaster wagons in the mid-1930s.

Atlas Toy Mfg. Corp. Based on West 17th Street, New York City, Atlas made stuffed toy animals, including the characters "Tubby Dog," the "Ping Pong" Pekinese, and "Trixie Cat" in the 1920s. The firm continued manufacturing through the prewar years, moving to West 21st Street after the war.

"Atlasphere" inflatable globe see *Alvimar Mfg. Co.*

Atkins & Co. Active in the 1910s and '20s, the first games produced by Atkins & Co. may have been the "Atkins Real Baseball" and "Cortella," both of 1915.

"Atomee" water gun see *Park Plastics Co.*

Atomic Industries, Inc. This Milwaukee, Wis., firm made the "Dynamic" gun, a "trigger-action repeating bubble gun," of the early 1960s.

"Atomic Machine Gun" see *Gladen Enterprises.*

"Atomic Mobile Unit" see *Ideal Novelty & Toy Co.*

"Atomic Pistol" The "Atomic Pistol" introduced by Daisy Mfg. Co. in 1948 was made from the prewar tooling and dies for the "Buck Rogers Disintegrator" pistol by the same company.

Attwell, Mabel Lucie An illustrator first prominent in the early 1900s, Mabel Lucie Attwell's designs found their way into toy form through Chad Valley, a Birmingham, England, company that started making dolls in 1917. Attwell designed the "Bambina" line of dolls. Her doll lines are noted for having an unusually high percentage of boy dolls: 50 percent. Attwell (1879-1964) enjoyed great popularity in Britain, with her images of chubby-faced children appearing on numerous cards and posters. She began illustrating books for the Raphael Tuck Company in 1910. Notable books include Tuck editions of Alice in Wonderland in 1910, Andersen's Fairy Tales in 1914, and Kingsley's The Water-Babies in 1916.

"Atwo" see *American Toy Works.*

Atwood Momanus Tabletop ninepins were once a popular pastime, as evidenced in part by Atwood Momanus' "Bilt Rite Miniature Bowling Alley" of the 1930s.

"Aub-Rubr" see *Auburn Rubber Co.*

"Auburn" The prewar "Auburn" coaster wagon was made by U.S. Toy Co.

Auburn Rubber Co. Considered the number one manufacturer of rubber toys, Auburn Rubber Company of Auburn, Ind., began its toy-making days in 1935, although it had been in business since 1912. Both the Auburn Rubber and Double Fabric Tire Corp. names were used before 1935.

The company started with toy soldiers, and expanded its range the next year with the coffin-nosed Cord sedan, the first of many toy vehicles, all now highly prized by collectors.

A

In addition to cars and toy soldiers, the company produced farm equipment, western figures, farm animals, pull-toys, toy tool kits, horseshoe games, emergency vehicles, trucks, airplanes, construction equipment, and motorcycles.

Its ads read: "Really new! Will not mar furniture. Unbreakable. Washable ... Cute as a bug's ear!" It also advertised itself as a safe plaything for children "who enjoy their toys with their mouths as well as their hands." "Designed with plenty of juvenile Sales Appeal," Auburn Rubber boasted of its late '30s line of molded all-rubber toys.

The line by 1939 included racers, automobiles, airplanes, trucks, tractors, farm implements, baseball players, soldiers, farm animals, brick building blocks and sponge rubber blocks, available in both bulk and boxed sets. The former sold in the 5- to 50-cent range, while the later sold for prices from 50 cents to $1. Auburn ceased producing toys during wartime. Most of the more distinctive figures Auburn released were the creative offspring of Roycroft-influenced illustrator Edward McCandlish, including the soldiers, farm animals, circus animals, and items for infants. The latter, although often not emphasized in discussions of Auburn, have charm and interest. McCandlish created sets of pull-toy animals on wheels, all of rubber, with a larger-scale animal in the front of the line, with small versions in tow. The "Hop Bunnies," "Hen and Chicks," and "Scottie Dogs" were set on octagonal wheels, to make their motions more interesting as they were pulled. He also created some uniform-sized Easter toys that could also be pulled in trains, the "Easter Egg Bunny" and "Easter Egg Chick."

After using rubber for nearly two decades, in 1953 Auburn introduced vinyl, with the motorcycle of that year being possibly the first. By 1955 the toy line was mostly vinyl. The two fire engines were the last of the rubber vehicles. Probably its most familiar toys are its toy tractors, featuring well-detailed farmer drivers at the wheel. In 1960, after moving to Deming, N.M., the firm's products were rubber and soft vinyl toys and novelties, sponge blocks, animals, building blocks,

farm implements, and automobiles and other vehicles. It went out of business in 1969.

Auburn Rubber Co. made this farm set in the 1950s.

Aucoin This company rests its claim to fame on its 1978 "KISS on Tour Game."

"Aunt Jemima" This famous advertising character has gone through numerous toy incarnations, beginning with several paper doll cutouts in the 1890s. In 1905, the R.T. Davis Milling Co., owners of Aunt Jemima Pancake Flour, issued the first Aunt Jemima cloth doll. More followed later that decade. While the 1890s family of Aunt Jemima had more members with different names, the family of the 1900s as issued in cloth-doll form included Jemima, her husband Uncle Moses, and their children Diana and Wade. The milling company was renamed the Aunt Jemima Mills Co. in 1914. In 1924, after war-related difficulties, the company issued a new series of cloth dolls that proved greatly popular. In 1929, three years after being purchased by Quaker Oats, a new set of cloth dolls were issued. Subsequently no new sets were offered until 1950, when the family reappeared as cloth-style dolls made of plastic fabric. Although primarily in the business of selling food, the milling company apparently owed its survival at several critical junctures to the success of its dolls.

"Aunty Bimbo" stuffed animals prewar, see *American Made Toy Co.*

Aurora Plastics Possibly the biggest name in model kits, Aurora produced an enormous number of kits from the '50s through the '70s. The firm was based in West Hempstead, N.Y. Early kits emphasized vehicles, including airplanes, missiles, helicopters, bombers, ships, military vehicles, warships, and historic ships. The firm also made "HO" accessories, radio kits, and plastic gliders.

In 1958, Aurora issued a number of kits that indicated an increasing sensitivity to currents in American pop culture. New models included "Black Fury," "Steve Canyon," and a variety of "Three Musketeers" kits. In the 1960s, a list of Aurora's figural kits reads like an American popular-character who's who. The year 1961 saw the appearance of the "Frankenstein" monster, followed in 1962 by "Dracula" and the "Wolfman," and in 1963 by "Creature From The Black Lagoon" and "Phantom of the Opera." The monster theme came into full flower in 1964 with the first appearances of the "Hunchback of Notre Dame," the "Addams Family Haunted House," "Godzilla," "Dr. Jeckyll as Mr. Hyde," and "King Kong." "The Bride of Frankenstein" appeared in 1965.

Superheroes also figured largely in the line-up, beginning with "Superman" in 1963. "Superboy" appeared in 1964, and "Wonder Woman" in 1965. In 1966, "Captain Action," "Captain America," and the "Hulk" all made their first appearances. The decade also included a famous series of "Batman"-related models. The caped crusader himself first appeared in 1964, with "Robin" and the "Batmobile" following in 1966, the "Batcycle" and "Batplane" in 1967, and the "Batboat" in 1968.

Other character models in the '60s included, in 1965, "Alfred E. Neuman," and in 1966, "Godzilla's Go-Cart," "King Kong's Thronester," "Man from U.N.C.L.E." figures, and two "Lost In Space" kits. "Tarzan" appeared in 1967, followed in 1968 by "Chitty Chitty Bang Bang" and the "Land of the Giants Space Ship," and in 1969 by the "Fantastic Voyage 'Voyager.'" The 1970s kits of interest included "Vampirella" in 1971, the "USS Enterprise" and "Mr. Spock" in 1972, and the Japanese monsters "Ghidrah" and "Rodan" in 1975.

In the '70s, Aurora also ventured into the world of games, and produced two "ABC Monday Night Football" games, among others.

Ausley Industries, Inc. Founder Robert C. Ausley saw his toy-making company Ausley Industries through two periods. The first, 1943-48, saw production of lead "home-cast" soldiers. In the second, and perhaps more creative period, the company produced cowboys and Indians with movable arms, made in plastic injection molds. Ausley ended production in 1950.

Austin & Craw Austin & Craw issued the "Tit Tat Toe, Three in a Row" game of 1896.

Austin Art Studios This Omaha, Neb., firm made gauze and rubber Halloween masks, costumes, and skeletons in the Boomer years. It used the "Austomatic Process" trademark.

"Authors" Indicative of a more literate time, games that involved identifying authors and their works were popular in the 1800s. The earliest may have been the card game simply entitled "Authors," as many of them were, released in 1861 by Whipple & Smith. In the 1890s, companies including J.H. Singer, Clark & Sowdon, McLoughlin Bros., and Parker Bros. issued Authors card games.

Auto-Bike Co. This Cincinnati, Ohio, company produced prewar bicycles, velocipedes, baby walkers, and coaster wagons.

"Auto-Builder" see *Structo Mfg. Co.*

Auto Buff A series of Ford models in 1:43-scale, built in the U.S. and produced in small numbers.

"Auto-Carts" late prewar, see *Auto-Wheel Coaster Co.*

"Auto Cycle" late prewar, see *Arnold, Schwinn Co.*

"Auto-Glide" late prewar, see *The Cushman Motor Works.*

Auto-Pilen A Spanish company, Auto-Pilen manufactured some of the "French Dinky" toy vehicles between 1974 and 1981,

A

after production had ceased at the French plants making the toys.

Auto Play Co. Auto Play Co. issued the "Auto Play Baseball Game" in 1911, one of the earliest such sport games.

Auto-Wheel Coaster Co., Inc. Based in North Tonawanda, N.Y., Auto-Wheel Coaster made wood and steel items, including carts, scooters, "Red Racer" wagons, pedal cars, baby walkers, steering sleds, bob sleds, and stake wagons. It issued coaster wagons in both wood and all steel. The company continued through the Boomer years, also manufacturing hand cars, spring-top sleds, and "sled strollers."

The "Aero-Flyer Stake Wagon" was made in the 1960s by Auto-Wheel Coaster Co.

Autobridge, Inc. Established in the late 1930s, Auobridge issued games including "Autobridge." It was located on Second Avenue, New York City.

Autocraft Co. Based in Steubenville, Ohio, this late 1930s company issued the "Autocrat" model-building sets, which were wood whittling sets.

"Autograph Pals" see *I.S. Sutton & Sons.*

"Autograph Pets" see *Collegiate Mfg. Co.*

Automatic Cradle Mfg. Co. see *Lullabye Furniture Corp.*

Automatic Recording Safe Co. Based in Chicago, Ill., in the late 1930s, Automatic Recording Safe made various

home saving banks, including items for the juvenile market.

Automatic Rubber Co. This Columbia, S.C., company made prewar "boys' toys," including the "Zip Zip Shooter."

"Automatic Toy" see *William F. Goodwin.*

Automatic Toy Co. The Automatic Toy Co. of Staten Island, N.Y., produced tin wind-up toys from the 1930s through '50s. Its best-known toy is the Auto Speedway of the '30s, featuring two racing cars on an oval track. Automatic also produced space toys, including friction rocket ships and a Space Shooting Range. Its games included the "Cross Country Racer" of 1940.

"Automite" see *Wen-Mac Corp.*

automobiles, juvenile Often called "juvenile automobiles" by the prewar toy industry, miniature model cars with electric motors were a premium item in the early 20th century. The leading manufacturer was American-National Co., who was producing juvenile autos in the 1920s. Other manufacturers, following American-National's lead in the 1930s, included Garton Toy Co., the Gendron Wheel Co., the Murray Ohio Mfg. Co., Skippy Racers, and the Toledo Metal Wheel Co.

The field greatly expanded in the postwar years. Some firms specialized in racecars, as did Hedstrom-Union Co., while others issued "Go-Karts," including New Monarch Machine & Stamping Co. Others specialized in tractors, including Barnett & Son, the Great Lakes Tractor Co., Midwest Industries, and Strunk Equipment Co. While most companies used gas engines, some relied on electric motors, including Grant & Grant and the Power Car Co. Several manufacturers, including Arnold-Dain Corp. and Chief Industries, specialized in assembly kits.

Because of significant interest in box-car and coaster racing, some manufacturers of coaster autos, such as Ramrod Products, considered their products "juvenile autos," as opposed to pedal cars. Other Boomer-years manufacturers included American Machine

& Foundry Co., Berbro Mfg. Co., Balke & Conroy, Blazon, Fair-Craft Corp., Family Fun Kit Co., Garton Toy Co., Hamilton Steel Products, Lange Plastics Co., Julius Levenson, Misner Corp., the Murray Ohio Mfg. Co., and Simplex Mfg. Corp.

automobiles, miniature The world was introduced to the world of the miniature toy automobile by Dowst Mfg. Co., who issued in 1911 a die-cast limousine measuring 2 inches long. This die-cast toy car, the beginning of a miniature automobile dynasty for Dowst under the "Tootsietoy" name, and the inspiration for countless imitations, stayed in production until the eve of the Great Depression.

By the mid-1930s, most manufacturers involved in die-cast production, usually classed as manufacturers of "pewter toys," were making small toy cars. Besides their small size, these were distinguished from the larger steel and tin toys, some of the them mechanical toys and others ride-on goods, by their simplicity, having for pieces only a body, axles, and tires—or sometimes even only a single cast piece without moving parts. While iron toy manufacturers were also making toy cars, they were generally of a larger scale.

As Dowst and other manufacturers had discovered in the late 1800s, the die-casting process provided the possibility of vastly greater detailing in the cast object than did any available iron-casting process. Besides Dowst, "pewter" manufacturers soon after the Depression included Novelty Casting Co., Peter F. Pia, Savoye Pewter Toy Mfg. Co., and Tiny-Tot Toy Co. In addition, myriads of small businesses and individuals cast car toys with handheld molding sets, using every possible variety of improvised lead and zinc alloys.

By the late prewar years, the making of auto miniatures was a growing concern for manufacturers including Barclay Mfg. Co., C.A.W. Novelty Co., Durable Toy & Novelty Corp., Karson Mfg. Co., Lorraine Metal Mfg. Co., Manoil Mfg. Co., the Newton Junior Corp., C. Sidney Payne, Tommy Toy Mfg. Corp., and Williams Kast Art Co. At the same time,

rubber manufacturers were adding vehicles at a slightly larger scale to their toy lines. In the postwar years, while die-cast materials continued to be the primary ones for toy car production, vinyl, acetate, polyethylene, and other new plastics grew in importance. These materials were used much as were the metal alloys.

Manufacturers in the Boomer years were myriad, and included AMT Corp., Ace Products, Action Tri-Play Toys, Alabe Crafts, Amloid Co., Argo Industries Corp., Auburn Rubber Co., Dowst, Eldon Mfg. Co., Fisher-Price Toys, Greyshaw of Georgia, the Hubley Mfg. Co., Irwin Corp., Jak-Pak-Inc., Lapin Proucts, Lido Toy Corp., Jack Manoil Co., Monogram Models, Multiple Products Corp., Pal Plastics, Payton Products, Plasticraft Mfg. Co., Plastic Toys Corp., Product Miniature Co., Renwal Toy Corp., Revell, Thomas Mfg. Corp., Totebrush, U.S. Plastics Corp., and Webo Toys.

automobile models The manufacture of model automobile kits became a major industry in the 1950s and '60s, when companies including AMT Corp., Associated Hobby Mfrs., Berkeley Models, Cavacraft Model Airplane, Comet Model Hobbycraft, L.M. Cox Mfg. Co., Elmar Products Co., General Molds & Plastic Corp., the Hubley Mfg. Co., Jo-Han Models, Monogram Models, Pagliuso Engineering, Polk's Model Craft Hobbies, Product Miniature Co., Pyro Plastics Corp., A.J. Renzi Plastic Co., Scientific Model Airplane Co., Strombeck-Becker Mfg. Co., and U.S. Plastics Corp. issued kits for both contemporary and historic cars.

automata, or automatons The automaton is a mechanical figure capable of independently performing multiple complex movements, once set in motion. They can be mechanically jointed figures, or toys on any scale, driven by any kind of mechanism. Automata appear to be about as old as civilization. Even the ancient Egyptians seem to have had figural contrivances designed to work in ways mysterious to the viewer.

A

The automata most familiar to us by that name were first popular in Europe in the 1400s as parts of elaborate clocks, some within churches and others operating in the open air for the edification of general towns-folk. By the 1500s, automata became a part of court and upper-class life. Clockmakers found a new expertise in creating clockwork figures that could perform relatively elaborate actions. While earlier automata had generally been water-powered, these depended on the spring motors already familiar from the manufacture of clocks. Many of these early automata were realistic figures with wax or bisque heads, with the most complex European examples capable of tasks ranging from dipping pens in ink and "writing" letters to playing miniature pianos.

The wind-up toys and electrically powered toys of the American 19th and 20th centuries can technically be considered automata. Generally the wind-up and battery-operated robots are accepted as such. Oddly enough, the postwar plastic and vinyl dolls capable of various actions are usually not seen in this light.

"Autoperipatetikos" see *Joseph Lyon & Co.*

"Ava Gardner" paper dolls 1949-52, see *Whitman Publishing Co.*

The Avalon Hill Co. Active from the late 1950s through the Boomer years, Avalon Hill released numerous games for adults based on sports, military, or economic competition, including such titles as "Beat Inflation" in 1961, "Blitzkrieg" in 1965, and "Pro Golf" in 1982. In 1976 it released the Robert Heinlein-inspired game, "Starship Troopers." The firm was based in Baltimore, Md.

Avalon Mfg. Co. This postwar Brooklyn, N.Y., firm issued numbered oil painting sets, mosaic-by-number sets, and "Shellcraft" sets.

"Avenger" cap pistol postwar, see *Kilgore Mfg. Co., Inc..*

"The Avenger" submachine gun see *Cordelco Industries.*

Averill Manufacturing Co. Averill Manufacturing made rag dolls from 1913 through the 1930s, initially using the designs of Georgene Averill. After the Averills left the company in 1923, the company made a line of dolls based on the designs of artist Grace Drayton, including the black doll "Chocolate Drop" and the "Dolly Dingle" series dolls. In the late 1920s the "Madame Hendren" dolls were among the company's lead products. In 1938, Averill issued the dolls "Sweets," "Snooks," and "Peggy Ann," based on the designs of illustrator Maude Tausey Fangel.

"Avon" puzzles postwar, see *Milton Bradley Co.*

Ay-Won Toy & Novelty Corp. Ay-Won was an important distributor of games and toys in the 1920s through the prewar years, based on Broadway, New York City.

"Ayanel" dolls see *A. & L. Novelty Co.*

E.B. Ayers, Jr. This Ocean Grove, N.J., company made prewar dollhouses.

J.C. Ayling Co. Based in Springfield, Ill., this prewar company made the "Jolly Boy" folding kites and "Ayling's" cloth kites.

Edmund B. Ayres, Jr. Edmund B. Ayres, Jr., of Lynbrook, Long Island, New York, produced dollhouses in the late 1930s.

Ayvad Water-Wings, Inc. A company based in Hoboken, N.J., before the war, Ayvad made water-wings, water-rings, and water-dogs.

Azco Products Corp. Soldier sets were among the specialties of this 1950s and '60s Pawtucket, R.I., manufacturer of games, toys, and banks.

Bb

"B.K.B." toys prewar, see *William P. Beers Co.*

b.o. see *battery-operated toys.*

B. & L. Broom Corp. A Boston, Mass., firm established in the late 1930s, B. & L. Broom Corp. made toy brooms and whisk brooms.

"B. & R." see *Behrend & Rothschild.*

B. & S. Mfg. Co. Located in Newark, N.J., B. & S. Mfg. Co. manufactured doll items including trunks, outfits, and baby bottles, and embroidery, sewing and novelty play sets in the late 1930s.

B. & S. Specialty Co. Based on Mercer Street, New York City, this mid-1930s company made doll shoes.

"B Line" toys see *Processed Plastic Co.*

BW Molded Plastics Plastic toys, including trucks, autos, racers, and trains, and infants' items were manufactured by this Pasadena, Calif., firm from the early 1950s into the '60s.

"Babe-Bee" model engine see *L.M. Cox Mfg. Co.*

babies Colonists led by Sir. Richard Grenville handed out "babies" among their peacemaking gifts to Roanoke Island and North Carolina Indians. At the time, the word "babies" could refer to dolls, even though the dolls represented adult figures, not baby figures. The term was used in this sense until around 1750. In the 20th century, the word was widely used in proper names for dolls, as in "Baby Adele" from Cameo Doll Co. and the "Baby Lucy" dolls by Maxine Doll Co., in the 1930s. All were baby dolls, however.

"Babs" "Babs" was a name used for several prewar dolls, including one from Horsman Dolls and another from Richard G. Krueger.

"Babsie," by Alexander Doll Co., was an early talking doll.

Baby Barry Toy Co. Dolls and stuffed toys were made by this West 21st Street, New York City, company in the Boomer years. Its line included the "Bombo" clown stuffed doll, 32 inches tall, of 1955.

Baby Bathinette Corp. Maker of infants' bathinettes, this Rochester, N.Y., company also made doll bathinettes and items for the play yard in the 1930s. In the Boomer era, Baby Bathinette continued issuing the "Bathinette" combination bath and table, and playpen canopies.

"Just Like Mother's..."
1930s doll bath and
accessories, Baby
Bathinette, Corp.

"Baby Beans" Mattel's "Baby Beans" line of 12-inch bean-bag dolls was issued in 1971. It included "Bedsie Beans," "Booful Beans," and "Bitty Beans." The "Bean Pals" animal toys followed in 1972, and "Bean Puppets" and "Bean Pets" in 1973.

"Baby Big Eyes" 1950s, see *Ideal Novelty & Toy Co.*

"Baby Brite" see *De Luxe Reading Corp.*

baby carriages see *carriages, baby.*

"Baby Darling" The "Baby Darling" and "Baby Glee" rubber dolls were made by

Miller Rubber Products Co. in the 1930s. The "Baby Darling" doll crib was made by S. & G. Mfg. Co.

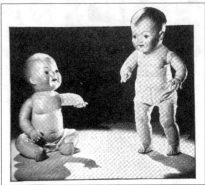

"Baby Glee," Miller Rubber Products, Co., 1930s.

"Baby Dear" 1960s, see *Vogue Dolls.*

Vogue Dolls' 1960s "Baby Dear."

"Baby First Step" 1968, see *Mattel.*

"Baby Glee" see *"Baby Darling."*

"Baby Grows Up" 1978, see *Mattel.*

baby houses In the early 1800s, doll houses were often called "baby houses."

"Baby Huey" The baby giant character of Harvey Famous Name Comics appeared in relatively few toy forms, the most prominent being puppets by Pride Products.

"Baby Jumbo" toys prewar, see *American Made Toy Co.*

Baby Line Furniture Corp. Based in Los Angeles, Calif., Baby Line made 1930s cribs, nursery chairs, high chairs, toy chests, and play yard items. In the Boomer years it continued emphasizing its nursery line, adding wardrobes.

"Baby Peggy" wooden toys prewar, see *Playskool Institute.*

"Baby Prince" velocipede prewar, see the *Colson Co.*

"Baby Sing-A-Song" 1969, see *Mattel Inc..*

baby swings see *swings, baby.*

"Baby-Tenda" The "Baby-Tenda" was an 1870s-era rocking horse that moved on a stable base, issued by a Dr. Walker.

"Baby-Trix" see *Uneeda.*

"Baby Walk 'n' Play" 1970, see *Mattel.*

baby walkers see *walkers, baby.*

"Babyland" furniture see *Gem Crib & Cradle Co.*

"Babyland" soft dolls see *M.&S. Doll Co.*

Bachmann Bros., Inc. Bachmann manufactured train accessory buildings, hobby kits, and plastic party goods from the 1950s through the Boomer years. Its "Plasticville" line became especially famous.

backgammon Prewar manufacturers of this traditional game included P. Becker & Co., Beulah Toy & Novelty Co., Milton Bradley Co., the Carrom Co., Cluff Cover Co., Cutler & Saleeby, Cuyahoga Lumber Co., the Embossing Co., Ferguson Bros. Mfg. Co., Hassenfeld Bros., W.C. Horn Bro. & Co., Novelty Bookbinding Co., Parker Bros., Pattberg Novelty Corp., Arthur Popper, William Rott, Selchow & Righter Co., Totty Trunk & Bag Co., and Transogram Co. One variant was a 1930s four-handed backgammon game, "Cross Gammon," by Robert-Gordon Toy Co.

Bacon Bros., Inc. Bacon manufactured animated musical toys in the 1950s and '60s. It was based in Boston, Mass.

John Badal Co. This Philadelphia, Penn., firm manufactured Boomer-era skip ropes, trike and bike noisemakers, lettered jacks and ball games, and doll hanger and clothespin sets.

"Badger" The "Badger" trademark was used on prewar children's vehicles by the Garton Toy Co. Garton also made the "Badger Playmate" gymnasium set.

Badger Basket Co. Doll cradles, bassinets, carriages, and hampers were the specialty of this Edgar, Wis., firm in the Boomer years.

Badger Cutouts, Inc. The "Pup-Pet" die-cast animals of the late 1950s were issued by this Maspeth, Long Island, N.Y., firm.

badminton Badminton was reaching new levels of popularity in the prewar years. Manufacturers included American Toy Works, Bersin Playthings, Milton Bradley Co., Benny Bratchet, General Sportcraft Co., Indian Archery & Toy Corp., Ken-Wel Sporting Goods Co., Marks Bros. Co., Munro Athletic Products Co., Parker Bros., Rollin Wilson Co., Jack Schaefer, Transogram Co., Jon Weber Manufactory, and Westminster Sports. A wholly different array of manufacturers were producing the yard game by the mid-Boomer years: A.H. Delfausse Co., Del Rey Plastics Corp., E. & L. Mfg. Co., Educational Products, Empire Plastic Corp., Famous Keystone Kits Corp., General Sportcraft Co., Gerber Plastic Co., Indian Archery & Toy Corp., Jaymar Specialty Co., Regent Sports Co., The Toy Tinkers, Trio Mfg. Co., and Wilson Sporting Goods.

Eugene B. Baehr & Sons A prewar manufacturer of school bags and brief cases, Eugene B. Baehr, based on East 22nd Street, New York City, also made dice, serpentines, and chess sets. By the late 1930s the company included marbles among its products.

Max Baer, Max Baer, located on West 26th Street, New York City, issued stuffed toys in the late 1930s.

Max Baer stuffed toy, 1930s.

Baer & Strasburger, Inc. This Broadway, New York City, firm made "Little Giant" pool tables and metal games in the 1920s.

bagatelles Perhaps the most prominent of prewar bagatelle manufacturers were the threesome of Gotham Pressed Steel Corp., Lindstrom Tool & Toy Co., and Northwestern Products. Other prewar American manufacturers included American Games Co., American Maid Artcraft Studios, Arcade Mfg. Co., Cuyahoga Lumber Co., Bar Zim Toy Mfg. Co., Durable Toy & Novelty Corp., Ferguson Bros. Mfg. Co., Gropper Onyx Marble Co., Johnson Store Equipment Co., Marks Bros. Co., M.H. Miller Co., Pattberg Novelty Corp., Rich-Illinois Mfg. Co., the Waddell Co., Robert Wolff Woodcraft Corp., and World Metal Stamping Co. Bagatelles in postwar years were produced by firms including Bar Zim Toy Mg. Co., T. Cohn, Henry Katz, Louis Marx & Co., and Northwestern Products.

Bailey & Bailey Both manufacturer and importer, Bailey & Bailey, on East 22nd Street, New York City, issued prewar cradle toys, soft toys, celluloid toys and novelties, tin toys, and wood toys.

The W.J. Baker Co. The W.J. Baker Co. of Newport, Ky., issued prewar baby walkers, pedal cars, and handcars. By the late prewar years it also manufactured roller skates.

Baker Mfg. Co. This Columbia, Penn., Boomer-years company specialized in kitchen, garden, tool, and golf sets in packages, boxed jackstone sets made of iron as late as 1960, and the "Doodle Bake."

B

The Bakers-Clevercraft Shoppe This prewar Pasadena, Calif., outfit specialized in "wooden tap dancing dolls."

balance toys Balance toys were toys using weights or counterweights to achieve their effects, with examples known from early Asia and from Europe by the 16th century. The counterweight is often a swinging weight located above or below the toy. Some of the more common examples were found in bell toys and baby toys, the roly-poly being perhaps the best known. The "Weebles" were the most prominent balance toys of the later 20th century, although others were manufactured. The Japanese "Daruma" dolls were often made as balance toys.

balance wheel The balance wheel, as found in horse-drawn vehicle toys, is the small wheel attached to the lowermost front hoof of the horse or to a shaft descending from the horse's body, or between the horses in the case of a multi-horse toy. The wheel was made in rotating and stationary forms.

Baldwin Mfg. Co., Inc. This Brooklyn, N.Y., firm issued mechanical toys, action toys, and games in the late 1930s.

The Ball & Socket Mfg. Co. Based in West Cheshire, Conn., this late 1930s firm issued metal toy furniture and toy kitchen gadget sets.

L.G. Ballard Mfg. Co. L.G. Ballard of Topeka, Kans., issued a "Chinese Checkers" game in the late 1930s.

balloons Toy balloons and novelty balloons played an important part on the prewar toy scene, with the Oak Rubber Co. appearing to be the leading manufacturer. Its line was characterized by decorated and shaped balloons, with some based on licensed characters, including Disney's "Mickey Mouse." Other prewar manufacturers included American Toy Airship Co., Anderson Rubber Co., Barr Rubber Products Co., Braley Midland Co., the Eagle Rubber Co., the Faultless Rubber Co., H. Fishlove & Co., the Maple City Rubber Co., the Mohican Rubber Co., Pacific Balloon Co., Perfect Rubber Co., S.F. Perkins Aerial Adv. Kite & Zeppelin Balloon Co., the Pioneer Rubber Co., M. Pressner & Co., Rex Rubber & Novelty Co., the Toycraft Rubber Co., United Balloon Co., the Western Reserve Rubber Co., the Wooster Rubber Co., and Yale Rubber Co. The A.C. Gilbert Co. also made balloon construction sets. By the late prewar years, Gordon Novelty Co., Howe Baumann Balloon Co., Lee-Tex Rubber Products Corp., Rex Rubber & Novelty Co., the Toycraft Rubber Co., the Western Reserve Rubber Co., and Yale Rubber Co. joined their ranks. A number of these prewar rubber manufacturing firms, including Anderson, Barr, Braley Midland, Eagle, Faultless, Gordon, Lee-Tex, Maple City, Mohican, Oak, and Pioneer, survived to remain major balloon manufacturers through the Boomer years. Other major balloon makers of the 1950s and '60s included Ashland Rubber Products Corp., Bayshore Industries, the Beistle Co., Dipcraft Mfg. Co., Everly Associates, the Fli-Back Sales Corp., Gem Party Favor Co., Jaybar Products Co., the National Latex Products Co., Orange Rubber and Plastics Corp., Tillotson Rubber Co., United Industries, and Van Dam Rubber Co. The new category of plastic balloon manufacturers included Brian Specialties and Jaybar.

Balloons were the prewar and postwar specialty of The Barr Rubber Products Co.

balls Balls made of various materials have proved satisfying playthings for undoubtedly thousands of years. In the American toy world, the invention of the vulcanizing process greatly increased the options for ball manufacturers. Even the introduction of early plastics changed the industry scene by making the manufacture of the modern table-tennis ball feasible. Prewar manufacturers included Anderson Rubber Co., Barr Rubber Products Co., Da Costa Toy Co., Eagle Rubber Co., the Faultless Rubber Co., Miller Rubber Products, Pennsylvania Rubber Co., Rex Rubber & Novelty Co., Schavoir Ruber Co., the Seamless Rubber Co., Sponge Rubber Products Co., the Toycraft Rubber Co., and C.B. Webb Co. For an example of varieties manufactured, see the *Faultless Rubber Co.* The Boomer years saw the increasing introduction of plastic into the ball manufacturing world. Some rubber manufacturers still major players included Barr, Faultless, and Seamless. Newly ascendant in the 1950s and '60s were Bayshore Industries, Cupples Co., Eyerly Associates, the Fli-Back Sales Co., Frank Plastics Corp., Gerber Toys, Milton A. Jacobs, King Solomon Products, Lee-Tex Ruber Products Corp. of California, Ohio Plastic Co., Pennsylvania Athletic Products, Plastic Toys Corp., Product Miniature Co., Tillotson Rubber Co., U.S. Fiber & Plastics Corp., Vantines, and W.J. Voit Rubber Corp.

Alvimar Mfg. Co. made this "New York World's Fair 'See-Thru' Ball" in 1964.

"Ballyhoo" The "Ballyhoo" name was in common use in prewar times. Examples from the 1930s include a Marks Bros. Co. bagatelle game, a Samuel Gabriel Sons & Co. board game, and an Einson-Freeman Co. puzzle, all having this same name.

The Balsa Novelties Co. Based in Brooklyn, N.Y., Balsa Novelties issued wood specialties including the "Glider-Gun" for shooting gliders in the late 1930s.

Bambino Products Corp. A company capitalizing on the biggest sports phenomenon of its time, this company produced Bambino, a baseball game, in 1934. It was based on South Jefferson Street, Chicago, Ill.

Bancroft-Rellim Corp. This Boston, Mass., manufacturer of the Boomer years issued toy chests, doll auto beds and seat, and baby swings.

The Bandalor Co. Pedro Flores formed this Rockford, Ill., firm in the 1930s to manufacturer yo-yos, after Donald F. Duncan bought the Flores Yo-Yo Corp.

bandalore tops see *yo-yo*.

"Bang" paper caps see *Kilgore Mfg. Co., Inc.*

"Bang" pistol prewar, see *The Dent Hardware Co.*

E.C. Bangert Co. Based in Falls Creek, Pa., this prewar company made novelties and toy guns.

banks Money and banks may have gone together from the beginning, if we are to take the baked clay banks discovered in ruins of Pompeii as evidence. Whether or not banks were characteristic items of childhood from ancient times may remain forever unknown. Certainly in 19th century America, however, banks for children were commonplace, with cast-iron versions especially common. Prewar manufacturers of savings banks included Arcade Mfg. Co., Banthrico, Behrend & Rothschild, Brodhaven Mfg. Co., J. Chein & Co., the Dent Hardware Co., Dudley Lock Corp., Durable Toy & Novelty Corp., Jerome Geffen, the Gong Bell Mfg. Co., Grey Iron Casting Co., Hoge Mfg. Co., the Hubley Mfg. Co., the Kenton Hardwqare Co., Kingsbury Mfg. Co., Nicol & Co., John Nutry, E.H. Roberts Corp., the J. & E. Stevens Co., "Uncle Sam's" Registering Savings Bank Co., White-Hill Co., the A.C. Williams Co., and Zell Products Corp. With the introduction of plastics and vinyls to toy manufactur-

B

ing, the number of firms manufacturing banks greatly increased. The ranks of figural banks were especially enriched. Manufacturers included Athol Comb Co., Azco Products Corp., Bayshore Industries, Bellevue Products, George Borgfeldt Corp., Bower Mfg. Co., A.N. Brooks Corpo., Brumberger Sales Corp., C. & G. Toy Co., Cherry Valley Mfg. Corp., J. Chein & Co., Cordelco Industries, Crestline Mfg. Corp., Del Rey Plastics Corp., Durable Toy & Novelty Corp., Eldon Mfg. Co., Fillum Fun, Five Star Industries, Goody Mfg. Co., Grey Iron Casting Co., Harrison's Mfg. Co., House of Puzzy, International Plastic Co., and Irwin Corp. Others included Milton A. Jacobs, Jak-Pak-Inc., Kalon Mfg. Corp., Henry Katz National Sales Organization, Keen-Eye Co., the Kirchhof Patent Co., Knickerbocker Plastic Co., Lapin Products, Logan Specialty Mfg. Co., M. & L. Toy Co., Merry Mfg. Co., Moonglow Plastic Jewel Corp., Ohio Art Co., Pet Toy Co. of New Hampshire, Plasticraft Mfg. Co., Randing, Rapaport Bros., A.J. Renzi Plastic Co., Riemann Seabrey Co., Royal Tot Co., Royalty Designs, Sollmann & Whitcomb, Spare-Time Game & Toy Co., Suburban Toy & Mfg. Corp., Superior Toy & Mfg. Co., Sidney A. Tarrson, Tibbetts Industries, Tigrett Industries, Tudor Metal Products Corp., United Metal Products, U.S. Plastics Corp., Vantines, and Worcester Toy Co. For more information see also *banks, dime register; banks, mechanical; banks, still.*

This "Rabbit Bank" was made by Knickerbocker Plastic Co., in the 1950s.

banks, dime register In the 1930s and '40s, a variety of tin manufacturers issued dime banks. They generally measure 2-1/2" square, with rounded corners. Often they featured a small window with a counter behind it, which registered the total amount as each dime was inserted. The banks could hold up to 50 dimes, or $5.00, with the bank opening automatically when the top amount was reached. Many featured popular cartoon characters, including Superman, Popeye, Captain Marvel, Little Orphan Annie, and such Walt Disney characters as Mickey Mouse and Snow White.

banks, mechanical While mechanical banks date back to the late 18th century in the U.S., production in great numbers awaited the later 19th century, when companies including the J. &. E. Stevens Co. began larger scale manufacture. Among the most desirable mechanical banks are "Bowling Alley" by Kyser & Rex in 1879, "Breadwinners" by J. & E. Stevens in the 1880s, "Bureau" by J. Serrell in 1869, "Darky Fisherman" by Shephard Hardware in 1891, "Fowler" by J. & E. Stevens in 1892, "Freedman's" by Jerome Secor in 1880, "Frog in Den" or "Toy Toad" by Jason Fallows in 1871, "Girl Skipping Rope" by J. & E. Stevens in 1890, "Jonah and Whale on Pedestal" by J. & E. Stevens in 1890, and "Red Riding Hood" by an unknown manufacturer in the 1880s.

banks, still A term used in contrast to "mechanical bank," "still banks" or "stills" refers to coin banks, usually of the cast-metal variety, without moving parts. Tinplate banks predominated from the 1870s to the '90s, with important manufacturers including Schlesingers, George W. Brown Co., William Fallows, and Althof Bergmann. Cast-iron still banks were highly popular from the late 19th century into the 1930s, with major producers including A.C. Williams Co., the J. & E. Stevens Co., Hubley Mfg. Co., and Kenton Hardware Co. Important early still banks include a number of character items, including "Andy Gump" by Arcade Mfg. Co., "Buster Brown and Tige" by Williams in the 1900s, "Foxy Grandpa," "Mutt and Jeff" by Williams, and the "Campbell Kids." Buildings, animals, and historic figures were also common subjects for still banks, with the latter including Benjamin Franklin, Boss Tweed, Charles Lindbergh, General Pershing, and George Washington.

S. Sunny Banks, Inc.

Action games including badminton were the specialty of this Boomer-era manufacturer, based in the Fifth Avenue Building.

Banner Plastics Corp.

One of the most important manufacturers of smaller plastic toys from 1946 on, Banner issued toy cars, trucks, trains, boats, and a simple but popular circus train. In the mid-1950s, the line included the 29-piece "Star Dust Tea Set," the combination metal and plastic "Banner Blocks," and the "Metro Truck Assortment," which included news, laundry, and ice cream panel toy trucks. Its "Train Accessory Unit" consisted of a loading platform, railroad station, luggage carriers, trees, telephone and light poles, and a variety of standing and sitting figures. By the early '60s, the line included tea seats in hard plastic, polyethylene and metal; cookware and housekeeping sets; plastic pots and pans; trucks and automobiles in metal and plastic; sand pails in plastic and metal; beach, bath, and garden toys; railroad trains and accessories; boats in hard and soft plastic; educational toys; infant toys; piggy banks and novelty banks; toy jewelry; military toys; small plastic dolls; push and pull toys; space helmets; Christmas filled stockings; and small goods assortments. The firm used trade names including "Bannertone" and "Bannerware." It was located in Paterson, N.J.

Banner Plastics Corp. made this "American Express" metal toy truck in the 1950s.

Bantam-Lite, Inc.

Bantam-Lite of West 27th Street, New York City, made flashlights, including the "Popeye Action Flashlight," for the postwar juvenile market.

Bantam U.S. Toys

Soft toys, rattles, and infant novelties were specialties of this West 34th Street, New York City, firm in the Boomer years.

Banthrico

A prewar company based on West Lake Street, Chicago, Banthrico made die-cast savings banks and advertising novelties. It is best known for die-cast banks in the shapes of cars, which it issued into the Boomer years.

Bantam Products see *United States Stuffed Toy & Novelty Co.*

Banton Bros.

Based in Newport, Maine, this prewar company produced ten pins and wooden games.

"Bar-K-L" holsters see *Mount Vernon Mfg. Co.*

Bar Zim Toy Mfg. Co.

Based on Fourth Avenue, New York City, Bar Zim made a wide variety of prewar toys and novelties from wood, tin, and other materials, including bagatelles, educational toys, savings banks, musical toys, noisemakers, Halloween toys, puzzles, whistles, and kindergarten toys. By the late 1930s it was also issuing nailing sets, party games, table tennis, Chinese checkers, and 1939 World's Fair games and novelties. During wartime, the firm continued with a line of xylophones, miniature pocket games, peg and nailing box sets, play tables, bowling alleys, games, puzzles, banks, flutes, and spelling and numbering boards. In the Boomer years, Bar Zim, now based in Jersey City, N.J., continued a line of educational toys, peg board sets, party games, puzzles, kindergarten toys, wood and metal toys, musical toys including xylophones, and spelling and counting boards.

W.A. Barber, Inc.

A manufacturer of juvenile rolltop desks and rocking horses, W.A. Barber of Brattleboro, Vt., was successor to Smith Wood Products.

"Barbie"

Mattel's "Barbie" of 1959 was based on German doll "Lilli," who represented a clever and sexually savvy young German panel-cartoon figure. Mattel's doll

B

was a fashion, or "high-heel," doll, in essence a three-dimensional paper doll. Although given a lukewarm greeting by the toy industry, "Barbie" became immensely popular. She was followed in 1961 with her boyfriend "Ken"; in 1963 with best friend "Midge"; and in 1964, little sister "Skipper" and "Ken" buddy "Allan." In 1964, "Barbie" appeared in the variations "Miss Barbie" and "Fashion Queen Barbie," with sculpted hairstyles to allow wig changes. In 1965, Mattel introduced "Skipper" friends "Skooter" and "Ricky"; in 1966, "MODern" cousin "Francie," and small twin sister and brother "Tutti" and "Todd"; and in 1967, "Francie" friend "Casey," and "Tutti" playmate "Chris." In 1967, "Barbie" acquired a "Twist 'n Turn" waist, and a more youthful face. The talking version was introduced in 1968. Also in 1968, Mattel introduced "Barbie" friends "Stacey," from England, and "Christie," who was black. Personality dolls appeared in the line with 1968's "Twiggy" and 1969's "Julia," the TV nurse. Later introductions included "P.J.," in 1969; "Brad," in 1970; "Fluff" and the sun-tanned "Malibu" versions of "Barbie" dolls, in 1971; "Steffie," "Tiff," and "Miss America" in 1972; and "Kelley" in 1973.

Barclay Mfg. Co. Based in North Bergen, N.J., Barclay was arguably America's leading producer of slush-metal toys, especially miniature soldier and civilian figures, vehicle toys, and "Build and Paint Auto" sets. Founded in 1923 by Beon Donze and Michael Levy, Barclay introduced its first line of toy soldiers in 1932. It became the largest U.S. producer of toy solders up to World War II. By the late prewar years, miniature automobiles and other vehicles had become a major part of its toy line. The company closed its doors in 1971.

Barclay Mfg. Co., Inc. A 1930s company of nearly the same name as the famous slush-metal toy manufacturer, Barclay Mfg. Co., Inc., based in Muncie, Ind., produced metal kitchen cabinets and table and chair sets for children.

"Barclays" This word is sometimes used not only for the toy lead soldiers made by Barclay Mfg. Co., but also (in a looser sense) to the Barclay-copy soldiers produced in soft plastic by Ajax and Thomas, and even the lead soldiers made by Frank Krupp after he left Barclay to found All-Nu. To a limited degree the word is used for general slush-metal toys. Since most slush-metal toys were issued without company markings, collectors have a tendency to attribute them to Barclay, it having been the highest-profile American producer.

Bardell Mfg. Corp. A Steger, Ill., firm, Bardell made toy and juvenile furniture, building blocks, inflatable toys, and chalkboards in the Boomer years. It also made wading pools and ice-skating rinks.

Barden & Robeson Corp. This Penn Yan, N.Y., company made postwar doll bassinets and doll cradles.

Bargreen Mfg. Co. Located in Everett, Wash., in the late 1930s, Bargreen issued games including the "Skoup" ball game.

barking dogs In the mid-1800s "barking dogs" referred to toy dogs with what was probably a small bellows and squeaker mechanism. Toys of this and similar natures continued to be successful into the 20th century, with such items appearing as the "Barking Scottie" fur animal toy by J.S. Heyman and the "Barky Buddy" pull-toy by Fisher-Price Toys.

H.F. Barnes Co. A publisher based on West 31st Street, New York City, Barnes published books for the juvenile market, including *The Book I Made Myself* of 1939, an educational book toy.

Barney & Berry A Springfield, Mass., firm, Barney & Berry manufactured ice skates in the mid-1800s.

S.O. Barnum and Son Founded in 1845 in Toledo, Ohio, this foundry made cast iron wheel toys, which the Barnums sold in their own store.

Baron, Alexander Based in Brooklyn, N.Y., and a specialist in "dog furnishings," Alexander Baron also made holster sets in the late 1930s.

H. Baron Co., Inc. Games for adults were the specialty of this East 19th Street, New York City, firm in the postwar years.

Baron Metal Toys Co. Established on Madison Street, New York City, in the late 1930s, Baron made sand pails, horns noise-makers, and other metal toys.

barouches Barouches were a kind of carriages sometimes made in juvenile form in the 1800s. A barouche had a high driver's seat, two bench seats facing each other in the shallow body of the vehicle, with C-springs giving it suspension. A folding top rising from behind the rear seat gave protection against the elements.

Barowe, Inc. Based on Lake Shore Drive, Chicago, Ill., Barowe was a prewar maker of geographic globes.

The Barr Rubber Products Co. One of the famous Ohio rubber companies, this Sandusky, Ohio, firm advertised itself as "the World's Largest Toy Balloon Plant" in the 1920s, manufacturing balloons, rubber balls, and rubber toys. By the 1930s its line included produced rubber toy balloons, hollow rubber balls, sponge balls, latex animal toys, and novelties. Its line expanded by the end of the decade to include toy sporting goods. The "Bartex" trade name was used on its latex animal toys. The company continued into the Boomer years, emphasizing its line of balloons and rubber balls.

The "Junior All-American Sport Kit" by Barr Rubber Products Co. mid-1950s.

"Barrel of Fun" see *The Leister Game Co.*

"Barrel of Monkeys" see *Lakeside Industries.*

"Barrow" blocks prewar, see *Fisher-Price Toys.*

Barry Products Pipe-cleaner art kits were the specialty of this postwar Chicago, Ill., firm.

Barry Toycraft Co. Barry Toycraft made juvenile metal adjustable ironing boards, and electric and non-electric irons. It was based in Street Paul, Minn., in the postwar years.

Barth Stamping & Machine Works A Cleveland, Ohio, company, Barth produced jig saw puzzles.

Bartholomew Babies Bartholomew Babies were dolls associated with London's Bartholomew Fair. Some were apparently imported to America by the last decade of the 17th century.

baseball The sport called "Baseball" began to resemble the modern sport by the 1850s. Early manufacturers of baseballs and bats included Philip Goldsmith, Harrison Harwood, Hawes of Towanda, E.I. Horsman, Peck & Snyder, A.J. Reach & Co., A.G. Spalding & Bro., and Wright & Ditson. In the period before the war the separation of "serious" sport and traditional games was growing ever wider, if not to nearly the degree found today. In the 1930s the game remained above all a game. Manufacturers of baseballs and related equipment included W.F. Bradley Lumber Co., E.C. Brinser's Sons, the Faultless Rubber Co., P. Goldsmith Sons Co., H. Harwood & Sons, Hutchinson Bros. Leather Co., Indiana Handle Co., Ken-Wel Sporting Goods Co., Lannon Mfg. Co., McKinnon Leather Products Inc., the Moneco Co., National Sporting Goods Mfg. Co., A.J. Reach, Roy Bros., Harry Schallman, Thompson & Fox, Tobert Sporting Goods, Rolling Wilson, Wilson-Western Sporting Goods Co., and Zenn Beck Bat Co.

basketball Family games based on the sport of basketball were common in the Boomer years. Manufacturers included Cadaco-Ellis, Cherry Valley Mfg. Corp., De Marco Toy Co., E.E. Fairchild Corp., Gardner & Co., Gotham Pressed Steel Corp., Lido Toy Co., Logan Specialty Mfg. Co., Midwest Metal Stamping Co., N.Y. Toy & Game Mfg. Corp., Northwestern Products Co., Tudor Metal Products Corp, and West-Craft Novelty Co.

Bass Educational Toy Co. Based in Norristown, Penn., Bass specialized in prewar drawing kits, including "Sketchie" and the "E-Z Draw" pantograph board.

Bassett-Lowke, Wenman J. An importer and retailer based in Northampton, England, Wenman Bassett-Lowke was the first to establish a mail-order business in toys, mailing his first catalogs with tipped-in photographs, in 1899. In addition to promoting German and French lines of toys including Gebruder Maerklin, Gebruder Bing, and Georges Carette, he commissioned companies to produce British toy designs. His catalog was issued through the 20th century.

Bastian Bros. Co. A Rochester, N.Y., company, Bastian Bros. produced celluloid toys and novelties, baby rattles, pin wheels, and toy airplane propellers in the 1930s and '40s.

"Bat Masterson" The NBC-TV character "Bat Masterson" inspired numerous toys in the late 1950s and early '60s, including a cane, gun and holster set by Carnell Mfg. Co., coloring book by the Saalfield Publishing Co., western sets by John Henry Mfg. Co., hats by Arlington Hat Co., game by Lowell Toy Mfg. corp., and plastic figures by Hartland Plastics and Multiple Products Corp.

Bates, J.C. Bates was a silversmith working around 1860 in Northfield, Mass., who advertised toys.

"Bathinette" The Baby Bathinette Corp. of Rochester, N.Y., enjoyed enough success with its baby and doll "Bathinettes" in the 1930s that it defended its patents in court in 1938, successfully. The "Bathinette" was a device having a raised bath table with a folding surface parallel to one edge.

battery-operated toys Battery-operated toys had their origins early in the century, when Knapp Electric experimented with using wet-cell batteries to power toy automobiles. Self-contained dry cells became common enough by the mid-1920s to encourage numerous manufacturers to experiment with the battery-operated toy, although attempts to produce what would have been expensive toys were hampered by the Depression. Battery-operated toys became most common and most popular after World War II, made not only by American manufacturers but a number of highly energetic firms in Occupied Germany and Japan. Some of the prominent character battery-operated toys of the postwar years include "Barney Rubble and Dino," Louis Marx & Co., 1963; "Charlie Weaver Bartender," Rosko, 1960s; "Frankenstein Monster," T-N (Japan), 1960s; "Fred Flinstone and Dino," 22", Marx, 1960s; and "Tarzan," San-Co (Japan), 1960s. Some of the most desirable battery-operated toys, however, were inventive toys reflecting widespread interest in the future, science fiction, and space travel. Many were robot and robot-like toys, including "Atomic Robot Man," (Japan), late 1940s; "Big Loo," Marx, 1961; "Fighting Robot," Horikawa Toys (Japan), 1966; "Great Garloo," Marx, 1961; "Mr. Atomic," Cragston (Japan), 1960s; "Saturn Robot," Taiwan, 1970s; and "Son of Garloo," Marx, 1960s. Other imaginative toys played upon the popularity of the flying saucer concept, including "King Flying Saucer," Japan, 1960s, and "UFO-XO5," M-T Co. (Japan), 1960s. Many also reflected the active U.S. space program of the 1960s, including "Apollo, U.S.A., N.A.S.A.," K.K. Masutoku Toy Factory (Japan), 1960s; "Apollo Spacecraft," Alps Shop Ltd. (Japan), 1960s; "Apollo-X Moon Challenger," Nomura Toys Ltd. (Japan), 1960s, "Cape Canaveral Series 2000 Kit," Marx, 1960s; "Man in Space Astronaut," Alps (Japan), circa 1960; "N.A.S.A. Space Saucer," Hong Kong, 1960s; and "Space Capsule," Horikawa (Japan), 1960s.

Baumgarten & Co., Inc. "Toys That Print & Paint" served as motto for the 1920s stamp and stencil sets issued by Baumgarten, located in Baltimore, Md.

Bausch & Lomb Optical Co. Bausch & Lomb of Rochester, N.Y., began manufacturing microscopes and microscope kits for the juvenile market in the prewar years, when educational and scientific sets were growing in popularity.

Bay State Model Airplane Co. Based in Lynn, Mass., this prewar company specialized in model airplanes, gliders, and kits.

Bayless Bros. & Co., Inc. Bayless Bros. was a prewar doll manufacturer in Louisville, Ky.

Bayshore Industries A Boomer-years manufacturer based in Elkton, Md., Bayshore made balloons, masks, squeeze toys, "bend-me" toys and novelties, bowling alleys, ten pins, games, pre-school toys, make-up kits, play balls, and joker and novelty items.

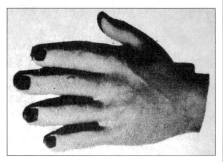

This "Giant Rubber Hand" was a Bayshore Industries toy from the 1950s.

The L.H. Bazuin Co. Based in Grand Rapids, Mich., in the late 1930s, Bazuin made hobby horses and wind-mill novelties, as well as Christmas tree stands.

Bburago This Italian company began manufacturing die-cast toy cars, especially "Formula One" race cars, in the mid-1970s.

J.P. Beach, An early game publisher, J.P. Beach issued "The Jolly Game of Goose" in 1851.

Frederick H. Beach, A prewar manufacturer based on West 42nd Street, New York City, Frederick H. Beach made juvenile punching bags, wood toys, die-cut puzzles, paint box kits, and doll cradles, as well as games for adults. Beach published the board

games "Sippa Fish" in 1936, "After Dinner" in 1937, "Fun Kit" in 1939, "Oldtimers" in 1940, "Scrambles" and "Stunt Box" in 1941, and "Take it and Double" in 1943. It released the activity game "Balloonio" in 1937. The firm became Frederick Beach & Co., Inc., in the postwar years, maintaining offices in the Fifth Avenue Building. It continued to specialize in games for children and adults, and hobby albums.

Henry S. Beach, Based in El Paso, Texas, Henry S. Beach issued Eskimo dolls and stuffed toy animals and birds in the late 1930s.

The Beacon Hill Craftsmen This late 1930s Beacon, N.Y., firm issued bow and arrow sets, and targets.

Beacon Hudson Beacon Hudson released at least two 1930s board games, "Open Championship Golf Game" and "World's Championship Golf Game."

Bear Products Co. Located in Chicago, Ill., Bear Products Co. issued toys and premiums on a special-order basis in the later 1930s. Its line included the "Popeye" acrobats.

Ray A. Beard Co. Based in Los Angeles, Calif., Ray A. Beard issued the "Forty-One" game in the mid-1930s.

A.E. Beck Mfg. Co. In the 1930s and '40s, A.E. Beck specialized in wooden items, including toy sail boats, juvenile furniture and toy furniture, jump ropes, bassinets, ironing boards, blackboards, and miscellaneous toys. Beck was based in Herrick, Ill.

Beck Products Co. A Pittsburgh, Penn., firm, Beck Products issued "Majik" ink and chemical trick toys in the late 1930s.

P. Becker & Co. A maker of toy trunks and the "Dolly Travel" line, this Chicago, Ill., company, based on West Monroe Street, also made table tennis sets and related items in the 1930s and '40s.

The Beckley-Ralston Co. This late 1930s Chicago, Ill., firm made the "Doodle-bug" hand-operated tri-cars.

Beco Mfg. Co. This Brooklyn, N.Y., company made electric games and toys in the mid-1930s.

Beco Plastics Co. see *Sidney A. Tarrson Co., Inc.*

Bedford Plastics, Inc. Jewelry sets, cosmetic kits, games and school kits were specialties of this Boomer-era Brooklyn, N.Y., firm.

Bee Bee Doll & Toy Mfg. Co. Based on West 21st Street, New York City, Bee Bee made dolls and stuffed toys in the 1950s and '60s.

"Bee-Bee" talking doll 1939, see *Mid-West Doll Mfg. Corp.*

"Bee-Line" see *The Beistle Co.*

"Beech Bonanza" see *Wen-Mac Corp.*

Beehler Arts The "Virga," "Play-Mates," "Kim," and "Hi-Heel Teen" dolls of the Boomer years were made by this West Street, New York City, firm. Beehler also made doll clothes.

William P. Beers Co. William P. Beers of Somers, Conn., made prewar novelty dolls, and stuffed animals and dolls.

"Beetleware" see *Bryant Electric Co.*

"Beginners' Luck" paint-by-numbers see *Craftint Mfg. Co.*

Behrend & Rothschild Based on East 23rd Street, New York City, Behrend & Rothschild made prewar metal novelties, mechanical toys, and registering banks. Its line included some leather items, including wallets and change holders, by the late 1930s, as well as banks having Walt Disney character designs.

Behrens Mfg. Co., Inc. Behrens manufactured hats and other paper goods for occasions including Halloween, New Years, and Street Patrick's Day. It was based on Blondell Avenue, New York City, in the postwar years.

The Beistle Co. In the 1920s through the prewar years, Beistle manufactured Valentines, Halloween paper novelties, Easter baskets, paper hats, and Christmas paper novelties. The Shippensburg, Penn., company added games in the 1930s. Its prewar Valentine cards included both folders and comic cards, and its Christmas items, artificial trees. The Beistle Co. also made "Mural-print" Mother Goose decorations, nursery wall sets, and paper hats. Since it depended on unrestricted materials, Beistle's line was largely unaffected by World War II. In the postwar years, Beistle Co. expanded its line to include cardboard toys, paper dolls, paper pop-guns, prize package toys, and numerous holiday novelties.

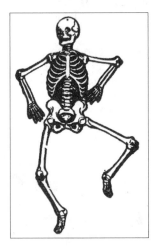

Cutout skeleton by The Beistle Co., 1950s.

Belcher, J. A Boston publisher, Belcher published *The History and Adventures of Little Henry*, an early toy book of the variety that featured a series of figures with a changeable head to move between them. The same publisher may also have been responsible for The *History of Little Fanny* from the same period. See *Little Fanny.*

Dora Bell Dress Co. Based in Miami, Fla., this firm issued ready-cut doll clothes in the late 1930s.

J.C. Bell, A 19th century publisher, J.C. Bell issued the 1980 board game "Uncle Sam's Baseball Game."

Bell Plastics Co. "Davy Crockett" tomahawks and knives were specialties of this Brooklyn, New York City, company in the 1950s and '60s. The firm also made plastic games, charms, novelties, and puzzles.

Bell Products Co. This St. Louis, Mo., firm made electric toys and educational toys in the Boomer era. It also manufactured transistor radios and some plastic toys.

bell toys Bell and chime toys were popular in the later 19th and early 20th century. Often consisting of a simple bell suspended between wheels, and sometimes of ornate construction, these toys made sounds of varying musicality as pushed or pulled across the floor. Important prewar manufacturers included Bevin Bros. Mfg. Co., L.A. Boettiger Co., the Gong Bell Mfg. Co., the N.N. Hill Brass Co., W.H. Leaman Co., Richmond Bros. Co., and Seiss Mfg. Co. Many early manufacturers were also involved in the manufacture of bells for such wheel toys as pedal cars, velocipedes and bicycles. Related toys included toy telephones and pull-toys, especially those developed by the Fisher-Price Toys. Bells were also used on dolls and stuffed toys, usually the spherical, dangling variety also found on some baby rattles. Prewar suppliers included Richmond Bros. Co. Bell and chime toys continued to be made in the Boomer years, with manufacturers including Buddy "L" Toys, Fisher-Price Toys, Gong Bell, N.N. Hill Brass, Henry Katz Organization, and Metal Masters Co.

Bellevue Products Co. Toy safes and the "Sky View Observatory" were specialties of this Bellevue, Ohio, company in the Boomer years.

Bellitz, S. This 1920s Philadelphia, Penn., manufacturer made masquerade hair goods including wigs, beards and mustaches.

"Bellphone" see *N.N. Hill Brass Co.*

Belvidere Strap Co., Inc. A leather goods manufacturer, Belvidere Strap Co. of Brooklyn, N.Y., made prewar pistol and holster sets, toy watches, and "kiddie purses." It also specialized in souvenir novelties.

The Bemis Riddell Fibre Co. Established in the later 1930s in Sheboygan, Wis., Bemis Riddell issued doll and baby carriages, bassinets, and children's furniture, including rockers.

Benay-Albee Novelty Co., Inc. This postwar manufacturer of novelty and Western hats was located in Maspeth, N.Y.

Ben-Her Industries, Inc. A specialist in "Bend-Me" toys, Ben-Her also made "Howdy Doody" toys in the 1950s and '60s. It was located on West 42nd Street, New York City.

"Ben Hur" Inspired by an action-packed motion picture, "Ben Hur" items came into fashion in the postwar years. Available playthings included the "Ben Hur Chariot Race" game by Lowell Toy Mfg. Co., coloring books land story books by Abbott Publishing Co., a Roman chariot kit by Adams Action Models, and toys by Acorn Industries.

Bendix Paper Co. Located on Canal Street, New York City, Bendix produced lithographed labels and pictures used on toys and games in the late prewar years.

"Bendme" see *Bayshore Industries.*

"Bend-Me," see *Ben-Her Industries.*

W.R. Benjamin Co. Based in Granite City, Ill., W.R. Benjamin issued the "Makit" wooden construction toy of the late 1930s and '40s. It also issued a "giant frame top," a foot-propelled lawn "Ferris Wheel," and parts for air guns. "Makit," similar to "Tinker Toys" in concept, was issued in four sizes by the war years: "Beginner's," with 47 pieces; "Primary," with 85; "Super," with 175; and "Jumbo Makit," with 275.

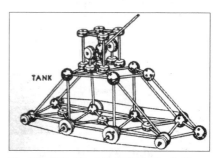

The "Makit Toy" tank by W.R. Benjamin Co.

Benjamin Electric Mfg. Co. The "Crysteel" furniture line, including juvenile furniture, of the 1920s was produced by this Des Plaines, Ill., company. The firm also went by the "Crysteel Works" name.

Benner Mfg. Co. This Lancaster, Penn., toy and furniture manufacturer specialized in items to "delight the kiddies" in the 1920s. Among its more unusual offerings was the 12-foot long "Jitney Coaster," which involved a wooden track, raised on one end, down which a 22-inch wooden car rolled. It also made seesaws, baby yards, spring horses, and baby walkers, and used the "Hy-Grade Toys" trade name. The firm became Benner, Inc., after the Great Depression, and was based in Mountville, Penn. The 1930s and '40s line included shooflies. In the post-war years, its lead items were shooflies in all styles, glider and spring rockers, "Rotating" see-saws, play yards, nursery chairs, high chairs, cribs, and travel cribs.

"Benningtons" Clay marbles with glaze are named "Benningtons," due to their resemblance to glazed works made by Bennington, Vt., potters. These marbles have "eyes," caused by the marbles being in contact with each other during firing. Most are brown.

P.J. Benrath Based in La Grange, Ill., P.J. Benrath issued the "31" card game of the late 1930s.

Benton, John Dean A silver and goldsmith working in Providence, R.I., Wilmington, Del., and Philadelphia, Penn., in the 1850s through '70s, Benton became famous for gold and silver models of railroad locomotives, ironclads (including the Monitor), and at least one steamer ship.

Benton Harbor Toy Co. This Benton Harbor, Mich., company produced prewar "popular priced" toy boats.

Berbro Mfg. Co. Based on Fifth Avenue, New York City, Berbro manufactured "Hot Rod Racers" in the 1950s-'60s, in both motorized and non-motorized forms.

Berea College Student Industries In the late 1930s, this Berea, Ky., company was formed to make soft dolls and animals.

Bergel of Hollywood, Inc. Stuffed animals and dolls with blinking eyes were the specialties of this Boomer-years company, based in Hollywood, Calif.

Bergen, Edgar Edgar Bergen's ventriloquist doll characters "Charlie McCarthy" and "Mortimer Snerd" became hot properties by the end of the 1930s, when companies including Fleischaker & Baum, Ideal Novelty & Toy Co., Kerk Guild, and Louis Marx & Co. were issued licenses to use their originally wooden likenesses. Edgar Bergen Interests of Hollywood, Calif., was licensor. Other companies arranging licenses by 1939 included Art Neckware Co., Bernson Silk Mills, George Borgfeldt Corp., Cohn & Rosenberger, Collegeville Flag & Mfg. Co., Columbia Proteletosite Co., E. Rosen Co., Eberhard Faber Pencil Co., Gilbert Clock Co., Samuel McCrudden Co., Marks Bros., Majestic Radio & Television Co., Pioneer Rubber Co., Plastic Novelties, Western Tablet & Stationery Corp., John C. Welwood Corp., White & Wykoff Mfg. Co., and Whitman Publishing Co.

"Mortimer Snerd" was one of the popular Edgar Bergen toys of the late 1930s.

Bergen Toy & Novelty Co., Inc.

Established in Carlstadt, N.J., in the mid-1930s by Charles Marcak, Bergen's initial line consisted of lead soldiers. Beginning in 1938, in cooperation with the injection-molding firm Columbia Protektosite Co., Bergen issued the "Beton" acetate soldiers, cowboys and Indians, and railroad figures. The line, rather than being hampered by materials restrictions in wartime, enjoyed healthy growth as the metal toy soldier manufacturers ceased production. Once Bergen moved to Hackettstown, N.J., after the war, it was producing all its own toys. The "Beton Toys" line included the "Dairy Farm and Cattle Range" and "Beton Circus" sets, U.S. Army infantry, and cowboys and Indians, sometimes sold with the slogan, "The World's Most Colorful Toy." These retained their popularity into the mid-1950s, by which time Louis Marx & Co. and other manufacturers had aggressively entered the world of plastic figure play sets. Bergen's assets were acquired by Rel Plastics in the late 1950s. The figures were also copied by other manufacturers.

Berger Playcraft Co. A company based in Two Rivers, Wis., in the late 1930s, Berger manufactured the "20th Century Bilder" construction toy and "Berger Bilder" blocks in several sizes appropriate for schools and home.

Berkeley Models, Inc. One of the leading model kit manufacturers of the 1950s and '60s, Berkeley was based in Hempstead, N.Y. It made model airplanes, miniature racecars, and modeling accessories and supplies.

Roy Berlin Co. Pogo sticks and stilts were specialties of this Los Angeles, Calif., firm in the Boomer years.

Bernhard Paper Favor Co. Based in Lima, Ohio, this company made prewar crepe paper character dolls, snapping mottoes, noise-makers, paper caps, and party novelties.

Bernson Silk Mills, Inc. Based on Madison Avenue, New York City, in the late prewar years, Bernson Silk Mills obtained a license to issue Edgar Bergen-related lounging pajamas, robes, and dresses.

Bersin Playthings, Inc. Based in the Fifth Avenue Building, Bersin made both juvenile and adult games, including construction toys, educational toys, "Playbird" badminton sets and accessories, quoits, shuffleboard, and target games, in the late prewar years.

Bersted's Hobby Craft, Inc. Rubber and plastic molds and kits to make plaster art model castings for hand painting were the specialty of this Monmouth, Ill., company, in the Boomer years.

Berwin Corp. Toy typewriters, educational toys, and metal toys were lead items for this Kenilworth, N.J., firm in the 1950s and '60s.

Best Art Products, Inc. This Brooklyn, N.Y., firm made postwar school and novelty crayons, chalk, and paint sets.

B

Best-Ever Products Co., Inc. Best-Ever was a postwar producer of stuffed toys, based in Brooklyn, N.Y.

Best Plastics Corp. Plastic toys, sewing kits and party favors were specialties of this Brooklyn, N.Y., company. Its toys, which included rubber-band powered speedboats, appeared from the late 1940s into the 1960s.

"Beton" see *Bergen Toy & Novelty Co.*

"Betsy Ballerina" see *DeJournette Mfg. Co.*

"Betsy Boo" cloth dolls prewar, see *Adler Favor & Novelty Co.*

"Betsy Green" toys prewar, see *Buffalo Toy & Tool Works.*

"Betsy McCall" A paper doll who originated in the pages of McCall's, "Betsy McCall" enjoyed unusual popularity during the Boomer years in both two and three dimensions, inspiring toys including dolls by American Character Doll Co., doll furniture by Strombeck-Becker Mfg. Co., miscellaneous items by Standard Toykraft Products, and "Betsy McCall's Pets" by Knickerbocker Toy Co. The American Character Doll Co. line was issued from 1957 to 1963. In 1964, Uneeda Doll Co. introduced a more up-to-date "Betsy McCall" fashion doll.

"Betsy McCall" was inspired by McCall's magazine.

Betsy Ross Electric Products Corp.

A prewar manufacturer of home and travel electric irons, this Johnson City, N.Y., company also produced toy irons into the 1940s.

B

"Betsy Ross" sewing machines see *Gibraltar Mfg Co.*

"Betsy Wetsy" see *Ideal Toy & Novelty Co.*

The Bettcher Stamping and Manufacturing Co. A Cleveland, Ohio, company, Bettcher made the "Buildal Builds All" toy of the 1920s, billed as "the construction toy that every child can understand."

"Betty Boop" In the 1930s, George Borgfeldt Corp. made miscellaneous Betty Boop toy specialties. Cameo Doll Co. also produced Betty Boop dolls, and the Ullman Mfg. Co. issued "Betty Boop's Movie Cartoon Lessons." Peltier Glass Co. issued "Betty Boop" marbles in the late 1930s.

"Betty Crocker" bake sets see *Ideal Novelty & Toy Co.*

"Betty Brite" The "Betty Bounce" and "Betty Brite" dolls appeared in the 1930s from Fleischaker & Baum.

"Betty Lou" toy bags and kits prewar, see *Ideal Products Mfg. Co.*

"Bettyware" see *Banner Plastics Corp.*

Beulah Toy & Novelty Co. This Brooklyn company issued the mid-1930s "Speller" and "Word Lotto" games. It issued the "Magnetik" backgammon, checkers and chess games through the prewar years.

Beverly Game & Novelty Co. Based in Beverly Hills, Calif., this company's products included "Cross-O-Grams" in the 1930s.

"Beverly Gray" books see *Grosset & Dunlap.*

Beverly Mfg. Co. A manufacturer producing felt goods, this Staunton, Va., company also made stuffed dogs in the 1930s.

Bevin Bros. Mfg. Co. Bevin Bros. of East Hampton, Conn., produced metal stampings, gongs, and bells for the toy trade in the 1930s.

"Bex" toys and games prewar, see *Metal Toy Co.*

"BFLO" toys prewar, see *Buffalo Toy & Tool Works.*

"Bi-Car" children's vehicle prewar, see the *W.J. Baker Co.*

"Bi-Kar" children's vehicle prewar, see *Hill Standard Corp.*

bicycles In prewar times bicycle manufacturing was a major business for companies across the country. Manufacturers included American National Co., Arnold, Schwinn & Co., Auto-Bike Co., the E.C. Brown Co., the Colson Co., Dayton Art Metal Co., the Emblem Mfg. Co., Excelsior Mfg. Co., Garton Toy Co., Gendron Wheel Co., D.P. Harris Hardware & Mfg. Co., Huffman Mfg. Co., Iver Johnson's Arms & Cycle Works, Junior Toy Corp., Metal Specialties Mfg. Co., Shelby Cycle Co., Skippy Racers, Steinfeld, W.A. Strohm & Bro., Toledo Metal Wheel Co., and Westfield Mfg. Co. By the late prewar years, firms joining their ranks included Allied Mfrs. of America, Cleveland Welding Co., Compax Mfg. Co., Monark Silver King, and the Murray-Ohio Mfg. Co. In the Boomer years, some earlier firms continued to thrive, notably Arnold, Schwinn & Co., Garton, Harris, Huffman, Murray, and Westfield. Newer firms included AMF Cycle Co., American Machine & Foundry Co., Barnett & Sons, Blake & Conroy, Blazon, Chain Bike Corp., Evans Products, Hedstrom-Union Co., Junior Toy Division, Julius Levenson, McBride & Oxford Mfg. Co., Midwest Industries, Ranger Cycle Co., Bert Scheuer, and Stelver Cycle Corp. Argo Industries Corp. made "water bicycles."

"The Taylor Sidewalk Cycle," 1920s.

"Bicypedes" see *Hedstrom-Union Co.*

Bieser, Charles W. see *American Soldier Co.*

"Biff" repeating cap pistol prewar, see *Kenton Hardware Co.*

The Biffit Co. Based in Alhambra, Calif., the Biffit Company issued a rubber ball and paddle game in the 1930s.

"Big Bad Wolf" Walt Disney's Big Bad Wolf character enjoyed great popularity in the 1930s, inspiring a variety of toys and playthings, including costumes by Sackman Bros. Co. and Wornova Mfg. Co., a Parker Bros. game, metal lithographed toys by Ohio Art Co., pop-up books by Blue Ribbon Books, rubber dolls and balls by Seiberling Latex Products Co., a stuffed toy by Knickerbocker Toy Co., and a wooden toy from the Toy Kraft Co.

"Big Bang" The "Big Bang" and "Big Dandy" toy cannon and pistols were made by the Conestoga Corp.

"Big Ben" The "Big Ben" name was used for several prewar children's vehicles, including a handcar by Hill Standard Corp. and a "truck wagon" by the Monarch Products Co. In the postwar years, it was used for puzzles by Milton Bradley Co., a tailless kite by the Hi-Flier Mfg. Co.

"Big Big" books see *Whitman Publishing Co.*

"Big Bill" cap pistol prewar, see the *Kilgore Mfg. Co.*

"Big Boy," 1920s see *Kelmet Corp.*

"Big Boy" The "Big Boy" prewar coaster wagons were made by American National Co. The same name was used in the 1930s by several other manufacturers as well. Hi-Flier Mfg. Co. used it for tailless kites; Milton Bradley Co., for paint and crayon sets as well as its "Quoit rope rings"; and A.C. Gilbert Co., for tool chests. Hi-Flier's "Big Boy" was issued through the Boomer years.

"Big Chief" While the Monarch Products Co. made the prewar "Big Chief" coaster wagons, the name was widely used elsewhere. In the 1930s the "Big Chief" name also appeared on bow and arrow sets from Rollin Wilson, glass marbles from the Rosenthal Co., Indian wigwam tents from the Blake Co., and a pistol from the Dent Hardware Co. The postwar "Big Chief" pistol was issued by Academy Die-Casting & Plating Co.

"Big Dandy" see *"Big Bang."*

"Big 4" coaster wagons prewar, see *White Coaster Wagon Works.*

"Big Little" books see *Whitman Publishing Co.*

"Big Load" toys prewar, see *American Mfg. Concern.*

"Big 6" Somehow the "Big 6" name proved popular in the 1930s, when a University Toy & Novelty Mfg. Co. game, a Goody Mfg. Co. repeating cap pistol, and a Wayne Toy Mfg. Co. target game all appeared under the name.

"Big Poly" see *Eldon Mfg. Co.*

"Big Stuff" single shot pistol prewar, see *Kilgore Mfg. Co., Inc.*

Big Time Toys, Inc. The "Bobbin-Dobbin" stick horses of the 1950s and '60s were made by this Houston, Texas, firm.

Big Top Games A Minneapolis, Minn., firm, Big Top was a games publisher in the Boomer years.

Bijou Toy Co. Based on West 19th Street, New York City, Bijou Toy Co. issued plush toys and infant novelties in the late 1930s. In the postwar years it continued as Bijou Toys, Inc.

"Bildkraft" toys prewar, see *Hustler Toy Corp.*

"Bill Ding" see *Strombeck-Becker Mfg. Co.*

Billie-Toy Mfg. Co., Inc. Wooden pull toys, educational toys, and magic sets were produced by this prewar New York City company, based on Broadway.

Billings, Inc. A Providence, R.I., company, Billings produced sand pails, sprinklers and shovels, sand sets, jump ropes, butterfly nets, tether tennis, and other activity toys in the 1930s and '40s.

Billy Boy Toy Co. Cast iron toy versions of such urban commonplaces as fire boxes, mail boxes, traffic signs, and fire hydrants were made by this Cleveland, Ohio, firm in the mid-1930s.

Bilnor Corp. In addition to wading and swimming pools, this Brooklyn, N.Y. firm made beach and bathtub toys and "surf riders," in the 1950s and '60s.

Bilt-Rite Baby Carriage Co., Inc. A Brooklyn, N.Y., company in the postwar years, Bilt-Rite manufactured baby carriages and doll carriages.

The Biltmore Mfg. Co. Biltmore, based in Cincinnati, Ohio, issued the "Dolly's Comfort" line of doll accessories in the late 1930s.

"Biltwell" wheel toys early 1930s, see *The Globe Co.;* late '30s, see *Garton Toy Co.*

Bilwin Co., Inc. This Briarcliff Manor, N.Y., company made the "Snow-Skeeters" snow skates of the Boomer years.

Bilz-Em Toys, Inc. Based in Port Huron, Mich., Bilz-Em Toys produced wooden construction sets in the mid-1930s.

Bimblick & Co. Wood bead dolls in the "Joy Doll Family" were 1920s products of this West 25th Street, New York City, firm. Bimblick also made ten pin sets.

Gebruder Bing Founded in 1866 by brothers Ignaz and Adolf Bing, this Nuremberg, Germany, toy firm became one of the most famous at the turn of the century and following decades. The company made a wide range of spring-driven toy cars, boats, and buses, with one of its most successful lines being the railroad systems it began making in 1882. A victim of the crash of 1929, the Maerklin toy train division was acquired by Karl Bub, and the toy boats line, by Fleischmann. See also *Georges Carette.*

Binghamton Sled Co. Based in Binghamton, N.Y., this firm manufactured sleds in the later 19th century. See *Henry R. Morton.*

Binley Cut Flower Holder Co., Inc. Shuffleboard and quoit boards were among this East 42nd Street, New York City, firm's line in the late 1930s. Binley also made table tennis equipment and tables.

Binney & Smith Co. Based on East 42nd Street, New York City, Binney & Smith issued "Crayola" crayons, "Grip-Fix" waterless paste, and "Artista" water colors before the war. "Gold Medal" became a major trade name for the company's chalks, water colors and crayons by the late 1930s. "Crayola" crayons became a staple in school rooms and play rooms across the country during the Baby Boom years, when the firm was also using the "Crayolet" trade name.

Binney & Smith Co., introduced "Crayola" crayons before World War II.

Birchcraft, Inc. Based in Waukesha, Wis., Birchcraft produced swings, wooden automobile toys, and doll beds in the 1930s.

Bissell Carpet Sweeper Co. Engaged in making functional carpet sweepers, this Grand Rapids, Mich., company also made toy versions in the prewar years and later. It used the "Little Queen" trade name for its housekeeping sets and sweepers from the '30s through the Boomer years.

Bissell's "Mother's Helper Toy Cleaning Set" was a favorite prewar toy.

"Black Beauty" Besides being the name of a famous fictional horse hero, "Black Beauty" was a trademark used on toys and playthings in the prewar years. Items under the name included a paint box from Milton

Bradley Co., police outfits from Dumore Belt & Novelty Co., and wheel goods from D.P. Harris Hardware & Mfg. Co.

"Black Sambo" see *"Little Black Sambo."*

blackboards Prewar blackboards are of considerable interest to collectors of juvenilia. Larger than small, hand-held or lap-held slates, many blackboards were held on easels, often with decorative or educational elements on the frame or on a separate board above the slate. Prewar manufacturers included American Mfg. Concern, A.E. Beck Mfg. Co., the Beistle Co., the N.D. Cass Co., H.G. Cress Co., Danzi Toy Mfg. Co., Drewry Bros., Fox Toy Co., Lehman Co. of America, Makatoy Co., Mason & Parker Mfg. Co., W. Howard Moudy, National School Slate Co., Playskool Institute, Richmond School Furniture Co., and Weber Costello Co. Dozens of firms made blackboards in the Boomer years, with notable names including Gotham Chalkboard & Trim Co., National School Slate, and Richmond.

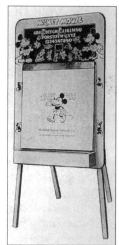

"The Mickey Mouse Blackboard" by Richmond School Furniture Co., 1930s.

Blackman Plastics A manufacturer of "HO" model train layouts and accessories, Blackman was based in Los Angeles, Calif., in the postwar years.

The Blake Co. This Rockford, Ill., company made prewar "Big Chief" Indian wigwam play tents.

Blake Industries, Inc. Animated rubber and latex toys were the specialty of this Boston, Mass., firm in the 1950s and '60s.

Blake Industries, Inc. This Detroit, Mich., company issued the "Bouncing Putty" of the Boomer years.

Blake Mfg. Co. Based in Clinton, Mass., Blake Mfg. Co. was a supplier to manufacturers of prewar juvenile wheel goods. Its products included window lights and hubcaps.

Bland Charnas Co., Inc. The Costume Division of this Brooklyn, N.Y., company made postwar masquerade costumes.

Blazon, Inc. An Akron, Ohio, firm, Blazon manufactured velocipedes, sand boxes, rocking horses, juvenile automobiles and tractors, bicycles, baby swings, roller coasters, and juvenile furniture in the Boomer years.

"Blendwell" crayons see *American Crayon Co.*

R. Bliss Mfg. Co. Founded in 1845 in Pawtucket, R.I., by Rufus Bliss, this early manufacturer first advertised toys in the early 1870s. The company was known for its use of lithographed paper on wooden toys, including architectural building blocks, dollhouses, boats, and trains. The company also made boys' tool chests, archery sets, and miscellaneous toys through 1914, when it was sold to Mason & Parker of Winchendon, Mass. Board games made by Bliss often had a topical nature, with many reflecting the country's active interest in the American West at the time. They included "Game of Attack," "The Game of Detective," "League Parlor Base Ball" and "Game of the Wild West" in 1889, "Game of the Dudes" and "Game of the Newsboy" in 1890, "Game of Shopping" and "Stanley in Africa" in 1891, "Runaway Sheep" in 1892, "Visit to the Farm" and "Game of the World's Columbian Exposition" in 1893, "Life in the Wild West" in 1894, and "Arena" in 1896.

Bloch Go-Cart Co. Manufacturers of "rustic furniture" and "invalid chairs," this Philadelphia, Pa., company also produced toys, baby carriages, and nursery furniture.

B

"Block City" see *Plastic Block City, Inc.*

Block House, Inc. An importer and manufacturer representative, Block House was the sole agent in the 1920s and '30s for "Richter Stone Blocks" and "Hausser Elastolin" soldier and animal toys. It was based on Fourth Avenue, New York City, moving to Broadway in the postwar years.

"Blockfast" see *Blockraft, Mfg. Co.*

"Blockhead" puzzles prewar, see *The Puzzle Makers.*

Blockraft Mfg. Co. Based in Grand Rapids, Mich., Blockraft made prewar toy construction blocks. By the late 1930s it was making "Zoocraft" animal sets and other educational toys. It may have used the "Essential Toys" slogan in wartime. Relocating to Cedar Springs, Mich., in the postwar years, Blockraft developed a full line that included construction blocks, "Primary" blocks, "Educator" blocks, magnetic trains, and educational toys. The firm's "Snap-N-Play" building blocks, introduced by the mid-1950s, differed from conventional building blocks in having small metal snaps attached to their sides, which added to their versatility. These were sold in boxes with the "Blockfast" trade name, and issued into the 1960s.

blocks, stone and composition Some building block toys were made of stone, fired clay, or composition. Prewar manufacturers included Block House, Meccano Co. of America, and Northwestern Products.

blocks, wood The first name in American wood blocks was Charles M. Crandall. Block manufacturers before the Great Depression included American Mfg. Concern, Milton Bradley Co., N.D. Cass Co., the Embossing Co., Samuel Gabriel Sons & Co., Halsam Products Co., J.L. Wright, the A. Schoenhut Co., and Scott Mfg. Co. The success of the idea of selling blocks in bags might be indicated by the existence by the 1930s of the "Bag of Blocks" from the A.I. Root Co., the "Bag O' Blocks" from the Ark Toy Makers, and the "Busy Blox," also packaged in bags, from the G.B. Lewis Co., among many others. Prewar manufacturers greatly expanded in number, to include the American Crayon Co., American Mfg. Concern, American Novelty Works, Ark Toy Makers, Blockraft Mfg. Co., Milton Bradley Co., the N.D. Cass Co., Crosman Bros. Co., the Embossing Co., Fisher-Price Toys, Fox Blocks Co., the Fox Toy Co., Furniture City Dowel Co., Samuel Gabriel Sons Co., Halsam, Hansen Wood Goods & Toy Mfg. Co., Hart Wood Products Co., Holgate Bros. Co., Hollywood Products Co., Ideal Products Corp., the Jackson-Guldan Violin Co., Richard G. Krueger, Kupper-Heidt Mfg. Co., J. Landowne Co., J.B. Lewis Co., the Mengel Co., Pendleton & Townsend, Henry Pilcher's Sons, the Playcraft Co., A.I. Root Co., the A. Schoenhut Co., Sheffield Toys, J.W. Spear & Sons, Tangle Wood Toys, the Toymakers, and Wordcraft. With the flood of newborns in the country in the 1950s and '60s, blocks sold well through the Boomer years. Makers of alphabet blocks included Blockraft, E.E. Fairchild Corp., Halsam, Kusan, and Twinzy Toy Co. Building blocks were made by a wide range of companies, of materials ranging from traditional wood to rubber, hard plastic, and soft plastic, sometimes in snap-together forms. Suppliers included American Toy & Furniture Co., Bardell Mfg. Corp., Milton Bradley, Brrr Products, Childhood Interests, A.H. Delfausse Co., Design Industries, Educator Playthings, Ellcraft Industries, Fisher-Price, the Fritzel Toys Corp., Samuel Gabriel, Gem Toys, and Gerber Plastic Co. Other makers of postwar building blocks were Goshen Mfg. Co., Greyshaw of Georgia, Halsam, Herald Toy Products Co., Holgate, Knickerbocker Plastic Co., Kohner Bros., Fred Kroll Asosciates, Kusan, Lapin Products, Lido Toy Co., M. & L. Toy Co., Metal Moss Mfg. Co., Plastic Block City, Plastic Toy & Novelty Corp., Playskool Mfg. Co., Sifo Co., Statler Mfg. Co., and Strombeck-Becker Mfg. Co. The venerable tradition of nested blocks, which went back to 1880s Crandall lines, continued with new versions in the 1950s and '60s by Fairchild, Samuel Gabriel, Gerber, and Plastic Toy & Novelty.

Fisher-Price "Creative Block Wagon," 1960s.

blood alleys see *taws.*

Blossom Doll Co., Inc. Located on East 20th Street, New York City, this prewar company made fabric dolls, mannequins, and doll hats, shoes, and stockings. By the late 1930s it was issuing "mammy" dolls and stuffed animal toys.

"Blox Kids" prewar, see *Holgate Bros. Co.*

"Blue Bird" Besides being used by the various companies bearing the name, "Blue Bird" was a widely used prewar trademark. It appeared on toy stoves and ranges from Grey Iron Casting Co., strollers from Auto-Wheel Coaster Co., furniture from N.D. Cass Co., and coloring kits from the Ullman Mfg. Co. The "Bluebird" wagons were also prewar, made by Steel Stamping Co.

The Blue Bird Co. Based in Baltimore, Md., the prewar Blue Bird Co. made small metal novelties for premium purposes.

Blue Bird Favor Co. A maker of paper novelties and decorations, this prewar company was based on Sigel Street, Chicago.

"Blue Boy" riding horse prewar, see *Whitney Bros. Co.*

"Blue Eagle" toys see *The Murray-Ohio Mfg. Co.*

"Blue Racer" wagon prewar, see *Auto-Wheel Coaster Co.*

Blue Ribbon Books, Inc. A publisher of juvenile books, located on Fourth Avenue, New York City, Blue Ribbon Books published Mickey Mouse pop-up and "waddle" books in the 1930s through an early license with Kay Kamen.

"Blue Ribbon" picture puzzles see *Madmar Quality Co.*

"Blue Ribbon" skates and wheel goods prewar, see *D.P. Harris Hardware & Mfg. Co.*

Blue Ridge Knitting Mills, Inc. This Walnutport, Penn., firm made knitted deluxe doll clothes in the 1950s-'60s.

Blue Ridge Novelties Doll beds and cradles, toy kitchen cabinets, and hand-made corn shuck dolls were made by this prewar Old Fort, N.C., manufacturer of children's furniture.

"Blue Streak" The Toledo Metal Wheel Co. used the "Blue Streak" trademark on prewar juvenile vehicles. In the postwar years, the name was used by Auto-Wheel Coaster Co. for a racer sled.

"Bluff" see *G.W. D'Arcey Co.*

The Stephen Blum Co. The Stephen Blum Co., on East 18th Street, New York City, produced doll outfits and doll carriage cover sets in the 1930s.

Blum Bros., Inc. Located on Wooster Street, New York City, this prewar paper box manufacturer made doll trousseau trunks in the 1930s.

Blum-Lustig Toy Co., Inc. This East 17th Street, New York City, firm made "French dolls in the flapper mode" in the 1920s.

H.J. Blumberg Co. Based on Broadway, New York City, in the late 1930s through the Boomer years, Blumberg manufactured dolls and novelties. The dolls were made of vinyl by the later 1950s. The firm also made doll clothing.

"Blutip" see *A. & J. Kitchen Tool Co.*

"Boat Boy" boats prewar, see *Patent Novelty Co.*

boat toys Boat toys could take almost any form, from simple pieces of wood barely whittled into shape to the most elaborate, floating models of historical ships that required only a miniature crew to make them complete. Extremely popular toys in prewar times, manufacturers of general boat toys included Abba International Products Co., American Maid Artcaft Studios, American Wunder Mfg. Co., O.B. Andrews Co., Benton Harbor Toy Co., Boucher Playthings Mfg. Corp., Buffalo Toy & Tool Works, the N.D. Cass Co., J. Chein & Co., Conestoga Corp., James A. Coulson, Fisher-Price Toys, Hansen Wood Goods & Toy Mfg. Co., Holgate Bros., the Hubley Mfg. Co., the Lindstrom Toll & Toy Co., Mantua Toy & Metal Products Co., Mason & Parker Mfg. Co., the Mengel Co., Miami Wood Products Co., Model Ship Supply Co., Ottawa Mfg. Co., Quoddy Boat, Rubbercraft Corp., the A. Schoenhut Co., Shoe Form Co., Skipper Mfg. Co., Thornecraft, Tillicum Sales Corp., and Weeden Mfg. Co. Boomer-era manufacturers included K. & B. Allyn Co., Alvimar Mfg. Co., Amerline, Amloid Co., Banner Plastic Corp., Bayshore Industries, Beaver Toys, Bilnor Corp., Cavacraft Model Airplanes, Comet Metal Products Co., Dowst Mfg. Co., Eldon Mfg. Co., Elmar Products Co., the Holiday Line, Ideal Toy Corp., Kestral Corp., Knickerbocker Plastic Co., Lido Toy Corp., Multiple Products Corp., Ohio Art Co., Pal Plastics, Payton Products, Renwal Toy Corp., Thomas Mfg. Corp., Tonka Toys, United Mask & Novelty Co., U.S. Fiber & Plastics Corp., Wolverine Supply & Mfg. Co., and Jay V. Zimmerman. See also *boats, construction kits; boats, mechanical and electrical; boats, sail.*

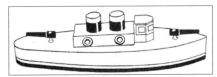

This 1930s toy boat by Tillicum Sales Corp. was simply one of many from the period.

boats, construction kits Model-building had become a popular endeavor by the 1930s, with boats often being the subject of choice. Many companies chose well-known ships for their kits, as did Megow's Model Airplane Shop, which produced "Santa Maria," "Seth Parker," "U.S.S. New York," "U.S.S. Lexington," and "Endeavor," in the mid-1930s. Other prewar manufacturers included Aero Model Builders Guild, Bildon Co., Boucher Playthings Mfg. Corp., the Boy Toymaker Co., Golden Aircrafts Corp., Paul K. Guillow, Ideal Aeroplane & Supply Co., Paul Jones, Model Ship Supply Co., Selchow & Righter Co., Selley Mfg Co., Thornecraft, and Ullman Mfg. Co. The great enthusiasm shown toward model kits of all kinds in the Boomer years extended to boat models. Manufacturers multiplied, with notable names including Aurora Plastics, Berkeley Models, Monogram Models, Multiple Products Corp., Pyro Plastics Corp., and Pyro Plastics Corp. Their number also included A-J Aircraft Co., Aristo-Craft Distinctive Miniatures, Associated Hobby Mfrs., Comet Metal Products Co., Comet Model Hobbycraft, Consolidated Model Engineering Co., L.M. Cox Mfg. Co., Crafco Corp. of California, Dumas Products, Hillcraft Industries, Ideal Aeroplane & Supply Co., Lindberg Products, D.N. Mallory, Polk's Model Craft Hobbies, the Royal Tot Co., Scientific Model Airplane Co., Sterling Models, and Strombeck-Becker Mfg. Co.

boats, mechanical and electrical

The development of efficient, small motors adaptable to toy use contributed to the explosion of electric-powered toys in the early 20th century. Children and adults felt a natural attraction to mechanical boat toys, which represented a step up from the age-old childhood pastime of floating whatever would float in a pool or pond. Prewar manufacturers included Boucher Playthings Mfg. Corp., Calcraft Co., Gobar Products, Keystone Mfg. Co., the Lindstrom Tool & Toy Co., the Lionel Corp., Richard Maerklin Toys, Mantua Toy & Metal Products Co., the Mengel Co., Miami Wood Products Co., Shoe Form Co., Skipper Mfg. Co., and the Straits Corp. By the late prewar years, Emmert-Hammes & Co., Hoge Mfg. Co., John G. Martin Jr., Steel Materials Co., and H. Walter Sykes

B

joined their number. These premium toys continued in popularity in the Boomer era, with manufacturers including J. Chein & Co., T. Cohn, Duban Shade Corp., Fleet Line Marine, Irwin Corp., John G. Martin, Oak Park Tool & Die Co., Ohio Art Co., Rel Mfg. Corp., and Wen-Mac Corp.

boats, sail Toy sailboats must have a history stretching back thousands of years, with all evidence sunk in the muds of ancient lakes and seas. The manufacture of toy sailboats increased steadily through the end of the 19th century. Manufacturers in the earlier post-Great Depression years included American Maid Artcraft Studios, A.E. Beck Mfg. Co., Boucher Playthings Mfg. Corp., the N.D. Cass Co., J. Chein & Co., Keystone Mfg. Co., Maine Yacht Corp., Ottawa Mfg. Co., Quoddy Boat, and Thornecraft. By the late prewar years, other manufacturers included John G. Martin Jr., Metcalf Mfg. Co., Passamaquoddy Boat Co., and Transogram Co. Despite the attractions of more complex toys being issued in the 1950s and '60s, manufacturers still found it worthwhile to issue sail boats through the Boomer years. They included American Toy Products, Berkeley Models, Cavacraft Model Airplanes, T. Cohn, Consolidated Toy Mfg. Co., Irwin Corp., John G. Martin, Pet Toy of N.H., Plasticraft Mfg. Co., and Sollmann & Whitcomb.

"Bobbing Tudy" toys prewar, see *Petrie-Lewis Mfg. Co.*

"Bobbsey Twins" Besides appearing in a famous series of books published by Grosset & Dunlap, the Bobbseys inspired playthings in the Boomer years, including the "Bobbsey Twins on the Farm" game by Milton Bradley Co. in the late 1950s, and a play house by Grosset & Dunlap.

"Bobby Bounce" dolls prewar, see *George Borgfeldt Corp.*

"Bobster" sled 1961, see *Garton Toy Co.*

Charles M. Boeckling Based in Peru, Ill., Boeckling made "Beck's Collapsible Sand Box" in the 1920s, an easily assembled device that came in both canopied and open versions.

Paul Boehland & Co. This Milwaukee, Wis., company produced tree decorations,

electrical lighting and "Fairy Crown" ornaments in the 1920s and '30s.

Boetsch Bros. This New Rochelle, N.Y., phonograph manufacturer included juvenile phonographs in its postwar line.

Louis A. Boettiger Co. Boettiger's "All-in-One" checkerboard was the company's mainstay in the 1920s. The board was a folding one, with a groove around the edges to hold the playing pieces for transport. Teethers under the "Baby Bite" trade name, pacifiers, and kiddie goggles were added to the line in the 1930s. The company was based on Leonard Street, New York City. In the Boomer years, based in Hewlitt, Long Island, N.Y., Boettiger issued infant toys, rattles, squeeze toys, crib exercisers, suction toys, and rubber swim goods.

Bogert & Hopper, Inc. A wood-turning business, this Varick Street, New York City, company produced toys including bubble blowers.

H. Boker & Co., Inc. In addition to the "Boycraft" construction sets, H. Boker & Co., located on Daune Street, New York City, made radio tools, sewing cases, and tool kits in the mid-1930s.

Bollinger, W.C. Established in Hanover, Penn., in the late 1930s, W.C. Bollinger specialized in children's rocking chairs.

Bo-Lo Co. This Atlanta, Ga., firm made "Bo-Lo" paddle ball toys in the late 1930s.

"Bonanza" The famous NBC hit of the late 1950s and '60s inspired numerous playthings, including a game by Parker Bros. and hats by Arlington Hat Co. in 1960. Toys later in the decade included puzzles by the Saalfield Publishing Co. and Milton Bradley Co., and a toy firearms outfit by Louis Marx & Co.

Bond, Stephen H. A manufacturer in New Bedford, Mass., Stephen H. Bond made toy boats, wind toys, and toy furniture in the 1930s.

Bongo Corp. The "Bongo Board," a balancing board of the 1950s and '60s, was made by this Fifth Avenue, New York City, company.

Bonney Forge & Tool Works An
Allentown, Pa., iron works, Bonney produced quoits in the 1930s and '40s.

Bonnie Bilt, Inc. In addition to wheel
goods and bicycle accessories, Bonnie Bilt made construction kits and Western toy sets in the Boomer era. It was located in Lawrence, Long Island, N.Y.

"Bonnie" books see *Samuel Lowe Co.*

"Bonnie" dolls prewar, see *Playmate Doll & Toys Co.*

Bonnytex Co. This postwar manufac-
turer made items for infants, including molded squeeze toys. It was based on Fifth Avenue, New York City.

Bonser Doll Co. Stockinette dolls for
infants, labeled "I am a Bonser Doll," were issued in the 1920s by this Mineola, Long Island, N.Y., company. In the earlier '30s the company changed its name to Bonser Products, calling its line of soft-body dolls and animal toys "The Bonsers."

"Bookmite Stories" books prewar,
see *Einson-Freeman Co.*

books, children's In America, children's
books go back at least to the 1640s, when John Cotton's *Spiritual Milk for Boston Babes, Drawn Out of the Breasts of Both Testaments*, first appeared. A question-and-answer book on religious doctrine, it stayed in print through the end of the century.

Publishers of children's books were often also producers of puzzles, paper dolls, and cutouts, as well as such items as stencil outfits, drawing and tracing books, coloring books, and toy books, all of which straddle the line between the "book" and the "toy." Prewar publishers included American Colortype Co., the Baltimore Salesbook Co., Blue Ribbon Books, Child Welfare Publishers, Cupples & Leon Co., M.A. Donohue & Co., Einson-Freeman Co., Samuel Gabriel Sons, the Goldsmith Publishing Co., Charles E. Graham & Co., Greenberg, the Harter Publishing Co., William G. Johnston, the Lezius-

Hiles Co., M.S. Publishing Co., Macrae Smith Co., David McKay Co., McLoughlin Bros., Peerless Engraving Co., the Platt & Munk Co., the Reilly & Lee Co., Rosebud Art Co., the Saalfield Publishing Co., Simon & Schuster, Stecher-Traung Lithograph Corp., Stoll & Einson Games, Sweeney Lithograph Co., Whitman Publishing Co., John C. Winston Co., and World Syndicate Publishing Co. Dozens of companies competed in the children's publishing field in the Boomer years, with notable names including the Gelles-Widmer Co., Grosset & Dunlap, Merrill Co. Publishers, the Platt & Munk Co., Rand McNally & Co., the Saalfield Pub. Co., Whitman Publishing Co., and Wonder Books.

books, coloring By the Boomer years,
coloring in coloring books became a nearly universal childhood experience. The publication of a wide variety of television serial and cartoon tie-ins made these books especially attractive. The lines of the Saalfield Publishing Co. and Whitman Publising Co. were especially prominent. Other postwar publishers included the Belmont Press, Creston Crayon Co., Eberhard Faber Pencil Co., Fun Bilt Toys, Grosset & Dunlap, Jack Built Toy Mfg. Co., Jak-Pak-Inc., Merrill Co. Publishers, the Platt & Munk Co., Stephens Publishing Co., and the Watkins-Strathmore Co.

boomerangs Sold as toys in the prewar
years, boomerangs were available from manufacturers including Abba International Products Co., Aluminum Goods Mfg. Co., and American Boomerang Co. In the Boomer era, the Alox Mfg. Co., Block House, and General Sportcraft Co. supplied the toys.

Boone, Daniel see *"Daniel Boone."*

George Borgfeldt & Co., George Borgfeldt Corp. Founded in 1881 by
George Borgfeldt with Marcell and Joseph Kahle in New York City, George Borgfeldt & Co. started as an importer and wholesaler of toys, including comic novelty tin wind-ups under the "Nifty" trademark. Still a toy importer in the 1930s, by which time it was known as the George Borgfeldt Corp., the company obtained an early license with Kay Kamen to produce Disney character toys and

novelties. Based on East 23rd Street, New York City, it sold general toys and the "Bye-Lo Baby" doll, among many other lines. Besides European and Japanese dolls, its imports included Steiff products. In the late '30s it obtained a license to issue Edgar Bergen related metal banks. The company continued well into the Boomer years, closing in 1962. In its last years, besides toys and dolls, it was emphasizing Easter and Halloween goods and tree ornaments.

Joseph Borzellino & Son
A small Atlantic City, N.J., company, Borzellino made games including "The Soldier on Fort" war game in the 1930s. Late in the decade it issued a combined "Soldier on Fort" and checkers board.

"Boston" chalk
see *Standard Crayon Mfg. Co.*

Boston Globe
The publisher of the famous Boston newspaper also published at least one game, the "Boston Baseball Game," in 1906.

"Boston Spinner" toys
prewar, see *A.M. Samour Mfg. Co.*

Boston Stilt Co.
This Boston-based company made adjustable stilts before the war.

H.E. Boucher Mfg. Co.
Based on Lafayette Street, New York City, Boucher manufactured "Toys That Are More Than Just Toys" in the 1920s, including sail boats, motor boats, engines, trains, construction sets, and locomotives. As Boucher Playthings Mfg. Corp., the company continued issuing miniature powerboats, sailboats, fittings, marine engines, and scale model ship supplies through the prewar years. It was based on Lafayette Street, New York City.

"Boulevard"
The "Boulevard" name was used on prewar velocipedes and baby carriages made by American National Co.

"Bouncing Putty"
see *Blake Industries.*

Bouton-Woolf Co., Inc.
A 1920s and '30s toy and game importer, Bouton-Woolf, located on West 24th Street, New York City, issued dolls, toys and novelties for the 5-cent-to-dollar stores. Its line included "Phyllis" dolls in the earlier '30s, and "Miss Babette" in the later 1930s.

The Bower Mfg. Co.
"Half Pint" coin banks and glass bowl banks were specialties of this Goshen, Ind., manufacturer in the Boomer years.

Bowers & Hard
A publisher in the early 1900s, Bowers & Hard issued the board games "Vanderbilt Cup Race" in 1906 and "Teddy's Bear Hunt" in 1907.

The Bowlet Co.
Based in Indianapolis, Ind., in the 1930s and '40s, the Bowlet Co. was known for its eponymous miniature adult bowling game.

The George H. Bowman Co.
This Cleveland, Ohio, manufacturer issued the "Like-Mother's" toys of the 1920s, including toy stoves and toy aluminum sets. The company also made the "Bowman" wheel-toy line.

bows and arrows
The bow and arrow toy was of high interest to prewar children. Safety laws saw to the swift decline and then disappearance of the toy in later years. Prewar manufacturers included the Archers Co., Bredenberg Bros., Glen Novelty Co., Indian Archery & Toy Corp., King Mfg. Co., Marks Brothers Co., Outdoor Amusement Co., A.S. Payne, F.D. Peters Co., Selchow & Righter Co., L.E. Stemmler, Rollin Wilson, and Woodcraft Equipment Co.

"Little Scout" arrow set, Rollin Wilson Co., 1950s.

"Boxville" 1920s, see *Superior Paper Box Co.*

"Boy Chemist" chemistry outfits, prewar, see *Sequoia Sales Co.*

Boy Craft Co. Plastic construction kits were the specialty of this Skokie, Ill., company in the 1950s and '60s.

The Boy Toymaker Co. This Brooklyn, N.Y., manufacturer produced the "Boy Boat Builder," "Nail-a-Toy" and "Historical-Model-Maker" educational sets in the 1930s. See *The M. Carlton Dank Toy Corp.*

Boyce-Meier Equipment Co. Located in Bronxville, N.Y., Boyce-Meier issued a toy sextant and adding toy in the late 1930s.

"Boycraft" construction blocks prewar, see *H. Boker & Co.*

"Boycycle" tricycle see *Steinfeld.*

The Boyd Specialty Co., Inc. The "Moon Rocket" and launcher, "Gizmo" flying saucers and launcher, and other plastic flying toys were 1950s-'60s specialties of this Columbus, Ohio, company. It also made boxed games, an ice cream machine, beads, puzzles, and premiums.

Boynton & Co. A Chicago, Ill., firm established in the later 1930s, Boynton issued games including "Tek-No-Krazy" and "Battleship," as well as novelty figures.

"The Boy's Own Toy-Maker" Subtitled "A Practical Illustrated Guide to the Useful Employment of Leisure Hours," E. Landell's 1860 book gave directions for building toys ranging from toy model vehicles and buildings to the "thaumatrope" optical toy. Taking the practical view that a child who learns to work materials has an advantage over one who does not, Landell invoked the Baconian adage, "Knowledge is power," and promoted leisure play as beneficial to individuals and society.

"Boy's Pal" coaster wagon prewar, see *Sheboygan Coaster & Wagon Works.*

boxing gloves Boxing as an activity for children was not only popular among children but also met with general parental approval in prewar times. Widespread, heightened enthusiasm for boxing continued into the early days of television. Most manufacturers of adult boxing gloves also made miniature versions for children. Prewar manufacturers included P. Goldsmith Sons Co., Hutchinson Bros. Leather Co, Ken Wel Sporting Goods Co., McKinnon Leather Products, the Moneco Co., A.J. Reach, and Wilson-Western Sporting Goods Co.

"Bozo" This famous clown, played by countless individuals on early television programs across the country, started off as a Capitol Records novelty record which struck chords with America's early Boomer kids. A wide variety of tie-ins were issued, with licenses initially controlled the Bozo Products Division of Beechwood Music Corp. The early "Bozo the Capitol Clown," issued through at least 1960, was made by Renall Dolls.

H.G. Brace & Co. This Seattle, Wash., firm issued the "Game of '49" in 1939.

Milton Bradley Co. Milton Bradley Co. was founded by Milton Bradley in 1861 in Springfield, Mass. It used the slogan, "Maker of the World's Best Games." Business began for Milton Bradley with his moral game, "The Checkered Game of Life" of 1860. He quickly branched into educational games, books, kindergarten teaching aids, school supplies, card games, and toys. "The Checkered Game of Life" was reissued in 1911, and the famous and greatly updated "The Game of Life" in 1960. Games of the 1870s included card game "Trips of Japhet Jenkens and Sam Slick" in 1871, and board games "Bamboozle, or the Enchanted Isle" in 1876 and "Squails" in 1877. The 1880s saw the appearance of card games "Excursion to Coney Island" and "Game of Costumes and Fashions," and board games "Bradley's Circus Game" in 1882, "Trip to Washington" in 1884, and "Halma" in 1885. The "Fairyland Game" also appeared in the '80s. The 1890s games included "Game of Old Mother Hubbard," "Swing a Peg" and "Table Croquet." The activity game "Conette" and "ADT Messenger Boy" both appeared in 1890, followed by board games "Columbus" in 1892, "The Gypsy Fortune Telling Game" and "Hippo-

B

drome Circus Game" in 1895, and "Go Bang" in 1898. "Mammoth Conette" also appeared in 1898.

The 1900s saw the appearance of timely and popular board games including "Bradley's Telegraph Game" and "Tourist, a Railroad Game." Other board and activity games included "Buying and Selling Game" in 1903; "Across the Yalu," "Game of Beauty and the Beast," "The Cadet Game," "The Fortune Teller," "Fox Hunt," "Hurdle Race," "Motor Cycle Game," and "Through the Locks to the Golden Gate" in 1905; "The Auto Game" in 1906; "Game of Bottle Imps" and "The North Pole Game" in 1907; "Turn Over" in 1908; and "Fire Fighters Game," "Jack and Jill," and "Game of Robinson Crusoe" in 1909. Card games of the decade included "Down the Pike with Mrs. Wiggs at the St. Louis Exposition" in 1904, "Cinderella" in 1905, "Wyhoo!" in 1906, "Golliwogg" in 1907, and "Game of Nations" in 1908. The 1910s saw the company's level of activity in the games world increase to an even greater degree, with popular card games "Grandma's Game of Useful Knowledge," "Home History Game" and "Game of Snap" appearing, along with activity game "Spin It" and board games "Game of India," "Little Boy Blue," "Little Jack Horner," "Race for the Cup," "Game of Steeple Chase," "Three Bears," and "Three Little Kittens." That decade began with a flurry of new titles. Card games in 1910 included "Crow Cards" and "Game of the Lost Heir." New board games included "Bicycle Race," "Cabin Boy," "Canoe Race," "Fast Mail Game," "The Happy Family," "Game of Old Mrs. Goose," "Peter Rabbit Game," "Toy Town Bank," and "Toy Town Conductors Game." New games later in the decade included "Honey Bee Game" in 1913, "'Round the World Game" in 1914, "The Game of Advance and Retreat" and "War of Nations" in 1915, and card game "Game of Goat" in 1916. The 1920s again showed increased activity, with new and popular titles including "American Boy Game," "Cross Country Marathon," "Game of Mail," "Movie-Land Lotto," "The Moving Picture Game," "The Overland Limited," "Game of Tiger Tom," and "Uncle Wiggily's New Airplane Game." The company used the slogan,

"The World's Best Games." Other games of the decade included "Saratoga Horse Racing Game" and "Walking The Tightrope" of 1920, "Cinderella" in 1921, "Barney Google and Spark Plug Game" in 1923, and "Andy Gump, His Game" and "Genuine Steamer Quoits" in 1924. In 1925, "Baseball and Checkers," "On the Mid-Way," "Game of the Transatlantic Flight," and "Walk the Plank" board games appeared, as well as card games "Peter Coddle's Trip to New York" and "Game of Twenty Five." "Babe Ruth's Baseball Game," "Radio Game," "Ring My Nose," and "Game of Stop, Look and Listen" appeared in 1926. 1927 saw the appearance of "The Game of Air Mail," "Flight to Paris," "Flivver," "Little Orphan Annie Game," "Moon Mullins Automobile Race," and "Toonerville Trolley" board games, and the "Walt and Skeezix Gasoline Alley Game" of cards. "Tiddley Golf Game" and the appropriately entitled "Down and Out" activity game appeared in 1928.

In the aftermath of the Great Depression, Milton Bradley again emerged as one of the leaders in the world of games. The company increasingly embraced cartoon and radio characters for game inspirations. Important titles of the decade including "Chester Gump Hops Over the Pole," "Fast Mail Railroad Game," "Fire Department," "The Gumps at the Seashore," "Harold Teen Game," "Little Orphan Annie Shooting Game," "Nebbs on the Air, a Radio Game," "Game of the Nebbs," "The Outboard Motor Race," "Pop the Hat," "Game of Scouting," "Skeezix and the Air Mail," "Skeezix Visits Nina," "Smitty Game," "Smitty Speed Boat Race Game," "Smitty Target Game," "Snug Harbor," "Game of Three Blind Mice," "Touchdown," "Game of Voyage Around the World," and "Winnie Winkle Glider Race Game." The company also enjoyed success with "Little Orphan Annie" and "Popeye" paint boxes. By mid-decade the company was running at full steam, listing as its specialties games including "Harlem," "Scavenger Hunt," "Check and Double Check," "I-Go," "Renju," "Rumme," "Spoof," "Round About Dolls," "Roulette," "Pirate and Traveler," and "Three Musketeers." By this time the company was producing a full "Bradley Line" which

B

included crayon sets, painting outfits, Bingo, Lotto, building blocks, nested blocks, kindergarten games, target games, chess and checker boards, picture puzzles, table croquet, table tennis, backgammon, dissected maps, board games, card games, soldier sets, party games, and adult games. Other successes of the 1930s—their sheer number indicates how large the Springfield, Mass., manufacturer had become—included "Endurance Run" in 1930; "Through the Clouds" in 1931; "Jolly Clown Spinette" and "Game of Skippy" in 1932; "Horse Racing" and "Three Men in a Tub" in 1935; "Easy Money," "Fibber McGee," "G-Men," and "Three Men on a Horse" in 1936; "Bull in the China Shop," "Carnival," "Charlie Chan," "Dr. Busby" and "The Game of Tom Sawyer" in 1937; "Chester Gump Game," "Go to the Head of the Class," "Snow White and the Seven Dwarfs," and "Vox-Pop" in 1938; and "Blackout," "Game of Friendly Fun," "Pinocchio the Merry Puppet," and "Town Hall" in 1939. In the late 1930s, the firm's leading titles included the question-and-answer game "Go to the Head of the Class," the 'glamorous' horse-race game "King of the Turf," the pirate board game "Plunder," and 'merry puppet' game "Pinocchio." Its lead titles for the youngest children were "Animal Ball Game," "Friendly Fun Game," "Jolly Picnic Game," and "Rainbow Game."

While still an active manufacturer, the titles issued in the early 1940s reflected the slowdown the industry as a whole experienced with the onset of World War II. "Fibber McGee and the Wistful Vista Mystery" and "Winko Baseball" appeared in 1940, "Box Hockey" and "Raggedy Ann's Magic Pebble Game" in 1941, "Ice Hockey" and "Adventures of Superman" in 1942. In wartime, the firm issued "great games in tune with the times," in its own words, including "Air Raid Warden," "Trade Winds, the Merchant Marine Game," "Battle of the Tanks," "Spotta," "Men of Destiny," "Fighting Marines," "Ferry Command, the Flying Fortress Game," and the 'booming seller,' advertised as 'today's game of thrills,' "Blackout." The company also continued issuing painting sets, picture puzzles, blocks, toys, and the "Tillicum" line of toy wooden boats. Milton Bradley enjoyed continued success in the

Boomer years, with its core products including adult and children's games, puzzles, anagrams, building blocks, checkers, crayons, cutouts and paper dolls, darts and dart games, farm sets, finger paint sets, hammering sets, looms, modeling clay, preschool toys, and water color sets.

The familiar Milton Bradley logo.

Fred K. Braitling, Inc. In the 1920s, specializing in real hair and mohair wigs "in all fashionable styles," Braitling used the "American Toys" trademark and "Dolly Dimple" trade name. Besides wigs it was making doll shoes, slippers, and stockings, using both genuine and artificial leather. The firm, having been established in 1869 in Bridgeport, Conn., used the "60 Years of Knowing How" slogan. The company continued making doll shoes and other accessories, including doll skates, in the 1930s. In the late prewar years its line expanded to include doll furniture.

Braley Midland Co., Inc. Based in Catlettsburg, Ky., Braley Midland manufactured toy rubber balloons and balloon novelties from the 1930s through the Boomer years.

Charles Brand, Based on West 7th Street, New York City, Charles Brand issued fur tails, which were popular adornments for use on caps and bicycles, and "lucky rabbit paws," in the late prewar years.

Louis P. Brantz Co. A Philadelphia, Penn., firm, Louis P. Brantz issued doll carriages, high chairs, cribs, and wheel goods. It was established in the late 1930s.

Benny Bratchet, Ltd. Located on East 9th Street, New York City, this company issued the 1939 "Benny Bratchet" stuffed dog.

Brauer Brothers, Inc. A prewar St. Louis, Mo., company, Brauer brothers manufactured play cowboy equipment.

Braun Mfg. Co., Inc. A Chicago, Ill., firm, Braun issued "Red Wing Nok-Down" archery sets in the late 1930s.

"Brave Eagle" "Brave Eagle" items included plastic figures by Hartland Plastics and playsuits by Sackman Bros. Co. in the 1950s and '60s. Licensing rights were controlled by Roy Rogers Enterprises.

Braymer Stuffed Toys, Inc. The "Braymer Prestige Line" featured long-pile plush stuffed toys in the 1950s and '60s. An affiliate of Columbia Toy Products Co., it was based in Kansas City, Mo.

Bredenberg Bros. Based in Champlain, N.Y., this prewar company made bows and arrows, doll bassinets, and sports equipment. In the later 1930s Bredenberg Bros. focused on hockey sticks, skis, toboggans, and paddles.

"Brer Rabbit" In the 1930s, Winchester Toy Co. made a "Brer Rabbit Bunny" stuffed toy, and Parker Bros. made a "Brer Rabbit" ring-toss game.

Charles A. Brewer & Sons Brewer, located on Harvard Avenue, Chicago, manufactured 1930s and '40s punch board games.

The Brewer-Titchener Corp. A Cortland, N.Y., company, Brewer-Titchener supplied manufacturers of prewar juvenile wheel goods. Its products included hub caps.

Breyer Molding Co. This Chicago, Ill., firm became the most famous name in medium-sized horse toys in the 1950s and '60s, gaining respect for its devotion to accuracy in depicting horse and other animal breeds. Earlier models were made of a glossy, hard plastic. The firm was established in 1950.

"Bri-Tone" crayons see *Imperial Crayon Co.*

Bricky Corp. Bricky issued construction toys, stuffed animals, felt dolls, toy theaters, and novelties. It was based in Brooklyn, N.Y., in the late 1930s.

"The Bride" "The Bride" and "The Bridegroom" were among the most popular of the paper dolls issued by McLoughlin Bros. in the last decade of the 19th century. The bride's wardrobe included a variety of gowns, while the groom's included both civilian and dress military clothing.

"Bridge & Turnpike" see *Kenner Products Co.*

"Bridge Builder" construction toy see the *Tec-Toy Co.*

Bridge Master, Inc. This Fifth Avenue, New York City, firm issued the "Four Aces" solitaire-bridge board of the late 1930s.

Bridgomatic, Inc. Located on West 34th Street, New York City, this firm issued its bridge game in the late 1930s.

"Brik Sets" prewar, see *The Meccano Co. of America.*

"Briktor" "Briktor" was a prewar trademark used on mechanical and electrical toys made by A.C. Gilbert Co.

The Brinkman Engineering Co. In the 1920s, Brinkman Engineering issued table-top skill games including "Basby Rack" shooting game, "Bowling Alley," "Shoot the Moon," and miniature rubber-cushion pool tables, as well as a line of toy telephones. The firm was based in Dayton, Ohio. Its game line included "Hurdle," "Animal Cage," "Whirlpool," and a baseball game by the mid-1930s. By late in the decade it had added junior medicine kits, and "Derby Winner."

E.C. Brinser's Sons, Inc. Based in Richmond, Va., E.C. Brinser was a manufacturer of prewar baseball bats.

S. Briskie The prewar company S. Briskie, located on Broadway, New York City, made play suits under the "Ruff N' Ready" trademark, with designs for Indian, cowboy, fireman, baseball player, and policeman costumes. It also made Halloween costumes.

William Britains Ltd. A London, England, firm established in 1893 by William Britain. Britains introduced and specialized in the three-dimensional hollow-cast lead soldier. It produced faithful replicas of more than 100 British Army regiments in its first decade. After becoming the world's largest producer of lead toy soldiers, Britains changed its production from lead to plastic in 1966.

Britannia Ware The term referred to toy dishes and housewares made of a metal of greater hardness than pewter, in the mid-1800s.

The Brittain Products Co. The "Dennis the Menace" bat and ball set of the early 1960s was issued by this Cuyago Falls, Ohio, manufacturer of puzzles, tops, pull toys, and practice golf balls. Its miscellaneous products included the "Drinking Rocket," introduced in 1955, a spill-proof drinking container shaped as a rocket ship.

Broadfield Air-Models Balsa gliders, remote-control field box kits and airplane supplies were specialties of this Ashland, Mass., firm in the postwar years.

Broadfield Glider Co. Based in Hempstead, N.Y., Broadfield Glider produced prewar gliders, construction kits, and balsa wood boomerangs.

Broadway Toy Mfg. Co., Inc. Located on W. Houston Street, New York City, Broadway made postwar musical toys, and fur and plush toys.

Brockton Mfg. Co., Inc. The "Dolly-Pak" doll accessories and doll luggage of the mid-1950s were issued by this Brockton, Mass., company. The line included miniature traveling, hat bag, shoe bag, garment bag, and diaper bag sets.

Brockton Plastics, Inc. This Brockton, Mass., company made Boomer-era plastic toys and hoops.

Brodhaven Mfg. Co. Located on Wooster Street, New York City, Brodhaven produced prewar jump ropes, lariats, banks, and wood dolls. By the late 1930s it was manufacturing knitting dolls, crayon-filled dolls and novelties, quoits, and ten pins.

"Broken Arrow" Tie-in's for the "Broken Arrow" character, licensed by M.R.W. Associates, were relatively few, but included hat ensembles by Newark Felt Novelty Co.

Brookglad Corp. This postwar doll manufacturer was based in the Fifth Avenue Building, New York City.

Brooks Co. Based in Brighton, Mass., Brooks Co. manufactured prewar games and "Shadow Pictures."

A.N. Brooks Corp. Banks and juvenile lamps were specialties of this postwar Chicago, Ill., firm.

Brooks Shoe Mfg. Co. This Philadelphia, Penn., manufacturer of "Little League" shoes and juvenile bowling shoes also made roller and ice skates in the 1950s and '60s.

"Brookside" crayon outfits prewar, see *Milton Bradley Co.*

The Brothers Mfg. Co. Based in Brooklyn, N.Y., this postwar firm made toy carpet sweepers and housecleaning sets, and kitchen sets.

Brown, Frederick This Boston, Mass., publisher issued John Greene Chandler's "The Game of Coquette and Her Suiters" and the boxed cut-outs "The American National Circus" in 1860. Brown also pushed Chandler-illustrated books "The Good Little Pigs Library" and "The Rock-a-Bye Library."

Brown, Herbert O. Based in Fairfield, Maine, Herbert O. Brown issued a "pipe organ doll display" featuring Shirley Temple, in 1939.

Arthur Brown & Bro., Inc. The "Jon Gnagy 'Learn to Draw'" art sets and paint-by-number sets of the Boomer era were made by this West 46th Street, New York City, company.

B

George W. Brown & Co.
George W. Brown was the first firm to produce clockwork toys, doing so as early as the 1850s. The company was founded in 1856 by George W. Brown and Chauncy Goodrich in Forestville, Conn. Its line included boat toys, wheeled vehicles, animal platform toys, horse-drawn vehicles, and bell toys, made of painted tin. George W. Brown produced a wide variety of mechanical wind-up toys, including paddling steamboats, railroad locomotives, a girl pushing a double hoop, a girl riding a velocipede, and a girl pushing a baby carriage, the last based on W.F. Goodwin's "Automatic Toy." Others included circus wagons, horse-drawn toys, the "Automatic Waltzer" pair of dancing figures, a "Machine Shop," and small animals. Although the company merged with J. & E. Stevens Co. in 1868, the original name continued in use until around 1880. See *American Toy Co.*

Brown & Eggleston
A maker of carriages and cabs in the 1850s, Brown & Eggleston also made hobbyhorses, children's carriages, and a kind of Irish Mail with a horse's head in the front.

The E.C. Brown Co.
The E.C. Brown Co. of Rochester, N.Y., made the "Velo-King" children's vehicles in the 1930s, including velocipedes, tricycles, bikes, scooters, and the "Velo-King Air Line" velocipedes.

The Les Brown Co.
This Naperville, Ill., firm made children's upholstered furniture, rocking and wheel horses, and miscellaneous toys in the late 1930s. In the postwar years it specialized primarily in upholstered juvenile furniture.

Brown County Folks
Located in Brown County, Ind., this prewar company produced "Abigail" and other character dolls, children's furniture, and wood toys.

"Brown-Eye" dolls
see *Remco Industries.*

The Brown Industries, Inc.
The "Air-O-Shoot," one of many 1920s flying toys, was issued by this Cincinnati, Ohio, firm.

The Brown Mfg. Co.
Based in Clinton, Mo., the Brown Mfg. Co. took part in the late 1930s Chinese checkers craze with its wood "Game of Chinker-Chek."

Brown, Taggard & Chase
This Boston, Mass., publisher issued early John Green Chandler paper dolls from 1857. The firm used the slogan, "Hurray for the Little Folks," on the envelopes holding the dolls and clothing.

"Brownie"
The "Brownie" name was used on roller skates from F.D. Kees Mfg. Co. and a game from M. H. Miller Co.

"Brownie" velocipedes
see *The Colson Co.*

Brownie Bill Nursery Timer Co.
This La Crosse, Wis., company's combination alarm and nursery clock was issued in the late 1930s.

Brownlee & Shaw, Inc.
A Chicago, Ill., firm, Brownlee & Shaw issued "Table Mibs" marble game in the late 1930s.

Brrr Products
Based in Hasbrouck Heights, N.J., Brrr Products' postwar line included giant blocks, animal costumes, and fibreboard toys including teepees.

Brumberger Sales Corp.
Postwar manufacturers of electric phones and slide and stereo viewers, Brumberger also manufactured mailbox savings banks and "Western Union" telegraph signal sets. It was based in Brooklyn, N.Y.

The Brunswick-Balke-Collender Co.
This Chicago, Ill., firm made the "Brunswick Junior Playmate" and pocket billiard tables in the 1920s. It continued making toy billiard tables into the mid-1930s.

"Bryan" toys
see *Ohio Art Co.*

Bryant Electric Co.
A manufacturer of children's dishes and "Hemcoware," this Bridgeport, Conn., company obtained an early license in the 1930s from Kay Kamen to produce Walt Disney character toys. Its toys, which were issued by its Hemco Plastics Division by the late 1930s, grew to include children's "Beetleware" tea sets and infant feedings sets, again including Disney designs.

Karl Bub Founded in 1851 by Karl Bub, this Nuremberg, Germany, firm specialized in clockwork tin transportation toys, including trains. Karl Bub's early practice of enameling his toys was changed later to lithography. In the 1920s and '30s, many Karl Bub toys reached the American market through F.A.O. Schwartz, the company's exclusive distributor. The firm continued in operation until 1966.

I.L. Buchan & Co. Established in Benton Harbor, Mich., in the late 1930s, Buchan issued "White Wing" Indian dolls and souvenirs.

bubble blowers Bubble blowers and bubble pipes are probably as old as soap. Prewar manufacturers included American Bubble Pipe Co., Bogert & Hopper, Milton Bradley Co., Du Point Viscoloid Co., J. Lesser Toy Mfg. Co., Jack Pressman & Co., Ray Laboratories, J.W. Spear & Sons, and Transogram Co. Undoubtedly spurred by developments in plastics technology, the number of manufacturers expanded in the Boomer years. Their number included the Alox Mfg. Co., Atomic Industries, Chemical Sundries Co., Elmar Products Co., Jak-Pak, Lido Toy Corp., Mace Plastics Corp., Manhattan Kreole Products, Merry Mfg. Co., Riemann, Seabrey Co., Starliter Co., and Waterbury Companies. Transogram also remained active in the field.

"Buck Jones" The Western movie star Buck Jones, at the height of his popularity in the earlier 1930s, authorized use of his name on the "Buck Jones Special" by Daisy Mfg. Co. The 1934 gun was the third character gun toy produced by the company. A 1937 radio program called "Hoofbeats," featuring Buck Jones, also led to some premium items, including pins, rings, and badges.

"Buck Rogers" The Buck Rogers franchise took off with the popularity of the science-fiction comic strip of the early 1930s. Early items included books from Whitman Publishing Co., casting sets from Rapaport Bros., chemical sets from Porter Chemical Co., a game from Lutz & Sheinkman, helmets and holsters from Daisy Mfg. Co., chemistry sets by Gropper Mfg. Co., and play suits from Sackman Bros. Especially notable early toys

were the "Buck Rogers Rocket Pistol," and the "Disintegrator" and "Liquid Helium" pistols, from Daisy Mfg. Co. The "Buck Rogers Rocket Ship Fleet" was made by John F. Dille Co., and the "Buck Rogers 25th Century Rocket Ship," by Louis Marx & Co. Radio premiums were issued by Kellogg's in the years 1932-33; by Cocomalt, 1933-35; and Cream of Wheat, 1935-36.

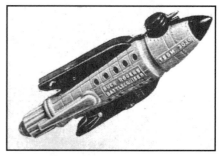

"Buck Rogers Battlecruiser," by Dowst Mfg. Co.

Buccheister Films, Inc. Based in Ridgefield Park, N.J., in the late 1930s, Buccheister produced "Movie Master" 8 and 16 mm. films, including films for the juvenile market.

"Buckee Horse" prewar, see *Janesville Products Co.*

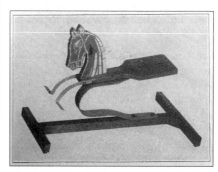

"Buckee Horse," 1920s.

"Buckeye" see *Kenton Hardware Co.*

"Buckin' Bronk" exerciser see *Excel Specialty Co.*

"Bucking Bob" horse see *Charles & Victor Goldstein.*

"Bucking Broncho" see the *Frank F. Taylor Co.*

B

"Bucking Horse" holster and gun

prewar, see *Keyston Bros.*

Buckingham Sports Co. Based on
Lafayette Street, New York City, in the late
1930s, Buckinham specialized in table tennis
and badminton.

The Buckstaff Co. One of the major pre-
war manufacturers of toy furniture, doll beds,
and doll high chairs, the Buckstaff Co. of Oshkosh, Wis., also manufactured a complete line
of infant and juvenile furniture. Both appeared
under the "Buckstaff" trademark.

"Buddie" The "Buddie Bikes" and "Bud-
die Walkers" of the 1930s were made by Garton Toy Co.

"Buddy Kar" prewar, see *The Frank F. Taylor Co.*

Buddy "L" Mfg. Co., Buddy "L" Corp. The Moline Pressed Steel Co.,
founded in 1910 by Fred Lundahl in East
Moline, Ill., entered toy making in 1921,
beginning with a pressed-steel pickup truck.
Lundahl named the firm's toys "Buddy 'L'"
after his son. By mid-decade, the company
had a line of some 30 trucks and road-con-
struction toys. In the later 1930s the company
added printing presses to its line. The company's toy division's name was made Buddy
"L" Manufacturing in 1930, and Buddy "L"
Wood Products or Buddy "L" Victory Toys
during wartime. "Buddy 'L' Steel toys,
famous for a generation, are out for the dura-
tion," the firm said. In the Boomer years it
was Buddy "L" Quality Toys Division,
Moline Pressed Steel Corp. It later became
Buddy L. Corp. See also *sand toys.*

"Buddy 'L' logo, 1930s.

"Buddy" pistol prewar, see *The Dent The Hardware Co.*

"Buddy" wagons see *Sheboygan Coaster & Wagon Works.*

"Buddy" wheelbarrows see *American-National Co., The*

Buell, Marjorie Henderson see *"Little Lulu."*

T. Buettner & Co., Inc. Girls' crafts and
toys were specialties of this Boomer-era Chicago, Ill., manufacturer.

"Buffalo Bill" The quasi-historical figure
of "Buffalo Bill" was a creation of dime nov-
elist E.C.Z. Judson, who wrote under the
name Ned Buntline. While William Cody
existed and enjoyed some exploits in the
West, Judson gave him his more famous
name. The pop-hero's star rose again in the
Boomer years with a Screen Gems motion
picture. "Buffalo Bill" items resulting
included cap pistols by Academy Die-Casting & Plating Co., leather-cased plastic toy
canteens by Spraz Co., and pistol holsters by
Mt. Vernon Mg. Co.

Buffalo Educational Games Co.
Established in Buffalo, N.Y., in the late
1930s, this firm made dart baseball and dart
football games.

"Buffalo" kazoo see *Kazoo Co., Inc.*

Buffalo Malleable Iron Works, see
Pratt & Letchworth.

Buffalo Metal Furniture Mfg. Co.
This Buffalo, N.Y., firm made juvenile
twisted-wire furniture in the mid-1930s.

Buffalo Toy & Tool Works A major
prewar manufacturer of toys, Buffalo Toy &
Tool Works was founded in 1924, with early
toys including lightweight pressed steel airplane and automobile toys, and carousel toys.
It was based in Buffalo, N.Y., with offices in
the Fifth Avenue Building. By the end of the
'20s the company had added "Dolly's
Washer" and "Little Miss Wash-Tub." Its pre-
Great Depression line also included rifles,
shooting galleries, Ferris wheels, seesaws,
racers, sweepers, pull-toys, and six "Instant-
Wind" toys. In the 1930s the firm was mak-

B

ing mechanical toys including "Electric Lite" toys, racers, zeppelins, laundry sets, "Cleanette" sets, and toy household items including sweepers and washing machines. The "Modern Miss" set included tub with washboard and wringer, hamper, stool, and rack dryer; the "Washette" set, the tub and washboard, crank-turned washer and wringer, and dryer; and the "Tiny Tot" set, the tub, washboard, and dryer. The "De Luxe Mangle" was an electrically powered wringer. The company added ten pins games and surprise package toys by the end of the decade. The firm closed in 1968.

"Tiny Tot" laundry set, Buffalo Toy & Tool Works, 1930s.

Bugle Toy Mfg. Co. A novelty company based in Providence, R.I., Bugle Toy made paper and tin horns, noisemakers, and miscellaneous party and carnival goods. It also made "Swagger Sticks" in 24, 30 and 36 inch lengths, in the 1920s and '30s. The "Parade Canes" were issued in the late prewar years.

"Bugs Bunny" The star of Warner Bros. Pictures, Bugs Bunny appeared in a variety of Boomer-era playthings, including books by Whitman Publishing Co., magic slates by Watkins-Strathmore Co., masquerade costumes by Collegeville Flag & Mfg. Co., plush toys by Bijou Toys, stick-ons by Colorforms, and film cards by Tru-Vue Co.

R.H. Buhrke & Co. Located on Fullerton Avenue, Chicago, Buhrke manufactured prewar leather holsters and play cowboy equipment.

"Build-A-Town" toys prewar, see *Central Wood Products, Inc.*

"Build-A-Truck" wooden toys prewar, see *Playskool Institute, Inc.*

"Build-Over" construction sets prewar, see *Central Wood Products, Inc.*

"Builder Blocks" see *Holgate Bros. Co.*

"Builder" building toy see *Chaspec Mfg. Co.*

building blocks see *blocks, stone and composition,* and *blocks, wood.*

building toys see *construction toys.*

This 1940s building set was made by Constructo Co.

"Buildoblox," prewar see *Strombeck-Becker Mfg. Co.*

"Builds Boys As Well As Toys" slogan see the *M. Carlton Dank Toy Corp., The*

Built-Rite Toys Warren Paper Products Co. used the "Built-Rite" trade name for its toys in the 1930s, and established Built Rite Toys as a separate division by the early '40s. Its wartime line included military toys made of fiberboard, including armored cars, army tanks, jeeps, trucks, and mounted guns, as well as forts with soldiers. The firm also continued issuing its earlier line, including garages, miniature villages, nativity sets, airport sets, and dollhouses. In the postwar years, the firm made dollhouses and furniture, picture puzzles, railroad accessory sets, games and puzzles, activity games and toys, doll cutouts, sewing cards, and crayon and chalkboard sets. It was based in Lafayette, Ind.

Bull's Eye Pistol Mfg. Co. Based in Rawlins, Wyo., this company made the "Bull's Eye" target pistol in the 1930s. The "Sharpshooter" appeared late in the decade.

"Bull's Eye" see *Daisy Mfg. Co.*

"Bully Pixy" felt dolls prewar, see *Mizpah Toy & Novelty Corp.*

"Bumpa" toys prewar, see *Milton Bradley Co.*

"Bunco" A popular name, "Bunco" was used in the 1930s for a card game by Parker Bros. and dice games by the Marbelite Co. and Weber Manufactory.

"Bunny" The Frank F. Taylor Co. used the prewar "Bunny" trademark on its juvenile vehicles and sidewalk cycles. The name was also used on some items by Gibbs Mfg. Co., including a wheelbarrow, cart, and push-toy in the 1930s.

Bunny Bear, Inc. Baby travel and play items, as well as "Carry Cribs," made up the line of postwar manufacturer Bunny Bear, based in Everett, Mass.

"Bunny Boo" rocking toy prewar, see *H.C. White Co.*

"Bunny Kuddles" stuffed animals prewar, see *Knickerbocker Toy Co., Inc.*

Burd Model Airplane Co. Burd was established in Baltimore, Md., in the late 1930s.

Cornelia Burdette, Cornelia Burdette introduced the "Terrible Terries" pipe-cleaner animals in the late 1930s. Her firm, based on Broad Street, New York City, also issued Easter and Christmas novelties.

Burg, Prudence & Priscilla This Syracuse, N.Y., firm issued paper dolls in the late 1930s.

Lorenzo Burge, Lorenzo Burge issued the 1844 board game, "The New Game of the American Revolution."

Burgess, Stringer & Co. A children's publisher located in New York City, Burgess, Stringer & Co. issued "The National Game of the Star Spangled Banner" in the wake of the success of W. & S.B. Ives in publishing games. The game was typical of the prevalent patriotic amusements.

Burgess Vibrocrafters, Inc. This Grayslake, Ill., firm made the "Jig Saw, Jr.," a colorful electric child's jig saw introduced in 1955.

The J.E. Burke Co. Based in Fond du Lac, Wis., the J.E. Burke Co. made prewar and Boomer steel home and public playground equipment.

John E. Burleson Mfg. Co. The "Battle Stations!" naval game of the 1950s-'60s was made by this Arlington, Va., firm.

Burlington Basket Co. Wicker and splint toy baskets, cradles and doll baskets were prewar products of this Burlington, Iowa, company.

"Burlington Zephyr" Early versions of this streamlined train were made by American Flyer Mfg. co. and Western Coil & Electrical Co.

Burnham Mfg. Co. Burnham, located in Charles City, Iowa, made prewar coaster wagons, barrows, scooters, and pedal bikes.

A.A. Burnstine Sales Organization

Burnstine's games included "Kan-U-Go," "Hop Chek," "Flying G-Men," "4 Aces Kard Jong" and "World Peaceways Soldiers of Peace," in the late prewar years. It was based in the Fifth Avenue Building, New York City.

"Burp Gun" Mattel made a hit of this toy gun by advertising it on the "Mickey Mouse Club" show in 1955. The gun, measuring 23-1/2 inches long, fired one to 50 shots at a time, with loud noise and smoke. It used Kilgore perforated caps.

Harcourt Burrage Co. This Providence, R.I., firm issued the "Artistic Toy Boats," combined water and pull toys, in the 1920s. Burrage's line included bathtub toys, "Old Time Sailors," ten pins, pull toys, and puzzles. It was based in Providence, R.I.

Burroughs, Edgar Rice As the author of the famous "Tarzan" and Mars novels, Edgar Rice Burroughs provided inspiration for countless childhood playthings and books in the prewar and postwar years. By the late 1930s, he had set up Edgar Rice Burroughs, Inc., to administer the issuing of "Tarzan" rights.

The Burrowes Corp. A manufacturer of pool tables, this Portland, Maine, company also made toy versions from the 1930s through the Boomer years.

Burt-Griffith Mfg. Co. This Denver, Colo., firm issued the "Bee-Gee" games of the mid to late 1930s, including the "Bee Gee Baseball Dart Target" of 1935.

Burton Playthings, Inc. "Happy Kids" coloring books were produced by this Lexington Avenue, New York City, company in the mid-1930s.

Bushnell, E.W. The Philadelphia manufacturer of E.W. Bushnell issued juvenile wheel goods in the mid-1800s, including "velocipede coaches, gigs, cabs, barouches, and boys wheelbarrows." The firm became Bushnell & Tull.

"Business Leaders" see *Metalcraft Corp.*

"Buster Brown" Radio shows featuring "Buster Brown," the advertising character of the Brown Shoe Co. of St. Louis, Mo., hit the Airwaves in the late 1920s and again during wartime through the early 1950s, when the program became a TV show. Premiums included a 5-inch rubber "Froggy, the Gremlin," issued by Rempel Mfg. Co. Larger versions were available in stores. Other items in the late 1940s included "Buster Brown Gang" tab-buttons and bandanas, and a paddleball game.

"Buster" crayons see *The Standard Crayon Mfg. Co.*

"Buster" pistol, prewar, see *The Dent Hardware Co.*

"Buster" wheelbarrows prewar, see *The Steel Stamping Co.*

"Busy Betty" toys see *The Hoge Mfg. Co.*

"Busy Busy Day" activity games see *Milton Bradley Co.*

James H. Butler & Co. Based in Berwick, Maine, James H. Butler & Co. produced wood and metal toys and novelties in the mid-1930s, including "wiggly animals" and toy autos and trucks.

Butler Bros. New York City's Butler Bros. was founded in 1876. It became one of the country's largest wholesale distributors of toys in the prewar years, maintaining sample houses in many major U.S. cities. It continued in operation into the postwar years.

Butler Toy Division This division of Products of Georgia, Inc., based in Louisville, Ga., issued educational wood puzzles, "Bang-A-Peg" sets, "Jr. Medic Play Stretchers," and hardwood "Play-Blox" in the 1950s. The firm also specialized in folding wood and aluminum "Kiddie" chairs.

Butterfield Toy Co. Butterfield Toy Co. issued paper pulp tunnels and trenches for toy railroads. It was founded in the late 1930s in Villa Park, Ill.

Butterfly Art Jewelry, Inc. This Brooklyn, N.Y., firm made ant houses, butterfly nets, and butterfly mounting kits.

"Button in Ear" stuffed animals see *Margarete Steiff & Co.*

Butts, Alfred Alfred Butts released the game "Criss-Cross Words" in 1938.

"Buzz Barton" The first promotional air rifle by Daisy Mfg. Co. was the "Buzz Barton" of 1934, named for a then-famous circus hero, only 15 years old at the time. Daisy used the "Buzz Barton" name on air rifles, six shooters, and holster sets.

buzz toy, also buzzing toy A buzz toy consisted of a small disk, usually of metal, with two holes or notches, through which strings could be run. With the strings taught, the disk could be wound, and then released to spin and produce a buzzing noise. The edges were often cut in a saw-blade manner to create the buzzing sound. Known from ancient times, buzz toys are also known from 18th century America, examples of which sometimes have the saw-blades bent in alternating right and left directions, to increase the buzzing sound. The toy was often hand-made, and often made from a coin.

"Buzzy Bee" see *Fisher-Price Toys, Inc.*

"Bye-Lo" baby dolls prewar, see *George Borgfeldt Corp.*

C.A.W. Novelty Co. Established in the late 1930s in Clay Center, Kans., C.A.W. Novelty issued molded plastic and pewter, or slush-metal, toys, including automobiles, airplanes, and trucks.

C. & G. Toy Co. The "Coca-Cola" combination dispenser and bank of the mid-Boomer years was produced by this Lyons, Ill., firm.

"C.B.G." see *Cuberly, Blondell, Gerbeau.*

"C-D" see *Cleveland Model & Supply Co..*

"C-K" toys prewar, see *Katagiri Bros.*

"C-T-K" tool chests see *Chicago Tool & Kit Mfg. Co.*

The C-K-R Co. Based in Cleveland, Ohio, the C-K-R Co. made stilts, sand shovels, and juvenile furniture in the 1930s.

cab In farm toys, the cab is the enclosure around the operator's platform on a tractor.

"Cabana" play tent, see *J.W. Johnson Co.*

"Cabin Blocks" construction toy see *Ideal Products Corp.*

cabinet, toy see *kitchen tixtures, toy.*

Cadaco, Ltd. A game company based in San Leandro, Calif., Cadaco made games including "Foto-Electric Football in 1930, "Foto world" in 1935, "Elmer Laydon's Scientific Fooball Game" in 1936, "Touchdown" in 1937, and "Transport Pilot" in 1938.

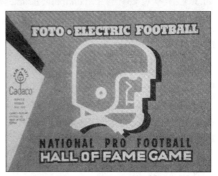

The "Foto-Electric Football Game" was made by Cadaco, Ltd.

Cadaco-Ellis, Inc. A company established in Chicago, Ill., by 1939, Cadaco-Ellis issued board games, football and basketball games, aeronautical and travel games, fortune-telling and mind-reading games, movie games, party packs, and Fourth of July novelties. Its titles included "Telepathy" in 1939, "Yankee Doodle!" in 1940, and "Ethan Allen's All-Star Baseball Game" and "Varsity Football Game" in 1942. Through the Boomer years, Cadaco-Ellis both manufactured and packaged quiz games, math games, party games, educational toys and games, "Tripoley," and spelling boards.

"Caddy Cart Croquet" see *Garton Toy Co.*

Cadillac Specialty Co. Based in Detroit, Mich., this prewar company manufactured shooting games and rubber band pistols and rifles.

Cadillac Wagon Co. Coaster wagons were postwar products of this Detroit, Mich., company.

Cahill, Thomas Based in West Chester, Penn., in the late 1930s, Thomas Cahill issued game boards.

Calcraft Co. The "Biff-It Ball," "Calcraft" racing boat, and "Hollywood Sky Rider" were 1930s products of this Glendale, Calif., company. It introduced its "OrkinCraft" later in the decade. The company's line also included hand looms, yarn reels, and rug looms by the late '30s.

W.J. Caley & Co. A Philadelphia, Penn., firm, W.J. Caley issued the "Botanee Box" in the late 1930s, a set for making artificial flowers.

California Stuffed Toys This Boomer-era manufacturer was based in Los Angeles, Calif.

California Toy Craft Co. This San Francisco, Calif., firm issued the late 1930s "Jane Withers" racing hoop.

Callen Mfg. Corp. The "Cap Grenade" cap exploders of the 1950s and '60s were issued by this Maywood, Ill., corporation.

Calumet Carton Co. Based in Harvey, Ill., in the later 1930s, Calumet issued boxed party games for children.

Cam-Cast A small U.S. manufacturer of die-cast promotional trucks in the '50s, Cam-Cast produced 1/50-scale van trucks for Western Auto, North American Van Lines, and Pillsbury's, among others, and oil tanker trucks for Gulf, Marathon Oil, and Sunoco.

Cambridge Paper Box Co. Blocks and jigsaw puzzles were among the products of this Cambridge, Mass., firm in the late 1930s.

"Camelback" bicycle prewar, see *Arnold, Schwinn & Co.*

"Camelot" see *Parker Bros. Inc.*

Cameo Doll Co. A maker of novelty and character dolls, Cameo was located in Port Allegany, Penn. In the Boomer era it specialized in "Kewpies," vinyl dolls, stuffed dolls, and novelty dolls. It used the slogans "Lasting Charm" and "Gift of a Childtime," and the trade name "Pink Magic" for its vinyl dolls. The "Peanut" dolls were fully jointed, drinking, wetting and crying dolls.

Cameo Doll Co. made this "Kewpie" doll in the 1960s.

"Cameoware" see *Worcester Toy Co.*

Cameron Precision Maker of the "Rodzy Standard," a steel, gas-powered hot rod, in the late 1940s, this company was based in Sonoma, Calif.

"Canasta" see *Whitman Publishing Co.*

Canastota Sherwood Stamping Corp. Based in Canastota, N.Y., this prewar firm made roller skates, adjustable doll roller skates, and novelties.

"Candy Land" see *Milton Bradley Co.*

candy stores see *fruit stores.*

cannons, toy The cannon as an American toy seems to have arrived with the Civil War. Ellis, Britton & Eaton, who were manufacturers of children's carriages and wagons, added a toy cannon to its line around 1859. A spring cannon, it could fire a marble some 60 feet. Charles M. Crandall issued "Henry's Artillery" in 1875, regarded as a precursor to the cannon toy he patented in 1877. In the earlier 20th century, manufacturers included Conestoga Corp., the Hubley Mfg. Co., Kenton Hardware, Co., and the Kilgore Mfg. Co. By the 1930s, manufactures included Conestoga, Dowst Mfg. Co., the Gibbs. Mfg. Co., Grey Iron Casting Co., Hubley, W.P. Johnson Co., Kenton, and Richard Maerklin Toys. In the late prewar years, the main companies issuing cannon toys were American Metal Toys, Conestoga, the Dill Co., Grey Iron, and Richard Maerklin. In addition to Conestoga and Dowst, postwar producers included Multiple Products Corp., Louis Marx & Co., and Ny-Lint Tool & Mfg. Co.

This toy cannon was produced by the Dayton Toy & Specialty Co. in the 1920s.

Canvas Products Co.
Bouncing devices and wading pools were the specialty of this St. Louis, Mo., firm in the Boomer years.

"Cap Grenade" see *Callen Mfg. Corp.*

cap canes An unusual western toy, cap canes were toy canes equipped to set off caps when banged on the ground. They were issued in the 1950s and '60s.

cap pistols see *pistol caps*

"Capital" banks see *Kalon Mfg. Co.*

Capital Toy Co., Inc.
Capital made the "Ceetee" mama dolls of the 1920s. It was located on West Broadway, New York City.

Capitol Novelty Co.
This manufacturer of stuffed animals was located on West 18th Street, New York City, in the late 1930s.

Capitol Publishing Co., Inc.
This Boomer-era publisher of children's and infants' toy books also issued activity boxes, hobby kits, and nature and science kits. Based on Broadway, New York City, Capitol had an exclusive distributing arrangement with Golden Press.

Capitol Records Distributing Corp.
Capitol's line of children's records in the late 1940s and '50s included colorfully jacketed titles using movie, TV and cartoon characters, including "Woody Woodpecker." The famous "Bozo" clown started off as the singing "Bozo, the Capitol Clown."

Cappel MacDonald & Co.
Active in wartime, this Dayton, Ohio, firm made "Teach-A-Tot" wooden construction toys and "Tru-Walk" toys in the early 1940s.

caps Paper caps for use in cap guns and other cap toys were initially the product of the fireworks industry, which was well-established in America by the 1830s. Some toy firms did become major manufacturers, including Kilgore Mfg. Co. and Andes Foundry Co. in prewar times, and Kusan and others after the war.

Kilgore Mfg. Co. made disc caps in the 1950s.

"Captain Kangaroo"
A popular TV figure among very young children from 1954 through the Boomer years and later, Bob Keeshan's "Captain Kangaroo" character inspired toys including banks and activity toys by Admiral Toy Corp., card table and "Treasure House" tents by H. Wenzel Tent & Duck Co., "Dabbles" by Dangles, "fun kits" by Barry Products, hand puppets by the Rushton Co., and hats by Newark Felt Novelty Co.

"Captain Kidd's Castle"
Charles M. Crandall issued this popular game in the late 1800s.

"Captain Marvel"
Making his first appearance in *Whiz Comics* in Feb. 1940, Captain Marvel sold more comic books than did Superman. Numerous Premiums appeared, including buttons, decoders, and flying toys.

"Captain Midnight"
The aviator hero of the 1940s inspired numerous radio premiums, issued by Skelly in 1939-41, and Ovaltine through the '40s into the 1950s. Playthings ranged from the 1939 "Captain Midnight's Trick and Riddle Book" to rings, "Detect-O-Scopes" and the famous "Code-O-Graph" line of decoder badges, issued 1940-42 and 1945-49.

C

"Captain Video" The 1949-1956

Dumont TV science-fiction show inspired premiums including plastic "Captain Video Space Men," which appeared in packages of Post's Raisin Bran cereal. Premiums also included tab buttons and rings, including one which launched "flying saucers."

Based on the Dumont TV show, Milton Bradley made the "Captain Video Game" in 1952.

Captive Flight Devices Founded in

Abington, Penn., in the later 1930s, this company issued the "Captive Model Autogiro," and construction kits.

"Capt'n Handy" kits see *Hillcraft Industries*

Cara, Inc. This Chicago, Ill., firm made

both stuffed animal toys and foam-filled toys in the 1950s and '60s.

Carb Mfg. Corp. "Carbcraft" washable

soft dolls and animals were made by this Broadway, New York City, corporation in the 1930s.

Carbondale Toy & Novelty Mfg.

Co. Dolls and doll parts were specialties of this Carbondale, Penn., firm in the Boomer years. It also made railway tunnels, Christmas decorations, and vinyl advertising novelties.

"Card-Buildo" Stoll & Einson Games

issued the "Card-Buildo" building set in the 1930s, while Einson-Freeman co. issued the "Card-Structo" set.

card games Educational card games came

about as early as the 1600s in England, as a means of teaching of grammar. Card games proved of great popularity once introduced in America. In the 19th century, they were issued in great variety. They were sometimes categorized as either religious games, which were often question-and-answer games on scriptural subjects, or "Vernacular Cards," on non-religious topics covering the gamut: "Geographical," "Philosophical" (pertaining to "Natural Philosophy in all its branches"), "Astronomical," and "Botanical." In the early 1800s, a popular game was "Conversation Cards," in which each player had to converse about the subject printed on the card that came up. The first best-selling card game was "Dr. Busby," issued in 1843 by W. & S.B. Ives. See also cards, playing.

cardboard and paper toys Although

not the most permanent of materials, both cardboard and paper have been important in the toy industry from at least the early 19th century. Toy soldiers, vehicles, buildings and dolls were all made. Prewar manufacturers included American Colortype Co., American Toy Works, O.B. Andrews Co., Bildon Co., the Central Paper Box & Printing Co., Chicago Die Cutting Co., Converters, Dennison Mfg. Co., Einson-Freeman Co., Erie Paper Box Co., E.E. Fairchild Corp., Samuel Gabriel Sons & Co., Gibraltar Corrugated Paper Co., Charles E. Graham & Co., the Harter Publishing Co., V.M. Kearley Mfg. Co., Maryland Toy & Games Corp., Milprint Products Corp., the F.L. Purdy Co., the Saalfield Publishing Co., the Tuco Work Shops, Universal Toy & Novelty Mfg. Co., Whitman Publishing Co., and Wolverine Supply & Mfg. Co. Prewar manufacturers of cardboard and paper toys had an advantage over other manufacturers when World War II rationing restricted the kinds of materials available for non-military use. See also *games; paper dolls; toy books.*

The Cardice Game Co. The "Cardice"

game for adults of the later 1930s was issued by this Duane Street, New York City, firm.

Cardinal Doll Corp. This West 48th

Street, New York City, corporation issued stuffed toys in the postwar years.

Cardinal Mfg. Co. Based in Brooklyn, N.Y., Cardinal specialized in games for children and adults.

Cardinal Parfums, Inc. A Brooklyn, N.Y., firm, Cardinal Parfums made "Kiddie Dress-Up" kits and bath kits in the 1950s and '60s.

Cardinal Products Corp. This Boomer-era manufacturer's line included checkers, dice, Chinese tile games, dominoes, and carnival wheels. It was based in Brooklyn, N.Y.

Cardinell Corp. A specialist in art sets, Cardinell issued mid-1930s items including "Young American" drafting sets, "artists outfits," drawing boards, and games.

cards, playing The New England Colonies resisted the notion of playing cards as a valid entertainment. By 1770, however, the pastime was welcomed across most of the colonies, even in the Puritan hotbed that Boston was. Playing cards, which were an invention that can be in greatest likelihood be attributed to the ancient Asians, came to be a dominant game through the 18th and 19th centuries. In contrast, card games, which were games developed with cards other than the traditional pack of cards, were characteristic of the 19th century, hitting their first high point with "Dr. Busby."

Cardwood Products Corp. Upholstered juvenile rockers, chairs, toy chests and doll rockers were the specialty of this postwar Webster Avenue, New York City, firm.

"Careers" see *Parker Bros.*

Georges Carette With the backing of Gebruder Bing, French citizen Georges Carette founded a toy-making company in Nuremburg, Germany, in 1886. Specializing in vehicle toys, mostly lithographed, he became best known for his electric streetcar and model train toys. He also made tin mechanical cars and boats. As a French citizen, Carette was deported from Germany in 1917, which ended the firm.

Carey-McFall Co. The "Master" home ice-skating rink and wading pools were made by this Boomer-era firm, based in Philadelphia, Penn.

Caribbean Mfg. Co. Taking advantage of the popularity of shell art in the Boomer years, Caribbean issued "Shellcraft" and "Pearlcraft" costume jewelry hobby kits. The firm was based in Sarasota, Fla.

Carling Co. This San Francisco, Calif., firm issued the "Carlo" games for adults in the later 1930s.

Carlisle & Finch Co. Carlisle & French Co. of Cincinnati, Ohio, established in 1895 by Robert Finch and Morton Carlisle, introduced the first successful electrically run toy railroad system in this country, in 1897. The company also distributed toys, including among its wares the first toy automobile, made by Knapp Electric in 1900. Carlisle & Finch made toys through 1915, although it manufactured marine lighting through the 20th century.

W.F. Carman Co. Located on Fifth Avenue, New York City, W.F. Carman made novelties in the 1930s.

Carnell Mfg. Co. Carnell made pistol and holster sets, using the "Just Like the Real Thing" slogan for its "Roundup" leather holsters in the 1950s and '60s. Based in Brooklyn, N.Y., it issued the "Official Dragnet Holster Set" of 1955, and the "Maverick" guns of 1960.

carnival goods An important source of toys, although not necessarily of the best quality, was the carnival, which had a greater impact on prewar and early postwar times than it does in our contemporary world. Some important toy makers manufactured carnival goods, including T. Cohn, the Kirchhof Patent Co., and Marks Bros. Co. Other manufacturers of prewar carnival goods and toys included S.S. Adams Co., American Merri-Lei Corp., Bugle Toy Mfg. Co., the Clever Idea Paper Novelty Co., Dessart Bros., the A.A. Faxon Co., Gottlieb Paper Products Mfg. Corp., Oscar Leistner, Theodore Metzeler, Albert P. Meyer & Co., the National Flag Co., "Old Glory" Mfg. Co., Pulp Reproduction Co., C.A. Reed Co., St. Louis Confetti Co., Seiss Mfg. Co., B. Shackman & Co., and United Pressed Products Co.

Carnival Toy Mfg. Corp. Musical string toys and plastic guns were specialties of this Bruckner Boulevard, New York City, firm in the Boomer years. It also made Christmas tree ornaments.

Jean Caro Products Co. A Freeport, Ill., company, Jean Caro made toy mops, dusters, and sweepers, and toy brush sets in the 1930s and '40s.

Carolina Washboard Co. Toy washboards were among this Raleigh, N.C., firm's line in the late 1930s.

Caron Novelty Co. A Leominster, Mass., company, Caron Novelty made prewar doll beds.

Francis W. Carpenter, Francis W. Carpenter of Port Chester, N.Y., produced cast-iron horse-drawn vehicles, including the well-known "Tally-Ho," in the 1880s. While Carpenter sold his patent rights and inventory to Pratt & Letchworth around 1890, he continued producing individual toys through the first decade of the 20th century.

The Carpenter Mfg. Co., In addition to making such Christmas items as icicles and tinsel garlands, this Norwich, Conn., company made jump ropes and toy cords in the 1930s.

Carpenter's Novelty Shop Based in Providence, R.I., Carpenter's Novelty Shop made lead toys, soldiers, and novelties in the 1930s.

carpet runners see *floor trains.*

carpet sweepers, toy Toys that evoked the new age of convenience that dawned in the 1920s and '30s were as popular among children as the actual "labor-saving" devices were among their parents. Toy carpet sweepers were among the toys touted as helping train children for adult life. Prewar manufacturers of the toy included Bissell Carpet Sweeper Co., Buffalo Toy & Tool works, the Gong Bell Mfg. Co., Gotham Pressed Steel Corp., Hoge Mfg. Co., Indiana Ox Fibre Brush Co., Jean Caro Products Co., Ohio Art Co., and Patent Novelty Co. In addition to toys by Bissell and Ohio Art, postwar examples were issued by American Metal Special-

ties Corp., the Brothers Mfg. Co., E. & L. Mfg. Co., Henry Katz, Kiddie Brush & Toy Co., Fred Kroll Associates, and Norstar Corp.

Carriage & Toy Co. A manufacturer of juvenile furniture, Carriage & Toy Co. of Baltimore, Md., made doll and baby carriages, children's rockers, and fibre furniture in the 1920s and '30s.

carriages, baby Carriages for babies were made in America by the 1820s, by Benjamin P. Crandall. The prewar manufacturers of baby carriages and "go-carts," many of which in themselves are of interest to toy collectors, were usually also manufacturers of doll carriages. In postwar times, as companies grew increasingly specialized, this grew decreasingly true. Important prewar manufacturers included American National Co., the Bemis Riddell Fibre Co., Bloch Go-Cart Co., Carriage & Toy Co., the Gendron Mfg. Co., Gendron Wheel Co., Geneva Mfg. Co., Charles & Victor Goldstein, Hartman Mfg. Co., C.H. Hartshorn, the Hedstrom-Union Co., Heywood-Wakefield Co., Jacobs & Kassler, Kozekar, Kuniholm, Lloyd Mfg. Co., the Marlin Carriage Co., Perfection Mfg. Co., the Frank F. Taylor Co., H.N. Thayer Co., the Toledo Metal Wheel Co., Uhlen Carriage Co., F.A. Whitney Carriage Co., and Whitney Reed Co.

J.B. Carroll Co. Based in Chicago, Ill., from the late 1930s through the Boomer years, J.B. Carroll issued advertising novelties. In 1960 it issued "Miss Airlanes," a magnetic paper doll.

The Carrom Co. The Lundington, Mich., producers of "Carrom" and "Crokinole" combination game boards issued "Jockey" and "The Lew Fonseca Baseball Game" in the 1920s. Carrom was also making folding bridge tables and chairs, "official Ping-Pong" tables, and folding tables for chess, checkers and poker by the mid-1930s. The Carrom Co. also made portable doll houses, "official" Ping-Pong tables, and the "Racketeer" game. Establishing a strong presence in the industry before the war, it maintained a display room in the Fifth Avenue Building. At the end of the 1930s, the Carrom Co. introduced "Baseball," "Football," "Hockey" and "Creeper" skill games, and "Horse Racing," "Astrology," "Battleship" and "Show-Me" games of chance. The company became Carrom Industries, Inc., by the war years, when its line included "Commando," "Kikit," "Gusher," and "Carrom Board" games, "Lok-Blok" and "Arkitoy" wood construction sets, poker tables, and dart boards. In the Boomer years, "Carrom" and "Crokinole" continued to be its leading titles, along with bowling games, dartboards, and "Kikit," "Fox Hunt," "Nok-Hockey" and "Gusher" games.

Carron Mfg. Co. Based on South Aberdeen Street, Chicago, Ill., Carron Mfg. Co. made 1930s electric pencil sets, wood burning outfits, and leather burning sets. By the end of the decade it was issuing electric embossing sets, battery-operated and non-battery telephones, crystal radio sets, a three-dimensional painting set, chime pianos, and Christmas tree ornaments. In the 1950s and '60s, Carron emphasized electric phonographs, in both "acoustical" and amplified 3-speed models.

cars, toy see *automobiles, miniature.*

C.E. Carter Co. This Girard, Penn., firm issued multicolored tops in the later 1930s.

Carter Craft, Inc. The "Dizzy Doodler" game of the early 1960s was issued by this Plano, Texas, firm.

Carter Tru-Scale Machine Co. This Rockford, Ill., firm specialized in miniature metal scale-model farm machinery, scale-model steel trucks, and die-cast trucks and farm toys in the 1950s and '60s.

cartoon characters The widespread use cartoon character images, whether from the newspapers, comic books or film, was a characteristic of prewar toys that continued through the rest of the 20th century. Because of the wide name-recognition comic characters enjoyed, the licensors of rights to their use became influential in the prewar toy world. The most influential was undoubtedly Kay Kaymen, responsible for licensing products based on the already incredibly popular Walt Disney characters. Other prewar licensors included Columbia Pictures Corp., for

"Scrappy"; John F. Dille Co., for "Roy Rogers"; Famous Artists Syndicate, for characters including "Dick Tracy"; Fleischer Studios, for "Betty Boop"; King Features Syndicate, Inc., for characters including "Jiggs," "Popeye," "Barney Google," "Katzenjammer Kids," "Krazy Kat," "Tillie the Toiler," and "Toots and Casper"; Stephen Slesinger, Inc., for "Alley Oop," "Dan Dunn," "Ella Cinders," "Winnie-the-Pooh," and "Tailspin Tommy"; and Fred A. Wish, Inc., for "Skippy." In the postwar years a number of new characters appeared, with CBS Films licensing Terrytoons characters; William C. Erskine, "Little Lulu"; Felix the Cat Productions, the "expected suspect"; Harvey Famous Name Comics, characters including "Joe Palooka," "Humphrey," "Little Max," "Sad Sack," "The Hi-School Gang," "Little Dot Polka," "Casper," "Little Audrey," "Buzzy," "Baby Huey," Herman & Katnip," and "Spooky." Kennedy Associates held licensing rights for "Ferd'nand," "Peanuts," and "Poor Pitiful Pearl." King Features enjoyed continued success with "Jiggs," "Popeye," "Barney Google," "Katzenjammer Kids," and "Flash Gordon." Red Ryder Enterprises continued enjoying the popularity "Red Ryder" established before the war. Screen Gems issued rights for "Huckleberry Hound," "Ruff & Reddy," and "Mister Magoo"; and Warner Bros. Pictures, for characters including "Bugs Bunny" and "Daffy Duck."

"Cartoy" see *Carriage & Toy Co.*

carts see *wagons, wheelbarrows toys*

Cartwright's Wooden Toys & Signs Established in Memphis, Tenn., in the later 1930s, this firm made wooden pull-toys and wooden toy letters.

"Casey Jones" The Screen Gems "Casey Jones" character inspired some 1950s and '60s playthings, including a coloring book by the Saalfield Publishing Co.

cash registers Toy cash registers were popular among both prewar and postwar children, being a staple in "playing store." Prewar manufacturers included Durable Toy & Novelty Corp., Kingsbury Mfg. Co., "Uncle

Sam's" Registering Savings Bank Co., and World Metal Stamping Co.

"Casper the Friendly Ghost"

Licensed by Harvey Famous Name Comics, "Casper the Friendly Ghost" appeared in numerous Boomer-era playthings, including card games by Ed-U-Cards Mfg. Corp., plastic inflatable toys by Alvimar Mfg. Co., costumes by Collegeville Flag & Mfg. Co., and puppets by Pride Products, Inc.

N.D. Cass Co. A manufacturer of prewar furniture ranging from bassinets to pool tables, N.D. Cass Co. was also known for its wooden toys, including toy cars, trucks, dollhouses, and toy barns. Some were clockwork mechanicals. Its games included the "Bowling Alley" activity game of 1921. By the eve of the Great Depression, Cass was advertising having 500 numbers in its "Cass Toys" line—"everything worth while in wooden toys." In the 1930s, its products included rocking horses, ten pins, tool chests, pool tables, toy pianos, toy furniture, blackboards, and ironing boards, as well as table and desk sets, nursery chairs, high chairs, and bassinets. N.D. Cass maintained offices in the Fifth Avenue Building and factory in Athol, Mass., where the company was founded in the 1890s. The company continued in operation through the postwar years as N.D. Cass Sales Co., when its specialties were toy pianos and spinets, blackboards, juvenile and doll furniture, rocking and spring horses, shooflies, musical and colonial rockers, peg tables, doll trunks and suitcases, "K.D." toy chests, play pens, and sandboxes. In addition to its Athol factory, it based a second in Brent, Ala.

"Cast-A-Toy" lead soldier sets see *Marks Bros. Co.*

cast-in driver In some toys, especially in cast iron, cast aluminum, and some of the earlier die-cast toy tractors, racers, and autos, the driver/operator is part of the main casting. See *separate driver.*

cast-in name The name on some cast-metal models appears as raised or recessed lettering.

cast-iron banks see *banks.*

cast-iron toys American cast-iron toys were first made shortly after the Civil War. Perhaps the best known of the early companies was Ives. Dent, Hubley, Kenton, and Wilkins were early companies that continued into the 20th century. Companies that followed included Arcade, Champion, Kilgore, and A.C. Williams. Toy companies who had minor involvement in cast-iron toy production included Freidag, Grey Iron, Judd, and North. Unfortunately for collectors, many cast-iron toys have no markings. This is true of even such major manufacturers as Hubley.

cast-iron toys—reproductions Many cast-iron toys have been reproduced as decorator items. Other cast-iron toys have been produced in recent decades which may not strictly be reproductions, but which have been passed off as "old" even so. Aside from seeking expert advice, what is a person to do? Collectors note that old molds used fine-grained sand, which led to a smooth iron surface in the original toys. The pieces tend to be well matched, with edges meeting tightly. Modern castings also tend to be thicker than old ones.

"Cast Iron Toys That Sell" slogan, 1920s, see *The Hubley Mfg. Co.*

"Cast-Rite" see *Rapaport Bros.*

F.C. Castelli Co. A manufacturer of juvenile metal furniture in the late prewar years, with its lead item the "Rock-A-Swings," this Philadelphia, Penn., firm turned to the manufacture of armaments in wartime. Castelli returned to its original line after the war, and issued the "Jet Ride," a three-wheel, chain-driven Irish Mail, in 1955.

Castello Fencing Equipment Co. In addition to adult sports equipment, Castello, based on East 11th Street, New York City, issued toy fencing sets in the late 1930s through the Boomer years.

Casterline Bros. Mfg. Co. A Milwaukee, Wis., firm, Casterline made Eskimo dolls and stuffed animals in sheepskin and plush including dogs, pandas, penguins, and bears, in the later 1930s.

Castle Films Located on Rockefeller Plaza, New York City, Castle Films began issuing 8 and 16 mm movie films in the late 1930s. In the Boomer years, the firm continued specializing in films for toy projectors, issuing science fiction films, "Abbott & Costello" comedies, and "Woody Woodpecker" and other cartoons.

Castle Products, Inc. A manufacturer of liquid bubble soap in the postwar years, this Hialeah, Fla., firm also made plastic sleighs and Christmas bells.

casting sets The makers of the molds or "moulds" for casting lead toys supplied both child toy-makers and other manufacturers, in prewar times. Manufacturers included Ace Toy Mold Co., the A.C. Gilbert Co., Home Foundry Mfg. Co., Metal Cast Products Co., also known as Make-A-Toy Co., Rapaport Bros., Henry C. Schiercke, and Williams Kast Art Co. Although Metal Cast Products continued in operation into the 1950s, Rapaport remained the main Boomer-era producer of these sets. It used the "Cast-Rite" trade name.

castings A number of prewar metal casting companies, including some whose main trade consisted of complete toys, made parts for other toy manufacturers. Such suppliers included Arcade Mfg. Co., Freidag Mfg. Co., Grey Iron Casting Co., Hubley Mfg. Co., Kenton Hardware Co., Novelty Casting Co., Peter F. Pia, and United States Lock & Hardware Co. Another prewar parts casting company which apparently did not market its own toys was Doehler Die Casting Co., located on Fourth Avenue, New York City.

cat's cradle A universal game known from ancient times, in America it was known among the Navajo before European settlement. The name derives from "cratch cradle," "cratch" coming from the French *creche*, a crib or manger.

"Cat's Eye" see *Peltier Glass Co.*, also *Berry Pink, Inc.*

Cavacraft Model Airplanes Model airplanes, boats and race cars were 1950s and '60s specialties of this Philadelphia, Penn., firm.

"Cavalcade" see *Selchow & Righter Co.*

Frank Cavanaugh Associates The "Frank Cavanaugh's American Football Game," issued from 1955 into the 1960s, was produced by this Detroit, Mich., firm.

Cawood Mfg. Co. This Beverly Hills, Calif., firm made "The Junior Scout," a 50-cent propeller-driven balsawood airplane, in the 1920s. Unlike many of its contemporaries, the "Scout" had a simple stick body without realistic body modeling.

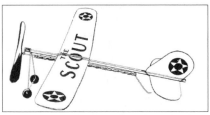

The "Junior Scout" toy airplane by Cawood Mfg. Co.

Cayo Mfg. Co. This Buchanan, Mich., firm issued tin whistling yo-yos in the 1930s, under the "Ka-Yo" name. Cayo made the tin yo-yos for the Donald F. Duncan.

cedar chests, toy Children who played with dolls and had doll outfits naturally needed someplace to safely stow extra clothes. Cedar chest companies and other manufacturers happily met the need with toy versions of their full-size products. Prewar manufacturers of toy versions included the N.D. Cass Co., the Davis Lumber Co., McGraw Box Co., the Mason & Parker Mfg. Co., Nussbaum Novelty Co., the Pilliod Cabinet Co., Tennessee Red Cedar & Novelty Co., and Totty Trunk & Bag Co.

celluloid see *celluloid toys, and cellulose nitrate.*

Celluloid Corp. A manufacturer of transparent wrappings and containers, this East 40th Street, New York City, firm also made celluloid toys and dice in the mid-1930s. By late in the decade its only toy items, aside from boxes and containers, were dice.

C

Celluloid Mfg. Co. Established in 1875 in New Jersey, John Wesley Hyatt's manufacturing company started using scrap material to make dolls in 1880. Celluloid Mfg. Co. was later bought by Celanese Corp. of America.

celluloid toys Then leaders in the industry, German toy makers made the first celluloid dolls in 1878, even though celluloid was an American invention. John Hyatt's Celluloid Mfg. Co. took up doll production two years later. Mainly rattles and floating bathtub toys, celluloid toys were made from around 1890 into the 1950s, when increasing controversy over the material's flammability drastically decreased demand, and as plastics with lowered flammability came into more widespread use. Prewar manufacturers of celluloid toys included Arrow Specialty Co., Bastian Bros. Co., Adam Bernhard, Celluloid Corp., DaCosta Toy Co., Du Pont Viscoloid Co., Engineering Service Corp., the Insel Co., Irwin Novelty Co., Katnips, Richard G. Krueger, Noveloid Co., Louis Sametz, and Zadek-Feldstein Co.

cellulose acetate Developed in 1911 as a less flammable alternative to celluloid, cellulose acetate was primarily used for film. New formulations in the 1950s were widely used in toys.

cellulose nitrate The first durable, easily manufactured plastic, John Wesley Hyatt (1837-1920) invented cellulose nitrate in 1869. Although others had experimented with the compound, Hyatt's formulation of linters, the short fibers that cling to cotton seeds, wood pulp, nitric acid, and camphor was tough and resisted cracking. He patented and trademarked it under the name Celluloid in 1870.

"Cellupon" toys prewar, see *Pulp Reproduction Co.*

Centerbar Corp. Located in South Natick, Mass., Centerbar made toy table and chair bridge sets and toy dinette sets in the mid-1930s. Its emphasis shifted to doll furniture, color design blocks, and games by the end of the decade.

Central Paper Box & Printing Co., The Based in Philadelphia, Penn., this prewar company made the Radio game, "punch cards," and anagrams in the 1930s.

Central Wood Products, Inc. A manufacturer of juvenile furniture based in Vancouver, Wash., Central Wood Products made sand toys, "Build-Over" construction sets, "Air Speeder" swings, and "Cute Cut" doll furniture in the 1930s and '40s.

"Century" dolls see *Doll Corporation of America.*

"Century Flyer" prewar, see *Wood & Metal Products Co.*

A Century of Progress The 1933 World's Fair, the second held in Chicago, Ill., produced a toy that is a great favorite with collectors: the "Greyhound Lines A Century of Progress" bus, produced in several versions by Arcade Manufacturing Co. Arcade also produced a "Century of Progress" Yellow Cab. One of the most notable toy introductions of the year, Lionel Corp.'s "Streamline Train" based on the Union Pacific Railroad "Train of Tomorrow," was an attraction at the fair, in the Transportation Building.

ceramic toys Potters were responsible for some of the toys available in Colonial and early United States households. While ceramics have been used for toy tea sets and doll faces, hands, and feet through the 20th century, in earlier times potters made a wider variety of playthings. Toys recorded from the 1800s in ceramic include doll heads, toy dishes, animal-shaped banks, animal and bird figural toys, bird-shaped whistles, animal-shaped bells, and infant rattles.

The Cerling Co. The "Scatback" game of the Boomer years was produced by this Chicago, Ill., firm.

Chad Valley This venerable British firm was founded in 1849 by Joseph and Alfred Johnson as a printing business, which they renamed Chad Valley in 1897 when they built a new factory near Birmingham. They began making toys around this time, and started issuing dolls in 1917. Chad Valley established a name for tin-plate and clockwork toys, and in the late '40s also introduced a line of die-cast vehicles with clockwork motors, mostly at 1/50 scale. Some were used as promotional models for automobile dealerships. Produced into the '50s, the line featured a number of Rolls-Royce and Commer vehicles, most of them highly valued by collectors. As a manufacturer of rag dolls, Chad Valley is famous for having engaged the talents of several well-known illustrators in the 1920s, including Norah Wellings, Hilda Cowham, and Mabel Lucie Attwell. Character dolls from the company included "Golliwog," "Red Riding Hood," "Tango Tar Baby," "Pixie," "Pierrot," "Peter Pan," and "Little Black Sambo." Louis Wolf was the distributor to the United States.

Chaffee & Selchow A publisher of board games in the late 1800s, Chaffee & Selchow's titles included "Parlor Golf" in 1897; "The Bell Boy Game," "The Bicycle Race Game," "The Cowboy Game," "Merry-Go-Round," "Old Maid," "Old Mother Goose," "Game of Red Riding Hood," "Turnover," and "The Young Athlete" in 1898; "The ABCdarian," "Dewey at Manila," "Lee at Havana," "Miles at Porto Rico," "Roosevelt at San Juan," "Game of Tiger Hunt," "The Vassar Boat Race," and "War and Dimplomacy" in 1899; and "Game of Cat" and "The Skating Race Game" in 1900. In 1913, "Pana Kanal, the Great Panama Canal Game," was issued.

Chain Bike Corp. This Rockaway Beach, N.Y., corporation manufactured bicycles under the "Ross" name, as well as tricycles, motorbikes, and other juvenile wheel goods in the Boomer years.

"Challenger" The "Challenger" name was used both for prewar coaster wagons by the Monarch Products Co. and for sleds made by Standard Novelty Works.

"Champ" coaster wagons see *Garton Toy Co.*

"Champ-ette" sleds see *Kalamazoo Sled Co.*

"Champion" A widely used trade name, "Champion" appeared on a variety of prewar toys, including coaster wagons from both Kalamazoo Sled Co. and Toledo Metal Wheel Co. A "Champion De Luxe" sled also appeared from Kalamazoo Sled Co. The name was also used for a combination game board from Milton Bradley Co., rubber-tired roller skates from Kingston Products Corp., a target from Gem City Specialty Co., target games by Wayne Toy Mfg. Co., and trains by American Flyer Mfg. Co. Kalamazoo Sled also used the trade name in the postwar years, as did many other firms.

Champion Agate Co. This postwar Pennsboro, W.V., firm made marbles. To help keep things confusing, Peltier Glass Co. also used "Champion" as a trade name in the postwar years.

The Champion Hardware Co., variety of cast-iron toy vehicles, including airplanes, autos, Mack trucks, motorcycles, wrecking cars, racers, and oil and gas trucks were made in the 1930s by this Geneva, Ohio, company. Champion also made toy stoves, pistols, combination safes, and express wagons in the years 1930-36, as well as cast-iron parts for other toy makers. Founded in 1883 by John and Ezra Hasenpflug, Champion remained in business until 1954.

Chancy Toy & Novelty Corp. Based in Brooklyn, N.Y., Chancy made prewar pistol and holster sets, chaps and vests, and basemen's mitts. Under its postwar name Chancy Toy & Sporting Goods Corp., the firm continued to emphasize pistol and holster sets.

Chandler, John Greene Born in Petersham, Mass., in 1815, John Greene Chandler was a commercial wood engraver and lithographer, with early works including illustrations for *Grandmother's Toy Book* in 1838, and *Chicken Little* in 1840. The latter was published by W.J. Reynolds of Roxbury, Mass. Chandler joined his brother in establishing the firm S.W. Chandler & Bro. Chandler's 1854 "Fanny Gray: A History of Her Life" is considered the first American paper doll. The artist followed this successful book with a series of paper dolls for Brown, Taggard & Chase of Boston, Mass., in 1857. These paper dolls came in a paper envelope with several sets of clothing, usually costing 10 to 15 cents. The envelopes bore the slogan, "Hurray for the Little Folks." In 1859 Chandler designed a card with an animated

Santa Claus, bearing Clement C. Moore's famous verses on the reverse. Chandler's "The Game of Coquette and Her Suiters" and the boxed cutouts "The American National Circus" were published in 1860 by Frederick A. Brown.

Chandler Mfg. Co. The "Hurst" gyroscope tops were made in the Boomer years by this Indianapolis, Ind., firm. See L.J. Hurst Mfg. Co.

Chandler Plastics The "Wild Bill Hickock Teepee" of 1955 was issued by this Bleecker Street, New York City, firm.

"Changeable Charlie" see *Gaston Mfg. Co., and Halsam Products Co.*

The Chapin-Stephens Co. Roller skates were products of this prewar Pinie Meadow, Conn., firm.

The Chapman-Sargent Co. Colonial doll beds were made by this Cleveland, Ohio, firm in the 1930s.

Character Molding Corp. Action-puzzle take-apart toys were Boomer-era specialties of this Brooklyn, N.Y., firm. Designs included jeeps, tanks, guns, rockets, trucks and hot rods.

Character Novelty Co. A manufacturer of stuffed animals, Character Novelty was located on East 22nd Street, New York City, in the mid-1930s, moving to Fifth Avenue by the end of the decade, then to the Fifth Avenue Building in the postwar years. It maintained a factory in South Norwalk, Conn.

Charles, William A publisher based in New York City and Philadelphia, William Charles published reissues of English toy books in the years 1810-25.

"Charlie Chaplin" While some might guess Shirley Temple if asked the name of the film star to inspire the most toys and dolls, the odds appear to be weighted a little in Charlie Chaplin's favor. Chaplin certainly had an impressive variety of toys made with his name involved, beginning during his first stardom in the silent films up through at least the 1980s. In the 1910s through the '30s, a heady variety of Chaplin figures, dolls, wind-up toys, mechanical figures, and rolling bell-

toys appeared from many companies, some of them unidentified—perhaps to avoid licensing fees and royalties at the time. Some of the toy Chaplins rode tricycles, some twirled canes, and one even whistled "How Dry I Am." Not only American toy-makers leapt on the Chaplin bandwagon. German, French and Spanish toy-makers quickly joined their ranks. Pirate versions abounded. A French manufacturer sold a series of dolls in the later 1910s and early 1920s, which included some with a good likeness of Chaplin, going by the name of "Charlot." The widespread popularity of not just Charlie Chaplin the film star but Charlie Chaplin the popular icon gave a foretaste of the overwhelming effect of the American film industry would have on world culture later in the century. Other doll versions have included a 1916 rag doll from Dean's Rag Book Co. of England, a number of early dolls by Boucher, the 9-inch composition figure by Mark Hampton Co., and the 15-inch composition and cloth doll by the Louis Amberg Co. More recent Chaplin toys have been widely varied in nature, and have included the 1971 "Charlie's Back" doll from Milton Bradley,

"Charlie McCarthy" see *Bergen, Edgar*

Charm Toys, Inc. This Ruleville, Miss., firm made stuffed toys and dolls in the 1950s and '60s.

Chase, M.J. The "Chase Stockinet" rag dolls of the 1920s through the prewar years were made by this Pawtucket, R.I., firm.

Chase Bag Co. The Chase Bag Company, based in Reidsville, N.C., entered the world of toymaking only after a century of manufacturing experience as a maker of "gunny sacks" for various food products. In 1963, Chase accepted a request to produce "Jolly Green Giant" cloth dolls, and enjoyed such success it decided to move aggressively into this new area of manufacture. Today it ranks as one of the leading makers of advertising dolls, having produced such well-known advertising characters as "Mr. Peanut," "Bazooka Joe," "Ronald McDonald," "Tony the Tiger," and "Chiquita Banana."

C.F. Chase Game Co. The "Rose Bowl Tournament" parlor football game of the earlier 1930s was made by this St. Louis, Mo., company.

Chaspec Mfg. Co. The "Arnold" educational toys of the Boomer years made by this Greenwich, Conn., company.

The Chatfield-Clarke Co. Chatfield-Clarke Co. of Woodbury, Conn., made "Plus-Lite" white blackboards in the late 1930s, and through the war years.

"Chatty Cathy" One of the most famous dolls of the Boomer years, "Chatty Cathy," who talked by means of an internal record activated by pulling the "Chatty Ring" was introduced by Mattel in 1960. She was issued in her original version through 1963, when she had her repertoire increased. She appeared in a new version in 1970. "Chatty Cathy" was followed in 1961 with "Talking Matty Mattel," "Talking Sister Belle," and "Talking Casper the Friendly Ghost"; in 1962 with "Black Chatty Cathy," "Chatty Baby," "Talking Beany," "Talking Cecil the Seasick Sea Serpent," and "Talking Bugs Bunny"; in 1963 with "Charmin' Chatty," "Tiny Chatty Baby," and "Tiny Chatty Brother"; in 1964 with "Talking Bozo the Clown"; in 1965 with "Talking Woody Woodpecker"; and in 1966 with "Talking Baby First Step" and "Talking Mrs. Beasley." Mattel's talking toys proliferated soon after "Chatty Cathy's" introduction. The talking stuffed doll "Shrinkin' Violette" was introduced in 1964, along with the stuffed plush talking animals, the "Animal Yackers," "Larry the Talking Lion" and "Crackers the Talking Parrot." The "Talking Hand Puppets" line was introduced in 1965, followed in 1967 with the first "Talking Patter Pillows."

The Checkerette Co. This Tulsa, Okla., firm was making its "Checkerette" four-handed checkers game in the late 1930s.

checkers, chess, and dominoes The traditional games of checkers, chess and dominoes remained mainstays for game manufacturers from the mid-19th century into the 20th century. With wood pieces, and wood or cardboard boards in the case of checkers and chess, they were made by prewar companies including Beulah Toy & Novelty Co., Milton Bradley Co., Compo-Site, the Elkloid Co., the Embossing Co., Grand Rapids Dowel Works, Halsam Products Co., the G.H. Harris Co., Gaston Hollander, W.C. Horn Bro. & Co., Parker Bros., Pattberg Novelty Corp., F. W. Peterson Corp., Arthur Popper, Selchow & Righter Co., and Utility Wood Products Co.

"Checkers" Shotwell Mfg. Co. was the leading competitor for Cracker Jack Co. in the years leading up to the purchase of the former by the latter in 1926. It had an edge over Cracker Jack in consistently providing assorted prizes in its boxes of popcorn confection. Cracker Jack took over the idea, which provided the ticket to its commercial success and longevity. A number of promotional toys featured the "Checkers" name in the 1920s, including spinning tops, spinners, and game tops. Any number of miscellaneous die-cast, celluloid, paper and ceramic prizes of the time, however, were used in "Checkers" packages, just as they were used in the packages of Cracker Jack and many other confections. Shotwell Mfg. Co. was based in Chicago, Ill., and Brooklyn, N.Y.

Chee-Ki Corp. of California This Santa Monica, Calif., company made "Plastisol" squeeze toys and vinyl hand puppets in the postwar years.

J. Chein & Co. Julius Chein founded J. Chein & Co. in Harrison, N.J., in 1903. The firm became famous for its lithographed sheet metal toys in the 1930s, when it maintained offices in the Fifth Avenue Building. The company's line included mechanical toys, pull toys, drums, jazz sets, laundry sets, sparkling toys, sprinkling cans, musical toys, pails, shovels, boats, geographical globes, games, dice, banks, noisemakers, trick novelties, and tops. Its line in the 1950s and '60s continued to emphasize the sheet metal toys manufactured before the war, as well as doll furniture, and blackboards. In the 1970s, its last decade in the toy business, the company became known as Chein Industries, Inc.

"Chemcraft" see *Porter Chemical Co.*

Chemical Sundries Co. A Chicago, Ill., firm, Chemical Sundries made bean blowers, soap bubbles, plastic bubbles, Christmas glitter, and a movie-viewer game in the Boomer years. It also sold jumping beans.

chemistry sets The chemistry set became an important activity toy in the prewar years, with manufacturers including A.C. Gilbert, General Sportcraft Co., Kemkit Chemical Corp., J. Lesser Toy Mfg. Co., the Midgetlab Co., the Porter Chemical Co., Jack Pressman & Co., and Sequoia Sales Co. producing sets in the 1930s. The name most associated with chemical sets, A.C. Gilbert, enjoyed considerable success with them in the postwar years. Earlier sets tended to be made with wooden boxes, while sets of the '50s and '60s tended to have tin boxes.

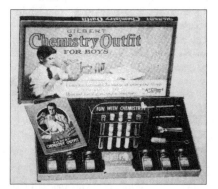

A.C. Gilbert made very successful "chemistry outfits" in the 1950s.

"Cherie" dolls prewar, see *Shaw Doll Co.*

"Cherokee" dart boards see *Indian Archery & Toy Corp.*

Cherry Valley Mfg. Corp. The "Fort Knox" savings bank safes of the 1950s and '60s were made by this Cherry Valley, Ill., corporation. It also made a junior basketball game and boy's baseball caddy.

"Cherub Babies" soft dolls see *Alexander Doll Co.*

chess, see *checkers, chess and dominoes.*

The Chessler Co., This Baltimore, Md., company made prewar masquerade costumes.

"Chester" see *"The Gumps."*

Chester Tool Co. The "Jr. Clockmaker" construction clock available in the Boomer years was made by Chester, based on Lafay-

ette Street, New York City. The firm also made electrical toys.

chests, cedar see *cedar chests, toy.*

chests, toy As the accumulation of toys became a more marked hallmark of childhood through the late 1800s and early 1900s, the idea of the "toy chest" rose in popularity. Several prewar companies issued chests made specifically for this use, including Baby Line Furniture, Strand Mfg. Co., Frank F. Taylor Co., the Toy Kraft Co., Transogram Co., and Ullman Mfg. Co.

"Cheyenne" "Cheyenne" items, licensed by Warner Bros. Pictures, were numerous in the late 1950s and '60s, with playthings including books by Whitman Publishing Co., games and puzzles by Milton Bradley Co., plastic figures by Hartland Plastics, and hats by Corona Hat Co. Daisy Mfg. Co. made outfits and holster sets, and a "Singin' Saddle" gun.

"Chicadee" construction kits prewar, see *Broadfield Glider Co.*

"Chicago" air rifle see *Markham Mfg. Co.*

Chicago Die Cutting Co. Based on West Lake Street, this mid-1930s Chicago, Ill., firm made rolling game products of wood and cardboard.

Chicago Metallic Mfg. Co. The "Betty Jane" juvenile tin baking sets of the later 1930s were made by this Chicago, Ill., firm.

"Chicago" printing presses see *Sigwalt Mfg. Co.*

Chicago Roller Skate Co. Roller skates were made from the 1930s through the Boomer years by this West Lake Street, Chicago, firm.

Chicago Table Tennis Co. Located on Milwaukee Avenue, this prewar Chicago, Ill., company made table tennis equipment and tables.

Chicago Tool & Kit Mfg. Co. Maker of tool chests, this West Superior Street, Chicago, company made juvenile tool chests and tool sets in the 1930s and '40s.

Chicago Toy & Doll Co. Latex, vinyl and plastic dolls were specialties of this firm. Despite its name it was based on Wooster Street, New York City.

Chicago Toy Co. This subsidiary of Chicago Musical Instrument Co. issued musical toys during World War II including "Bugle Boy," "Air Raid Siren," "Cataplane," and "Tonette." It also published "American Songster" and "Singing Storybooks."

Chicago World's Columbian Exposition One of the most important World's Fairs, the Chicago World's Columbian Exposition of 1893-94 had immense influence in shaping American and world culture in the years before the turn of the century. The world of toymaking was by no means left out. In one interesting conjunction, the Exposition saw the introduction of both the Linotype machine and a caramel-popcorn confection that sold like "cracker jack." The Linotype machine, which gave manufacturers access to inexpensive die-cast goods, was put into use by companies including Dowst Manufacturing and Cosmo. Such companies, incidentally, provided trinkets for confections including Checkers, Angelus Marshmallow, and Cracker Jack. Several doll companies have important Columbian Exposition connections, including Arnold Printworks and The Columbian Doll. The first toy premium ring was given out at this fair.

Chick Toys Established in the late 1930s in Richmond Hill, Long Island, N.Y., Chick Toys made doll beds, train tunnels, basinettes, and toy barns and barnyards.

chicken feet American Colonial children found playthings where they could, and managed to find some even among kitchen scraps. The exposed tendons on chicken and turkey feet could be pulled to make the toes open and close, making them a natural, if somewhat grisly to many of our sensibilities, mechanical toy.

"Chief" A widely used trade name, "Chief" was used on a prewar sled and a six-wheel coaster truck by Garton Toy Co., and a pistol by the Dent Hardware Co. "The Chief" was a velocipede by American National Co.

Chief Industries The "Mini-Midget" race car kits by this Dowagiac, Mich., firm assembled into either "pushmobiles" or motor-driven juvenile cars.

"Chieftain" roller skates see *Kingston Products Corp.*

"Child Guidance Toys see *Archer Plastics.*

Child Health Sand Co. Safety concerns about playthings were seriously considered in the 1930s, as is demonstrated by the existence of this Pinewald, N.J., company, which provided hygienic material for sand boxes or other recreational needs.

"Child Improvement Books" prewar, see *Child Welfare Publishers, Inc.*

child labor Child labor practices have exerted a heavy influence on the toy industry. As late as the mid-19th century, children went to work at age 6, and hundreds of thousands of children worked full-time by age 12. The enactment of laws limiting child labor proved a substantial boost to the toy industry, which worked assiduously, especially in the Boomer years, to extend the years during which children used toy manufacturers' products.

Child Life Toys, Inc. This Seattle, Wash., firm made Western wood dollhouses and doll house furniture in the Boomer years.

Child Welfare Publishers, Inc. Games, children's books, stencils, tracing books, and drawing and painting books were published by this Evanston, Ill., publisher in the 1930s and '40s.

Childhood Classics Soft dolls and toy animals, and musical dolls and animals, were specialties of this East 116th Street, New York City, company in the Boomer years.

Childhood Interests, Inc. Based in the Fifth Avenue Building, Childhood Interests made educational playthings of plastic and wood to be used in sequence from infancy through preschool and first grade, in the 1950s and '60s. They included cradle toys, pull toys, push toys, the "Cradle Gym," the "Cradle Bounce," "Color Xylo," "Pound-A-Way," and "Play Pen Rail Train."

Children's Day Children's Day was designated as being the third Saturday in June of each year. The day became a focal point for summer toy merchandising. How differently the event looked in the early 20th century from how such a day might look in the 21st century is made clear by this remark from a 1934 trade publication: "Children's Day offers dealers a splendid opportunity to make their toy departments hum with yuletide activity during early June. The release of children from schools makes it a logical time to promote all kinds of toys."

"The Children's Farmyard" An early farm play set of cutout figures, "The Children's Farmyard" was published by Kellogg & Bulkeley in the 1850s.

"The Children's Magazine," An early periodical aimed at a youthful audience, *The Children's Magazine* first appeared in 1789.

George A. Childs, Childs issued the 1895 "The Game of Football" board game.

Child's Wonderland Co. Decorative art transfers and pictorial maps for children's rooms were made by this late 1930s Grand Rapids, Mich., firm. It also issued a cardboard construction set.

"Chilton Ware" see *Aluminum Specialty Co.*

chime toys see *bell toys.*

china China tea sets for children were imported from Europe to America from about 1800. Metal and pottery sets began overtaking china sets in popularity several decades into the 19th century.

"Ching Chow" see *"The Gumps."*

"The Chipmunks" Items based on the popular "The Chipmunks," licensed by MCA, included balloons by Van Dam Rubber Co., games and activity sets by Hassenfeld Bros., Halloween costumes by J. Halpern Co., harmonicas by Plastic Injecto Corp., hobby craft sets by Hollywood Shell & Toy Co., jumping beans and novelty plastic rings by Karl Guggenheim, books by Golden Press, musical plush toys by Commonwealth Toy & Novelty Corp., hats by Spec-Toy-Culars, holster sets by Esquire Novelty Corp., playsuits by Sack-man Bros., rubber squeeze toys by Bayshore Industries, stuffed toys and puppets by Timely Toys, and wall plaques and stuffed novelties by Christy Mfg. Co.

Chongka Games The "Chongka" game was made by this eponymous San Francisco, Calif., firm in the 1950s-'60s.

Chris Mfg. Co. This Modesto, Calif., company made the "Biff-A-Ball" inflatable and "Pan-O-Ramic" balls of the Boomer years.

Christmas In New England, church leaders correctly saw the observation of Christmas as a bow to pagan and non-Christian influences, and so forbade its observance. A five shilling fine was levied on festive miscreants. By the end of the Revolution, the tide of non-Puritan immigrants effectively canceled the force of the taboo against observing Christmas. While some Christmas gift giving did take place in earlier 1700s America, it did not become common practice until later. From the Revolution through the 1850s the practice gradually grew. Often, Christmas presents could be bought either before or after Christmas Day, with "Christmas presents" and "New Year's presents," being to some degree interchangeable. Some retailers simply advertised "holiday presents."

These glass Christmas Tree ornaments were produced in the 1920s.

Christmas candles Candles on Christmas trees remained a common holiday sight into the 1930s, when electric lights were starting to have a strong sales impact at Christmas time. Many makers of prewar Christmas candles happened also to be the country's crayon makers. They included the American Crayon

Co., the Art Crayon Co., Creston Crayon Co, Fox Co., Globe Crayon Co., Homeland Mfg. Co., the Mack-Miller Candle Co., Republic Tool Products Co., Standard Oil Co., and Will & Baumer Candle Co.

Christmas cards The exchanging of cards in the holiday season first became common in the 1840s. The now commonplace greetings of "Merry Christmas! Happy New Year!" came into use by 1850.

A Christmas Carol This classic Charles Dickens novel, still a part of children's experience of the holiday, first appeared in 1843.

Christmas fancy goods A term used in the 1800s for general decorations, as opposed to toys.

Christmas lights The introduction of the idea of putting lights in the window is attributed to the Irish.

Christmas snow see *artificial snow.*

Christmas stockings The tradition of Santa filling stockings with toys is an early one. "Children, select your largest stockings," advised early toy seller E.C. Ferre, proprietor of Ferre's Depot of Middletown, Conn., in 1846. Capitalizing on the tradition, companies learned to manufacture pre-filled stockings, usually of mesh to allow the candies and toys inside to be seen, as well as toy-filled "suitcases." Prewar manufacturers included Ammidon & Co., G.W. Morris, George E. Mousley Inc., and S. Thanhauser. The latter advertised its stocking as "a real toy for the kiddies' supreme enjoyment." Filled stockings continued to be popular through the Boomer years, with Dillon-Beck Mfg. Co., best known for its plastic toy cars, among the manufacturers. Postwar companies producing stockings already filled with toys included Allison's, Banner Plastics Corp, Crown Novelty Co., Dillon-Beck, Jak-Pak-Inc., Lawrence Industries, George E. Mousley, the Richards Co., Royal Crest Products Co., S. Thanhauser, and Thomas Mfg. Corp.

"Christmas Story" wood toys prewar, see *Holgate Bros. Co.*

Christmas tree The practice of having a Christmas tree inside the home caught on only slowly in America, becoming more common by the 1840s. The Christmas tree's introduction from Germany to England directly into Queen Victoria's court by Prince Albert made the custom popular in England and America. Earlier German immigrants may also have brought the tradition with them to this country.

Christmas tree, artificial Factory-made trees gained in popularity during those decades of "convenience" and the "labor-saving" device, the 1920s and '30s. Prewar manufacturers included the Beistle Co., Biltwell Brush Co., Arthur W. Hahn, North Ridge Brush Co., Rossig Corp., and Tienken Tree & Novelty Corp. Aluminum Christmas trees, more commonly known from the Boomer years, appeared as early as the 1930s, from companies including Flower Products Co.

Christmas tree decorations Decorations on the trees of wax tapers, baskets of sweetmeats, drums, dolls, fifes, fiddles wooden and candy horses, needle cases, and pincushions became common by the late 1840s. The decorating of Christmas trees was an activity associated in most children's minds with anticipations of gifts of toys. While the early practice of hand-made tree decorations never entirely died out, many companies, some with ties to the toy industry, began manufacturing various decorations and ornaments. By the 1930s, when it had become big business, firms included Adco Electric Mfg. Co., American Merri-Lei Corp., Associated Mfrs. Co., Paul Boehland & Co., George Borgfeldt Co., Bouton-Woolf Co., Carpenter Mfg. Co., Douglas Mfg. Co., Etges Mfg. Co., the George Franke Sons Co., R.E. Gebhardt Co., Heseltine & Co., the Hy-Sil Mfg. Co., the Keydel Co., Kirchen Bros., the Kirchhof Patent Co., Oscar Leistner, Metal Goods Corp., National Tinsel Mfg. Co., the Ohio Art Co., Paper Novelty Mfg. Co., M. Pressner & Co., Reynolds Metals Co., Carl Silverman, Strauss-Eckardt Co., Tahyer Mfg. Co., Tinsel Corp. of America, W. & F. Mfg. Co., B. Wilmsen, and Louis Wolf & Co. Several prewar companies specialized in the Christmas tree fence, including Bush Mfg. Co., A.W. Drake Mfg. Co., Grey Iron Casting Co., Homeland Mfg. Co., the Massillon Wire Basket Co., S. & G. Mfg. Co., and Woerner's Mfg. Works.

Christmas tree lights Electrical "lighting outfits" for the Christmas tree became prevalent by the 1930s. Manufacturers included Adco Electric Mfg. Co., Associated Mfrs. Co., N. Goldman & Co., Liberty Outfit Mfg. Co., J. Morris & Co., Noma Electric Corp., Ozan Products Co., Pass & Seymour, Raylite Trading Co., and Thomas Import Co. With the advent of cheap commercial plastics in the 1950s, electrically lit decorations and figures appeared more widely, leading to the large, electrically lit plastic Santas and snowmen placed in front yards by the 1960s.

Noma Electric Corp. Christmas lights from the 1930s.

Christmas tree stands Christmas tree stands were made of a variety of materials and in a variety of patterns, some undecorated and others colorfully lithographed with Christmas or other decorations. Important prewar manufacturers of Christmas tree stands, many of which are of interest to collectors, include Ace Mfg. Co., Arcade Mfg.

Co., Albert P. Danner, the Dayton Casting Co., Everts Folding Tree Stand, Freidag Mfg. Co., Grey Iron Casting Co., the Littlestown Hardware & Foundry Co., Marion Craftsmen Tool Co., Rapaport Bros., Roland P. Place Co., Twin City Iron & Wire Co., and Youngstown Tool & Mfg. Co.

Christy Mfg. Co. Fur cats and kittens, autograph animals, and "Dim Wit" novelties were postwar specialties of this Fayetteville, N.C., firm.

Chromatic Printing Co. This Philadephia, Penn., publisher issued paper dolls in the 1870s.

"Chummy Bunny" rocker see *The Delphos Bending Co.*

"Chummy-3-Coaster" The Mengel Co. made the "Chummy-3-Coaster" and "Chummy-4-Coaster" wagons in the 1930s.

"Chunky" books prewar, see *McLoughlin Bros.*

Cimko Innovations Doll accessories were the specialties of this postwar Brooklyn, N.Y., firm.

Cincinnati Game Co. Active in the late 1800s, Cincinnati Game Co. published "Illustrated Mythology" in 1896, and "Game of Birds," "Flags," and "Flowers" in 1899. Early 1900s games included "Game of Fortunes" and "Fractions" in 1902, "Our National Life" in 1903, "Astronomy" in 1905, and "Game of Yellowstone" in 1910.

Cincinnati Fly Screen Co. Based in Cincinnati, Ohio, this firm made outdoor recreational play houses for children in the 1930s, including the "Play-Bild" houses, stores, and garages.

"Cinderella" Since the "Cinderella" story has been traced to ancient Chinese sources, the pedigree of "Cinderella" toys is undoubtedly a long one. In American toy history, 19th century items included a "Cinderella, or Hunt the Slipper" game by McLoughlin Bros. in 1887, and a "Cinderella" game by Parker Bros. in 1895. In the 20th century, prewar items included a board game by Stoll & Einson Games and a playhouse by Hettrick

Mfg. Co. A greater proliferation of playthings followed the release in 1950 of Walt Disney's *Cinderella* animated full-length feature. Boomer playthings included 1950 watch by Timex and wristwatch by U.S. Time; 1950s hand puppets by Gund Mfg. Co.; '50s-'60s coloring books by the Saalfield Publishing Co.; dolls by Nancy Ann Storybook Dolls and Uneeda Doll Co.; and 1965 paper dolls by Whitman Publishing Co. Particularly fitting playthings were doll shoes by Queen City Plastics, and dish washing and housecleaning sets by Norstar Corp.

"The Cinnamon Bear" A holiday-time radio serial that aired from 1937 through the 1950s, "The Cinnamon Bear" inspired tab buttons, coloring books, and stuffed toy animals.

"Circus" scroll-cut puzzles prewar, see *Milton Bradley Co.*

"Circus Cycle" see *Wham-O Mfg. Co.*

circus toys With the rise of the circus as a popular entertainment in the mid to later 1800s, circus toys naturally enjoyed similar popularity. Among the earliest toys were stuffed toy elephants, undoubtedly made by many manufacturers, and Charles M. Crandall's interlocking wooden "Acrobats," which prefigured the series of toys now better known among toy collectors, the A. Schoenhut Co.'s "Humpty Dumpty Circus" of the 1920s and '30s, comprised of "unbreakable jointed wooden animals and figures—the greatest and one of the best playthings every invented for children." Another firm successful with circus-themed toys was J. Chein, working in lithographed sheet metal, in the 1930s. Other prewar manufacturers included Fisher-Price Toys, Grey Iron Casting Co., Howard Toy & Novelty Co., Miami Wood Specialty Co., Playskool Institute, the Toy Kraft Co., and Toy Mfg. Co. Perhaps the most popular postwar circus toy was the "Super Circus," an elaborate play set with large tin big-top tent, plastic structures, and numerous, well-detailed soft plastic figures depicting sideshow attractions, clowns, acrobats, animals, and audience members, made by Louis Marx & Co. Other manufacturers included Allison Studios, Atlanta Novelty Mfg. Corp., George Borgfeldt Corp., Fisher-Price Toys, Hale-Nass Corp., Kusan, and Softskin Toys.

"Cisco Kid" The Saalfield Publishing Co. made a 1950s puzzle set based on this radio star of the 1940s and '50s. Sackman Bros. Co. made "Cisco Kid" suits, chaps and vests in the 1950s and '60s.

Andre Citroen The firm eponymously named for its founder, Andre Citroen, and established in 1919, began producing toy versions of its real automobiles in 1923, as promotional items. Eventually the line of miniatures included models by other auto brands. The company's name is typically stenciled on the underside of the models.

Civil War The Civil War spurred changes in the toy-manufacturing world, prompting the introduction of the first toy cannon by Ellis, Britton & Eaton. Toy guns also received new impetus, with the first American patent for a toy gun being issued in 1859. In the post-Civil War years, toy manufacturers turned increasingly to mechanical toys, toy automatons, steam engines, and banks. Croquet playing was also a post-Civil War fad.

"Clambroth" These opaque marbles are made of white or other color glass, with thin, evenly spaced swirls on their surface.

"Clancy the Laughing Clown" see *the Rushton Co.*

Clare Creations, Inc. Stuffed toys were made by this Fifth Avenue, New York City, postwar firm.

D.P. Clark, The firm of D.P. Clark of Dayton, Ohio, was founded in 1898 by David P. Clark. The company specialized in producing sheet-steel novelty toys and toy automobiles, using frictional and flywheel mechanisms. In 1909 the company became Schieble Toy & Novelty.

E.O. Clark, Active in the late 1890s and early 1900s, E.O. Clark issued games including "The Charge," "The Hippodrome," "The Owl and the Pussy Cat," "Game of Robinson Crusoe for Little Folks," "The Scout," and "Game of Steeple Chase."

Clark & Martin A game publisher, Clark & Martin issued the "New Baseball Game" in the 1880s.

Clark & Sowdon Clark & Sowdon issued games in the 1890s including "Rip Van Winkle" and "Yacht Race." The company issued titles including "Tete-a-Tete" and "Game of Wang" in 1892, "Authors Illustrated" in 1893, "Chessindia," "Hunting the Rabbit," and "Paws & Claws" in 1895, and "The Game of Rough Riders" in 1898. Late games included "The Game of Golf" in 1905.

Clark, Austin & Smith This publisher issued the "Nellie" paper dolls, and others, in the 1890s.

Clark Toy Mfg. Co. A Morehead, Ky., company, Clark Toy made bean shooters and "cap bursters" in the 1930s.

Clark Treat Toy Co. Aquehonga Animated Pull Toys were the leading product of this Staten Island, N.Y., company in the 1930s.

Clarke, G.P. New York inventor G.P. Clarke developed a creeping doll in 1871, the same year a "Creeping Doll" was patented by R.J. Clay.

Clarke Mfg. Co., Inc. Based in New Haven, Conn., Clarke Mfg. Co. made inflatable boats, playballs, and balloon accessories in the 1930s.

The Clarolyte Co., Inc. Based in Long Island City, N.Y., Clarolyte made infants' plastic toys and novelties in the Boomer years.

Classy Products Corp. Official "Roy Rogers" and "Dale Evans" items were the lifeblood of this Woodside, N.Y., company in the 1950s and '60s. Its licensed line included cap pistols, holster sets, scabbards, lassos, and cuff sets.

clay see *modeling clay.*

Clay, R.J. New York City inventor R.J. Clay invented and patented a "Creeping Doll" in 1871. It crept on its hands and knees when its clockwork mechanism was activated. Clay also patented another "Toy Automaton" in 1873, and a "toy for producing a crying sound" in 1872.

clay marbles see *marbles*

"Claymaster" see *Creston Crayon Co.*

"Clayola" see *Binney & Smith Co.*

"Clayrite" see *Milton Bradley Co.*

"Cleanette" cleaning sets see *Buffalo Toy & Tool Works.*

Cleinman & Sons, Inc. Toy rings, badges, watches, jewelry, and beauty sets were specialties of this Cincinnati, Ohio, postwar firm.

Clement Toy Co. A wood turning company specializing in items for the toy trade, Clement produced its own toy carts in the 1930s.

"Cleveland" bicycles see *Westfield Mfg. Co.*

Cleveland Model & Supply Co. Model airplane kits and supplies were produced by this prewar Cleveland, Ohio, company. By the late 1930s the firm was issuing both airplane and railroad kits, and was using the "Cleveland-Designed" trade name on its scale model supplies. In the postwar years, the firm specialized in airplane kits and gliders, and was known as Cleveland Model Products Co.

Cleveland Welding Co. Established in Cleveland, Ohio, in the later 1930s, Cleveland Welding Co. made bicycles.

Clever Things The "Beacon Beanie" flashing beanies and "Space Conquerer" rocket were made by this Cincinnati, Ohio, company in the 1950s-'60s.

Click Products Co. Cowboy chaps were made by this West 14th Street, New York City, firm in the late 1930s.

clicker Clickers were metal toys designed for the pleasure of children and the irritation of adults, usually made of two pieces of sheet metal, one often shaped like an insect or frog, and the other a flat "tongue" of metal underneath. Pressed with thumb or finger, the tongue resisted being bent to a certain degree, then bent with a sharp "click." The simplest clicker toys were made of a single piece of metal, as in the metal Cracker Jack clicker in the shape of a guitar pick. Clickers were also often called "crickets."

Climax Industries The "Kid-O" modeling dough and "Doh-Mix" modeling material of the early 1960s were made by this Cleveland, Ohio, firm.

Climax Rubber Co. Located on Broadway, New York City, this prewar company made rubber novelties and doll accessories, including rubber pants, bathing caps, and capes.

climbing monkeys Climbing monkey toys were popular toys in the prewar years. The German company Lehmann introduced a great many toys which featured figures that appeared to cling to a string with hands and feet, and which would then appear to swiftly climb up when the bottom string was pulled. The company made human figures as well as monkeys, and made similar toys of men climbing palm trees or the bases of windmills. Lehmann's climbing monkey was named "Tom," while Ferdinand Strauss's toy was "Trixo." The most common climbing monkey in prewar times was "Zippo, the Climbing Monkey," by the Louis Marx Co. These companies likely issued the toy under other names. A "Climbing Mickey Mouse" toy was also made in the 1930s by Dolly Toy Co.

Popular in the prewar years, this "Climbing Monkey" was made by Louis Marx & Co.

"Climbing Tractor" prewar, see *Animate Toy Co.*

The Clinton Toy Corp. Based in North Haven, Conn., Clinton made a line of airplane flying toys in the 1920s, including seaplanes, land planes, and transports, costing $3.00 to $12.00, gliders costing a dime to a dollar, and construction kits costing $1.00 to $6.00.

"Clipper" coaster wagon prewar, see *Gendron Wheel Co.*

"Clipper" roller skates see *Kingston Products Corp.*

"Clipper" velocipedes see *The Monarch Products Co.*

clockwork A key-wound mechanism involving a spring coil that provides power for some toys. See *motors, spring.*

clocks, educational The educational toy clocks became widely popular in the Boomer years, the most notable examples being made by Fisher-Price Toys. Other manufacturers included F.P.I., the Hubley Mfg. Co., the Lux Clock Mfg. Co., Sifo Co., Talking Devices Co., Tot Guidance, and Vantines. Toy timepieces were by no means new to the Boomer years, toy watches having been made as early as the 1920s, by S. Lisk & Bro.

Clover Games Co. Based on West 15th Street, New York City, in the 1930s and '40s, Clover Games issued titles including "Bagdad, the Game of the East," of 1940.

"Clue" "Clue," an extremely well-received mystery game first released in the later 1950s by Parker Bros., is one of the most characteristic game titles of the Boomer years. It may have been inspired by British evening party games, in which guests would play "murder suspects." Among other possible predecessors is the mystery party game "Clues," a 1930s product of the Ullman Mfg. Co.

Cluff Cover Co., Inc. This unusual 1930s company specialized in making table covers with game surfaces, for bridge, "Crown & Anchor," "Four Handed Checker," backgammon, "Sweepstakes," and contract bridge. It also made complete backgammon sets. The company, based on West 55th Street, New York City, in the mid-1930s, moved to West 19th Street later in the decade, and changed its name to Cluff Fabric Products, Inc.

"Co-Ed" bicycle see *Chain Bike Corp.*

Co-Operative Displays, Inc. The wartime "Sil-O-Models," which were official recognition training models of leading combat aircraft, were issued by this Cincinnati, Ohio, company.

Coast Electric & Mfg. Co. Coaster wagons, scooters and "two-wheel cars" were made by this prewar Portland, Ore., company.

C

"Coaster Blocks" preschool toys
prewar, see *Fisher-Price Toys, Inc.*

coaster brakes Coaster brakes are a form of bicycle brake in which reverse motion of the pedals causes the brake to close against the rear wheel hub or rim. Resumed forward motion releases the brake. A prewar manufacturer specializing in making these brakes for other wheel goods manufacturers was the New Departure Mfg. Co. of Bristol, Conn.

"Coaster King" wagons see *Auto-Wheel Coaster Co, Inc.*

coaster wagon see *wagon, coaster.*

The Coburn Co. Swivel-action jumping ropes were the postwar specialty of this Whitewater, Wis., company.

Coburn Mfg. Co. Located on West 20th Street, New York City, Coburn Mfg. Co. made wood cut outfits and "Film Fun" paint sets in the mid-1930s.

"Coca-Cola" While playthings related to the famous soft drink were not so prevalent in the Boomer years as they would become by the post-Boomer years, they nevertheless were far from uncommon, especially with the large variety of toy "Coca Cola" bottle trucks issued in different scales by firms including Buddy "L" Toys, Louis Marx & Co., Lesney Products Co., and anonymous Japanese tin-litho firms. Among the more notable toys were toy soft-drink dispensers by Trim Molded Products Co. and C. & G. Toy Co., the latter being a combination dispenser and bank.

"Coca-Cola Dispenser" by Trim Molded Products Co., 1960s.

Coe & Sniffen Coe & Sniffen of Stratford, Conn., manufactured ice skates in the mid-1800s, patenting an improved skate in 1859.

coffin In the practical-minded 1800s, all the typical appurtenances of American life found their way into toy versions. Even wood toy coffins, apparently made so children could play at imitating the relatively common event of child death, are known from the century.

S. Cohen & Son A Philadelphia, Penn., maker of novelty cloth and felt caps, S. Cohen & Son was making policeman, cowboy, aviator and sea captain outfits in the early to mid-1930s. It added "G-Man" outfits by the end of the decade, when it was issuing its costumes under the "Boys-D-Lite" trade name. The company also made silver foil icicles.

Cohn & Rosenberger Based on West 34th Street, New York City, Cohn & Rosenberger obtained a late '30s license to issue Edgar Bergen related jewelry.

Joseph Cohn Co. Based on Bleecker Street, New York, in the late 1930s, Joseph Cohn made lithographed metal toys.

T. Cohn, Inc. A specialist in tin toys, T. Cohn of Brooklyn, N.Y., made metal toys including sand pails and noisemakers in the 1920s. By the '30s, the line included a wide variety of drums, tambourines, kazoos, sand and snow shovels, lithographed metal sand pails in all sizes, tin horns designed for different occasions, and games including "Pocket Size Bagatelle" and "Pokerette." In the late 1930s T. Cohn issued a large selection of "Popeye" items including sand pails, sprinkling cans, sand toys, and sand sets. In postwar years, it issued play sets and lithographed sheet-metal toys.

"Col-O-Rol" blocks see *Playskool Institute, Inc.*

Colbert & Bretz Founded in Elkhart, Ind., in the later 1930s, Colbert & Bretz made the "Walk-Ski," which was an attachment to go over skate blades.

Colby, L.J. A publisher in the late 19th century. L.J. Colby issued the "Literature Game" board game in 1897.

Colby Bros. Founded by George J. and Edwin A. Colby in Waterbury, Vt., in the 1850s, Colby Bros., started business making willow carriages, doll carriages, and baskets. After the Civil War, the company added sleds and wagons to its line. George Colby and L.H. Thomas patented a toy boat in 1866. The firm was purchased in the 1870s by Montpelier Mfg. Co., which continued making "Colby" wheel goods for some years.

Albert Coles & Co. Albert Coles began his silversmithing business in 1835 in New York City. His early production included baby rattles. The company continued operating through much of the century.

F.A. Colford Co. A Washington, D.C., company, F.A. Colford made doll furniture in the 1930s.

Collector Models, or Collector Series Usually models with special inscriptions placed there with the collector in mind, these models commemorate often special events. Although the assumption is often made that these models will increase in value, in part due to the attached notion of the model being a limited edition, this is not always the case.

Collegeville Flag & Mfg. Co. A maker of flags and decorations, this Collegeville, Penn., company also made prewar masquerade costumes and children's play suits, including Edgar Bergen related outfits and "The Lone Ranger" at the end of the 1930s. The suits cost from 49 cents to $5.00. The firm continued through wartime with flags, play suits, costumes, and Santa outfits. In the Boomer years, Collegeville continued to emphasize the same specialties, issuing numerous costumes based on TV, comic and movie characters. In 1960 it introduced the innovation of the "Mask-O-Rama" costume, billed as a one-size-fits-all costume. Among its prominent 1960s products were the "Yellow Submarine" costumes, for which it held exclusive rights.

The Lone Ranger costume was a popular product by Collegeville Flag & Mfg. Co. in the prewar years.

Collegiate Mfg. Co. "Personality Pets" and "Autograph Pets," popular toys of the 1950s and '60s, were issued by this Ames, Iowa, firm. Collegiate also made "Cheer-Up and Her Family," and other felt-crafted products.

Collette Mfg. Co. A maker of juvenile sporting goods, this Amsterdam, N.Y., company manufactured beach balls, playballs, soccer balls, and swimming tubes in the 1930s and '40s.

Collingbourne Mills, Inc. Based in Elgin, Ill., Collinbourne Mills made "Playtime" embroidery sets in the earlier 1930s, adding the "Kiddie's Knitting Knob" later in the decade.

W.Q. Collins Co. A juvenile furniture manufacturer in the 1930s, based in Rockport, Ind., W.Q. Collins also made toddler wagons and "toddler wheel chasers." Miniature sewing cabinets, vanity tables and bureaus were among its furniture items.

Colonial Earphone Co. The "G-Man Detect-I-Phones" of the late 1930s was issued by this West 42nd Street, New York City, firm.

Colonial Moulded Plastics Co., Inc. The "Space-Nik" spinning satellite and "Ka-Zoom" of the early 1960s were produced by this Wilkinsonville, Mass., manufacturer.

coloring books Coloring books and coloring sets became common as wax crayons gained in popularity. Among collectors, many of the postwar coloring books and sets relating to television characters have the greatest interest. Whitman Publishing Co. and the Saalfield Publishing Co. were especially active in this area. See *crayons.*

Colorforms Based in Norwood, N.J., Colorforms became famous in the Boomer years for its activity sets, led by its vinyl "Stick-On" toys. Many of these sets were based on licensed characters, including "Popeye," "Bugs Bunny," "Betsy McCall," "Roy Rogers," "Three Stooges," "Emmett Kelly," "The Jetsons," and "Captain Kangaroo." Colorforms' puzzles likewise depicted popular characters, including "Bat Masterson," "Three Stooges," and "Emmett Kelly." The firm also made games, including the skill game "Flip It!" and baseball game "Play Ball!" Its coloring sets including such crayon sets as "Girls, Girls, Girls," and such colored pencil sets as "Color the Presidents" and "Three Stooges." Also in the line were "Paint-It-Yourself Greeting Cards" and "Likwi-Chalk." The firm made craft sets such as "Metal Tapping," "Walletcraft," "Totem Pole Paint Set," and "Stagecoach Woodcraft," and Christmas kits and "Paint-It-Yourself" cards.

Colorgraphic, Inc. This subsidiary of the Meyercord Co. of Chicago, Ill., made the "Young Patriot" cardboard military plays sets during World War II. They included Army and Navy "Young Patriot" sets, construction sets, the "Invasion Set," "Build Your Own Army Machines," and "Sculpture-ettes."

Colorville Toy Co. Based in Des Plaines, Ill., Colorville issued miniature railway systems in the 1920s.

The Colson Co. Based in Elyria, Ohio, the Colson Co. obtained the Kay Kamen license in the 1930s to issue Disney velocipedes. The "Mickey Mouse Velocipede" showed the mouse's body on the fender, with his feet appearing to move as the pedals were turned. It also made the "Fairy" line of velocipedes, scooters, sidewalk bikes, baby bikes, auto coasters, handcars, sport racers, 3-wheel speed bikes, and the "Flyer" and "Colson" bicycles. By the late 1930s, when it had added "Commander" bicycles, it was known as the Colson Corp.

The Colson Co. issued the "Mickey Mouse Velocipedes" in the 1930s.

"Columbia" bicycles and velocipedes see *Westfield Mfg. Co.*

Columbia Products Corp. Based in Brooklyn, N.Y., Columbia Products issued Walt Disney character kiddie bags, school bags and pencil bags in the late 1930s, along with San Francisco World's Fair designs.

Columbia Protektosite Co. A Carlstadt, N.J., company, Columbia Protektosite made plastic toys for companies including Bergen Toy & Novelty Co., from the late 1930s into the 1950s. It obtained a late 1930s license to issue "Charlie McCarthy" monocles. During the war, it continued a line of plastic novelties, tea sets, household novelties, and sun glasses.

Columbia Stamp Works Besides making rubber type and stamps for hand-printing sets, this South Dearborn Street, Chicago, Ill., company made junior police badges in the 1930s.

Columbia Toy Products A Kansas City, Mo., firm, Columbia Toy Products made stuffed toys from the later 1930s through the Boomer years. One of its more popular items in the latter period was "Mr. Bim the Monkey," a combination vinyl-and-plush stuffed figure of the kind the Rushton Co. specialized in. The firm's line included a full line of Easter plush toys.

The Columbian Doll, Emma Adams named her line of rag dolls after the famous Columbian Exposition, after winning a

Diploma of Merit at that World's Fair. One of the dolls, named "Miss Columbia," "toured" the world on behalf of various children's charities, together with a double sent along in case of mishap. The two dolls are housed in the Wenham Museum in Massachusetts. Before 1900, the dolls were marked "Columbian Doll, Emma E. Adams, Oswego Centre, N.Y." After 1906 the mark recognized Marietta Adams Ruttan, Emma's sister, as manufacturer. Production ended around 1910.

The Columbian Exposition, see *Chicago's World Columbian Exposition*

"The Columbian Sailor" see *Arnold Printworks.*

Comalan, Inc. The "Homer Lock Blocks" of the late 1930s was issued by this Homer, N.Y., firm.

Come Play Products A Worcester, Mass., company, Come Play made juvenile garden sets, housekeeping toys, ball and jack sets, jump ropes, and juvenile snow shovels, in the Boomer years.

"Comet" A widely used trademark, "Comet" was the name for Toledo Metal Wheel Co.'s all-steel coaster wagon and Kingston Products Corp.'s roller skates in the 1930s. The name was also used for checkers by Halsam Products, marbles by Master Marble Co., and at least two pistol toys: an "airplane glider cap shooter" by Kilgore Mfg. Co. and a single-shot pistol by the J. & E. Stevens Co. The postwar "Comet" sleds were made by Garton Toy co.

Comet Model Airplane & Supply Co., Inc. Model airplane kits, gliders, and supplies were 1930s specialties of this Chicago, Ill., company. Calling itself Comet Model Hobbycraft, Inc., in the postwar years, it issued a full line including balsawood flying scale model airplane construction kits; plastic scale model airplanes; plastic ready-to-fly airplanes; balsa-wood scale-model boat construction kits; and cars and car kits. Comet's all-balsa airplane kits included "Gliders," "Flying Scale," and "Struct-O-Speed E-Z-to-Build Models," priced from 10 cents to $1.29 in the mid-Boomer years. The all-plastic sets cost slightly more, roughly

one to three dollars. Its premier items were the "Read-to-Fly U-Control Gas Models," which included a variety of jets and airplanes, and a Jaguar-type racing car, priced from $.95 to 14.95.

"Commander" At least two "Commander" wagons were issued in prewar years. Garton Toy Co. issued a coaster wagon under the name, and the Monarch Products Co., an express wagon.

"Commodore" coaster wagon see *American-National Co.*

Commonwealth Plastics Corp. This Leominster, Mass., corporation was founded in 1935. In the Boomer years it issued plastic whistles, dollhouse items, toys, and dolls.

Commonwealth Toy & Novelty Co. Fur and plush stuffed toys were made by this West 27th Street, New York City, firm in the mid-1930s. It later moved to East 19th Street, and added "Mickey Mouse" portable tennis tables by the end of the decade. The "Feedme" line of animal toys, including bears and rabbits, were advertised as the "world's only eating animals" in 1939, when the company was also beginning to manufacture a line of soft washable animals. In the postwar years, it specialized in the washable plush stuffed and fur animals, as well as doll muffs and musical toys. It was based on West 18th Street in the 1950s and '60s.

Community Craft Weavers, Inc. This Broadway, New York City, firm made stuffed dolls and toys in the late 1930s. It continued the line in the Boomer years as Community Craft Toys.

Comon-Tatar, Inc. Plastic ball puzzles and peg games, molding kits, and boxed games for children and adults were postwar specialties of this Blasdell, N.Y., company.

Compax Mfg. Co. Founded in the later 1930s on West 55th Street, New York City, Compax made folding bicycles under the "Air Liner" trade name.

Compo-Site, Inc. A Newark, N.J., firm, Compo-Site made checkers and poker chips in the 1930s and '40s.

C

composition Composition, a cheap material often used in toys of the 1800s, was generally a papier-mache, often with sawdust and resins added. See also *molded pulp toys.*

"Concentration" game see *Milton Bradley Co.*

"Concentration" kindergarten toys prewar, see *Holgate Bros. Co.*

The Conde Nast Publications, Inc. Based in the Graybar Building, New York City, this publisher issued "Tiny Vogue" doll clothes patterns in the 1930s.

The Conestoga Corp. The Conestoga Corp. became famous in the 1920s for its "Big-Bang" line of "Safe Celebrators." The line featured field and heavy artillery, Navy gun-boats, Army tanks, and pistols. The 11-inch "Big-Bang Bombing Plane," touted as having "a real BANG when you push the plunger—each BANG spins the propeller," was released just before the Great Depression. Based in Bethlehem, Penn., Conestoga continued to manufacture toy pistols, gun-boats, army tanks, "Ro-To-Tops," and lasso games into the 1930s. By the end of the decade it had added roller coaster toys, the "Air-E-Go-Round," lasso-games, binoculars, and "non-skid toy train track silencers." Conestoga continued releasing the "Big-Bang" cannons through the Boomer years, and continued to bill them as "Safety Celebraters." A line that cost in the $1.00 to $5.50 range in the 1920s, cost $3.95 to $14.95 in the 1960s.

The "Big Bang Bombing Plane" was issued in 1929 by The Conestoga Corp.

Conestoga wagons While pioneers were exploring the West in the real craft, children of the East enjoyed miniature "Conestoga wagons" produced by wheel-goods manufacturers.

"Conette," 1890s see *Milton Bradley Co.*

The Congress Tool & Die Co., Inc. The "Min-I-Scale" scale model trains in "O" gauge of the late prewar years were made by this Detroit, Mich., firm.

Connecticut Leather Co. This Hartford, Conn., company issued "Davy Crockett Indian Fighter Moccasins" in 1955. They were "do-it-yourself" kits with adhesive "Davy Crockett" medallions.

Connecticut Telephone & Electric Corp. Toy telegraph and telephone sets were among the 1930s products of this Meriden, Conn., corporation. By the end of the decade it discontinued the telegraph toys.

Connor Lumber & Land Co. Based in Laona, Wis., Connor made juvenile furniture in the late prewar years. In the Boomer years it also made toy chests, and doll playpens, cribs, cradles, and beds. One of its products was the licensed Walt Disney-related "Zorro" toy chest of 1958.

Consolidated Toy Mfg. Co. Based in Lawrence, Mass., Consolidated made postwar doll furniture, games, and sailboats.

Construct-A-Plane Co. Based in Brooklyn, N.Y., this company made model airplanes, kits, and supplies in the 1930s.

construction toys One of the most important types of toy prevalent from the mid-19th century through the 20th century is the construction toy, epitomized in many minds by "Erector" sets, "Tinkertoys," or "Lincoln Logs." Construction toys had their first popular appearance on the American scene in the 1860s, in the form of not only the versatile interlocking wood blocks made by Charles M. Crandall but also log-cabin construction sets made by French and Wheat, of New York City, and Vermont Novelty Works. The notion of their educational value helped construction toys become one of the most popular items from many manufacturers.

Leading manufacturers in the 1920s included American Original Toys, the Bettcher Stamping & Mfg. Co., "Erector" set manufacturer A.C. Gilbert Co., G.B. Lewis Co., Mt. Carmel Mfg. Co., Meccano Co., and the A. Schoenhut Co. By the 1930s the number of manufacturers had grown into the dozens. Among their names were such familiar ones as J.L. Wright, maker of "Lincoln Logs"; Gilbert; the Toy Tinkers, maker of "Tinkertoys"; and Structo Mfg. Co., whose "Structo" name first referred to a "practical toy and model constructing outfit" akin to the "Erector." Other prewar manufacturers worked in everything from wood to steel, and frequently involved electrically driven motions or functions. They included Ajax Hardware Mfg. Co., American Wunder Mfg. Co., Apollometal Artcraft Co., Bilz-Em Toys, H. Boker & Co., Boucher Playthings Mfg. Corp., the Boy Toymaker Co., Central Wood Products, Constructrad, the Dorfan Co., the Embossing Co., Federal Dry Battery Corp., Fox Blocks Co., Gadget Products Corp., A.C. Gilbert Co., Robert Keller Ink Co., Knapp Electric, Knapp-Monarch, G.B. Lewis Co., the Lyons Mfg. Co., Master Makers, the May-Kit Co., the Meccano Co. of America, Miniature Homes Co., More-Craft Sales Co., Rite Mfg. Co., the A. Schoenhut Co., Seiss Mfg. Co., Selfbilt Toy Co., Stanlo Toy Div., Steel Builder Co., the Tec-Toy Co., the Toymakers, Wisconsin Toy Co., and Woodcraft Novelty Co.

Postwar manufacturers included a few familiar names from earlier decades, including Gilbert, Structo, and the Toy Tinkers. The "original Lincoln Logs" were still manufactured in Chicago, but as a division of Playskool Mfg. Co. Other Boomer-era companies, whose numbers were enriched through the introduction of plastics to manufacturing possibilities, included Blockraft, Bonnie Bilt, Built-Rite Toys, Chaspec Mfg. Co., Chester Tool Co., Comet Metal Products Co., Comet Metal Products Co., Design Industries, Dowst Mfg. Co., Fisher-Price Toys, Gem Color Co., Geodestix, Gibbs Automatic Moulding Corp., Greyshaw of Georgia, Halsam Products Co., Holgate Toys, Husky Toy Co., Irwin Corp., Jack Built Toy Mfg. Co., Henry Katz, Kenner Proucts Co., Kohner Bros., Lawson & Lawson, Mirinco Toys, Models of Industry, Modern Research Development, Morlin Co., Multiple Products Corp., Northwestern Products Co., Ny-Lint Tool & Mfg. Co., Plastic Block City, Poynter

Products, Rig-A-Jig Toy Co., Royal Tot Co., Steven Mfg. Co., Strombeck-Becker Mfg. Co., Thomas Mfg. Corp., Tonka Toys, Toycraft Corp., Vanguard Toy Co., and the Vogel Mfg Co.

Constructrad, Inc. Radio construction sets were popular in the 1930s. This Washington Street, New York City, company made sets for both short- and long-wave radios, and advertised them as "for boys and grownups."

"Contack" see *Parker Bros., Inc.*

Continental Model Airplane Co. This Brooklyn, N.Y., firm made model airplanes in the late 1930s.

Continental Plastics Corp. This Hollis, N.Y., firm made rack items, including "Laverne and Shirley" toys in the 1970s.

Continental Sales Corp. Active in the late 1930s, Continental Sales Corp. of Milwaukee, Wis., issued bowling, football, and baseball board games. Titles included "Ward Cuff's Football Game" of 1938.

Continental Toy & Novelty Co. This firm based on East 17th Street, New York City, manufactured the "Continental" line of quality stuffed animals in the 1920s. Continental used the "Toys of Distinction" slogan.

Convent Doll Corp. A Bayonne, N.J., firm, Convent made dolls in the late 1930s.

Morton E. Converse Co. Morton Converse founded his wooden toy manufacturing company in 1878, initially under the name Mason & Converse, and by 1883 under the Morton E. Converse Co. name. His Winchenden, Mass., factory, called "Toytown Complex," gained recognition as the largest wood toy factory in the world. The company was known for Noah's arks, alphabet blocks, and doll furniture, many with lithographed decorations. The game "Faba Baga, or Parlor Quoits" was issued in 1883. In the 1890s Converse made steel toys with clockwork mechanisms. In the 1920s, as the Morton E. Converse & Son Co., the company was issuing a full line of toys and juvenile items, including bassinets, beds, blackboards, building blocks, cedar chests, chimes, cradles, doll houses, doll yards, drums, games, toy stores,

C

toy pianos, pool tables, "Razzle Rattler," swings, ten pins, tool chests, wagons, toy yachts, and card table sets. It used the "Standard Toys That Give Satisfaction and Bring Results" slogan, and the "Johns-Manville" trade name on some of its furniture. Converse continued in business until 1934.

Converters, Inc. Converters was a Cambridge, Mass., manufacturer of prewar paper board toys and novelties.

Conway Co. Based in Skokie, Ill., this firm made small toy delivery trucks in the 1940s and '50s, for promotional purposes. They were used for Wrigley's Spearmint Gum and Kraft Cheese, among other promotions.

"Coo-Coo" games see *Herbert Specialty Mfg. Co.*

cooking utensils, toy see *kitchen utensils, toy.*

Cooney, J.F. Based in Flushing, N.Y., J.F. Cooney issued the "Blocko" game of the late 1930s.

coonskin caps see *tails, animal.*

Ben Cooper, Inc. This Brooklyn, N.Y., firm made some of the most famous masquerade costumes and Halloween suits in the Boomer years, the former under the "Famous Names" trade name, and the latter under the "Ben Cooper" name. Its Halloween costume line featured Walt Disney characters, "Huckleberry Hound," "Quick Draw McGraw," "Terrytoon" characters, and CBS and NBC TV stars. Its "King-size Mask Parade" costumes were oversized, one-size-fits-all outfits. By the early 1960s, "glitter and glow" costumes were popular. Masks were sold both with and without suits. Ben Cooper also made Santa Claus outfits.

"Cootie" The "Cootie" name was first used by James R. Irvin & Co. for a prewar puzzle game. The most famous game by this name, however, was issued by W.H. Schaper Mfg. Co., Inc. A plastic assembly game and toy, "Cootie" appeared in unchanged form from 1949 through the Boomer years.

One of America's famous games— "Cootie" by W.H. Schaper Mfg. Co.

"Copprotect" air rifle shot see *Daisy Mfg. Co.*

"Cor-Cor" toys see *Corcoran Mfg. Co.*

coral Polished coral was a favored material for early European and American baby toys, because of its durability and smooth surface. It was used especially in teethers and rattles.

Cordelco Industries, Inc. Plastic piggy and other banks, gun replicas, cap tommy guns, pull toys and banjos were specialties of this postwar Los Angeles, Calif., firm.

Corcoran Mfg. Co. A leading manufacturer of pressed steel toys in the 1920s through '40s, Corcoran made toy autos, buses, Pullmans, freight cars, scooters, and dump, delivery, fire and advertising trucks. Based in Washington, Ind., it made a specialty of large, pressed-steel riding toys, including automobiles and trains.

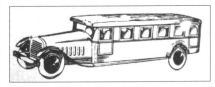

This "Interurban Bus" was a pressed steel toy made by Corcoran in the 1920s.

Corey Game Co. Corey Game Co. of Everett, Mass. began in the late 1930s with games including "Strategies, Game of Armies" and "Suffolk Downs." By wartime the firm was located in East Boston, Mass. Its line included the titles "Blockade," "Yankee Trader," "Raffles," "United States Trading,"

"Hippety-Hop," "Pirate's Island," and "Chinese Chess." It also made nested blocks. New in 1943 were "Air Attack," "Thing-A-Jigs," "Klondike Gold," and "Kongo-Kapers." "Aldjemma" was released in 1944.

Corgi Toys Mettoy Playcraft Ltd. of Swansea, South Wales, founded in 1943, established Corgi Toys in 1956. The line featured miniature toy vehicles in metal and plastic.

Cork-Craft, Inc. The "Sink-It" basket ball game of the late 1930s was issued by this Chicago, Ill., firm.

cornhusk doll see *dolls, cornhusk.*

Corona Hat Co. Cowboy hats, doll hats and novelty hats were specialties of this postwar Lynbrook, N.Y., company. Its cowboy hats went under the "Corona Corral" trade name.

Coronet Carriage Co., Inc. Based in Boston, Mass., Coronet made Boomer-era doll carriages.

Coronet Toy Mfg. Co. Stuffed toys comprised this Seattle, Wash., firm's postwar line.

Corral Toys, Inc. Based in the Fifth Avenue Building, Corral issued postwar pistol and holster sets.

Cortland Furniture Co. Boomer-era doll carriages, strollers, furniture and rockers were specialties of this Lexington Avenue, New York City, firm. Cortland also made toy chests.

Cosmopolitan Doll & Toy Corp. The "Ginger Dolls" of 1950s and '60s were made by this Jamaica, Long Island, N.Y., corporation.

"Cosmic" kites see the *Hi-Flier Mfg. Co.*

Cosmo Mfg. Co. Founded in 1888, Cosmo began using linotype die-casting methods after its introduction at the Columbian World's Exposition of 1893. A maker of trinkets, charms, and premiums, by the 1920s Cosmo was the major supplier for "Cracker Jack" and "Checkers" premiums. Nathan

Shure, owner of Cosmo, purchased Dowst Mfg. Co. in 1926.

Cosom Industries, Inc. This postwar Minneapolis, Minn., company issued games and plastic play balls in the Boomer years.

E. Joseph Cossman & Co. Influential throughout the Baby Boomer comic book-reading public, Cossman issued such enduring novelties as the plastic "Spud Gun" and "Uncle Milton's Ant Farm," the latter an invention of Milton Levine. Cossman was based in Hollywood, Calif.

costumes see *masks*, also *masquerade costumes.*

S.H. Couch Co., Inc. Based in North Quincy, Mass., Couch made "Handifone" toy telephones in the 1930s.

Coulson, James A. This prewar Seattle, Wash., manufacturer made toy boats, dollhouses, and doll's "overstuffed furniture."

counter An early word, used in the 1700s, for dice or blocks inscribed with letters or figures. See *blocks.*

Country Town Products, Inc. Based in Bridgeport, Penn., Country Town issued Boomer water riding toys and games.

Couturier Dolls This 1950s and '60s division of Horsman Dolls specialized in fashion dolls. Its offices were in the Fifth Avenue Building.

"Cowboy Ge-Tar" see *Mattel.*

"Cowboy King" pistol see *Academy Die-Casting & Plating Co.*

cowboy outfits and equipment Helped in no small part by the popularity of Western movies, the manufacture of cowboy outfits and equipment became big business by the 1930s. Prewar firms included Brauer Bros., S. Briskie, R.H. Buhrke & Co., Chancy Toy & Novelty Corp., Collegeville Flag & Mfg. Co., Dumore Belt & Novelty Co., Feinberg-Henry Mfg. Co., Keyston Bros., Leather Products Co., Lendzion Leather Goods Co., A.C. Morand Corp., the Mordt Co., Sackman Bros. Co., Trojan Sporting Goods Co., the William C. Waugh Co., and Wornova Mfg. Co. By the late prewar years, Click Products Co., Jacobson & Co., Kronheimer Co., Lincoln Novelty Co., the Mode Novelty Co., Peppy Mfg. Co., and Radio Hat Co. joined their ranks. The enthusiasm for all things Western grew during the first decade of the Boomer era, assisted in no small part by the various Western heroes of TV, not least of them Davy Crockett. Manufacturers increased in number, bolstered not only by character possibilities but also by the introductions of new plastics and manufacturing processes. Their number included Arlington Hat Co., Benay-Albee Novelty Co., Classy Products Corp., Corona Hat Co., John R. Craighead Co., Criterion Toy & Specialty Co., Dumore Belt & Novelty Co., Esquire Novelty Co., Empress Varieties Mfg. Corp., Fun Duds, Hale-Nass Corp., J. Halpern Co., Milton A. Jacobs, John-Henry Mfg. Co., Keyston Bros., Leslie-Henry Co., Melvin G. Miller Co., Newark Felt Novelty Co., Niscott Mfg. Co., Park Plastics Co., Pilgrim Leather Goods Co., Promotion Toys Co., Sackman Bros. Co., George Schmidt Mfg. Co., Seneca Playsuit Co., Service Mfg. Co., Smart Style, Tracies Co., and Western Novelties Mfg. Co.

cowboys and Indians Consensus arose either among children of the Boomer years or toy manufacturers that such a category as "cowboys and Indians" existed, and that the category referred to the bags or boxes of plastic figures that depicted exactly those two groups. The leading manufacturer was Louis Marx & Co., who filled countless play sets in seemingly unlimited combinations and recombinations through the 1950s and '60s. Others of the many manufacturers included Dell Plastics Co., Elmar Products Co., Lido Toy Co., Multiple Products Corp., Payton Products, Plastic Toys Corp., Stuart Toy Mfg. Co., and Tim-Mee Toys.

Cowles, A.B. In addition to birdhouses, this Rochester, N.Y., company made cardboard doll houses in the 1930s.

Cowles' Novelties Based in Rush, N.Y., in the Boomer years, Cowles specialized in doll-dressing kits.

L.M. Cox Mfg. Co. Cox achieved prominence in the Boomer years for its gasoline-powered airplanes, engines and accessories. It adapted its knowledge to developing a line of gas-engine model racecars and boats, many of them, including the famous "Prop Rods," propeller-driven racecars. It also made engine fuel.

During the Boomer years, L.M. Cox Mfg. Co. was well known for its "Prop Rods," like the "Thimble-Drome" shown here.

"Cozy Cart" see *Kozekar.*

"Cozy Corner" books, see *Whitman Publishing Co.*

Cracker Jack Co. A confection born and named in the 1890s, "Cracker Jack" appeared in tubs, not boxed packages, until 1899. Coupons to be redeemed for prizes were issued in the early 1910s, to be replaced by the toys themselves in 1912. The firm changed from its original name of Rueckheim Bros. & Eckstein to Cracker Jack Co. in 1922. Based in Chicago, Ill., the firm established offices in Brooklyn, N.Y., in the 1910s. Cracker Jack was bought by Borden Foods, Inc., in 1963. The prize toys offered in packages of "Cracker Jack" ranged from paper dolls, cards of riddles, pin-back buttons, and celluloid and die-cast novelties in the early years, to tin, ceramic, die-cast and paper toys in the prewar years, and to plastic figures in the postwar years. See also *"Checkers."*

"Cracker Jack" stuffed dogs prewar, see *H. & J. Toy Mfg. Co.*

"Crackerjack" painting books see *The Saalfield Publishing Co.*

"Cradle Gym" A popular toy of the 1940s and through the Boomer years designed to stimulate eye and hand coordination in infants, the "Cradle Gym" saw precedent among the American Indians. Pawnee Indians invented an early version, with a wooden hoop fixed to the head of the cradleboard, above the baby's head. Brightly colored beads strung on the hoop attracted the baby's attention. The particular "crib exerciser" named "Cradle Gym" was made by Childhood Interests, which also made the "Cradle Pal."

"Cradle-Time Twinzies" cloth animals see *Twinzy Toy Co.*

cradles, doll see *doll beds.*

Crafco Corp. of California
Miniature plastic ship model kits and balsa flying model airplanes were postwar specialties of this Goleta, Calif., firm.

Craftint Mfg. Co.
Based in Cleveland, Ohio, Craftint issued the successful "Beginners' Luck" paint-by-number sets of the 1950s. In 1955 the firm expanded its craft and hobby offerings by acquiring the Artists Materials Divisions of Devoe & Reynolds Co. of Louisville, Ky. The firm continued issuing art and craft kits through the Boomer years.

"Craftor Builder" prewar, see *Irvin, James R. & Co., Inc.*

"Craftsman" blocks see *Holgate Bros. Co.*

John R. Craighead Co.
This Denver, Colo., company made postwar Western holster sets and cowboy accessories.

Cramco, Inc.
A Philadelphia, Penn., firm, Cramco made doll high chairs, baths, and TV chairs in the 1950s and '60s.

Crandall, Benjamin Potter
The first Crandall to be involved in the toy manufacturing trade, Benjamin Potter Crandall was born in Hopkinton, R.I., after 1800. His first shop, in Westerly, R.I., specialized in two-wheel, but essentially axle-less basswood baby carriages and some toys. The carriage was regarded as the first such manufacturer in America. He moved his business to Madison Street, New York City, in 1841, and was joined in it by his four sons, including Jesse Armour Crandall. From its simple origins, the company's carriages developed into four-wheeled, stylish buggies and strollers with springs and fringed tops. The "oscillating axle" developed for these carriages, with independent suspension on each wheel, was later adopted by automobile manufacturers. The company went on hiatus during the Civil War. Crandall re-established the business with sons Charles Thompson and William Edwin, while Jesse set up a firm focusing more on toys than carriages in Brooklyn.

The related firms worked and advertised together in ensuing years. After Benjamin Potter Crandall died in the 1870s, the sons continued the business, concentrating on carriages but also issuing toys. Through the years the firm was an important innovator and manufacturer of sleds and children's sleighs, doll carriages, rocking horses, shooflies, velocipedes, and the "Obelisk Building Blocks."

The "Cricket" developed from B.P. Crandall's desire to improve on rough rocking horses being imported from Germany. The German version consisted of flat board sides with curved bottom rocking edges, a flat top, and the suggestion of a horse's head. Crandall changed the toy by carving legs in the sides and adding rocking-chair rockers. Under the name "Cricket" it proved a good seller for the firm. The Crandalls developed a version with stuffed body for realism, a move soon copied and exported to America by European manufacturers, and then focused on wood-body rocking horses. Jesse Crandall developed the spring horse and shoofly.

The Crandall factory may have made the first velocipedes in America, issuing three-wheeled children's vehicles in the early 1840s. New versions kept appearing from its doors through the 19th century, including the "American Trotter," with sulky seat behind a front horse's head, the "American Speeder," akin to the Irish Mail, and the "Cantering Tricycle," which gave the child the sensation of horse-riding motions. The developments were collaborations between father B.P. Crandall and son Jesse, the former having patents in the 1860s and the latter in the 1870s and '80s, with one in 1886 involving an improved treadle to increase the velocipede's speed.

"Obelisk Building Blocks" were devised in the 1880s by Charles T. Crandall after seeing the popular attraction "Cleopatra's Needle" in Central Park.

Crandall, Benjamin Potter, Jr. One of Benjamin Potter Crandall's four sons, Benjamin Potter Jr. invented and patented a combination sleigh and carriage in 1870 for the family company.

Crandall, Charles M. Charles M. Crandall of Montrose, Penn., and Waverly, N.Y., was one of the most important American manufacturers of playthings in the 19th century. Born in 1833, he established his first business in Covington, Penn., around 1867, moving to Montrose, Penn., in 1875, and Waverly, N.Y., in 1888. One of his most famous toys were the flattened, rectangular "Crandall's Building Blocks," issued around 1867, having ends that could be joined in a dove-tail manner. Crandall's instructional materials with the blocks showed how to make buildings or even a model bicycle. One of his most popular introductions was "Crandall's Great Show—The Acrobats," of 1874. These jointed wooden figures with elaborate lithographed costumes and faces had block-shaped feet and hands that could join together, or interlock with long wooden sticks. The toy was issued as part of the "Crandall's Building Blocks" line, which also included the popular "District School House" and "Treasure Box." One of Crandall's greatest successes was the puzzle "Pigs in Clover," which turned into a nationwide fad when introduced in 1889.

Crandall, Charles Thompson Son of Benjamin Potter Crandall, Charles T. Crandall invented "Obelisk Building Blocks."

Crandall, Jesse Armour Born in the same year as Charles M. Crandall, 1833, he entered the carriage trade in his father's New York factory. His first invention came at age eleven, when he devised a machine to evenly drill spoke holes in carriage wheels. In the 1860s and 1870s he held various patents relating to the carriage trade, including one for the first folding carriage. In the 1860s and '70s, however, his focus had turned to toy production. Sometime during the Civil War, when the family business went on a tempo-rary hiatus, he taught convicts in an Ohio state prison to make toys. Afterwards he established a factory in Brooklyn, N.Y., where he created a number of innovative toys and games. During his years working for his father, Benjamin P. Crandall, and on his own, Jesse Crandall's inventions included the shoofly, the spring horse, nested blocks, the return ball, and the "Sandometer," a combination work desk and self-contained play area with sand and sand toys. He contributed many inventions to the development of carriages, velocipedes, hand-cars, croquet, toy guns, and sleighs. His games included "Chinaman Party," "Dude Party," "Elephant Party," and "Barnum's Greatest Show."

Crandall, William Edwin A son of Benjamin Potter Crandall, William Edwin held some of the firm's patents for carriage and perambulator improvements in the 1870s.

Crandall of Montrose see *Crandall, Charles M.*

Louis Crandall Toys, Inc. The "Neighborhood Times" newspaper kit of the 1950s-'60s was a product of Louis Crandall Toys, a Phoenix, Ariz., company.

"Crane" bathroom sets see *Arcade Mfg. Co.*

Crane & MacMahon, Inc. This Street Marys, Ohio, firm made croquet sets in the 1930s.

"Crashmobile" friction car see *Action Tri-Play Toys Co.*

cratch cradle see *cat's cradle.*

Crawford Furniture Mfg. Co. In the mid-1930s, this Waco, Texas, company obtained a license through Kay Kamen to produce Disney-theme tents and camp furniture.

Crawford Mfg. Co. Stuffed fabric toys, stuffed hobby horses, rocking toys, nursery chairs, and nursery hassocks were made in the 1930s by this Richmond, Va., company.

crawler Usually used of a toy that is a vehicle with treads. A bulldozer is a crawler with a front blade.

"Cray-O-Tone" see *United Crayon Co.*

"Crayel" crayons see *Standard Crayon Mfg. Co.*

Crayoff Mfg. Corp. Washable crayons, finger paints, and poster paints were this Pasadena, Calif., firm's postwar products.

"Crayola," "Crayolet" see *Binney & Smith.*

"Crayonex" see the *American Crayon Co.*

crayons While the "Crayola" brand name has cast almost all other manufacturers of wax crayons into the shade, the number of companies that have made crayons and crayon sets through the years is by no means small. Binney & Smith Co. introduced its first packages of colored wax crayons in 1905. Various other kinds of crayons were already used at the time, however. Over the next quarter of a century companies to offer Binney & Smith competition included some of the most prominent names in the toy business. Manufacturers included the American Crayon Co., the Art Crayon Co., Milton Bradley Co., Creston Crayon, Samuel Gabriel Sons & Co., Globe Crayon Co., Goody Mfg. Co., the Mack-Miller Co., Marks Bros. Co., New Jersey Crayon, Parker Bros., Peterson Mfg. Co., Prang Co., Jack Pressman & Co., the Saalfield Publishing Co., Standard Crayon Mfg. Co., Standard Toykraft Products, Stoll & Einson Games, Texcraft Toy Products, Transogram Co., the Ullman Mfg. Co., and Weber Costello Co.

In the late prewar years, manufacturers joining their ranks included American Art Clay, American Toy Works, Brodhaven Mfg. Co., Eagle Pencil Co., Hassenfeld Bros., Imperial Crayon Co., McLoughlin Bros., Mack Specialties, New Jersey Crayon Co., and Roebuck Publishers.

Crayon manufacturing grew into even greater importance in the Baby Boomer decades. Many of the prominent prewar names remained in the business, including Binney & Smith, American Art Clay, American Crayon, Art Crayon, Milton Bradley, Creston, Imperial, Pressman, Standard Toykraft, Transogram, and Weber-Costello. Others included Advance Crayon & Color Corp., American Artists' Color Works, Best Art Products, Built-Rite Toys, Colorforms, Crayoff Corp., Gem Color Co., Harett-Gilmar, Jack Built Toy Mfg. Co., Henry Katz, Peerless Playthings Co., Reliance Pen & Pencil Corp., Rosebud Art Co., United Crayon Co., Venus Pen & Pencil Corp., and Welded Plastics Corp.

Milton Bradley's "Crayrite" crayons competed with Binney & Smith's "Crayola" brand in the 1950s.

"Crayrite" see *Milton Bradley Co.*

crazing The lines that appear in the old paints on old toys are called "crazing" lines; or the toy is referred to as "crazed," or as having a "crazed" surface or "crazed" paint. Similar aging lines found in the glaze of ceramics and china, including toys made of these materials, are referred to in the same way.

Creative Enterprises, Inc. This postwar Westport, Conn., company issued paint-by-number kits, and educational kits and toys.

Creative Products, Inc. Based in Pittsfield, Maine, Creative Products issued the Boomer-years "Woody Wisdom" educational and novelty wood toys.

"Crescent" bicycles see *Westfield Mfg. Co.*

Crescent Gun Co. This Saginaw, Mich., firm made the "Dewey" air rifle in 1899, following Dewey's victory at Manila Bay.

Crescent Model Aircraft Co. This model airplane company based in Brooklyn, N.Y., in the 1930s.

"Cresco" see *Creston Crayon Co.*

"Cressco" see *H.G. Cress Co., Inc.*

C

H.G. Cress Co. Educational items made up a heavy proportion of this Troy, Ohio, company's production in the 1920s and '30s. It issued "Cressco" educational boards, spellers, readers, wall blackboards, and number boards, as well as spelling slates and games. The company also made drawing sets in the '30s, and "Free Glide" shuffleboard and "Skiddle" equipment.

Crestline Mfg. Corp. Crestline made postwar cast-metal banks, toys, and novelties. It was based in Brooklyn, N.Y.

Creston Crayon Co., Inc. Located on Park Avenue, New York City, Creston began making candles and school crayons in the mid-1930s. In the Boomer years, its line emphasized crayons and chalk, blackboards, slate sets, blackboard erasers, painting sets, coloring books, and modeling clay.

cricket A term used by Kirchhof, and presumably other toy makers, for "clickers," a kind of noisemaker.

"Cricket" see *rocking horse.*

"Cricket" records see *Pickwick Sales Corp.*

Crisloid Plastics, Inc. Games for adults, dice and dominoes were Boomer-era specialties for this Providence, R.I., company.

Criterion Bell & Specialty Co., Inc. A Brooklyn, N.Y., manufacturer of bells and Christmas tree decorations, Criterion also specialized in bell and chime toys in the Boomer years.

Criterion Toy & Specialty Co. Like Criterion Bell & Specialty Co., this firm was located in Brooklyn, N.Y., in the 1950s and '60s. It manufactured metal toys and novelties.

"Crokinole" The "Crokinole" trademark was used by several prewar companies, including combination gameboards from both the Carrom Co. and Milton Bradley Co. There were also "Crokinole" wigs for dolls by Rosen & Jacoby.

B.R. Cromien, In the 1930s, this Rockaway, N.J., company made dressed dolls, doll outfits, and sewing sets.

C.K. Cropper & Co. A manufacturer of nursery specialties, this Waterloo, Iowa, company made both children's and toy furniture in the mid-1930s.

croquet The popularity of the 1800s post-Civil War hit of croquet continued well into the next century, especially as the growing Middle Class cultivated its taste for the manicured lawn. Prewar manufacturers included the N.D. Cass Co., Crane & MacMahon, Dieterman & Jones, Garton Toy Co., Indiana Handle Co., Newton & Thompson, H. Rademaker & Sons, Roy Bros., South Bend Toy Mfg. Co., Thompson & Fox, and Transogram Co. The number of postwar manufacturers speaks eloquently of the degree to which croquet maintained its hold in the world of outdoor family recreations through the Boomer years. One firm, Skowhegan Croquet of North Anson, Maine, appears to have begun as one of the many Northeatsern wood-turnings manufactucturers of the early 20th century, being founded in 1909. Croquet was likely always among its products. In the Boomer years it issued "Playday" sets, made of kiln-dried rock maple. Others included Bayshore Industries, Blake & Conroy, T. Cohn, Creative Products, E. &. L. Mfg. Co., Garton Toy Co., General Sportcraft Co., Harett Gilmar, Irwin Corp., Milton A. Jacobs, Jaymar Specialty Co., Julius Levenson, Pet Toy of N.H., Pressman Toy Corp., H. Rademaker & Son, Randall Wood Products, Red Robin, Regent Sports Co., A.J. Renzi Plastic Co., Riemann, Seabrey Co., Sheldon Mfg. Co., Solmann & Whitcomb, South Bend Toy Mfg. Co., the Rollin Wilson Co., and Withington.

Croquet first became popular in America after the Civil War.

croquet, table Table croquet became a popular pastime in the early heyday of family games, in the latter 19th century. Most early games manufacturers seem to have issued sets, including Milton Bradley Co. and McLoughlin Bros. See also *trock.*

William Crosby William Crosby, a publisher in the mid-1800s, issued "The Game of the Races" in 1844.

Crosby, Nichols & Co. Boston publisher in the 1850s, Crosby, Nichols & Co. published Chandler's *Fanny Gray* in 1854. It was located on Washington Street

Crosby Products Co. Kiddie golf sets and novelties were made by this Wyandotte, Mich., company in the 1930s.

Crosman Brothers Co. Based in Portland, Maine, Crosman Brothers Co. made the "Kiddle Blox" building blocks of the 1920s. By the '30s, Crosman added "Kiddie Frates," which was a toy freight train, wood sand sand pails, and the "Fourway Kiddie Slide" to its line.

"Crown" bicycles see *D.P. Harris Hardware & Mfg. Co.*

Crown Can Co. A division of Crown Cork & Seal Co., Crown Can Co. of Philadelphia, Penn., made toy ice cream freezers in the late 1930s.

"Crown" dominoes prewar, see *The Embossing Co.;* postwar, see *Halsam Products Co.*

Crown Novelty Co. Jacks sets, holster and handcuff sets, doll bottles and bagged toys were specialties of this postwar Bronx, N.Y., company.

Crown Toy Mfg. Co. In the late 1930s, Crown Toy of Brooklyn, N.Y., issued Walt Disney character banks, statuettes, and "gloves dolls."

Crusader Enterprises The "Crusader" coin-operated mechanical horse, introduced in the 1950s, was a product of this Memphis, Tenn., company.

"Crusader Rabbit" This cartoon figure inspired 1950s-'60s playthings including coloring books by the Saalfield Publishing Co.; plastic sword, shield and hat by Vinfloat Industries; and "recolor" books by Fun Bilt Toys.

"Cry Baby" doll see *E. I. Horsman Co., Inc.*

Cuboker Co. This Baltimore, Md., firm issued the "Cuboker" game of the late 1930s, and dice games.

"Cuddle" animals postwar, see *Knickerbocker Toy Co., Inc.*

"Cuddle Kewpies" prewar, see *Richard G. Krueger.*

"Cuddle-Up" squeeze toys see *Bayshore Industries.*

Culver Mfg. Co. Leather craft kits, including the moccasin making "U-Mak-A-Moc," were products of this Erin, Tenn., company in the Boomer years.

Edward Cumings Co. Based in Flint, Mich., Edward Cumings made table tennis sets in the late prewar years.

A.B. Cummings Co. This Attleboro, Mass., company made toy moving picture machines in the 1930s.

Cupples & Leon Co. A publisher on Fourth Avenue, New York City, Cupples & Leon's line included juvenile and comic cartoon books in the 1930s through the Boomer years.

Cupples Co. A St. Louis, Mo., firm, Cupples made postwar rubber and vinyl inflated balls.

Currier & Ives The Einson-Freeman Co. based prewar puzzles on the works of these famous American lithographers.

G.H. Curry Mfg. Co. A Los Angeles, Calif., company in the 1930s, Curry made lead toys and novelties "from 5 to 25 cents."

"Curtain-Wall Builder" see *The Toy Tinkers, Inc.*

Cushing, Loring Associated with Tower Toy Co., Cushing made doll furniture and toys in the 1800s.

The Cushman Motor Works Based in Lincoln, Neb., this manufacturer began manufacturing motor scooters as early as the late 1930s, with the "Auto-Glide" being an early model.

B.L. Custer Co. This Marietta, Ga., company specialized in doll accessories including "Dolsox," Christmas stockings, and plastic toys in the Boomer years.

custom, or custom-made "Customs" are specially made models, usually in small numbers. Usually this means the toy or model was not made on an assembly line. The word can also be used in reference to a die-cast or other model of a customized car, however.

Custom Stuffed Toy & Novelty Co. Plush stuffed toys were the product of this postwar Wooster Street, New York, company.

customize In model building, one "customizes" a model by adding elements not in the original model kit. Manufacturers have realized the importance of customizing within the model-building hobby, and typically produce some kits intended and even advertised as being suitable for customizing.

cutouts Cutouts were toys similar to paper dolls issued on flat sheets of paper or board. Some were issued to make standing play sets. A common form involved flat images which could be placed on the appropriately shaped blank spaces on a pictorial mat, making many cutouts kin to picture puzzles, especially the frame-tray puzzle.

The Beistle Co. made these embossed Halloween cutouts in the 1950s.

"Cute Cut" doll furniture see *Central Wood Products, Inc.*

"Cutie" trade name see *New York Toy & Game Co.*

Cutler & Saleeby, Inc. Based in Springfield, Mass, the firm issued board games in the 1920s and '30s, including the early "India Bombay" and 1927's "Ski-Hi New York to Paris."

Cuyahoga Lumber Co. Table tennis tables, backgammon boards, and sand boxes were among this Cleveland, Ohio, company's products in the 1930s.

Walter Czuczka This Mount Vernon, N.Y., manufacturer produced postwar preschool toys, as well as farm animal and wild animal toy sets.

Dd

D. & D. Industries, Inc. Baby rattlers, crib and cradle toys, and infants' toys were specialties of this Leominster, Mass., firm in the Boomer years.

"D.R.G.M." The marking "D.R.G.M." is often mistaken for an identifying mark. Standing for "Deutsches Reiches Gebrauchmuster," it may be taken as an indicator that the toy's provenance is Germany, but not any particular toy manufacturer in that country.

"D.S." Dessein, Germany.

Dabs Corn Games "Radio" and "Bingo" corn games for the home or concessions were mid-1930s products of this Asbury Park, N.J., company.

Arthur V. DaCosta A manufacturer of infant toys, especially balls, Arthur V. DaCosta of Providence, R.I., made a name for itself with the "Cry Ball." "They cry as they roll—they roll as they cry," advertisements of the 1920s promised. The company also made the "Water Ball," "Dura Ball," and "Jingle Ball." The "Cry Ball" became the "Crying Bawl" of the 1930s, when the firm changed its name to DaCosta Toy Co., Inc. The company also made infant toys, Pyralin toys, water balls, and "Cry Balls" in the '40s.

Dadan Inc. "The Big Board," a stock market game of the mid-Boomer years, was issued by this Watertown, N.Y., company.

Daddy Scott, Inc. Besides garden and lawn ornaments, this Marblehead, Mass., company made wooden toys, windmills, and novelties in the 1930s. By the end of the decade it was specializing in advertising displays.

"Daintie Doll" wooden toys prewar, see *Essenel Co.*

"Daisy" "Daisy" was a widely used trademark in prewar toys. Gibbs Mfg. Co. issued "Daisy" carts and wagons, Roy Bros., "Daisy" croquet, and Dowst Mfg. Co., "Daisy" dollhouse furniture. George Borgfeldt Corp. used the name on a dolls line, American Crayon Co., on "color boxes," the Seiss Mfg. Co. on flashlights, Schacht Rubber Mfg. Co. on horseshoe games, and the Massillon Wire Basket Co. on toy fences.

Daisy Mfg. Co. The most famous name in toy guns and rifles, Daisy manufactured toy firearms ranging from water pistols and pop guns to air rifles, the popular "Red Ryder" guns, and "Buck Rogers" ray-guns.

The Plymouth Iron Windmill Co., was founded in 1882 to make iron windmills. It made its first "Daisy" air rifle, on a design invented by Clarence J. Hamilton, in 1888. Surprised by the success of the rifle, in 1889 the company gave up manufacturing windmills. By 1890, the company was seeing sales five times larger than sales it had seen from its windmills. The company became Daisy Mfg. Co. in 1895.

Daisy introduced the first repeater in 1900, and a lever-action gun in 1901. In 1913, Daisy introduced "Daisy Pump Gun" and the first metal water pistol, "No. 8 Water Pistol," both invented by C.F. Lefever. The "Military Model No. 40" appeared in 1916 at the unprecedented high price of $5.00.

Daisy Mfg. Co. is probably the most famous name in toy guns and rifles.

Two company officials bought 90 percent of Markham Air Rifle Co.'s stock in 1912. Markham's name changed to King Mfg. Co. in 1928. Daisy bought all King's stock in 1931, and continued the "King" line.

In 1934, Daisy introduced promotional guns, first the "Buzz Barton 1,000 Shot Special," followed by the "Buck Rogers Rocket Pistol" and the "Buck Jones Special." Daisy introduced the "Golden Eagle" air rifle in 1936, and the first air pistol, the "Targeteer," in 1937, and in 1939 entered into an arrangement with artist Fred Harman to produce guns bearing Harman's cowboy character's name, "Red Ryder," which would become Daisy's most famous gun. Daisy produced the "Superman Krypto Ray-Gun" and the military "Defender" rifle before the onset of World War II. In wartime years, the firm produced a few wooden guns, resuming production of metal guns in 1946.

By the mid-1950s, its tie-in toy holster sets included "Annie Oakley" and "Ramar of the Jungle," in addition to "Red Ryder."

The firm moved to Rogers, Ark., in 1957. In 1959-60 the company, at least on paper, changed hands twice, and emerged as Daisy-Heddon Sales Co., Inc. in 1960.

Daisy's postwar line included the "Atomic Pistol" of 1948, the "Noisemaker Gun" of 1952, and the "Spittin' Image" in 1962. The company also made targets and shooting games, including the "Red Ryder Whirli-Crow Target Game" of the 1940s.

Daisy made this "Buck Rogers Rocket Pistol" in 1934.

"Dale Evans" More than being a mere female counterpart to cowboy star Roy Rogers, Dale Evans was a widely popular star in her own right. Playthings inspired by her screen character included cowgirl suits by Sackman Bros. Co., hats by Miller Bros. Hat Co. and Sackman, holsters by Classy Products Co., and plastic figures by Hartland Plastics.

Dale Radioplane Co. Founded in Long Beach, Calif., in the later 1930s, Dale Radioplane made electric remote control airplanes and folding-wing gliders.

Lawrence N. Daleiden & Co. Based in Chicago, Ill., Daleiden specialized in lithographed paper Christmas cribs in the late 1930s.

Dan-D Mfg. Co. This Dayton, Ohio, firm manufactured the "Dan-D" airplanes and gliders of the 1920s, in six models. The flying toys were made of balsa wood, with rubber-band motors and solid wood propellers. The company also made toy furniture including kitchen cabinets and a "Chifferobe."

"Dancerina" 1969, see *Mattel, Inc.*

dancing jack Word for jumping jack, probably 1700s-1800s.

Dandee Doll Mfg. Co. Based in Philadelphia, Penn., Dandee made postwar character dolls, drink-and-wet dolls, and novelty and nun dolls.

"Dandy" A common prewar trademark name, "Dandy" coaster wagons were made by Sheboygan Coaster & Wagon Works, and "Dandy" dump trucks by the Lehman Co. of America. The name was also used on musical toys by Marks Bros. Co. and paint boxes by Milton Bradley Co.

"Dandy the Duck" see *Rempel Mfg. Co.*

Dandy Toy & Novelty Co., Inc. "The Dandy Line" of stuffed toys in the 1920s was made by this Brooklyn, N.Y., company.

The logo for Dandy Toy & Novelty Co.'s stuffed toys, 1920s.

Dandy Toys Based on East 20th Street, New York City, Dandy Toys made Boomer-era plastic dolls and animals.

"Daniel Boone" Although Daniel Boone is usually regarded as a postwar icon, "Daniel Boone" toys appeared in prewar times as well, including cabin logs from Woodcraft Novelty Co. and tents from W.E. Hettrick & Sons. Postwar playthings included "Daniel Boone Cabins" by Rustic Furniture Co. and leather-encased plastic toy canteens by Spraz Co., in the 1950s-60s. Tie-in items increased by the mid-1960s, thanks to a television show featuring Fess Parker in the pioneer hero's role. Playthings included "Daniel Boone Wilderness Trail" game by Transogram Co., plastic figure by Remco Industries, film viewer by Acme Toy Corp. in 1964; and card game by Edu-U-Cards in 1965.

The M. Carlton Dank Toy Corp. "The Boy Toymaker" of the 1920s was made by this Brooklyn, N.Y., firm. The "Boy Toymaker" construction toy was sold with the slogan, "Builds Boys As Well As Toys." Carlton Dank's line of "Joy Toy" outfits also included "The Boy Boat Builder," "'Spirit of Boyhood' Airkraft Builder," "Zeppelin Konstructor," "Mot-O-Boat Konstructor," "Junior Art-Kraft," "Glide-O-Plane" gliders, "Strip-O-Wood Model Maker," "Kite-Kraft Builder," and "Educational Metal-Kraft." The firm became the Boy Toymaker Co. in the post-Great Depression years. See also *Handicraft Creators.*

Danlee Co. Gun and holster sets, cowboy vests and lassos were among the leather specialties of this postwar Van Nuys, Calif., company. Danlee also made marbles and marble bags, and jack and ball sets.

Danzi Toy Mfg. Co. Doll bath tables and dressing tables were made by this Cleveland, Ohio, company in the 1930s.

"Dapper Dan" see *Smethport Specialty Co.*

Dapping, William Active in the early 1900s, William Dapping issued "The Great American Baseball Game," a board game, in 1906.

G.W. D'Arcey Co. The early-1960s game of "Bluff" was produced by this Pittsburgh, Penn., firm. The Saalfield Publishing Co. reissued the game in 1964.

Darling Doll & Toy Corp. This mid-1930s doll manufacturer was located on West 17th Street, New York City.

A.R. Darling Electric Co. In the mid-1930s, this Indianapolis, Ind., company made toy transformers and motors.

Darrow, Charles Brace In 1934, Charles Brace Darrow set up business on Westview Street, Philadelphia, to produce and market his "'Monopoly' adult game." He sold "Monopoly" through Wanamakers. The famous department store had enough success with the game to attract the notice of Parker Brothers, who had initially turned down Darrow when he first offered the game.

F.E. Darrow, Franklin Elijah Darrow of Bristol, Conn., manufactured dolls of steamed and pressed rawhide in the 1860s.

Dart Board Equipment Co. Based in Philadelphia, Penn., from the late 1930s through the Boomer years, this firm made darts, dartboards, and table-tennis tables. It used the "Deco" trade name on its darts and dart games.

Dartmore Corp. Plastic inflatable toys were specialties of this postwar Brooklyn, N.Y., firm.

darts Darts and dart games have remained one of the more durable entertainments in America. Prewar manufacturers included Apex Mfg Co., Glen Novelty Co., Karl Guggenheim, Indian Archery & Toy Corp., Joseph Koenig, Marks Bros. Co., New England Mfg. Co., A.S. Payne, Henry H. Sheip Mfg. Co., and Toohey Mfg. Co. In the Boomer years several dozen manufacturers made darts, dart toys and dart games, including such diverse companies as the Alox Mfg. Co., T. Cohn, Knickerbocker Plastic Co., Lido Toy Co., and Park Plastics Co.

Joseph Davidson A manufacturer of juvenile furniture in the late 1930s, Davidson made baby and doll carriages, desks, and rockers. The company was also a representative for manufacturers of wheel goods.

E.W. Davies Aircraft Co. The "All Print" model airplane construction kits of the early to late 1930s were made by E.W. Davies Aircraft Co. of San Francisco, Calif.

The firm also made the "Davies-Dwarf-Model" gas motor gliders, and supplies for model airplanes.

A.A. Davis The firm of A.A. Davis of Nashua, N.H., specialized in novelty toys in the 1860s and perhaps 1870s. The toys included small, lithographed figures of celebrities, small animals, and small butterflies with moving parts that were mounted in small protective cases. One figure was "Magic Major General Grant."

H. Davis Co. Based on Broadway, New York City, in the late prewar years, H. Davis issued games and basket-weaving sets. As H. Davis Toy Corp., located in Brooklyn, N.Y., Davis continued issuing adjustable looms, embroidery sets, and sewing sets, as well as ring toss and a magnetic fish game, in the Boomer years.

Davis Lumber Co. Based in Martinsville, Ind., this company made juvenile rockers, chairs, and cedar chests in the 1930s and '40s.

Davis Products, Inc. Inflatable plastic water animals, balls, rings, toys, and pools were among this Van Nuys, Calif., firm's specialties in the Boomer years. It also made steel-wall rigid pools.

Rees Davis Studios Rees Davis Studios of Chicago, Ill., issued soft dolls, stuffed animals, floating bath toys, and novelties in the late 1930s.

"Davy Crockett" The first children's tale based on the historical character may have been one that appeared in 1833, entitled *Sketches and Eccentricities of Col. David Crockett of West Tennessee*. The postwar explosion of Davy Crockett tie-in toys and playthings was triggered by Walt Disney's airing of "Davy Crockett, Indian Fighter," on its "Disneyland" TV show, and by its subsequent release of a movie based on the TV series. The many items in 1955 included complete costumes by Bland Charnas Co.; "Davy Crockett with Horse" by Payton Products; "Dispatch Cases" and powder horns by Neptune Plastics; holster sets combined with Hubley flint-lock guns, by Service Mfg. Co.; and "Davy Crockett Badgers with Raccoon

Fur" by Nadel Co. The later "Davy Crockett" bicycle was issued by Hedstrom-Union Co.

Davy Crockett Enterprises, Inc. This Baltimore, Md., firm issued "Davy Crockett" clothing, and unsuccessfully attempted to trademark the words "Davy Crockett, Frontiersman," on clothing, in the wake of Walt Disney's TV and movie success with the character.

"Dawn" De Luxe Reading Corp. issued "Dawn" dolls in the late 1960s and early '70s. A 6-inch fashion doll, "Dawn's" companions included "Daphne," "Denise," "Dinah," "Gary," "Jessica," and "Maureen."

Dayton Art Metal Co. Dayton Art Metal advertised its Mono-Rail type racing toy auto, which came with either spring or electric motor, in the mid-1930s. Based in Dayton, Ohio, it also manufactured streamline bicycles, electric motors, and skis.

Dayton Friction Toy Works Founded in 1909 by David P. Clark, this Dayton, Ohio, firm made toys until 1935. The company used the trade name "Gyro" for its pressed-steel friction toys with a horizontal flywheel, for which it received a patent in 1926. By the end of the '20s it was using the "Double Friction Toys" name for its line.

Dayton Friction Toy Works produced this 18-inch "Victoria Coupe" in the 1920s.

The "Freight Engine" by Dayton Friction used a patented horizontal flywheel for propulsion.

"Dayton" line see *Dayton Toy & Specialty Co.*

The Dayton Toy & Specialty Co. A manufacturer of sheet-metal toys, this Dayton, Ohio, company made "Son-ny" wagons, wheelbarrows, carts, scooters, trucks and velocipedes. The Dayton line of "Son-ny" wheel goods enjoyed considerable success in the late 1920s, with Dayton unable to keep up with demand in 1928, and introducing new heavy steel cannons ("instead of the frail tin and lead ones") in 1929. Its line at the end of the decade included the No. 1 Dump Truck, No. 6 U.S. Army Truck, No. 7 Anti-Aircraft Truck, No. 60 Cannon with two "Saf-ty" shells, and No. 66 Cannon & Caisson, with 8 "Saf-ty" shells. All but the cannons appeared under the "Son-ny" trade name.

The "Son-ny" line continued in popularity into the mid-'30s. It included three sizes of "De Soto" streamlined coaster wagons, "Knee-Action Coaster" wagons, and "Mammoth Flyer" coaster wagons. Its "drawn bed" wagons, or express wagons, were as inexpensive as 25 and 50 cents. The firm also was making wheelbarrows in all sizes, standard scooters, and new streamlined scooters.

This toy truck by Dayton Toy & Specialty Co. was made in the 1920s.

The "Son-ny" U.S. Army Truck was another steel toy by Dayton Toy & Specialty Co.

De Luxe Reading Corp. The maker of "Topper Toys," De Luxe Reading initially produced toys only for the food-store trade until 1962, when it built what it boasted was the largest toy plant of its kind, in Elizabeth, N.J.

Its early products included the "Johnny Seven" line, led by the "Johnny Seven O.M.A. (One Man Army)" gun, which combined into one toy a grenade launcher, anti-tank rocket, armor-piercing shell, anti-bunker missile, repeating rifle, tommy gun, and detachable automatic pistol. The line also included a "Combat Phone Set" and "Micro-helmet," plus the vehicle toy sets "Armored Battalion," "Fire Brigade," "Service Station," "Speed Set," and "Task Force."

The doll line of De Luxe Reading featured "Penny Brite," a girl doll with cheerful appearance measuring 8 inches tall. The line included "Kitchen Dinette," "Travel," "Beauty Parlor," "Bedroom" and "School Room" sets of doll furniture and accessories. "Baby Brite" was the baby doll of the line, although she was paradoxically larger, measuring 13-1/2 inches tall. When "Dawn," a fashion teenage doll, appeared in the late 1960s, she was smallest of the three, at 6 inches.

In the late '60s the firm also introduced the "Johnny Lightning" cars, to compete with Mattel's "Hot Wheels."

"De Luxe" roller skates see *Kingston Products Corp.*

De Marco Toy Co. The "Mr. Basketball" game of 1960 was made by this Bloomington, Ill., firm.

"De Soto" Charles M. Crandall published this popular game in the late 1800s.

"De Soto" coaster wagon see *Dayton Toy & Specialty Co.*

"De Witt" speed boats see *Shoe Form Co., Inc.*

Clyde Dean Ink Co. Located in Chicago, Ill., Clyde Dean made "painting outfits with pictures to color" in the earlier 1930s.

"Deanna Durbin" Licensing rights in the late 1930s were handled by Mitchell J. Hamilburg Co. Playthings included dolls by Ideal Novelty & Toy Co.

D

decal Transparent paper or cellophane-like material used in toys and models of various kinds, sometimes simply bearing the trade name or model number, but often bearing design elements important to the toy. In model-building, some decals are water-transfer while others are self-adhesive. In Hot Wheels collecting, the decals or side decorations are called the "tampo."

decalcomanias Prewar manufacturers included American Decalcomania Co., Inc. of Chicago, Ill.; the Commeford Co. of Brooklyn, N.Y.; the Meyercord Co. of Chicago, Ill.; National Decalcomania Corp. of Philadelphia, Penn.; Palm Bros. Decalcomania Co. of Cincinnati, Ohio; Palm, Fechteler & Co. of East 26th Street, New York City; William F. Schweikert & Co. of Cleveland, Ohio; Universal Toy & Novelty Mfg. Co.; and L.C. Wells of East 26th Street, New York City.

Decker & Decker Manufacturers in the late 19th century, Decker & Decker issued "A Game of Characters" in 1889 and "Bible Characters" in the 1890s.

"Decor-Ables" stuffed animals see *Peter Pan Toys.*

Decor Plastic Mfrs. Plastic games and Halloween light-up decorations were specialties of this postwar Syracuse, N.Y., firm.

"Decorated China" Glazed clay marbles decorated with lines, usually in geometric patterns, are called by this name.

Decorative Cabinet Corp. Based on Fifth Avenue, New York City, in the late 1930s, Decorative Cabinet made the "E-Z-Do Rol-A-Dor" doll closet.

Dee-Lane Dolls A firm based in Kansas City, Mo.; in the late prewar years, Dee-Lane issued hand-made dolls.

Deeks Mfg. Co. The "Fungun" marksmanship sets were products of this Camden, N.J., company in the earlier 1930s.

"Defender" air rifle see *Daisy Mfg. Co.*

"The Defender" cap pistol see *Cordelco Industries, Inc.*

James DeHart, This Winston-Salem, N.C., company published the "Monday Morning Coach Football" game in the mid-1930s.

DeJournette Mfg. Co. Cardboard dolls, designing books, drawing boards, and games were specialties of this postwar Atlanta, Ga., company. Among its leading items was "Betsy Ballerina" of the mid-1950s, a ballerina paper doll that came with costumes, cardboard stage, and changes of scenery.

DeKalb Toys Based in De Kalb, Ill., DeKalb made rockers, nursery stools and carts, rockers and sand boxes in the Boomer years.

Del Rey Plastics Corp. Del Rey specialized in polyethylene banks and toys, including sand sets and action toys, in the 1950s and '60s. Based in the Fifth Avenue Building, the company issued packaged toys for chains and supermarkets.

Dell Distributing Co. Dell manufactured character squeeze toys including "Huckleberry Hound" and Walt Disney characters in the 1950s and '60s. It was located on Third Avenue, New York City.

Dell Plastics Co., Inc. Plastic toys, dolls, doll furniture, dish sets, pots and pans, horse and rider sets, stage coaches, covered wagon sets, Alaskan toys, canteen and mess kit sets, and pre-school toys were made in the 1950s and '60s by this Brooklyn, N.Y., company.

The Delphos Bending Co. Based in Delphos, Ohio, this company produced shooflies, animal rockers, gliders, swings, and baby swings, among other furniture and recreational equipment from the 1930s through the Boomer years. Its line in the mid-1930s included the "Chummy Bunny," "Ducky Doo" and "Dapple Grey Pony" rockers; the "Mother's Choice Moderne Streamline Baby Rockers," a shoofly; "Standard Merry-Go-Round," with three horse-headed sets that traveled around a circular metal track; and the "Moderne Table and Chair Set." The firm used the name "Happy Land Playthings" for its line, and claimed to be the "world's largest manufacturers of bentwood products." In the 1950s and '60s its trade names included "Hi Prancer" molded spring horses and "Teeter Tot" shooflies. Delphos also made toy chests.

The "Dapple Grey Pony" rocker was made by The Delphos Bending Co. in the 1930s.

Delta Clay Co. Based in Oakland, Calif., in the late 1930s, Delta Clay made clay sets and clay-modeling tools.

Delta Electric Co. A Marion, Ind., company, Delta produced electric lanterns, lights, lamps and horns for juvenile and toy vehicles in the 1930s and '40s.

Deluxe Game Corp. Based in Richmond Hill, Long Island, N.Y., this firm manufactured service station play sets in the late 1940s and early '50s.

DeLuxe Game Corp. This Kingston, Penn., manufacturer of postwar playground equipment also made games, spring horses, paint-by-number artist easels, and hammer-and-nail sets in the 1950s and '60s.

DeLuxe Woodcraft Co., Inc. Rocking and swinging horses were specialties of this Racine, Wis., firm in the postwar years.

Demerritt-Fisher Co. Juvenile, nursery and play-yard furniture were produced by this Keene, N.H., company in the earlier 1930s.

Denis Crib, Inc. Doll beds, bassinets, play yards and bunk beds were specialties of this Holyoke, Mass., firm in the 1950s and '60s.

Elsie Denney Hawaiian dolls and doll clothes patterns led this Honolulu, Hawaii, firm's line in the Boomer years.

Denning Mfg. Co. Snow gliders were the primary product of Denning, located in Cleveland, Ohio, in the mid-1930s. Names and types included "Skee Skates, "Speed Skees," saddle coasters, and scooter bobs.

Dennis Play Products "Dennis the Menace" playthings, including puppets, cloth and vinyl dolls, "Moonmaster" rockets, "Whiffenpoofs," and batons were produced in the 1950s and '60s by this Menlo Park, Calif., company.

"Dennis the Menace" Although Dennis Play Products issued many "Dennis the Menace" items, it did not issue all of them. A bat and ball set appeared from Brittain Products Co.; activity sets, from Standard Toykraft Products and Colorforms; and puzzles, "Tiddley Winks" and books by Whitman Publishing Co.

Dennison Mfg. Co. A long-lived company, Dennison, based in Framingham, Mass., made crepe paper doll cutouts in the 1930s, in addition to novelties and Christmas paper items.

Reginald Denny Industries, Inc. Based in Hollywood, Calif., in the late 1930s, Reginald Denny manufactured flying model airplanes.

Denslow, W.W. A famous illustrator, Denslow (1856-1915) was the first illustrator of *The Wonderful Wizard of Oz*. He produced some of his own "Oz" tales.

The Dent Hardware Co., A major name in cast-iron toys, Dent, based in Fullerton, Penn., was founded in 1895 by Henry H. Dent. It made toys until 1937, and continued in the business of making cold-storage equipment into the 1970s. Dent's toy line included vehicles with balloon type rubber wheels, including various kinds of trucks, steam shovels, roadsters, tractors, fire engines, hook and ladders. The "Pioneer" fire truck, Ford Tri-Motor, and large hook-and-ladder trucks were popular items. Dent also made aluminum toys, repeater pistols, penny-toy tools, jackstones, banks, and toy ranges, and assembled box assortments, including "Toyland Treasure Chests" in the 1930s.

"The Deputy" Licensed by MCA, "The Deputy" items appeared from several manufacturers in the late 1950s and early '60s, including games and puzzles by Milton Bradley Co., hats by Arlington Hat Co., holster sets by J. Halpern Co., and miscellaneous toys by 20th Century Varieties.

"Deputy" repeater see *Kilgore Mfg. Co., Inc.*

Derekum Industries Derekum, located in Chicago, Ill., manufactured decalcomania transfers in the late 1930s.

"Des-Arts" line see *Dessart Bros., Inc.*

Deshler Broom Factory In addition to the adult item, this Deshler, Neb., company also made the toy version in the 1930s and '40s.

Design Industries The Boomer-era "Play Squares" design and building blocks and "Play Spaces" building toy were made by this Pittsburgh, Penn., company.

Dessart Bros., Inc. Santa Claus outfits, masks, paper hats, wigs, beards, and moustaches were the mainstay of Dessart Bros., located in Brooklyn, N.Y., in the earlier 1930s. By the end of the decade the company had added noisemakers, serpentines, and paper party favors to its line. Its wartime line consisted of masks, hats, hair goods, and noisemakers. In the Boomer years, the firm issued a similar line of gauze, rubber and vinyl masks, Santa Claus outfits, party hats and novelties, and masquerade costumes and hair goods.

Detroit Gasket & Mfg. Co. This Detroit, Mich., firm issued late 1930s dartboards.

Detroit Wood Products A division of Monnier Lumber Co. of Detroit, Mich., Detroit Wood Products made doll cradles and bath tables, shuffleboard sets, adjustable stilts, golf tees, jigsaws, and tennis tables in the 1930s. By the end of the decade it was emphasizing its shuffleboard and tennis table specialties.

Dewes & Smith Based in St. Louis, Mo., Dews & Smith made 1930s disk games and novelties.

"Dewey" air rifle see *Crescent Gun Co.*

Dewey Doll Co. A prewar doll maker, Dewey was based in Summit, N.J.

Dexter Corp. Based in Portland, Maine, Dexter issued banks, toy forts, doll and toy furniture, and wooden trains in the late 1930s.

"Dial" typewriter see *Louis Marx & Co.*

Diamond Game Co. This Greenfield, Mass., company issued the "Diamond" baseball game in the mid-1930s.

Diamond Toy Co. In addition to the "Jimmie Foxx" baseball game, Diamond Toy Co., based in Wilmington, Del., issued the "Postal Telegraph" signal box, a mechanical quoits game, and the "Pin-Zoo educational pastime" in the 1930s. In the late prewar years its primarily specialty was producing pinwheels.

dice Used for games since ancient times around the globe, dice have been dated to the first millennium B.C. from Egypt. These early examples were six-sided carved stones. Dice were known to American Indians in the simple form of fruit pits colored white on one side, and black on the other. For manufacturers, see *games, adult.*

"Dick Tracy" The cartoon detective Dick Tracy enjoyed popularity before and after the war, in and out of the comic pages of the country's daily newspapers. Prewar "Dick Tracy" items included books from Whitman Publishing co., a game by Einson-Freeman Co., a fingerprint set by Jack Pressman & Co., and a "Dick Tracy Siren Gun" by Louis Marx & Co. In the boomer years, items included dress hats by Miller Bros. Hat Co.; tin friction cars and plastic cars by Louis Marx & Co.; and handcuff sets by John-Henry Mfg. Co.

"Dickens Dolls" see *Alexander Doll Co.*

Dickerman & Co., Inc. Based in East Granville, Vt., Dickerman & Co. issued wooden peg tops, ring toss, and toy croquet sets in the mid-1930s.

J.A. Dickerman Co., Inc. In addition to children's furniture, this Gardner, Mass., company made doll carriages in the earlier 1930s. See *Thayer Co.*

die-casting An outgrowth of the Linotype machine, an invention for casting type, which was introduced in the Chicago World's Columbian Exposition of 1893-4. In the toy world, the word is closely linked to the name Samuel Dowst, founder of the company that became Tootsietoy. See *metal-alloy toys.*

This "No. 432 M.G. Sports Car" by The Hubley Mfg. Co. is an example of die-casting from the 1960s

die-cutting The companies that cut dies for other toy makers served a vital function. Prewar specialists included Connecticut Tool & Engineering Co. of Bridgeport, Conn., Danly Machine Specialties, Inc., of Cicero, Ill., the Hoggson & Pettis Mfg. Co. of New Haven., Conn., and Revere Products Corp. of Phoenix, N.Y.

Diemer, Walter, Harry, and William see *The American National Co.*

Dieterman & Jones This Jonesville, Mich., company manufactured indoor and outdoor shuffleboard sets, table tennis sets, and croquet sets in the mid-1930s.

"Dig" see *Parker Bros., Inc.*

Diggerator Co. The "Diggerator" was a hand-operated toy resembling a power-shovel, issued in the mid-Boomer years by this Seattle, Wash., company.

The Dill Co. Based in Baltimore, Md., in the late 1930s, the Dill Co. made action wood pull toys, dollhouses, forts, cannons, garages, gas stations, and railroad stations. It also made fiber and cardboard specialties.

John F. Dille, Co. A West Madison Street, Chicago, company, Dille controlled Buck Rogers rights in the 1930s and '40s, and produced Buck Rogers display pieces for Christmas shows.

Dille-McGuire Mfg. Co. This Richmond, Ind., company made a junior lawn mower in the 1930s.

Dillon-Beck Mfg. Co. The "Wannatoy" line of plastic toys was produced from the later 1940s into the 1960s by this firm. It was based in Irvington, N.J., in the early Boomer years, and later in Hillside, N.J.

dime registers see *banks, dime register.*

"Ding Dong School" Licensed merchandise for TV's "Ding Dong School" ranged from bells by N.N. Hill Brass Co. to an Irish Mail by Steger Products Mfg. Co. Other licensed items included "Kid-O" modeling compound by Climax Industries, "Pipe Cleaner Art" by Barry Products, and "Play Rhythm Set" by Gardner & Co.

"Dingle-Dangle" stuffed toys see *Gund Mfg. Co.*

Dinky Toys see *Meccano.*

Dipcraft Mfg. Co. Balloons and modeling material were specialties of this postwar Pittsburgh, Penn., firm.

"Discoverer" trains see *American Flyer Manufacturing Co.*

The Discus Co. Based in Weymouth, Mass., the Discus Co. made indoor bowling games for all ages in the 1930s and '40s.

disk In farm toys, the implement towed behind the tractor having many wheel-like blades used to break up soil. These range from heavy rubber versions made by Auburn to die-cast versions by Hubley and more elaborate steel models by Carter Tru-Scale.

Walt Disney Enterprises The notation "Walt Disney Enterprises" appears on Walt Disney character-related playthings issued from the mid-1930s through 1939, licensed by Kay Kamen, whose name may also appear on toys.

D

Walt Disney Productions Walt Disney Productions issued the licenses for toys, games and other playthings using Disney characters from the release of *Pinocchio* in 1939 through the 1980s. For prewar licenses, see *Kay Kamen, Inc.*

Licenses in the postwar years went to firms including the Oak Rubber Co., for balloons; Tigrett Industries, banks; Auburn Rubber Co., beach and swim items; Samuel Gabriel Sons & Co., blocks and pre-school games; Whitman Publishing Co., books; Gardner & Co., dart game; Uneeda Doll Co., dolls; Halsam, "Early Settlers Logs"; Gund Mfg. Co., "Hand Puppetettes"; Benay-Albee Novelty Co., hats; Esquire Novelty Corp, holster sets and rifles; Stahlwood Toy Mfg. Co., infant toys; Kestral Corp., inflated toys; Jaymar Specialty Co., jigsaw puzzles; Econolite Corp., lamps; the Watkins-Strathmore Co., "Magic Slate" games and puzzles; Ben Cooper, masquerade costumes and masks; American Mirror Works, "Mirror-action" toys; Hollywod Film Enterprises, motion picture films; Multiple Products Corp., musical toys; Transogram Co., paint sets and crayon boxes; Aldon Industries, plastic cut-outs; Louis Marx & Co., ramp walkers; Plastic Playthings, rattles; Bayshore Industries, rubber figures; National Leather Mfg. Co., school bags and novelties; Dell Distributing, squeeze toys; Gund Mfg. Co., stuffed toys; Lido Toy Co., target sets and tracing sets; the Gong Bell Mfg. Co., telephones, rider toys, rocking toys, and push toys; Tru-Vue Co., 3-D color film cards; Jaymar Specialty Co., wood pull toys; Bantam-Lite, wrist flashlights; Tudor Metal Products Corp., xylophones; and M. Shimmel Sons, "Year of the Duck" items.

See also *individual characters,* also the *"Mickey Mouse Club."*

"Disneyland" The Walt Disney family theme park "Disneyland," which opened in 1955, inspired as many playthings as any individual character out of the Disney universe. "Disneyland" items from the later 1950s and '60s included "Disneyland Beach 'N Garden" sets by Eldon Mfg. Co., blocks by Halsam Products Co., feeding sets by Hankscraft Co., games by Transogram Co.,

pin-ups by Dolly Toy Co., the "Disneyland Quiz" by Jacmar Mfg. Co., and the "Disneyland Stage Coach" by Strombeck-Becker Mfg. Co. Miscellaneous playthings were issued by Whitman Publishing Co. and Pressman Toy Corp.

Jamcar Mfg. Co. responded to the opening of Walt Disney's family theme-park with "Disneyland Electric Quiz" in the 1950s.

"Walt Disney's True-Life Adventures" Walt Disney's television "True-Life Adventures" programs inspired various playthings, including books by Whitman Publishing Co., cards by Russell Mfg. Co., and games by Jacmar Mfg. Co.

Display Food Co. Founded in Street Paul, Minn., in the late 1930s, Display Food manufactured miniature artificial foods, party favors, and trick food novelties.

dissected maps An educational toy popular in early 19th century and on, dissected maps were jigsaw geography puzzles. By the 1800s maps were available in this manner for the U.S., Europe, Asia, Africa, Great Britain, and South America.

dissected pictures "Dissected" was used in the 19th century as "jigsaw" would be later. By the early 1800s a variety of subjects were being treated in this puzzle format.

distant control Lionel Corp. used the term "distant control" in the 1930s for the remote control made possible by its transformers.

Distinctive Products Inc. Miniature golf sets were the specialty of this late 1930s Wrightsville, Penn., firm.

Distinctive Juvenile Mfg. Co. This Perkasie, Penn., company made postwar juvenile rockers, toy chests, and sand boxes.

"Dione Quintuplets" The "Dione Quintuplet" phenomenon of the 1930s inspired a variety of playthings, including cutout books by Whitman Publishing Co., dolls by Alexander Doll Co., and movie films by Pathegrams.

"Dixie" car see *Janesville Products Co.*

"Dixie Flyer" velocipedes see *The Monarch Products Co.*

"Dixie Thriller" sled-type coaster wagon see *Rainey Mfg. Co.*

Joseph Dixon Crucible Co. Based in Jersey City, N.J., Dixon obtained license through Kay Kamen in the 1930s to issue Disney pencils and pencil boxes.

Dixtoy Co. Dixtoy specialized in "wind toys" and wind-toy games in the 1920s. The "Jolly Clown Wind Game" resembled a round fan on a short handle, with pinwheel eyes. The "Wind Mill Clown" and "Dancing Clown Wind Toy" involved small figures connected to the pinwheel mechanism, held on longer, more typical pinwheel sticks. Dixtoy was based in Canton, Ohio.

In the 1920s, Dixtoy Co. made a variety of "wind toys" including the "Jolly Clown Wind Game."

Dobsaw Enterprises The "Pale-face Tepee" of the 1950s-'60s was issued by this Washington, D.C., company.

H. Hudson Dobson, Based in Fifth Avenue Building, H. Hudson Dobson manufactured wooden pull toy boats. Dobson was also a representative for English toy firms.

John W. Dobson, Based in Flushing, N.Y., this prewar company made the "Daddy's Helper" toy wheelbarrow.

doctor and nurse kits Toy doctor and nurse kits and bags became popular in prewar times, with manufacturers including Fleischaker & Baum, Hale-Nass Corp., Jackson-Guldah Violin Co., and Wickery Toy Mfg. Co. prominent in their production. Others manufacturing by the late prewar years included Brinkman Engineering Co., James McGowan Associates, Transogram Co., and Wicker Toy Mfg. Co. Hassenfeld Bros., a pencil and pencil-box manufacturer, entered the ranks of toy manufacturers before World War II by making doctor and nurse kits, and became one of the leading companies in the field in the Boomer years. Other postwar manufacturers of doctor and nurse kits included Merry Mfg. Co., Ozan Products Co., Peerless Playthings, Pressman Toy Corp., A.J. Sirls Products Corp., and Transogram. Interesting variations on the toy doctor or nurse kit were the similar accessories made for dolls. See *doll hospital* supplies.

"Dr. Busby" The first best seller among children's card games, "Dr. Busby" sold phenomenally when introduced by W. & S.B. Ives in 1843. More than 50,000 copies of the game were sold in its first year. It was designed by Anne W. Abbott of Beverly, Mass. The game sold more than 50,000 copies in its first year, and continued to be popular for some years. Later versions were issued by J.H. Singer and J. Ottmann Lithography. In the 1890s, McLoughlin Bros. issued a similarly named "Game of Dr. Fusby." In the 1930s, both Milton Bradley Co. and Parker Bros. issued "Dr. Busby" games.

"Dr. Doolittle" The popular Hugh Lofting books occasionally inspired toys and games, including the 1930s "Dr. Doolittle's Picture Matching Game" by Milton Bradley Co.

"Dr. Seuss Zoo," snap-together animals see *Revell, Inc.*

Dodge, Mary Mapes The acknowledged leader among juvenile fiction authors in the later 1800s, Mary Mapes Dodge found lasting fame with *Hans Brinker of the Silver Skates,* published in 1865. Its popularity was undoubtedly helped by American's recent enthusiasm for the sport of ice-skating, which rose markedly in the 1850s and '60s. Dodge also edited the magazine *St. Nicholas,* founded in 1873, until her death. Collections of her magazine writing appeared as *Baby Days* in 1876 and *Baby World* in 1884. She was born in 1831 in New York City, and died in 1905.

Dodge Mfg. Corp. This Oneida, N.Y., corporation made coaster wagons in the earlier 1930s.

"Dodger" steering sleds see *Sheboygan Coaster & Wagon Works.*

Charles William Doepke Mfg. Co.

Known for its heavy pressed-steel vehicles manufactured and widely sold in the earlier postwar years, Doepke used the "Model Toys" trade name for the excellent reason that its toys were faithful reproductions of construction vehicles and fire-fighting trucks. Made of high-grade steel, these toys were designed to withstand the roughest play. Their quality worked against them, in the end, since the lower-cost, lower-quality toys made by other pressed-steel manufacturers commanded the market. The line was introduced immediately after World War II, and continued into the mid-1950s.

Doepke's primary line consisted of the "Wooldridge H.D. Earth Hauler," the "Barber-Greene" bucket-loader, the "Jaeger Concrete Mixer," the "Adams Diesel Roadgrader," the "Unit Mobile Crane," the "Euclid Earth-Hauler Truck," the "American LaFrance Pumper Fire Truck," the "Caterpillar D6 Tractor and Bulldozer," and the "American LaFrance Aerial Ladder Truck." New in 1955 was the "Jaguar Sports Car Kit," to be assembled at home, and the "Searchlight Truck," with battery-operated searchlight and steerable front wheels. In the mid-1950s two of the firm's lead items were the "Rolybird," a three-wheeled pedal helicopter with tubular steel frame, and the "Yardbird," a platform on wheels that moved around a railroad-like track. Although more like a hand-car in

appearance, the "Yardbird" used a bicycle-style propulsion system, but was designed for hand-cranking instead of pedaling.

The Charles William Doepke Mfg. Co. made the "Yardbird," a train-like vehicle hand-cranked around a track.

"Doerfler" model yachts see *Maine Yacht Corp.*

"Doh-Mix" see *Climax Industries.*

Dolclos Products Corp. Doll clothes, shoes, and novelties were specialties of this Broadway, New York City, company in the Boomer years.

doll In general usage, the word "doll" replaced the term "babies" by the mid-18th century. Dolls may have originated as adult religious articles, which were taken over by children at the end of ceremonial rites. See *Kachina doll.*

In America, doll manufacturing seems to have picked up when general toy manufacturing did, with the first doll patent in the U.S. having been issued in 1858. See *dolls, wood; dolls, rag; etc.*

This 1950s doll was produced by Royal Doll Mfg. Co.

Doll, George Owner of one of the most famous early toy stores, George Doll established "The Temple of Fancy" in 1837 on Third Street in Philadelphia, moving it in 1844 to 106 N. Second Street He was joined in the business by his brother, John, and son, also named John.

Doll, John Born in 1847, John Doll worked at his father George Doll's toy store from age 17, taking over business in 1879. In 1880 he started Wanamaker's first toy department. Considered the "Dean of Toy Buyers," Doll was the first buyer to travel abroad to obtain toys for American stores.

doll beds Doll beds, bassinettes and cradles rank among the most popular of doll accessories. While many turners and furniture factories turned them out anonymously in the 19th century, many manufacturers were making them a major part of their toy output by the prewar years. Manufacturers included the Bemis Riddell Fibre Co., Benner, Birchcraft, Blue Ridge Novelties, Bredenberg Bros., Burlington Basket Co., Caron Novelty Co., N.D. Cass Co., the Chapman-Sargent Co., Detroit Wood Products Div., Harold W. Dow, Drewry Bros., the Dur-A-Bilt Co., Forest County Lumber Co., the Franklin Studio, L. Hopkins Mfg. Co., K. & B. Novelty & Mfg. Co., Lehman Co. of America, Lullabye Furniture Corp., Martin Metal Bed Co., Menasha Woodenware Corp., the Mengel Co., Perfection Mfg. Co., W.C. Redmon Sons & Co., Rockford Eagle Furniture Corp., S. & G. Mfg. Co., the A. Schoenhut Co., Storkline Furniture Corp., Marvin R. Suther and Whitney Bros. Co.

doll carriages Doll carriages, strollers and go-carts have long been important accessories for "playing house." Many cart and carriage builders from the mid-1800s on made doll versions along their full-size products. By prewar times, in addition to wood and wicker version, many doll carriages were being made by metal-stamping firms.

Important prewar manufacturers included All Metal Products Co., the American National Co., the Bemis Riddell Fibre Co., Carriage & Toy Co., Joseph Davidson, J.A. Dickerman Co., the Gendron Wheel Co., Gotham Pressed Steel Corp., Hartman Mfg. Co, C.H. Hartshorn, the Hedstrom-Union Co, Heywood-Wakefield Co., the N.N. Hill Brass Co., Jacobs & Kassler, Junior Toy Corp., Kozekar, Lloyd Mfg. Co., the Marlin Carriage Co., Muskin Mfg. Co., Perfect Mfg. Co., L.B. Ramsdell Co., O.W. Siebert Co., South Bend Toy Mfg. Co., H.N. Thayer Co., the Toledo Metal Wheel Co., Uhlen Carriage Co., Welsh-Hartman Co., Whitney Bros., F.A. Whitney Co., and World Metal Stamping Co.

D

Toy doll carriages were often just smaller versions of a company's full-size line.

The "Doll-E-Cradle" was produced by American Metal Specialties Corp. in the 1950s.

This folding doll cart was produced in the 1920s.

doll clothing   see *doll outfits.*

Doll Corporation of America In the
1920s, Doll Corporation of America offered
two lines of dolls, the "Century" dolls, which
were considered a "quality line at a price,"
and "Domec" dolls which were the "'price'
dolls of quality."

doll dies and molds Several prewar
companies specialized in making doll dies
and molds, including S.G. Ecker Co., on West
Broadway, and Manhattan Modeling & Chas-
ing Co., on Grand Street, New York City.

The Doll District, See *"The Toy Dis-
trict."*

doll eyes   see *eyes, doll and animal.*

doll faces Specializing had grown to such
a degree by the prewar years that some companies had a specialty in producing doll faces.
Such firms included Crescent Hill Novelty
Co., M. Fluegelman, and Rosen & Jacoby.

doll hair Specialists in producing doll hair
included the prewar firms Joseph Benn
Corp., Eastyarn Inc., H.A. Loeb & Co., and
E. Mittestaedt.

doll hospital Playing hospital grew to be
such a significant area of child play that toy
manufacturers actively catered to it by the
1930s, with a significant number busily making what the industry called "doll hospital
supplies." Prewar manufacturers included
Fred K. Graitling, Foulds & Freure, Karl
Ohlbaum & Son, Quaker Doll Co., Renown
Doll Wig Co., A.H. Wohlleben, and J.W.
Wood Elastic Web Co. Companies active in
the postwar years included Arranjay Wig
Co., Dollspart Supply Co., Jacks Fixit Service, Meyer Jacoby & Son, Premier Doll
Accessories Co., and Renown Doll Wig Co.

dollhouse Unlike many other doll items,
the dollhouse was typically not an accessory
to a doll or dolls, although small dolls might
be accessories to a dollhouse.

Important prewar manufacturers of doll-
houses included O.B. Andrews Co., E.B.
Ayers, the Carrom Co., James A. Coulson,
A.B. Cowles, William G. Johnston, Model
Doll House Co. New Process Corp., the F.L.

Purdy Co., Purves Products Co., Rochester
Folding Box Co., the A. Schoenut Co., Stoll
& Einson Games, Terre Town Toy Trades-
men, the Tolerton Co., Toy Furniture Shop,
Vista Toy Co., Warren Paper Products Co.,
and Wicker Toy Mfg. Co.

Dollhouses of the postwar years were made
by companies including Arandell Products
Co., Argo Industries Corp., Built-Rite Toys,
Child Life Toys, T. Cohn, Family Fun Kit
Co., Fibre-Bilt Toys, Flagg Doll Co., Hall's
Lifetime Toys, Jayline Toys, Louis Marx &
Co., Plastic Art Toy Corp., Rich Industries,
South Bend Toy Mfg. Co., and the S.J. Weg-
man Co.

doll outfits Although the manufacture of
doll clothing was usually the province of the
doll maker, during the prewar specialization
of toy manufacturers, many developed specialties in making doll clothing and other outfit specialties.

An example might be provided by Canastota
Sherwood Stamping Corp, which developed
the specialty of manufacturing the doll roller
skate. Doll stockings were another specialty,
being made by Apollo Knitting, Arcadia
Hosiery, and Blossom Doll companies.

Doll shoes, yet another specialty, were made
by ArtNovelty Doll Shoes Co., B. & S. Specialty Co., Blossom Doll Co., Karl OhlBaum
& Son, and Peerless Doll Shoe Co. Progressive Novelty Co. made both doll stockings
and shoes, while Fred K. Braitling made
these and also the doll roller skates.

Prewar companies specializing in general
doll outfits included Aetna Novelty Co., the
Stephen Blum Co., Climax Rubber Co., B.R.
Cromien, Dolls' Tailors Co., the Dolly's
Dressmaker, Foulds & Freure, the Franklin
Studio, M. Hardy, Harris Raincoat, Hygrade
Fabric Co., M.L. Kahn, Lodge Textile works,
Minerva Toy Co., Molly-'Es Doll Outfitters,
the Newman Co, Nichols Mfg. Co., Park
Avenue Doll Outfitters, Rilington Toy Nov-
elty Co., M. & S. Shillman, Tailored Craft
Novelty Co., Totsy Mfg. Co., Toy Knitted
Sportwear, and Vogue Doll Shoppe.

doll voices   see *voices. doll and animal*

Dollcraft Novelty Co. Based on West 25th Street, New York City, by the late 1930s, Dollcraft made soft dolls, including a "Lone Ranger" doll. In the Boomer years, located on Lafayette Street, Dollcraft specialized in plush toys, "Lazy Baby" dolls, and dancing dolls.

dolls, baby Baby dolls became popular only in the later 1800s, after the Montanaris of London introduced the first infant or baby dolls at London's Crystal Palace Exposition in London, in 1851. Some of these expensive wax creations became available in the United States. Their impact was great enough to inspire a flood of baby dolls made of bisque, wax over papier-mâché, china, or other materials.

dolls, black In the socially self-aware, or at least self-conscious, 1950s and '60s, some firms made a point of issuing black dolls, even though in some cases these were indistinguishable in their nature from prewar "mamie" dolls. These companies included Allied-Grand Doll Mfg. Co., Arcadia Doll Co., Flagg Doll Co., Francesse Doll Co., Jolly Toys, Mattel, Rosette Doll Co., and the Sun Rubber Co.

dolls, cloth see *dolls, soft.*

dolls, composition and other materials Dolls with composition heads were widely made in the early to mid 19th century. Some of the heads were given an outer coating of wax. Often heads of composition or other materials were imported, and attached to cloth bodies either by craftspeople or individuals at home. The material continued to be important through the 1800s and the first half of the 1900s, with some use still occurring in the Boomer years.

Doll makers of the earlier 20th century, many of whom produced composition dolls, as well as soft and ceramic dolls, included Acme Toy Mfg. Co., Adler Favor & Novelty Co., Louis Amberg & Son, American Character Doll Co., American Stuffed Novelty Co., Arranbee Doll Co., Atlantic Toy Mfg. Co., Atlas Doll & Toy Co., Averill Mfg. Corp., W. Bimblick, Blum-Lustig Toy Co., Bonser Doll Co., Capital Toy Co., Century Doll Co., M.J. Chase Co., Doll Corp. of America, Domec Toys, European Doll Mfg. Co., Marshall Field & Co., Fleischaker & Baum, Gem Doll Corp., Gerling Toy Co., E. Goldberger, Hoest & Co., E.I. Horsman Co., Ideal Novelty & Toy Co., Kirsh & Reale, Lenci Dolls, Live Long Toys, Marks Bros. Co., Maxine Doll Co., National French Fancy Novelty Co., the Nelke Corp., Overland Products Corp., Paramount Doll Co., Penn Stuffed Toy Co., M. Pressner & Co., Primrose Doll Co., Katherine A. Rauser, Regal Doll Mfg. Co., Reisman, Barron & Co., Royal Toy Mfg. Co., the Rushton Co., S. & H. Novelty Co., The A. Schoenhut Co., Shaw Doll Co., Strauss-Eckardt, Toy Products Co., Twistum Toy Factory, Uneeda Doll Co., Unique Novelty Doll Co., and Yagoda Bros. & Africk.

dolls, cornhusk A probable invention of American Indians, dolls made of corn husks were treasured American Colonial and pioneer toys. It was also called cornshuck doll, and likely by other folk names. A prewar manufacturer of the dolls was Blue Ridge Novelties.

dolls, fashion In 18th century usage, London milliners and dressmakers made "fashion dolls" which were designed to display new baby fashions in mantuas and nightgowns. Many were imported to America. These were also called "Flanders Babies." In the Boomer years of the 20th century, "fashion dolls" or "glamour dolls" were conspicuously stylish, adult-modeled dolls.

dolls, leather While most 19th century doll bodies were made of cloth, leather was also used. Leather dolls with composition heads were advertised as early as the 1820s in Philadelphia.

dolls, mammy "Mammy dolls" or "colored mammy dolls" were black fabric dolls of adult women figures.

"Dolls of All Countries" see *Admiration Toy Co., Inc.*

Dolls of Hollywood Dolls, hand puppets and squeeze toys were specialties of this Boomer-era Santa Monica, Calif., firm.

dolls, paper Paper dolls became popular among privileged European and Colonial families in the 1760-'80s. These dolls were cardboard cutouts of men and women with moveable arms and legs, and with numerous paper costumes that could be changed. In France they were called *pantins*, and in America, "protean figures." See also *toy books.*

The first to appear in a magazine, which later became a common source for them, was a figure to be cut out and pasted onto cardboard, with costumes, in the Nov. 1859 *Godey's Lady's Book.* Magazines including *Good Housekeeping* and *Ladies' Home Journal* followed suit. Publishing paper dolls became big business by the later 19th century, with publishers active in the field including Milton Bradley Co.; Clark, Austin & Smith; the Chromatic Printing Co.; Kimmel & Forster; Selchow & Righter; Frederick A. Stokes & Co.; Samuel Gabriel Sons & Co.; and Peter G. Thomson.

Since many of the late 19th and earlier 20th century paper dolls were made by book publishers and other printers, see also *cardboard and paper toys.*

With all the toy innovations of the Boomer years, one would have thought such traditional playthings as cutouts and paper dolls would have fallen by the wayside. Yet the opposite seems to have been the case, with the toys reaching renewed levels of popularity in the 1950s and '60s. The most important publisher of traditional toy books and paper dolls was Whitman Publishing Co.

The most innovative may have been Colorforms, whose durable vinyl activity sets were cutouts brought into the age of plastics. Other manufacturers using new postwar materials in their toys included Aldon Industries, who made "3-D" plastic cutouts, and Trim Molded Products Co., which made cutouts with plastic dolls.

Other Boomer-era manufacturers were the Beistle Co., Milton Bradley Co., Built-Rite Toys, J.B. Carroll Co., Cohn-Hall-Marx, De Journette Mfg. Co., Samuel Gabriel Sons & Co., Great Lakes Press, Jak-Pak-Inc., Jaymar Specialty Co., Merril Co. Publishers, Platt &

Munk Co., the Saalfield Publishing Co., Stencil-Art Publishing Co., and Stephens Publishing Co.

dolls, plastic Vinyl, latex, and plastic became the primary doll-making materials in the Boomer years.

To sample a few representative companies gives an idea of the range of these toys. They include A. & H. Doll Mfg. Corp., which made dolls in sizes from 6 to 26 inches, with the company having a reputation for "big dolls," an aspect of its line it tended to emphasize with capital letters. These large vinyl creations had such names as "Marcie," "Donna," "Gigi," and "Gigi's Li'l Sister."

Juro Novelty Co. used the new materials in its "Juro Celebrity Dolls," which included Paul Winchell's "Jerry Maoney" ventriloquist doll and Dick Clark's "Autograph Dolls" and "Dancing Dolls."

Margon Corp. enjoyed success with its "Margon Moving Eyes," which were doll eyes that rolled and automatically centered themselves. These pudgy-cheeked baby and child dolls made by Margon also featured attractive, curled lashes by 1960.

The famous Nancy Ann Storybook Dolls Company adapted to the times, and started making its miniature dressed dolls with hard plastic bodies and heads. Although advertised as being "for fashion, for glamour, for quality," in those glamour-driven days, the "Storybook Dolls" were not fashion dolls in the sense "Barbie" was, being less conducive to the constant changes of clothes and accessories, and more rooted in one or another particular "Storybook" character.

Roberta Doll Co. issued the "Roberta Ann" line of full-jointed plastic dolls of all types. It divided its baby dolls into "Drink, Wet, and Tear" baby dolls, "Newborn Infants," and "Christening Babies." Older-age dolls were "Sweater," "Colored," "Bride," "Formal," and "High Heel Glamour" dolls. The line included the large plastic dolls popular at the time, measuring 30 and 36 inches, some of them with the "walking" feature.

Uneeda Doll Co. never seemed to lack for gooey doll names, a fact unchanged in its vinyl and plastic Boomer years, when such dolls as "Dollikin," "Yummy," "Dewdrop," "Tinyteens," "Twinks," "Sis," "Purty," "Prithilla," "Debteens," "Chubby," and "Baby Bumpkins" were popular. The firm also made licensed dolls, including Walt Disney's "Polyanna."

Admiration Toy Co. made the "Lady Alice Dolls," with vinyl and plastic doll bodies. The line of walking dolls, high-heel dolls, and baby dolls measured from 6 to 12 inches high, and sold for prices from 39 cents to $2.98 in the mid-Boomer years.

Vogue Dolls enjoyed considerable success with its family of "Ginny Dolls." Wide-faced, relatively small dolls, "Ginny," "Ginnette," "Jill" and "Jeff" made up one of the more popular dollhouse casts of characters of the Boomer years, especially in the 1950s and earlier '60s. Vogue also made redheaded, green-eyed dolls named "Brikette" and "Li'l Imp," and the "Arranbee Dolls." As befitted its name, the company considered its dolls "Fashion Leaders in Doll Society."

Flagg Flexible Dolls made "Dollhouse Dolls," which it described as "the most perfect, most lifelike miniatures available— exactly scaled to fit the rooms and furnishings of standard doll houses." These were hand-painted, dressed bendy figures, capable of being bent "in every natural position," the company promised, without mentioning the various unnatural ones that bendies invariably suffered through in the 1960s. The company also made 7-inch "Dancing Dolls."

The list of companies making dolls in the Boomer years is enormous, making the task of any who might wish to assemble a representative collection an imposing one. It also makes more difficult the identification searches of those with ambiguously labeled or unlabeled dolls.

For that not insignificant number of you with supreme dedication, however, here is your preliminary assignment sheet. For this list I have not attempted to separate those who stuck to their prewar composition guns—it seems possible there were a few—from those who fully adapted to the plastics revolution.

A.B.C. Toys, A. & L. Novelty Co., Ace Toy Mfg. Corp., Active Doll Corp., Adanta Novelties Corp., Alexander Doll Co., Allied-Grand Doll Mfg. Co., American Character Doll Co., American Mfg. Concern, Arcadia Doll Co., Arranbee Doll Co., Artistic Doll Co., Asbury Mills, Astor Doll & Toy Mfg. Corp., Baby Barry Toy Co., Banner Plastics Corp., Bee Bee Doll & Toy Mfg., Beehler Arts, Best Plastics Corp., H.J. Blumberger Co., George Borgfeldt Corp., Brookglad Corp., Cameo Doll Products, Carbondale Toy & Novelty Mfg. Co., Charm Toys, Chicago Toy & Doll Co., Commonwealth Plastics Corp., Cosmopolitan Doll & Toy Corp., Couturier Dolls, Cowles' Novelties, Dandee Doll Mfg. Co., Dandy Toys, Dell Plastic Co., Elsie Denny, Dennis Play Products, Doll Bazaar Mfg. Co., Dollcraft Novelty Co., Dolls of Hollywood, Dollspart Supply Co., Dollyana, Dorothy Creations, Dream Girl, Sam & Herbert Drelich, Effanbee Doll Co., Elite Creations, Ellanee Doll Co., Elmar Products Co., Empire Doll Co., Etone Doll Co., Eugene Doll & Novelty Co., Francesse Doll Co., French Doll Co., Gerling Toy Co., Ruth Gibbs, Goldberger Doll Mfg. Co., Grant Plastics, Charles Gregor Creations, Horsman Dolls, the House of Puzzy, Hungerford Plastics Corp., Ideal Toy Corp., International Plastic Co., Irwin Corp., J-Cey Doll Co., Jolly Toys, K-B Doll Corp., Kimport Dolls, Knickerbocker Plastic Co., Libby-Majorette Doll Corp., Lido Toy Co., M.C. Doll Co., M. & S. Doll Co., Manomatic Novelty Corp., Mattel, Megahorn Co., Midwestern Mfg. Co., Minerva Toy Co., Morden Doll Corp., W.J. Murphy Co., Nasco Doll, Natural Doll Co., Novelty Dolls, P. & M. Doll Co., P.M.A. Dolls, Paulmar Novelties Co., Pensick & Gordon, Plakie toys, Practi-Cole Products, Princess Anna Doll Co., Red Seal Novelty Co., Renall Dolls, Renwal Toy Corp., Richwood Toys, Riemann Seabrey Co., Rose Mary Dolls Mfg. Co., Rosette Doll Co., Royal Doll Mfg. Co., Sayco Doll Corp., Schranz & Bieeber Co., B. Shackman & Co., Sherman Doll & Toy Co., Skippy Doll Corp., Standard Doll Co., Sterling Doll Co., Sterling Plastics Co., the Sun Rubber Co., Thomas Mfg. Corp., Top-Flite Dolls, Valentine Dolls, Vantines, Wagner Parade of Dolls, Wipco,

D

and I.B. Wolfset & Co. Bear in mind, this list is not a complete one.

dolls, rag Rag dolls seem to date from around 1840, in America. See *dolls, soft.*

dolls, rubber Early dolls with rubber heads have been dated to the 1820s-'40s, made of gutta-percha or India rubber. Goodyear patented his vulcanizing process in 1844, after which his more elastic version of the substance appeared with increasing frequency in the world of dolls.

Prewar manufacturers included American Character Doll Co., Arranbee Doll Co., Climax Rubber Co., Fleischaker & Baum, E. Goldberger, Horsman Dolls, Ideal Novelty & Toy Co., Miller Rubber Products Co., Regal Doll Mfg. Co., the Schavoir Rubber Co., Seiberling Latex Products Co., and Thornecraft.

Postwar manufacturers, who were making the shift toward vinyl through the 1950s and '60s, included Allied Grand Doll Mfg. Co., Bantam U.S. Toys, Eastern Moulded Products, Flagg Doll Co., Jolly Toys, Manomatic Novelty Corp., Morden Doll Corp., Nasco Doll Co., Rempel Mfg., and, most especially, the Sun Rubber Co.

The "Sunbabe" dolls were made by Sun Rubber Co. in the 1950s.

dolls, soft Soft dolls, a standard category in the doll industry, included cloth and rag dolls. The earliest American mention of a rag doll appeared in connection with a Boston witch trial, in which rag dolls found in the laundry, presumably put there by the children, were thought to have been used by the laundress for bewitching those children. The

"witch" was executed. Later interactions between adults and children's dolls in America have been less dire.

For doll manufacturers in the pre-Great Depression years, see *dolls, composition and other materials*

Prewar manufacturers include such prominent names as American Character Doll Co., Horsman Dolls, Knickerbocker Toy Co., Lenci-Lenart Import, and the Rushton Co.

Other prewar manufacturers included Adler Favor & Novelty Co., American Doll & Novelty Co., Arrow Novelty Co., Arts & Crafts Studio, Atlanta Playthings Co., William P. Beers Co., Blossom Doll Co., Bonsser products, Brown County Folks, Carb Mfg. Corp., M.J. Chase, Fairfield Novelties, Fleischaker & Baum, Georgene Novelties, M. Hardy, Harvard Toy Works, Kat-A-Korner, Kerk Guild, Richard G. Krueger, Mizpah Toy & Novelty Corp., Frank Plotnick Co., Ross & Ross, S. & H. Novelty Co., Sayco Doll Corp., Scovell Novelty Mfg. Co., Sterling Doll Co., Sweeney Lithograph Co., H.H. Tammen Co., Tiny Tot Studio, and Tru-Craft Novelty Co.

Their number increased by the late prewar years, and also included A.B.C. Toys, Alexander Doll Co., American Character Doll Co., the Artistic Toy Co., Atlas Toy Mfg. Co., Bantam Products, Berea College Student Industries, Bricky Corp., Community Craft Weaters, Crown Toy Mfg. Co., Rees Davis Studios, Dollcraft Novelty Co., the French Doll Makers, Gund Mfg. Co., Horsman Dolls, Junel Novelties, Kaklar Cloth Toy Co., Knickerbocker Toy Co., Maybro Mfg. Co., Molly-'Es, Morehead Character Doll Co., Phe-Lena Novelty Creators, the Rushton Co., Twinzy Toys, and Victory Doll Co.

Georgene Novelties, already prominent in the prewar years, emerged as one of the main contenders on the postwar stage, due in part to its licensing arrangements involving storybook and cartoon characters. Georgene was the exclusive licensed manufacturer for "Raggedy Ann" and "Raggedy Andy" dolls, and also made "Little Lulu," "Nosy Rosy," "Yum Yum," "Sunflower Sue," and "Lazy Bones" dolls.

Other major manufacturers of the Boomer years included A. & L. Novelty Co., Alexander Doll Co., American Foam Latex Corp., Arcadia Doll Co., Arrow Fur Co., Asbury Mills, Atlanta Novelty Mfg. Corp., Atlanta Playthings Co., George Borgfeldt Corp., Cameo Doll Products Co., Childhood Classics, Christy Mfg. Co., Community Craft Toys, Dollcraft Novelty Co., Eden Toys, Flagg Doll Co., Gund Mfg. Co., Harrison's Mfg. Co., Knickerbocker Toy Co., Richard G. Krueger, M. & S. Doll Co., Esther Miller Doll Creations, My-Toy Co., Plakie Toys, Rose Mary Dolls Mfg. Co., Royal Doll Mfg. Co., Sayco Doll Corp., Softskin Toys, Standard Doll Co., Stuart, I.S. Sutton & Sons, Twinzy Toy Co., and I.B. Wolfset & Co.

dolls, walking Walking dolls appeared surprisingly early, with the first appearing around 1827, soon after "sleep eyes" first appeared. J.S. Bronner patented in 1863 a "toy automaton, or walking doll," which moved forward with blocky movements. William F. Goodwin patented in 1868 a more realistic walking doll that pushed a carriage. Being able to use the wheeled carriage for stability allowed the mechanical motions to be made more realistic. Both worked by means of clockwork mechanisms.

dolls, wax Dolls of wax, which allowed more delicate sculpting of the faces, were popular in the mid-1800s. They were usually imported. Dolls of wax may have been the first to have moving eyes, in the later 1820s. The most expensive wax dolls of the time had rooted hair.

dolls, wind-up see *dolls, walking.*

dolls, wishbone A Colonial American toy, the wishbone doll was made by attaching a small wax head to the top of a wishbone from a chicken or turkey, which was then dressed.

"The Dolls with the Golden Heart" see *Fleischaker & Baum.*

dolls, wood Wood must rank with the most venerable substances used in making dolls, even though evidence of stone dolls goes back much farther into prehistory. In pre-Colonial America, American Indians made dolls of wood, clay, and leather, as well as other plant materials.

An important early innovator in the history of the American wood doll was Joel Ellis of Springfield, Vt., who designed a hard-maple doll with mortise and tenon joints, which allowed arms and legs to be fixed in different positions. The head was wooden, shaped in steel molds with steam and pressure, while the hands and feet were metal. Improvements by George Sanders, also of Springfield, and others led to the wooden dolls manufactured by Mason & Taylor from 1879 into the 1880s.

In the 1800s, some dolls with porcelain, rubber or composition heads might have had wooden arms, hands, or legs.

Prewar manufacturers of wooden dolls included Artwood Toy Mfg. Co., Brodhaven Mfg. Co., Cameo Doll Co., Essenel Co., Jaymar Specialty Co., Joy Doll Co., Kiddie-Crafters, Noveloid Co., J.W. Pickering & Son, the Toy Tinkers and Tryon Toy-Makers & Wood-Carvers. By the late prewar years, firms joining their number included Alexander Doll Co., Associated Syndicate, Henry S. Beach, Brodhaven Mfg. Co., Embree Mfg. Co., M. Hardy, Marks Bros. Co., Playskool Institute, President Novelty & Jewelry Co., O. Schoenhut, Stepin Sam Co., and Toy Furniture Shop. While some of these later firms were entering at the nursery toy level, others were responding to the late 1930s popular demand for tap-dancing dolls, which were being made of wood.

Dolls' Tailors Co. Makers of doll dresses and outfits, this Milwaukee, Wis., company also made the "Wel-Drest" baby dolls in the 1930s.

Dollspart Supply Co. Based on East 19th Street, New York City, Dollspart manufactured postwar doll hospital supplies, doll wigs, and doll jewelry.

"Dolly Ann" toy kitchen sets prewar, see *The Washburn Co.*

Dolly Dear Accessories This Rives, Tenn., company issued dollhouse accessories in the 1950s and '60s.

D

"Dolly Dingle" A paper doll, "Dolly Dingle" was associated with *Pictorial Review* in the later 1800s.

Dolly Toy Co. Based in Dayton, Ohio, Dolly Toy Co. made Easter pull toys, "Reg'lar Fellers" kites, "Sky Boy" kites, and "Fibro" doll furniture in the earlier 1930s. In that decade it also obtained license through Kay Kamen to issue "animated Mickey Mouse toys." By late in the decade the company was emphasizing Easter pull toys and miscellaneous holiday novelties.

In wartime, the line consisted of Easter novelties, Halloween pumpkins, "Fibro" toys, Christmas tree houses, and candy boxes.

In the Boomer years, having moved to Tipp City, Ohio, the company focused on nursery pin-ups, nursery lamps, and novelties.

Dollyana, Inc. Miniature dolls, baby dolls, drink and wet dolls, walking dolls, and teen-age dolls were specialties of this Passaic, N.J., company in the Boomer years. It also made doll outfits.

"Dollydear," prewar see *Fitmore Mfg. Co.*

"Dollyduds" see *Lodge Textile Works.*

The Dolly's Dressmaker Ready-cut doll outfits, complete with sewing supplies, were made by this Massillon, Ohio, company in the 1930s.

Dollywood Studios, Inc. A Hollywood, Calif., firm, Dollywood made dolls including the "Defense Dolls" of the early 1940s, including "Soldier," "Sailor," "Marine," "Aviator," and "Nurse" models.

"Domec" dolls see *Doll Corporation of America.*

dominoes The game of dominoes arose in ancient Asia. The most distinctive early American dominoes game was Charles M. Crandall's 1881 "Noah's Dominoes." The playing blocks had the usual domino markings on one side, and lithographed images of wild animals on the other, with half of an animal on each side in the domino manner. For manufacturers, see *checkers, chess, & dominoes.*

"Donald Duck" Walt Disney's irascible sailor-suited duck appeared in early toy form as "Donald the Duck," as in the mid-1930s stuffed toy by Richard G. Krueger. By the late 1930s he was firmly established as "Donald Duck," with a number of playthings to his name.

Toys and playthings included banks by Behrend & Rothschild and Crown Toy Mfg. Co., chime toys by N.N. Hill Brass Co., "Flip-Flap" and "Pop-Up Kritter" pull toys by Fisher-Price Toys, a Parker Bros. game, a "Man-Egg-Kins" figure by Paas Dye Co., masquerade costumes by A.S. Fishbach, painting and sewing sets by Standard Toykraft Products, pencil sharpeners by Plastic Novelties, rubber toys by Seiberling Latex Products Co., sleds by S.L. Allen & Co., stamping sets by Fulton Specialty Co., stuffed toys by Knickerbocker Toy Co. and Richard G. Krueger, toys and novelties issued by George Borgfeldt Corp., sand toys by Ohio Art Co., and xylophones by Fisher-Price Toys. "Donald's Nephews" stuffed toys were also issued by Knickerbocker in the 1930s.

Postwar items included bean bags by Gardner & Co., dart game by Empire Plastic Corp., and "Math-Magic" by Jacmar Mfg. Co.

During World War II, Dollywood Studios made these "Defense Dolls."

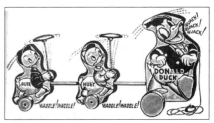

The "Donald and Nephews" pull-toy by Fisher-Price Toys, 1940s.

The "Donald Duck Cart" made in the 1940s, was another Fisher-Price wood toy.

Donaldson Bros. Active in the late 19th century, Donaldson Bros. published the "Bicycle Game," an 1896 board game.

Donar Products Corp. The "Weave-It" sets of the late 1930s were issued by this Medford, Mass., firm.

Dongan Electric Mfg. Co. Toy transformers for railroad systems were the prewar product of this Detroit, Mich., company.

"Donna Reed" "Donna Reed" paper dolls were made by the Saalfield Publishing Co. Licensing rights were controlled by Screen Gems.

M.A. Donohue & Co. An important prewar and postwar publisher, Donohue of Chicago, Ill., was issuing a full line of painting books, toy books, and "Linennear" and board juvenile books by the 1920s. One of its most prominent titles was the "Raggedy Ann and Andy" series of books. The firm was affiliated with the Goldsmith Publishing Co.

Donze, Leon see *Barclay Mfg. Co.*

"Dopey" see *"Snow White and the Seven Dwarfs."*

Dorco Rubber Corp. Rubber toys, floats, and rubber sundries were made by this Fourth Avenue, New York City, corporation in the 1930s.

The Dorfan Co. Based in Newark N.J., with offices in the Fifth Avenue Building, Dorfan made "modern electric" trains in the 1920s, including engines with "a really remarkable take-apart engine." It made both electrical and mechanical trains into the 1930s.

"Doris Day" "Doris Day" appeared as a Whitman Publishing Co. character in books. Licensing rights to her name were controlled by MCA.

Dorothy Creations, Inc. Latex, vinyl, and high-heel dolls were products of this Chicago, Ill., firm in the Boomer years.

Dot & Peg Productions The "Young American Designer" paper doll kit of the war years was issued by this Chattanooga, Tenn., company. The toy included a "Fashion Show" stage for the dolls.

Dot Games This postwar baseball game manufacturer was based in South Haven, Mich.

Double Fabric Tire Corp. Founded in 1910, this company changed its name to Auburn Rubber Crown Cord around 1915. See *Auburn Rubber Co.*

"Double R Bar Brand" see *"Roy Rogers Enterprises."*

Doughboy Industries, Inc. Based in New Richmond, Wis., Doughboy made large inflated plastic toys, beach balls, swim rings, and toys in the Boomer years.

"Bobo the Clown" was one of Doughboy Industries' toys in the

"Dough Boy" single-shot cap pistol prewar, see *Kilgore Mfg. Co., Inc.*

Lyle Douglas This Dallas, Texas, firm issued trick and joke novelties from the later 1930s through the Boomer years.

Douglas Co., Inc. Washable lambskin and plush stuffed toys were the specialty of this Keene, N.H., company.

Douglas Plymouth Corp. The "Hobby-Art" paint-by-number sets of the 1950s and '60s were issued by this Manitowoc, Wis., company.

Dover Mfg. Co. Specializing in electric household toys, this Dover, Ohio, company made toy electric sad irons and waffle irons in the 1930s.

Harold W. Dow, In addition to children's furniture, bassinettes and strollers, this Warner, N.H., company made prewar wooden toys and games.

Dowae Toys, Inc. A Springfield, Mass., manufacturer, Dowae issued a line of flying toys in the 1930s including gliders and long-distance prop-driven toys. Lead items included the "Dowae Midget Flyer," the sling-propelled "The Stunt Plane" and "Dowae Albatross," "The Sail Plane," and the prop-driven "The Junior Transport" and "The Senior Transport," the latter being 32-inches long.

Dowis Football Game Co. Responsible for the "Huddle All-American Football Game," issued from 1931 into the mid-'30s, Dowis was based in Atlanta, Ga.

"Dowmetal" speed planes see *Roland P. Place Co.*

Dowst Mfg. Co. Brothers Charles and Samuel Dowst, trade-journal publishers, saw the Line-o-Type machine being demonstrated at the Chicago World's Columbian Exposition of 1893. Although the machine was designed to cast type for printing, the Dowsts saw its potential for other applications. Being publishers of the *National Laundry Journal,* the Dowst Bros. Co. first used the machine for making collar buttons and promotional trinkets, including miniature sadirons. By the turn of the century his company, based in Chicago, Ill., was focusing almost entirely on die-casting.

A major turning point came in the years 1910 and 1911, after years of making miniature objects used as premiums by various companies, including Rueckheim Bros. & Eckstein. In 1910, Dowst Bros. Co. made several size models of Louis Bleriot's "aeroplane" which flew over the English Channel in 1909. It followed these toys with its 2-inch "Limousine," a fairly generic depiction of a contemporary luxury car. In 1914 the firm manufactured its first miniature car openly modeled on an existing car, its "Flivver," or 1914 Model T Ford convertible. This toy is considered the first die-cast model miniature of a real car made in America. It remained in production at Dowst until 1926. The names "Tootsie Toy" and "Tootsietoy" had started appearing on the firms toys by the early 1920s, the name itself reflecting the birth of a girl into the extended Dowst family, whose nickname was "Tootsie." The name was trademarked in 1924.

Two years later, Nathan Sure bought Dowst Bros. Co. and moved it adjacent to his Cosmo Toy & Novelty Co. He named the resulting firm Dowst Mfg. Co., a name it retained until the early 1960s.

By the early 1930s, the "Tootsietoy" line of metal automobiles, airplanes, dollhouse furniture, trains, and "5-cent and 10-cent goods" had high visibility in the toy world. The firm's line expanded to include toy "Buck Rogers" spaceships, toy dishes, "Basketball in Miniature," vending machine novelties, advertising novelties, and standard and special game markers, by the late 1930s.

In the Boomer years, Dowst's "Tootsietoy" line included die-cast metal automobiles, trucks, airplanes, construction toys, farm toys, road-building toys, military toys, educational toys, party favors, doll accessories, bird feeder sets, and miniature novelties.

In 1961 the company bought the toy division of Strombeck-Becker Mfg. Co., and changed its name to Strombecker Corp.

This "Auto-Gyro" was one of Dowst's offerings in 1934.

"Dozy Animals" see *Gund Mfg. Co.*

Dr. see *"Doctor,"* alphabetized as spelled out.

"Dragnet" A popular TV show in the 1950s-'60s, "Dragnet" inspired merchandise including jailer keys and handcuff sets by John-Henry Mfg. Co. Licensing rights were controlled by MCA.

"Dragon" checkers see *Halsam Products Co.*

"Dragon-Fly" airplanes and gliders see *Western Aircraft Mfg. Co.*

W.W. Drake Mfg. Co. The Drake toy trick horse, a walking toy named "Stroller," and the toy glider "The Flying Fish" were lead items in W.W. Drake's line in the mid-1930s. The company was based in Hazleton, Penn.

draisine A German invention in the early 19th century, the draisine was a two-wheeled device on which one moved by pushing one's feet against the ground. A Scottish inventor added pedals in 1839, in a move giving rise to the bicycle and velocipede.

Edward O. Drane & Co. This Chicago, Ill., firm made postwar puzzles, magic tricks and joke novelties.

Draper-Maynard Co. Mickey Mouse athletic goods including baseballs, bats, and gloves were made by this Plymouth, N.H., company in the mid-1930s.

Draw-Graph Mfg. Co. Located on South Michigan Avenue, Chicago, Ill., this firm made the mid-1930s "Draw-Graph" drawing outfit, adding a metal pantograph later in the decade.

"Draw-Mor" see *New Draw-Mor Mfg. Co., The*

drawing devices and toys Drawing devices and drawing toys, which ranged from pantographs to the "Hoot-Nanny" and "Spirograph," were important activity toys through most of the 20th century.

Prewar sets included "Draftsman, Jr." and "Hoot-Nanny" from Howard B. Jones,

"Drawcraft" pantograph by Texcraft Toy Products, "Draw-O-Graph" drawing set by Bernard-Edward Mfg. Co., "Drawing Teacher" instructive play material by Milton Bradley Co., "Drawing Teacher" pantograph by the Drawing Master Co., and the "Draw-Mor" drawing device by New Draw-Mor Mfg. Co.

Other prewar manufacturers included the Aman & Sandman Box & Lumber Co., Bass Educational Toy Co., Cardinell Corp., Draw-Graph Mfg. Co., Federal Stamping & Engineering Co., Majestic Art Novelty Co., Plaza Mfg. Co., and Standard Crayon Mfg. Co. Manufacturers in the later prewar years also included American Toy Works, Burgess Battery Co., Embree Mfg. Co., Northwestern Products, Playgames, and H. Walter Sykes. Undoubtedly the most famous drawing toy of the Boomer era was "Spirograph," a mechanical kit akin to the metal "Hoot-Nanny" device, but made of plastic by Kenner Products Co. Introduced in the 1966-67 season, "Spirograph" became one of the enduring yet characteristically "Boomer" toys of the last part of the century.

Other Boomer companies included De Journette Mfg. Co., Eberhard Faber Toy & Game Co., Karbon Kopee, Metal Moss Mfg. Co., Norton Products, Rennoc Games & Toys, Scheuer Sales Corp., Skil-Craft Corp., and Venus Pen & Pencil Corp. Northern Signal Co. issued the "Hoot-Nanny," formerly made by Jones.

Drawing Master Co., The All-steel adjustable pantographs, a popular drawing toy in the 1930s and '40s, were made by this Cleveland, Ohio, company.

"Dreadnaught" steering sleds see *Garton Toy Co.*

"Dreadnought" cannons see *Harvill Corp.*

Dream Girl, Inc. This postwar doll company was based in Brooklyn, N.Y.

"Dreamie" animals and dolls see *Gund Mfg. Co.*

Leopold Dreifuss A prewar San Francisco, Calif., company, Dreifuss made

"Paint-O-Graphs" paint sets for children in the mid-1930s.

Dremel Mfg. Co. One of several companies that followed the lead of Gilbert and Structo, Dremel Mfg. Co. of Racine, Wis., made an "electric motor erecting set" in the mid-1930s.

Lyle S. Drew A wood-turning company, this Union, N.H., company made prewar wooden toys. By the late 1930s its line included wooden boats, train sets, and milk delivery sets.

Drewry Bros. One of many New England wood-turning companies, Drewry Bros. of North Weare, N.H., made wooden toy carts, wagons, toy bassinets, novelties, and blackboards in the earlier 1930s.

dribbler "Dribbler" was a nickname used for British toy locomotives made from the 1840s through to the turn of the century, of solid brass. Powered by steam, they tended to leave a trail of water behind them as they ran, giving rise to the name.

Dritz-Traum Co., Inc. Based on East 26th Street, New York City, Dritz-Traum issued the "Peggy" manikin doll, which came packaged with "real McCall Dressmaker" patterns and sewing accessories, during the war years. The firm's subsidiary, Heirloom Needlework Guild, produced the "Cuddle Cut-Ups" kits for making stuffed animals.

"Drive 'Em" toys prewar, see *Keystone Mfg. Co.*

Dry-a-Line Co. A Milwaukee, Wis., company, Dry-a-Line Co. was making sheepskin stuffed animals in the 1930s.

William F. Drueke Based in Grand Rapids, Mich., Drueke issued games and novelties in the late 1930s. The firm became William F. Drueke & Sons, Inc., in the postwar years. It specialized in games for children and adults, puzzles, gavels, and novelties.

drum, toy The first tin drum toys, imported from Europe, appeared in American shops by the late 18th century. As domestic tin production increased in the next century, domestically made versions became common. By the 19th century, manufacturers seem to have developed the practice of issuing drums in regular sizes, with diameters of roughly 6", 8", and 10" being standard. Manufacturers in the earlier 20th century included N.D. Cass Co., T. Cohn, and Morton E. Converse & Son Co. Although many seem to have left their toys unmarked, prewar manufacturers included Acme Can Co., the N.D. Cass Co., J. Chein & Co., T. Cohn, Gotham Pressed Steel Corp., Fred Gretsch Mfg. Co., the Master Package Corp., Noble & Cooley Co., the Ohio Art Co., and Stoer Mfg. Co.

Tin and other drum toys maintained their popularity into the Boomer years, with manufacturers including Bayshore Industries, Block House, George Borgfeldt Corp., Chein, Emenee Industries, Carl Guggenheim, Noble & Cooley, Ohio Art, Riemann, Seabrey Co., and White Eagle Rawhide Mfg. Co.

Estelle Toy Co. released the "Little Warrior War Drum" set in the 1950s-60s.

duals Refers to the dual wheels in some farm toys, usually in the rear but sometimes on both front and rear axles.

Duban Shade Corp. Electric boats were specialties of this postwar Honeoye Falls, N.Y., firm. Its toys included "Dragonfly," "Falcon," "Swamp-Scooter," and "Sea-King."

J.A. Dubuar The 1894 air gun "Globe" was issued by J.A. Dubuar, of Northville, Michigan.

"Duchess" hoops see *The Gibbs Mfg. Co.*

"Duckart" The Toy Kraft Co. issued the "Duckart" toys in the 1930s. It also used the

"Duckie" trademark on its box cart and cradle bed.

"Ducky Doo" rocker see *The Delphos Bending Co.*

Dudley Lock Corp. A lock-making firm on West Randolph Street, Chicago, this company made mid-1930s toy vault banks with combination locks.

Duit Publishing Co. Based on Hudson Street, New York City, this publisher issued anagram and word games, and "Alpha Lotto," in the earlier 1930s.

"Duke Harry" rocking horse see *Moulded Products.*

Dumas Products In addition to powerboat models and airplane kits, Dumas made the "Roll-A-Hoop" in the postwar years. It was based in Tucson, Ariz.

Dumore Belt & Novelty Co. As did many early 20th-century leather-goods manufacturers, Dumore, located on Greene Street, New York City, made toy holster sets, cowboy outfits, cowboy chaps and vests, and police outfits, of both leather and artificial leather. In the late '30s the company added "G-Man" outfits. In the Boomer years, located on East 19th Street, it also made Indian headdresses, tomahawks, and sheath and knife sets. It used the "Indian Chief" trade name on its headdresses and Indian holster sets, and "Bronco Buster" on its cowboy sets. The company was founded in 1922.

Dun-Rite Toy Mfg. Co. A Brooklyn, N.Y., manufacturer, Du-Rite made Boomer-era doll cradles, carriages, and high chairs, as well as Easter baskets.

Donald F. Duncan, Inc. A Chicago, Ill., company, Duncan was formed in the late 1920s. The famous "Duncan Yo-Yo-Man" first appeared in 1929. Donald Duncan was introduced to the idea of the Philippine yo-yo through the displays of Pedro Flores, a yo-yo carver and performer who helped inspire the first American fad for the ages-old toy in the 1920s. By the mid-1930s, Duncan advertised making "toy specialties," premium goods, and "yo-yo tops." By late in the decade it was

using the "Hi-Li" and "Gold Seal" trade names.

This Duncan "Genuine Beginners Yo-Yo" appeared in the 1950s.

Duplex Mfg. Corp. Duplex of Sherman, N.Y., issued metal toy garages in the late 1930s.

DuPont Viscoloid Co., Inc. In the 1920s, this firm's "celluloid toys of every description" were made by Viscoloid's Pacific Novelty Division, based on Fifth Avenue, New York City. In the earlier 1930s, the Pyralin Products Department of DuPont Viscoloid, located in the Empire State Buildling, made toy animals, baby rattles and floating toys of its "Viscoloid," its name for celluloid.

Dupli-Craft Co. Based in Mountain View, Calif., Dupli-Craft issued toy duplicators and relevant supplies in the late 1930s.

The Dur-A-Bilt Co. A maker of juvenile and nursery furniture, this Brooklyn, N.Y., company made doll carriages, cradles, bassinet and swings in the 1930s and early '40s.

Durabilt Steel Locker Co. Durabilt, based in Aurora, Ill., made steel tennis tables and equipment in the earlier 1930s.

Durable Gelatin Roll & Supply Co. Located on West 17th Street, New York City, this company made the 1930s Junior Printer printing toy.

Durable Toy & Novelty Corp. The "Uncle Sam's" name was used by this firm for coin register banks from its establishment in 1907. The firm was located on Fourth Avenue, New York City, by the 1920s, moving offices to the Fifth Avenue Building in the 1930s. It issued its "Uncle Sam's" register banks in three-coin and single-coin models,

D

"Uncle Sam's" store register, and the "2-in-1" combination and savings bank. Durable also made book banks, "Radio Questionaire," electrical games, "Uncle Sam's" movie projector, and "Duracolor" films. During wartime, Durable issued an "Uncle Sam Bank," featuring a standing "Uncle Sam" figure beside the non-mechanical bank, out of "non-critical composition." The firm also issued the "Knapp Electric Questioners" during the war. "Uncle Sam's" banks remained in production in the postwar years.

The wartime non-mechanical bank by Durable Toy & Novelty Corp. featured a standing Uncle Sam and was made of "non-critical composition."

"Duracolor" films see *Durable Toy & Novelty Corp.*

Durgin & Palmer Durgin & Palmer issued the 1885 board game "Durgin's New Baseball Game."

Durham Mfg. Co. This Muncie, Ind., firm made all-metal juvenile table and chair sets in the late prewar years.

Duro Metal Products Co. Based in Chicago, Ill., Duro Metal manufactured a motor-equipped juvenile workshop.

Dutch influence see *Santa Claus, bowling games, Easter eggs, skates, sleds, Maypole, golf, tick-tack, trock.*

Dutch Novelty Shops Fittingly located in Holland, Mich., Dutch Novelty Shops made wooden shoes for dolls and wood toys in the late 1930s.

E.P. Dutton & Co. A publisher based on Fourth Avenue, New York City, Dutton issued juvenile books for all ages in the prewar years.

"Dyaltype" transformer see *American Flyer Manufacturing Co.*

"Dy-Dee Baby" In the earlier 1930s, Fleischaker & Baum offered the world its "Dy-Dee Baby." By the end of the decade, the "Dy-Dee" line had grown to include the "Dy-Dee-Ette," "Dy-Dee-Kin," "Dy-Dee Lou" and "Dy-Dee-Wee" dolls, with doll carriages, layettes, and accessories available. "Dy-Dee Baby" continued to be made through the Boomer years. By 1960 the names of the baby's friends included "Dydee Ellen" and "Dydee Jane," with "Dydee Louise" joining "Dydee Lou," and with the names of these more mature dolls being un-hyphenated. By then, too, Fleischaker & Baum had become Effanbee Doll Co.

Dyer Products Co. Dyer made the "Marble Minder" with marbles, of the mid-Boomer years. It was located in Canton, Ohio.

$2⁶⁹

A wicker doll carriage from the 1920s.

E.&L. Mfg. Co. Housecleaning and household toys were specialties of this Boomer-era Park Avenue, New York City, firm. It made carpet sweepers, brooms, sewing and embroidery sets, dishes, and nursery sets, as well as croquet and badminton equipment.

E. Metal Co. see *American Soldier Co.*

"E.P.L." see *Earnest Lehmann Co.*

"EZ" cap pistol see *The Hubley Mfg. Co.*

"E-Z-Do" Division This division of the Decorative Cabinet Corp., on Fifth Avenue, New York City, made postwar toy chests.

"E-Z Fly" kites see *Hi-Flier Mfg. Co.*

"E-Z-Fly" kites, 1920s see *George D. Wanner Co.*

E-Z Pack Bag & Cover Co. Based in Brooklyn, N.Y., in the late 1930s, E-Z pack made toy trench bags and ironing board covers.

"Eagle" air rifle see *Daisy Mfg. Co.*

Eagle Doll & Toy Co. This doll company was based on Green Street, New York City, in the mid-1930s.

Eagle Lock Co. Based in Terryville, Conn., Eagle Lock issued the late 1930s game "Screwy."

Eagle Pencil Co. This East 14th Street, New York City, firm manufactured crayon sets and pencil boxes in the late 1930s, in addition to mechanical pencils and fountain pens.

Eagle Rubber Co. One of a number of Ohio rubber manufacturing firms, Ashland's Eagle Rubber Co. made inflated and sponge balls, toy balloons, and novelty toys in the 1930s. By late in the decade it was using the "Eagletex" trade name. In the Boomer years, it manufactured a diverse line of goods

including "Eagle" brand toy balloons, inflated and sponge playballs, playground balls, and sports balls.

"Earth Invaders" figurines see *J.H. Miller Mfg. Co.*

earth mover The vehicles used for hauling dirt. As in life-size construction vehicles, the earth mover may be either a tractor-trailer mechanism or simply the earth-moving trailer. Famous toy versions include the vinyl version of the 1950s-'60s by Auburn Rubber, and the 1950s Heileiner by Doepke.

East Coast Studios Dolls and doll novelties were 1930s and '40s products of this Atlantic City, N.J., company.

Easter baskets Many manufactures of "fiber toys" and favors in the prewar years issued Easter baskets. Some postwar firms who made it a specialty included Bayshore Industries, the Beistle Co., Dun-Rite Toy Mfg. Co., Jaybar Products Co., and Living Plastic Displays.

Easter eggs The introduction of the use of Easter eggs is attributed to the Dutch. One manufacturer's name associated with the decorative food items was Belmont Industries, a postwar source of Easter egg colors.

Easter grass While not exactly a toy, Easter rabbit toys and candies in the postwar years would have been hard to imagine without the presence of artificial Easter grass. The artificial grass was a prewar tradition, with at least one manufacturer, Kuhmarker Waxed Paper Co., Inc., located on West 26th Street, New York City, having it as a specialty in the 1930s.

Eastern Moulded Products This Norwalk, Conn., firm specialized in packaged rubber toys and novelties in the Boomer years.

E.C. Eastman E.C. Eastman published the 1863 card game "The Commanders of Our Forces."

Eastman Mfg. Co., Inc. Based in Union City, Penn., this firm made juvenile and nursery furniture in the 1920s through the prewar and wartime years. In the Boomer years, specializing in juvenile desks and desk sets, it issued roll-top, flat-top and "modern" models.

"Easy-Bake Oven" see *Kenner Products Co.*

"Easymount" velocipedes see *The Frank F. Taylor Co.*

Eau Claire Cold Storage Corp. This juvenile furniture manufacturer was located in Eau Claire, Wis., in the 1930s.

Eberhard Faber Pencil Co. This famous Brooklyn, N.Y., pencil manufacturer obtained a license in the late 1930s to issue Edgar Bergen related pencil boxes and pouches.

Eberhard Faber Toy & Game Co., Inc. Based in Wilkes-Barre, Penn., with a Fifth Avenue Building showroom, Eberhard Faber made paint sets, coloring books, activity boxes, and kaleidoscopes, in addition to pencils and pencil boxes, in the Boomer years.

Victor Eckardt Mfg. Co. Besides carpenter sets and tool chests, this East 22nd Street, New York City, firm made push animals on wheels, dressed dolls, novelty doll items, and junior police outfits in the 1930s and '40s. The firm became Victor Eckardt Toy Co., Inc., by the war years, when it issued dolls, stuffed toys, and tree ornaments.

"Eclipse" croquet sets see *Garton Toy Co.*

Eclipse Game & Puzzle Co. Games and puzzles were specialties of this Chicago, Ill., company.

Econolite Corp. While novelty and juvenile animated lamps were the main products of Econolite, based in Los Angeles, Calif., in the 1950s and '60s, the company also made vinyl tub toys, play balls, and beach balls.

Ed-U-Cards Mfg. Corp. Educational games for children, with many character-related card games among them, including the "Howdy Doody Dominoes" of the mid-1950s, were familiar Ed-U-Cards products in the Boomer years. The corporation was based on Duane Street, New York City, in the 1950s, moving to Long Island City, N.Y., by the 1960s.

"Ed Wynn Fire Chief" game 1930s, see *Selchow & Righter Co.*

Eden Toys, Inc. This West 34th Street, New York City, firm made postwar infants' toys and stuffed toys.

Edison Wood Products One of a number of Wisconsin furniture makers specializing in juvenile and nursery items in the 1930s, this New London company also made toy furniture.

Edmunds-Metzel Co. see *Hafner Mfg. Co.*

Educational Block & Game Co. Based in Grand Rapids, Mich., this late 1930s firm issued lithographed blocks, including alphabet blocks.

Educational Card & Game Co. A 1920s firm, Educational Card & Game issued "Heroes of America" and "Bid-A-Word."

Educational Cards, Inc. This Detroit, Mich., firm made the "Word" rummy card game of the Boomer years.

Educational Electronics Co. Radio kits, wireless broadcast kits, electronic kits and transistor kits were specialties of this Chicago, Ill., company.

Educational Films Corp. of America Based on Rockefeller Plaza, New York City, in the late 1930s, Educational Films made "Film Featurettes" for 8 mm. projectors.

Educational Laboratories A Denver, Colo., firm, Educational Laboratories made target games and "anteriums" in the late 1930s.

Educational Laboratories Located in Elmhurst, Ill., this late 1930s firm made "Air Pressure" laboratory sets.

"Educational Letters" see *The A.I. Root Co.*

Educational Products This Chicago, Ill., firm made junior photography outfits in the late 1930s.

Educational Products, Inc. Tether tennis, pogo sticks and stilts were among the outdoor childhood sporting goods made by this firm in the 1950s and '60s. Based in Newark, N.J., the company also made playground equipment.

educational toys Manufacturers grew increasingly interested in the educational value of toys through the later 19th century, especially through the efforts of such conscientious souls as Milton Bradley. By the early 20th century, companies who expressly included "educational toys" in their lines included American Mfg. Concern, Baumgarten & Co., H.E. Boucher Mfg. Co., Milton Bradley Co., N.D. Cass Co., M. Carlton Dank Toy Corp., the Embossing Co., Geographic Educator Coirp., Ideal Book Builders, "Lincoln Logs," Meccano Co., Parker Bros., Porter Chemical Co., the A.I. Root Co., Scott Mfg. Co., Transogram Co., and Waldorf Toy Corp.

"Educator" blocks see *Kupper-Heidt Mfg. Co.*; postwar, see *Blockraft Mfg. Co.*

Educator Playthings, Inc. This Laingsburg, Mich., company made play houses, doll beds, blocks, and child-size plywood kitchen appliances in the 1950s and '60s.

"Educraft" line see *Martini Artists Color Laboratories.*

Bernard Edward Mfg. Co. Located on West Randolph Street, Chicago, this company made pantograph drawing boards in the mid-1930s.

The Edwards Mfg. Co. "Whippet Derby" racing games in board, metal, and felt were issued in the 1930s by Edwards, of Cincinnati, Ohio.

"Eegee" dolls see *E. Goldberger.*

Effanbee Doll Co., Inc. Based in the Fifth Avenue Building in the Boomer years, Effanbee made the "Dy-Dee" dolls, trousseau sets, and accessories, as well as "The Most Happy Family," "My Fair Baby," "Mickey Boy" dolls, and "Mary Jane," "Twinkie," "Sweetie Pie" dolls. The firm also made "Fluffy" and "Tiny Tubber" vinyl miniatures, soft dolls, and novelties. See *Fleischaker & Baum.*

"Effanbee Durable Dolls" "Effanbee" was a line from doll-makers Fleischaker & Baum, popular by the 1920s. Hit items of the line in the prewar years included "Dy-Dee Baby," "Patsy" dolls, and "Patsy" nurse and doctor kits.

"Eggbert" pre-school toys see *Strombeck-Becker Mfg. Co.*

Einson-Freeman Co. Einson-Freeman Co.'s products made up a line of cheaper toys and games, sold in the ten- to 25-cent range, which were offered alongside the products of Stoll & Einson, which produced items in the 50-cent to dollar range. The "Funland Books and Games" were Einson-Freeman's, while "Playjoy Books and Games" were Stoll & Einson's. Einson-Freeman also made "Par-T" masks based on cartoon and movie characters. The executive office for the two companies was in Long Island City, N.Y.

The firm's games included "Dick Tracy Detective Game" and "Three Little Pigs Game" in 1933, "Star Ride" in 1934, "Electric Baseball," "Pioneers of the Santa Fe Trail," "The Game of Socko the Monk" and "Tom Sawyer on the Mississippi" in 1935, and "Stop & Go" in 1936.

The Elastic Tip Co. Elastic Tip issued its "pistol game which is absolutely harmless" in the 1920s and '30s. The pistols, which shot suction-cup darts, came with targets lithographed in red, white and blue. A Boston, Mass., manufacturer, Elastic Tip continued making its "vacuum tipped pistols" into the mid-1930s.

elastolin Elastolin is a kind of composition material manufactured in Germany, molded around wire supports. The toys tend to have a poor survival rate.

"Elastolin" The "Elastolin" line from Germany was imported and distributed by Block House in the 1920s and '30s.

The Eldae Co. Indoor kiddie tents were late 1930s products of this Detroit, Mich., firm.

Eldon Mfg. Co. This Los Angeles, Calif., company manufactured Boomer-era polyethylene toys, including vehicle toys, and beach toys.

"Eldredgette" sewing machine see *National Sewing Machine Co.*

Electric Eye Co. The "Electric Eye Kit" was the leading product of this Park Row, New York City, company in the mid-1930s. The company also made checkerboards.

Electric Game Co., Inc. Based in Holyoke, Mass., Electric Game Co. made electric baseball and football games and the "Electroquest" electric test game in the mid-1930s. Lead titles included the "Quest-O-Light" electric question-and-answer game and "Electric Bridge" in the late '30s. The firm's line included football, baseball, basketball and hockey electric games by the war years. Later products included the battery-operated "Electric Brainstorm Beanie," introduced in 1955, and "Electric Build-It" and "Electric Jack Straws." The firm continued into the 1960s.

The "Electric Baseball" game of the 1950s was produced, fittingly, by the Electric Game Co., Inc.

"Electric Questioner" see *Knapp Electric, Inc.;* postwar, see *Jacmar Mfg. Co.*

electric toys In the early 20th century, toy manufacturers increasingly embraced the possibilities offered by electricity and electrical motors, using the power source for everything from toy car headlights to buzzers in question-and-answer games. Undoubtedly the most famous electric toys were the trains made by such companies as American Flyer Mfg. Co., the Dorfan Co., and the Lionel Corp. Other manufacturers active by the late 1920s included Knapp Electric and Metal Ware Corp.

Many other companies explored electricity as a means of enhancing or even making possible new toys. Some announced their new specialty in their names: Adco Electric Mfg. Co., American Electric Toy & Novelty Co., Connecticut Telephone & Electric Corp., Delta Electric Co., Electric Eye Co., Electric Game Co., Signal Electric Mfg. Co., and Western Coil & Electrical Co.

Other prewar manufacturers of electric toys included Beco Mfg. Co., Boucher Playthings Mfg. Corp., Diamond Toy Co., the Dover Mfg. Co., Elmwood Button Co., the Excel Mfg. Corp., M.M. Fleron & Son, A.C. Gilbert Co., the Gong Bell Mfg. Co., Kingston Products Corp., Leland-Detroit Mfg. Co., Mantua Toy & Metal Products Co., E.K. Manuel & Co., National Company, A.G. Redmond Co., John P. Ryan Co., Tucker Toys, and Woodhaven Metal Stamping Co.

In the postwar years, companies included Bell Products Co., Brumberger Sales Corp., Cadaco-Ellis, Chester Tool Co., R.E. Dietz Co., Educational Electronics Co., Electric Game Co., Irwin Corp., Jacmar Mfg. Co., Keystone Ferrule & Nut Co., Kilgore, Kohner Bros., Fred Kross Associates, Maco Toys, Louis Marx & Co., Metal Ware Corp., Ny-Lint Tool & Mfg. Co., Remco Industries, Structo Mfg. Co., Tigrett Industries, Toytronic Development Co., Western Coil & Electrical Co., and Woodhaven Metal Stamping Co.

Tudor Metal Products Corp. made the "Electric Horse Race Game" in the 1960s.

"Elf" books see *Rand, McNally & Co.*

"Elfago Baca" The Walt Disney character Elfago Baca inspired such playthings as a "Shootin' Outfit" and holster sets by Daisy Mfg. Co., and hats by Benay-Albee Novelty Co., in the late 1950s and '60s.

Elgo Plastics, Inc. Elgo was maker of the plastic "Skyline" construction sets for Halsam in the 1950s and '60s.

Elgo Rubber Products Co. This Philadelphia, Penn., company manufactured Boomer-years rubber quoits.

Elite Creations, Inc. Based in Long Island City, N.Y., Elite creations made Boomer-era miniature and vinyl dolls.

Elka Toys Stuffed toy animals of plush and fur were postwar products of this West 24th Street, New York City, company.

Elkay Mfg. Corp. Elkay, located in the Fifth Avenue Building, issued the "Speed Clock" toy speedometer and "Postal Telegraph Jr." in the late 1930s. It also manufactured phonographs, telephones, and model airplane kits. In the Boomer years it issued magnetic toys and the "Tri-Signal" telegraph set.

Leigh A. Elkington Musical toys including whistles, fifes and flageolets were made by this prewar East 34th Street, New York City, firm. In the postwar years, based on Park Avenue and using the name L.A. Elkington, its line also included megaphones, castanets, brass finger cymbals, batons, and other musical items.

The Elkloid Co. Elkloid, of Providence, R.I., made dice, dominoes, poker chips and games in the 1930s and '40s.

Ellanee Doll Co. This postwar doll manufacturer was based in Brooklyn, N.Y.

Ellenville Wood Novelty Co. This Ellenville, N.Y., company made "rustic novelties," including toys, in the 1930s and '40s.

Elliott & Evans, Inc. The "Lady-Like" line of play fashions for children were postwar specialties of this Fort Lauderdale, Fla. company.

Elliot, Greene & Co., Inc. This West 37th Street, New York City, firm manufactured looms for making beaded articles, in the late 1930s.

C.C. Elliotte Corp. The unusual "Loco-Beel," a locomotive scooter, was made by this Richmand, Va., corporation in the mid-1930s.

Ellis, Britton & Eaton Established in 1859 in Springfield, Vt., this firm made baby carriages and perambulators. The firm was soon better known for the name of its manufacturing plant. See the **Vermont Novelty Works.**

Ellis, Joel T.A. The senior partner in the 1859 firm of Ellis, Britton & Eaton, Joel Ellis provided much of the invention behind the company's success. Among his innovations was the "tumbling barrel," a large drum turned by a belt. Filled with small wooden pieces needed for carriages or toys, the slow tumbling replaced hand sanding. In 1873 he patented a doll joint and formed a separate company to manufacture dolls. The hard-maple doll had mortise and tenon joints, which allowed arms and legs to be fixed in different positions. The head was wooden, shaped in steel molds with steam and pressure, while the hands and feet were metal. The doll sold poorly, possibly due to the depression that year. Joel Ellis died in 1888. See also **Vermont Novelty Works,** and **Mason & Taylor.**

Elm City Toy Mfg. Co. Juvenile printing presses were manufactured in the late 1930s by this New Haven, Conn., company.

Elmar Products Co. Plastic action toys, tops, bubble pipes, and novelties comprised this 1950s-60s line. It included spring-powered racecars. The firm was based on West 24th Street, New York City.

Jerry Elsner Co., Inc. Elsner, based on Brook Avenue, New York City, in the Boomer years, specialized in fur toys and novelties.

The Elmberg Co. One of many prewar Wisconsin specialists in juvenile furniture, Elmberg also made juvenile tool chests and

E

wood toys and novelties in the 1920s and earlier 1930s.

Elmwood Button Co. A Stratford, Conn., company, Elmwood made the "Radio Rex" battery-operated toy in the mid-1930s.

"Elsie the Cow" The Borden's advertising figure of "Elsie the Cow" was featured in several toy and plaything forms, including sand pails by Sollmann & Whitcomb, and coloring books by the Saalfield Publishing Co.

Elssler, Fanny In the 1840s, popular paper dolls based on this famous ballerina were imported from Europe.

"Elvis Presley" The popular 1950s and '60s rock singer gave the inspiration for playthings including toy guitars by Emenee Industries, and hats by Magnet Hat & Cap Co.

Theodore J. Ely Mfg. Co. Based in Girard, Penn., Ely manufactured steel and mechanical toys in the 1930s. By the postwar years it was specializing in toy pianos, toy chests, and musical novelties, as well as corkboards and green chalkboards.

"Em-Gee" see *Molly-'Es Doll Outfitters, Inc.*

"Embeco," see *Milton Bradley Co.*

Embee Distributing Embee issued "Bringing Up Father Game," a 1920 board game.

Emblem Mfg. Co. A bicycle manufacturer, Emblem issued bikes under the "Emblem," "Pierce," "Greyhound," and "Speedwell" trade names, as well as velocipedes and sidewalk bicycles. It was based in Angola, N.Y., in the 1930s and '40s.

embossed Having raised or indented features, as in the raised grill of a tin tractor, or raised trade name on hubcaps on a pressed-steel truck.

The Embossing Co. In the 1920s, the Embossing Co. of Albany, N.Y., established itself with a line of checkers, dominoes, house building blocks, "Wonderwood" flowers, construction sets, "Transit" toys, doll furniture, and "Everedy Modelling Material." Its line of blocks included "Toy Blocks," "Sta-built Blocks," "Color Cubes," "Designing Sets," and "Home Building Blocks." In 1929, on the verge of the Great Depression, the company expanded its line with new ABC blocks, "Modern Educational Blocks," "Prism Color Sets," and games.

In the 1930s, Embossing made "Sky-Hy" blocks, "Ensign" blocks, house-building blocks, and other construction toys. The company divided its goods between "Toys that Teach" and games and puzzles for adults. It also continued making modeling outfits, wooden pull toys, dominoes, anagrams, puzzles, games, designing sets, checkers, and spelling boards in the prewar years.

Its titles included the board games "Flapper Fortunes," "Neck and Neck," "Tit-Tat-Toe," and a "Vest Pocket Checker" set in 1929, "Bottoms Up" in 1934, "Frisko" in 1937, and "Anex-A-Gram" in 1938. 1940s titles included "Jack-Be-Nimble" and "Sniff."

In the war years, the firm was able to continue a line of educational toys, embossed alphabet and animal blocks, dominoes, checkers, and game kits. The Embossing Co. became a part of Halsam Products Co. in the 1950s.

The Embossing Co.'s logo from the 1920s.

Embree Mfg. Co. Based in Elizabeth, N.J., Embree manufactured "Kopeefun Kit," which was a toy book with "magic copying paper," as well as tap-dancing dolls and wooden toys in the late 1930s. The "Kopeefun" kits continued in popularity into the Boomer years.

embroidery and sewing sets Activity toys and sets have played an important part in most childhoods. Many were designed with heuristic goals in mind, none more so than the embroidery and sewing sets that helped teach children needlecraft. While the line becomes blurred between what is a toy and what is a home craft, many toy manufacturers, including such prominent ones as Milton Bradley Co. and Parker Bros., were actively involved in the production of these kits. Because of the nature of the designs the children worked on, both kits and the finished products have appeal to collectors.

In the 1920s, companies producing sets included American Toy Works, Parker Bros., Katherine A. Rauser, Standard Solophone Mfg. Co., Transogram Co., Ullman Mfg. Co., and Theodore Yonkers.

Manufacturers by the earlier 1930s included American Toy Works, Bouton-Woolf Co., Collingbourne Mills, B.R. Cromien, Makatoy Co., the Massillon Wire Basket Co., Minerva Toy Co., Jack Pressman & Co., J.W. Spear & Sons, Standard Toykraft Products, Transogram, Ullman, and Universal Toy & Novelty Mfg. Co.

Emenee Industries, Inc. Emenee billed itself as the world's largest manufacturer of musical toys and instruments, in the Boomer years. Some of its lead items were character related, as in the "Gene Autry Cowboy Guitar with Automatic Player" and "Arthur Godfrey Uke Player with Flamingo Ukulele," of 1955. The firm used the words "Golden" and "Silver" in its names, although the instruments were plastic. It was based in the Fifth Avenue Building.

Emerson Mfg. Co. Based in Hooksett, N.H., Emerson was a prewar maker of juvenile desks and "novelty furniture."

Emerson Radio & Phonograph Corp. The "Mickey Mouse" midget radio of the mid-'30s was made by this Eighth Avenue, New York City, corporation.

Emerson-Steuben Corp. This Brooklyn, N.Y., firm made prewar dolls and novelties.

Emmert-Hammes & Co. Based in Warren, Mich., Emmert-Hammes made the "Flyin' Fool" all-aluminum flying airplanes, airplane kits, gliders, and mechanical boats in the later 1930s. The items were priced 10 cents to $1.95.

Empay Corp. Located on Lafayette Street, New York City, Empay made metal toys and games in the 1930s.

"Empeco" toys, see *Metal Package Corp.*

"Empire" bicycles see *Steinfeld, Inc.*

Empire City Toy & Novelty Co. "Fur stuffed toys" were made from the 1930s through the Boomer years by Empire City. Based on West 27th Street, New York City, before the war, it was located on West 25th Street in the postwar years.

Empire Doll Co. Empire Doll Co. was based in Brooklyn, N.Y., in the 1950s and '60s.

"Empire" electric accessory toys see *The Metal Ware corp.*

"Empire" pencils see *Hassenfeld Bros.*

Empire Plastic Corp. Empire Plastic's toys included polyethylene riding toys for younger children, including bus and tractor ride-ons. It also made dart games, water guns, and sports sets. The firm was based in Pelham Manor, N.Y.

"Empire" steam engines see *The Metal Ware Corp.*

"Empress" toys see *M. Pressner & Co.*

"End of Day" Glass marbles with only a single pontil mark are called "End of Day" marbles.

"Enduro" crayons see *Standard Crayon Mfg. Co.*

Engineering Service Corp. In addition to weaving sets and art metal giftware, this Albany, N.Y., corporation made prewar celluloid puzzle novelties.

engines, toy The production of toy engines became important in the early 20th century. Weeden Mfg. Co. and Metal Ware Corp. were making steam and electric engines by the end of the 1920s. In the 1930s, manufacturers included American Toy Airship Co., Boucher Playthings Mfg. Corp., the Kenton Hardware Co., Knapp Electric, Richard Maerklin Toys, the Metal Ware, and Weeden. The firms A.B.C. Products, American Electrical Products Co., Jensen Mfg. Co., and Marion Electrical Mfg. Co. joined their ranks by the late prewar years. Two of these firms, Jensen and Metal Ware, were still actively producing toy steam engines by the mid-Boomer years.

Postwar manufacturers of steam engines included Jensen Mfg. Co. and the Metal Ware Corp. Manufacturers producing gas engines included K. & B. Allyn Co., L.M. Cox Mfg. Co., Frazier Model Engineering Laboratories, Herkimer Tool & Model Works, Polk's Model Craft Hobbies, the Testor Corp., and Wen-Mac Corp.

enigmatical cards "Enigmatical cards" was an early 1800s term for what seem to have been "trivia" or question-and-answer cards. See *card games.*

Enos-Leonard Mfg. Co. The "Bala-roo" game was the leading mid-1930s product of this Wakefield, Mass., company. Besides games it also issued wooden toys and novelties.

"Ensign Blocks" see *The Embossing Co.*

Enterprise Model Aircraft & Supply Co., Inc. Model airplanes were the postwar specialty of this Mineola, N.Y., company.

Samuel Eppy & Co., Inc. Eppy made plastic charms and charm postcards in the 1950s and '60s. The Jamaica, N.Y., firm also made candy lollipops.

Equitable Paper A specialist in "holiday surprise bags," Equitable was based in Long Island City, N.Y. The firm concentrated on Halloween and Christmas.

"Erector" construction sets see *A.C. Gilbert Co.*

Ero Mfg. Co. Located on West Monroe Street, Chicago, Ill., Ero produced leatherette stuffed animals and dolls.

The Ertl Co., Inc. Founded in Dubuque, Iowa, by unemployed foundry worker Fred Ertl, Sr., the Ertl Co. began in 1945 as a family business. Ertl had learned sand-casting techniques in Germany. His son, Fred Ertl, Jr., began actively managing the company as early as 1948. The firm moved to Dyersville, Iowa, and grew to become the premiere 20th-century manufacturer of toy farm equipment, which it based on the original blueprints for machinery and vehicles built by such companies as John Deere and International Harvester. In the post-Boomer years, Ertl manufactured die-cast promotional toy banks based on vintage model vehicles. Fred Ertl, Jr., was also instrumental in the effort to establish toy safety standards within the industry.

Eska Eska, based in Dubuque, Iowa, made chain-drive juvenile tractors and farm equipment in the 1950s and '60s. Its materials included cast aluminum.

"Eskimo" The "Eskimo" trademark was used by several prewar companies. Garton Toy Co. used it for steering sleds, while United Electric Mfg. Co. used it for motorized jigsaws and vacuum cleaner toys.

Esquire Novelty Corp. The "Pony Boy" cap pistol of the 1950s and subsequent decades was manufactured by this Jersey City, N.J., firm. Esquire also made "Wells Fargo," "Restless Gun," "Shotgun Slade," "Black Pirate," "Rin Tin Tin," "Lone Ranger," and "Tonto" guns, rifles, holsters, and Western accessories. The company was purchased in the early 1970s by Strombecker Corp.

Essay Mfg. Co., Inc. Toys, games and novelties were postwar products of this Quincy, Mass., company.

Essenel Co. The "Daintie Doll" and wooden toys were made in the 1930s and '40s by this Providence, R.I., firm.

Essex Rubber Co. Based in Trenton, N.J., Essex produced rubber quoits, playballs, and swimming tubes in the 1930s and '40s.

Estelle Toy Co. Vital ingredients for cowboy-and-Indian playtime, tom-tom drums "Injun" feathered headdresses, and play tents were made by this Honeoye Falls, N.Y., company in the 1950s and '60s.

"Little Brave Tom-Toms" from Estelle Toy Co., 1950s-60s.

E. B. Estes Starting in 1847, E.B. Estes established wood-turning plants in Maine, New Hampshire, Vermont, Massachusetts, New York, and Pennsylvania. Estes made wooden dumbbells, baseball bats, croquet sets, Indian clubs, toy clothespins, polo and hockey sticks, and toy cart wheels, continuing in business into the 20th century.

Estes Industries Based in Penrose, Colo., Estes established itself in the 1960s in the field of working model rockets, developing a line of nearly 50 rocket kits by the end of the decade. In 1969 the company merged with Damon Engineering of Needham Heights, Mass., which expanded the Estes line into scientific educational products. One of Estes' kits produced the "Camroc," which took a photo from the air before returning to the ground.

Estey Organ Corp. In the late 1930s, this Brattleboro, Vt., firm made miniature reed organs for the juvenile market.

Eugene Doll & Novelty Co. This doll manufacturer was based in the Fifth Avenue Building in the Boomer years.

Eureka Doll Mfg. Co. This manufacturer of the "Eureka Dolls" of the 1920s and '30s was located on West Houston Street, New York City.

Eureka Mfg. Co. see *American Soldier Co.*

Eureka Mfg. Co., Inc. Eureka's postwar specialties were flannel Christmas stockings and "Santa Pak" bags. It was located in Taunton, Mass.

European Doll Mfg. Co. A Doll District firm, European issued character dolls, felt dolls, infant dolls, pillow dolls, mama dolls, and flapper dolls in the 1920s. Anita Novelty Co. was a subsidiary.

Evans and Liddle, Inc. Manufacturer of toy brooms, this Evans and Liddle was located in Lockport, N.Y., in the 1930s and '40s.

S.W. Evans & Son Play equipment including the "Evans Roll-E-Coaster" and see-saw were Boomer-years products of this Philadelphia, Penn., company.

Evans Doll Mfg. Co. This doll maker was located on East 4th Street, New York City, in the late 1930s.

Evans Products Co. The "Evans" velocipedes and bicycles of the 1950s and '60s were made by this Plymouth, Mich., company.

Evansville/C-K-R Division Evansville/C-K-R, a division of the American Fork & Hoe Co., issued juvenile garden sets, snow shovels, and sand shovels, in the late 1930s. It was based in Cleveland, Ohio.

"Everbest" Christmas stockings see *Thanhauser, S.*

"Everbrite" Christmas decorations see the *Carpenter Mfg. Co.*

"Everdur" see *Schavoir Rubber Co.*

Everest Mfg. Co. Musical toys and games were postwar products of this Linden, N.J., company.

Everlast Toy Co. Based in Tacoma, Wash., Everlast made juvenile furniture and wooden toys in the 1930s and '40s.

"Evergleam" aluminum Christmas trees see *Aluminum Specialty Co.*

The Everwear Mfg. Co. The prewar, mid-1930s "Happy Time" play apparatus for home use was made by this Springfield,

E

Ohio, firm. The postwar "Happi Time" toys are not related.

Excel Leather Mfg. Co. Based on West 19th Street, New York City, Excel made footballs and sporting goods in the later 1930s.

Excel Mfg. Corp. A Muncie, Ind., corporation, Excel made toy electric toasters and toy drawing boards in the mid-1930s.

Excel Projector Corp. Excel Projector, based in Chicago, Ill., issued 16mm and 8mm projectors and screens in the late 1930s.

Excel Specialty Co. Maker of the mid-1930s "Buckin' Bronk" hobbyhorse, Excel Specialty was located on East 44th Street, New York City.

"Excelloid" dolls and toys see *George Borgfeldt Corp.*

Excelsior Mfg. Co., Inc. A prewar manufacturer of bicycles, sidewalk bicycles, and exercisers, Excelsior was based in Michigan City, Ind.

Exclusive Movie Studios, Inc. This Chicago, Ill., company issued 16mm and 8mm films and projectors in the late 1930s.

"Exclusive Right" toys mid-1930s, see the *Hubley Mfg. Co.*

exercisers In the later 19th and earlier 20th centuries, exercisers were items designed to keep young children active. As often as not they were some variation on the hobby or spring horse. Prewar manufacturers included the American National Co., Appleton Toy & Furniture Co., Cameo Doll Co., Excel Specialty Co., Gordon Toy & Mfg.

Co., Kiddie Gym, Lloyd Mfg. Co., Pines Winterfront Co., the Republic Toy Products Co., and the A. Schoenhut Co. See *spring horse.*

Expert Doll & Toy Co. Expert, on West 22nd Street, New York City, made prewar "stuffed animals of all descriptions." The "Wagglers" of the late 1930s were toy animals with a concealed wire trigger that made the toys' heads and legs move when held up. Based on West 21st Street in the Boomer years, Expert specialized in popular-priced Easter novelties, rabbits, bears, and dogs.

Exposition Doll & Toy Mfg. Co. Located on Wooster Street, New York City, Exposition was a doll manufacturer.

express wagons see *wagons, coaster and express.*

eyes, doll and animal Many collectors of early dolls and stuffed animals faced considerable difficulties in identifying their finds, hampered by the absence of identifying tags and the rarity of original catalogs. Oftentimes they will compare characteristics between known and unknown items, in hopes of making educated guesses as to provenance. An additional difficulty faces such collectors: manufacturers bought many parts ready-made, including doll heads, faces, hair, teeth, wigs, shoes, hands, arms, feet, legs, and even bodies. Eyes for dolls and toy animals were a specialty of a number of companies by the prewar years. Manufacturers included C. Luthard of Brooklyn, N.Y., Marks Bros. Co., Margon Corp., Karl Ohlbaum & Son, G. Schoepfer, and J.W. Schoepfer.

The Embossing Co. logo, 1940s.

F.L. Doll Co. This prewar doll company was based on Cherry Street, New York City, in the mid-1930s.

F.M. Engineering Co., Inc. This Minneapolis, Minn., firm made mechanical toys, including the "Moby Dick" mechanical whale, in the 1950s and '60s.

F.P.I., Inc. A postwar Providence, R.I., manufacturer of novelty blackboards and magnetic boards, F.P.I. also made wood and metal animal and figural toys, and games.

Fable Toy Co. Based in Brooklyn, N.Y., Fable Toy made stuffed toys and novelties in the Boomer years.

factory mint As a collector's term, "factory mint" reflects the fact that toys sometimes emerged from the factory with flaws. Often packed loose in boxes, or sold loose in bins at dime stores, new toys might not emerge "mint," but might safely be described as "factory mint." It is a forgiving term.

Fair-Craft Corp. This Boomer-years West Haven, Conn., firm made juvenile autos and midget cars, as well as kits and parts for building motorized and coaster cars for children.

"Fairblox" construction blocks see *Ideal Products Corp.*

E.E. Fairchild Corp. "All-Fair," E.E. Fairchild's brand name, was famous in the toy world from 1926 through the prewar and postwar years. Based in Churchville, then Rochester, N.Y., Fairchild made games, puzzles, action wood pull toys, and premium merchandise. Its slogan, "Our Work is Child's Play," was later purchased for use by Fisher-Price Toys.

In the Boomer years the corporation continued its focus on picture puzzles for children and adults, children's card games, checkers and checkerboards, bingo, board games and "poly bagged" rack items.

The firm's games included 1920s titles "Fortune Telling," "Mumbly Peg," and "Strike-Out." "X-Plor-US" appeared in 1922; "Tutoom, Journey to the Treasures of Pharaoh," in 1923; "Auto Race Jr." and "Toonin Radio Game," in 1925; "Animal & Bird Lotto," "Match 'Em," "Witzi-Wits," and "Game of the World Flyers," in 1926; "The Way to the White House," in 1927; "Hi-Way Henry" and "Stop and Go," in 1928; and "The Capital Cities Air Derby," "Speedem Junior Auto Race Game," and "Tip the Bellboy," in 1929. The titles "Baseball Game," "Our Gang Tipple Topple Game," and "Stop and Shop" appeared in 1930; "Bean-Em," "Busto," "Flap Jacks," "Glydor," "Jav-Lin," "Sky Hawks," and "Watch on De Rind," in 1931; "Bow-O-Winks," "Cities," "Dim Those Lights," "Jaunty Butler," and "Simba," in 1932; "WPA—Work, Progress, Action," in 1935; "Buck Rogers in the 25th Century" and "Skippy, a Card Game," in 1936; "Frank Buck's Bring 'Em Back Alive Game," in 1937; and "Patch Word," in 1938. "Ko-Ko the Clown," "Monkey Shines," and "Treasure Hunt appeared in 1940, and "Cargo for Victory" and "Game of International Spy," in 1943.

"Tip the Bellboy" was a 1929 game by E.E. Fairchild.

Fairchild's "Way to the Whitehouse" game made its debut in 1927.

Fairfield Novelties, Inc. A prewar maker of soft stuffed dolls, stuffed novelties, and lithographed stuffed dolls, Fairfield was based in Atlantic City, N.J. In the later 1930s it changed its name to Fairfield Products Corp.

Fairway Novelty Co. Located on East 18th Street, New York City, Fairway Novelty made plush animals and stuffed toys in the late prewar years.

"Fairy Craft" speed boats see *Shoe Form Co., Inc.*

"Fairy Land" picture puzzles prewar, see *Parker Bros., Inc.*

"Fairy Princess" doll furniture prewar, see *American Crayon Co.*

"Fairy" vehicles see *The Colson Co.*

"Fairyland" cooking sets see *Aluminum Goods Mfg. Co.*

Fairyland Toy Co. Stuffed plush animal toys were specialties of this postwar Minneapolis, Minn., company.

Fairyland Toy Products, Inc. Based in the Fifth Avenue Building, Fairyland was a postwar source of doll shoes.

Faith Mfg. Co. A manufacturer of "trophy ash receivers," this North Crawford Avenue, Chicago, Ill., company also made miniature autos in the 1930s.

"Falcon" "Falcon" was a widely used prewar trademark. American Mfg. Concern used it with its "Falcon Toys That Last" trademark

and motto, and its "Falcon Buddy" snow skates. "Falcon" cameras were made by Utility Mfg. Co., and the "Falcon" tri-motor plane vehicle was made by Toledo Metal Wheel Co.

Falcon Model Airplane Co. Based in Portland, Ore., Falcon made model airplane construction sets and supplies in the 1930s.

false faces The prewar toy industry sometimes used the term "false faces" for masks.

Family Fun Kit Co. The "Family Fun Kits" of the 1950s and '60s were made by this Alderwood Manor, Wash., company.

Famous Keystone Kits Corp. Juvenile tool sets and toy fishing sets were among this Chicago, Ill., company's products in the Boomer years. It also made badminton sets.

Famous Products Corp. Based in Wilmington, Del., Famous Products made the "Hockey-Skate-Coaster" in the late 1930s.

Fan Craze Publishers of card games, Fan Craze issued the 1904 "Fan Craze Card Game" and "American League" game.

farm sets Sets of toys or paper cutouts meant to represent life on the farm in miniature must have existed in the 19th century. By prewar times several manufacturers were involved in making arrangements of figure, vehicle, and animal toys to evoke the rural scene. Prominent among them were Acme Toy & Novelty Co., Arcade Mfg. Co., Hansen Wood Goods & Toy Mfg. Co., Holgate Bros. Co., the E.M. Nichols Co., Strombeck-Becker Mfg. Co., and J.L. Wright, Inc.

Arcade and Wright remained active in the area into the late prewar years. Chick Toys, the E.M. Nichols Co., Herman Grunow, Remotrol Co., Valley Novelty Works, and Warren Paper Products were also manufacturing farm sets at the time.

The height of farm-set manufacture came in the Boomer years from the Louis Marx Co. from the 1950s through the '70s. Marx issued complex sets with tin barns, silos, and sheds, and plastic people, animals, fences, tools, and vehicles. Auburn Rubber Co., the Ohio Art

Co., and other manufacturers of rubber and plastic goods also issued noteworthy farm sets in the postwar years.

They included Allison Studios, Milton Bradley Co., Built-Rite Toys, Carter Tru-Scale Machine Co., Dowst Mfg. Co., the Hubley Mfg. Co., Lansing Co., Lee Aluminum Foundry & Mfg. Co., Multiple Products Corp., Tonka Toys, and Webo Toys.

These popular farm animals from Ohio Art Co. were first issued in the 1950s.

Farmer Electric Maps

Farmer Electric Maps This Washington, D.C., firm manufactured electric map and picture map games in the late prewar years.

J.K. Farnell & Co., Ltd.

J.K. Farnell & Co., Ltd. This London, England, manufacturer issued the "Alpha" soft toys available in America in the 1920s.

fashion doll

fashion doll see *dolls, fashion.*

fast hitch

fast hitch In farm toys, this identifies a tractor-implement hitching system which involved two attachment points, instead of the usual one. The term was introduced by International Harvester. The system was popular in the '50s.

The Faultless Rubber Co.

The Faultless Rubber Co. One of many Ohio rubber companies in the 1930s, Faultless, based in Ashland, made a wide variety of balls for sports as well as balloons and novelties. By the late prewar years its categories had grown: "Balls - croquet, golf, baseballs, dog, tennis and playground balls, sponge balls, jack and return balls, valve balls, inflated play balls; sponge rubber blocks, rubber novelties of all kinds." It continued issuing balls and ball games through the Boomer years.

favors and souvenirs

favors and souvenirs On the whole, due to their usual low quality and the difficulty of attributing manufacture, party favors and souvenirs tend to be of limited interest to collectors of toys and general childhood items. Significant exceptions, however, can be found among the tin favors, noisemakers, clickers and horns, especially as made by such quality manufacturers as the Kirchhof Patent Co. Collectors also take keen interest in almost anything manufactured by Dowst Mfg. Co., who produced both tin and die-cast items used as premiums, favors and, undoubtedly, souvenirs. Even the famous Arcade Mfg. Co. of Freeport, Ill., was involved in the production of favors and souvenirs.

Companies active in the earlier 20th century included Adler Favor & Novelty Co., Langfelder, Homma & Hayward, Max Schnetter & Co., and B. Shackman & Co.

In the prewar years, manufacturers included S.S. Adams Co., Adler Favor & Novelty, American Merri-Lei Corp., Bankograph Co., Bernhard Paper Favor Co., Blue Bird Favor Co., the Clever Idea Paper Novelty Co., the A.A. Faxon Co., H. Fishlove & Co., Gordon Novelty Co., International Souvenir & Import Co., Kashner Novelty Corp., Oscar Leistner, Marks Bros., Theodore Metzeler, Newton & Thompson, Rainbo Paper Favor Works, C.A. Reed Co., Russell-Hampton, St. Louis Confetti Co., the Seiss Mfg. Co., B. Shackman & Co., Sydnawey Co., United Pressed Products Co., Van Housen's Favor Co., and W. & F. Mfg. Co.

The Faxon, A.A., Co.

The Faxon, A.A., Co. Halloween items were among the goods produced by the A.A. Faxon Co. of Philadelphia, Penn. The company also made carnival goods and horns.

"Featherweight Toys"

"Featherweight Toys" see *F.W. Woolnough Corp.*

Feature Games

Feature Games This postwar games company was based in Cedar Rapids, Iowa.

Federal Screen & Weatherstrip Mfg.

Federal Screen & Weatherstrip Mfg. The 1930s "Playball" baseball game was made by this Cleveland, Ohio, manufacturer.

The Federal Rubber Co. A firm based in Cudahy, Wis., in the 1920s, Federal manufactured "High-Grade" brand tires for juvenile vehicles, rubber pedals, and white tubing.

Federal Stamping and Engineering Corp. Making activity sets for more technical-minded youth, this prewar Brooklyn, N.Y., company made the "Grapho-Scope" sketching device and radio crystal sets. By the late 1930s the company had added the "Jecta-Scope" sketching device, "Micro Science-Scope" projecting microscope, and microphones.

The "Grapho-Scope" sketching toy from Federal Stamping and Engineering Corp.

Federal Toy Co. see *American Toy Co.*

"Federal" wax crayons see *Standard Crayon Mfg. Co.*

"Feedme" animals see *Commonwealth Toy & Novelty Co.*

Feinberg-Henry Mfg. Co. Part of New York City's 1930s leather goods industry, this West 23rd Street company made holster sets and novelties at mid-decade, adding ranch outfits and cowboy suits by the late prewar years. In the late '30s it produced "Lone Ranger" outfits, watch fobs, hats, wallets, and pistol holster sets. The firm continued its toy line into the war years, with "Gene Autry" gun and holster sets, "Lone Ranger" play suits, and "U.S. Army" and "U.S. Marine" outfits.

Felder Bros., Inc. Based on Broadway, New York City, in the mid-1930s, Felder Bros. made pistol holster sets and leather novelties.

"Felix-the-Cat" A widely popular prewar animated cartoon figure, "Felix-the-Cat" appeared in a variety of toy forms. George Borgfeldt Corp. made toys and dolls; McLoughlin Bros., crayon and paint books; and E. Simon's Sons, masquerade costumes. Gund Mfg. Co. also made a "Felix Movie Cat" stuffed toy in the earlier '30s.

By the late prewar years Felix's name tended less often to appear in hyphenated form. Playthings included the books by McLoughlin Bros., as well as films by Novelty Film Co. and masquerade costumes by E. Simon's sons.

Boomer year playthings included banks by Sollmann & Whitcom, dolls by Cameo Doll Products Co., swim rings and play balls by Dartmore Corp., and miscellaneous items by M. Shimmel Sons.

Fellowcrafters, Inc. In addition to poker and game tables, Fellowcrafters made toy boats and bowling games. It was based in Boston, Mass., in the late 1930s.

felt toys Felt proved a useful material for a variety of toys, especially art and sewing sets. Probably the prewar line with greatest visibility were the "Felt-O-Gram" toys made by Poster Products and distributed by the famous publisher Reilly & Lee Co. In "The Felt-O-Gram Line of Toys" children could find alphabets, family figures, and circus sets. Other prewar manufacturers included Hustler Corp., Kingston Products Corp, Newton Mfg. Co., Poster Products, and Scrambled Eggs.

Fenner Game An early 1900s publisher, Fenner issued the 1908 "Game of Batter Up."

"Ferdinand Strauss" toys 1930s, see *The Mechanical Toy Co.*

"Ferdinand the Bull" Early toys and playthings included balloons by Oak Rubber Co.; banks and hand puppets by Crown Toy Mfg. Co.; bell and chime toys by N.N. Hill Brass Co.; books by Whitman Publishing Co.; Chinese checkers by Parker Bros.; masquerade costumes by A.S. Fishbach; mechanical toys by Louis Marx & Co.; pencil sharpeners by Plastic Novelties; rubber toys by Seiberling-Latex Products Co.; sand toys by Ohio Art Co.; soft toys by Knickerbocker Toy Co.; stamping and coloring sets by Fulton Specialty Co.; stuffed toys by Ideal Novelty & toy Co. and Richard G. Krueger; toys and novelties by George Borgfeldt Corp.; and wood toys by Fisher-Price Toys.

"Ferdinand the Bull" pull-toy from The N.N. Hill Brass Co., 1939.

Ferguson Bros. Mfg. Co. Specializing in juvenile and gaming furniture before the war, this Hoboken, N.J., company made combination backgammon and chess boards and tables, game sets, bagatelles, and nursery items.

Ferre's Depot An early toy store, Ferre's Depot was founded by E.C. Ferre in Middleton, Conn., in 1828.

"Fibber McGee" game see *Milton Bradley Co.*

fiber toys see *molded pulp toys.*

Fiberoid Doll Products Co. Based on Broadway, New York City, Fiberoid made prewar doll heads, legs and arms.

"Fibo-Bilt" doll houses prewar, see *Playskool Institute, Inc.*

Fibre-Bilt Toys This division of Atlantic Container Corp., based in Long Island City, N.Y., made postwar corrugated fibre play houses and doll houses, as well as costumes and toys.

"Fibro," prewar see *Dolly Toy Co.*

Ficks Reed Co. Children's rockers were made by this earlier 1930s Cincinnati, Ohio, company.

Fidelity Felt Co. Fidelity, based in Philadelphia, Penn., manufactured felt track ballast for miniature railways in the later 1930s.

Marshall Field & Co. Not only a major retailer for domestically produced toys, Marshall Field was an active importer of dolls, toys, and games.

Field Mfg. Co. Plastic police whistles were among this postwar firm's line, which emphasized games for adults and poker chips. It was based on Fifth Avenue, New York City.

field hockey see *hockey, field.*

Field Mfg. Corp. A prewar Peoria, Ill., company, Field Mfg. made the "Riot-us" party game and dice games.

"Fifteen" This puzzle, a national fad before "Pigs in Clover" was a hit, involved moving fifteen squares around a sixteen-square board to restore them to proper order. The game was issued by a firm named Gem, with Selchow & Righter the distributors. In the 1930s it was produced by the Embossing Co., and in the 1950s-'60s by the Plas-Trix Co.

The Fifth Avenue Building Where Broadway crosses Fifth Avenue at Madison Square in New York City is the Fifth Avenue Building, 200 Fifth Avenue, which has had associations with the toy trade from prewar times. In the 1930s it held the sample displays of more than 200 leading toy manufacturers.

Filipino tops see *yo-yos.*

"Filipino Twirlers" see *Goody Mfg. Co.*

Fillum Fun, Inc. A variety of toys, including "Glo-Irons," toy projectors, Indian headdresses, and banks were Boomer-era products of this East 107th Street, New York City, company.

Finecraft Industries Finecraft made doll baths in the Boomer years. It was based in Lawrence, Mass.

"Finger Dings" see *Remco Industries, Inc.*

F

finger paints Finger paints were a distinctively Boomer toy, and a source of unutterable joy to the children who felt wholly liberated to be dealing with non-toxic paints by the fistful. Many of the leading crayon and paint companies became involved in production. They included Admiral Toy Corp., Advance Crayon & Color Corp., American Art Clay Co., American Artists' Color Works, Binney & Smith, Milton Bradley Co., Craftint Mfg. Co., Crayoff Mfg. Corp., Hassenfeld Bros., Fred Kroll Associates, the Morilla Co., Pressman Toy Corp., Rosebud Art Co., Standard Toykraft prdoucts, Transogram Co., and Welded Plastics Corp.

fingerprint and handprint sets As an activity toy, fingerprint and handprint sets had enough popularity to encourage several manufacturers to issue them. Prewar manufacturers included New York Toy Game Co., Jack Pressman & Co., Scientific Publications, and Sequoia Sales Co. In the late prewar years, Ranger Co. and Transogram Co. also issued sets. Postwar manufacturers included Hale-Nass Corp. and N.Y. Toy & Game Corp.

"Fingertip" puppets see *Wilkening Mfg Co.*

Finch, Robert see *Carlisle & Finch Co.*

fins "Fins" is an alternate and possibly never very widespread word for "flashing."

"Fire Chief" A widely used name in the prewar years, "Fire Chief" was used for two lines of velocipedes in the 1930s, one from Gendron Wheel Co. and the other from the Colson Co. The "Fire Chief" roller skates of the '30s were issued by Louis Marx & Co. The designation was also used for various "Fire Chief" juvenile autos and toy cars from various manufacturers, including Skipper Mfg. Co., Gendron Wheel Co., and the Hoge Mfg. Co.

For children playing fireman, a useful accessory was the "Fire Chief" houses made by Gibraltar Corrugated Box Co. The "Fire Chief" juvenile autos and pedal cars of the postwar period appeared from manufacturers including Midwest Industries, the Power Car Co., and Steger Products Mfg. Co. "Fire Chief" helmets were common plastic items from several manufacturers, including Irving L. Hartman Co.

FIRE CHIEF 264

The "Fire Chief" pull-toy by the Gong Bell Mfg. Co. was one of several toys bearing the name.

"Fire Fly" The "Fire Fly" trademark was used by both S.L. Allen & Co. and Toledo Metal Wheel Co. for prewar coaster wagons.

"Fire Opal" agates see *Akro Agate Co.*

"Firemite" rifle see *Peerless Playthings Co., Inc.*

fireplace toys see *kitchen utensils, toy.*

"Fireside" stuffed toys prewar, see *Knickerbocker Toy Co., Inc.*

"Fireside Series" games see *McLoughlin Bros.*

fireworks Since originating in ancient Asia, the fireworks industry seems to have thrived. Besides the entertainment provided by the fireworks themselves, the industry has directly supplied the toy industry through production of caps for cap guns.

"First Birthday" baby doll see *Nancy Ann Dressed Dolls, Inc.*

first edition In toys, the term refers to a first-state production model. The term is usually only employed when it occurs on the toy or doll itself, as a designation by the manufacturer for the collector. As such it is more a merchandizing than a collector term.

A.S. Fishbach, Inc. Playsuits and masquerade costumes were the specialty of this prewar East 22nd Street, New York City, company. By the late 1930s the company had moved to West 20th Street, and was issuing Walt Disney character play suits and masquerade costumes.

F

Fisher & Matson Co. Based in Park Ridge, Ill., this company made dart baseball games and the "Bowl-A-Dart" bowling game in the 1930s.

Fisher, Herman Guy Born Nov. 2, 1898, in Unionville, Penn., Herman Guy Fisher studied marketing and commerce at Pennsylvania State University. He worked for Alderman-Fairchild Co. in the later 1920s, a company that was beginning to make games. E.E. Fairchild Corp. was formed after a split of the company, with Fisher as vice president and general manager from 1926 to 1930. After an unsuccessful attempt to buy Fairchild, Fisher created Fisher-Price Toys with Irving Price, then mayor of East Aurora, N.Y., and Helen M. Schelle. Fisher served as president and general manager from 1931 until 1966, and as chairman of the board until 1969. He died in 1975.

Fisher-Price Toys, Inc. Fisher-Price Toys was founded in 1931 in East Aurora, N.Y., near Buffalo. The earliest toys were the "Doctor Doodle" and "Granny Doodle," both duck pull-toys, "Drummer Bear," "Lookee Monk," "Barky Puppy," and "Bunny Scoot." A series of wind-up "Go'N Back" wooden walking toys included a mule, bear, and elephant. The "Pop-Up Kritters" included dinosaur, stork, giraffe, and the long-lived cat, "Tailspin Tabby." The "Woodsy-Wee Pets," "Woodsy-Wee Circus Toys" and "Woodsy-Wee Zoo" consisted of a wooden train of animals, connected by hooks and eyelets.

In the mid-'30s, in addition to wooden push and pull toys and the "Pop-Up Kritters," the company was advertising "Bak-Up" mechanical walking toys, circus toys, beaded novelty toys, and pre-school educational toys. By the late 1930s, it had obtained licenses to issue "Popeye" and Walt Disney "Pinocchio," "Mickey Mouse," and "Donald Duck" items. The company made few toys during wartime, devoting the bulk of its production capacity to war work.

In the Boomer years, Fisher-Price continued its earlier emphases, issuing action wood pull toys and plush toys, building blocks, circus toys, infant toys, musical toys, pre-school educational toys, and Easter toys. It introduced plastic elements to its toys in 1950, with "Buzzy Bee." Based in East Aurora, N.Y., it maintained offices in the Fifth Avenue Building.

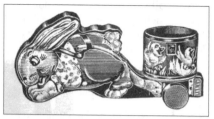

Fisher-Price pull toy, "Bunny Cart," from the 1940s.

The 1961 "Safety School Bus" was a favorite by Fisher-Price.

H. Fishlove & Co. This manufacturer of favors and novelties was based in Chicago, Ill., from the earlier 20th century through the Boomer years. One of Fishlove's more interesting novelty toys of the 1920s was a mechanical top designed for 10-cent retail, being a glass jar in top shape. Inside were candy, toys, jacks, or ball-and-jacks sets. Halloween favors and "Witchcraft favor sets" were leading products in the 1930s, along with favors, balloons, and "jokers." Fishlove still gave top billing to its glass "long-spinning tops filled with toys, candy, marbles, or jacks and balls". The company was flourishing by the late prewar years, issuing "Peek-A-Boo" glasses, "Hotcha Girls" novelty dolls, dancing "Three Little Pigs," the "Scratch Me" pups, and live souvenir turtles.

Fitmore Mfg. Co. Located on Bleecker Street, New York City, Fitmore made children's and doll bath tables.

Five Star Industries, Inc. Plastic toys including banks, bat and ball sets, bowling sets, and duckpins were Boomer-years products of this Hoboken, N.J., company.

"Fix-It" toys see *Ideal Novelty & Toy Corp.*

F

Flagg Doll Co. Flexible plastic dolls of a scale to fit doll houses were this Jamaica Plaine, Mass., company's postwar specialty. Flagg also made doll outfits and dollhouses.

"Flamingo" self-tuning ukuleles

see *Emenee Industries, Inc.*

Flanagan, A., Co. An early game company, A. Flanagan released "Helps to History" in 1898 and the "Geography Game" in the 1910s.

Flanders Babies see *dolls, fashion.*

flannel boards Flannel boards were used in both educational and home play settings in the Boomer years. One of the leading manufacturers, the Saalfield Publishing Co., issued a "Flannel Board Play" line, which included a "Mr. and Mrs. Flannel Board" set. Other manufacturers included H. Davis Toy Corp. and Educaid Mfg. Co.

flash cards Among the most important educational toys of the Boomer years, as well as being among the most inexpensive, were flash cards, which helped children learn numbers, letters, arithmetic, reading, and foreign languages. Manufacturers included Milton Bradley Co., Built-Rite Toys, Ed-U-Cards Mfg. Corp., E.E. Fairchild Corp., the Gelles-Widmer Co., and Russell Mfg. Co.

"Flash" repeating pistol see *The Hubley Mfg. Co.*

"Flash Gordon" The "Flash Gordon" character of King Features Syndicate inspired toys from Bar Zim Toy Mfg. Co. and coloring books by the Saalfield Publishing Co.

flashing When die-cast toys emerged from the mold, they would typically have "flashing" or "flashings," which were thin ridges of metal made by seepage between the flat surfaces of the molds. Usually toy makers removed the flashing. In home-cast toys it would be worn down through play, if not sanded off. Presence of flashing on a toy may indicate a recent casting from home-cast molds.

"Flashy the Frog" see *Rempel Mfg. Co.*

flats "Flats" are essentially two-dimensional toy lead soldiers, being so thin that they seem no more than embossed or painted vertical sheets of metal. Being made of a minimum of raw material, flats were always inexpensive toys. The "comic book flats" were similar toys made of plastic and usually sold through comic book ads, in the postwar years.

"Flatsy" Ideal Novelty and Toy Co. issued "Flatsy" dolls from 1968 to 1970. These were bendy toys of posable soft vinyl, issued in 2, 5 and 8-inch sizes.

Flatto Ribbon Corp. Flatto Ribbon, located on Madison Avenue, New York City, issued "Shirley Temple" and "Movie Star" hair bow ribbons in the late 1930s.

Fleck Industries This Jenkintown, Penn., firm made "Magic Mirror" movies and records in the 1950s and '60s.

"Fleet Flyer," prewar see *Wolverine Supply & Mfg. Co.*

Fleet Line Marine, Inc. Electrically powered model boats and motors were postwar products of this Van Nuys, Calif., firm.

Fleet Mfg. Co. A postwar manufacturer specializing in swimming and pool items, Fleet also made hoops and two-egg incubators. It was based in Glendale, Calif.

"Fleetliner" stroller-carriage see *Thayer.*

"Fleetwing" see *Auto-Wheel Coaster Co., Inc.*

Fleischaker & Baum One of the firm's successes of the pre-Depression years was "Bubbles," or "Little Miss Bubbles," in the Effanbee line. Fleishchaker & Baum advertised its products as "the Dolls with the Golden Heart," since they wore small gold hearts on necklaces.

An extremely successful doll manufacturer widely known for its "Effanbee" trademark, Fleischaker & Baum operated out of offices in the Fifth Avenue Building. Lines in the Effanbee line in the earlier 1930s included such "infant walking, talking, sleeping and unbreakable dolls" including "Bubbles," "Patsy," "Patsy-Ann," "Patsykin," "Patsy-ette," "Patsy Joan," "Patsy Lou," "Mary Lee," "Mary Ellen," "Mary Jane," "Betty Brite," "Betty Bounce," "Betty Bee," "Lamkin Lovums," "Tousle Head," "Sugar Baby," "Skippy," "Grumpykins," "Patsy Fluff," "Patsy Babykin," "Kali-Ko-Kate" and "Kali-Ko-Pete," "Kot'n-Tale Kate" and "Pete," "La-Z Kat," "Dy-Dee Baby," "Patsy Tiny-ette," and "Patsy Babyette." It was also mak-ing "Patsy" nurse and doctor kits.

By the late prewar years, its "Bubbles," "Dy-Dee Babies," "Betty," and "Patsy Family" lines of "Effanbee Durable Dolls" were con-tinuing strongly, as were most of its individ-ual dolls. New items included nurse and doctor kits, "Dancing Lady and White Horse Inn (Tyrolean)" dolls, "Charlie McCarthy," "Clippo the Marionette," "America's Chil-dren," "Dewees Cochran's Portrait Dolls," "Anne Shirley Dolls," and "Wonder Babies."

The firm managed to keep producing dolls during wartime, with its lead "Effanbee Dolls" names being "Sweetie Pie," "Sugar Pie," "Junior Miss" dolls, "Dy-Dee" layettes and bathinettes, "Tousle Tot" dolls, "Tommy Tucker," "Little Lady" dolls, "Brite-Eyes" baby dolls, and "Pat-O-Pat" dolls. The war-time line also included sewing sets, "Work-Shop" puppets, "Clippo" marionettes, and doctor and nurse sets. See *Effanbee Doll Co.*

"Bubbles" was one of Fleischaker & Baum's most popu-lar toys.

H. Fleisig, Inc. A paper box company, this Lafayette Street, New York City, firm also made some doll items, including doll trunks, in the earlier 1930s.

M.M. Fleron, & Son, Inc. The "Sig-naler" Official Boy Scout line, including radio, blinker, and telegraph, were 1930s and '40s products of this Trenton, N.J., company.

Fletcher & Goldsmith Wolf Fletcher made dolls from about 1875, with Philip Goldsmith joining as a partner soon after the founding of the Covington, Ky., business. The dolls had cloth bodies and composition heads. Wolf Fletcher sold out his interests in the company in 1878. In 1888, Goldsmith patented a corset-body doll, which proved extremely popular. Goldsmith also made bisque baby dolls, using a machine imported from Germany.

At Goldsmith's death in 1894, his sons ceased doll production. They concentrated on baseball manufacture, moving the business in 1898 to Cincinnati, Ohio.

Fletcher Game Co. Based in Chicago, Ill., Fletcher issued "Personology" handwrit-ing games and bridge games in the late 1930s.

"Flexible Flyer" The "Flexible Flyer" sleds were made by S.L. Allen & Co. The company used similar trademarks on many of its other products, including "Flexy Quoit Kit," the "Flexy Racer," a sled on wheels, and "Flexy Whirl," a see-saw merry-go-round.

"Flexible Playdolls" see *Flagg Doll Co.*

"Flexoplane" sleds see *Carriage & Toy Co.;* postwar, see *American Acme Co.*

"Flexy Racer" see *S.L. Allen & Co.*

The Fli-Back Co. Established in the later 1930s, this High Point, N.C., firm issued the "Fli-back" paddle and ball games. The firm also used a second name, the Sock-It Co., in the late '30s.

In the Boomer years, as the Fli-Back Sales Corp., the company's line included sponge balls, return balls, baseballs, decorated inflated balls, toy rubber footballs and bas-ketballs, return and spinning tops, balloons and balloon sticks, toy wood rolling pins, and its "Fli-Back" paddle ball games.

Fli-Bal, Inc. The "Fli-Bal" game of the 1950s and '60s was made by this Kansas City, Mo., firm.

"Flicker-Fun" see *Wonder-Art Enter-prises.*

Flinch Card Co. Established in 1902 in Kalamazoo, Mich., this company's "Flinch" game was among the best-selling games of the early 20th century. "More simple than Authors, more scientific than Whist," the company's ads proclaimed. Flinch Card Co. lasted into the 1930s. Other titles included "Bourse, or Stock Exchange" in 1903, "Competition, or Department Store" in 1904, and "Roodles" in 1912. "Flinch" became a staple title in the Parker Bros. line through the Boomer years.

"Flip-Flop Friends" see *Jack Built Toy Mfg. Co.*

"Flip-Flop" stuffed animals see *Master Industries, Inc.*

"Flivver Family" wheel goods see *Lullaby Furniture Corp.*

"Float-Me" toys prewar, see *Marks Bros. Co.*

Flobell Doll Co. Based on West 21st Street, New York City, Flobell was a prewar doll manufacturer.

Floda Mfg. Co., Inc. The "Dolly's Boudoir" set of the mid-1930s was produced by this West 23rd. Street, New York City, firm.

floor runner see *floor trains.*

floor trains Floor trains were push or pull toy versions of trains for use on the floor. Made with standard vehicle-toy wheels instead of railroad-system wheels that mimicked the real thing, they used no tracks. Many early train toys, made of cast iron and wood as early as the 1850s, were floor trains.

"Floppipets" stuffed animals prewar, see *Adler Favor & Novelty Co.*

"Flor-El-Lyn" dolls see *The Franklin Studio, The.*

Flores, Pedro see the *Yo-Yo Mfg. Co.,* also *The Bandalor Co.*

Florida Playthings, Inc. Based in Street Petersburg, Fla., this 1930s company made wood action toys, pull toys, and sand toys.

"Flossie Flirt" dolls see *Ideal Novelty & Toy Co.*

"The Flower Garden" construction set see *The Toymakers.*

Flower Products Co. An electrically lighted aluminum Christmas tree was produced in the 1930s and '40s by this East 35th Street, Chicago, firm. Flower Products also made novelties.

M. Fluegelman, Inc. A supplier of pressed doll faces, hats and novelties to other manufacturers, Fluegelman was based on Sixth Avenue, New York City, in the 1920s and '30s.

"Fluffila" stuffed toys see *Coronet Toy Mfg. Co.*

"Fluffy" stuffed animals prewar, see *American Made Toy Co.;* postwar, see *Knickerbocker Toy Co., Inc*

"Fly-A-Way" airplanes and gliders see *Paul K. Guillow, Inc.*

"Flyaway" sleds and shooflies see *Pratt Mfg. Co.*

"Flyer" bicycles see *The Colson Co.*

"Flyin' Fool" airplanes prewar, see *Universal Sales Corp.*

"Flying Ace" see *Moen & Patton, Inc.*

"Flying Arrow" "Flying Arrow" and "Flying Cloud" were prewar coaster wagons made by The Globe Co.

"Flying Dutchman" juvenile car see *Hill-Standard Corp.*

"Flying Eagle" coaster wagons see *Radio Steel & Mfg. Co.*

"Flying Flash" coaster wagons see *Janesville Products Co.*

"Flying Fool," 1920s see *Flying Toy Co., Inc.*

"Flying Saucer" The Flying Saucer craze of the Boomer years inspired a variety of playthings, ranging from the "Flyin' Saucer," early version of the toy that became "Frisbee," to balloons by the Oak Rubber Co., circular sleds by Montello Products Co., guns by U.S. Plastics Corp. and Park Plastics Co., and a horseshoe game by Wham-O Mfg. Co.

Flying Saucers were everywhere in the Boomer years; even on this rattle by Stahlwood Toy Mfg. Co.

"Flying Scout" roller skates see *Chicago Roller Skate Co.*

"Flying Top" see *Daisy Mfg. Co.,* also *"Jack Armstrong."*

Flying Toy Co., Inc. Based in Chicago, Ill., in the 1920s, Flying Toy made a line of model toy airplanes that flew with gas motors. One of its more prominent items in the late '20s was the "Flying Fool," a pistol that launched a glider, using rubber-band power.

The Flying Toy Co. Flying toy planes and the flying "Dodo Mystery Bird" were made in the mid-1930s by this San Diego, Calif., company.

"Flying Yankee" motorboats see *Keystone Mfg. Co.*

flywheel A heavy wheel at the end of a crankshaft, designed to help an engine run smoothly. On early one- and two-cylinder engines, the flywheel is often exposed. On many toy tractors it is the "fifth wheel" or cylindrical extension of the engine located below and to the front of the driver.

"Foam-E-toys" see *Eden Toys, Inc.*

folders "Folders" were a kind of three-dimensional paper figure which were sold in flat folders, and which became their intended shape when opened. Common folders shapes included eggs, chicks and ducklings for Easter, or turkey bodies for Thanksgiving. Some greeting cards were made as folders.

Foliage Co. of America A manufacturer of postwar Christmas decorations, this Ludington, Mich., company also made toys.

Follender Wig. Corp. An East Islip, N.Y., company, Follender made dolls' wigs in the 1920s and '30s.

football As an American game, football was a game played by pre-Colonial American Indians. When adopted by early European settlers, it was played by girls and women, since it was seen as being inadequately rugged for the play of boys.

football games Board and table games based upon the field game of football were popular both before and after the war. Prewar manufacturers included Milton Bradley Co., Cadaco-Ellis, the Carrom Co., Electric Game Co., Northill Co., Novelty Research Artists, Parker Bros., Playgames, and Welna Distributing Co. In addition to Milton Bradley, Cadaco-Ellis, Electric Game and Parker Bros., postwar manufacturers included Frank Cavanaugh Assoicates, E.E. Fairchild Corp., Gotham Pressed Steel Corp., Lord & Freber, and Stars on Stripes. Tudor Metal Products made unquestionably the most famous of postwar football games with its "Tru Action Electric Football," which involved figures of football players, initially of metal and later of plastic, who moved across the lithographed metal field because of the metal board's vibrations.

Forest County Lumber Co. One of many Wisconsin juvenile furniture manufacturers in the 1930s, this Elcho, Wis., company made rockers, doll cribs, and doll bassinets.

"Forever Toys" see *Cardinal Doll Corp.*

The Forrest Mfg. Co. A Cleveland, Ohio, company, Forrest made the "Stark's ball gun" in the mid-1930s.

Forster Mfg. Corp. Steel gyroscope tops and toy telephones were this Pittsburg, Penn., corporation's main toy products in the 1930s and '40s. In the Boomer years, Forster emphasized take-apart educational toys, pull toys, and miniature rolling pins.

F

"Fort Knox" banks see *Cherry Valley Mfg. Corp.*

fortune-telling games
Fortune-telling games had a run of popularity in the later 1800s—for probably not the first time. Peoples' predilection for wanting to know the future without waiting for it, or to have "supernatural" guidance in the absence of any sure knowledge, has made the game of fortune-telling a perennially attractive one, whether or not the game-players take the game seriously.

The most famous fortune-telling game of the 20th century is undoubtedly "Ouija," introduced in 1890 by Kennard Novelty Co. and issued through the early 20th century and earlier Boomer years by William Fuld. Another early title was "Chiromagica," published by McLoughlin Bros.

Perhaps the best-know novelty of a fortune-telling bent is "Magic '8' Ball," introduced in 1946 by Alabe Crafts Co. The toy was a kind of reusable plastic fortune-cookie which gave varying degrees or neutral, affirmative and negative answers to questions.

Besides Fuld, prewar manufacturers of fortune-telling games included Cadaco-Ellis, Jada Novelty Mfg. Co., Margarete Ward Publications, O. Schoenhut, Selchow & Righter Co., and Edward Smith Mfg. Co. In addition to Fuld and Alabe, postwar manufacturers included Arlane Mfg. Co.

One of the most famous fortune-telling games is "Ouija," published in the 20th century by William Fuld.

Fortune Toy Corp.
The "Heartbeat Doll" of the mid-1950s was issued by this specialist in miniature dolls. The firm was based in the Fifth Avenue Building.

"Foto Electric Football" see *Cadaco-Ellis, Inc.*

Foulds & Freure, Inc.
Toys, dolls in varying sizes, and novelties were issued in the 1920s through the prewar years by this East 20th Street, New York City, firm, which called itself "The House of Doll Hospital Supplies" by the late '20s. It issued a doll hospital in the later '30s.

"4-5-6 Pick-Up-Sticks" see *O. Schoenhut, Inc.*

"Four Wheel Turn" coaster wagon
see *Wood & Metal Products Co.*

Fox Blocks Co., Inc.
Based in Pasadena, Calif., Fox Blocks made educational wooden building blocks in the 1930s. By the end of the decade it changed its name to Fox Blox Co.

Fox Co.
A Philadelphia company, Fox was a prewar manufacturer of toy guns, including the "Fox" double barrel breech-loading play gun, fifteen-shot repeaters, and the "Fox Ranger" repeating cannon of the mid-1930s. It also made "Kumbak" indoor golf.

A.H. Fox Gun Co.
Based in Philadelphia, Penn., in the 1920s, Fox made what it advertised as "the only play gun that shoots 'real shells'," the "Fox Double-Barrel Play Gun." The child could load realistic shells, from which small wooden balls were fired. "These shells resemble, in size and shape, real shot gun shells," the company said. "They load in the breech of the gun, as in a big gun." Its $3.00 price included two shells, ammunition, and bell target.

Fox Toy Co.
Based in Berea, Ohio, Fox Toy Co. issued early 20th century toys under the "Foxy Toys" name, specializing in steel slates and spelling boards in the 1920s. In the '30s its products included anagrams, "Foxy Blox," "Master Molder" sets, and "Klay Kast" sets.

"Foxy" or "Foxy Toys" see *Fox Toy Co.*

frame tray puzzle see *puzzles.*

Francesse Doll Co. Francesse's dolls were white and colored vinyl rooted-hair baby and teen-age dolls, manufactured in the Boomer years. The Street Petersburg, Fla., company also made plush toys, stuffed dolls, doll clothes, and musical toys.

Franco-American Novelty Co. The "Home Derby" game of the late 1930s was made by this Broadway, New York City, firm. Franco-American also made jokes, tricks, and novelty toys through the Boomer years.

Francis, Field and Francis see *Philadelphia Tin Toy Manufactory*

Frandine Mfg. Co. Based in Los Angeles, Calif., Frandine made rubber band guns and games in the late 1930s.

The George Franke Sons Co. A manufacturer of Christmas items, the George Franke Sons Co. of Baltimore, Md., made tinsel garlands, holiday boxes, and ornaments, in the 1920s, adding icicles and cellophane cord in the '30s. In the late prewar years Franke also made toy suitcases. Specialties in the postwar years included glass Christmas ornaments, lead icicles, and Christmas stockings.

Franklin Mfg. Corp. This Norwood, Mass., firm specialized in juvenile printing presses in the late 1930s.

Franklin Rubber Co. Based in Philadelphia, Penn., Franklin Rubber Co. made rubber quoit sets for indoor and outdoor play in the late 1930s.

The Franklin Studio Based in Covington, Ga., the Franklin Studio made mid-1930s wicker doll cradles and bassinets, jigsaw puzzles, and dolls.

"Frantz" toys and games see *Hustler Toy Corp.*

Frarol Mfg. Co. One of many Wisconsin prewar manufacturers of juvenile furniture, Frarol was based in Ontario, Wis.

Frazier Model Engineering Laboratories Model gasoline engines for model airplanes, racecars, and speedboats were the specialty of this Grand Rapids, Mich., com-

pany. It also manufactured "steam marine engines, atmospheric engines, and hot air engines."

Frederick Machine Works This Norwalk, Ohio, company made prewar coaster wagons.

Frederick Mfg. Co. Wood pull toys and novelties were produced by this prewar Butler, Penn., company.

Freidag Mfg. Co. Besides golf course equipment, Freidag, of Freeport, Ill., made prewar iron toys, juvenile golf sets and games, jackstones and jack sets, and Christmas tree holders.

French and Wheat A jobber or dealer operating 1859-1866 on Ann Street, New York City, French and Wheat may also have been a manufacturer. The company sold a log cabin construction toy.

The French Doll Makers This cloth doll manufacturer was located on West 24th Street, New York City, in the late 1930s. A firm called French Doll Co., located elsewhere on West 24th after the war, may have been related.

Ralph A. Freundlich, Inc. Based in Clinton, Mass., Freundlich made dolls, stuffed animal toys, and novelties in the 1930s and '40s.

friction motor A type of "impulse motor" used to power some toys, ranging from some of the earliest toy cars to some of the most recent fast-food toys.

friction wheel The flywheel is a centrally and internally positioned inertia wheel, usually activated by the motion of the rear wheels of a wheel toy, by a gear or spring connection. American toys used cast-iron friction wheels, while European toys used cast lead. Popular in the early 20th century, a great many friction toys made of cheaper materials appeared in the postwar years through the end of the 20th century, being often small car toys with plastic bodies and small metal flywheels.

Friedberger-Aaron Mfg. Co. Textile education toys were the specialty of this Phil-

F

adelphia, Penn., company, including the Wonder Weaver and Loomcrafter toy looms of the mid-1930s.

J.F. Friedel Co. This Syracuse, N.Y., issued games including "Game of Chinese Checkers" in the late 1930s.

Frisch Doll Supply Located on West Broadway, New York City, Frisch made doll heads with moving eyes and other doll parts in the mid-1930s.

"Frisky Pony" riding toys see *Rempel Mfg. Co.*

The Fritzel Toys Corp. Educational and nursery toys were specialties of this Randolph, Vt., firm in the Boomer years. It made wooden preschool toys, blocks, block wagons, hammer toys, floor toys, and pull toys.

"Frontier" "Frontier" was a popular word for trade names in the Boomer years, especially in the wake of the Davy Crockett fad of the mid-1950s and later. As such it is not particularly useful in hunting down the manufacturer of a toy. For instance, "Frontier" play clothes were manufactured by Seneca Mfg. Co.; "Frontier" six-shooter pistols, by Kilgore; and "Frontier" toy chests, by the Modern Crafts Co. Even such word combinations as "Frontier Scout" were used by more than one firm—in this case, Spraz Co. and Wonder-Art Enterprises.

Frostee Sno Ball Co. Christmas tree snowballs and artificial snow were specialties of this Chicago, Ill., firm in the late prewar years.

"Frosty Sno-Man Sno-Cone Machine" 1960s, see *Hassenfeld Bros. Inc.*

"Frozen Charlottes" Small dolls of bisque or china, "Frozen Charlottes" were simple, non-jointed, naked figures of girls standing or lying straight with arms at their sides. These were popularly associated with the New England ballad of a foolish girl who refused to hide her elegant gown beneath a coat while sleigh-riding with her fiance. She consequently froze to death. The small dolls were popular in the later 1800s.

fruit stores Fruit and candy stores were often the source for toys in the earlier 1800s, a tradition carried on to a limited degree by candy stores since then.

William Fuld William Fuld, a manufacturer based in Baltimore, Md., claimed the "Ouija" board of 1920 as an original invention, touting it as the "original 'Ouija' talking board" into the Boomer years. Based on popular mystical games of the late 19th century, "Ouija" was a substantial hit for the company, which also issued "Return Pool" and hand-decorated action pull toys in the 1920s. Fuld continued to make pool and billiard tables, wooden action toys, and games through the prewar years.

Fuld & Co., Inc. A prominent publisher of Valentines and Christmas cards from its establishment in 1893, Fuld was based on Broadway, New York City in the prewar years, moving to Fourth Avenue by the 1940s, and to Boonton, N.J. in the Boomer years. By the the 1930s and '40s its line included cutouts, mechanicals, and novelties.

S. & J. Fuller Fuller was a famous London publisher of toy books in the years 1810-35.

Fuller Mfg. Co. The "Pony Ride" merry-go-round of the Boomer years was manufactured by this Centerville, Iowa, company.

Fulton Bag & Cotton Mills Based in Atlanta, Ga., Fulton's products included juvenile tents in the late prewar years.

Fulton Specialty Co. In the 1920s, this firm's "Fulton Printing Toys" included the "Artistamp De Luxe Set," "Picture Makers," and its regular "Artistamp" series featuring "Famous Printer & Sign Writer," "Yankee Circus," "Wild West," and "Farm & Jungle." New in the late '20s was the "Our Army" set, which contained images of dirigibles, airplanes, and other military subjects. Its games included the board game "The Wizard" of 1921. Based in Elizabeth, N.J., Fulton specialized in printing-related toys through the prewar years, including hand operated toy printing presses in the 1930s. It obtained a license through Kay Kamen in the mid-'30s to issue Walt Disney character rubber stamps. In the Boomer years, still based in Elizabeth,

N.J., the firm adopted the new name, Fulton Marking Equipment Co.

"Fulton Speedster" coaster wagon
see *Hill-Standard Corp.*

"Fulton" toys prewar, see *Patent Novelty Co., Inc.*

Fun Bilt Toys, Inc. Based in Los Angeles, Calif., Fun Bilt issued postwar crayon "re-color" books, modeling clay sets, and photographic kits.

"Fun-E-Flex" wooden toys prewar, see *George Borgfeldt Corp.*

"Fun Fair" toys prewar, see *Wolverine Supply & Mfg. Co.*

"Fun Farm" see *Wham-O Mfg. Co.*

"Fun To Do" books see *The Platt & Munk Co., Inc.*

The Funck Co. This St. Louis, Mo., company made prewar juvenile furniture.

"Funland" see *The Einson-Freeman Co.*

"Funny Animals" see *Colorforms.*

"Funny Faces" construction toy see *Chaspec Mfg. Co.*

"Funzies" see *The Tracies Co.*

"Fur-Z" animals prewar, see *New York Stuffed Toys*

furniture, doll and toy Doll and toy furniture were likely among the earliest toys produced by American wood-turning companies, in the 1700s and 1800s. As an item of formal manufacture, however, they only slowly rose in importance.

By the earlier 20th century some firms were specializing in these toys' manufacture, including Arcade Mfg. Co., the N.D. Cass Co., Colorville Toy Co., Dolly Folding Kite Co., Dowst Mfg. Co., Keller Toy Mfg. Co., the Lehman Co. of America, the Mason Mfg. Co., Toy Corp. of America, and Vilas-Harsha Mfg. Co.

By the 1930s, however, toy and doll furniture became an important category for a great many more firms. Prominent companies included the Anchor Toy Corp., Arcade, N.D. Cass, Dowst, Hoge Mfg. Co., the Kilgore Mfg. Co., the A. Schoenhut Co., Strombeck-Becker Mfg. Co., and Transogram Co. Others included the American Crayon Co., Stephen H. Bond, the Buckstaff Co., Centerbar Corp., Central Wood Products, F.A. Colford Co., James A. Coulson, C.K. Cropper & Co., Dolly Toy Co., Drewry Bros., the Dur-A-Bilt Co., Gem Mfg. Corp., Hansen Wood goods & Toy Mfg. Co., Ralph T. Jones, Lambert & Latimer, Lehman Co. of America, A. Leipzig, Menasha Woodenware Corp., the Mengel Co., Mentzer-Read Co., Merriman Mfg. Corp., North Vernon Industries, Paper Products Co., Henry Pilcher's Sons, B. Shackman & Co., Star Novelty Works, Toy Furniture Shop, Tropical Industries, Wicker Toy Mfg. Co., and the Woodcraft Toy Studio.

Companies that made doll hammocks a specialty included E.R. Hutchison and International Mfg. Co.

In the postwar years, the introduction of plastics almost wholly changed the world of dollhouse and toy furniture. Some of the most typical lines of the times were produced by Louis Marx & Co., which made simple but realistic furniture of hard and soft plastic for its dollhouses, and Renwal Toy Corp., which used colorful hard plastics to create some of the most detailed furniture miniatures of the time.

Other doll and toy furniture of the Boomer years was manufactured by firms including American Mfg. Concern, American Metal Specialties Corp., American Toy & Furniture Co., Argo Industries Corp., Bardell Mfg. Corp., Blake & Conroy, Block House, Built-Rite Toys, Cardwood Products Corp., N.D. Cass Sales Co., J. Chein Co., Children's Furniture Corp., T. Cohn, the Connor Lumber & Land Co., Consolidated Toy Mfg. Co., Cortland Furniture Co., Cramco, Dell Plastics Co., Dolclos Products Corp., Elmar Products, Grand Rapids Juvenile, Hall's Lifetime Toys, Milton A. Jacobs, Julius Levenson, Lila-Lu Toys, Megahorn Co., William Moore Mfg. Co., New York Toy & Game Mfg. Corp., Renwal Toy Corp., Richwood Furniture, Riemann, Seabrey Co., Scandia-Custer Toy Corp., Sollmann & Whitcomb, Strombeck-

F

Becker, Sunny Toys, Toy Corp. of America, Transogram Co., Vogue Dolls, Well-Worth Mfg. Co., Whitney Bros. Co., and Wolverine Supply & Mfg. Co.

Manufacturers who specialized primarily in dollhouse-scale furniture included Block House, Built-Rite, Child Life Toys, Grandmother Stover's, Modern Furniture Co., New York Doll Accessories Corp., Plastic Art Toy Corp. of American, Pyro Plastics Corp., Rel Mfg. Corp., Renwal, B. Shackman & Co., and Strombeck-Becker Mfg. Co.

The "Jolly Twins Nursery Set" by Renwal; just one example of the many plastic dollhouse furnishings from the 1950s.

furniture, juvenile and nursery
The juvenile and nursery furniture of the 19th century and prewar years holds considerable interest to collectors of toys, dolls, and childhood items. Aside from the intrinsic interest of the furniture and its decoration and design, many of the manufacturers were also makers of shooflies, rocking horses, go-carts, and other items intermediate between toys and furniture.

In the earlier 20th century, prominent names in the field included Appleton Toy & Furniture Co., Baldwin Fibre Co., Benner Mfg. Co., Carriage & Toy Co., N.D. Cass Co., Morton E. Converse & Son Co., Eastman Mfg. Co., the Elmberg Co., the Lehman Co. of America, the Mason Mfg. Co., Mason & Parker Mfg. Co., Tennessee Red Cedar &

Novelty Co., Toy Corp. of America, Vilas-Harsha Mfg. Co., and H.C. White Co.

Prewar manufacturers included: the American National Co.; American Novelty Co.; Baby Line Furniture; A.E. Beck Mfg. Co.; Bloch Go-Cart Co.; Blue Ridge Novelties; Brown County Folks; the Buckstaff Co.; Carriage & Toy Co.; the N.D. Cass Co.; Central Wood Products; W.Q. Collins Co.; C.K. Cropper & Co.; the Dur-A-Bilt Co.; Eastman Mfg. Co.; Edison Wood Products; the Elmberg Co.; Everlast Toy Co.; Ferguson Bros. Mfg. Co.; Forest County Lumber Co.; Gem Crib & Cradle Co.; Monroe Hitz Co.; Jacobs & Kassler; Johnson, Randall Co.; Krebs, Stengle & Co.; Lambert & Latimer; Lehman Co. of America; Lloyd Mfg. Co; Lullabye Furniture Corp.; Mack Toy Works; Merriman Mfg. Corp.; Paragon Furniture Co.; Paris Mfg. Co.; Piedmont Mfg. Co.; Henry Pilcher's Sons; Porter Schreen Co.; Purves Products Co.; Readsboro Chair Co.; G.I. Sellers & Sons Co.; Sheboygan Coaster & Wagon Works; South Bend Toy Mfg. Co.; South Tamworth Industries; Storkline Furnishing Corp.; Totty Trunk & Bag Co.; Trimble; Uhlen Carriage Co.; Victor Woodturning Co.; F.A. Whitney Carriage Co.; H.C. White Co.; and the Woodcraft Toy Studio.

Furniture City Dowel Co.
A prewar wood-turning company, Furniture City Dowel of Grand Rapids, Mich., made wooden pull toys, soldier sets, trains, and building blocks.

Furniture Stylists, Inc.
This prewar Hoboken, N.J., company specialized in adult-oriented games, manufacturing decorated bridge tables and the games "Back to Prosperity," "Seeing Nellie Home," and "Crap-O-Lette" in the 1930s.

furniture, toy
see *furniture, doll and toy.*

"Fuzzy-Wuzzy" dolls
prewar, see *Bonser Doll Co.*

"Fyr-Kracker" cannon
see *Dayton Toy & Specialty Co.*

Gg

"G.&D." see *Grossett & Dunlap, Inc.*

"G.B.N." see *Gebruder Bing.*

G.C. & Co., or G.C.Co.N. see *George Carette.*

"G.E.M. Brand" George E. Mousley used this prewar trademark on the company's Christmas stockings and Easter novelties.

G.H.Q. Motors Based on East 149th Street, New York City, G.H.Q. Motors made airplane kits and miniature gasoline motors in the late 1930s.

"G.I. Joe" see *Hassenfeld Bros., Inc.*

"G.M.," or "G.M. & Co." see *Maerklin, Gebruder*

"G-Man" Toys and playthings of the late 1930s included the "G-Man Detect-I-Phone" by Colonial Earphone Co.; junior outfit by All Metal Products Co.; "G-Man Patrol" mechanical target game by Baldwin Mfg. Co.; machine gun and "Pursuit Car" toy auto by Louis Marx & Co.; siren whistle by John Lauterbach Co.; games by Milton Bradley Co. and Parker Bros. Co.; and fingerprint and detective sets by N.Y. Toy & Game Sales Co. The latter were issued well into the Boomer years.

"G.S." see *Garrett Sales Corp.*

"Gabby Goofies" see *Fisher-Price Toys, Inc.*

"Gabby Hayes" Playthings that tied in with this media figure included the "Gabby Hayes Carry-All" fishing set by Nassau Products Corp. and the "Gabby Hayes" line from John-Henry Mfg. Co.

Samuel Gabriel Sons & Co. Established in the 1910s and based in the Fifth Avenue Building, Samuel Gabriel Sons & Co. published prewar picture books in paper, linen, and "linenette," as well as "put-together books," juveniles, "Sewdress" dolls, paper dolls, painting and drawing books, painting and crayon sets, kindergarten pastimes, games for beginners, weaving looms, sewing sets, model clay, and mosaic sets. It designed its products "To Keep Busy the Little Hand and Little Head." It also manufactured toy books, wood and cardboard blocks, puzzles, model clay, and art sets. Titles included the activity games "The New Game of Shuffle-Board" in the 1920s and "Clown Winks" in the '30s, and board games "Across the Sea Game" and "Clipper Race" in 1930, "Bally Hoo" in 1931, "Ching Gong" in 1937, "Game of Black Sambo" and "Chee Chow" in 1939, and "Bird Lotto" in 1940. Other 1940s titles included "Dubble Up," "Good Things To Eat Lotto," "In and Out the Window," "Indians and Cowboys," "Jumping Jupiter," "Object Lotto," "Peter Rabbit Game," and "Snap-Jacks." The firm continued issuing a variety of paper, linenette, linen and wood pre-school toys, toy books, activity books, blocks, paper dolls, toys, games, and activity sets during World War II and the years following.

Gallant Knight Co. The "Gallant Knight" plastic chessmen and checkers, as well as game boards, of the 1950s and '60s were issued by this Northbrook, Ill., company. It was a division of Northbrook Plastic Card Co.

"Galloping Horse" juvenile car see *The Frank F. Taylor Co.*

The Game Co. The Game Co. was based on West 57th Street, New York City, in the Boomer years.

Game Makers Inc. Based in Long Island City, N.Y., Game Makers issued a line of action toys and games in the 1930s and '40s, including "Jig Chase," "Jig Race," and "Bomber Ball."

"Game of the States" see *Milton Bradley Co.*

game tables and boards The growth of leisure time in the 1920s and '30s led to the development of countless formalized leisure-time activities. Larger game outfits involving specially made tables became more popular, reflecting the fact that many games had become permanent fixtures in the middle-class family home. A number of manufacturers specialized in making game boards and game tables. Prewar companies included American Novelty Works, Louis A. Boettiger Co., Milton Bradley Co., the Carrom Co., Cluff Cover Co., Cuyahoga Lumber Co., Detroit Wood Products Div., Dieterman & Jones Co., E.E. Doe Mfg. Co., Electric Eye Co., E.E. Fairchild Co., Ferguson Bros. Mfg. Co., William Fuld, Gotham Pressed Steel Corp., Grand Rapids Dowel Works, Hassenfeld Bros., W.C. Horn Bro. & Co., Ivorycraft Co., Master Woodworkers, Novelty Bookbinding Co., N.L. Page & Son Co., Paris Mfg. Co., Parker Bros., Rochester Folding Box Co., William Rott, Selchow & Righter Co., Totty Trunk & Bag Co., and Transogram Co.

games While the classic games of chess and checkers are far older, games started appearing in modern board form in the 1820s. Some of the earliest, which were traveling games with educational intent, used pasteboard or cloth boards. The 1840s saw an explosion in the popularity of games in both card and board formats, after the great success of "Dr. Busby" and "The Mansion of Happiness" in 1843. By 1844 board games were being issued by numerous publishers. In the last half of the 19th century, important publishers included W. & S.B. Ives, McLoughlin Bros., Milton Bradley Co., and Parker Bros.

Through the earlier 20th century, the number of manufacturers involved in making games grew substantially. By the peak years just before the Great Depression, they included American Soldier Co., Apex Mfg. Co., the Arcade Mfg. Co., Baumgarten & Co., Charles M. Boeckling, Milton Bradley, M. Carlton Dank Toy Corp., Davis Brake Beam Co., Dixtoy Co., Durable Toy and Novelty Co., Elastic Tip Co., the Embossing Co., Flinch Card Co., William Fuld, Samuel Gabriel Sons & Co., Halsam Products Co., W.C. Horn Bros. & Co, Ideal Book Builders, Emil Kahn Co., Katagiri Bros., Klauber Novelty Co., Knapp Electric, John C. Lehne Sales Co., Madmar Quality Co., A. Master, McDowell Mfg. Co., the Mordt Co., Morrison Brushes, Parker Bros., Petrie-Lewis Mfg. Co., Radio Quiz Corp., Realistic Game & Toy Corp., the Reed Mfg. Co., Rosebud Art Co., the Saalfield Publishing Co., Schmid Bros., the A. Schoenhut Co., Selchow & Righter Co., J.W. Spear & Sons, Standard Solophone Mfg. Co., Statler Toy Corp., Stoll & Edwards Co., Stox, Thwaites, the Toy Tinkers, Traps Mfg. Co., Wilder Mfg. Co., Zulu Toy Mfg. Co., and Theodore Yonkers.

While postwar games centering on various television and cartoon figures are heavily collected, the most valued games tend to be those be these pre-Great Depression manufacturers, and by those active before World War II.

Parker Bros. Game "Jackstraws Improved" from the 1890s.

Despite the prewar period being shorter than the postwar, even collectors of older games face a daunting task, if for no other reason than that the numbers of companies publishing games in these years was, as you can see, enormous. Some certainly had higher profile, and form the focus for some collectors.

In the years after the Great Depression and before World War II, their number included such prominent names as Milton Bradley, Cadaco, Einson-Freeman/Stoll & Einson, E.E. Fairchild Corp., Fuld, Samuel Gabriel Sons, Hoge Mfg. Co., Knapp Electric, Lindstrom Tool & Toy, Parker Bros., the Reilly & Lee Co., Rich Illinois Mfg. Co., A. Schoenhut, Selchow & Righter, Standard Toykraft Products, the Toy Tinkers, Transogram, Whitman Publishing Co., and Wolverine Supply & Mfg. Co.

Even collectors focusing on an individual company may not make the task easy, since many companies issued such a large variety of titles over the years. For instance, Milton Bradley in the mid-1930s advertised having more than 600 items in the "Bradley Line."

The numerous other prewar manufacturers included Abbott Mfg. Co., Acme Toys, Advance Mfg. Co., America, American Maid Artcraft Studios, American Toy Airship Co., American Toy Airship Co., American Toy Works, Anderson Steam Vulcanizer Co., O.B. Andrews Co., Angelus Press, Apex Mfg. Co., Arcade Mfg. Co., Arney Amusement Devices, and Arrow Mfg. Co.

Additional companies included Bambino Products Co., Banton Bros., Bar Zim Toy Mfg. Co., the Beistle Co., Beverly Game & Novelty Co., the Biffit Co., Billie-Toy Mfg. Co., Billings, Joseph Borzellino & Son, Charles A. Brewer & Sons, Brinkman Engineering Co., Brooks Co., Cadillac Specialty Co., Cardinell Corp., the Carrom Co., the Central Paper Box & Printing Co., C.F. Chase Game Co., Chicago Die Cutting Co., Child Welfare Publishers, the Conestoga Corp., Deeks Mfg. Co., James DeHart, Dewes & Smith, Diamond Game Co., Diamond Toy Co., Dickerman & Co., the Discus Co., Harold W. Dow, Dowis Football Game Co., Durable Toy & Novelty Corp., the Edwards Mfg. Co., the Elastic Tip Co., Electric Game Co., the Embossing Co., E.E. Fairchild Corp., Federal Screen & Weatherstrip Mfg. Co., Fisher & Matson Co., Gem City Specialty Co., Goody Mfg. Co., Gotham Pressed Steel Corp., the Herbert R. Gottfried Co., Paul K. Guillow, the Harter Publishing Co., the Hatfield Co., Herbert Specialty Mfg. Co., Hipwell Mfg. Co., Hustler Corp., James

R. Irvin & Co., Ivorycraft Co., and Johnson Store Equipment Co.

Others included Katagiri Corp., Kenilworth Press, the Lawn Shuffle Co., Lederer Mfg. Co., the Lezius-Hiles Co., Lubbers & Bell Mfg. Co., Lutz Sheinkman, M.S. Publishing Co., McDowell Mfg. Co., McGavin Specialties Co., Marks Bros., Marx, Hess & Lee, Maryland Toy & Games Corp., A. Master, Metal Toy Co., Michigan City Paper Box Co., the M. H. Miller Co., Moorman Game Co., W. Howard Moudy, National Games Co., New England Mfg. Co., Newton & Thompson Mfg. Co., New York Toy & Game Co., Nok-Out Mfg. Co., Northwestern Products, "Old Rivals" Game Co., Original Game & Novelty Co., the Paddle Tennis Co., Pavick's Mfg. Co., A.S. Payne, Peerless Engraving Co., Pigskin, Playgames, Jack Pressman & Co., Psychic Baseball Club, Harry E. Pulver, Radio Sports, Rippon Co., Rochester Folding Box Co., "Rolling the Green," Rosebud Art Co., Walter L. Rothschild, Russel Mfg. Co., Schacht Rubber Mfg. Co., "Sherms," Shu-Quoi Games Co., J.M. Simmons & Co., J. W. Spear & Sons, Standard Playing Card Co., the Stickless Corp., Sweeney Lithograph Co., Syndicate Products Co., Tactical Game Co., Thornecraft, Toohey Mfg. Co., Toy-In-Action Corp., the Toymakers, Transo Products, the Turner & Seymour Mfg. Co., James W. Tyson, Unique Novelty Co., United States Playing Card Co., Universal Toy & Novelty Mfg. Co., Warner Mfg. Co., Weber Manufactory, Whitman Publishing Co., the Wilder Corp., and Wilson Mfg. Co.

While it might not have seemed surprising to those able to observe the economic upheavals of the time, the list of manufacturers active in the game business in the later Great Depression years has relatively little overlap with the list of manufacturers emphasizing games in the late 1930s. I will list these, since comprehensive views of the prewar years is of significant interest to many collectors. I will not follow this with a comprehensive list of Boomer-era game manufacturers, however, since the panoptic view is less useful to Boomer-era collectors than more detailed, broken-down listings.

G

Late prewar manufacturers included Acme Toys, Leonard Adams Studios, All Metal Products Co., Alwill Projecto Corp., American Electrical Products Co., American Toy Works, Apex Mfg. Co., Arcade Mfg. Co., Arrco Playing Card Co., Artwood Toy Mfg. Co., Associated Syndicate, Baldwin Mfg. Co., L.G. Ballard Mfg. Co., Balsa Novelties Co., Bar Zim, Bargreen Mfg. Co., Bear Products Co., P.J. Benrath, Bersin Playthings, Billings, Binley Cut Flower Holder Co., Bo-Lo Co., Borzellino, Boynton, J.G. Brace & Co., Milton Bradley, Charles A. Brewer, Brinkman, Brown Mfg. Co., Brownlee & Shaw, Buffalo Toy & Tool Co., A.A. Burnstine Sales Organization, Burt-Griffith Mfg. Co., Cadaco-Ellis, Calumet Carton Co., Carrom, Centerbar Co., Child Welfare, Clover Games Co., Conestoga, Continental Sales, Corey Game Co., H. Davis & Co., Diamond Toy Co., the Discus Co., Harold W. Dow, William F. Krueke, Durable, Eagle Lock Co., Embossing, Fairchild, Fairway Mg. Co., Farmer Electric Maps, Fellowcrafters, the Fli-Back Co., Franco-American Novelty Co., Frandine Mfg. Co., J.F. Friedel Co., Fuld, Samuel Gabriel, Give-A-Party, Glolite Corp., Goody Mfg. Co., Goosmann Mg. Co., Gotham, Gropper Mfg. Co., Herbert Specialty Mfg. Co., Herion Fan Co., Hoge, Ivorycraft Co., Jaymar Specialty Co., Johnson Store Equipment Co., Karson Mfg. Co., Kerger Co., Knapp, John C. Kohaut, Kraftoy Corp., M.V. Krieg, John Lauterbach Co., the Lederer Co., Lindstrom, E.S. Lowe Co., Lubbers & Bell Mfg. Co., A. Lutz, Lynco Corp., James McGowan Associates., Marks Bros., John C. Martin Jr., Lawner Martin Co., Louis Marx & Co., A. Master, Metalectric Corp., Midwest Products Co., Charles E. Miller, National Games Co., Newton & Thompson Mfg. Co., N.Y. Toy & Sales Co., and Northwestern Products.

Others included Oznam Products, the Paddle Tennis Co., Parker Bros., Patent Engineering Co., Peltier Glass Co., Play Equipment Co., Jack Pressman, Products Mfg. Corp., Radio Games Co., Ravely & Co., Recreation Equipment Co., Red Circle Mfg. Co., the Reilly & Lee Co., Rex Accessories Co., Rex Mfg. Co., Rhyme-A-Lings, Rich Mfg. Co., Ring-A-Pin Co., "Rolling the Green," Rosebud Art, Roy Toy Co., Russell Mfg. Co., Schacht Rubber Mfg. Co., O. Schoenhut, the A. Schonehut Mfg. Co., Selchow & Righter Co., J.H. Sessions & Son, Sheboygan Specialty Co., "Sherms," Shower Mfg. Co., J.M. Simmons & Co., Edward Smith Mfg. Co., J.W. Spear & Sons, Standard Novelty Co., Standard Toykraft Products, Stoner Corp., Ferdinand Strauss Toys, Sweeney Lithograph Co., the Target Co., Toy Creations, the Toymakers, Transogram, Triad Mfg. Co., Tudor Metal Products Corp., the Turner & Seymour Mfg. Co., Unique Novelty Co., U.S. Playing Card Co., United Toy & Novelty Co., Universal Game Co., Universal Toy & Novelty Mfg. Co., Valley Novelty Works, Vermont Plywood Co., Volume Sprayer Co., Wabash Industries, Jon Weber Manufactory, Whitman Publishing Co., the Whittier Craftsmen, Windy Boat, Van A. Wirt, and Wolverine Supply & Mfg. Co.

"The Literary Game of Quotations" from Parker Bros., 1890s.

games, adult Games designed for adult players comprised a part of the toy industry increasingly distinct from childrens' games manufactured in the prewar years. While many of the largest manufacturers, such as Milton Bradley Co., the Embossing Co., Parker Bros., Selchow & Righter, and Wolverine Supply & Mfg. Co., made both kinds of pastimes, many made primarily one or the other.

Prewar manufacturers included the Alphadice Co., American Games Co., O.B. Andrews Co., Barrowe, Frederick H. Beach, Ray A. Beard Co., the Bowlet Co., Chicago Table Tennis Co., Cluff Cover Co., H.G. Cress Co., Dabs Corn Games, Charles Brace Darrow, Dieterman & Jones, Duit Publishing Co.,

Durabilt Steel Locker Co., the Elkloid Co., Enos-Leonard Mfg. Co., Field Mfg. Corp, Flinch Card Co., Furniture Stylists, General Sportcraft, the Herbert R. Gottfried Co., Hollywood Games, W.C. Horn Bro. & Co., Imperial Methods Co., Jig-Cross Novelty Co., Kardolette, N.J. Magnan Corp., Marks Bros., Meccano Co. of America, Modern Brands, Morris-Systems, L. Oppelman, N.L. Page & Son, Pattberg Novelty Corp., Arthur Popper, Rochester Folding Box Co., Walter L. Rothschild, William Rott, John Samuels, Simon & Schuster, J.W. Spear & Sons Co., Story & Clark Piano Co., Strand Mfg. Co., Tilley & Sherman, Traps Mfg. Co., United States Playing Card Co., the Waddell Co., Weber Manufactory, Westminster Sports, and Wilder Corp.

Prewar manufacturers of two of the vital ingredients for many such games, dice and poker chips, included Celluloid Corp., Compo-Site, the Elkloid Co., the G.H. Harris Co., Ivorycraft Co., the Marbelite Co., Pattberg Novelty Corp., Arthur Popper, William Rott, United States Playing Card, Utility Wood Products Co., and Van Dyke Products.

Milton Bradley's "Game of Life" from the 1960s.

games, miniature see *pocket games.*

"Gang Busters" A popular radio show, stage show, and show attraction at the New York World's Fair, "Gang Busters" was a minor 1939 hit. The exclusive licensor Bernard L. Schubert issued rights for items including a target range by Baldwin Mfg. Co.; books by David McKay Co. and Whitman Publishing Co.; game by Lynco Corp.;

holster sets by Feinberg-Henry Mfg. Co.; make-up kits by Miner's; and toys by Louis Marx & Co.

Logo for the 1939 hit show, "Gang Busters."

"Gang" pistol prewar, see *The Dent Hardware Co.*

garage and gas station toys A natural consequence of the popularity of toy cars and trucks was the development of garage and gas station toys. While some garages were relatively simple toys with the simplest of roofs, walls, and raising or opening doors, some of the gas station toys were complex affairs, especially in the postwar years. Marx made some of the most remarkable, with tin-litho buildings on tin-litho platforms, plastic accessories, plastic garage mechanics, and plastic cars. The first were made in prewar times by companies including Acme Toy & Novelty Co., Cincinnati Fly Screen Co., Gibbs Mfg. Co., Gibraltar Corrugated Paper Co., Grey Iron Casting Co., Keystone Mfg. Co., the F.L. Purdy Co., Rich Illinois Mfg. Co., Terre Town Toy Tradesmen, and the John C. Turner Corp. By the late prewar years, the Dill Co., Duplex Mfg. Co., Manufactured Specialties Co., Transogram Co. and the John C. Turner Corp. joined their ranks. Garages and gas stations were manufactured by numerous postwar companies, including Built-Rite Toys, T. Cohn, Louis Marx & Co., and Renwal Toy Corp.

garden sets Toy garden tools have a popularity going back into the 1800s, without countless smaller wood and iron-working firms issuing them as penny toys or as working miniatures. By the years before the Great Depression, manufacturers including them in their lines included Arcade Mfg. Co., Kirch-

G

hof Patent Co., and Transogram Co. All three continued producing sets through the prewar years, being joined in the 1930s by Holgate Bros. and Kingsbury Mfg. Co. Other prewar manufacturers included the C-K-R Co., Gardner Screw Corp., Hamilton Steel Products, Jaymar Specialty Co., the Kirchhof Patent Co., the Sabin Machine Co., and Waterbury Button Co.

In the Boomer years, toy garden tools were often made of wood and tin, but increasingly appeared in combinations of wood and plastic, and finally all plastic. Manufacturers included Baker Mfg. Co., T. Cohn, Come Play Products, Eldon Mfg. Co., Fillum Fun, Hamilton Steel Products, Irwin Corp., the Kirchhof Patent Co., Kroll Trading Co., Moen & Patton, Ohio Art Co., Radio Steel & Mfg. Co., Revere Mfg. Co., Suburban Toy & Mfg. Corp., Syracuse Toycraft Co., Transogram Co., and Worcester Toy Co.

Gardner & Co. This postwar Chicago, Ill., company specialized in skill, action and educational games and toys, dart games, bean bag games, basketball games, rhythm sets, TV games, party games, preschool games and toys, card games, spinner games, dice games, tambourines, bagged toys, and premium and promotional items.

Gardner Screw Corp. Besides general hardware, this East 17th Street, New York City, firm also made a variety of metal toys in the prewar years. The "Good Scout's Delight" line of wood and metal toys included toy handcuffs, toy money, shovels, a change maker, and a police badge in the 1920s. The "Juvenile Police Combination" was a set with club, badge, and handcuffs. Gardner continued the "Good Scout's Delight" line into the 1940s.

The "Good Scout's Delight Juvenile Police Combination."

Garrett Sales Corp. This Garrett, Ind., firm made toy cars under the "Garrett Lasting Toys" line of hard-rubber toy vehicles in the 1970s. The company also went by Rubber Toys Unique, and the toys, by the name "Rubbur Cars."

Garton Toy Co. A Sheboygan, Wis., manufacturer, Garton was one of the prominent names in juvenile toy vehicles. It established itself in the 1930s and '40s with pedal cars, coaster wagons, "Buddie Bikes," "Buddie Kars," wagons, velocipedes, Badger scooters, wheelbarrows, steering sleds, croquet sets, baby walkers, sidewalk cycles, and sandboxes, as well as outdoor furniture and lawn hose reels. Through the Boomer years, Garton issued much the same line, adding outdoor and indoor golf sets and water skis.

The "Hot Rod" was a Garton Toy Co. pedal car from the 1950s.

Garton's "Delivery Cycle"

gas engines see *engines, toy.*

gas station toys see *garage and gas station toys.*

"Gasoline Alley" The famous "Gasoline Alley" cartoon strip of the 1920s, by Frank King, featured the characters Uncle Walt, Skeezix, and Rachel. They inspired playthings including crayon books and paint books by McLoughlin Bros, and crayons and a "Walt and Skeezix" board game by Milton Bradley Co. The "Skeezix and Pal" store display to help sell associated products were made by Adler-Jones Co.

B. Shackman & Co. released these "Gasoline Alley" figures in the 1920s.

Skeezix   Uncle Walt

Gaston Mfg. Co. Based in Cincinnati, Ohio, Gaston issued the "Changeable" block toys of the 1950s, including "Changeable Charlie." See also *Halsam Products Co.*

Gat" repeating pistol see *The Hubley Mfg. Co.*

W.W. Gavitt W.W. Gavitt issued the 1903 card game, "Gavitt's Stock Exchange."

Gay Stuffed Toy & Novelty Co. Based on West 24th Street, New York City, this manufacturer specialized in teddy bears in the early 20th century, in plush and long pile mohair. The firm also made cats, dogs, and miscellaneous animal toys. By the 1930s, it also made soft toys for infants and Easter rabbits. The company continued these emphases through the Boomer years, often using the "Gay Toys" trade name.

Gayla Industries A Houston, Texas, firm active in the Boomer years, Gayla issued the "Keep Guided Plastic Kites" line, which sold in the $1.00 to $3.50 price bracket. Its kites included "Sky Raider," "Sky King," "Invader," "Lancer," "Firebird," and, most importantly for many children of the time, "Bat Kite."

Gebruder Bing see under *Bing.*

Gebruder Maerklin see under *Maerklin.*

"GEE" line of stuffed animals see *Gund Mfg. Co.*

"Gee Gee Horsee" exerciser see *Appleton Toy & Furniture Co.*

"Gee Wee" games see *Vera Toys.*

Geebee's Co. A Charlotte, N.C., company, Geebee's made a combination sled and see-saw in the late 1930s.

The Gelles-Widmer Co. This St. Louis, Mo., company specialized in learning games for school and home, including the "Dolch Play-Way" reading and arithmetic games, in the Boomer years. It also made "Parent-Teacher Aids" and flash cards.

"Gem" A widely used prewar trademark, "Gem" appeared on a bank from Behrend & Rothschild, mops from Arcade Mfg. Co., and science kits from Bausch & Lomb Optical Co. American Bubble Pipe also made a "Gem Bubbler."

Gem City Specialty Co. Gem City, located in Erie, Penn., specialized in outdoor games, including jump ropes, rubber ring toss, and the Champion crack shot target game. It also issued the "Gem City Champion" indoor golf game in the mid-1930s.

Gem Color Co. Wood construction sets, art sets, and mineral sets were among this Paterson, N.J., company's specialties in the postwar years.

Gem Crib & Cradle Co. This manufacturer of infant and juvenile furniture was based in Gardner, Mass., in the late 1930s through the Boomer years.

Gem Doll Corp. Based on Greene Street in the Doll District, Gem was a 1920s manufacturer.

Gem Electric Mfg. Co. Gem Electric, on Broome Street, New York City, entered the Christmas tree lighting business in the late 1930s. It moved to Brooklyn, N.Y., in the Boomer years.

Gem Mfg. Corp. A manufacturer of juvenile furniture, this Bascom, Ohio, corporation also made toy ironing tables, toy clothes racks, complete toy laundry sets, and

G

other toy doll furniture in the 1930s and '40s. It specialized in toy bassinets and cradles in the Boomer years.

Gem Party Favor Co. A Philadelphia, Penn., company, Gem supplied birthday party supplies, games, balloons and surprise packages in the 1950s and '60s.

Gem Toys, Inc. This Boomer-years specialist in wooden blocks and pull toys was based in Azusa, Calif.

"Gemco" sulkies prewar, see *Geneva Mfg. Co.*

The Gendron Mfg. Co. Gendron, of Toronto, Ontario, Canada, was one of two companies with the "Gendron" name involved in the manufacture of juvenile vehicles. Its products in the earlier 1930s included coaster wagons, velocipedes, pedal cars, scooters, sleigh autos, doll carriages, baby carriages and baby sleighs. Gendron also made nursery furniture.

The Gendron Wheel Co. The Gendron Wheel Co. of Toledo, Ohio, issued the "Pioneer Line" of the 1920s, featuring juvenile autos, velocipedes, scooters, tot bikes, handcars, wagons, bicycles, doll and baby carriages, and baby walkers. It employed the slogan, "The Children's Vehicle Line That Sets the Pace." Gendron's line in the 1930s included coaster wagons, all-steel wagons, toy automobiles, tot bikes, and barrows. The company also made playground equipment and "invalid chairs" in the 1930s and '40s. Located in Perrysburg, Ohio, in the Boomer years, Gendron emphasized the manufacture of playground equipment, steel gyms, slides, and sandboxes.

"Gene Autry" As a movie cowboy, Gene Autry began his long-lived popularity in the 1930s. Early toys and playthings in the late '30s included books by Whitman Publishing Co.; cowboy hats by Mode Novelty Co.; cowboy outfits by Keyston Bros.; repeating cap pistol and game by Kenton Hardware Co.; doll by R.A. Freundlich; and "singing" lariat and paper bang gun by Spotswood Specialty Co. Tie-in items continued to be popular in the Boomer years. "Gene Autry" playthings included films by Hollywood Film

Enterprises, books by Whitman, and a guitar with "automatic guitar player" by Emenee Industries.

The "Gene Autry Repeating Cap Pistol" by the Kenton Hardware Co., late 1930s.

"General Electric" The "General Electric Appliance Replicas" of the 1950s and '60s were manufactured by Structo Mfg. Co. The "General Electric" irons of the same period were made by Nassau Products Corp.

General Electric Co. As did many other manufacturers, General Electric entered the business of manufacturing electric Christmas tree lights and ornaments in the later 1930s. It was fittingly located on 1 Plastics Avenue, Pittsfield, Mass., at the time.

General Fibre Co. This postwar St. Louis, Mo., company made toy railway tunnels.

General Fibre Products Co. Based in Fitchburg, Mass., this firm made doll trunks and children's suitcases in the 1950s and '60s.

General Graphics Corp. Inflatable world globes were Boomer-era products of this Clifton, N.J., company. The firm used the "Georama" trade name.

The General Industries Co. Based in Elyria, Ohio, in the 1920s, General Industries made the "DeLuxe Phonograph" for children. These hand-cranked machines measured 17-1/2 inches high, in the late '20s console version. The smaller "Genola" was a table-top model with no cover.

General Molds & Plastics Corp. The "Andy Gard" line of plastic toy vehicles and battery-operated toys were produced by General Molds & Plastics, a specialist in polyethylene toys and in producing molds for the toy trade in the 1950s and '60s. The firm also issued Civil War, Cowboy, and Indian plastic figures. It was based in Leetsdale, Penn.

General Playground Equipment, Inc.
This Kokomo, Ind., firm made equipment for both public and private playgrounds, as well as beach and swimming pool items, in the late 1930s through the Boomer years.

General Shaver Corp.
A division of Remington Rand, Inc., General Shaver made a standard design, standard construction toy typewriter in the late 1930s and '40s. It was based on Fourth Avenue, New York City.

General Sports Equipment Co.
This Schenectady, N.Y., firm was making baseballs in the late 1930s.

General Sportcraft Co.
Apparently both importer and manufacturer, General Sportcraft's line included chemical sets in the mid-1930s. Its imports emphasized English games and products. By late decade it focused exclusive on sports and games, the latter including shuffleboard and deck tennis. In the Boomer years, General Sportcraft issued equipment for a variety of sports, as well as action games and toys including carpet and lawn bowls, boomerangs, quoits, croquet, and pogo sticks.

General Trains, Inc.
Based on West Lake Street, Chicago, Ill., General Trains made streamlined electric trains and tracks in the 1930s.

General Wheelbarrow Co.
The "Little General Boybarrow" was a popular 1930s item from this Cleveland, Ohio, manufacturer.

Geneva Mfg. Co.
Based in Geneva, Ill., this prewar manufacturer made children's sulkies, furniture, ironing boards, and novelties.

Geodestix
Structural kits and assembled model structures were 1950s and '60s products of this Spokane, Wash., company.

Geographic Educator Corp.
Based in Long island City, N.Y., this game firm's "Geo Bloc-O-Graphy World Puzzle" of the 1920s was a combination globe and take-apart puzzle. The firm also issued the "Neo-Golf," "Bowl-O-Pool" and "Nock-Em-Off" games.

Georgene Novelties, Inc.
A leading name in the doll industry, Georgene made soft dolls and animals. It was based on East 21st Street, New York City, in the 1930s, moving offices to the Fifth Avenue Building by the end of the decade. In the Boomer years it continued as a leader in the cloth doll specialty. Georgene held an exclusive license to issue "Raggedy Ann" and "Raggedy Andy" dolls. It also issued dolls including "Little Lulu," "Nosy Rosy," "Yum Yum," "Sunflower Sue," and "Lazy Bones."

Georgene Novelties, Inc. released the "Little Lulu" dolls in the 1960s.

"Gerber Babies"
Seven companies issued promotional baby-food dolls since 1936, when the first rag dolls were issued by an unidentified company. Manufacturers issuing the dolls included Sun Rubber, in the years 1955-58; Arrow Rubber & Plastic Corp., 1965-67; and Atlanta Novelty, in the late 1970s and 1980s.

Gerber Plastics Co.
Based in St. Louis, Mo., Gerber made plastic toys including badminton and tennis equipment, baby toys, preschool toys, and sandbox toys, in the 1950s and '60s.

The Gerling Toy Co.
A manufacturer based on West 21st Street, New York City, in the 1920s, Gerling made mama dolls, boudoir dolls, "Dancing Dollies," and "Winsome Babies," as well as novelties, premiums and carnival items. In the Boomer years, located on Broadway, Gerling's specialties continued to be dolls and animal toys.

G

"Giant," trademark see the *American-National Co.*

"Giant Books" see *Whitman Publishing Co.*

Giant Grip Mfg. Co. An Oshkosh, Wis., firm, Giant Grip made pitching horseshoes in the late 1930s.

"Giant Horse" blocks prewar, see *American Crayon Co.*

"Giant Magnet" see *Smethport Specialty Co.*

Giant Mfg. Co. Based in Council Bluffs, Iowa, Giant issued the "Junior" line of playground equipment and supplies of the 1930s and '40s.

"Giant Play Logs" see *Poynter Products, Inc.*

Giant Plastics Corp. Plastic bows and arrows, peg games, Indian sets, play puppet sets, and rack merchandise were specialties of this Park Avenue, New York City, firm in the Boomer years.

"Giant Series" picture puzzles see *Milton Bradley Co.*

"Giant" wheelbarrows see *The Steel Stamping Co.*

Ruth Gibbs Based in Flemington, N.J., Ruth Gibbs made "Miss Moppet" dolls and wardrobes in the 1950s and '60s.

Gibbs Automatic Moulding Co. This postwar Henderson, Ky., firm specialized in construction toys.

The Gibbs Mfg. Co. Gibbs Mfg. Co. was founded in 1884 in Canton, Ohio, by Lewis E. Gibbs as a manufacturer of plows. Gibbs added toys to the production line in 1886. Gibbs was manufacturing a line of games and pull toys at least 150 strong by the 1920s, with numbers including the "Waddle-Duck" and "Pretty Polly" pull toys, the ring-tossing "Hoop-ee" game, and the "Bing Ball" skill game. The company's products in the earlier 1930s included mechanical spinning tops, wagons, wood toys with lithographed paper decorations, metal toys including sand toys, games, jigsaws, and novelties. Prominent in the prewar years, it continued manufacturing through the postwar period.

Gibbs Mfg. Co.'s "Bing-Ball" ball-catch game from the 1920s.

The "Waddle Duck" was a Gibbs Mfg. Co. pull-toy.

Gibraltar Corrugated Paper Co., Inc. This mid-1930s North Bergen, N.J., company made toys and games of corrugated paper.

Gibraltar Mfg. Co., Inc. The "Betsy Ross" toy sewing machines of the Boomer years were manufactured by this Jersey City, N.J., company.

Gibraltar Mfg. Co., Inc. made the "Betsy Ross Sewing Machine" in the 1960s.

"Giddy-Ap" spring horses see *DeLuxe Woodcraft Co., Inc.*

"Gigi" line see *A. & H. Doll Mfg. Corp.*

Gilbert Clock Co. Based in Winsted, Conn., this firm obtained a late 1930s license to issue Edgar Bergen related clocks.

A.C. Gilbert Co. A.C. Gilbert is best known as the manufacturer of the "Erector" set, a popular construction toy that involved metal struts, platforms, wheels and pulleys, which a child could use for construction projects, using appropriately scaled tools. The company first offered the toy in 1913. Sets built in the years 1913-1962 are of primary interest to collectors.

Albert C. Gilbert started in New Haven, Conn., as a manufacturer of box magic sets, however, in 1908. The "Erector" sets brought his company instant success. At the beginning of World War I, the company bought out Richter Anchor Block and the American affiliate of Meccano. In 1914 it started manufacturing toy automobiles and trucks, and scientific toys. In 1916 its line included the "Meteor Game," an activity game.

By the end of the '20s and the beginning of the Great Depression, Gilbert's line was led by its "Improved Erector," electrically driven zeppelins and airplanes, and new tool chests and chemistry sets.

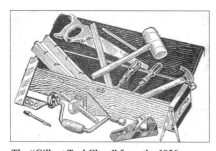

The "Gilbert Tool Chest" from the 1920s.

In the 1930s, the company was well established, maintaining offices in the Fifth Avenue Building and selling not only the famous construction toy but also electrical sets, tool chests, chemistry sets, puzzles, magic sets, the "Kaster Kit," an "Electro Plater" kit, jigsaws, motors, and the "Pak o' Fun Movy Sho." In 1938 it acquired American Flyer Mfg. Co., and subsequently kept the name for the line of trains active.

By the late prewar years, Gilbert was making electrical sets, glass blowing kits, mineralogy sets, microscopes, an electric eye kit, telephone and telegraph sets, puzzles, and motors, in addition to the items introduced earlier. Its line in the 1950s and '60s was of a similar nature, emphasizing "Erector" sets, "American Flyer" trains in "S" and "HO" gauges (until the line was sold to Lionel Corp. in 1966), tool chests, chemistry sets, microscopes, puzzles, and motors.

The company's founder, Alfred Carlton Gilbert (1884-1961), was an interesting character in his own right, being a medical doctor and a Gold Medalist at the 1907 World Olympics in London. He served as the first president of the Toy Manufacturers Association of the U.S.A. See also *Kelmet Corp.*

A.C. Gilbert's "Mysto Magic" set from the 1950s.

Gilbert Toy & Novelty Co. This Brooklyn, N.Y., firm made "Tobie" dolls in the late 1930s.

Marty Gilman, Inc. Plastic inflatable toys were Boomer-years specialties of this Gilman, Conn., company.

Gilmark Merchandising Corp. Small-scale cars, trucks and military vehicles were specialties of this earlier 1950s firm, based in New York City. Gilmark also made a variety of rocket and space cars.

"Ginny" dolls see *Vogue Doll Shoppe.*

"Giraffe Gym" see *The Goshen Mfg. Co.*

Girard Model Works, Inc. Frank E. Wood's company, the Toy Works, founded in 1919 in Girard, Penn., became Girard Model

Works, Inc. in 1922, and later Girard Mfg. Co. Manufacturing spinning tops, skates, banks, a "Walking Porter" toy, steel autos, trucks, and trains, the company made Louis Marx a commissioning agent in the late 1920s, and for several years used the Marx name on toys it produced, alongside its own line. For this period, Girard and Marx toys were indistinguishable, although some Girard toys bore the slogan, "Making Childhood's Hour Happier." An activity game from Girard's last decade is the "Japanese Ball Game" of the '30s. The "Joy Line" of toy trains were of particular importance, produced by Girard for Marx under a commission sales agreement. They first appeared in 1927 or '28. The line was completely taken over by Marx after Girard declared bankruptcy in 1934.

Company logo for Girard Model Works, Inc.

"Girder and Panel" see *Kenner Products Co.*

Gits Plastic Games An early manufacturer of plastic games, Gits issued "adult games for morale" during the war years. Besides chess, its games included "Helios" and "Polygon."

Give-A-Party This Chicago, Ill., firm issued the "Newspaper Party" game of the late 1930s.

"Gizmo" launcher and flying saucers see the *Boyd Specialty Co., Inc.*

Glad Toy Co. Based in the Fifth Avenue Building, New York City, Glad Toy made postwar fur stuffed animals.

Gladen Enterprises, Inc. A postwar manufacturer of bicycle accessories, Gladen of Bay City, Mich., also made plastic machine gun toys.

Glanson Co. This Fifth Avenue, New York City, company made postwar cribbage boards under the "Brooks" and "Triumph"

names, and "Sidney S. Lenz" canasta and bridge scoreboards.

"Glantz's" stuffed toys see *Expert Doll & Toy Co.*

glass toys Glass was used as a material for 18th century toys. Henry William Stiegel's Mannheim, Penn., glass works was producing glass toys in the 1760s. Glass balls, beads, and glass toy dishes continued to be manufactured for children into the 19th century.

"Glassonix" marbles see *Peltier Glass Co.*

Glen Novelty Co. "Bristle" archery and dart games were produced by this Glens Falls, N.Y., company in the 1930s.

"Glide-A-Tot" baby jumper see *The Frank F. Taylor Co.*

"Glide-O-Plane" gliders see *The Boy Toymaker Co.*

Glider Skate Mfg. Co. Glider skates for use on snow or ice were the specialty of this Chicago, Ill., firm in the late 1930s.

"Gliderole" sled see *Auto-Wheel Coaster Co., Inc.*

"Glitter Glo" costumes see *Ben Cooper.*

"Glitterama" plastic Christmas trees see *Lapin Products, Inc.*

"Glo-Ranges" electric ranges prewar, see *The Metal Ware Corp.*

"Globe" air rifle see *J.A. Dubuar.*

The Globe Co. Based in Sheboygan, Wis., the Globe Co. made coaster wagons, scooters and velocipedes in the 1930s, as well as disc wheels and stamped metal parts for wheel toys. It touted the "one piece body—no seams, no rivets, no joints, no welds" of its "Globe Racer" wagon. The company was successful enough to maintain permanent showrooms on West 29th Street, New York City. The company also made dolls and the "Ideal" doll display stands.

The "Globe Racer" wagon was produced by The Globe Co. in the 1930s.

Globe Crayon Co. Besides chalk and wax crayons, this prewar Brooklyn, N.Y., company made art sets and watercolors. By the late 1930s and '40s it was manufacturing chalk and blackboard sets, and modeling clay.

Globe Rubber Products Co. This postwar manufacturer of "Swim King" swimming accessories also made quoits and ice sports supplies. It was based in Philadelphia, Penn.

"Globe Series" picture puzzles see *Milton Bradley Co.*

"Globe Trotter" doll trunks prewar, see *McGraw Box Co.*

Globe-Union Mfg. Co. Based in Milwaukee, Wis., this company made roller skates and sled skates from the 1930s through the Boomer years, with a production hiatus during wartime. It used the "Globe" trade name."

globes, geographical Geographical globes became specialties for manufacturers of educational toys and tin toys by the later 1930s. Prewar manufacturers included J. Chein & Co., Pioneer Rubber Co., Replogle Globes, and Weber Costello Co. In the Boomer years, Alvimar Mfg. Co., Barnett & Son, Chein, George F. Cram Co., Ohio Art Co., Rand, McNally & Co., Replogle Globes, Sterling Plastics Co., and Weber Costello all issued them as educational items and toys. Occasionally the globes were parts of games, as in Replogle's "Globe Race" of the mid-1950s, in which magnetic airplanes traveled around the metal globe. General Graphics

Corp. was issuing what may have been the most unusual examples by the late 1950s: inflatable geographic globes.

glockenspiele A glockenspiele is a percussion instrument with tuned metal bars played with two mallets or hammers. Many toy versions are called xylophones despite having metal bars; and many have bars tuned to a simple major scale, rather than a chromatic, 12-note scale.

The Glolite Corp. Besides electric stars and "electric altars," Glolite made electrically illuminated miniature Christmas trees under the "Candlelight" and "Glolite" trade names in the late 1930s and '40s. The firm continued to emphasize Christmas light sets and illuminated holiday decorations through the Boomer years.

Gloria Toy Co., Inc. Plush toys and novelties were postwar specialties of this Broadway, New York City, company.

"Glyde Pony" see *Rich Illinois Mfg. Co.*

"Go" A Japanese game, "Go" was made available in prewar America by Parker Bros. and Katagiri Corp. The latter called it "Go Chinese Game."

"Go-Bi-Bi" walker-stroller prewar, see *The Frank F. Taylor Co.*

go-cart (1) more typical meaning (2) See "standing stool." For manufacturers, see *carriages, baby.*

"Go-Dink" scooter prewar, see *Garton Toy Co.*

"Go to the Head of the Class" see *Milton Bradley Co.*

Gobar Products Based in Elkhart, Ind., Gobar made the mid-1930s "Mystery Boat." The company specialized in mechanical boats, toy guns, and "ten cent novelties."

Godey's Lady's Book In 1859, this women's periodical became the first magazine to publish paper dolls in its pages.

"Gogoose" see *Janesville Products Co.*

G

"Gold Medal" The trademark "Gold Medal" was used by several prewar companies. Transogram Co. used it for its line of toys and games, while D.P. Harris Hardware & Mfg. Co. used it on its skates, bicycles and other wheel goods.

"Gold Star" see *The Brothers Mfg. Co.*

E. Goldberger The "Eegee" dolls were the product of this Brooklyn, N.Y. firm in the 1920s through the '40s. The line continued in prominence through the Boomer years. The company was called Goldberger Doll Corp. by the war years, and Goldberger Doll Mfg. Co., Inc., in the Boomer years.

Logo for Goldberger's "Eegee" dolls.

Golden Aircrafts Corp. This prewar Dallas, Texas, corporation made "Ski-Ryder" model aircraft and boat construction kits.

"Golden Arrow" racer The large pressed-steel "Golden Arrow" racers of the 1920s and '30s, measuring about 21" long, are among the most famous toys manufactured by Kingsbury Mfg. Co. They have a distinctive appearance, with tail fin and flattened body extending to the sides. Major H.O.D. Segrave raced the state-of-the-art racer "Golden Arrow" at the record speed of 231-1/2 mph. on March 11, 1929. Kingsbury, which had already successfully produced the "Sunbeam" and "Bluebird" racers in large toy form, obtained exclusive rights to manufacture a toy version of the "Golden Arrow," and issued them by that summer.

"Golden Arrow" wagon see *Rainey Mfg. Co.*

"Golden Eagle" air rifle see *Daisy Mfg. Co.*

"Golden Eagle" jigsaw puzzles see *Parker Bros.*

"Golden Fleece" stuffed toys prewar, see *Winchester Toy Co.*

"Golden Hour Collection" puzzles prewar, see *Samuel Gabriel Sons & Co.*

Golden Needle Corp. This Brooklyn, N.Y., company issued Boomer-era sewing and knitting sets, manicure sets and children's jewelry.

Golden Press, Inc. Books and records for children were this Fifth Avenue, New York City, firm's specialty in the Boomer years. The "Little Golden Books" series were among the most popular children's books of the time, being a uniform edition of color-illustrated story books for young readers. Many tied in to popular movies and TV shows and cartoons. Disney titles, ranging from Walt Disney's "Davy Crockett" to "Cinderella," were especially popular. Golden Press issued a popular series of pocket-size guide books, most of them with a natural history focus.

Golden Triangle Toy Co. Doll carriages and strollers, hobbyhorses, stick horses, and plastic toys were specialties of this postwar Pittsburgh, Penn., company.

"Goldilocks and the Three Bears" A folk tale of extreme popularity, "Goldilocks and the Three Bears" inspired a variety of playthings. One of the earliest American items was "Goldenlocks and the Three Bears," published in 1890 by McLoughlin Bros. Later examples from the prewar period include the A.I. Root Co.'s "Three Bears" adding board, Charles E. Graham & Co.'s "Three Bears Kut-Outs," Holgate Bros. Co.'s "Three Bears" log cabin and "Goldilocks and the Three Bears" wooden toy, Milton Bradley Co.'s "Three Bears" puzzle box, and Harter Publishing Co.'s "Three Bears" shadow play. Postwar playthings included "Goldilocks & 3 Bears Fingertip Puppets" by Wilkening Mfg. Co., and the "Goldilocks" game of 1955 by Cadaco-Ellis.

Sanitoy's "Goldilocks" stuffed doll, 1950s.

The Goldsmith Publishing Co. Located

on South Dearborn Street, Chicago, Ill., Goldsmith was an active publisher on inexpensive editions for children during the first half of the century and through the Boomer years. It published fiction, Christmas giveaway books, and valentines.

P. Goldsmith Sons Co. Based in Cin-

cinnati, Ohio, the P. Goldsmith Sons Co. issued 1930s juvenile sporting goods with a "Reg'lar Fellows" theme. It used the "Sports Joys for Real Boys" slogan.

Philip Goldsmith's Sons This Coving-

ton, Ky., firm manufactured sporting goods in the later 1800s, especially baseballs.

Charles & Victor Goldstein A special-

ist in juvenile vehicles, this Brooklyn, N.Y., company made children's bikes and scooters, scooter cycles, the "Baby-Pal Car," "Rambling Rob" and "Bucking Bob" horses, and beach carriages in the 1930s.

golf The introduction of golf is attributed to the Dutch. Early golfers used a mixture of wooden and iron clubs and leather balls packed with steamed feathers. The most important American manufacturer, A.G. Spalding & Bros., began importing and manufacturing clubs in the 1890s. Juvenile golfing equipment was a minor category for toy manufacturers until the Boomer years, when a number of companies issued sets. They included Baker Mfg. Co., Bayshore Industries, Blake & Conroy, T. Cohn, E. & L. Mfg. Co., Empire Plastic Corp., Garton Toy Co., Lapin Products, Moen & Patton, N.Y. Toy & Mfg. Corp., Transogram Co., Withington, and Wolverine Supply & Mfg. Co.

golf games Board and other family games based on golfing appeared frequently once the outdoor game established itself, with titles appearing from the 1890s through the 1930s from companies including Milton Bradley Co., E.O. Clark, Clark & Sowdon, McLoughlin Bros., the A. Schoenhut Co., and J.H. Singer. Postwar manufacturers included Big Top Games, Coleco Toy Products, Parris Mfg. Co., Pet Toy Co. of New Hampshire, Sabas & Carney, and Signal Game Co.

Golfette This Chicago, Ill., firm issued the late 1930s "Golfette" card game.

The Gong Bell Mfg. Co. A famous

name in toys for younger children, Gong Bell made hardware bells, cast-iron and wood bell push and pull toys, and toy telephones before and after the war. The firm's toys of the 1920s included the "New Television Plaphone," "Improved Fire Alarm," "Whirl-Ring Monoplane," "Pedal Pete," and "Jingling Jim." In the late prewar years, its line emphasized push-and-pull toys, toy mowers and lawn sweepers, toy phones, hobby toys, puzzle blocks, rider toys, and doll furniture. It continued production of some wood toys during the war. Gong Bell's 1950s-'60s pull toys included "Granny Goose," "Bruin Band," Fuzzy Fireman," "Loco-Trix," "Dancing Bears," "Drum Major," "Jumbo Jim," and "Kitty Bell Toy." Its telephone toys included "Dial Plaphone," "Speedphone," "Pay Bank Phone," "Upright Dial Phone," "Electric Bell Phone," and "Hand Phone with Voice." Founded in 1886, Gong Bell was surprisingly enough located in the same city, East Hampton, Conn., as another well-known manufacturer of bell and chime toys, N.N. Hill Brass Co.

PIGGY TRUCK 256

The "Piggy Truck" from the Gong Bell Mfg. Co.

G

"Goo-Goo" Radio celebrity Joe Penner made famous not only the phrase, "Wanna Buy a Duck?" but also the duck itself, named "Goo-Goo." The Rushton Co., makers of "Mawaphil Soft Dolls" at the time, issued a "Goo-Goo" duck in time for Penner's first talking picture, "College Rhythm," in the fall of 1934. Thornecraft issued a rubber squeeze doll; and Franco-American Novelty Co., "Goo-Goo" eye glasses.

Rushton Co. issued this "Goo-Goo" duck, seen with radio celebrity Joe Penner, in 1934.

Good Doll & Toy Co., Inc. This manufacturer in the Doll District was active in the late 1930s.

Good-Lite Electric Mfg. Co. One of many manufacturers in the burgeoning business of producing electric Christmas tree outfits in the late 1930s, Good-Lite was based in Bridgeport, Conn. It continued in operation through the Boomer years.

"Good Luck" coaster wagons see *Frederick Machine Works.*

"Good Scout" wagons see *Sheboygan Coaster & Wagon Works.*

Goodenough and Woglom A firm active near the end of the Great Depression, Goodenough and Woglom issued "Bible Quotto" in 1932, and "Bible Lotto," "Bible Rhymes" and "Hymn Quartets" in 1933.

Goodrich, Chauncey see *George W. Brown & Co.*

Goodwin, William F. A New York City inventor, William F. Goodwin patented the 1866 "Automatic Toy," which was made by several 19th century manufacturers, including George W. Brown & Co. The figure was a walking doll with realistic action, balancing

itself by leaning into the baby carriage it pushed.

L.A. Goodman Mfg. Co. Juvenile wall plaques were among the specialties of this Chicago, Ill., firm in the 1950s and '60s. It also made illuminated Christmas decorations, and lamps.

"Goody" 1920s, see *Shulman & Sons.*

Goody Mfg. Co. Based on East 16th Street, New York City, Good made educational games, coloring sets, and novelties in the 1930s and '40s. In the Boomer years the company's line emphasized novelty pencil boxes, checkerboard sets, magic toys, educational games, and coloring sets.

"Goodyear" erasers see *The Rosenthal Co.*

Goodyear Rubber Sundries Co. In the 1930s, this New Haven, Conn., company was making rubber play balls.

"Goofy" games see *Herbert Specialty Mfg. Co.*

"Googlies" This 1967-68 line of 14-inch stuffed animals included "Googli Kitty," "Puppy," "Bunny," and "Bear," in its first year, and "Googli Pig" and "Elephant," in its second. The line was issued by Mattel.

"Gooseberry" marbles Marbles that are like "Clambroths" but made with a translucent core are "Gooseberries."

Goosmann Mfg. Co. This Grand Rapids, Mich., company issued the "Rub-Er-Shot" marksman outfit and "Junior Hockey" game in the late 1930s.

Gopher Game Co. This Forest Lake, Minn., manufacturer issued Boomer-era games.

Gordon Mfg. Co. Based in Philadelphia, Penn., Gordon made the "Health Rider" exerciser, having a steel base and horse seat at the end of the heavy metal spring. The firm, under the name Gordon Toy & Mfg. Co., continued making the "Health Rider" through the 1930s and '40s. In the Boomer years, again called Gordon Mfg. Co., the firm

G

made gym sets, hobbyhorses, and playground equipment.

Gordon Motor Crib Co., Inc. The "Gordon Motor Crib" of the 1920s was a bassinet designed to serve efficiently in the touring car and sedan, and then to become a carriage when added to a rubber-tired carriage base. The company was based on Bridge Street, New York City.

Gordon Novelty Co. Based on Broadway, New York City, Gordon Novelty made party favors, premium items, and novelties in the 1930s and '40s. In the 1950s and '60s, its line also included balloons and masks.

Gordon Toy & Mfg. Co. see *Gordon Mfg. Co.*

The Goshen Mfg. Co. This Goshen, Ind., specialist in outdoor furniture was producing juvenile items, including swings, teeter-totters, slides, and sandboxes, by the late prewar years. It continued the line through the Boomer years.

Gotham Industries "Little Miss Muffet" tea sets were postwar products of this Broadway, New York City, company. Gotham also made plastic bowling games and "Duraflector" Christmas ornaments.

Gotham Pressed Steel Corp. Originally called Gotham Stamping & Die Corp., and located on E. 24th Street, New York City, Gotham made drums, horns, noisemakers, megaphones, and siren horns in the 1920s. The company moved to Wales Avenue, New York City, and issued through the 1930s and early '40s doll carriages, drums, games, toy carpet sweepers, toy dust pans, bagatelles, novelties, horns, and noisemakers, as well as pool and billiard tables.

Gotham's titles included the board and activity games "Carl Hubbell Mechanical Baseball," "Ching-Ka-Chek" chinese checkers, "Ride 'Em Cowboy," "Jackie Robinson Baseball Game," and "Jungle Hunt." Gotham also made table ice hockey games, skip ball, roulette, "National Handicap" pool tables, and the "Trike Shot" bagatelle. In the late '30s Gotham obtained a license to issue Walt Disney character toy cleaning sets, through Kay Kamen.

In the Boomer years, now located at 133rd Street and Cypress Avenue, Gotham issued action games including "Electro-Magnetic" football and baseball games, "Electric Basketball," "Push-Button Magnetic Baseball," "Big League Hockey," and pool and bumper pool tables, in both floor and table models.

Gotham Stamping & Die Corp. see *Gotham Pressed Steel Corp.*

"Gothic" crayons see *The Art Crayon Co.*

The Herbert R. Gottfried Co. An Erie, Penn., company, Herbert R. Gottfried manufactured toy pianos and pipe organs in the mid-1930s, as well as games and novelties.

Sidney Gottheimer, Inc. Fitted doll cradles, bassinettes and baskets were postwar products of this West 15th Street, New York City, firm.

Gottlieb Paper Products Mfg. Co. A prewar specialist in Christmas bells, garlands and serpentines located Brooklyn, N.Y., Gottlieb became I.W. Gottlieb Paper Specialties Corp. by the late 1930s.

Gould Mfg. Co. This 1920s Oshkosh, Wis., manufacturer made nursery toys, wheel goods, juvenile furniture, wooden action toys, and novelties.

J.H. Grady Mfg. Co. A St. Louis, Mo., company, Grady manufactured prewar indoor and sports balls. It was using the "Duro-Seam" trade name by the late 1930s.

Charles E. Graham & Co. A Newark, N.J., publisher, Graham published toy books in the 1920s, and "Uncle Wiggly" picture books in the 1930s. Other items included coloring books, puzzles, paint books, and scrapbooks.

William J. Graham This Lowell, Mass., firm issued jump ropes, cowboy lariats, tinsel cords and kite twine in the late 1930s.

"Grako Kid" see *Graton & Knight Co.*

G

Gramercy Stamp Co. Gramercy started its successful business in supplying postage stamps and stamp collecting outfits to young collectors in the late 1930s. It was based on West 16th Street, New York City.

Grand Rapids Dowel Works This Grand Rapids, Mich., wood-turning company produced chessmen, chess and checker boards, golf tees, cribbage boards, and wood novelties in the 1930s and '40s.

Grand Rapids Juvenile, Inc. Juvenile and doll furniture were this Grandville, Mich., firm's postwar specialty.

Grand Rapids Toy Furniture Co., Inc. Based in Grand Rapids, Mich., this postwar company manufactured doll furniture, peg tables, alphabet stools, stick horses, and plastic toys.

Grand Wig & Novelty Co. Doll and costume wigs were among this West 17th Street, New York City, company in the 1930s.

Grand Wig Co., Inc. Besides wigs and beard sets, this Fifth Avenue, New York City, company issued doll accessories, doll hospital supplies, and Santa Claus outfits in the Boomer years.

"Grandmama's" 1880s, see *McLoughlin Bros.*

Grandmother Stover's, Inc. This Columbus, Ohio, company specialized in dollhouse miniatures.

Grant & Grant The "Wee Folks Wagon," an electric auto for children, was a 1950s-60s product of this Los Angeles, Calif., company.

Grant Plastics, Inc. Based in Townsend, Mass., in the Boomer years, Grant Plastics made dressed and undressed dolls.

Graton & Knight Co. This Worcester, Mass., firm issued the "Grako Kid" holsters of the mid-1950s. These came with memberships in the company's "Grako Kid Wrangler's Club."

Gray Bros., Inc. Based in Plano, Ill., Gray Bros. produced "five and ten cent toys" in the earlier 1930s.

"Gray Ghost" This CBS Films hero inspired 1950s-'60s playthings including paint sets by Transogram Co., and gun and holster sets by Carnell Mfg. Co.

Grayco Products, Inc. Character lamps for children were the specialty of this late 1930s Chicago, Ill., firm.

Great American Plastics Co. This Fitchburg, Mass., company issued the "Glows-Mobile" plastic toy car of the late 1940s, with battery-operated light.

Great Lakes Press This Rochester, N.Y., company published paper dolls and costumes in the 1950s and '60s.

The Great Lakes Tractor Co. The "Vanguard" gas-powered juvenile autos of the 1950s-'60s were produced by Great Lakes Tractor of Cleveland, Ohio.

Grebnelle Novelty Active in the 1910s, Grebnelle issued "Championship Baseball Parlor Game," a 1914 board game.

Greenberg Publisher, Inc. The "How Smart Is Your Baby" educational toy set was issued in the mid-1930s by this Fourth Avenue, New York City, firm. It also published Tony Sarg books through the 1930s and early '40s.

Greenfield Wood Letter Co. The "Diamond" baseball game of the late 1930s was produced by this Greenfield, Mass., company.

greenhouse toys Toy greenhouses, a kind of gardening toy, were a 20th century equivalent of the enclosed terrariums that fascinated the Victorians. Prewar manufacturers included Arrow Mfg. Co., the Meccano Co. of America, and Wolverine Supply & Mfg. Co.

"Greenie Stik-M" caps see *Mattel, Inc.*

Wolf Greenspan & Sons Based in Brooklyn, N.Y., Wolf Greenspan & Sons made children's wicker furniture and toy clothes baskets in the 1930s and '40s.

Greenville Mfg. Co. Based in Brooklyn, N.Y., Greenville manufactured playsuits, holster sets, and masquerade costumes in the late prewar years.

greeting cards Greeting cards were sometimes also toys. Many valentines, especially in the 20th century, had simple mechanical actions, or else were "folders," which were a combination of the ideas of card and toy.

Albert. A. Gregg Albert A. Greg produced the "Gregg Football Game," a 1924 board game.

Gregg Mfg. Co. Toboggans and skis of hickory and birch wood were made in the 1930s by this Street Paul, Minn., company.

Greiner, Ludwig A German immigrant, Ludwig Greiner manufactured dolls in the mid-19th century in Philadelphia, Penn. He obtained a patent on his method of making composition doll heads.

The Fred Gretsch Mfg. Co. Musical toys and juvenile instruments were the specialty of this Brooklyn, N.Y., company. In the 1930s it made children's drums and drum outfits, toy band instruments, harmonicas, kindergarten rhythm band instruments, and ukuleles, as well as rolling hoops. It was using the "Hill Billy" trade name on band sets in the later 1930s and '40s.

Grey Iron Casting Co. Based in Mount Joy, Penn., Grey Iron is best known to collectors as a producer of metal toy soldiers. It used the slogan "Guaranteed Iron Toys" in the 1920s. Specializing in iron toys, the company also produced jackstones, banks, golf clubs, Christmas tree holders and fences, stoves and ranges, sad irons, toy tools and tool sets, machine guns, and the "Tint-Em Toy" paint sets by the earlier 1930s. the "Clever Clown" circus sets appeared late in the decade. Founded in 1900 under the name Brady Machine Shop, the company made its first toys in 1903. Its toy soldier lines included the "Grey Klip Armies" line of toy soldiers, manufactured 1917-1941, "Greycraft Models" figures in the 1930s, the "Iron Men" series in 1936, and "Uncle Sam's Defender" in 1938. The company was forced to cease toy production during World War II. The company was still in business in the mid-

Boomer years, producing iron toys, jackstones, cast iron stoves, toy tools and tool sets, and toy soldiers at a time when almost all other companies had turned to plastic.

"Grey Klip Armies" see *Grey Iron Casting Co.*

"Greycraft Models" figures see *Grey Iron Casting Co.*

"Greyhound" juvenile vehicles see the *Emblem Mfg. Co.*

"Greyhound" coaster wagons see *Hamilton Steel Products.*

"Greyhound" roller skates see *Moen & Patton, Inc.*

Greyshaw of Georgia, Inc. Greyshaw, located in Atlanta, Ga., produced a variety of Boomer-era toys, including blocks, toy cars, trunks racers, target shooters, infants' toys, building sets, and rack merchandise.

Grier Mfg. Co. This Greenville, S.C., company, founded in the later 1930s, issued baseballs, softballs and playground bats.

Grimm's Fairy Tales This famous collection of traditional tales was first published in 1815.

A. Gropper A. Gropper released the "Hunting in the Jungle" activity game in the 1920s.

M. Gropper & Sons Gropper's line of "National" onyx marbles included the "National Prima Agates," "National Cerise Agates," and "National Milkie Agates" in the 1920s. Based in the Fifth Avenue Building, with factory in Brooklyn, N.Y., the firm changed its name to Gropper Onyx Marble Co. in the 1930s. The line expanded to include croquet, quoits, sand sets, toy cash registers, soldier sets, animal sets, target games, and bagatelles in the earlier 1930s. By the end of the decade it changed its name again to the Gropper Mfg. Co., Inc., adding "Woodbuilt" construction sets, knitting and weaving kits, tennis sets, and wood spinning tops.

G

Gropper Bros. The Gropper Bros. and A. Gropper Corp. of the 1920s were related businesses, both operating out of 225 Fourth Avenue, New York City. Gropper Bros. manufactured wood spinning tops, "Ball Bearing" tops, "Buster Spring" tops, and "Full Rubber Cushion" tops, among some 40 other items. At the same time, A. Gropper Corp. manufactured wood and metal toys, noisemakers, tea sets, soldier sets, and animal sets.

The Jerome Gropper Co. Located on East 22nd Street, New York City, Jerome Gropper issued postwar wood spinning tops, Filipino tops, marbles, wooden pull toys, jack sets, and pinwheels.

Gross-Given Mfg. Co. A Street Paul, Minn., company of the late 1930s, Cross-Given manufactured the "Sandy" picnic table and sand box combination, a descendant of Jesse Crandall's "Sandometer."

Grossett & Dunlap, Inc. An important prewar and postwar publisher of juvenile and children's books, Grosset & Dunlap's licenses included "Snow White" in the late 1930s. In the Boomer years, the Broadway, New York City, publisher issued numerous games, toys and activity sets, including "ActiviToys," "Beginner's Stamp Outfit," "Bobbsey Twins Play House," "Jolly Jump-Ups," "Notch-Ems," and "G. & D. Activity Boxes." Its numerous book lines and children's titles included "Big Treasure Books," "Squeekum Book," "Treasure Coloring Books," "Wonder Books," "Wonder Play Books," and "Tap-A-Tune Music Book." Book series of the 1950s-60s included the "Bomba," "Bobbsey Twins," "Honey Bunch," "Thornton W. Burgess," "Tom Corbett, Space Cadet," "Ken Holt," "Maida," "Chip Hilton," "Tom Quest," "Rick Brant," "Hardy Boys," "Lone Ranger," "Dana Girls," "Connie Blair," "Vicki Barr," "Nancy Drew," "Judy Bolton," "Cherry Ames," "Beverly Gray," and "Tom Swift, Jr." series.

Grossman Stamp Co. Grossman, located on West 24th Street, New York City, competed with Gramercy Stamp Co. in the late prewar years in issuing stamps for young collectors, collecting outfits, and albums. It continued through the Boomer years from a new location on Sixth Avenue

Grove & Grove This Chicago, Ill., firm issued archery sets in the late 1930s.

Grove-Tex Industries Based in Waco, Texas, Grove-Tex issued postwar play money, educational items, and trick spinning rope.

The Johnny Gruelle Co. This Princeton Junction, N.J., company issued postwar "Raggedy Ann" and "Ragged Andy" books, and owned the character copyrights to Gruelle's creations.

Herman Grunow Fibre and composition play items including hand-finished castles, tunnels, forts, doll houses, farm sets, and Christmas cribs were produced by this late 1930s manufactured, based on North William Street, New York City.

Karl Guggenheim, Inc. This Boomer-era manufacturer of children's jewelry and novelties also issued bongo drums and jumping beans. Guggenheim was located on Union Square, New York City.

"Guild" puzzles and playing cards see *Whitman Publishing Co.*

Paul K. Guillow, Inc. The "Fly-A-Way" airplanes and gliders were made by this prewar Wakefield, Mass., company. Guillow also made airplane construction sets, and the "Crash" and "Flying for Fun" aviation games of the earlier 1930s. The "Fun-Doo" puzzle appeared in the late '30s. The line of "Fly-A-Way" gliders and airplane construction sets continued through wartime. In the postwar years, Guillow continued its emphasis on ready-to-fly gliders and motorplanes, die-cut balsa flying and shelf model airplane construction kits, and gas-engine model kits.

Gulliver's Travels Although not originally intended as a tale for children, *Gulliver's Travels,* first published in England in 1726, soon became a favorite among younger readers.

"The Gumps" The famous 1920s and '30s cartoon strip "The Gumps," by Sidney Smith, featured the characters Andy Gump,

Chester, and Ching Chow. Playthings included the "Andy Gump" toy auto by Arcade Mfg. Co. in cast iron, and in die-cast metal by Dowst Mfg. Co. Arcade also made a cast-iron bank. Milton Bradley Co. issued "Andy Gump, His Game," in 1924. In the '30s, Milton Bradley also released "The Gumps at the Seashore," "Chester Gump Hops Over the Pole," and "Chester Gump Game," the last one appearing in 1938.

gun toys Through the latter 19th and the 20th centuries, gun toys have been popular, led by the air-guns and pop-guns manufactured by such firms as Daisy Mfg. Co. and King Mfg. Co.

Manufacturers active in the earlier 20th century included American Original Toys, the Art Metal Works, Buffalo Toy & Tool Works, Daisy, A.F. Fox Gun Co., Remington Arms Co., and Savage Arms Co.

In the prewar years, companies emphasizing toy guns in their lines included All-Metal Products Co., Forrest Mfg. Co., Fox Co., Grey Iron Casting Co., J.C. Manufacturing Co., W.P. Johnson Co., Paul Jones, McClure & Wilder, McDowell Mfg. Co., Marks Bros. Co., the Massillon Wire Basket Co., the Tec-Toy Co., and the Toy Craftsmen.

Gun toys were a diverse lot in the Boomer years, due in part to the introduction of plastics, and to the imaginative frenzy of toy makers faced with unprecedented levels of competition. The manufacturers included Ack-Ack, Aid's, Bar Zim Toy Mfg. Co., Beaver Toys, the Beistle Co., George Borgfeldt Corp., Buddy "L" Toys, Carnival Toy Mfg. Corp., J. Chein & Co., Cordelco Industries, E. Joseph Cossman & Co., Daisy, Essay Mfg. Co., Esquire Novelty Co., Gladen Enterprises, Goody Mfg. Co., the Hubley Mfg. Co., Irwin Corp., Jak-Pak, Henry Katz, Kenn-Eye Co., Kilgore, Knickerbocker Plastic Co., Kusan, Langson Mfg. Co., Leslie-Henry Co., Lido Toy Co., Lindberg Products, M. & L. Toy Co., Maco Toys, Louis Marx & Co., Mattel, Model Weapons, Moonglow Plastic Jewel Corp., W.J. Murphy Co., Nichols Industries, Pal Plastics, Park Plastics, Parris Mfg. Co., Peerless Playthings Co., Plasticraft, Playtime, Pyro Plastics Corp.,

Ray Plastic, Renwal Toy Corp., Rubbermaticgun Corp., George Schmidt Mfg. Co., Slammer Gun Co., Steven Mfg. Co., Suburban Toy & Mfg. Corp., Tigrett Industries, Tru-Matic Toy Co., and Woodhaven Metal Stamping Co.

Gund Mfg. Co. Stuffed toy animals and novelties were the mainstays in Gund's early success from its formation in the late 1890s. In the 1920s and earlier '30s it issued the "Gee" line of mechanical stuffed toys, including monkeys, horses and penguins. Based on West 20th Street, New York City, its line included Easter novelties, Scotties, soft-faced dolls, Airedales, "Animals-on-Wheels," Sealyhams, Terriers, Comic Characers, "Poochie the Popularity Pup," and novelties by the late prewar years. The firm continued production during wartime, issuing the "Dreamie" and "Percale Cuddle" lines of bears, cats, and pandas. In the Boomer years, Gund continued to specialize in soft-body dolls and stuffed animals. It also issued a variety of Walt Disney toys and hand puppets, "Popeye" toys, and musical stuffed toys. One of its successes in the later 1960s was the novelty toy "Bag Full of Laughs." The firm employed the "Gunderful" trade name.

The "Percale Cuddle Panda" was released by Gund Mfg., Co.

"Gunsmoke" One of the more popular CBS TV programs of the late 1950s and early '60s, "Gunsmoke" inspired playthings including coloring books by Whitman Publishing Co., games by Lowell Toy Mfg. Co., hats by Arlington Hat Co., holster sets by J.

G

Halpern Co., plastic figures by Hartland Plastics, and target games by Park Plastics Co.

gutta percha Gutta percha was a nonelastic rubber used in toys in the earlier 1800s, before the patenting of the vulcanizing process.

Guy Fawkes Day Observed on November 5, Guy Fawkes Day resembled Halloween in spirit. Generally boys ran around shouting and ringing bells and carrying their "old men" dolls, making the event one displeasing to Puritan colonists.

Gym Junior Co. This firm, based in Weehawken, N.J., in the 1930s and '40s, issued the "Gym Junior" apparatus.

"Gypsy" and "Gypsy Jr." fortune-teller sets see *Alabe Crafts, Inc.*

The Gibbs Mfg. Co. made the "Hoop-EE" ring toss game in the 1920s.

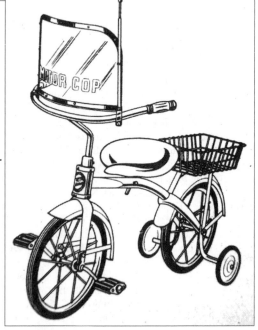

Garton Toy Co. made this "Motor Cop Sidewalk Bicycle" in the 1950s.

H.&J. Toy Mfg. Co. This Brooklyn, N.Y., company made teddy bears and stuffed animals in the 1930s.

The H.&P. Mfg. Co. The "improved type kaleidoscope toy," the "Wonderscope," was made in the 1930s by this Cleveland, Ohio, company.

H.&W. Kite Co. "Hywon" kites were made in the 1930s and '40s by this Decatur, Ill., company.

"H.F. & Co." see *H. Fishlove & Co.*

Hafner Mfg. Co. In the 1920s Hafner of Chicago, Ill., was known for its "Overland Flyer" mechanical trains. Hafner Mfg. Co. of Chicago, Ill., issued mechanical toy railway systems in the 1930s.

One of Hafner's popular "Overland Flyer" trains from the 1920s.

Arthur W. Hahn This Lafayette Street, New York City, brush manufacturing firm made the "Street Nick Christmas Trees" line of the 1920s, consisting of stylized, conical artificial trees flecked with artificial snow in eleven sizes ranging from 4 to 42 inches high. Hahn continued making artificial Christmas trees in the 1930s and '40s.

"Halco" see *J. Halpern Co.*

Hale-Nass Corp. Based on East 21st Street, New York City, Hale-Nass made aviation helmet outfits, target sets, toys, and novelties in the 1930s. In the postwar years, based on Broome Street, the firm specialized in hand-cuffs, badges, whistles, walkie-talkie sets, conchas, police and detective sets, motorcycle police sets, emergency outfits, fingerprint sets, western and sheriff outfits, and whistling lassos.

Clyan Hall Sturditoys Workshops The "Hollywood Derby" racing game of the late 1930s were made by this Corona del Mar, Calif., manufacturer. Clyan Hall also made educational toys and children's furniture.

Hall's Lifetime Toys This Chattanooga, Tenn., company issued Boomer-era doll beds and furniture, and a folding doll house.

Halperin Co. A Philadelphia, Penn., company, Halperin manufactured the "Junior" air gun of 1894.

J. Halpern Co. Based in Pittsburg, Penn., Halpern made prewar masquerade costumes. In the later 1930s and '40s it also manufactured dolls and fireworks. By the 1950s, the firm was firmly established as a manufacturer of holster sets, making western, space, military, Canadian Mountie, and Indian sets. Its line in the earlier Boomer years also included Halloween costumes, Santa suits and wigs, play suits, sparklers, and "Sky Fliers." It also made paper caps for toy pistols. The costume and play suit line was embracing numerous popular characters by the late '50s, including "Droopy the Dog," "Charlie Chan," and "Mighty Mouse." The firm used the "Halco" and "Superb Halco Brand" trade names on its products.

J. Halpern's 1950s costume, "Black Cat."

"Witch" was another popular 1950s Halloween outfit by Halpern.

Halsam Products Co.

A major name in wood toys before and after the war, Halsam of Chicago, Ill., emphasized blocks, checkers, dominoes, and pull toys in the earlier 1930s. It obtained an early Kay Kamen license to issue Walt Disney toy building blocks. By the end of the decade, some fifteen years before the existence of the theme park, it was issuing alphabet spelling blocks under the "Disneyland" name, as well as "Mickey Mouse" and "Hi Lo" safety blocks.

"Mickey Mouse" Safety Blocks by Halsam — an early Disney-licensed toy.

While the company never abandoned its focus on wooden blocks, by the late 1930s it also had strong lines in its "American Logs," a log-building construction toy whose popularity endured well into the Boomer years, and "American Brick Blocks," a brick house construction toy which enjoyed even greater success in the later 1950s and '60s in its "American Plastic Bricks" incarnation.

In wartime, Halsam continued its lines of "American Safety Blocks," "American Logs," "American Bricks," checkers and dominoes, as much diminished side lines to its defense-oriented work.

In the Boomer years, its line featured alphabet, Walt Disney, and "Hi-Lo" safety blocks; "American Logs" and "American Bricks"; checkers and dominoes; "Blockville" building sets. Halsam also entered into two exclusive sale representation agreements, one with Elgo Plastics, Inc., which produced "American Plastic Bricks," the deluxe skyscraper construction set "American Skyline," plastic checkers, and "Pegboard Playtiles"; and with the Embossing Co., which produced "Magna," "Crown," and "Lone Star" dominoes, plastic chess sets, and game kits. The firm's relationship with Elgo Plastics started in the early 1940s.

The company's relationship with Walt Disney continued, as exemplified by its "Walt Disney Early Settlers Logs," a version of its "American Logs" introduced in 1958.

The Halsam Products Co. logo.

Hamburg Puppet Guild

Established in Hamburg, N.Y., in the late 1930s, Hamburg Puppet Guild produced dressed and strung puppets, books of puppet plays, stages, and a sculpting set for modeling puppet heads.

Hamilton Steel Products Hamilton, based on West 74th Street, Chicago, Ill., was making coaster wagons and garden sets in the earlier 1930s, adding scooters and wheelbarrows by the end of the decade. In the Boomer years, its line still featured wheel goods, with coaster wagons, scooters, wheelbarrows, pedal bikes, juvenile jeeps, plastic automobiles, tractors, and trailers. Hamilton also made juvenile garden sets.

The "Greyhound" was one of Hamilton Steel Products' 1930s coaster wagons.

Hamilton-Meyers An 1890s publisher, Hamilton-Myers issued the 1890s board games "Chevy Chase," "Toboggan Slide," and "The Game of the Trolley Ride."

Hammatt & Sons The "Diabolo" tops of the Boomer years were products of this Anaheim, Calif., company. Hammatt also made flying discs, games, and shuffleboard.

hammer and nail sets An unforgettable toy even though most are played with at an age poorly remembered by the adult mind, nailing and hammering sets consisted of three objects: the hammer, something to hammer, and something into which to hammer it. The toy is usually regarded as a preschool or kindergarten one, even though many people find the joy of hammering never entirely dies.

Prewar examples included the "Hammer-Bench" by E.E. Fairchild Corp., "Hammer-Nail" sets by Playskool Institute, "Nail-A-Toy" hammer set by the Boy Toymaker Co., "Nailcraft" nailing sets by Transogram Co., and "Nail 'Em" sets by Artwood Toy Mfg. Co.

Other manufacturers included Anchor Toy Corp., Bar Zim Toy Co., Quick Sales Mfg. Co., the A.I. Root Co., and Toyline Mfg. Co.

Perhaps the most important postwar manufacturers were Playskool Institute and Holgate Bros. Co. Others included Bar Zim Toy Co., Childhood Interests, De Luxe Game Corp., the Fritzel Toys Corp., Henry Katz, Northwestern Products, and Pressman Toy Corp.

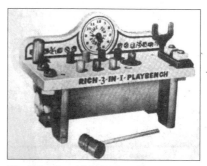

The "Play Bench" by Rich Industries, 1950s.

"Hammer-Bench" preschool toy see *E.E. Fairchild Corp.*

"Hammer-Nail" sets and tables see *Playskool Institute, Inc.*

Hampton Publishing Co. Hampton of Chicago, Ill., specialized in pre-school toy and activity books of washable cloth and linen, in the postwar years.

handcars Sometimes called the "Irish Mail," handcars were a variety of juvenile automobiles given propulsion by arm, back and hand power. The body of the vehicle tended to be an open framework with a seat on which the child sat, with feet positioned to give her or him leverage when pulling back on the handles. Doing this propelled the craft forward. Since a child could put her or his entire body into the effort, these could usually travel at a much better clip than they could on pedal cars, which used only leg power. Prewar manufacturers included the W.J. Baker Co., the Colson Co., the Gendron Wheel Co., Hill-Standard Corp., and the Toledo Metal Wheel Co. In the Boomer years, manufacturers included Auto-Wheel Coaster Co., Hubline, and Plastic Block City.

"Hand Kraft" toys see *The Toy Kraft Co.*

hand puppets see *puppets.*

handcuffs A necessity for toy police and detective outfits, handcuffs became more typical toy items in the 1930s and through the Boomer period, with manufacturers including Hale-Nass Corp, John-Henry Mfg. Co., Talbot Mfg. Co., and 20th Century Varieties.

Handicraft Creators, Inc. This firm sold the "Carlton Dank's Creative Craftoys" line of craft kits, including tapping, metal embossing, "Feltcraft," and leathercraft sets, in the earlier to mid-1950s. It was based in Brooklyn, N.Y.

Handikraft, Inc. Handikraft, established in Chicago, Ill., in the later 1930s, was one of several companies that capitalized on the growing interest in wood-burning sets and accessories, metal tapping sets, flower-making sets, games, construction toys, kindergarten pastimes, and spelling boards.

"Handifone" see *S.H. Couch Co.*

C.A. Handy Based on N. Kildare Avenue, Chicago, Ill., Handy was manufacturer of table tennis sets.

Hankscraft Co. This Reedsburg, Wis., manufacturer of lamps and nightlights also made plastic educational toys in the Boomer years.

Hansen Wood Goods & Toy Mfg. Co. Based in Reno, Nevada, Hansen was making wood pull toys, jump ropes, noisemakers, toy boats, farm sets, "De Luxe" animal racers, doll furniture, blocks, and preschool toys in the 1930s.

"Happy Days" yard play goods prewar, see *Hill-Standard Corp.*

"Happy Family" game late 1800s, see *Charles M. Crandall.*

"Happy Hooligan" An early comic character, the Happy Hooligan made several notable appearances in games and toys. In the mid-1930s, Milton Bradley Co. issued a "Happy Hooligan" game, while McLoughlin Bros. issued a paint box and a *Happy Hooligan Toddle Book.*

Happy Hour A division of Street Paul Plastic Products of St. Paul, Minn., Happy Hour made three-dimensional sculpted plastic games in the 1950s-'60s.

"Happy Hour" painting sets see *The Ullman Mfg. Co.*

Happy Products, Inc. This postwar Eynon, Penn., firm made washable terry cloth and denim, foam-stuffed toys.

"Happyland" picture puzzles see *Milton Bradley Co.*

"Happyland Playthings" see *The Delphos Bending Co.*

Hard Mfg. Co. Doll bed mattresses were the specialty of the ironically named Hard Mfg. Co. of Buffalo, N.Y., in the mid-1930s.

Lester Harding Lester Harding, established in Philadelphia, Penn., in the late 1930s, made "self-walking" miniature animals, including elephants and penguins.

Hardware & Woodenware Mfg. Co. see *National Novelty Corp.*

Hardy Different Toys Based on West 29th Street, New York City, Hardy Different Toys made musical novelties in the Boomer years, including animal toys.

M. Hardy, Inc. Based on West 25th Street, New York City, M. Hardy made soft stuffed toys, animals, and dolls, doll clothes, and infant novelties in the 1930s and '40s.

Hardy Plastics and Chemical Corp. Plastic toys, including stagecoaches, were early 1950s products of this Brooklyn, N.Y., company.

Harett Gilmar, Inc. "Bugs Bunny," "Circus Boy," and "Jingle Dingle," among others, appeared on this Far Rockaway, Long Island, N.Y., firm's board games, educational games, activity sets, and action toys in the 1950s and '60s. Harett Gilmar also made "Looney Tunes" and "Circus Boy" wipe-off and coloring sets, as well as rack toys and games, and junior sporting goods.

Harman Toy. Co. Stuffed toys were made in the mid-1930s by Harman of Brooklyn, N.Y.

Harmonic Reed Corp. "Roy Rogers" harmonicas and toy musical instruments were among this Rosemont, Penn., firm's products in the 1950s and '60s. Harmonic Reed made "Harmotone" musical toys, "Tic Tac Toe" game, and the "Mystery Maze" puzzle. Its "Spitz Jr. Planetarium" was part of its "Star Master" line of "scientific toys for the Space Age," issued through much of the 1950s. Others included "Junior Telescope," "DeLuxe Telescope," "Giant Telescope," astronomy sets, and "Portable Junior Planetarium."

harmonica Besides being a musical instrument, child-sized harmonicas have long been a common toy and novelty item. They have ranged in quality from the fine productions in metal and wood from M. Hohner to the tiny hard-plastic variety found in postwar gumball machines or Christmas stockings. Another prewar manufacturer was Fred Gretsch Mfg. Co. of Brooklyn, N.Y. M. Hohner, Inc. was located on Fourth Avenue, New York City.

Plastic Injecto Corp. was one of the larger postwar manufacturers of harmonicas and related musical instruments, such as the "Piano-Key Blow Accordion," and the red plastic "Hot Potato," a simple ocarina. Its double-sided red plastic harmonica "Big Twin" had 20 holes and 40 reeds. In its more standard harmonica line, its instruments included "Rock 'n Roll," "Companion," "Carnival Band," and "Circus Band," retailing for 39 to 59 cents in the mid-Boomer years. Other Boomer-period manufacturers included Emenee Industries, Harmonic Reed Corp., William Kratt Co., Lapin Products, and Proll Toys.

"Harmony" see *Continental Plastics Corp.*

The Harmony Co. Musical instruments by this North Lawndale Avenue, Chicago, Ill., company, including the 1930s and '40s pocket-size ukulele and toy banjo ukulele.

"Harold Teen" The "Harold Teen" daily strip by Carl Ed in the late 1920s and early '30s inspired a variety of games and toys, including a crayon and paint book by McLoughlin Bros. and a Milton Bradley Co. game. Adler-Jones Co. of Chicago, Ill., had the interesting specialty of producing "Harold Teen" retail display fixtures.

D.P. Harris Hardware & Mfg. Co. Based on Chambers Street, New York City, D.P. Harris manufactured prewar bicycles, velocipedes, and roller skates. In the Boomer years its "Rollfast" line of roller skates included both beginner's models, under the names "Lil' Pal," "Prep," and "Cub," and full-size models, named "Roamer," "Overland," "Peerless," and "De Luxe."

H.E. Harris & Co. The "Honor-Bilt" line of stamps and collector outfits and albums of the Boomer years were made by this Boston, Mass., company.

G.H. Harris Co. A Brooklyn, N.Y., company, G.H. Harris specialized in composition poker chips, including ones advertised as "noiseless," but also made checkers and novelties in the mid-1930s.

Morton H. Harris, Inc. see Marksman Products.

Harris Raincoat Co. Taking advantage of its area of expertise, this Seventh Avenue, New York City, firm also made "Dolly Raindear rainy day outfits" for dolls in the 1930s.

Harris Toy Co. Harris produced cast-iron toys in the years 1887-1913, and also acted as jobber for the manufacturers Dent Hardware Co., Hubley Mfg. Co., and the Wilkins Toy Mfg. Co.

Harrison's Mfg. Co. This Harrison, Maine, firm issued postwar wood toys, games, dolls, and novelties.

Harrop Ceramic Service Co. Besides plaster molds and specialties, Harrop, of Columbia, Ohio, was offering modeling clay and modeling sets in the 1930s.

Hart Publishing Co. A postwar publisher of children's and toy books, Hart was located on Fifth Avenue, New York City.

The Hart Vance Co. This postwar game manufacturer was based in St. Louis, Mo. It also made pocket calculators.

H

Hart Wood Products Wooden construction blocks were among this Pittsburgh, Penn., company's prewar products.

Harter Publishing Co. In addition to educational and coloring books for children, this Cleveland, Ohio, company made educational games and puzzles in the 1930s and '40s.

The Hartford Steel Ball Co. Based in West Hartford, Conn., Hartford issued the mid-1930s "Tu-Weeler" roller skates. It also made steel and metal balls used in games.

Hartland Plastics Hard-plastic figures of western TV heroes and their horses were the stock-in-trade of this Hartland, Wis., firm in the Boomer years. Hartland also made standing figures of TV gunfighters and Major League baseball stars.

Hartman Mfg. Co. Along with baby swings and strollers, Hartman, of St. Louis, Mo., made doll strollers and buggies from the 1930s through the Boomer years.

C.H. Hartshorn, Inc. A maker of baby carriages and furniture, this Gardner, Mass., manufacturer made doll strollers and buggies in the 1930s and '40s. By the late '30s it had added velocipedes to its line. In the postwar years, as Hartshorn, Inc., it specialized in children's upholstered furniture.

Hartwig Studios, Inc. see *Tots Toys.*

"Harva" rubber toys see *Julius Schmid, Inc.*

Harvard Electric Co. A Chicago, Ill., company, Harvard Electric made whistles in the earlier 1930s.

Harvard Mfg. Co. Table tennis sets and balls were made by this Cambridge, Mass., company in the mid-1930s.

Harvard Toy Works Based in Malden, Mass., Harvard made stockinette and rag dolls in the late 1930s.

Harvey House Based in Irvington, N.Y., Harvey House issued postwar toy books and nature kits.

Harvill Corp. The "Dreadnought" cannons of the 1950s and '60s were manufactured by this Los Angeles, Calif., company.

Harwood, Harrison A manufacturer of baseballs, Harrison Harwood established a factory in Natick, Mass., in 1858. In 1855 he had developed a ball covering consisting of two elongated peanut-shaped pieces of leather over the yarn filling, which enabled the ball to last longer under the bat before splitting open.

H. Harwood & Sons, Inc. Based in Natick, Mass., Harwood was a prewar manufacturer of indoor and playground balls, with an emphasis in baseballs especially pronounced in the later 1930s and through the Boomer years.

"Hasbro" see *Hassenfeld Bros., Inc.*

Hasenpflug, John and Ezra see *The Champion Hardware Co.*

W.E. Haskell, Inc. Home and playground "Climb-A-Round" sets were issued in the late prewar years by this Springfield, Mass., firm. The "Climb-A-Round" consisted of a circular climbing and sliding pole apparatus.

Hassenfeld Bros., Inc. Hassenfeld Bros., Inc., of Providence, R.I., started as a manufacturer of pencils and related goods before venturing into the toy field. The transition to toy company was a slow one. In the mid-1930s Hassenfeld was making "school companions," "My Pal" drawing sets, and such commonplace games as checkers and backgammon. The "Gilt Edge" crayon and paint sets were issued in the late 1930s. Most importantly, it introduced doctor and nurse kits, which sold well enough for the firm to venture further into toy making.

In wartime, the firm issued "Junior WAAC" and "Junior Air Raid Warden" sets, the "De Luxe Junior" doctor and nurse kits, and "Dolly's Homemaker Set." It also issued the play set of three-dimensional figures for Army, Navy and Air Corps units, "Uncle Sam Fighterset." The wartime line also included paint and crayon sets, doctor and nurse sets, pencil boxes, school bags, scrapbooks, photo albums, and pencils.

In 1952, Hassenfeld Bros. introduced "Mr. Potato Head," advertising it on Jackie Gleason's TV show. The original toy and the series of related toys it spawned, starting with "Mrs. Potato Head" in 1953, remained popular through the Boomer years. The plastic potato was introduced in 1964.

Hassenfeld Bros. used the "Hasbro Toys" trade name on its toys by the early '50s. Its line featured oil painting sets, "Jr. Miss" cosmetic cases and sewing kits, doctor and nurse kits, "Beaux Arts" paint sets," the "Let's Play Conductor" game, "Jolly Hobby" finger-painting sets, "Teach-a-Toy" stenciling sets and plastic educational maps.

The company introduced "G.I. Joe," billed as "America's Movable Fighting Man," in 1964 with advertising on NBC. It brought Hassenfeld Bros. $5.3 million in sales in 1964. The first figures, 12 inches tall, were the "Action Soldier," "Action Sailor," "Action Marine," and "Action Pilot." Talking "G.I. Joes" were introduced in 1967. The "Adventure Team" series was issued from 1970 to 1976. It included "Black Adventurer," "Air Adventurer," "Talking Astronaut," "Sea Adventurer," "Talking Team Commander," and "Land Adventurer." The large-size figures were discontinued in 1976.

"Mr. Potato Head," one of Hassenfeld Bros.' most popular toys, was introduced in 1952.

The Hatfield Co. Based in Greens Fork, Ind., Hatfield made prewar parlor baseball, basketball and football games.

hats Beyond their utility, hats have a long history as playthings, with novelty, play and costume hats of paper and other materials becoming major items for American manufacturers in the early to mid-20th century. While paper cone hats with nursery rhyme and other childhood motifs brightly illustrated on the sides are popular among collectors of earlier childhood items, the hats with the highest profile in the toy industry in the prewar and postwar periods were the character promotional or tie-in hats, often but not always relating to western figures. Corona Hat Co., for instance, issued felt western hats tying in with "Rawhide," "Cheyenne," "Lawman," and "Sugarfoot" in the 1950s-'60s. Another Boomer-era manufacturer, Arlington Hat Co., held rights to issue hats for "Paladin," "Wagon Train," "Wells Fargo," "Bonanza," "the Rebel," "Hotel de Paree," "Johnny Ringo," "Bat Masterson," "The Rifleman," "Maverick," and "Gunsmoke."

Hausser Elastolin see *Elastolin.*

"Have Gun, Will Travel" The CBS Films show inspired numerous western-related playthings in the 1950s and '60s, including hats by Arlington Hat Co., holster sets by J. Halpern, plastic figures by Hartland Plastics, and miscellaneous tie-in items by 20th Century Varieties.

Hawes Mfg. Co. Founded in the 1830s by Londoner George Hawes, this manufacturer of wooden toys was based in Newark, N.J., with a factory in Monroeton, Penn. The business moved to Tonawanda, Penn., in 1887, where it stayed in operation into the early 20th century.

Hawk Model Aeroplane Co. Established in Chicago, Ill., Hawk Model Aeroplane was making model railroad construction kits in the late 1930s. In the Boomer years, it shortened its name to Hawk Model Co., although its core business remained 1/4-inch scale plastic model airplane assembly kits. In the later 1960s, the firm issued more car models, including "Car Classics" in 1/24th scale, and the "Weird-Ohs" line, which included "Digger the Wayout Dragster," "Daddy the Suburbanite," "Davey the Motorcyclist Road Blaster," and "Huey Hut Rod."

H

The "Huey Hut Rod" by Hawk Model Aeroplane Co., 1960s.

A 1940s puppet by Hazelle's Marionettes.

"Hawk" pistol prewar, see *The Hubley Mfg. Co.*

"Hawkeye" cap pistol see *Kilgore Mfg. Co., Inc.*

"Hawkeye" doll cradles prewar, see *Burlington Basket Co.*

Hawkins, G.H. The firm established on Canal Street, New York City, of G.H. Hawkins issued a walking doll in 1868, based on a patent by William F. Goodwin. The toy was Goodwin's "Automatic Toy," which used a spring mechanism.

Hawley Products Co. A St. Charles, Ill., paper goods firm in the 1930s and '40s, Hawley's products included pressed paper hats for Halloween.

R.M. Hay Co. Based in Stamford, Conn., R.M. Hay issued infants' toys, kindergarten beads, and bubble sets in the late 1930s.

"Hayco" see *R.M. Hay Co.*

Hazard, Willis P. Willis P. Hazard issued the 1853 card game, "Conquest of Nations."

Hazelle's Marionettes Established in Kansas City, Mo., in the late 1930s, Hazelle's issued marionettes, theaters, kits, and plays. Under the new name Hazelle, Inc., in the postwar years, the firm continued to specialize in marionettes, hand puppets, and puppet stages.

Hazel Novelty & Cabinet Co. "Strand's" toy chests of the 1950s-60s were manufactured by Hazel, of St. Louis, Mo.

Heaney Laboratory The educational toy "Training Plane" and wooden juvenile exerciser "Spunk & Andy Roc-A-Bot" were 1930s products of this Long Island, N.Y., firm.

"Heap Big Injun" archery set see *Withington.*

Heathe Model Airplane Co. This model airplane firm operated in Brooklyn, N.Y., in the 1930s.

"Heavy Artillery" Issued in 1875, Charles M. Crandall's "Heavy Artillery" was considered an expensive toy in its time at two dollars, but enjoyed popularity for a number of years. It was followed by Crandall's toy cannon.

"Heavy Duty" coaster wagons see *The American-National Co.*

"Heavy Duty Poly" see *Eldon Mfg. Co.*

The Hedstrom-Union Co. This Gardner, Mass., nursery furniture manufacturer also specialized in wheel toys, including doll carriages, velocipedes, and sidewalk bikes, in the 1920s and '30s, as well as children's rockers. It was making the "H.C. White" kiddie car and walker by the late 1930s. In the Boomer years, Hedstrom-Union moved to Fitchburg, Mass., with a factory also in Dothan, Ala. Its line continued to emphasize velocipedes, doll carriages and strollers, and sidewalk bikes, in addition to baby carriages and strollers and playground equipment.

Heider Mfg. Co. Based in Carroll, Iowa, Heider made prewar wood and steel coaster wagons.

"Heidi and her Friends" dolls see *Remco Industries, Inc.*

"Heidi" dolls see *Fleischaker & Baum.*

Heirloom Needlework Guild, Inc. see *Dritz-Traum Co., Inc.*

Helios Products Corp. Based on Broadway, New York City, Helios made toy train lamps in the mid-1930s.

J.B. Hellenberg Co. This Coldwater, Mich., firm made prewar Indian clubs and dumb bells.

Helm Fine Art Decorating Co. Cellophane kites were among the late 1930s products of this Baltimore, Md., manufacturer of Christmas trees and cellophane tree decorations.

Helm Products Helm made character items in the early '80s, including soap dispensers.

Helmet Corp. of America Novelty hats were the postwar specialty of this St. Louis, Mo., company.

"Help Yourself" books see *Whitman Publishing Co.*

Helvetic I. & M. Corp. An importer based on Fifth Avenue, New York City, Helvetic also manufactured musical toys and novelties and musical movement for toy manufacturers.

Hemcoware see *Bryant Electric Co.*

"Hennessy" building blocks see *Milton Bradley Co.*

"Henrietta" plastic egg-laying chicken see *Lapin Products, Inc.*

Herald Toy Products A division of Fred Hebel Corp. of Addison, Ill., Herald manuactured building blocks.

Herbert Specialty Mfg. Co. Besides advertising novelties of paper and light metal, Herbert, based in Chicago, Ill., made games, toys, punchboards, and puzzles in the 1930s and '40s.

Herberts Machinery Co., Ltd. A Los Angeles, Calif., firm, Herberts made the "Wizard Junior" line of small woodworking power tools in the late 1930s.

"Herby" see *"Smitty."*

"Hercules" steel toys prewar, see *J. Chein & Co.*

Herion Fan Co. The "Autogiro Roulette" and "Autogiro Put & Take" games of the late 1930s were issued by this Lexington Avenue, New York City, firm.

Herkimer Tool & Model Works The "O.K." miniature motors of the 1950s-'60s were products of this Herkimer, Ind., firm.

Walter L. Herne Co. Herne, of East 54th Street, New York City, issued the Boomer-era "Toys That Grow," and paint and craft sets.

"Hero" pistol prewar, see *The J. & E. Stevens Co.*

R. Herschel Mfg. Co. This Peoria, Ill., firm made coaster wagons in the earlier 1930s.

Heseltine & Co. Specialists in Christmas items, this Pittsburg, Penn., company was manufacturing illuminated icicles and stars in the mid-1930s.

The Hettrick Mfg. Co. A manufacturer of play tents and swimming pools, Hettrick of Toledo, Ohio, made playhouses and toy circus tents in the mid-1930s. By the end of the decade it also made small gliders. In the Boomer years, it continued its emphasis on play tents and playhouses, and also made swimming pools and "American" velocipedes. It made the "Roy Rogers" umbrella tent of the late 1950s.

W.E. Hettrick & Son This firm, based as was the Hettrick Mfg. Co. in Toledo, Ohio, in the 1930s and '40s, also made play tents, houses, and pools.

"Hexoblox" see *Strombeck-Becker Mfg. Co.*

J.S. Heyman A Los Angeles, Calif., firm, Heyman made fur animals in the 1930s. By

H

the end of the decade it advertised its dogs and rabbits of "fine yarn and Shetland floss."

Heywood-Wakefield Co. Based in Boston, Mass., this juvenile furniture manufacturer also made doll carriages in the 1930s and '40s.

The Hi-Flier Mfg. Co. In addition to its "Hi-Flier Kites," this Decatur, Ill., company made the "E-Z Fly Kites" line in the mid-1930s, and advertising kites. By the late 1930s it was producing "Strat-O-Flier" box kites and balsawood gliders. Both "Hi-Flier" and "Strat-O-Flier" were still leading trade names for the company in the Boomer years.

"Hi-Guy" tops see *Nissen Products Corp.*

"Hi-Ker" see *W.H. Schlee, Inc.*

"Hi-Liner" trucks and trailers see *C.J. Ulrich Co.*

"Hi-Lo" bicycles see *The Colson Co.*

"Hi-Lo" blocks see *Halsam Products Co.*

"Hi Prancer" spring horse see *Delphos Bending Co.*

"Hi-Speed Racer" coaster wagons see *The American-National Co.*

"Hi-Test" see *American Artists' Color Works.*

hidden-ball game In this American Indian game, a ball was hidden in one gourd of three, which were quickly shuffled around to confuse the watcher. The confidence man version using three upended shot glasses or cups is probably better known, through early Western movies.

hide-and-seek A game that goes back to at least the ancient Greeks, hide-and-seek may be a game known around the world. Among the American Indians, it was a training game for tracking. The game was also played by Colonial Americans.

Highland Sales Co. Associated with such famous game names as "Cootie" and "Tickle Bee," Highlander was an affiliate of W.H. Schaper Mfg. Co.

"Highlander" trains see *American Flyer Mfg. Co.*

The N.N. Hill Brass Co. The N.N. Hill Brass Co. was a leading manufacturer of iron toys, bell toys and chime toys, founded in 1889 in East Hampton, Conn. The company also made doll carriages and go-carts through the early 1900s and prewar years.

The company's 1920s toys included airplanes, telephones, reins, rattles, call bells, tea bells, chimes, and iron and steel toys. Its "Tea Wagon," advertised as "Just Like Mother's," was an enameled toy packed with a metal tea set. The "Improved Bellphone" appeared in 1929.

In the 1930s, through a licensing agreement with Kay Kamen, it featured images of Mickey Mouse, Minnie Mouse, and the Three Little Pigs and Big Bad Wolf, among other Disney characters, on its pull toys, chimes, toy telephones and reins. Mickey also appeared on the "Coin Bank French Telephone" in the mid-1930s, a combination telephone toy and savings bank. Through the 1930s and '40s the company was also making rattles, "child's leaders," jump ropes, tea bells, call bells, and bicycle bells. The firm's restricted line in wartime included toy telephones and wooden pull toys.

In the Boomer years, the firm continued its traditional specialties of bell and chime toys, telephones, hobbyhorses, and all styles of bells.

The N.N. Hill Brass Co. logo.

The "Just Like Mother's" miniature tea wagon, 1920s.

Hill-Standard Corp. An Anderson, Ind., playground equipment firm, Hill-Standard also made juvenile vehicles. It claimed the distinction of having originated and been the exclusive manufacturers of the "Irish Mail" since 1900. Hill-Standard also called the toys "the rowing machine on wheels." It printed the "Irish Mail" name on the vehicle seats. In the mid-1930s, apparently its last years, the firm issued a "Streamline Irish Mail."

The "Streamline Irish Mail," Hill-Standard Corp., 1930s.

"Hill Toys" see *The N.N. Hill Brass Co.*

Hillcraft Industries Hillcraft of Traverse City, Mich., issued ship-building model kits in the 1950s and '60s that used styrofoam as the building material.

Hillerich & Bradsby Co., Inc. Established in Louisville, Ky., in the late 1930s, Hillerich & Bradsby Co.'s early products included the "Louisville Slugger" bats and "Grand Slam" golf clubs, which continued to be its lead trade names through the Boomer years.

"Hippety-Hop" pogo sticks see *Rapaport Bros.*

Hipwell Mfg. Co. A prewar Pittsburg, Penn., game company, Hipwell made the "Five-in-one Electric Miami Greyhound Derby" and "Safety First Auto Traffic Race."

"The Hive" *The Hive* was an early magazine aimed at children, published by W. & S.B. Ives in the 1800s.

"Ho-Bo" tops prewar, see *Florida Playthings, Inc.*

"Hobble Wobble" pull toys see *Softskin Toys, Inc.*

"Hobby Chime" bell toys see *The Gong Bell Mfg. Co.*

Hobby-Craft, Inc. Based in Chicago, Ill., Hobby-Craft issued rubber-molding sets for casting plaster figures in the late 1930s.

hobbyhorse The hobbyhorse toy was known as far back as ancient Greek times.

H

Hobby Model Mfg. Co. Based in the Fifth Avenue Building, Hobby Model issued late 1930s airplane construction sets.

hockey Hockey is a wintertime game and sport that has enchanted children for years. Before World War II, when the activity was still more fun game than serious sport, manufacturers of the hockey sticks included Avoca Mfg. Co., Bredenberg Bros., C.A. Lund Co., Northland Ski Mfg. Co., F.W. Peterson Corp., Southern Metal Products, Central Paper Box Co., Erie Paper Box Co., H. Fleisig, the George Franke Sons Co., Kroeck Paper Box Co., Schultz-Illinois-Star Co., the Strouse, Adler Co., and Transogram.

hockey, field An early version of this game was played by American Indians.

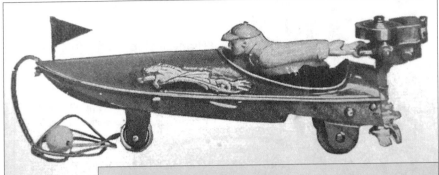

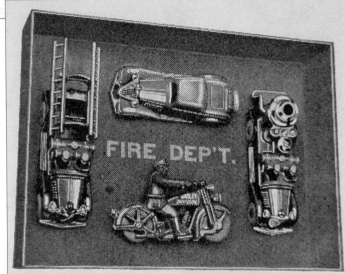

Hubley's "Sea Horse" motorboat, 1929.

In the 1930s, Hubley released the "Fire Department" and "Auto Assortment"

Hodgman Rubber Co. The "Funflotes" beach inflatable toys, introduced in the late 1930s, were produced by this Framingham, Mass., company. Hodgman continued manufacturing inflatable swim floats through the Boomer years.

H.J. Hoenes Co., Inc. The "Viking" steel toys of the 1930s were made by this Cleveland, Ohio, firm. It also made electric lighted steel toys.

Hoffman Lion Mills Co., Inc. Based on West Broadway, New York City, Hoffman made jump ropes in the 1930s, adding lariats to the line by the late prewar years. In the 1950s and '60s, its line also included toy clothesline and clothes pin sets, kite twine, and bell novelties. It was based in Fall River, Mass., in the Boomer years.

Hoge Mfg. Co., Toy Division Hoge made electric and mechanical trains, transformers, sewing machines, register banks, miniature kitchen furniture, carpet sweepers, target games, mechanical toys, steel toys, and children's games in the 1920s and '30s. Based on East 21st Street, New York City, its toys were reportedly manufactured by Girard and distributed by Henry Katz. The company's best-known items were its "Popeye Tru-To-Life Mechanical Rowboat" of 1935, and the more commonly found "Fire Chief" car, also of the '30s. In the late '30s, Hoge's line also included the "Educational Play Pictures" machine, washing machines, toy machine guns, and toy boats.

M. Hohner, Inc. The famous Hohner name appeared on prewar and postwar juvenile musical items, including harmonicas and accordions. It was based on Fourth Avenue, New York City.

Hohwieler Rubber Co. Based in Morrisville, Penn., Hohwieler issued hockey pucks and rubber quoits games from the late 1930s through the Boomer years.

Holgate Bros. Co. Located in Kane, Penn., Holgate established itself as one of the leading manufacturers of wooden toys. In the 1930s it made nursery, school, and kindergarten play materials, and educational building blocks. Its line included wooden play sets based on "Mother Goose" subjects, which featured wooden buildings, people and animals. "Mother Goose Play Tray," "The Old Woman Who Lived in a Shoe," "Goldilocks and the Three Bears," and "Red Riding Hood" were among the titles. Among its block-toy innovations were "Kindergarten Blocks" and the smaller "Junior Blocks," sold in wooden play wagons, and "Jerry Blocks," which built toy trains and tunnels. It also made nested blocks. By late in the decade its trade names included "Bingo Bed," "Junior Blocks," "Color Cones," the "Blox-that-Lox" train, and "Little Loom." In the war years, Holgate issued bag of blocks, sand toys, beads, push-and-pull toys, wooden trains, baby toys, and "Bingo Bed." In the 1950s and '60s, as Holgate Toys, Inc., a division of Playskool Mfg. Co., the firm continued to specialize in educational play materials for pre-schoolers, or "grow-up toys." The company still issued many items from its earlier line, as well as wooden puzzles and poly-bagged rack toys.

"The Old Woman Who Lived in a Shoe" play set from Holgate Bros. Co., 1930s.

The Holiday Line, Inc. A Boomer-years manufacturer of swimming pools and beach accessories, this Brooklyn, N.Y., company also made plastic toys, play balls, and stuffed toys.

Gaston Hollander Gaston Hollander of Long Island City, N.Y., made prewar checkers, chess, and backgammon pieces.

hollowcast, or hollow cast Many of the slush-metal or pot-metal toys made by manufacturers of toy soldiers and other figures used a hollowcast method, in which the molten lead alloy was poured into the mold and then poured out again, leaving only a thin layer of cooled metal to hold the shape of the mold. Using hollowcast methods allowed toymakers to issue toys more cheaply. They could also ship the resulting lead toys more cheaply. Barclay Mfg. Co. and Britains were among the firms using the method.

Holly-Ho Toy Mfg. Co. Glider horses and juvenile furniture were postwar specialties of this La Crescenta, Calif., company.

Hollywood Film Enterprises, Inc.

This Hollywood, Calif., firm issued 16-mm and 8-mm motion pictures, many for the children's market, in the later 1930s and '40s. Its line included westerns, comedies, novelty films, and animated works featuring characters including "Mickey Mouse," "Donald Duck," and "Oswald Rabbit." In the Boomer years the company specialized in 8-mm silent motion picture films.

Hollywood Games Inc. Based in Hollywood, Calif., this company made "Intel," a game for adults, in the mid-1930s. It changed its name to Hollywood Games Co. by the end of the decade.

"Hollywood Imp" stuffed dolls

prewar, see *The W.R. Woodard Co.*

Hollywood Products Co. This prewar Hollywood, Calif., company made "Hollywood" building blocks.

"Hollywood Real Life Toys" see

Scovell Novelty Mfg. Co.

Hollywood Shell & Toy Co. This Hollywood, Calif., company issued "Shellcraft," "Playcrafts" and copper-craft kits in the Boomer years.

The Holmquist-Swanson Co. This Chicago, Ill., firm made infant furniture and play yards in the 1930s and '40s, using the "Swan" trade name.

holster, toy pistol see *pistol holster, toy.*

Home Foundry Mfg. Co. Based in Baltimore, Md., this prewar manufacturer's "Home Foundry" casting set made a variety of toy objects, most notably toy soldiers. By the late 1930s the company had found significant success by catering to the growing interest in wood-burning sets. It issued the "sensational patented Air-Flow Wonder Pen," an electrical burner that came in sets with pre-printed boards cost from $1 to $5. It used similar "pens" in the "Home Foundry Electric Metal Tap Outfits" with "the sensational new electric tapper," and the "Home Foundry Sand Pen Sets." The company still issued casting sets, and continued releasing new molds to help maintain interest

Home Game In the early 1900s, Home Game issued the card games "Game of Five Hundred, "Bird Center Etiquette," and "Bunco."

Homeland Mfg. Co. A prewar Baltimore, Md., firm involved with electric light items for Christmas, Homeland also made similar products to go with toy train tracks in the 1830s and '40s.

T. Homer T. Homer was an 1830s American manufacturer of dissected maps and pictures, tin toys, and dollhouse furniture.

"Honey Bunch" books see *Grosset & Dunlap, Inc.*

Honold Mfg. Co. This Sheboygan, Wis., firm manufactured all-steel coaster wagons and scooters in the 1920s.

C.I. Hood A late 19th century manufacturer, C.I. Hood issued "Hood's Spelling School" game in 1897 and "Hood's War Game," a card game, in 1899.

"Hoop-La" hoops see *Brockton Plastics, Inc.*

hoop toys An activity that is centuries old—if not more—hoop-rolling long had a connection to barrel-making, which involved the production of great quantities of curved pieces of wood. In its most formal guise— and it was never a formal activity—the child would have a long stick with a short crosspiece tacked onto the farther end, which she or he would use for propelling the hoop down the street. Hoop-rolling was played in America from Colonial times. It had its own fads, including one in the 1800s that apparently made being a pedestrian in Philadelphia hazardous.

The activity that led to the hula-hoop, in contrast, may have originated in non-Western cultures. The famous Wham-O "Hula Hoop," the center of the immense popular phenomenon of 1958, was apparently inspired by a health exercise popular in Australia that involved spinning hoops around the body by gyrating the hips.

Although most were of anonymous manufacture, a few prewar toy companies included rolling hoops in their manufacturing lines. Selchow & Righter made the "Hoopla" hoop and stick game, and the Fred Gretsch Mfg. Co. the "Woozle Hoops" rolling hoops, in the 1930s. Others included California Toy Craft Co., Lobdell-Emery Mfg. Co., and Noble & Cooley Co. In the postwar years some firms still made rolling hoops, including Dumas Products, Gibbs, Mfg. Co., and McDonald Burglar Bar Works. Most, however, concentrated on hip-spinning hoops. Manufacturers included American Thermoplastics Products Corp., Brockton Plastics, Fleet Mfg. Co., Irwin Corp., Jak-Pak-Inc., James Industries, Lancaster Toy Co., F.D.Peters Co., Plastic Block City, Rapaport Bros., William Spitz & Sons, Universal Tubing Co., and West Georgia Mills.

"Hoosier" vehicles see *Hill-Standard Corp.*

"Hoosier-Kraft" juvenile furniture see *Merriman Mfg. Corp.*

"Hoot Gibson" outfits see *Wornova Mfg. Co.*

"Hoot-Nanny" see *Howard B. Jones;* postwar, see *Northern Signal Co.*

Hoover Products, Inc. The "Plakies" infant's toy of the late 1930s was made by this Youngstown, Ohio, company.

"Hopalong Cassidy" Merchandise based on the movie and TV cowboy "Hopalong Cassidy" was popular in the 1950s and early '60s. It included art sets by Transogram Co., cowboy suits by Herman Iskin & Co., guns and hosters by R. & S. Toy Mfg. Co., and stationery by Whitman Publishing Co.

"HOPE B," marking see *R. Bliss Mfg. Co.*

Hopkins Mfg. Co. This Boomer-era Emporia, Kans., company made the "Space Trainer" exercising toy.

L. Hopkins Mfg. Co. Based in North Girard, Penn., Hopkins made doll beds, bassinets, and high chairs in addition to baby play yards in the 1930s and '40s.

Hoppy Taw Corp. The "Hoppy Taw" game of the 1950s-'60s was a product of this Salt Lake City, Utah, company. It also issued games "Hop-Top," "Dynaland," and "Gambolee."

Hop Scotch, Inc. The "Hippity Hoppity" hop scotch game of the Boomer years was produced by this Park Avenue, New York City, company.

hopscotch A known back at least to the ancient Greeks, the game of hopscotch was played in the Colonies, and remained an active part of American childhood from that time.

W.C. Horn Bro. & Co. W.C. Horn of Newark, N.J., was a manufacturer of albums for every purpose, scrap books, desk files and stationer's specialties in the early 20th century. The firm also made games by the 1920s, with its titles including chess, checkers, backgammon, cribbage, chess, dominoes, "Rhum Trays," "Tit-Tat-Toe Hurdle Peg," and "Double Dummy Bridge." It continued manufacturing games through the 1930s and the postwar years.

Horn Wagon Co. An Akron, Ohio, company, Horn Wagon made 1930s coaster wagons with balloon tires.

hornbooks Hornbooks were small rectangles of wood with hands, looking much like square table-tennis paddles, on which was fastened a printed sheet with letters and syllables. This paper was then covered by a thin layer of transparent horn to protect the paper. Hornbooks were widely used in schools in Colonial times, until primers became commonplace.

H

horns, toy While for adults horns are primarily musical instruments, among children they start as more primarily items for the production of noise, an activity as beloved of 19th and 20th century children as of 21st. Most miniature horns were made anonymously by tinware companies, and were not only common toys but early decorations for Christmas trees, once they became prevalent at Christmastime. Horns came to be made in cardboard and paper as well as tin and other metals, with colorful paper horns becoming as common a toy for both child and adult observances of the New Year as the tin ones. Prewar manufacturers of paper horns included Bugle Toy Mfg. Co., Dessart Bros., A.A. Faxon Co., Marks Bros., and G.C. Willett & Co. Bugle Toy Mfg. Co. naturally also made tin toy horns. Others included Chicago Metallic Mfg. Co., T. Cohn, Gotham Pressed Steel Corp., Keller Toy Mfg. Co., the Kirchhof Patent Co., and Seiss Mfg. Co.

E.I. Horsman Co., Inc. This famous manufacturer was founded by E.I. Horsman, who made baseballs in his school years well before establishing his toy and doll business in 1864. In addition to indoor games and amusements, which were the firm's original focus, Horsman began manufacturing croquet sets when they became a fad, later adding archery and tennis sets as they gained popularity.

E.I. Horsman's board, card, and skill game titles included "Letters" in 1878, "Snap" in 1883, "Halma" and "Ring-A-Peg" in 1885, "Basilinda" and "Tiddledy Wink Tennis" in 1890, "Magnetic Jack Straws" in 1891, "Trilby" in 1894, and "Watermelon Frolic" in 1900.

Horsman had early imported dolls, and entered manufacturing with rag dolls. In 1909 he obtained sole rights to manufacture a "Billiken" doll, which appeared with a "Can't Break 'Em" head and cloth body. The doll sold extremely well, although "Sister Billiken" did not match it, being perhaps a little too grotesque. About the same time Horsman introduced "Baby Bumps," which may have been the first baby doll modeled by a sculptor of a real baby. Horsman followed "Baby Bumps" with a series of "Art Dolls" also modeled from life, and, in 1911, with

"the Campbell Kids," by arrangement with the soup company.

The line of dolls by Horsman, whose firm was located on Broadway, New York City, continued through the 1920s, when its line featured baby dolls including "Baby Dimples" and "Dolly Rosebud," and in the '30s, when the company changed its name to Horsman Dolls, Inc., and established offices in the Fifth Avenue Building. The "Tinie Baby" line of baby dolls was introduced in the mid-1930s.

The success of the firm carried through the Boomer years. The line included "Love-Me" baby, "Baby Precious" doll with bonnet, "Pram Baby," "Draft Dodger Doll" in flannel sleeping outfit, and "Baby Precious" doll with hat and coat, by the mid-1950s.

horse toys see *rocking horse, shoofly, spring horse.*

horseshoes Prewar manufacturers of pitching horseshoes included Marion Craftsman Tool Co., Ohio Horse Shoe Co., Street Pierre Chain Co., Smith Rubber Horseshoe Co., Seamless Rubber Co., and Wolverine Supply & Mfg.

Horton Handicraft Co. This Hartford, Conn., firm issued "Hortoncraft" leather hobby kits in the late 1930s.

"Hot Wheels" The Mattel response to the popularity of Lesney Products' "Matchbox" line of toy miniature cars made its debut in 1968. The speed-performance orientation of the line, emphasized by Mattel's release of plastic track for racing the cars, quickly caught the buying public's fancy. Early models were often based on the fanciful designs of Ed Roth and other hot-rod designers. The line included such numbers as "The Red Baron," "Custom Firebird," "Classic Nomad," "Turbofire," "TwinMill," "Volkswagen Beach Bomb," and the "Deora."

Hotel McAlpin The Hotel McAlpin, located on Broadway at 34th Street, New York City, was the official Toy Fair Hotel as early as the 1930s. It was referred to as the "Headquarters for the Toy Industry." Temporary and permanent exhibits supplementing permanent salesroom exhibits in the Fifth Avenue Building appeared in the McAlpin.

housecleaning toys Housecleaning toys have long enjoyed the bright light of approval because of their very practicality: toy brooms did, after all, work effectively at doing what they needed to do. Child-size brooms likely appeared wherever and whenever adult-size ones did, throughout history. Colorful sets that included attractively lithographed tin dustpans and tin sweepers became popular before the war, and flourished afterwards as well. They have won the affection of collectors despite their having a lower profile than the tin mechanicals of the time. Prewar manufacturers who made various kinds of toy housecleaning utensils included Buffalo Toy & Tool Works, Deshler Broom Factory, Evans & Liddle, Gotham Pressed Steel Corp., Jean Caro Products Co., Kiddie Brush & Toy Co., Light Buoy Industries, Liquid Veneer Corp, N.Y. Association for the Blind, Ohio Art Co., and Patent Novelty Co.

houses, play see *playhouses.*

Charles W. Howard Based in Albion, N.Y., Howard made toy trucks, trailers, furniture, and circus items, as well as sand boxes, in the 1930s. By the late '30s the company was called Howard Toy & Novelty Co.

"Howdy Doody" In the early to mid-1950s the "Howdy Doody Show" was as much cultural phenomenon as NBC TV show. While the most famous toys are the marionettes by Peter Puppet Playthings, the show inspired many smaller toys including bubble pipes by Lido Toy Co., card games by Russell Mfg. Co., crayons by Milton Bradley Co., "Doodle" slates by the Stickless Corp., plastic figures by Tee-Vee Toys, plastic inflatable roly-polys by Kestral Corp., and ukeleles by Emenee Industries.

Howe Baumann Balloon Co. This Newark, N.J., company made toy balloons and novelties in the late 1930s.

Hub Mfg. Co. A manufacturer of wading pools, this postwar Salem, Mass., firm also made blocks, doll baths, doll diaper bag kits, and toy ironing boards.

Hub Products Co. Hobby horses were the product of this late 1930s Jackson, Mich., firm.

"Harley Davidson Motorcycle Toy"

The Hubley Mfg. Co. Founded in 1894 in Lancaster, Penn., by John E. Hubley, Hubley Mfg. Co. was one of the great names in cast-iron toys before the war. In 1909 it purchased the Safety Buggy Co. factory. At the time it produced cast-iron toys, horse-drawn wagons and fire engines, circus trains, and cap guns. When the Great Depression hit, the firm survived by emphasizing the production of smaller, cheaper toys.

Two important toys of the 1920s were the No. 16 "Indian Motorcycle" and No. 17 "Harley Davidson Motorcycle," both cast-iron toys released in 1929, measuring 9 inches long with "imitation motor exhaust" The company boasted proudly of these toys: "Flashy colors, clicking wheels, rubber tires, demountable riders ... They're real! These little fellows have all the snap and class of the big machines."

Hubley's 1930s output emphasized toy autos, buses, and trucks. The company also made banks, cap pistols, circus and fire toys, gas ranges, toy kitchen items, wheel toys, airplanes, motorcycles, and motorized toys.

"Indian Motorcycle Toy"

H

Two sets which were popular in the late Great Depression years were the "Hubley Fire Department," with pumper, ladder truck, fire chief's car, and motorcycle; and the "Auto Assortments," which contained from five to ten sedans, roadsters, and coupes. The 1934 "Airflow Chrysler" was also an important prewar toy.

Metal restrictions brought about by the advent of World War II brought Hubley's toy production to a halt in 1942.

In the postwar years the firm's toys included die-cast and plastic toys, metal cap pistols and rifles, and leather holster sets. Die-cast production had already begun to supplant cast-iron production as early as 1936, due to the increasing cost of shipping and increased competition from overseas manufacturers. Die-cast took a leading role after the war, and continued in importance after the company was purchased by Gabriel Industries in 1965. "Hubley" die-cast toys were produced into the '70s, when Gabriel, a division of CBS, retired the name.

Hubley's 1960s die-cast toy, "No. 453 Tow Truck."

Cap guns were also a Hubley item, like this "Colt .38 Six Shooter" from the 1950s.

Hubline Division A division of Hub Tool Mfg. & Machine Co., Hubline made the "Hum Main-Liner Irish Mail" of the 1950s-60s.

"Huckleberry Hound" The famous cartoon dog inspired numerous playthings in the early 1960s, including banks and target games by Knickerbocker Plastic Co., a "Spin-O" game by Bardell Mfg. Co., squeeze toys by Dell Distributing, and stuffed toys by Knickerbocker Toy Co.

Huffman Mfg. Co. The "Aircrafted" bicycle was a 1930s product of this Dayton, Ohio, company.

Fred A. Huffman Mfg. Co. This Farmington, N.M., company introduced the "Ride-A-Hopper" Plastic riding toy in 1969.

"Huffy Puffy Train" see *Fisher-Price Toys, Inc.*

"Hula Hoop" see hoop toys; *Wham-O Mfg. Co.*

"Hula" masquerade outfits see *American Merri-Lei Corp.*

Hull & Stafford A 19th century tinware manufacturer based in Clinton, Conn., Hull & Stafford issued brightly painted tin toys including mechanical wind-ups, pull toys, doll house furniture, and horse-drawn vehicles. The firm, originally Hull & Wright, made toys from about 1870. See *Union Mfg. Co.*

Hum-A-Tune Co. The "Hum-A-Tune" novelty of the late 1930s was produced by this St. Paul, Minn., firm.

Humble Mfg. Co. Humble, based on Madison Avenue, New York City, produced "Mono-Blade" single-runner sleds in the late 1930s.

"Humdinger" toys and games see *Schmid Bros.*

"Humpty Dumpty Circus" One of the most famous of toys by the A. Schoenhut Co. was its "Humpty Dumpty Circus" of the 1920s and '30s. Undoubtedly inspired by Charles M. Crandall's "Acrobats" of the previous century, Schoenhut's circus figures, made of jointed wood, had hands and feet with grooves, which allowed them to perch in different poses on their circus equipment. The sets, made in different scales, included circus people, animals, and vehicles.

The "Humpty Dumpty Circus" was a famous A. Schoenhut toy from the 1920s.

Hustler Toy Corp.'s "Peppy Pup" was an early remote-controlled wood toy.

Hunefeld & Co. Based in Cincinnati, Ohio, Hunefield made wagons and other juvenile vehicles in the 1930s.

Hungerford Plastics Corp. Flexible vinyl squeeze-toys and dolls were specialties of this Boomer-era company, based in Morristown, N.J.

Hunter, J.H. In 1899 J.H. Hunter issued the board game, "Great American War Game."

"Hurray for the Little Folks" see *Brown, Taggard & Chase.*

L.J. Hurst Mfg. Co. This Indianapolis, Ind., company made gyroscope tops from the mid-1920s to the '40s. In the postwar years, "Hurst" gyroscopes were issued by Chandler Mfg. Co.

Husky Toy Co. This Grand Rapids, Minn., firm made a tractor construction toy in the 1950s-60s.

Hustler Toy Corp. This Sterling, Ill., manufacturer issued games, toys, construction sets, and the "Action Toy Builder" in the 1920s. Its early game titles included "Baseball, the Great American Game" and "Intercollegiate Football" in 1923. In the 1930s, the firm shortened its name to Hustler Corp. Its line included wooden action toys, games, pre-school felt sets, and the "Speed King" roller skates. Its "Peppy Pup" was a jointed wooden toy dog with rubber wheels in its feet, whose actions could be controlled by a simple mechanical remote-control device. The "Speed King" line became its most important product in the Boomer years.

Hutchinson Bros. Leather Co. By the 1930s this Cincinnati, Ohio, company had established its specialty in leather footballs, boxing gloves, and other sports equipment, which it continued issuing through the prewar and the postwar years.

Hutchinson, E.R. Based in Elmira, N.Y., Hutchinson made doll's couch hammocks in the 1930s.

"Hy-Grade Toys" see *Benner Mfg. Co.*

"Hy-Speed" carts and wagons see *The Steel Stamping Co.*

"Hy-Speed" roller skates see *Moen & Patton, Inc.*

Clara Hyde Toys, Inc. This Memphis, Tenn., company made wooden pull toys, stick horses, ironing boards and juvenile table and chair sets in the late 1930s.

hydraulic Some pressed-steel toy trucks, especially dump trucks of the '50s, bear the designation "hydraulic." In part they are called this because the originals did use hydraulic power. Usually, too, they have some mimicry of the hydraulic system under the dumper part of the truck, consisting of a tube and plunger, which may give some resistance when the dumper is lowered because of air compression. The power for dumping is supplied by a spring mechanism.

Hygrade Fabric Co. A manufacturer of rubber specialties, this Broadway, New York City, company made prewar beach sport balls.

H

Halloween party favors from the 1920s.

A 1950s Halloween costume by J. Halpern, Co.

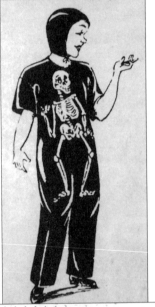

"Rainbow Blocks" by Halsam Products Co., 1920s.

Ii

I-S Unlimited, Inc. The "Bali" word card game of the 1950s-60s was published by this East 38th Street, New York City, company.

ITC Modelcraft ITC was the division of Ideal Toy Corp. manufacturing hobby model kits in the Boomer years. Its best selling kit in the late 1950s was "Tyrannosaurus Rex," which assembled a mounted skeleton of the dinosaur.

ice skates see *skates, ice.*

"Icecycle" see *Kingston Products Corp.*

Ideal Aeroplane & Supply Co., Inc. Established in 1911 and based on West 19th Street, New York City, by the 1920s, this firm issued the "Ideal Model Airplanes" construction kits, the most popular model being the "New York-Paris Monoplane." The company continued issuing airplane toys and construction toys in the earlier 1930s, adding model boats by the end of the decade, and model trains by the war years. In the Boomer years, Ideal's line also included "HO" trains.

Ideal Book Builders This Chicago, Ill., publisher issued an extensive series of boxed "Child Improvement Outfits" in the 1920s. Titles included "Building Fun," "Funny Face Games," "Wonder Speller," "Picture Mosaics," "Wonder Nature Stories," "Word Pictures," "Ideal Speller," "Wonder Garden," "Animal Wonderland," "Bird Wonderland" and "Garden Speller."

Ideal Mfg. Co. In addition to its specialty of wheel chairs, Ideal Mfg. Co. made play yard equipment in the late prewar years.

"Ideal Model Airplanes" see *Ideal Aeroplane & Supply Co.*

Ideal Novelty & Toy Co. One of the most prominent toy manufacturers for much of the 20th century, Ideal was founded in 1903 in Brooklyn, N.Y. Founders Rose and Morris Michtom specialized in stuffed toys and dolls, making their name with the original "Teddy Bear." In the 1910s, its line included stuffed figures of the popular comic character, "Mr. Hooligan," and a doll portrait of the sailor boy "Admiral Dot." In 1918 the company introduced its "Sleeping Dolls," with composition heads and patented sleeping eyes.

In the 1920s, Ideal Novelty & Toy Co. pioneered "flirting, sleeping, rolling eyes" in "unbreakable dolls," with the lead doll being the "Ideal Flossie Flirt" dolls, introduced in the 1910s and popular into the 1930s. Ideal's dolls were manufactured with rubber arms and legs. The company advertised the limbs for being "natural-feeling," and for having "no paint to crack or peel; they suffer no splitting or chipping, and do not discolor."

In 1925 the firm introduced a series of "Hush-a-Bye Baby" dolls, in seven sizes.

By the late 1920s, ideal issued "Flossie Flirt" in six sizes, and "Tickletoes" in four sizes. "Baby Smiles" was another popular doll. Ideal's newest popular dolls just before the Great Depression were "Peter Pan" and "Wendy" dolls.

"Flossie First" was one of Ideal Novelty & Toy Co.'s most popular dolls in the 1920s.

By the 1930s its "Ideal" doll line included jointed, all-rubber dolls; stuffed body dolls with rubber arms and legs and flirting eyes; sleeping, walking, mama dolls; infant dolls; and all-composition wig dolls. The company enjoyed massive success with its "Ginger" dolls, with the "double action glass-like eyes and lashes," and then with its "Shirley Temple" dolls.

The "Betsy Wetsy" nursing, drinking and wetting dolls, made of rubber with outfits and layettes, were the company's lead product by the late '30s, along with "Snow White" and "Dwarf" dolls, "Shirley Temple" dolls, trunks, and outfits, and the "Ideal" dolls line, with rubber arms and legs and flirting eyes. The "Idenite" dolls trade name was also used. Ideal also issued Edgar Bergen character hand puppets.

Ideal continued through the war years with a line of dolls, stuffed toys, plastic toy dishes, and plastic toy boats.

In the Boomer years, the company changed its name to Ideal Toy Corp. Specializing in dolls, stuffed toys, inflatable toys, puppets, pre-school toys, plastic and metal toys, and mechanical toys, the firm had a number of successes with its innovations, including the plastic "Fix-It" toy vehicles and "Robert the Robot" of the mid-1950s; "Mr. Machine" of 1960; "Robot Commando" of 1961; "Tammy," "Odd Ogg," and "King Zor" of 1962; and the famous "Mouse Trap Game" of 1963.

Its doll line in the Boomer years included the aptly named "Plassie" of 1945; "Baby Ruth" and "Magic Skin Boy" of the early 1950s; "Saucy Walker," "Baby Big Eyes," "Magic Lips Doll," and "Posie," in the mid-'50s; "Patty Playpal" and "Peter Playpal" in 1960; "Shirley Temple as Heidi," also in 1960; and the 42-inch tall "Daddy's Girl," again in 1960. "Mitzi" was Ideal's response to Mattel's "Barbie." More enduring was "Tammy," introduced in 1962. Also popular in the 1960s was the line of "Tiny Thumbelina" baby dolls.

In 1961, Ideal Novelty & Toy Co. released its "Robot Commando" toy.

"Ideal" printing presses see *Sigwalt Mfg. Co.*

Ideal Products Corp. "Lokblok" construction blocks, "Merri-Go Walkers," and strollers were among the 1930s products of this Hammond, Ind., corporation.

Ideal Products Mfg. Co. A Pittsburg, Penn., company, Ideal Products Mfg. Co. made "The Dolly Kit," "Miss Dixie," and other toy bag kits for prewar children.

Ideal Toy & Novelty Mfg. Co. Construction toys, tricks and joke novelties were made in the late 1930s by this Boston, Mass., firm.

"If Made of Metal We Make It," trademark see *J. Chein & Co.*

"Ignatz Mouse" The popular cartoon mouse appeared in several attractive toys in the 1930s, including an "Ignatz Mouse Cycle Rider" by J. Chein & Co. and a stuffed toy by Knickerbocker Toy Co.

The Illfelder Corp. The 1930s "Soljertoys" line was issued by this West 22nd Street, New York City, importer. Illfelder also specialized in soft toys, dolls, and animal toys. By the late 1930s it had changed its name to Illfelder Importing Co.

Illinois Clay Products Co. The 1930s and '40s "Plastoy" modeling clay was made by this Joliet, Ill., company.

Illinois Specialty Co. Based in Tuscola, Ill., this 1930s and '40s company made toy ironing boards and toy electric irons.

"Imp" juvenile skates see *Chicago Roller Skate Co.*

"Imperial" A popular word for trademarks, prewar occurrences included baby walkers by the Frank F. Taylor Co., croquet sets by Harold Kinne, and sleds by Auto-Wheel Coaster Co.

Imperial Crayon Co. Established in Brooklyn, N.Y., in the late 1930s, Imperial Crayon made chalk and crayon sets, adding modeling clay and paint sets in the Boomer years.

Imperial Crown Toy Corp. Plastic, latex and vinyl popular-priced dolls were the specialty of this mid-1950s Brooklyn, N.Y., firm.

Imperial Knife Co. Located on Broadway, New York City, Imperial Knife issued character, scout, and 1939 World's Fair knives in the late prewar years.

Imperial Methods Co. The Game of Twenty Grand was made by this Forest Park, Ill., company in the mid-1930s.

imports, toys Toys in Colonial America were largely imported. The first formal imports of toys occurred as early as 1695. Dolls were likely among the first shipments from Europe.

"Indestructo" books see *Samuel Gabriel Sons & Co.*

India rubber see *rubber toys.*

Indian Archery & Toy Corp. Besides professional archery equipment and accessories, this Evansville, Ind., firm made archery sets for children, aqua planes, surfboards, and rope-spinning lariats, in the 1920s. It employed the "Indian Play-Things" trade name. The company's focus expanded to include aerial toys, dart games, stilts, and badminton sets in the 1930s and '40s. For its archery sets it issued attractive jungle animal targets. The firm concentrated on archery sets, darts, badminton sets, shuttlecocks, and stilts in the postwar years.

Indian Archery & Toy Corp. issued jungle animal targets for its children's archery sets.

Indian Artcraft This postwar Fort Lauderdale, Fla., firm specialized in Indian tom-toms, tomahawks, and totem poles.

Indian Bead Co. Established on York Avenue, New York City, in the late 1930s, this firm made bead sets.

"Indian Chief" gun see *Fox Co.*

Indian Leather Holster Co. Based on Grand Street, New York City, this firm made holster sets in the 1930s and '40s, and through the Boomer years.

"Indian swirl" marbles These swirls are made of black glass with outer bands of colored glass. See also "Joseph swirl."

Indian toys and novelties Toys based on American Indian clothing and culture were widespread in the Boomer years, due in great part to the popularity in all things western. Manufacturers included Dumore Belt & Novelty Co., Estelle Toy Co., Fillum Fun, Giant Plastics Corp., Indian Artcraft, Leeds Sweete Products, Meier & Frank Merchandise Co., Metropolitan Flag Mfg. Corp., W.G. Murphy Co., Niscott Mfg. Co., Pawnee Bill's Indian Trading Post, Sollmann & Whitcomb, Spraz Co., and Thrift Novelty Co. The popularity of such goods had grown through the earlier 20th century, with many items made by leather goods and costume manufacturers.

Indiana Desk Co. This Du Bois, Ind., firm made juvenile furniture in the late 1930s.

Indiana Handle Co. A Paoli, Ind., company, Indiana Handle made croquet sets and baseball bats in the 1930s and '40s.

Indiana Ox Fibre Brush Co. Juvenile sweeper sets were among the products of this 1930s and '40s Seymour, Ind., company.

"Indianland" figures see *Multiple Products Corp.*

infant toys As items of historical and collector interest, infant toys appeal because of their association with babies and toddlers. Since most people have no memories of these earliest years, the main nostalgic appeal is of a parental nature. Prewar manufacturers included Artwood Toy Mfg. Co., Atlanta Playthings Co., Bailey & Bailey, L.A. Boettiger Co., Da Costa Toy Co., Du Pont Viscoloid Co., M. Hardy, Irwin Novelty Co., Richard G. Krueger, Mistress Patty P. Comfort, Noveloid Co., the Rushton Co., and the Toy Tinkers.

Infant Toys Co. Based on West 21st Street, New York City, Infant Toys made doll clothing of "Pliofilm" in the late 1930s.

inflatable plastic toys Undoubtedly one of the new categories of Boomer-era toy production was that of inflatable plastic toys, which weren't just beach toys but also Easter, Christmas, Halloween, and general playroom playthings. Manufacturers included Alvimar Mfg. Co., whose inflatable toys in the 1950s and '60s included "Casper the Friendly Ghost" and "Lassie Wonder Dog." Other firms included Bardell Mfg. Corp., Dartmore Corp., Davis Products, Doughboy Industries, Eyerly Associates, the Holiday Line, Ideal Toy Corp., Kestral Corp., Lo-E Mfg. Corp., Monroe Fabricators, Paradies Playthings, Plastic Heat Sealing Co., Plastikaire Products, U.S. Fiber & Plastics Corp., Urb Products Corp., and W.J. Voit Rubber Corp.

This early inflatable toy Mickey Mouse was produced by Seiberling Latex Products Co., in 1934.

"Inflatoys" see *Alvimar Mfg. Co. Inc.*

The Insel Co. Based in Arlington, N.J., Insel made 1930s and '40s Pyroxylin baby rattles and teething rings, in addition to other baby items.

"Instant Insanity" A puzzle hit of the late 1960s for Parker Bros., "Insant Insanity" featured a row of four, four-colored plastic blocks to be rearranged to show all four colors on each side of the stack. See also *"Soma."*

"Instructo" laundry sets see *N.D. Cass Co.*

"Interlox" puzzles see *Madmar Quality Co.*

International Chain & Mfg. Co. This York, Penn., firm made "Gym Dandy" child's swings, trapezes and flying rings for indoor and outdoor use in the late prewar years.

International Mfg. Co. This Boston, Mass., manufacturer made juvenile furniture and the "Kiddy" swings in the 1930s and '40s.

International Plastic Co. Based on Third Avenue, New York City, this postwar firm specialized in infants' toys, balls, banks, dolls, plastic toys, pre-school toys, pull toys, rattles, and stuffed toys.

International Souvenir & Import Co., Inc. This Brooklyn, N.Y., company made novelties, paper hats, and souvenirs before the war.

"Invincible" repeating cap pistol prewar, see *Kilgore Mfg. Co.*

Irish Mail "Irish Mail" is used as a category name for handcars, but was also used as a trademark name for prewar handcars by Hill-Standard Corp. In the Boomer years, the name was used by Hubline, Plastic Block City, and Steger Products Mfg. Corp.

A. & P. Irmischer & Co. The "Mak-A-Lamp" construction set of the late 1930s was manufactured by this Chicago, Ill., company.

iron toys In addition to cast-iron quoits, which were likely made by all foundries from

Colonial times on through the 1800s and earlier 1900s, early cast-iron toys included sadirons for girls, used for pressing doll clothes. Often they came with a cast-iron trivet. Examples of toy sadirons are unknown from the earlier 1800s. By the mid-1800s, miscellaneous iron toys were being manufactured, including iron stoves, wheel toys, and toy garden tools. Before the widespread use of steel and aluminum in toys, iron was used in such items as skates and velocipedes. Iron was also the primary material used in early jackstones, through the prewar period.

Manufacturers still making iron playthings of various kinds in the 1930s included Arcade Mfg. Co., Billy Boy Toy Co., the Blue Bird Co., the Champion Hardware Co., the Dent Hardware Co., Freidag Mfg. Co., Grey Iron Casting Co., the N.N. Hill Brass Co., the Hubley Mfg. Co., the Kenton Hardware Co., Kilgore Mfg. Co., Kilgore Toys, the Littlestown Hardware & Foundry Co., Manoil Mfg. Co., National Sewing Machine Co., Nicol & Co., W. L. Sherwood, the J. & E. Stevens Co., United States Lock & Hardware Co., and the A.C. Williams Co. By the mid-Boomer years, the only manufacturer still specializing in iron toys was Grey Iron Casting Co.

Iron Products Corp. Based in LaCrosse, Wis., this company made the "Whiz-a-Long" snow scooter in the 1930s.

"Ironmaster" trains see *American Flyer Mfg. Co.*

irons, toy see *sad irons, toy.*

Irvin, James R. & Co., Inc. In addition to comic Christmas cards, this prewar Chicago, Ill., company made games, toys, and jigsaw puzzles.

"Irving Jaffe" roller skates 1930s, see *The John C. Turner Corp.*

Irwin Corp. Based on West 20th Street, New York City, Irwin made mechanical toys, celluloid infant's toys, moving picture projectors, cameras, and films in the late 1930s. In the Boomer years, it specialized in plastic toys, mechanical toys, dolls, pinwheels, tea sets, animals, roly-polys, floating toys, toy

autos, whistles, and Easter novelties. One of its more unusual toys was the large plastic "Dandy the Lion," of 1963.

Herman Iskin & Co., Inc. Iskin, established in 1910, specialized in exclusive TV cowboy and cowgirl playsuits in the postwar years. It also issued "Seneca" frontier playsuits and "Pla-Master" playsuits. It was based in the Fifth Avenue Building, New York City, in the Boomer years.

"It" doll see *Amberg Dolls.*

E.R. Ives & Co., Ives Corp., Ives and Blakeslee & Co. Founded by Edward R. Ives in 1868, E.R. Ives & Co. made baskets and toys in Plymouth, Conn., until 1870, when he moved the company, now Ives Corp., to Bridgeport, Conn. In 1872, Ives joined Cornelius Blakeslee, a brother-in-law, to form Ives and Blakeslee & Co. The "Ives" name became a famous one in the toy industry, being attached to a large variety of cast-iron and clockwork toys. After much of a decade of success manufacturing mechanical trains and electric trains in the 1920s, the company fell victim to the Great Depression, and was forced into bankruptcy in 1928-29. Lionel Corp. and American Flyer Mfg. Co. jointly took over the company's assets. Lionel then assumed complete interest in Ives, moving production to Irvington, N.J. Lionel produced train toys with the Ives name into 1931. Some "Lionel-Ives" train toys appeared until 1933.

W. & S.B. Ives A mid-1800s publishing company, Ives found itself with a hit on its hands when it issued "Dr. Busby" in 1843, the first bestseller in card games. The company also issued one of the most successful early board games, "Mansion of Happiness," in 1843. The game was reissued by Parker Bros. in 1886. Based in Salem, Mass., the publisher also issued the 1844 "The Game of Pope or Pagan" and 1845 "Characteristics," and published the children's magazine *The Hive.*

"Ives Toys Make Happy Boys (since 1868)" trademark, see *Ives Corp.*

I

"Ivoroid" game playing pieces prewar, see *Parker Bros.*

ivory Ivory has long seen use as a suitable material for teethers. By the 1800s, ivory was also used for billiard balls, whistles, bagatelle balls, checkers, dominoes, backgammon men, dice, and jackstraws.

Ivorycraft Co., Inc. A prewar game company based in Long Island City, N.Y., Ivorycraft specialized in dice varieties in the mid-1930s. By the late prewar years it was issuing poker chips, dominoes, checkers made of the plastic Catalin, and the "Ancient Game of Mandarins."

Hill-Standard's "Streamline Irish Mail," 1930s.

Gebruder Bing made this Model Steam Roller in the 1910s.

J.&H. Metal Products Co. A division of Taylor-Shantz Co. of Rochester, N.Y., this company made "Homecraft" juvenile woodworking tools and sets in the 1930s and '40s.

J. and J. Mfg. Co. Based in Texarkana, Texas, this prewar company made "Boom-Rang" toy airplanes.

J.&S. Products A Los Angeles company that probably operated in the '50s, J.&S. Products produced a toy car, roughly nine inches long, consisting of a solid chassis (even the windows are solid) above a pair of wheel assemblies which are attached to a single point below the chassis via a steel spring, which provides suspension. The toy features black rubber wheels on metal hubs.

J.C. Mfg. Co. This Jackson, Mich., company made "The American Boy" play guns of the 1930s and '40s.

J-Cey Doll Co., Inc. This postwar Brooklyn, N.Y., firm specialist in vinyl dolls was apparently affiliated with its neighbor company, J-Cey Toy Mfg. Co., also of Brooklyn, a specialist in stuffed toys.

"J. Fred Mugs Game" 1955, see *Samuel Gabriel Sons & Co.*

J.P.T. Stuffed Toy Co., Inc. This postwar specialist in stuffed toys was based in Brooklyn, N.Y.

J.W.K. Industries In the 1950s and '60s, this Douglassville, Penn., company issued toy gasoline pumps, electric traffic signals, traffic play signs, pre-school wood magnetic toys, and "Trainer Toys" wheel goods accessories.

"Jack & Jill" A popular trademark, "Jack & Jill" was used on a number of prewar playthings, including Milton Bradley Co. games, American Crayon Co. paint boxes, Maple City Rubber Co. balloons, and the Hettrick Mfg. Co.'s playhouses. Globe-Union Mfg. Co. also issued "Jack-N-Jill" sled skates. In the Boomer years, the eternally tumbling nursery-rhyme characters continued appearing on numerous playthings, including "Jack & Jill" bubble blowers by Manhattan Kreole Products; dolls by Nancy Ann Storybook Dolls, Asbury Mills, and Uneeda Doll Co.; and double-runner sled skates by Sollmann & Whitcomb. The variant name "Jack-N-Jill" appeared on kiddie seats by National Production Co., sled skates by Globe-Union, and a "TV-Radio" by Fisher-Price Toys.

"Jack Armstrong" "Jack Armstrong, the All-American Boy," first aired in 1933 as a daily radio serial. His adventures, at first of a domestic and school nature, expanded to world-spanning scope in the years after the Depression, and turned in a patriotic direction during World War II. After the war, the show became "Armstrong of the SBI." The series lost popularity and left the air in 1951. "Jack Armstrong" premiums included rings, cast and sports photos, patches, pedometers and whistles. One of the more important "Jack Armstrong" promotions involved a box-top mail-in deal from General Mills in Minneapolis, Minn., in 1935-36. The 300,000 children sending in box tops received Daisy Mfg. Co.'s "Flying Top," a gun that shot a spinning disk into the air, in a package that announced it as "Jack Armstrong's latest invention." Daisy had introduced the "Flying Top" in 1935. It was called the "Wee-Gyro" in promotional materials.

Jack Built Toy Mfg. Co. A firm based in Burbank, Calif., in the Boomer years, Jack Built made coloring books, train sets, crayons, puzzles, and activity books.

The "Color and Re-Color Set" by Jack Built Toy Mfg. Co., 1950s.

jack-in-the-box Wooden jack-in-the-box toys were manufactured in America from the early 1800s. Papier-mache was often used in these early toys. The faces were strikingly painted, sometimes in clown-like patterns, and sometimes in patterns strongly evocative of traditional African face-painting or mask-painting.

"Jack Rabbit" velocipedes see *The Frank F. Taylor Co.*

"Jack Stack" see *The Toy Tinkers, Inc.*

"Jackbilt Playthings" prewar, see *Rochester Folding Box Co.*

jacks see *jackstones*.

"Jack's Pony" exerciser see *The Republic Tool Products Co.*

The Jackson-Guldan Violin Co. A Columbus, Ohio, manufacturer, Jackson-Guldan made toy violins, wooden blocks, building blocks, peg boards, and toy doctor cases in the earlier 1930s. It was specializing in toy violins by the late prewar years.

jackstones Jackstones go back at least to the ancient Greeks. Also known as knucklestones. In prewar America, jackstones or jacks were often made of cast-iron, with diecast metal becoming the usual material of choice through the Boomer years. Although plastic became the predominant material by the late 20th century, metal jacks remained available, sometimes as nostalgia items.

Prewar manufacturers included Arcade Mfg. Co., the Dent Hardware Co., Freidag Mfg. Co., Grey Iron Casting Co., Kilgore Mfg. Co., the J.&E. Stevens Co., and U.S. Lock &

Hardware Co. In the late prewar years, Ohio Plastic Co. and Piqua General Supply Co. joined their ranks.

In the Boomer years, manufacturers included the Alox Mfg. Co., Arandell Products Co., Jan Badal Co., Baker Mfg. Co., Come Play Products, Crown Novelty Co., Danlee Co., Grey Iron Casting Co., the Jerome Gropper Co., Jak-Pak-Inc., Lee Products Co., Nadel & Sons, Ohio Plastic, Riemann, Seabrey Co., M. Shimmel Sons, the J.&E. Stevens Co., and Wells Mfg. Co.

Jacmar Mfg. Co. Jacmar of Brooklyn, N.Y., issued Boomer-era electric educational games, parlor games, hobby kits, novelties, rack merchandise, electric and non-electric wall plaques, puzzles, and decorations. Jacmar's line, which it advertised as the "World's Largest Line of Electrical Games," included titles released before the war by Knapp Electric.

Jacob, Joseph Owner of an 1800s hatchet factory, Jacob made toy tools and novelties for the Tower Toy Guild.

Jacobs & Kassler The "Kiddiejoy" line of the 1920s and earlier '30s was issued by this importer and distributor, who specialized in dolls, toy tea sets, and juvenile furniture. The firm was located at various addresses in New York City.

E.H. Jacobs Mfg. Co. The "Sportcraft" whittling sets of the late 1930s were issued by this Danielson, Conn., firm.

Jacobson & Co. Based on Bond Street, New York City, in the late 1930s, Jacobson issued cowboy hats, carnival hats, and hat souvenirs. As Jacobson Co. in the postwar years, based in Elmhurst, N.Y., the firm specialized in New Year's, Halloween, Street Patrick's Day, doll, cowboy, and fireman hats.

Meyer Jacoby & Son, Inc. In addition to doll and costume wigs, this firm made Santa wig and beard sets, and undressed plastic dolls. It was based on West 20th Street, New York City, in the 1950s-60s.

Jacrim Mfg. Co. This Boston, Mass., company manufactured the "Seaworthy" toy yachts and "Flying Yankee" motor boats of the

1920s. After the Great Depression the "Jac-rim" line was issued by Keystone Mfg. Co.

Jada Novelty Co. Jokes, tricks and puzzles were specialties of this late 1930s Pittsburgh, Penn., company.

Jago Novelty Co., Inc. "Western Frontier" holster sets were specialties of this postwar Brooklyn, N.Y., company.

Jak-Pak-Inc. A Milwaukee, Wis., company, Jak-Pak-Inc. issued such Boomer-period toys as "Pla Doubles," "Pow'r Pop" guns, "Pow'r" dart guns, multi-colored jacks and ball sets, make-up sets, jump rope, peashooters, and whistles.

James Industries, Inc. James Industries was founded in 1946 by Richard and Betty James to sell their spring toy, "Slinky." The Paoli, Penn., firm thrived through the Boomer years issuing the original toy and its variant forms, including "Slinky Train," "Slinky Dog," and "Slinky Worm." Although usually the animals were advertised as the "Slinky Dog" and "Slinky Worm," and so forth, in their early years they occasionally appeared under other names. The names "Suzie, the Lovable Slinky Worm," "Tommy, the Slinky Pup," and "Loco, the Slinky Train," appeared in 1955. Other toys included "Slinky Soldiers," "Slinky Seal," "Slinky Handcar," "Slinky Spiral," "Slinky Glasses," "Slinky Playmolder," and "Slinky Swamp Buggy."

"Jane Powell" books see *Whitman Publishing Co.*

"Jane Russell" dolls see *The Saalfield Publishing Co.*

Janesville Products Co. Based in Janesville, Wis., this company's prewar output included wood coaster wagons, scooters, "Skudder" cars, the "Humpty Dumpty" motion toy, children's vehicles, and "Roly Rider" spring toys. It remained known for quality coaster wagons through the remainder of the century.

japanner In the 19th century, before the development of a separate toy industry in America, tin manufacturers, often using the term "japanners" to refer to the manufacture

of painted or printed tin, were among the country's toy makers.

japanning "Japanning" refers to the decorative surface applied to early American and European tin items, involving several layers of paint finished with a coating of lacquer. In France, a more inexpensive technique involved a varnish and paint mixture that was "burned on" in alcohol, then baked, achieving a similar hard translucence.

Harry Jaspan This Philadelphia, Penn., company issued the "Official Ace" darts in the late prewar years.

Jawin Mfg. Co., Inc. Jawin, of Brooklyn, N.Y., was a specialist in wheel goods in the late 1930s.

The Jay & Jay Co. The "Zit-Zingo" travel game of the 1950s-60s was issued by this East 43rd Street, New York City, company.

"Jay Bee" dolls prewar, see *Bouton-Woolf Co., Inc.*

Jaybar Products Co. Bubble solution for bubble blowers was the specialty of this postwar Brooklyn, N.Y., company. It also made plastic balloons, party baskets, and serpentines.

Jayline Mfg. Co., Inc. Electric trains and hobby accessories for "O," "HO," and "OO" scales were specialties of this firm in the early 1940s. During wartime, Jayline issued a variety of play sets of cardboard, including "Camouflage," which used a farm layout of buildings, fences, and trees, and incorporated military figures and vehicles: "A peaceful countryside becomes a field of action," the company suggested. Its other sets included "Motorized Attack Force," "The Jayline Air Attack Force," "Navy Set," and a "Noah's Ark." The company also made doll houses and furniture. Jump ropes, lariats, tops, metal dollhouses, jigsaw puzzles, stencil sets, and Christmas items were postwar specialties of this Philadelphia, Penn., company, when its name became Jayline Toys, Inc.

Jaymar Specialty Co. Games by this Brooklyn, N.Y., company included the "What's My Name?" board game of the 1920s and "Katzenjammer Kids Hockey"

J

skill game issued in the '40s. Through the prewar years, Jaymar specialized in wood and other toy and novelties, jointed wood dolls, jointed cardboard dolls, educational toys, and cast-iron toy tool and garden sets. In the 1950s and '60s, the company made toy pianos, wood and plastic pre-school toys, jigsaw puzzles based on Walt Disney and other characters, building blocks, educational toys, paper dolls, activity toys, badminton sets, croquet sets, and wood inlaid puzzles. In the Boomer years it maintained offices in the Fifth Avenue Building, New York City.

Jeanette Toy & Novelty Co. Founded in 1898 in Jeanette, Penn., this company specialized in lithographed tin toys, including trays, tea sets, and figural glass candy containers, in the early years of the 20th century. It also issued games, including the "Brownie Auto Race" board game of the 1920s.

Jee-Bee Toy Creations This postwar Kansas City, Mo., company made stuffed toys.

Jefferson Electric Co. Based in Chicago, Ill., this 1920s firm issued the "Jefferson Universal Toy Transformer" for electrical train outfits.

Jefferson Mfg. Co. Musical toy instruments were the specialty of this Boomer-era Philadelphia, Penn., company.

Jefferson Mfg. Co.'s "Texan Jr. Guitar" from 1964.

Jeffrey Toy Mfg. Co. This Chicago, Ill., firm made exerciser spring horses and shooflies in the Boomer years. It also issued wire puzzles, swings, and telescopes.

Jenkintown Steel Co. The "Swyngomatic" baby swings of the 1950s-60s, as well as the "Lullamatic Jr." toy cradles, were products of this Jenkintown, Penn., company.

"Jenny Wren" doll houses and furniture prewar, see *The Elastic Tip Co.*

Jensen Mfg. Co. This Jeannette, Penn., firm made electric steam engines and equipment in the late prewar years. In the Boomer years, it shifted to making model steam engines, and "miniature power plants."

"Jerry Blocks" see *Holgate Bros. Co.*

"Jerry Pets" see *Jerry Elsner Co.*

Jeschke Wire & Specialty Co. Jeschke, based in Crawfordsville, Ind., made toy scissors and wire forms in the late 1930s.

"Jet Hawk" bicycle see *Midwest Industries.*

Jet Jumper Mfg. Corp. Besides such outdoor activity sets as tetherball and volleyball, Jet Jumper made pogo sticks. It was based on West 29th Street, New York City, in the Boomer years.

"Jet Racer" Irish mail see *Midwest Industries.*

"Jet Ride" Irish Mail see *F.C. Castelli Co.*

"Jet Rocket Space Ship" see *The S.J. Wegman Co.*

"Jet" roll caps see *J. Halpern Co.*

"Jet" skates see *Moen & Patton.*

jewelry, children's In the accessory-minded 1950s and '60s, the manufacturing of children's jewelry became an important segment of the toy industry. Manufacturers included Banner Plastics Corp., Cleinman & Sons, Elegant Button & Novelty, Golden Needle Corp., Carl Guggenheim, Jay Ell Products Co., and President Novelty & Jewelry Co. A great many kits for assembling jewelry also appeared, from numerous firms including Hassenfeld Bros. and Standard Toykraft Products.

"Jewels for Playthings" see *Kilgore Mfg. Co., Inc.*

J

jews-harp Found back to the 18th century in America. Sensitivity about the name caused it to be designated "mouth harp" and "jaw harp" in the later 20th century.

Jiffy Plastics Mfg. Co. The "Kid-Doo" snow sled in the shape of a snowmobile was introduced in 1969 by this Tecumseh, Mich., company.

Jig-Cross Novelty Co. Based in Richmond, Va., Jig-Cross made the prewar Jig-Cross games and the Automatic-Instruction board.

Jig-O-Pin Products Corp. Established in Detroit, Mich., in the late 1930s, Jig-O-Pin produced toy blocks and puzzles.

"Jig Saw, Jr" see *Burgess Vibrocrafters, Inc.*

"Jig Wood" picture puzzles prewar, see *Parker Bros., Inc.*

"Jigleets" bird and animal puzzles see *Wordcraft.*

"Jim Bowie" Another historical figure who became a media hero in the Boomer years, "Jim Bowie" playthings included 3-D color film cards by True-Vue Co., and plastic figures by Hartland Plastics.

Jimmy Allen Flying Club The Jimmy Allen Flying Club released a metal premium ring in the 1930s with a vertical propeller superimposed above a pair of wings, similar to the symbol used by Captain Midnight.

"Jimmy Bounce" toys see *Petrie Lewis Mfg. Co., Inc.*

"Jimmy Durante Uke" see *Emenee Industries.*

Jingl-Blox Toy Mfg. Co. "Jingl-Blox" were issued in the 1930s by this Cincinnati, Ohio, company.

"Jingle Blox," postwar see *Gerber Plastic Co.*

"Jingle" stuffed animals prewar, see *National French Fancy Novelty Co.*

"Jitney" The "Jitney" name was used by at least two companies for prewar wagons: Benner, and Lullabye Furniture Corp.

Jo-Ann Musical Toys, Inc. This Dayton, Ohio, company issued educational xylophones in the late 1930s.

Jo-Han Models, Inc. Jo-Han, a manufacturer of scale model miniature cars in the 1950s and '60s, was based in Detroit, Mich.

"Joanne Woodward" paper dolls see *The Saalfield Publishing Co.*

Jock-O Co. The "Jock-O" monkey hand puppet of the late 1930s was made by this Chicago, Ill., company.

"Joe Palooka" "Joe Palooka" playthings in the Boomer years included a "Bop Bag" by Ideal Toy Corp. and boxing gloves, gym sets, striking bags, and training sets by B.&M. Sportoy Co.

"John Gilpin" game late 1800s, see *Charles M. Crandall.*

John-Henry Mfg. Co. "Dick Tracy" handcuffs and handcuff sets, and "Dragnet" jailer keys and handcuff sets, were issued in the 1950s-60s by John-Henry, based on Grand Street, New York City. The firm also made badges and goggles.

"Johnny Lightning" see *De Luxe Reading Corp.*

"Johnny One-Shot" wrist holster and pistol see *Kilgore Mfg. Co., Inc..*

"Johnny Seven" see *De Luxe Reading Corp.*

C.J. Johnson Co. Besides lawn and beach furniture, this Bradford, Penn., company made coaster wagons, scooters, sled-guards and sleds in the early 20th century, continuing in operation through the prewar years.

Iver Johnson's Arms & Cycle Works Based in Fitchburg, Mass., this company made baby walkers, scooters, velocipedes, junior cycles, and juvenile bicycles in the 1930s and '40s.

J.W. Johnson Co. Based in Chicago, Ill., Johnson made children's tents from the 1930s through the Boomer years, when it moved to Bellwood, Ill. Its line included the "Planet Patrol" tepee tent and "Robin Hood" tent in the 1950s-60s.

J

Nestor Johnson Mfg. Co. Based in Chicago, Ill., Nestor Johnson made skates and children's snow shoes in the 1930s and '40s. It was using the "Snow Glider" trade name for its snowshoes earlier in the decade, and for its tubular ice skates in the late '30s.

Johnson, Randall Co. This Traverse City, Mich., company made fibre, maple, and bentwood juvenile furniture in the 1930s and '40s.

Johnson, Smith & Co. This Detroit, Mich., firm manufactured electric train construction sets, blank cartridge pistols, and books in the late 1930s.

Johnson Store Equipment Co. In addition to table golf, shooting games and bagatelles, this Elgin, Ill., company made animal walking toys in the earlier 1930s. Its 1933 baseball board game "Bambino" remained popular through the decade. By the late '30s its line included table golf, shooting games, action toys, and the "Five Pins" bowling game.

William G. Johnston Co. Based in Pittsburgh, Penn., this prewar publisher made children's books and "cardboard toy houses in book form."

Jolly Blinker Corp. This postwar Brooklyn, N.Y., company made vinyl and polyethylene plastic infant toys, water balls, music balls, swing toys, suction toys, and carriage and crib toys.

"Jolly Jingle Joys" floating toys see *Bayshore Industries.*

"Jolly Kitchen" sets see *Aluminum Goods Mfg. Co.*

Jolly Toys, Inc. Based on Fifth Avenue, New York City, Jolly Toys specialized in baby dolls, and rubber and plastic dolls.

"Jollytime" dominoes see *Milton Bradley Co.*

"Jon Gnagy" art sets see *Arthur Brown & Bros.*

Howard B. Jones Based in Chicago, Ill., in the 1930s and early '40s, Howard B. Jones made a predecessor to the Boomer toy "Spirograph," a mechanical drawing toy

called "Hoot-Nanny, the Magic Designer." The toy was issued after the war by Northern Signal Co.

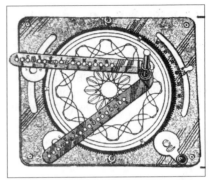

The "Hoot-Nanny" was a mechanical drawing toy by Howard B. Jones.

Paul Jones, Inc. Based in Mishawaka, Ind., Paul Jones issued toy soldiers, glider airplanes, construction toys, horse racing and marble games, shooting games, rubber-band guns, toy pistols, sailboat construction kits, and "Pop Pop" boat toys in the 1930s.

Ralph T. Jones Fine dollhouse furniture was made from the 1910s through the end of the '30s by this prewar Hingham, Mass., company. Jones, which was associated with the Tower Toy Guild, also made playroom equipment.

Jones & Bixler Co. Charles A. Jones and Louis S. Bixler founded Jones & Bixler Co. in Freemansburg, Penn., in 1899. The company made the "Red Devil Line" of cast-iron automobile toys in 1903, when the company became part of National Novelty Corp. The toys of Jones & Bixler and Kenton Hardware, also part of the National Novelty Corp. trust, are considered indistinguishable for the years 1909-1913. The company continued until 1914.

"Joseph swirl" marbles Black glass marbles with white swirls are sometimes called "Joseph" swirls.

Jotto Corporation The "Jotto" word game of the 1950s and '60s was published by this East 22nd Street, New York City, company.

"Joy," imprint see *Artwood Toy Mfg. Co.*

"Joy Bee Dolls" see *Bouton-Woolf Co., Inc.*

Joy Doll Co. Based on West 24th Street, New York City, Joy Doll made wood and soft dolls and novelties in the 1930s. It changed its name to Joy Doll Corp., and address to West 17th Street, New York City, by the late 1930s.

"The Joy Doll Family" see *Bimblick & Co.*

"Joy Family" beaded dolls see *Artwood Toy Mfg. Co.*

"Joy Line" vehicles see *Gem Crib & Cradle Co.*

"Joy-Toy" outfits see *The Boy Toymaker Co.*

"Jr." see *"Junior."*

Judd Toy Co. Based in Rochester, N.Y., with factory in Waterloo, N.Y., Judd manufactured wooden wheel goods and toys during World War II.

Judsen Rubber Works, Inc. Judsen, based in Chicago, Ill., in the late 1930s, issued rubber pitching horseshoes and "Skee-Zee" roller skate ankle pads.

"Judy Bolton" books see *Grosset & Dunlap, Inc.*

The Judy Co. The Judy Co. of Minneapolis, Minn., was established in the late 1930s with a line of building blocks, peg boards, and puzzles. Its line by wartime included "Judy Puzzle Inlays," and "Judy's Farm," a farm play set with buildings, wooden animals and vehicles, and fencing and posts. The "Judy Juniors" inlay puzzles were introduced in 1943. In the postwar years it issued farm play sets with rubber animals, people, and vehicles.

"Jumbo" crayons see *The Ullman Mfg. Co.*

"Jumbotyre" bicycles see *Shelby Cycle Co.*

jump rope, or jumping rope A venerable game, jumping rope was known in Colonial times. Turners frequently made jump-rope handles as a sideline. The idea that dozens of companies may have been manufacturing the handles in any particular decade of the 1800s is not a far-fetched one. Earlier prewar companies that listed jump ropes as a specialty included the Alox Mfg. Co., A.E. Beck Mfg. Co., Billings, Brodhaven Mfg. Co., the Carpenter Mfg. Co., Gem City Specialty Co., Hansen Wood Goods & Toy Mfg. Co., the N.N. Hill Brass Co., Hoffman Lion Mills Co., Leather Products Co., the Mordt Co., Newton & Thompson Mfg. Co., Nitram Mfg. Co., J.W. Spear & Sons, and the Toy Tinkers. Manufacturers that joined their number by the late prewar years included Anderson Rubber Co., Artwood Toy Mfg. Co., William J. Graham Co., Meyer Rubber Co., and Piqua General Supply Co. The many companies who issued jump ropes in the Boomer years included firms using new materials, including American Thermoplastics Products Corp. and Plastic Block City.

jumping beans Jumping beans were a novelty that fascinated millions of children in the Boomer years. The most prominent were probably the "Mexican Jumping Beans" imported by Alamos Distribution Corp., packaged in two-tone plastic boxes, the lid being clear to reveal the beans within, and sold on easel display cards that sat on 7-11 and Woolworth's counters across the country. Other companies issuing the vegetable toy included Chemical Sundries Co., Karl Guggenheim, and M. Shimmel Sons. The "beans" were seeds of the Yerba de la Flecha tree of Mexico's Sonoran desert, which jumped if they contained larvae of a moth. The larvae remained active for up to two months.

"Jumping Horse" exerciser see *Cameo Doll Co.*

jumping-jack Popular in Europe, wooden jumping-jacks were manufactured in America from the early 1800s.

J

"Jumping Jack" toy from the 1920s.

"Jumping Jitney" prewar, see *The Wayne Toy Mfg. Co.*

Junel Novelties, Inc. Established on East 11th Street, New York City, in the late 1930s, Junel made soft dolls and novelties.

"Junglegym" see *Playground Equipment Co.*

"Junior" air rifle see *Halperin Co.*

"Junior Bronco" spring horse see *Wirsig Products Co.*

"Junior Caster Sets" see *Rapaport Bros.*

"Junior Chef" see *Argo Industries, Corp.*

"Junior Craftsman" paint and crayon sets see *Milton Bradley Co.*

"Junior Craftsman" workbench and tools see *The Mordt Co.*

"Junior De Luxe" skates see *Chicago Roller Skate Co.*

"Junior Elf" books see *Rand, McNally & Co.*

"Jr. Miss" cosmetic and sewing sets see *Hassenfeld Bros.*

"Junior No-Roll" crayons see *Milton Bradley Co.*

"Jr. O" roller skates see *Kingston Products Corp.*

"Junior Patrol" pistol outfits see the *Mordt Co.*

"Junior Police" and "Junior Sheriff" holster sets see *Adolph Schwartz.*

"Junior" roller skates see *Kingston Products Corp.*

Junior Toy Corp. This Hammond, Ind., corporation made prewar tubular velocipedes, scooters, doll buggies, and pedal cars. By the late 1930s and '40s it was using the "Sky Line" trade name on its streamlined velocipedes and pedal cars. During wartime the line continued, presumably made with non-restricted materials. The firm continued into the Boomer years as Junior Toy Division.

"Junior Transfer" coaster wagons see *Lullabye Furniture Corp.*

"Junior" wagon Both Dayton Toy & Specialty Co. and Sheboygan Coaster & Wagon Works issued prewar "Junior" wagons.

"Jupiter Rocket" bank see *Superior Toy & Mfg. Co.*

"Jupiter Rocket" space toy see *Gladen Enterprises, Inc.*

"Jupiter" transformer see *Dongan Electric Mfg. Co.*

Juro Novelty Co. Based on East 18th Street, New York City, this doll manufacturer issued a line of "Juro Celebrity Dolls," including Paul Winchell's "Jerry Mahoney" and "Knucklehead," and Dick Clark's "Autograph" and "Dancing Dolls."

"Just Like Mother's" toy furniture see *Lehman Co. of America, Inc.*

"Just-Lyk" dolls prewar, see *Natural Doll Co., Inc.*

K.&B. Novelty & Mfg. Co. Maker of juvenile furniture and swings, this Kansas City, Mo., company also made prewar toy airplanes and doll furniture. It added marble games to its line by the late 1930s.

K.&O. Models, Inc. Based in Van Nuys, Calif., K.&O. Models issued the "Fleet Line" plastic boats of the 1950s, with battery-operated outboard motors.

K-B Doll Corp. The "Barbara Jo" dolls of the 1950s and '60s were issued by this West 23rd Street, New York City, company.

"K.B.N." see *Karl Buba.*

"K-Line" see *Kestral Corp.*

"K-Pop Gun" see *Kusan, Inc.*

Ka-Klar Cloth Toy Co. Based in Manchester, Conn., in the late 1930s through the Boomer years, Ka-Klar manufactured stuffed animals and soft dolls.

"Ka-Yo" see *Cayo Mfg. Co.*

"Ka-Zoom" musical rocket see *Colonial Moulded Plastics Co., Inc.*

Kachina doll Religious objects used by some Southwestern American Indians, Kachina dolls were carved of wood and brightly painted. They were used as play dolls after having served a religious function.

Emil Kahn Co. This manufacturer made "Riot-Us," billed as "the greatest 10-cent party game out," in the late 1920s. Emil Kahn was located on Broadway, New York City.

M.L. Kahn Based on East 19th Street, New York City, Kahn specialized in dolls' knit goods, dresses, and novelties in the 1920s through the prewar years.

Kaklar Cloth Toy Co. see *Ka-Klar Cloth Toy Co.*

Kalah Game Co. The "Kalah" game of the 1950s and '60s was the lead product of this Molliston, Mass., manufacturer of table, educational, and adult games.

Kalamazoo Sled Co. This Michigan specialist in folding hammocks and lawn furniture also made sleds and novelties through the prewar years, using the "Champion" trade name. It introduced the "'Victory' Model Rocket Racer," an all-wood sled, in 1943. In the Boomer years its toy specialty remained sleds and baby sleds. The firm used the "Kal-Kasual" trade name on its furniture.

kaleidoscope The kaleidoscope is a popular optical toy involving a tube through which the viewer gazes to regard radially-symmetrical mirror duplications of the items or images held on the farther end of the tube. These items tumbled and changed the pattern seen, being contained in a section of tube that fit loosely around the viewing tube, the "head," that could be turned with the hand.

The original kaleidoscopes used pieces of colored glass trapped between two panes, in the turning heads. By the Boomer era, colored pieces of plastic were common inclusions.

Invented in the 1800s by Scottish scientist Sir David Brewster, they remained popular through the later 19th and 20th centuries.

Earlier prewar manufacturers of kaleidoscopes included the H. & P. Mfg. Co., P.H. Kantro Industries, Petrie-Lewis Mfg. Co., and Quincy Paper Box Co. In the late prewar years, Quincy remained active, joined by Petrie-Lewis Mfg. Co. and Valley City Novelty Co.

In the Boomer years numerous versions appeared, including a distinctive line by Steven Mfg. Co., a company that billed itself as "Manufacturer of World Famous Kaleidoscopes." Steven's No. 400 "Deluxe" came with four interchangeable heads.

Other postwar manufacturers included H. Davis Toy Corp., William F. Drueke & Sons, Eberhard Faber Toy & Game Co., Orange Rubber and Plastics Corp., Tri G Co., and Whirley Corp.

Kalon Mfg. Co. Kalon of Brooklyn, N.Y., made dime register and television banks, games, and toy washing machines in the 1950s and '60s. "Kalomatic" was a Kalon trade name.

Kay Kamen, Inc. In the 1930s, Kay Kamen was the exclusive representative for Walt Disney Enterprises. Based on Seventh Avenue in New York City, Kamen also had offices in Chicago, Toronto, London, Paris, Milan, Copenhagen, Madrid, Lisbon, and Sydney. Relatively few companies obtained licenses to manufacture early "Mickey Mouse" and "Three Little Pigs" merchandise. By later in the decade, "Donald Duck," "Snow White & Seven Dwarfs," "Ferdinand the Bull" and "Pinocchio" were popular licenses.

Early to mid-1930s deals with toy companies resulted in toy building blocks by Halsam Productions, movie projectors by Keystone Manufacturing, stuffed dolls by Knickerbocker Toy Co., metal toys and sand toys by Ohio Art, balloons by Oak Rubber, and rubber dolls and toys by Seiberling Latex Products. Deals with children's publishers resulted in pop-up and "Waddle" books by Blue Ribbon Books, paint books by Saalfield Publishing Co., and popular-priced books by Whitman Publishing Co.

Other companies holding early Disney licenses through Kay Kamen included Andrews Co. for play houses, George Borgfeldt Corp. for general toys, Bryant Electric Co. for children's dishes and "Hemcoware," Colson Co. for velocipedes, Crawford Furniture Mfg. Co. for tents and camp furniture, Joseph Dixon Crucible Co. for pencils and pencil boxes, Dolly Toy Co. for animated "Mickey Mouse" toys, Fulton Specialty Co. for rubber stamp sets, N.N. Hill Brass Co. for metal pull toys, King Innovations for purses, Richard G. Krueger for nursery toys, Marks Brothers Co. for games, toys, and paint sets, David McCay for story books, Reliance Pic-

ture Frame Co. for framed pictures, Richmond School Furniture Co. for blackboards, Sackman Brothers Co. for play suits, Standard Brief Case Co. for children's briefcases, Straits Corp. for lamps, metal boats, and airplanes, U.S. Lock and Hardware Co. for jack sets, Wornova Mfg. Co. for costumes, and Zell Products Corp. for toy banks.

Licenses by the late 1930s included Adler Favor & Novelty Co. for party favors, Alexander Doll Co. for dolls, S.L. Allen & Co. for sleds, Aluminum Goods Mfg. Co. for dishes and cooking utensils, American Toy Works for target games, Behrend & Rothschild for banks, Milton Bradley Co. for games, Bryant Electric Co. for "Beetleware" dishes, Commonwealth Toy & Novelty Co. for a portable tennis set, Crown Toy Mfg. Co. for banks, glove dolls and statuettes, Emerson Radio & Phonograph Corp. for radios, A.S. Fishbach for costumes, Fisher-Price Toys for pull toys, Gotham Pressed Steel Corp. for toy cleaning sets, Richard G. Krueger for dolls, Louis Marx & Co. for mechanical toys, Naylor Corp. for tapping sets, Odora Co. for toy chests, A.G. Palmer Supply Co. for party favors, Parker Bros. for games, Pontiac Spring & Bumper Co. for spring riding toys, Storkline Furniture Corp. for nursery furniture, Standard Toykraft Products for painting and sewing sets, Whitman Publishing Co. for games in addition to books, and J.L. Wright for "Plaster Kaster" sets.

KamKap, Inc. Based on Broadway, New York City, KamKap made postwar toy cash registers, a talking toy switchboard, xylophones, marimbas, and surveyor sets.

Kamm Games Kamm Games issued the 1940s board game "Casey on the Mound."

Kampes Dolls, Inc. Based on Fifth Avenue, New York City, Kampes made the mid-1930s "Kamkin Kiddies," which included a boy, a girl, and a baby.

Kansas Toy & Novelty Co. Based in Clifton, Kans., this specialist in slush-metal toys produced miniature airplanes, autos, racers, trucks, tractors, and steam rollers in the mid-1930s.

Kant Novelty Co. Based in Pittsburgh, Penn., Kant Novelty issued noisemakers, favors, and paper hats in the late 1930s.

P.H. Kantro Industries Based in Portage, Wis., Kantro produced kaleidoscopes in the 1930s.

Kapri Mfg. Co. In addition to such juvenile furniture items as rockers and TV chairs, Kapri made hobbyhorses in the 1950s and '60s.

The Karavan Based on Fifth Avenue, New York City, in the 1930s, the Karavan may have been both manufacturer and importer, specializing in Russian toys including nested dolls and eggs, carved animals, carved and painted mechanical toys, and children's furniture.

Karbon Kopee Kompany Based in Boston, Mass., this firm made Boomer-era "Karbon Kopee" drawing kits.

Kardollette, Inc. Based on E. 42nd Street, New York City, this firm issued the mid-1930s "Kardolette" roulette and "CuKu Bridge" games.

Karson Mfg. Co. Established on Broadway, New York City, in the late 1930s, Karson manufactured metal toys, games, and novelties.

The Kashner Co. From the earlier 20th century through the prewar years, Kashner issued novelties including snapping mottoes and paper hats. In the 1930s and '40s the company was known as Kashner Novelty Corp. It was based on Broadway, New York City.

"Kast-A-Toy" see *Ace Toy Mold Co.*

"Kast-Art" miniatures see *Williams Kast Art Co.*

"Kaster Kit" outfits see *A.C. Gilbert Co.*

Kat-A-Korner Kompany, Inc. Kat-A-Korner, based in Nashville, Tenn., made oil cloth and soft-body dolls and animal toys in the 1930s.

Katagiri Bros. Based on East 59th Street in the 1920s, New York City, Katagiri Bros.

was an important importer of mechanical toys and novelties. Its toys included the mechanical "Branko Acrobat," featuring a celluloid boy figure on a wire trapeze powered by a spring motor. In the earlier 1930s the company was based on Fourth Avenue

Katnips, Inc. Based in Providence, R.I., Katnips made celluloid novelties and rubber toys in the 1930s.

"Katy Flyer" hand car see *Hill-Standard Corp.*

Henry Katz & Co., Inc. This Fourth Avenue, New York City, manufacturer produced the "Katz Toys" line of the 1920s. One of its leading toys was the "Coney Island" mechanical amusement park toy, and "Grand Central," a 1928 mechanical toy. Katz also made "Zepcraft" zeppelin toys and "Commander" airplanes, electric trains, sewing machines, register banks, and noisemakers, as well as white enamel kitchen furniture and rubber-cushioned pool tables.

Henry Katz & Co. logo.

Henry Katz National Sales Organization In the 1950s and '60s, Henry Katz National Sales represented manufacturers of steel, mechanical, and plastic toys.

"Kay Stanley's Cake Mix Sets" see *Plastic Block City, Inc.*

Kayanee Corp. of America The "Sewmaster" sewing machines of the 1950s and '60s were products of this Broadway, New York City, firm. In the mid-Boomer years the company issued a line of 17 models, priced from $2.98 to $19.98. Some were battery-operated, while others used A.C.

Kaye Novelty Co. Describing itself as the world's largest manufacturer of pin-wheels, this 1950s Brooklyn, N.Y., company also issued toy airplanes, flying birds, parasols, batons, and party hats and favors.

The Kaymar Corp. The Toddler, which was a combination jumper, walker, go-cart and pull-cart, was made by this St. Louis, Mo., company in the 1930s.

"Kayo" see *"Moon Mullins."*

Kaysam Corp. of America Soft vinyl infants' toys, novelties, and bath toys were the specialty of this Paterson, N.J., company in the Boomer years. It also made vinyl and latex parts for doll manufacturers.

Robert Kayton Co. Based on West 26th Street, New York City, Robert Kayton issued a "Snow White" table garden and Walt Disney character lawn figures in the late 1930s.

Kazoo Co., Inc. In addition to kazoos, this Eden, N.Y., company made horns, noise-makers, and advertising novelties. Touting itself as the "oldest and largest kazoo manu-facturers in the world," and issued the No. 19 "Old Reliable," initially in one color and in two-color versions by the late 1920s. It also manufactured the No. 7 "Miniature Saxo-phone Kazoo," and the No. 35 "Kazoo Bell Noise Maker." The No. 717 "Large Saxo-phone Kazoo" of the late '20s had "melodi-ous tone—plays real jazz." In the 1930s the firm also made musical bubble makers and vest-pocket cigarette rollers.

kazoos Besides Kazoo Co., the Kirchhof Patent Co. made these buzzing metal instru-ments, both before and after World War II. Other postwar manufacturers included Rie-mann, Seabrey Co. and Spec-Toy-Culars.

V.M. Kearly Mfg. Co. Corrugated board was used for toys by the 1930s, with V.M. Kearly of West 22nd Street, New York City, manufacturing arks, play stores, and toy kitchen cabinets, ranges, and refrigerators. The company also made some steel toys, including an electric washing machine and play stores.

Keen-Eye Co., Inc. The "Keen-Eye" pad-dle and ball toys and "Piggy Jack" banks of the Boomer years were products of Keen-Eye, based in Butler, Wis. The firm also made tops, guns, dart games, and novelty toys.

F.D. Kees Mfg. Co. Based in Beatrice, Neb., in the 1930s and '40s, F.D. Kees manu-factured "Brownie" and "Kees" roller skates, and "Kees" ice skates.

The Keezer Mfg. Co. Keezer's stuffed animals, issued in the Boomer years, were designed for the school, collegiate and gift shop trade. It was based in Plaistow, N.H.

Keiser-Fry The 1929 "Babe Ruth National Game of Baseball," a board game, was issued by Keiser-Fry.

Keller, J.W. Active in the late 19th century, J.W. Keller issued the 1894 "Hounds & Hares" board game.

Robert Keller Ink Co. The Kolorkraft Division of Robert Keller Ink Co. made the "Kopy-Kat" water color paint sets of the 1930s.

Keller Toy Mfg. Co. In the 1920s and '30s, Keller specialized in tin horns, fog horns, drum horns, noisemakers, sand toys including sprinkling cans and sand molds, and laundry sets. "Bean blowers" were added to the line in the later 1930s. The firm was based in Columbus, Ohio.

"Kelley Kar" see *Burnham Mfg. Co.*

Kellogg & Bulkeley A publisher based in Hartford, Conn., in the 1850s, Kellogg & Bulkeley issued toys including "The Chil-dren's Farmyard," a farm play set of cutouts.

Kelly Bros., Inc. This Gardner, Mass, firm issued juvenile furniture in the late pre-war years.

Kelman Co. Based in Brooklyn, N.Y., in the late 1930s, Kelman made sewing sets.

Kelmet Corp. The Kelmet Corp. of New York City produced large, pressed-steel trucks under the tradenames "Kelmet," "Big Boy," and "Trumodel" from 1923 through the 1930s. "Big Boy" trucks were based on the White Truck. Its line of construction toys on the verge of the Great Depression included a Dump Truck, Steam Shovel, Excavator, Universal Crane, "Coal Pocket," Aerial Trucks, "Trumodel Derrick," Army Truck, and Chemical Truck. Kelmet subcontracted much of its work, with A.C. Gilbert completing final assembly.

Kemkit Chemical Corp. Based in Brooklyn, N.Y., Kemkit made prewar chemistry sets.

"Ken Holt" series see *Grosset & Dunlap, Inc.*

Kenilworth Press, Inc. Located on East 46th Street, New York City, Kenilworth published "The Game of the Three Little Pigs," first released in 1933.

Kenner Products Co. Based in Cincinnati, Ohio, Kenner became one of the leading toy manufacturers of the Boomer years, enjoying success with such varied items in the later 1950s as "Presto-Paints," "Girder & Panel" and "Bridge & Turnpike" building sets, "Turn A Tune," "Battery Motor" play drill, "Fountain Brush" painting sets, "Zilly Zoo," "Nursery Birds," plastic toys, and infants' mobiles. Kenner motorized its construction toys in 1960, and introduced its "Show Time Projector" with "16 famous character shows in full color," which anticipated one of its more popular entries of the 1960s, the "Give-A-Show Projector." Other hits included the "Flintstone Building Boulders" of 1963, and the "Kenner Easy-Bake Oven" of 1964. The latter, using a light bulb for its heat source, was touted for its safety. It remained a popular toy for decades.

"Girder & Panel," one of Kenner's popular 1950s-60s toys.

"Keno Lotto" This popular game was produced by numerous manufacturers. In prewar times, Milton Bradley Co., Parker Bros., and Selchow & Righter all issued games under this name. J.M. Simmons & Co. also issued a "Keno-Bingo."

R.O. Kent Corp. Based on West 31st Street, New York City, Kent issued Boomer-era bicycle accessories.

The Kenton Hardware Co. F.M. Perkins began manufacturing a patented line of refrigerator hardware in 1890, in Kenton Ohio. The company began toy production in 1894 with a line of horse-drawn fire vehicles, toy stoves, and banks. The name became the Kenton Hardware Co. in 1900.

In the years 1903-1920 the Kenton name largely disappeared. In 1903, as part of the National Novelty Corp. merger, it produced toys under the name Wing Mfg. Co. After the break-up of National Novelty's trust, and several other takeover episodes, Kenton again emerged under its own name in 1920, and produced iron toys through the 1930s. Its line included banks, cap pistols, blank cartridge pistols, toy stoves and ranges, hook-and-ladder toys, automobiles, concrete mixers, airplanes, dirigibles, "Buckeye" ditchers, ladder toys, sand toys, and boxed assortments. A major manufacturer in the prewar years, Kenton maintained show offices in the Fifth Avenue Building, New York City.

Kenton continued in operation until 1952. A company called Littlestown Hardware &

Kenner Products Co. logo, 1960s.

iT's *Kenner*

iT's **FUN!**

Foundry acquired the tooling for many Kenton toy designs and issued them under the brand name "Utexiqual" until that foundry closed in 1982.

"Kentontoy" see *The Kenton Hardware Co.*

Kerger Co. Publisher of the "Varsitee" football playing cards in the late 1930s, this Gary, Ind., firm also issued the "21st Century Football" board game.

Kerk Guild, Inc. Besides "soap novelties," this Utica, N.Y., company made the "Lynda Lou" felt dolls of the 1930s and '40s. The firm also issued board games, including "The Van Loon Story of Mankind Game" and "A.A. Milne's Winnie-the-Pooh Game," both of 1931. In the late '30s, the company obtained a license to issue Edgar Bergen related soap figures.

Kestral Corp. A postwar firm based in Springfield, Mass., Kestral issued plastic inflatable toys, as well as pools. It used the "K-Line" trade name.

Kewaunee Equipment Co. Based in Kewaunee, Wis., this postwar juvenile furniture company also made some "movable" toys and doll high chairs.

"Kewpie" Artist Rose O'Neill introduced the "Kewpie" doll in the 1910s. The dolls apeared in the years 1914-1919 in the pages of *Good Housekeeping*. "Kewpie" dolls remained a phenomenon through the prewar years. The dolls' manufacturers included George Borgfeldt Corp., who made bisque dolls, and Richard G. Krueger, soft dolls, in the earlier 1930s. In the late prewar years, Schavoir Rubber Co. made rubber "Kewpies." Postwar rights to issue the dolls were held by Cameo Doll Products and Knickerbocker Toy Co. The latter issued soft dolls.

The Keydal Co. A manufacturer of electric angel chimes for Christmas trees, this Detroit, Mich., company was also known for the "Jipsy Kart" wagon in the 1930s.

Keyless Roller Skate Co. This Tecumseh, Mich., manufacturer was established in the late 1930s. Kingston Products Corp. also used the "Keyless" trade name on roller skates in the '30s.

Keyston Bros. Juvenile playsuits and pistol holsters were specialties of this San Francisco, Calif., company in the 1930s and '40s. In the Boomer years, Keyston emphasized cowboy, cowgirl and Indian suits, holsters, and western accessories. In the later 1950s, its leading holster sets included "The Arizonan," "The Colt," "Frontiersman," "The San Jose," "The Marshal," and "Texan .45." The holsters were made of steer hide.

Keystone Ferrule & Nut Co. A Burlington, Wis., firm, Keystone Ferrule & Nut manufactured 8 mm. toy movie projectors, Morse Code signal keys and electronic toys in the 1950s and '60s.

"Keystone" tool sets see *Famous Keystone Kits Corp.*

Keystone Mfg. Co. Founded in Boston, Mass., around 1920, Keystone was a major prewar manufacturer best known for its toy motion picture machines and "Keystone Moviegraph" comedy films for children. It also made movie cameras and the "Radioptican" postcard projector.

The company also made heavy steel toys, electric-motor boats, sailboats, spring-motor boats, wood toys, wood horses, and wagons. In the mid-1920s, through an arrangement with Packard Motor Co., it manufactured pressed-steel riding trucks based on Packard models. In competing with Buddy "L" in the large truck-toy category, Keystone introduced nickeled hub caps and radiator caps, engine crank, and transparent celluloid windshields. It also offered the option on its trucks of rubber tires and headlaps, for an extra 50 cents. The trucks could be steered, and had stop-and-go signal arms.

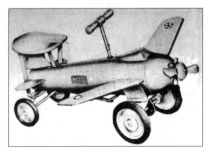

The "Ride 'Em Plane" was another Keystone Mfg. Co. offering.

Keystone Mfg. Co.'s "Ride 'Em Dump Truck," 1950s.

The "Radiopticon" projector from Keystone Mfg. Co., 1920s.

By the late '20s, the company's "Keystone Model Toys" line of heavy steel vehicles was 23 toys strong, and included a Steam Shovel, Aerial Ladder, Dump Truck, Hydraulic Dump Truck, Wrecking Car, U.S. Army Truck, Ambulance, "Koaster Truck," Dump Truck, U.S. Mail Truck, Police Patrol, Fire Truck, Truck Loader, and ride-on Locomotive.

In the earlier 1930s Keystone obtained a license from Kay Kaymen to produce early Walt Disney movie projectors. In 1934 the company introduced "Siren Riding Toys" with handlebars for steering and saddle riding seats, and, in 1936, the "Ride-Em" mail plane. By late in the decade, Keystone's line included dollhouses, soldier forts, masonite desks, sail boats, spring motor boats, wood toys, in addition to the projectors and heavy steel toys. During this time the company maintained offices in the Fifth Avenue Building.

Keystone's prices give a good example of toy prices in the late prewar years. Its projectors cost from $2.50 to $7.50; its rocking cradles,

equipped with Swiss music boxes, from $2.50 to $5.00; its juvenile desks, from $2.50 to $8.50; its ride-on trucks and other heavy steel toys, from $2.00 to $10.00; its sail boats, from 10 cents to $10.00; and its dollhouses, from $1.25 to $10.00.

During wartime, Keystone was able to manufacture toy sailboats, dollhouses, wooden war toys, and bowling alleys.

In postwar years, most of the company's toy output was based on Kingsbury Mfg. Co. tooling, which it obtained in the 1940s.

Keystone View Co. A Meadville, Penn., company, Keystone View Co. made stereoscopes, stereoscopic views, and lantern slides in the 1930s and '40s.

"Kid Cycle" see *The W.J. Baker Co.*

"Kid-Doo" see *Jiffy Plastics Mfg. Co.*

"Kid-O" modeling dough see *Climax Industries.*

"Kidd-E-Toys" see *American Metal Specialties Corp.*

"Kiddie" The H.C. White Co. used the "Kiddie" trademark on a variety of its prewar products, including its juvenile furniture. It also manufactured the "Kiddie-Kar," "Kiddie-Kart," "Kiddie-Koaster," "Kiddie-Kwacker" rocking toy, "Kiddie Pedal Kar", "Kiddie Planes," and "Kiddie-Skooter."

The 1920s "Kiddie-Kar" by H.C. White Co.

The *"Kiddie Tricycle"* was another pedal toy by H.C. White

"Kiddie Blox" see *Crosman Bros. Co.*

"Kiddie-Boggan" see *Northland Ski Mfg. Co.*

Kiddie Brush & Toy Co. This Jonesville, Mich., company made toy housecleaning sets, including "The Little Housekeeper," "Modern Maid," "Mother's Helpmate," and "Spic and Span" in the 1930s. By the late prewar years its line included dollhouses. "Susy Goose," a trade name for the firm's house cleaning sets, was introduced in the later '30s, and became the most prominent of the firm's trade names in the Boomer years. The line came to include the "Musical Tone" toy carpet sweepers, toy brooms, dish washing sets, laundry sets, doll bassinet sets, plastic figures and play sets, "Friendly Acres Dairy Farm" sets, and toy horses. The firm used the slogan, "Toys That Mold Character." In the early 1960s, the "Susy Goose Toys" line featured doll furniture for Mattel's "Barbie" line.

"Kiddie" floating toys see *DuPont Viscoloid Co.*

Kiddie Gym, Inc. This Newark, N.J., firm issued "Kiddie" gym sets, slides, sand boxes, see-saws, cycle swings, the "Ideal" swing car, and "Cal's Colt" in the 1930s and '40s.

"Cal's Colt" was a 1940s exerciser by *Kiddie Gym, Inc.*

"Kiddie Kar," postwar see *The Hedstrom-Union Co.*

"Kiddie Klay" see *Imperial Crayon Co.*

"Kiddie-Kollege" wooden toys prewar, see the *Playcraft Co., The*

"Kiddie Pal" dolls see *Regal Doll Mfg. Co.*

"Kiddie" phonographs prewar, see *Plaza Mfg. Co.*

"Kiddie Quiz" games see *Jacmar Mfg. Co.*

"Kiddiejoy" dolls and toys prewar, see *Jacobs & Kassler.*

"Kiddies" printing sets see *The Superior Type Co.*

"Kiddilac" autos see *Garton Toy Co.*

Kiddy Case Mfg. Co. Children's toy-carrying cases were the specialty of this Boomer-era Denver, Colo., company.

Kiddy-Crafters Kiddy-Crafters of Medford, Mass., advertised its "Modernistic" wooden toys in the 1930s. Its line included Noah's Arks, rocking horses, dolls, and nursery decorations.

"Kiddy Kapers" stuffed toys see *Elka Toys.*

"Kiddybird" autos see *Hamilton Steel Products.*

"Kiddykook" see *Aluminum Specialty Co.*

"Kiddytools" sets see *Grey Iron Casting Co.*

Kiddie Gym, Inc. This Newark, N.J., made "Kiddie" gym sets and sandboxes in the 1930s, as well as the "Ideal" swing car.

Kidee-Krome, Inc. This Boomer-years juvenile furniture manufacturer was based in Paterson, N.J.

Kilgore Mfg. Co., Inc.

A major toy manufacturer based in Westerville, Ohio, Kilgore began as a toy manufacturer in 1925 through the purchase of a kite-manufacturing business from the George D. Wanner Company. Kilgore made its name in cast-iron toys, however, which it introduced in 1928. Its line included toy trucks, cars, fire engines, cap guns, and cannons. It produced toy paper caps after its merger with Andes Foundry and the Federal Toy Co. under the aegis of American Toy Co. The prestigious Butler Bros. Co. became its biggest distributor. The 1930s Kilgore's line included single-shot and repeating cap pistols, using paper caps. It also made jackstones and toy vehicles with rubber tires. By the late '30s it was advertising play guns with "lustrous inlaid pearl grips," and "modern plastic toys." A major player in that decade, it maintained offices in the Fifth Avenue Building, New York City. During wartime, the company was forced to cease manufacturing not only its cap pistols and paper caps, but also its plastic toys. In the postwar years, Kilgore continued emphasizing toy cap pistols and paper caps, and added to its line mechanical and electronic toys and games.

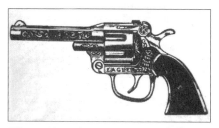

Kilgore Mfg. Co., Inc. released the "Eagle" cap pistol in the 1950s.

The "Hawkeye" was also a 1950s cap pistol by Kilgore.

"Kim Novak" paper dolls see *The Saalfield Publishing Co.*

Kimmel & Forster

This New York City publisher issued paper dolls including "The American Lady and Her Children," not a unique title in the late 1800s.

Kimport Dolls

This Independence, Mo., company made character dolls, "antique" dolls, American states dolls, and "dolls of all nations" in the 1950s and '60s.

"Kindergarten Kids" dolls see *Sayco Doll Corp.*

kindergarten and preschool toys

Kindergarten toys are among the most important in the development of children. While they often have a purposefully educational function, almost any toy at that age could not help but be educational, since wide-eyed children are willing to learn from almost anything.

Among the more famous kindergarten toys are the bench and hammer sets, made by companies including Holgate Bros. Co. and Playskool Institute, and the stacking "Bill Ding" clowns from Strombeck-Becker Mfg. Co.

Other prewar manufacturers specializing in kindergarten pastimes and goods included American Crayon Co., American Toy Works, Milton Bradley Co., the Embossing Co., Fisher-Price Toys, Samuel Gabriel Sons & Co., Hansen Wood Goods & Toy Mfg. Co., the Harter Publishing Co., George Leis, Parker Bros., the Playcraft Co., the Reliance Mfg. Co., Rippon Co., the A.I. Root Co., Saalfield Publishing Co., the A. Schoenhut Co., Sheffield Toys, J.W. Spear & Sons, Standard Toykraft Products, E. Steiger & Co., Transogram Co., the Ullman Mfg. Co., Whitman Publishing Co., and York & Troidl.

Among postwar companies, Playskool Mfg. Co. was perhaps the leader, manufacturing not only its own "Playskool" line of wooden educational toys but also other famous lines through its Lincoln Logs, Makit Toy, Appleton Juvenile Furniture, and Holgate Toys divisions.

Fisher-Price Toys, however, continued to issue an imaginative line emphasizing pull toys, push toys, and the kindergarten favorites

K

of the plastic "Snap-Lock Beads." See hammer and nail sets; blocks; rattles; shooflies.

"Kindersets" see *South Bend Toy Mfg. Co.*

"Kindograph" crayons see *The American Crayon Co.*

Jane King Doll Clothes This doll clothes manufacturer was established in the late 1930s in Baltimore, Md.

King Du-G Game Co. This Parsons, Kans., company issued the "King Du-G" game board of the late 1930s.

King Features Syndicate, Inc. King Features Syndicate was responsible for licensing some of the most notable cartoon characters of the 1930s to toy manufacturers, not least among them Popeye and his crew. King Features Syndicate properties also included Flash Gordon, Little Annie Rooney, Tillie the Toiler, Blondie, Barney Google, Just Kids, Jiggs and Maggie, Krazy Kat, Little Jimmy, Little Miss Muffet, Polly and Her Pals, Secret Agent X-9, Katzenjammer Kids, Tim Tyler, Toots and Casper, the Little King, Pete the Tramp, Henry, Mandrake the Magician, and Judge Puffle. King Features Syndicate was located on East 45th Street, New York City.

"King Harry" rocking horse see *Moulded Products, Inc.*

King Innovations Located in the Fifth Avenue Building in New York City, King Innovations obtained an early license from Kay Kaymen to produce "Mickey Mouse" and "Three Little Pigs" purses. The firm also issued licensed "Kewpie" dolls in the 1930s.

"King Flyer" coaster wagon see *The Monarch Products Co.*

King Mfg. Co. A Plymouth, Mich., company, King Mfg. Co. was the former Markham Air Rifle Co., its name having changed in late 1928. Daisy Mfg. Co. purchased the line in 1931, and continued issuing items under the "King" name. In the 1930s the line included popguns, water pistols, and toy bow and arrow sets.

King Mfg. Co. made the "Rapid Fire Pump Gun" in the 1920s.

"King-Pin" shovels see *The Conestoga Corp.*

"King Prancer" spring horse see *The Delphos Bending Co.*

"King" return top see *Lee Products Co.*

Kingman, Bradford In the 1850s, this Boston, Mass., manufacturer made children's carriages, rocking horses, sleds, toy pails, toy wheelbarrows, cradles, wagons, and a distinctive Irish Mail vehicle bearing a horse's head at front.

Kingsbury Mfg. Co. A high-profile toy manufacturer of the prewar years, Kingsbury Mfg. Co. had its origins in the late 1800s, with Wilkins Toy Co. In 1895, Harry T. Kingsbury bought Wilkins, combining it with Clipper Machine Works, which specialized in farm machinery and equipment. Kingsbury operated the company under the Wilkins name, introducing toy autos in the early 1900s, until the end of World War I, when he began to use his own name.

Kingsbury, based in Keene, N.H., specialized in copying famous models of aircraft, roadsters, trucks, and buses. In the 1920s, the "Kingsbury Motor Driven Toys" line featured famous race cars, first the "Sunbeam" and the famous, tail-finned "Bluebird," and in 1929 the toy racer that is Kingsbury's most famous toy, the "Golden Arrow." Kingsbury held exclusive rights to reproduce the record-breaking racer in toy form.

The famous "Bluebird" racer by Kingsbury Mfg. Co., 1920s.

In the 1930s, the company continued to produce electrically lighted, motor-driven toys as well as play-store scales and cash registers, and toy garden tools and garden sets. In addition to its racers, Kingsbury's offerings included the "Silver Arrow" flying planes. Also a maker of banks, Kingsbury produced the "Banclock" and "Motobank" five-coin registering banks. Kingsbury maintained offices in the Fifth Avenue Building, New York City, in the prewar years. With the onset of World War II, Kingsbury shifted production to war contracts, and sold its toy dies and tooling to Keystone Mfg. Co.

Kingsbury, as Kingsbury Machine Tool Division, became a subcontractor to the likes of General Motors, IBM, and General Electric, and never returned to toy production.

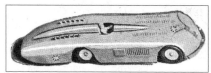

Kingsbury's line also included the "Sunbeam" toy racecar.

Kingston Products Corp.
Kingston Products Corp. of Kokomo, Ind., was founded as Kokomo Brass Works by Charles T. Byrne and James F. Ryan, to produce brass castings for the plumbing industry. Joining with other, kindred companies, Kingston Products Corp. was producing "Kokomo Toys" by the 1920s, having a separate Toy Division by the 1930s. Its line included toy racers, trucks, fire engines, and other transportation toys. It briefly produced electrically powered race cars in the late '20s, ceasing at the onset of the Depression. In the '30s the line included roller skates, "Little Lady" juvenile electric irons and ranges, the "Velva" doll and "Velva Craft" felt toys. Kingston used the "Keyless" trade name on its roller skates from the earlier 1930s, but apparently had no more than accidental connection to the Keyless Roller Skate Co. In the Boomer years, the Toy Division of Kingston Products Corp. continued to issue roller skates.

Kingsway, Inc.
"Florentine" chess sets, checkers, magnetic cribbage, and poker chip rackers were postwar products of this Chicago, Ill., company.

Kinne, Clarence and Harold
Clarence Kinne and Harold Kinne of Pawtucket, R.I., manufactured children's sleds, shooflies, croquet, tennis rackets, and athletic goods in the 1920s.

Kirby-Cogeshall-Steinau Co.
This Milwaukee, Wis., firm made wooden dice and paper poker chips in the late 1930s.

The Kirchhof Patent Co.
Based in Newark, N.J., Kirchhof was one of the premier prewar manufacturers of metal noise-making and musical toys of various kinds, including "crickets," or clickers, tambourines, kazoos, rattles and party horns. Its line included miniature garden tool sets, beach pails and shovels, snow and garden shovels, tops, junior badges, penny toys, premiums, and advertising novelties. Most of its toys and novelties sold in the 5- to 25-cent range. Kirchhof also made Christmas decorations.

The company was founded in 1852 by Charles Kirchhoff, a German builder of weaving machinery. The company also produced Braille printers and ticker-tape machines.

The company ceased making its novelty and noisemaker line during wartime. In the Boomer years, Kirchhof resumed issuing its penny toys, 5- and 10-cent toys, and 10- and 25-cent sand pails and shovels. The company especially emphasized items for special occasions, including Halloween, New Years, and carnivals. It employed the "Life of the Party" trade name.

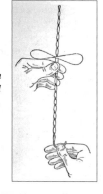

The aerial toy "American Ace Flyer" was produced by Kirchhof in the 1920s.

Kirkland, R.T. Based in Union City, Tenn., in the late 1930s, R.T. Kirkland made doll house accessories, including draperies, housewares, and table sets.

Kirsh & Reale, Inc. This Madison, Avenue, New York City, firm was sole American agent for the "Lenci Dolls," imported from Torino, Italy.

"Kit Carson" One of the pioneer figures to figure large in Boomer-era childhood imaginations, Kit Carson inspired such items as "Kit Carson" leather-cased plastic toy canteens by Spraz Co., and cap pistols by Kilgore.

kitchen fixtures, toy Toy stoves and cabinets were popular before the war, made of materials including cast iron, tin and cardboard, in a variety of miniature scales. Most, however, were in the scale appropriate to dolls rather than doll houses, and were frequently used for imaginary kitchens in which the child herself or himself would play.

Prewar manufacturers included Barclay Mfg. Co., Blue Ridge Novelties, the N.D.Cass Co., Harold W. Dow, the Elmberg Co., Hoge Mfg. Co., the Hubley Mfg. Co., V.M. Kearley Mfg. Co., Mack Toy Works, Mason & Parker Mfg. Co., Paper Products Co., the F.L. Purdy Co., G.I. Sellers & Sons Co., and South Bend Toy Mfg. Co.

In the postwar years, a great many doll-size kitchen appliances were issued in tin, especially by Wolverine Supply & Mfg. Co. In great vogue, however, were child-size kitchen appliances, conceived by manufacturers for the playrooms of the ideal suburban homes of the time. Some appeared in tin, and others in pressed board, all being sturdy versions of ovens, cabinets, refrigerators, sink units, and cupboards. Each major catalog or department store retailer had its own line of child-size kitchens with the store logos proudly displayed, sometimes combined with the brand name of the manufacturers of real appliances, perhaps in the hope that the children would then become adult consumers of the same products.

This toy refrigerator by Wolverine Supply & Mfg. Co. was introduced in the 1950s.

kitchen utensils, toy The making of miniature and play kitchenware brought companies famous for their "real" products into the company of toy manufacturers. Prewar manufacturers included A.&J. Kitchen Tool Co., Acme Can Co., Aluminum Goods Mfg. Co., Aluminum Specialty Co., Chicago Metallic Mfg. Co., the Dover Mfg. Co., the Excel Mfg. Corp., McKee Glass Co., Newton Mfg. Co., Parker Bros., Taplin Mfg. Co., the Wagner Mfg. Co., the Washburn Co., and West Bend Aluminum.

One of the most typical manufacturers of the Boomer years was Aluminum Specialty Co., whose "Kiddykook Chilton Ware" miniature utensils had widespread acceptance. Aluminum Specialty also made polyethylene tea sets, baking sets, and percolator sets.

Other postwar manufacturers included Argo Industries Corp., Baker Mfg. Co., the Brothers Mfg. Co., Criterion Toy & Specialty Co., Lido Toy Co., Louis Marx & Co., Mirro Aluminum Co., Revere Copper & Brass, Structo Mfg. Co., and Wirecraft Corp.

The "Revere Junior Kitchen Set" of the 1960s.

kites The flying of kites dates back to ancient times, being known in particular from early Asia. Popular in Colonial America and afterwards, kites were made of linen and later of paper or plastic. An 1850 illustration of childhood activities shows kites in the standard lozenge-like shape and also in octagonal form, with long tails of knotted rags and large, painted faces on the linen.

In the earlier prewar years a number of companies made a specialty of kites, including Acme Toys, American Balsa Wood Co., J.C. Ayling Co., Dolly Toy Co., H.&W. Kite Co., the Hi-Flier Mfg. Co., Marks Bros. Co., S.F. Perkins Aerial Advertising Kite & Zeppelin Balloon Co., and Wilder Corp.

In the late prewar years, the Alox Mfg. Co., Paul K. Guillow, Heim Fine Art Decorating Co., and Tissue Paper Products Co. joined their ranks.

Keeled, tailless kites or "bat" kites were an innovation of the Boomer period. Gayla Industries issued the "Keel Guided Plastic Kites," with individual kites including "Invader," "Firebird," and "Bat Kite."

Other Boomer manufacturers included Alox, Hi-Flier, Hoffman Lion Mills Co., Lancaster Toy Co., J.J. Murray, Novelty Kite Mfg. Co., and the Saalfield Publishing Co.

Kits Co. This Miamisburg, Ohio, firm made late 1930s "Sticker-Kit" sets of gummed stickers. In the postwar years, as Kits, Inc., the firm continued issuing boxed and plastic-wrapped cards, as well as toy archery sets.

"Kitty Clover" A paper doll by Sheila Young, "Kitty Clover" was associated with *Ladies' Home Journal* in the later 1800s.

"Kitty Kuddles" stuffed animals prewar, see *Knickerbocker Toy Co.*

Klasgo Mfg. Co. The "Magic Water Mill" and the "Magic Mill" assembly kit were products of Klasgo, based in Pittsburgh, Penn., in the 1950s and '60s. Klasgo also made water pumps.

Klauber Games, Inc. A specialist in action games for both children and adults, Klauber Games issued Boomer-era dart games; shuffleboard and bowling with linoleum alleys; golf chipping and putting games; ring toss; and "Keno." It was located in Chicago, Ill.

Klauber Novelty Co. This Chicago, Ill., firm's success of the 1920s was "Bridge Keno." The firm continued in the games business through the prewar years, and was issuing "Shufflette" home shuffleboard, "Spares and Strikes" home bowling game, "Gin Keno," which was "Gin Rummy" for 12 players, and "Bridge Keno," into the war years.

J. Klieger Fur Co. Based on West 27th Street, New York City, J. Klieger issued stuffed fur toys, as well as novelties, in the Boomer years.

"Klay Kast" outfits see *The Fox Toy Co.*

"Klondike" trains see *American Flyer Mfg. Co.*

Knapp Electric, Inc. Based in Indianapolis, Ind., Knapp Electric made a number of prewar electric toys, including the long-lived "Electric Questioner," "Electric Thriller," and "Three Wa Transmitter." The company also achieved distinction by issuing the first transportation toys powered by wet-cell batteries. In the late '20s, it produced "American Industry in Miniature," a complete, electrically-powered outfit that combined jigsaw, lathe, sander, and grinder, for which Knapp sold boxes of "White Pine Blocks" and "20 Boards" for the home construction needs of young manufacturers. In 1928 Knapp introduced a companion to the "Electric Questioner" for younger children, "The Tell Bell." Knapp touted it as "instructive, amusing, mysterious."

The company was founded in 1894, with the "Knapp Electric Questioner" a feature of its line from the beginning. The toy successfully retained its popularity. Rivaling it by the 1930s, however, was a wooden construction toy set called "Krazy Ikes," which built fanciful people and animals.

Other titles by Knapp Electric included "The Tell Bell" of 1928, "Auto Race Electro

Game" and "Football Knapp Electro Game Set" of 1929, "Electro Game Set" of 1930, and "Ges It Game" of 1936.

By the late 1930s the company had added scale model electric trains and toy motors to its line.

See also Whitman Publishing Co., which issued "Krazy Ikes" after the war, and Carlisle & Finch Co.

Knapp-Monarch Co. Like Knapp Electric a manufacturer of prewar electric toys, Knapp-Monarch's line included the "K-M Build-a-Motor" construction toy and toy electric irons.

"Knee-Action" coaster wagon see Dayton Toy & Specialty Co.

F.A. Knerr & Sons The "Teg" play board of the late 1930s was made by this Buffalo, N.Y., firm.

Knickerbocker Plastic Co., Inc. Based in North Hollywood, Calif., in the 1950s and '60s, Knickerbocker Plastic manufactured infants' and children's plastic toys. Its "Toys with Play-Appeal" included boats, beach toys, wheel toys, guns, pistols, rifles, water guns, target games, remote control toys, infant toys, banks, and doll stands. A prominent toy introduced in 1958 was the "Popeye Roly Poly Target," which featured "Popeye" character targets and a cork gun. Knickerbocker also introduced "Zorro" water pistols and target games in 1958. In 1960 it introduced a line of "Art Linkletter" pre-school toys.

Knickerbocker Toy Co., Inc. In the 1920s, Knickerbocker touted its line of high-grade stuffed animals as being "America's Premier." It included teddy bears, stuffed dogs and cats, stuffed monkeys and monkey hand puppets, and stuffed animal wheel toys including bears, horses, elephants, and various dog breeds.

Located on Fifth Avenue in New York City, Knickerbocker remained a specialist in stuffed animals and dolls in the 1930s, and obtained an early license from Kay Kaymen to produce Walt Disney-themed stuffed dolls. Both "Mickey Mouse" and "Minnie Mouse"

were leading sellers by the mid-1930s. By the late 1930s the company was based in the Fifth Avenue Building.

The firm maintained a wartime line of stuffed toys and doll novelties, including the "Sleepyhead Family." In the Boomer years, Knickerbocker maintained offices on Broadway, and a factory in Brooklyn, N.Y. Its line continued to emphasize stuffed animals and dolls, with the features of "safety locked-in eyes," washable fabrics with non-allergenic "feather foam." Featured items in the 1950s-60s included "Huckleberry Hound" toys, the "Sleepyhead" doll, "Cuddle Miniatures," "Betsy McCall's Pets," "Cuddle Bears," "Cuddle Cats," "Cuddle Pandas," "Kewpie" dolls, "Hollywood Hound," "Baby Santa," and "Quick Draw McGraw." Knickerbocker Toy Co. was taken over by Hasbro in 1983.

The "Zorro Water Pistol" by Knickerbocker Plastic Co., 1950s.

Knight Stuffed Toy Co. A late 1930s manufacturer of stuffed toys, Knight was based on West 18th Street, New York City.

Knight Table Tennis Co. Based in Brooklyn, N.Y., Knight issued shuffleboard and dart games as well as table tennis, in the postwar years.

"Knock-Em Flat" puzzles see *Puzzle Makers, The.*

knucklestones see *jackstones.*

"Koaster" trucks see *Keystone Mfg. Co.*

Thomas Kochka Thomas Kochka issued the 1899 game, "Patent Parlor Bowling Alley."

"Kocomotive" pull toy see *Kusan, Inc.*

Joseph Koenig Maker of "Tournament" French darts in the 1930s, Joseph Koenig of Philadelphia, Penn., also made "Kingson Hy-Lo" tops.

John C. Kohaut, Inc. Established in Newark, N.J., in the late 1930s, Kohaut made ring toss games, bocce balls, "Bicycle Polo," "Penguin Skittles," and shuffleboard.

"Koko the Clown" A popular prewar cartoon figure, Koko appeared in various toy and game forms, including the "Komikal Koko" doll of the 1930s by the Bakers-Clevercraft Shoppe.

Kokomo Brass Works see *Kingston Products Corp.*

Kokomo Stamped Metal Co. The "Redskin" skate was one of several issued by this Kokomo, Ind., firm in the 1920s. The company's skates were marked "KoKoMo."

Kokomo Stamped Metal Co. made the "Redskin" roller skates in the 1920s.

"Kokomo Toys" see *Kingston Products Corp.*

Kolor-Kraft Products, Inc. This Philadelphia, Penn., company made prewar paint sets. Its leading line in the 1930s was the "Kolor-Kraft Cut-Outs," which featured famous movie star and comic strip characters, including "Popeye," "Ed Wynn," "Max Baer," "Scrappy," "The Katzenjammer Kids," "Laurel and Hardy," "Joe Palooka," "Krazy-Kat," "Charley Chase," and "Little Annie Rooney." The sets sold for 10 cents, 50 cents, and a dollar.

"Kolorjax" jackstones and sets see *Grey Iron Casting Co.*

"Kombination" coaster wagon see *American Acme Co.*

"Komic" sets see *Artwood Toy Mfg. Co.*

Kooken, Olive Olive Kooken was a sculptor of figures for Barclay and Tommy Toy, notably sculpting the nursery-rhyme figures for the latter, including Old Mother Hubbard and Little Miss Muffett.

"Kopeefun" kits see *Embree Mfg. Co.*

Louis Koppe & Sons Located on Third Avenue, New York City, Louis Koppe & Sons manufactured doll beds and carriage outfits in the 1930s.

korloy A non-metallic material somewhat like cast iron.

Kozekar, Inc. "Kozekar" baby and doll carriages were made by this Minneapolis, Minn., company in the 1930s and '40s.

"Krack-Kannon" see *The Gibbs Mfg. Co.*

Kraftoy Corp. Based in Grand Rapids, Mich., in the late 1930s, Kraftoy made croquet sets and hammering toys.

Francis W. Kramer Studios, Inc. A mechanical display manufacturer established in the late 1930s in Chicago, Ill., Kramer also made toy railroad tunnels.

William Kratt Co. The "Kratt" harmonica and blow-accordion were made by this postwar Union, N.J., firm.

The Walter S. Kraus Co. A manufacturer of juvenile furniture in the late prewar years, Kraus was located in Woodside, N.Y.

"Krazy Ikes" see Knapp Electric, Inc., and Whitman Publishing Co.

"Krazy Kat" A popular cartoon figure, Krazy Kat appeared as a stuffed animal from Knickerbocker Toy Co., and was featured in both wood and metal toys by J. Chein & Co., in the 1930s.

Krebs, Stengel & Co. This juvenile furniture manufacturer used the slogan, "Desks

Like Dads Make Happy Lads," in the 1920s. It was located on East 32nd Street, New York City. Moving to Lexington Avenue, New York City, Krebs used the shortened slogan "Like Dad's" for its 1930s and '40s juvenile desk and chair sets.

Kreisler Sound Equipment Co. In the late 1930s, Kreisler developed and produced dolls equipped with talking and listening sound equipment. The company was based on West 20th Street, New York City.

M.V. Krieg Based in Riverside, Ill., M.V. Krieg published "question-pad party games" and sewing instruction booklets in the late prewar years.

"Kringle Society" dolls and toys see *Marshall Field & Co.*

Krischer's Mfg. Co., Inc. A Brooklyn, N.Y., metal-stamping company, Krischer's line included toy watches.

Kroll Trading Co. A Boomer-era specialist in plastic toys, Kroll made garden sets, sand toys, and swords. It was based on Greene Street, New York City.

"Kroma" outfits see *The American Crayon Co.*

Kronheimer Co., Inc. Established on Broadway, New York City, in the late 1930s, Kronheimer made cowboy outfits.

Richard G. Krueger Located on Broadway in New York City, Richard G. Krueger obtained an early license from Kay Kaymen to produce "Mickey Mouse" and "Three Little Pigs" nursery toys. The company also had rights to produce "Silly Symphony" characters and soft Rose O'Neill "Kewpies." Its toy line in the 1930s and '40s included celluloid toys, infants' celluloid rattles, floaters, rubber dolls and animals, water balls, "Cry Bawls," nested blocks, dressed dolls, soft animals, rattle-head dolls, and musical cradles. In the Boomer years, Krueger, based on West 34th Street, New York City, continued to emphasize infants' novelties and soft toys.

Kuatro Sales Corp. Based in Seattle, Wash., in the late 1930s, Kuatro issued games for adults including the "Kuatro" board game.

"Kubes" see *Kusan.*

"Kum Bak" yo-yo tops prewar, see *Mansfield Novelty Co.*

Kuniholm Mfg. Co. A prewar manufacturer of baby carriages and walkers in Gardner, Mass., Kuniholm also made children's vehicles, pedal cars, and scooters.

Kupper-Heidt Mfg. Co. Based in Lakewood, Ohio, Kupper-Heidt made "Educator" interlocked toy building blocks in the mid-1930s.

Kusan, Inc. With an active line of preschool toys in the 1950s, Kusan's toys included the pull-toy "Kasey the Klatter-Gator," "Koo Zoo" blocks, alphabet letters, toy guns, and infants' items. The Nashville, Tenn., company became well known for its plastic blocks, including transparent blocks with animal-shaped enclosures, and musical toys. Kusan also made scale model electric trains and accessories in the 1950s and '60s, including the "O" gauge "Kannon Ball Express," 40 inches long, in the mid-1950s.

"Kute Klothes" outfits see *Tailored Craft Novelty Co.*

Kyser & Rex Founded by L. Kyser and Alfred Rex in 1880, this Philadelphia, Penn., firm produced cast-iron toys and mechanical banks through 1884. Among its desirable banks are "Hindu with Turban," "Uncle Tom," "Chimpanzee," "The Organ Bank," and "Lion and Monkeys."

L.&J. Wood Products This postwar Burbank, Calif., company manufactured shooflies, as well as baby furniture.

L.&S. Novelties Established on West 27th Street, New York City, in the late 1930s, L. & S. Novelties made fur stuffed toys.

L.J.S. Sales & Mfg. Co. The "Fence" and "Triani" games of the 1950s-'60s were published by this Greenville, Ohio, firm.

"L-T" see *Lee-Tex Rubber Products Corp. of Chicago.*

L-u-c-e Mfg. Co. Toy luggage was this postwar Kansas City, Mo., firm's specialty.

La Mar Toy Co. Fur and plush toys and animals comprised this postwar Brooklyn, N.Y., firm's line.

"La Promenade" baby carriage see *American-National Co.*

La Velle Mfg. Co. A pre-Great Depression firm, La Velle issued a wide variety of games, toys, and puppets in its "La Velle Toys" line, including "Mystics," "Pla-Klay," "Pla-Wax," "Anchor Blocks," "Tiptop Boxing Game," "Little Dressmaker," "Patchwork Sampler," "Yale-Harvard Football," "Golf," "Nurse's Outfit," and "Compo-Art." Its puppet line included puppet and marionette theaters.

"Labcraft," "Labstock" see *The Porter Chemical Co.*

Lador, Inc. Based on West 32nd Street, New York City, Lador made musical toys in the 1930s and '40s. The company also made Christmas tree holders. By the late '30s it had moved to Fifth Avenue.

"Ladorable" musical toys see *Swiss Music Corp.*

lacrosse The most popular of games adopted from the American Indians, lacrosse was through the years modified to be less strenuous a game if still fairly true to the original. American Indians played with teams of from 30 to 40 players, typically men and boys, the games lasting an entire day. It was mainly a game for adults, with children playing in their own "leagues."

"Lady Dover" see *Dover Mfg. Co.*

"Lady Junior" see *Renner & Co.*

"Ladyfaire" costumes see *Waas & Son.*

O.J. Lafayette & Co., Ltd. Located in Laguna Beach, Calif., in the late 1930s, O.J. Lafayette issued "Dolls of All Nations," stuffed toys, and juvenile furniture.

Lafayette Toy Co. A mid-1930s manufacturer located on Prince Street, New York City, N.Y. Lafayette made mechanical novelties.

Lakeside Industries Based in Minneapolis, Minn., Lakeside issued "Gumby" and "Pokey" bendable rubber toys in the 1960s, as well as accessories. Lakeside also issued the popular "Barrel of Monkeys" game.

Lakeside Marble Co. A Milwaukee, Wis., company, Lakeside made clay marbles for games and toys in the mid-1930s.

Lakewood Mfg. Co. The "Arabian Pony" spring exerciser on wheels was issued by this Chicago, Ill., company in the late 1930s.

Lamaico Toys The "Rocket-Shute" parachute toy of the Boomer years was a product of Lamaico Toys, of Boulder, Colo.

Lambert & Latimer Juvenile and doll furniture was made by this prewar Leominster, Mass., company.

"Lambsy" wool toys prewar, see *Gund Mfg. Co.*

lamps Children's lamps for the nursery and playroom are often of considerable interest to toy collectors, since they often featured appealing illustrations, sometimes based on nursery rhyme or other characters. Prewar manufacturers included Aerolux Light Corp., Grayco Products, M. Hardy, and Sprague Mfg. Co. A new kind of children's light became popular in the postwar years: night-lights, which were miniature, low-wattage lamps giving a dim glow when inserted in the electric socket. Manufacturers soon learned to issue them in designs appropriate to the nursery and child's bedroom. Postwar manufacturers of nightlights included Alan-Jay Plastics, Gem Electric Mfg. Co., Lidco, William G. Minder Industries, and Radex Stereo Co.

Lan-Dee Mfg. Co. The "Lan-Dee" toy telephones of the late 1930s were made by this Chicago, Ill., company. Lan-Dee also made periscopes and pocket telescopes.

Lancaster Toy Co. Based in Lancaster, Penn., this Boomer-era firm issued batons, whips, canes, toys, games, and kites.

"Lancer" kite see *Gayla Industries.*

J. Landowne Co., Inc. The 1930s educational block toy "Tutor Toy" was made by this Fourth Avenue, New York City, N.Y., firm.

William Chauncey Langdon Based in New Orleans, La., This manufacturer produced "The Game of American Story and Glory," a patriotic board and card game, in 1846.

Lange Plastics Co. This Dubuque, Iowa, company issued toy horses, cars, tractors, and games, in the Boomer years. Lange also made plastic swimming pools.

Langfelder, Homma & Hayward, Inc. Based on Broadway, New York City, N.Y., this firm was an important importer of toys, baskets, tea sets, Easter novelties, Street Patrick's favors, Valentine's items, and Washington's Birthday favors in the 1920s through '40s. Its lines from Japan included "Nagoya" toy tea sets, and celluloid dolls and rattles.

Langson Mfg. Co. A Chicago, Ill., bowling alley manufacturer, Langson also made the "Ting-a-Ling" tops of the mid-1930s. In the late '30s it issued the "Nu-matic Paper Buster" gun, and the "Aerial Torpedo Cane." The "Paper Buster" gun series continued to lead Langson's product line during the Boomer years.

Lannom Mfg. Co. Based in Grinnell, Iowa, Lannom made balls for indoor and outdoor recreation in the 1930s and '40s.

Lapin Products, Inc. Established in the late 1930s on Varick Street, New York City, N.Y., Lapin made "Snow White and the Seven Dwarfs" hair barrettes and ornaments, as well as dice, poker chips, and molded toy parts. It was one of the first companies to issue toy cars in the new plastics being developed before the war. In the 1950s and '60s, when it was based in Newark, N.J., Lapin issued toy autos, plastic toys, musical toys, sand toys, and novelties.

"Laramie" Playthings inspired by NBC's "Laramie" included hats by Arlington Hat Co., and toy TV sets by R.&S. Toy Mfg. Co.

The Lareo Corp. The "Roy Rogers" lariats and "Trigger Trotter" jumping-horse platforms of the 1950s-'60s were issued by Lareo. The company was based in East Orange, N.J.

lariats Toy lariats were an essential part of playing cowboy, which became especially popular in the prewar years as a consequence of the popularity of Western movies, radio shows, and comic strips. Manufacturers included the Alox Mfg. Co., Brodhaven Mfg. Co., Indian Archery & Toy Corp., the Mordt Co., and Spin-O-Rop Co. In the late prewar years, William J. Graham Co. and Hoffman Lion Mills Co. joined their ranks. The constant presence of fancy lariat work on Boomer-era TV shows helped the continuing popularity of lariats as toys. Alox and Hoffman Lion Mills both continued issuing them into the Boomer years. Other manufacturers included Arandell Products Co., Classy Products Corp., the Coburn Co., Danlee Co., Dunmore Belt & Novelty Co., Grove-Tex Industries, Jayline Toys, the Lareo Corp., Nadel & Sons, M. Shimmel Sons, and West Georgia Mills.

"Lassie" The famous movie and TV collie inspired numerous Boomer-era playthings, including costumes by Collegeville Flag & Mfg. Co., toy dogs by Smile Novelty Toy Co., fiction books by Whitman Publishing Co., games by Lisbeth Whiting Co., jump ropes by West Georgia Mills, inflatable toys by Alvimar Mfg. Co. Other items included "Lassie & Timmy" coloring sets and paints by Standard Toykraft products, and "Lassie the Wonder Dog" rubber toy by Rempel Mfg.

"Latticino" see *transparent swirls.*

"Laughing Santa" talking toy see *Gund Mfg. Co.*

laundry sets Toy laundry sets were undoubtedly turned out by local turners in the 19th century. By prewar times they became regular items featured by toy manufacturers, including J. Chein & Co., the Ohio Art Co., Parker Bros., and Wolverine Supply & Mfg. Co. While some were doll-sized, others were child-sized. Washing boards, tubs, drying racks, and even washing machines, when those "labor-saving" devices came onto the scene, all appeared in miniature. Other prewar manufacturers included American Toy Works, Buffalo Toy & Tool Works, Gem Mfg. Corp., and Keller Toy Mfg. Co. The prevalent ideas of suburban consumer conformity in the 1950s and '60s encouraged the popularity of housekeeping toys such as these, and likely increased the numbers of coordinated sets available. Manufacturers included Ames Products Co., Arandell Products Co., Fillum Fun, Hoffman Lion Mills Co., Henry Katz, Kiddie Brush & Toy Co., Lo-E Mfg. Corp., Ny-Cal Co., Solmann & Whitcomb, Structo Mfg. Co., Wolverine Supply & Mfg. Co., and C.G. Wood Co.

"Laurel & Hardy" The comic duo of the silver screen doubtless inspired many childhood shenanigans. Toy manufacturers used their likenesses in some playthings, including the "Laurel & Hardy" game of the 1930s from Transogram Co.

John Lauterbach Co. The "Whistlekraft" game of the late 1930s was issued by this Philadelphia, Penn., firm.

LaVelle LaVelle issued the 1922 sports board games "Yale Harvard Football Game" and "Tip-Top Boxing."

"Lawman" Warner Bros. Pictures' "Lawman" inspired 1950s-'60s playthings including coloring books by the Saalfield Publishing Co., holster sets by J. Halpern Co., plastic figures by Hartland Plastics, and western hats by Corona Hat Co.

lawn mowers With the rise of the great American lawn in the later 19th century, lawn mowers came into vogue. As with every other novel device, toy versions came into demand. Prewar manufacturers, working in a variety of materials, included Arcade Mfg. Co., Dille & McGuire Mfg. Co., the Gong Bell Mfg. Co., the Hubley Mfg. Co., and Marion Craftsman Tool Co. In the late prewar years, Playskool Institute began issuing the toys. Postwar toys, which increasingly reflected America's fascination with power mowers, were made by American Toy & Furnishing Co., Chain Bike Corp., Gong Bell, Marilyn Products, Ohio Art Co., and Suburban Toy & Mfg. Co.

lawn ornaments While not precisely toys, many lawn ornaments were made by companies that made toys. The lawn ornaments designed for Christmas, including the plastic, internally lit Santas and snowmen that became popular in the 1960s, are of interest to collectors of both toys and Christmas items.

Lawn Shuffle Co., The The "Shuff-L-Lawn" outdoor game of the 1930s was made by this White Plains Avenue, New York City, company.

lawn swings see *swings.*

Lawner-Martin Corp. This game manufacturer was established in the late 1930s on Fifth Avenue, New York City, N.Y.

Lawrence Industries, Inc. In a variant on toy-filled Christmas stockings, which the company also issued, Lawrence manufac-

L

tured toy-filled comic puppets in the Boomer years.

Lawson & Lawson, Inc. This Seventh Avenue, New York City, firm made the "Jack's House" life-size construction toy in the 1950s-'60s.

lead soldiers see *soldier toys.*

lead toys see *slush-metal toys; casting sets; pewter toys.*

Leading Novelty Mfg. Co. Maker of prewar stuffed toys and animals, Leading Novelty was located on West 21st Street, New York City.

W.H. Leaman Co. Based in South Meriden, Conn., W.H. Leaman made wooden toys, rattles, pull toys, and bell toys in the 1930s and '40s.

leapfrog This unforgettable childhood activity involving children taking turns successively hopping over each other—one hunkers down, the other hops with the boost of the hands being placed on the lower one's back—is known from at least the 1700s.

"Leaping Lena" stuffed toy see *Master Industries.*

leather Leather has long proved a useful material for toy-makers, being used for the making of balls for at least 4,000 years. A leather ball stuffed with straw is known from Thebes, Egypt, that has been dated to 2160 B.C.

It proved especially useful in meeting the demand in prewar and postwar years for Western toys, including lariats, holsters, whips, hats, and general apparel. Artificial leather, or "leatherette," was used for some of these toys as early as the 1930s, and for such boxing toys as the "Yale Shadow Ball" in the '20s.

Prewar leather goods manufacturers who included toys in their lines included Alexander Baron, Belvidere Strap Co., Dumore Belt & Novelty Co., Economy Mfg. Co., Feinberg-Henry Mfg. Co., Felder Bros., Hale-Nass Corp., Louis Lefkowitz & Bros., the Mordt Co., Nitke Bros., and R.S. Pitts Mfg. Co. In postwar years, leatherette became an important material in making

stuffed or soft animals, by companies including R. Dakin Co.

While the number of firms using actual leather in toys drastically declined in the Boomer era, those who made play sets for tooling leather increased. In the years just before the war, only a handful of companies specialized in these kits, including Fellowcrafters, Horton Handicraft Co., R.S. Pitts Mfg. Co., and E.A. Sweet Co.

In the postwar years, in contrast, their numbers included Arrow Leather Goods Mfg. Co., Colorforms, Danlee Co., the Elliot-Morris Co., Horton Handicraft Co., Jewel Leather Goods Co., Pilgrim Leather Goods Co., Pressman Toy Corp., R. & S. Toy Mfg. Co., Rapaport Bros., and Lisbeth Whiting Co.

Leather Products Co. Juvenile cowboy equipment and jump ropes were made by this prewar Chicago, Ill., firm.

leatherette see *leather.*

"Leave It to Beaver" The popular 1950s television program inspired playthings including coloring books by the Saalfield Publishing Co.

Leavitt Mfg. Co. Leavitt, based in Urbana, Ill., made merry-go-rounds in the 1930s. Becoming Leavitt Corp. in the late 1930s, it also manufactured track athletic equipment.

Lebanon Paper Box Co. Established in the late 1930s in Lebanon, Penn., this firm made musical blocks.

Lectronik Heart-Beat This Madison, Wis., company manufactured the offbeat specialty of an electronic pulsating device to be used in dolls and stuffed toys, in the early 1960s.

The Lederer Co. Automated display figures, such as seen in store windows, were made in the 1930s by this W. 32nd Street, New York City, firm. By the late '30s it also made games. In the Boomer years, as the Lederer Industries, Inc., based in the Fifth Avenue Building, the firm made the "Ledco Santasprize" surprise packages. It also issued toys and games for promotions.

L

Lederer Mfg. Co. A prewar New Haven, Conn., company, Lederer Mfg. Co. made sidewalk tennis, wooden toys, and novelties.

Lee Fur Co., Inc. Fur toys were the specialty of this postwar West 27th Street, New York City, firm.

Lee Products Co. This Atlanta, Ga., company made tops, jackstones, pea shooters, and package toys in the Boomer years.

Lee Rubber & Tire Corp. The "Fling" combination game set of the 1950s-'60s were issued by this Conshohocken, Penn., company.

Lee-Tex Rubber Products Corp. Rubber toys, balloons, and premium specialties were produced by Lee-Tex, established in the late 1930s in Chicago, Ill. In the Boomer years it continued manufacturing balloons and balls, as well as "plastisol" toys.

Leeds Sweete Products A Chicago, Ill., company, Leeds Sweete Products issued Boomer-era figure casting sets, wood carving sets, crayon accessories, space toys, and "Diabolo" tops. It also manufactured Indian items including totem poles and "Kachina" dolls.

Lefever, Charles Frederick C.F. Lefever, known as Fred Lefever, invented the pump-action air rifle, which became Daisy Mfg. Co.'s "Daisy Pump Gun" of 1913. He also invented the first metal water pistol, which became the "No. 8 Water Pistol," also released by Daisy in 1913.

E. Leganger & Co. A late 1930s firm in Chicago, Ill., Leganger manufactured children's wicker rockers.

Lehman Co. of America, Inc. This Cannelton, Ind., company made juvenile, nursery and doll furniture in the 1920s. After the Great Depression, Lehman added stilts and play yards to its line. By the end of the decade it was producing musical rockers and cradles and the "Babyguard" high chairs.

Earnest Lehmann Co. Earnest P. Lehmann established his toy manufacturing company in 1881 in Brandenberg, Germany. His toys became well-known in American, being imported in large quantities from 1895 through the 1920s, with the exception of the years of World War I. The company specialized in fancily mechanical toys in lithographed tinplate.

Some typical clockwork Lehmann toys include "Tut-Tut," which shows an oversize man sitting in an early automobile, blowing on a horn, and "Zig-Zag," a rocking car suspended between two large wheels, in which two riders sit facing each other. Other Lehmann toys included the automobile "Oho," "Dancing Sailor," "Icarus," "Autobus," and the strolling "Lehmann Family," also known as "Walking Down Broadway." Lehmann also made the "Alabama Coon Jigger," which shows a dancer on a platform, and "Mandarin," which shows a Chinese figure being carried in a sedan chair by servants.

Lehmann died in 1934. Business continued for a few years under the direction of Lehmann's partner, Johannes Richter. The company was re-established in 1951, and produced toys through the rest of the 20th century.

John C. Lehne Sales Co. This Fifth Avenue Building firm issued "Rap-O," a combination racket and basket game of the late 1920s.

A. Leipzig, Inc. Established on East 26th Street, New York City, in the late 1930s, Leipzig manufactured toy furniture, clothes baskets, cradles, sewing stands, bassinets, and doll wagons.

George Leis Based in Vauxhall, N.J., George Leis made prewar educational preschool toys.

The Leister Game Co., Inc. Leister specialized in party goods, including games, game books, puppets, and novelty gifts. It was based in Toledo, Ohio, in the Boomer years.

Leland Detroit Mfg. Co. In addition to miniature wheelbarrows and express wagons, this Detroit, Mich., company made a Monorail electric elevated railway and toy electric motors in the 1930s.

"Lenci Dolls" see *Kirsh & Reale, Inc.*

L

Lendzion Leather Goods Co. Prewar cowboy and police outfits, lariats, pistols and holsters, and "Sam Brown" belts were made by this Chicago, Ill., leather goods company.

Lenora Doll Co. This doll manufacturer was based on West 18th Street, New York City, before the war.

Leslie-Henry Co., Inc. Based in Mt. Vernon, N.Y., Leslie-Henry specialized in issuing western accessories, especially items tied in to popular media shows of the Boomer years. Calling itself the "world's largest manufacturer of pistols, holsters sets, and Western toys," it issued "Bonanza," "Wagon Train," "Maverick," "Texas Star Ranger," "Young Buffalo Bill," and "U.S. Marshal" items. Leslie-Henry's line included holster sets, cap pistols, derringers, rifles, roll caps, die-cast toys, cowboy outfits, spurs, and boxed sets. The firm maintained offices in the Fifth Avenue Building.

Lesney Products This London, England, die-casting firm was founded in 1947 by the unrelated friends Leslie Smith and Rodney Smith, joined later by John "Jack" Odell. The firm issued occasional die-cast toys, including an elaborate "Coronation Coach," until 1953, when the "Matchbox" line of miniature toy vehicles made its debut. Lesney established a 1 to 75 numbering system for the toys. This line was split into a United States numbering system and a rest-of-the-world system in 1981. In 1982, Universal Group bought the toy line. It changed hands again in 1992, being bought by Tyco Toys, Inc., and most recently by Mattel in 1996.

J.M. Lesser Co., Inc. Doll accessories, including jewelry, were specialties of this 1950s-'60s Broadway, New York City, company.

J. Lesser Toy Mfg. Co. A Brooklyn, N.Y., manufacturer, J. Lesser made wooden soldier sets, bubble outfits, and "Magic" chemistry sets, in the 1930s.

Letchworth, William P. see *Pratt & Letchworth.*

"Letter Blocks" see *A.M. Shepard Co.*

"Letty Lane" A paper doll by Sheila Young, "Letty Lane" was associated with *Ladies' Home Journal* in the later 1800s.

Levin, Harry see *Levin & Modlin.*

Levin & Modlin Established in the late 1930s, this West 30th Street, New York City, firm made novelty fur animals.

Levy, Michael see *Barclay Mfg. Co.*

"Lew Lehr" "Lew Lehr" items in the late 1930s included a rubber doll by Schavoir Rubber Co., and "Lew Lehr's Funny Faces" and "Lew Lehr's Go-Zin-Ta" games by Jason MacGowan Associates. Licensing rights were controlled by Gruskin & Birnes.

Lewis & Scott Mfg. Co. Established in Plantsville, Conn., in the later 1930s, Lewis & Scott made bakelite molded kazoos, horns, bubble pies, sirens, police whistles, signal sets, holsters, and police and radio patrol sets and badges.

G.B. Lewis Co. The Arkitoy Toy Division of this Watertown, Wis., company issued "Arkitoy Play Lumber," a new wood construction toy in 1920s. The "Arkitoy" wood construction sets were issued into the mid-1930s. Its line also included "Busy Blox" and "Tru-To-Life" riding toys. G.B. Lewis Co. was established in 1863.

"Arkitoy Play Lumber" wood construction set by G.B. Lewis Co., 1930s.

Lewis Supply Co., Inc. Based on Warren Street, New York City, in the late prewar years, Lewis Supply provided wheels and repair parts for baby carriages and juvenile vehicles.

L

The Lezius-Hiles Co. This Cleveland, Ohio, publisher issued the phrenological game "Faces" in the early 1930s. It also published children's books.

Libby Doll & Novelty Co. Baby dolls, mama dolls, and novelties were the mainstays of this West 28th Street, New York City, company in the earlier 1930s. Its "Baby Elaine" and "Dolly Elaine" dolls were well established by late in the decade.

Libby-Majorette Doll Corp. Latex-vinyl dolls including high heel, bride, and walking dolls were postwar specialties of this West 21st Street, New York City, company. It also made drink-wet baby dolls.

"Library of Games" see *Russell Mfg. Co.*

"Library of Pocket Games" see *William F. Drueke & Sons.*

"Liddle Kiddles" Mattel issued the "Liddle Kiddle" dolls in the years 1966-71. The dolls measured from 3/4 to 4 inches. Some were based on nursery rhyme and storybook characters, including "Liddle Middle Muffet," "Liddle Red Riding Hiddle," and "Peter Paniddle." The "Lucky Locket Kiddles" were issued in the mid-1970s.

"Lido" slides and pools see *Muskin Mfg. Co.*

Lido Toy Co. Lido issued a diverse array of plastic toys in the 1950s and '60s, including bubble pipes, pick-up sticks, toy vehicles, tool sets, cowboy and Indian figures, plastic scissors, whistles, charms, soldiers, airplanes, train sets, target games, dart guns, pop guns, stencil sets, "Televiewer" sets, bagatelle games, and dishes. Lido also issued "Mickey Mouse," "Popeye," "Felix the Cat," and Harvey Comics-related toys. Its line also featured doll bottles and nursing sets, kitchen sets, layettes, doll tubs, horse and rider sets, and bowling pin sets.

"Life-Like" riding toys see *Rempel Mfg. Co.*

"Life Lyke" line see *American Doll & Novelty Co.*

"Life of the Party" balloons see *The Van Dam Rubber Co., Inc.*

"Life of the Party" products see *The Kirchhof Patent Co.*

"Lifetime" toys see *Coronet Toy Mfg. Co.*

Light Buoy Industries Toy housecleaning sets were made by this Brooklyn, N.Y., firm in the 1930s and '40s.

"Lightning" Standard Novelty Works made the prewar "Lightning Guider" sleds and "Lightning Wheel" coaster wagons.

"Lightning Draw" holster see *Ray Plastic, Inc.*

"Like Dad's" furniture see *Krebs, Stengel & Co.*

"Like Dad's" shovels see *Mirro Aluminum Co.*

"Like Mother" play hats see *Corona Hat Co.*

"Like-Mother's" 1920s see the *George H. Bowman Co.*

"Like Mother's" toy sets see *Mirro Aluminum Co.*

"Li'l Abner" Early toys and playthings based on this popular comic-strip figure included books by Whitman Publishing Co., marionettes by Robert Wilson, masquerade costumes by J. Halpern Co., comic puzzles by Transogram Co., and shooting gallery by Daisy Mfg. Co., in the late 1930s. "Li'l Abner" rights were controlled by United Feature Syndicate.

"Li'l Genius" school kits see *Bedford Plastics.*

"Li'l Imp" dolls see *Vogue Dolls.*

"Li'l Miss" see *Bedford Plastics.*

"Li'l Rancher" holster sets see *Chancy Toy & Sporting Goods Corp.*

"Li'l Raskal" electric trains see *Varney.*

L

"Li'l Stinker" game see *Schaper Mfg. Co.*

Lila-Lu Toys, Inc. The "Lila-Lu" doll and matching "Castro Convertible" doll sofa-bed of the 1950s-'60s were made by this Fifth Avenue, New York City, firm.

Lilliputian dolls This term was used for very small dolls in the late 18th century.

"Lincoln" The J.L. Wright Co. used its famous name on more than the "Lincoln Logs." Other prewar toys included the "Lincoln Barnyard," wooden barn with metal figures, "Lincoln Bricks," "Lincoln Log Historical Figures," "Lincoln Log" jigsaw puzzles, "Lincoln" playhouses, and "Lincoln Stones." It also made "Lincoln" birdhouses. In the 1930s, "Lincoln Logs and Allied Toys" was an alternate name for the J.L. Wright Inc. The company's main products were both its "Lincoln Logs" items and its "Brick and Lumber" building sets.

Lincoln Line, Inc. Based in Chicago, Ill., Lincoln Line made plastic toy cars and trucks in the early 1950s, including telephone and TV repair ladder trucks.

Lincoln Logs Division In the 1950s, J.L. Wright's famous toy company became a division of Playskool Mfg. Co. In addition to the "Lincoln Logs" sets, which are marked with a Lawndale Avenue, Chicago, Ill., address, the firm made "Tot Railroad" sets, "Peg Blox," and "Makit Toy" construction sets. Metal figures, traditional with earlier "Lincoln Logs" sets, continued to be issued into the early 1960s.

Lincoln Novelty Co. Cowboy suits and accessories were produced by Lincoln Novelty, based in the Fifth Avenue Building, New York City, in the late 1930s.

Lind, Jenny P.T. Barnum brought Jenny Lind to America for her great tour in 1850. Her visit was followed by a flood of "Jenny Lind" paper dolls made in Germany. The coloratura soprano inspired a song, a song book, and such items as "Jenny Lind" earrings and "Jenny Lind" candy kisses.

Lindberg Products, Inc. This Skokie, Ill., firm manufactured plastic construction sets making airplanes, boats, and missile launchers, in the 1950s and '60s. It also made toy guns. The firm was a subsidiary of Boy Craft Co.

The Lindstrom Tool & Toy Co. Lindstrom, based in the Fifth Avenue Building, New York City, with a factory in Bridgeport, Conn., made humming tops, climbing monkeys, dancing dolls, and mechanical boats in the earlier 1930s. Bagatelles were among its more popular toys. By the late '30s, the company was also issuing motion picture projectors and phonographs.

"Lindy" The most famous airplane pilot of the 1930s saw his name being put on countless toys and playthings, including excellent cast-iron replicas of his airplane by the Hubley Mfg. Co. and Arcade Mfg. Co. Other items included "Lindy" bicycles by Shelby Cycle Co., the "Lindy Flyer" coaster wagon by Radio Steel & Mfg. Co., the "Lindy" card game and "Lindy Hop Off" board game by Parker Bros., the "Lindyplane" by Gibbs Mfg. Co., and the "Lindy Special" coaster wagon by R. Herschel Mfg. Co.

"The Line Beautiful" juvenile vehicles see *American-National Co.*

"Line Crockery" Marbles of clay in which the main color is white with uneven bands of gray or blue running around the marble are referred to by this name.

"Linenette" picture books see *Samuel Gabriel Sons & Co.*

The Lionel Corp. Lionel electric and mechanical trains were among the leading American toys both before and after the war. Besides the trains themselves, Lionel's products included, in the years after the Great Depression, "Multi-volt" transformers, model railroad accessories, electric ranges for girls, and model boats with clockwork motors. In 1934 it produced the "Train of Tomorrow," exhibiting it at the Century of Progress Exposition. That year also saw the debut of the "Mickey Mouse Handcar," a 7-3/4 inch long handcar with Mickey on one side, and Minnie on the other.

By the late 1930s Lionel's line included electric trains in "O" gauge, "OO" gauge, Standard gauge, and the "027" and "060" Series, as well as mechanical trains. It also offered remote-control airplanes.

In wartime, Lionel made "Lionel War-Time Train Kits" of fiberboard, laminated board and wood. The set included engine, tender, and freight cars, and was neither electric nor mechanical, and was intended for younger children.

The corporation was based on East 26th Street, New York City, from the prewar years through the Boomer years, when its specialties were "O" gauge electric trains, scale-model locomotives and cars; the "027" and "Super 'O'" series; "Trainmaster" transformers; model railroad accessories; and an "HO" line. Attractions to its line of electric trains included horns, "Magne-Traction," working headlights, "knuckle" couplers, whistles, puffing smoke, and solid steel wheels.

The "Bild-A-Loco" engine from The Lionel Corp., 1929.

In 1934, Lionel released the "Train of Tomorrow."

Liquid Veneer Corp. Located in Buffalo, N.Y., Liquid Veneer included "Midget Mops" toys in its prewar line.

Lisk, S., & Bros. A prewar importer, this East 15th Street, New York City, firm also manufactured noisemakers and "liquid pistols," or water pistols in the 1930s and '40s.

Lissberger Mfg. Co. Besides its specialty of outdoor juvenile furniture and table tennis tables, Lissberger of Baltimore, Md., manufactured Boomer-era wood promotional toys, and sand boxes.

"Litho-Plate" see *Richmond School Furniture Co.*

lithography, paper and metal
Although a number of prewar toy manufacturers did their own lithography work, specialty lithographers working in both paper and metal did the work for many others. Prewar specialists serving the toy trade in paper and board lithography included Banner Lithography & Printing Co. of Rose Street, New York City; Grinnell Lithographic Co., West 31st Street, New York City; R.J. Kittredge & Co. of Chicago, Ill.; and U.S. Printing & Lithography Co. of Brooklyn, N.Y. Specialists in lithographing on metal included four Brooklyn, N.Y., firms: Brooklyn Metal Decorating Co., Burdick Co., Metal Lithographing Corp., and Tin Plate Lithographing Co. Metal Lithograph & Coating Corp. was based in Chicago, Ill. See also *tin-litho.*

"Little Angel," "Littlest Angel" see *Vogue Dolls.*

"Little Annie Rooney" Playthings tied in with this cartoon character included "Little Annie Rooney Toddle Book" by McLoughlin Bros. Licensing rights were controlled by King Features Syndicate.

"Little Archie" The cartoon figure "Little Archie" inspired playthings including coloring books by the Saalfield Publishing Co.

"Little Artist" sets see *Standard Toykraft Products, Inc.*

"Little Audrey" The Harvey Famous Name Comics cartoon figure "Little Audrey" inspired 1950s-60s items including dolls by Roberta Doll Co.

"Little Beaver" archery sets see *Withington.*

"Little Big Books" prewar, see *The Saalfield Publishing Co.*

L

"Little Black Sambo" Games and toys based on this popular children's book included the "Black Sambo" game by Stoll & Einson Games, the "Sambo" bean-bag game by Toohey Game Co., and "Sambo Five Pin" by Parker Bros., in the earlier 1930s. In the late prewar games, the "Game of Black Sambo" was issued by Samuel Gabriel Sons & Co., and the "Sambo" target game by All-Metal Products Co.

"Little Builders" blocks prewar, see *Furniture City Dowel Co.*

"Little Carpenter" chests see the *Mordt Co.*

"Little Colonel" see *"Shirley Temple."*

"Little Country Doctor" kits see *Transogram Co.*

"Little Craftsman" wooden toys prewar, see *Holgate Bros. Co.*

"Little Dolls for Little Tots" see *Rosette Doll Co.*

"Little Fanny" The first American toy book with the figure of "Little Fanny" may have been a Boston edition in the 1810s of *The History of Little Fanny,* possibly published by J. Belcher. The most famous American "Little Fanny" was lithographed by John Greene Chandler and published by Crosby, Nichols & Co. in 1854, at the beginning of the American paper-doll fad.

"Little Folks" The Lehman Co. of America made a variety of sets of "Little Folks" doll furniture in the 1930s, including the "Little Dreamland" bedroom furniture and "Little Lady" dining sets.

"Little Giant" The "Little Giant" trademark was widely used by prewar manufacturers. Games under the name appeared from Gotham Pressed Steel Corp., coaster wagons from Pressed Metal Products Co., electric motors from the Straits Corp., and wheelbarrows from Steel Stamping Co.

"Little Golden" books and records see *Golden Press.*

"Little Housekeeper" A trademark shared in the 1930s, housecleaning toys appeared from both Kiddie Brush & Toy Co. and N.D. Cass Co. under the name.

"Little Jimmy" Crayon and paint books by McLoughlin Bros. were among the "Little Jimmy" cartoon character items of the late 1930s. Licensing rights were controlled by King Features Syndicate.

"Little Laddie" wagons see *H.C. White Co.*

"Little Lady" Kingston Products Corp. used the "Little Lady" trademark for its kitchen toys, including electric ranges and irons. See also "Little Folks."

"Little Lulu" "Little Lulu" was a cartoon character of the 1930s through the Boomer years, drawn by "Marge," who was Marjorie Henderson Buell. Marge's "Little Lulu" cartoon character appeared in book form in 1935's *Little Lulu* (Curtis) and 1941's *Little Lulu on Parade* (David McKay). She first appeared in comic book form in 1945. Dolls were issued from the earlier 1930s through the prewar years by Sayco Doll Corp. In the Boomer years, playthings included coloring books by Whitman Publishing Co., costumes by Collegeville Flag & Mfg. Co., dolls by Georgene Novelties, and jump ropes by Arandell Products Co. The "Little Lulu Magic Slate Paper Saver" was issued by the Watkins-Strathmore Co.

"Little Marksman" target games prewar, see *The Hoge Mfg. Co.*

"Little Miss Autograph" see *Gund Mfg. Co.*

Little Miss Hi-Heels, Inc. Toy radios were specialties of this Boomer-era firm, based in Miami, Fla.

"Little Miss Muffet" The popular nursery-rhyme character appeared on numerous playthings through the years, often in combination with other nursery-rhyme figures. Earlier prewar items included cleaning sets by Patent Novelty Co., and jack sets by Arcade Mfg. Co. Later prewar items included "Beetleware" dishes by Bryant Electric Corp. In the postwar years, playthings included dolls by Nancy Ann Storybook Dolls, and tea sets by Gotham Industries.

L

"Little Mother" doll accessories
see *Alexander Miner Sales Corp.*

"Little Mother" doll carriages and strollers see *Muskin Mfg.Co.*

"Little Orby" see *Tigrett Industries.*

"Little Orphan Annie" The cartoon "Orphan Annie," introduced through the newspapers in the 1920s by Harold Gray, featuring the adventures of the blank-eyed girl Orphan Annie and her dog Sandy.

In the 1930s, related items included dolls from George Borgfeldt Corp.; crayon and paint books and a shooting game by Milton Bradley Co.; a cut-out doll by Samuel Gabriel Sons & Co.; a "metal doll" by Louis Marx & Co.; electric ranges by Metal Ware Corp.; embroidery and sewing sets by Jack Pressman & Co.; and a jacks set by Arcade Mfg. Co. The Adler-Jones Co., a specialist in such matters, made large "Little Orphan Annie" display units for retailers, to help sell the abundant merchandise. Mizpah Toy & Novelty Corp. also made a "Sandy" felt dog.

Late in the prewar years, playthings also included costumes by Collegeville Flag & Mfg. Co.; crayon and paint books by McLoughlin Bros.; dolls by Mizpah Toy & Novelty Co.; pastry sets, clothes pins, and a pulley & wash line set by Transogram Co.; shooting games by Milton Bradley Co.; and stamping sets by Superior Type Co.

In the early 1980s, Little Orphan Annie became simply "Annie," due to the release of the movie of that name. Associational items at the time used the old images of the Little Orphan Annie comics characters, almost always accompanied by the shortened name, "Annie." The larger part of the associational items seem to have been decorative or functional, rather than toys, although Knickerbocker issued a 15-inch cloth doll for the movie. In 1981, Parker Brothers released an "Annie—The Movie Game," of only minor interest to collectors. Aladdin issued two Annie lunch boxes, one of vinyl in 1981 and the second of steel in 1982.

"Little Pal" The "Little Pal" trademark was used by at least two prewar manufacturers. Plaza Mfg. Co. made portable phonographs under the name, and the Hoge Mfg. Co. made sewing machines. Hoge also made "Little Princess" sewing machines. The "Little Pal" trade name was also used by King Mfg. Co. in the 1950s-'60s.

"Little Play Nurse" kits see *Transogram.*

"Little Queen" housekeeping toys see *Bissell.*

"Little Rascals" The popular TV crew from "Little Rascals" appeared on numerous playthings, including squeeze toys by Bayshore Industries, coloring books by FunBilt Toys, and paper dolls by the Saalfield Publishing Co.

"Little Red Hen" books see *The Saalfield Publishing Co.*

"Little Red Hen" mechanical toy see *Baldwin Mfg. Co.*

"Little Red Riding Hood" One of the most popular of fairy-tale figures, "Little Red Riding Hood" inspired prewar toys including stuffed dolls by Knickerbocker Toy Co., and stamping sets by Fulton Specialty Co. A postwar doll was issued by Nancy Ann Storybook Dolls.

"Little Scout" coaster wagons see *R. Herschel Mfg. Co.*

"Little Shaver" dolls see *Alexander Doll Co.*

Little Star Novelty Corp. This postwar West 17th Street, New York City, company made stuffed toys.

"Little Tot" The "Little Tot" and "Little Tots" trade names were shared by several prewar companies. Plaza Mfg. Co. issued "Little Tot" record book, and the A. Schoenhut Co. issued "Little Tots" building blocks. The "Little Tots" name was also used by Richmond School Furniture Co. and Standard Toykraft Products.

"Little Women" Dolls based on the popular juvenile novel were issued by several companies. In the 1930s, Alexander Doll Co. issued "Little Women" dolls, and Whitman

L

Publishing Co. issued paper doll cutouts. The Alexander "Little Women" dolls remained popular into the Boomer years. See *Louisa May Alcott.*

"The Littlechap Family" Remco Industries introduced the "Littlechap" family of dolls in 1964. The family included "Dr. John Littlechap," wife "Lisa," and children "Judy" and "Libby."

Littlefield Mfg. Co. Littlefield's line of playthings in the 1920s ranged from the "Kangru-Springshu" to the games "Quarterback," "Over the Top," "Rollin' Sambo," "Defense of Covered Wagons," and "Shoot 'Em Down." The firm was based in Chicago, Ill.

The Littlestown Hardware & Foundry Co., Inc. A maker of cast-iron toys, the Littlestown (Penn.) Hardware & Foundry Co. made toy trucks, autos, and tools, as well as toy golf club sets and children's polo outfits in the mid-1930s. The company also made Christmas tree holders. By the end of the decade the company was specializing in tool chest toys, picks, rakes, toy golf club sets, and Christmas tree holders. See also *Kenton Hardware Co.*

Live Long Toys Live Long Toys made brightly colored, washable, soft stuffed toys based on animals and famous cartoon figures from cartoon strips including "Gasoline Alley," "Orphan Annie," and "Smitty" in the 1920s. The firm was located in Chicago, Ill.

"Lively Horseman" The "Lively Horseman" game was a popular item introduced in the late 1800s by Charles M. Crandall.

"Living Turtle Garden" see *Walter L. Herne Co.*

Lloyd Mfg. Co. This prewar Menominee, Mich., manufacturer of baby carriages and juvenile furniture also made doll carriages.

Lo-E Mfg. Corp. Plastic doll kits and toys sets were products of this West 21st Street, New York City, company in the 1950s and '60s.

"Load-N-Dump" toys see *Buddy "L" Toys.*

"Lock-A-Bead & Block" 1958, see *Lido Toy Co.*

Locke, John This famous philosopher's 1699 *Thoughts on Education* forwarded the influential argument that learning should be pleasant, or even a game. This perspective became important in the development of new toys and games through the 18th and 19th centuries, guiding such toy-making luminaries as Charles Crandall and Milton Bradley.

"Lockwood Stand-Ups" playwood dolls see *George Borgfeldt Corp.*

"Loco-Bell" scooter see *C.C. Elliotte Corp.*

"Loco Builder" see *Dorfan Co.*

Lodge Textile Works The "Dolly-duds" products of the 1930s were produced by this Albany, N.Y., firm. The line included doll blankets, doll underwear, and Red Riding Hood capes.

H.A. Loeb & Co. This Chicago, Ill., company made human-hair doll wigs in the 1930s and '40s.

log cabin toys The first set of wooden pieces to construct a miniature log cabin was produced around 1850. It came in a wooden box, with 94 pieces. In the 1860s sets were issued by French and Wheat, and Vermont Novelty Works. Prewar companies issuing log cabin construction toys included Wisconsin Toy Co., Woodcraft Novelty Co., and J.L. Wright, the latter the manufacturer of the famous "Lincoln Logs." Halsam Products Co. issued the "American Logs" sets popular in the late 1930s through the Boomer years.

Logan Electric Specialty Mfg. Co. Logan issued basketball games in the late 1930s. It was based in Chicago, Ill. In the postwar years, as Logan Specialty Mfg. Co., the firm continued manufacturing basketball games, horseshoe games, punching bag sets, and banks.

"Lok-A-Bloks" see *Childhood Interests.*

"Lokblok" blocks see *Ideal Products Corp.*

Loma-Jean Mfg. Co. This postwar La Verne, Calif., firm specialized in doll beds.

London babies The name "London babies" was used in late Colonial times for the dolls imported from England.

"Lone Eagle" coaster wagons see *R. Herschel Mfg. Co.*

Lone Ranger Since "the Lone Ranger" Western hero started in radio, interpretations of his appearance in toy and costume form had greater variety in the prewar than in the postwar years, when the combined force of TV and movies defined his image. Early costume manufacturers of "Lone Ranger" "cowboy suits" and "ranch outfits," such as Collegeville Flag & Mfg. Co. and Feinberg-Henry Mfg. Co., produced elaborate outfits unlike the simple costumes later seen. Feinberg-Henry also made "Lone Ranger" school bags, watch fobs, hats, wallets, and pistol holster sets in the late 1930s.

Other early toys and playthings included books by Whitman Publishing Co., caps by Penn Novelty Embroidery Co., cowboy hats by Jacobson & Co., soft dolls by Dollcraft Novelty Co., games by Parker Bros., "Silver" rocking horse by the Mengel Co., and pistol by Louis Marx & Co. The "Tonto" Indian headdress was issued by Jacobson & Co., and the "Tonto" soft ball by Dollcraft Novelty Co.

In the postwar years, "Lone Ranger" items saw no diminution of popularity. If anything, the opposite was true, with books and frame tray puzzles appearing from Whitman Publishing Co.; play suits, from Herman Iskin & Co.; games, from Parker Bros.; miscellaneous playthings, from 20th Century Varieties; novels, from Grosset & Dunlap; school bags, from National Leather Mfg. Co.; 3-D color film cards, from Tru-Vue Co.; western guitars, from Jefferson Mfg. Co.; and western accessories, from Esquire Novelty Co.

H. Wenzel Tent & Duck Co. issued "Lone Ranger" camp tents and umbrella tents, as well as a "Lone Ranger & Tonto Wigwam." Hartland Plastics also issued "Lone Ranger" and "Tonto" plastic horses and riders.

One of the many Lone Ranger items from the 1950s: "Lone Ranger Crayons" by Parker Bros.

Long, William William Long was a cabinet-maker and carver of rocking horses and "go-chairs," or wheelchairs, in late 18th-century Pennsylvania. Long may have been the first American manufacturer of the rocking horse.

"Long Boy" single-shot cap pistol prewar, see *Kilgore Mfg. Co.*

Long Island Mask Co. Based in Richmond Hills, Long Island, N.Y., this company made prewar masks, "luloups," dominoes, Santa Claus masks and costumes, and play hats. The company also made dominoes in the late prewar years. In the 1950s and '60s, its line included Halloween masks of cloth, vinyl and rubber; half masks; Santa Claus masks; costume hands, feet, and ears; party hats; and make-up sets.

"Look-In" iron toys see *The Hubley Mfg. Co.*

"Looky Chug-Chug" see *Fisher-Price Toys.*

"Loomcrafter" see *Friedberger-Aaron Mfg. Co.*

looms When looms were a more common household item than they are today, miniature versions for children were likewise in greater demand. Prewar manufacturers included Milton Bradley Co., Friedberger-Aaron Mfg. Co., Samuel Gabriel Sons & Co., Miniature Ship Models, Modeloom Co., the Morison Co., Ostlind Sales Co., and William Poenitz. By the late 1930s, companies entering the loom-making fray included Calcraft Corp., Donar Products Corp., Elliot, Greene & Co.,

L

Gropper Mfg. Co., Holgate Bros. Co., Oregon Worsted Co., Plume Trading & Sales Co., Standard Toykraft Products, Straits Mfg. Co., Structo Mfg. Co., Transogram Co., Valley Novelty Works, and Walco Bead Co. Even so, postwar production of the juvenile and toy versions was by no means insignificant. Companies active in the field included Ainslie Knitting Machine Co., Milton Bradley, the Brothers Mfg. Co., H. Davis Toy Corp., Pressman Toy Corp., Structo, and Transogram.

"Lorain" all-steel toys see the *Steel Stamping Co.*

Lord, Arthur S. The "Bonanza" game of the late 1930s was made by Arthur S. Lord, of E. 86th Street, New York City.

Lord & Freber, Inc. A Hollywood, Calif., firm, Lord & Freber issued baseball, football, and word games in the postwar years. Its line also included darts and dartboards, poker games, butterfly collecting kits, and pipe-cleaner craft kits.

Lorraine Metal Mfg. Co. Established in the late prewar years, this Fourth Avenue, New York City company made metal toys.

"Louisvile Slugger" see *Hillerich & Bradsby Co.*

"Lov-Le-Tex" dolls see *Alexander Doll Co.*

Lovable Toys, Inc. This Acworth, Ga., company issued plush toys and washable foam-stuffed chenille dolls and animals, in the Boomer years.

Love, Inc. "The Love Game" of the late 1930s was issued by Love, Inc., based in the Fifth Avenue Building, New York City.

"Love Me" baby doll see *Horsman Dolls.*

E.S. Lowe Co. Founded in the late 1930s on Sixth Avenue, New York City, E.S. Lowe Co. early emphasized the manufacture of "Bingo" games, casino equipment, game boxes, dominoes, backgammon, and games for adults.

In the early '40s, moving to West 20th Street and then into the Fifth Avenue Building, the company issued a number of game titles including "Pirate Ship" in 1940, "Airplane Speedway Game," "Cross Country," "Hornet," and "Land and Sea War Games" in 1941, "Baseball" and "Basketball" in 1942, "Horse Race" in 1943, and "The Jeep Board" in 1944.

In 1942 and '43, one of its hits was "The Bookshelf of Games," which in 1943 included eighteen pocket-size games for adults that sold from 50 cents to a dollar. Chess and Checkers were among the games, at the higher end of the price range. Besides the intense magazine advertising campaign, the popularity of the series could be attributed to their use as small gifts for service men abroad. The firm also issued lines of children's books, juvenile games, and Christmas cards through wartime.

Lowe's Boomer-era line continued with a focus on games for adults, including backgammon, "Chuck-A-Luck," poker racks and chips, dominoes, checkers, cribbage, roulette, dice and cups, Bingo, and Chinese tile games. It especially emphasized its chess line, with titles including "Chess Tutor" and "Renaissance Chess."

The firm also continued issuing boxed games, along the line of its "Bookshelf" games of the war years.

Samuel Lowe Co. This Kenosha, Wis., publisher was one of the leading publisher of children's books in the Boomer years.

Lowell Toy Mfg. Corp. Based in Long Island City, N.Y., Lowell was a postwar game manufacturer.

"Lu-Gee" toy guns see *Park Plastics Co.*

"Luger" dart gun see *Park Plastics.*

"Luger" plastic water pistols see *Knickerbocker Plastic Co.*

Lubbers & Bell Mfg.Co. Lubbers & Bell, of Clinton, Iowa, made board and skill games in the 1920s and '30s. Titles included "Blox-O" in 1923, "Toss-O" and "Zoo Hoo" in 1924, and "Puzzle-Peg" in the mid to late '30s.

"Lucky Boy" coaster wagon see *Auto-Wheel Coaster Co.*

"Lucky Boy" glass marbles see *The Rosenthal Co.*

"Lucky Ducky" action toys see *W.W. Drake Mfg. Co.*

lucky rabbit's foot see *rabbit's foot.*

Lucky Toy Co. Lucky Toy was based on West 21st Street, New York City, in the earlier prewar years, and on West 22nd Street by the late 1930s. It made the "Lucky" stuffed toys, promotional items, and stuffed novelties. The company relocated to Brooklyn, N.Y., in the postwar years. Its line continued with plush toys and novelties, musical plush toys, chain store items, and promotional and premium items. The toys were sometimes marked with an inverted horseshoe, and the words, "A Lucky Toy."

Ludlow Toy & Mfg. Co. Based in Ludlow, Vt., this firm manufactured doll carriages, toy carts and wheelbarrows from its founding in 1872 through the late 1880s.

Lujon Dolls Located on West 22nd Street, New York City, this company made "colored" and "suntan dolls" in the 1930s and '40s. By the late '30s it had changed its name to "Lujon Sun Tan Colored Doll Co.," with its salesroom on Broadway.

Lukas, John A Chicago, Ill., firm, Lukas made doll wigs in the 1930s and '40s.

"Lullaby Baby" doll see *Horsman Dolls.*

Lullabye Furniture Corp. Formerly Automatic Cradle Mfg. Co., Lullabye Furniture of Stevens Point, Wis., manufactured a line in the 1920s and earlier '30s featuring doll bassinets, scooters, wagons, and the "Flivver Family" of wheel goods. The "Flivver Family" included "Baby Flivver" walkers and strollers, "Baby Scoot Flivver" scooters, "Jitney" wagons, "Junior Transfer" coaster wagons, and "Kiddie Flivver" infant's vehicles, "Pointer" wagons, the "Row-Flivver," and the "Victory Flyer" sport

model wagon. The company appears to have given over production of wheel goods in the late '30s to concentrate on baby and juvenile furniture. It continued in operation through the Boomer years.

"Lullamatic Jr." toy cradles see *Jenkintown Steel Co.*

luloups A 1930s term for the black velvet mask, luloups was adapted from the French *les loups.*

Lumarith A form of celluloid acetate developed by the Celanese Corp. of America, Lumarith was capable of being compressed, extrusion molded and injection molded. As the second such plastic, after Tenite, it proved of importance in the toy industry. The "Lumarith" trade name was also used with electric Christmas tree lights from Louis Sametz.

"Lumimask" luminous masks see *Austin Art Studios.*

"Lunar-1" two-stage, remote-launching rocket see *Scientific Products Co.*

lunch boxes With the rise of functional lunch boxes in the 1950s and '60s, toy versions likewise acquired some popularity. They were made by manufacturers including Eastern Bag Mfg. Co., Fisher-Price Toys, and Ohio Art Co.

C.A. Lund Co. Recreational snow equipment was the specialty of this firm. Based in Hastings, Minn., it manufactured toboggans, snowshoes, skis and hockey equipment in the 1930s and '40s.

Lundahl, Fred see *Buddy "L" Mfg. Co.*

Lutz, A. The "Hi-Li" game of the late 1930s was produced by A. Lutz, of West 17th Street, New York City.

Lutz & Sheinkman, Inc. Located on Duane Street, New York City, Lutz & Sheinkman issued a Buck Rogers game in 1934.

"Lutz" marbles The "Lutz" or "Lutz-type" marble is a glass marble with the colored opaque strands of glass swirled on the surface, with gold-colored flakes often out-

L

lined by threads of white glass. "Lutz" marbles of clear glass are the most common.

"Luvable Skin" dolls see *Goldberger Doll Mfg. Co.*

Lux Clock Mfg. Co., Inc. The postwar "Pendulette" clocks, made for the juvenile market, were products of this Waterbury, Conn., firm. It also made "Minute Minder" timers.

D.W. Lynch Co., Inc. Shooflies and baby walkers were among this Lancaster, Penn., company's products, issued from the 1930s through the Boomer years. The firm also made nursery seats and chairs, and baby yards.

Lynco Corp. The "Gang Busters Game" of 1938 was the lead product of this Philadelphia, Penn., firm.

Joseph Lyon & Co. Lyon made the "Autoperipatetikos," literally "self-walker," of the 1860s. The doll, patented in 1862, was a small figure with papier-mache head and cardboard body, with a clockwork mechanism moving the feet.

G.E. Lyons Industries, Inc. Based in Hannibal, Mo., Lyons Industries made children's furniture, including sand boxes and peg-and-desk sets.

The Lyons Mfg. Co. Lyons, of Mt. Carmel, Conn., issued the "Rollster" roller skates in the mid-1930s. It also made miniature wood home building sets.

Kenner's "Spirotot" drawing toy, 1960s.

In 1923 Milton Bradley released the "Flivver Game."

L

Note: "Mc" and "Mac" are alphabetized as spelled.

M.&J. Knitcraft Co. This postwar Brooklyn, N.Y., company specialized in knitted doll clothing.

M.&L. Toy Co. Based in Union City, N.J., M.&L. issued toy guns, water pistols, blocks, clock banks, novelty glasses, bicycle accessories, and plastic novelties.

M.&S. Doll Co. Soft dolls, vinyl character dolls, and foam-filled terry cloth dolls and animal toys were specialties of this Fifth Avenue Building, New York City, firm in the Boomer years.

M.C. Doll Co., Inc. The "Emm-Cee" vinyl and plastic dolls of the 1950s and '60s, including character dolls, were this firm's products. It was located on Canal Street, New York City.

MPM Corp. The Viking Products Division of MPM Corp, based in Stoughton, Wis., in the 1950s and '60s, made sled and coaster wagon combinations.

M.S. Publishing Paint, drawing, cutout and novelty books were an important part of this Varick Street, New York City, publisher's line in the 1930s.

"Mac" games and toys see *McDowell Mfg. Co.*

Mace Plastics Corp. Bubble pipes and solution were among the Boomer-era products of this Mount Vernon, N.Y., firm. Mace also made Nativity sets, Easter items, and Christmas tree ornaments.

Mache Products Co. This Brooklyn, N.Y., firm made train tunnels and Christmas bells in the late 1930s.

Mack Mfg. Co. Based in Bowling Green, Ohio, Mack issued the "Tom Thumb" basketball set of the late 1930s.

The Mack-Miller Candle Co. Besides making candles, this prewar Syracuse, N.Y., company also made crayons.

Mack Toy Works Based in Yardville, N.J., Mack Toy Works made 1930s and '40s juvenile and toy furniture, and "house furnishing novelties."

"MacKenzie's Raiders" In the late 1950s and early '60s, "MacKenzie's Raiders" items included plastic figures by Hartford Plastics, and miscellaneous play accessories by John-Henry Mfg. Co.

Maco Toys, Inc. This Brooklyn, N.Y., firm made Boomer-era toy carbines, machine guns, automatic pistols, "Ack-Ack" guns, and electronic toys.

Macrae Smith Co. A Philadelphia, Penn., publisher, Macrae Smith issued children's books in the 1930s and '40s.

"Madame Alexander" dolls see *Alexander Doll Co.*

Madame Louise Doll Co., Inc. Established in Syracuse, N.Y., in the late 1930s, Madame Louise made dolls dressed in foreign and nun costumes.

Made-in-America Novelty Corp. In addition to 1939 New York World's Fair novelties, this company made kazoos, "Jazz-Kazoonets," and noisemakers in the late '30s. It was based on West 19th Street, New York City.

Madewell Chair Co. This Sheboygan, Wis., company made juvenile furniture, specializing in upholstered rockers in the 1930s and '40s.

Madmar Quality Co. This Utica, N.Y., firm was the premier producer of picture and map puzzles of the 20th century, surviving the Great Depression, World War II, and the intense competition of the Boomer years by maintaining the high level of quality in its line. Its products also tended to be more expensive than the competition. Early titles included the "Toy Town Picture Puzzle" series of the 1920s, and skill games "Disk" and "Crickets in the Grass" of the 1920s and '30s. The company was still issuing a line of hand-cut plywood puzzles in the 1960s.

"Mae West" In the 1930s, popular movie stars occasionally moved into the world of dolls and toys. Tru-Craft Novelty Co. was one to make "Mae West" dolls.

Gebruder Maerklin Beginning in 1859 in Goeppingen, Germany, Theodor and Caroline Maerklin manufactured tinplate doll kitchenware. When their sons took over the business in 1881, the name became Gebruder Maerklin. Production gradually broadened to include enameled tinplate boats, carousels, aeronautical toys, and especially clockwork toy trains. The company issued the first standardized tinplate train tracks in 1891.

In the earlier 20th century, the products of this famous firm, known as Maerklin Bros. & Co. by the 1920s, were sold in the "Maerklin Toys" line in America, their sales overseen by Richard Maerklin, who maintained show rooms in the Fifth Avenue Building, New York City, in the 1920s and '30s. Popular 1920s items included the elaborate "Flying Tops," which appeared in moth, butterfly, sunflower, and pinwheel designs.

The firm's line also included clockwork trains, model naval craft, steam trains, steam and electrical engines, steamers and steam yachts, artillery, model baths and bathrooms, cooking stoves and ranges, and musical choral tops. Maerklin switched production to plastic train sets in the 1950s.

Richard Maerklin Toys An earlier 20th century and prewar importer, Richard Maerklin Toys was sole U.S. agent for Maerklin Bros. trains and other toys, especially mechanical toys.

Maggie Magnetic, Inc. The popular "Whee-Lo" magnetic, track-running tops were 1950s and '60s products of this West 32nd Street, New York City, firm. Maggie Magnetic also made the "Maggie Boards," which were magnetic bulletin boards, and "Whee-Lo" related toys including the late '50s "Sputnik."

"Magi-Stix," 1955 see *Samuel Gabriel Sons & Co.*

"Magic" air gun see *Plymouth Air Rifles Co.*

"Magic Bowling Ball" see *Alabe Crafts.*

"Magic Designer" see *Northern Signal Co.*

"Magic '8' Ball" see *Alabe Crafts.*

"Magic Farmyard" see *Remotrol Co.*

magic lantern Magic lanterns were widely imported to the U.S. from Europe through the 1800s. An early alternate spelling was, "magic lanthorn." In the prewar years, American manufacturers of the diversion included Keystone View Co. of Meadville, Penn.

Magic Mould Mfg. Co. A Toledo, Ohio, company, Magic Mould issued prewar molding sets using water mix composition.

magic sets Just as children make an ideal audience for illusion shows, so children make excellent would-be illusionists. Nothing makes a child happier than the ability to fool another. Prewar manufacturers included S.S. Adams Co., Billie-toy Mfg. Co., A.C. Gilbert Co., Magical Manufactures, Petrie-Lewis Mfg. Co., and "Sherms."

"The Magic Flote," 1930s, see Magic Flote Novelty Corp. of Chicago.

M

"Magic Slate" see *Watkins-Strathmore Co.*

Magical Manufactures Based in the Fifth Avenue Building, New York City, in the 1930s and '40s, Magical Manufactures was responsible for "Houdini Magic" sets, tricks, and puzzles.

"Magna" dominoes see *The Embossing Co.*

"Magnetic Baseball" see *Remotrol Co.*

"Magnetic Circus" see *Smethport Specialty Co.*

"Magnetic Global Air Race" see *Replogle Globes.*

"Magnetic Guidance toys" see *J.W.K. Industries.*

Magnetic Hat & Cap Corp. "Mickey Mouse" and "Elvis Presley" hats were among the novelty hats and caps produced by this Boomer-era West 22nd Street, New York City, company.

"Magnetic Pic-Up-Stix" see *Steven Mfg. Co.*

magnets and magnetic toys Magnets, whether natural or manufactured, make good toys. Commercial magnet toys were available from the later 1800s. Prewar magnetic playthings included the "Magnetic Bubbles" by Rosebud Art Co., "Magnetic Checkers" by Beulah Toy & Novelty Co., "Magnetic Jack Straws" by Milton Bradley, and two "Magnetic Fish Pond" games, one each by Parker Bros. and Milton Bradley Co. Other manufacturers included H. Boker & Co. and U.S. Toy Co.

In the Boomer years, several clever magnetic toys rose to prominence, including the "Magnestiks" construction toy by Ohio Art, and the "Funny Face," "Dapper Dan," and "Wooly Willy" line of toys by Smethport Specialty Co., which used a magnetic wand to move iron-filings "hair" around the subject's hairless face. Perhaps the most notable is the "Whee-Lo" toy by Maggie Magnetic, a spinning plastic wheel or top with a magnetic axle, which "defies gravity," in the parlance

of the toy trade, by traveling over and under a steel track.

Other postwar manufacturers of toy magnets and magnetic toys included the Alox Mfg. Co., American Visual Aids, Bar Zim Toy Mfg. Co., Blockcraft, Milton Bradley Co., Elkay Mfg. Corp., Elmar Products Co., H. Fishlove & Co., Hale-Nass Corp., Henry Katz, Kohner Bros., Fred Kroll Assoc., Pressman Toy Corp., Remotrol Co., Roseburd Art Co., Steven Mfg. Co., and Sidney A. Tarrson.

The "Magnetic Globe Race" by Replogle Globes, 1950s-60s.

Sifo Co.'s "Magnetic Alphabet Board," 1960s.

Magnotrix Novelty Corp. Based on Park Row, New York City, Magnotrix issued magic tricks, joke novelties and puzzles in the late 1930s.

Magnus This East Orange, N.J., firm was established in the late 1930s to manufacture table tennis equipment.

Magnus, Charles In the 1850s, Charles Magnus published the card game, "The Sibyls Prophecy, Comic Leaves of Fortune."

M

"Mah Jong" sets The Chinese tile game of "Mah Jong" was issued by manufacturers beginning in the 1930s, with Parker Bros. being possibly the first Postwar companies included A.&L. Mfg. Co., Cardinal Products, E.S. Lowe Co., and Mastercraft Plastics Co. Companies played with the name as readily as they did with Chinese checkers, as in Lowe's "Mah Lowe."

Mahr-Bufton Co. This Minneapolis, Minn., firm made wheel goods in the late pre-war years, including "Trav-L-Eez" collaps-ible baby carriages. It also supplied wheels for juvenile vehicles.

Maine Yacht Corp. A maker of wood toys, this Dover-Foxcroft, Maine, company made "Doerfler" model sailing boats in the 1930s and '40s.

Majestic Art Novelty Co. Transfer drawing devices were made by this Chicago, Ill., company before the war.

Majestic Radio & Television Co. This Chicago, Ill., firm issued Edgar Bergen related radios in the late 1930s.

"Mak-Ur-Own" puzzle kits prewar, see *Harry E. Pulver.*

Makatoy Co. Activity sets made up most the prewar line of this Chicago, Ill., firm, including blackboards, stencil sets, painting sets, sewing sets, picture puzzles, and novel-ties.

Make-A-Toy Co. see *Metal Cast Prod-ucts Co.*

"Maker of the World's Best Games" see *M. Hou Bradley Co.*

"Making Childhood's Hour Hap-pier" see *Girard Model Works, Inc.*

Makit-Kit Co. Based in Evanston, Ill., in the late 1930s, Makit-Kit made scroll-saw kits with patterns on wood.

"Makit Toy" see *W.R. Benjamin Co.;* also *Lincoln Logs Division.*

"Malice" game see *Rennoc Games & Toys.*

Mam-A-Car Corp. An Elmhurst, Long Island, N.Y., company, Mam-A-Car made baby walkers and strollers, collapsible baby carriages, lawn cribs, and auto cribs in the 1920s. It employed the "Happiness on Wheels" slogan.

"Mambo" stuffed toys see *Bijou Toys.*

"Mammoth Flyer" coaster wagon see *Dayton Toy & Specialty Co.*

mammy dolls see *dolls, mammy.*

"Man-O-War" car mid-1930s, see the *Mengel Co.*

Mangold Toy Co. Stick horses and toy mops and brooms were postwar specialties of this Granbury, Texas, company. The com-pany was founded in 1940. By the '60s, the stick horses had plastic heads and bridles, cloth manes, and enameled sticks.

Manhattan Kreole Products, Inc. Liquid bubble-blowing sets were Boomer-era products of this Brooklyn, N.Y., company.

M. Manheim Co., Inc. A 1950s-'60s firm based in the Fifth Avenue Building, New York City, Manheim made toys, novelties, and Christmas decorations.

Manning Mfg. Corp. The "Zipees" roller skates of the 1950s and '60s were prod-ucts by Manning, of Chicago, Ill. The firm also made ice skates, slider skates, snow-shoes, "Roll-Barrow," and "Roc-N-Spin."

Jack Manoil Co., Inc. Based in Waverly, N.Y., Jack Manoil specialized in die-cast metal play cars and plastic toy cars, in the 1950s-'60s.

Manoil Mfg. Co., Inc. Based on Bleecker Street, New York City, and Waverly, N.Y., Manoil made hollowcast sol-diers, or "dimestore soldiers," and other toys before and after the war. Founded in 1937, its die-cast cannons were among its most popu-lar toys by the late '30s.

Manomatic Novelty Corp. Latex and vinyl dolls made up this Wooster Street, New York City, firm's postwar line.

M

Mansfield Novelty Co. Spinning tops and wooden crickets were made in the 1930s and '40s by this Mansfield, Penn., company.

Mansfield-Zesiger Mfg. Co. The postwar "Bambino" game was a product of this Cuyahoga Falls, Ohio, company. It also made the "Five Pins" bowling game.

"The Mansions of Happiness" A successful early game issued by W. & S.B. Ives in 1843, "The Mansions of Happiness" was a colorfully lithographed board game involving the movement of playing pieces from square to square. Typical of the times, the game was highly moral in tone. Parker Bros. issued a "Mansion of Happiness" board game in the 1930s.

Mantua Toy & Metal Products Co. Based in Woodbury Heights, N.J., Mantua made electric and steel toys, including boats, miniature motors, and pumps. In the 1930s it used the Triple "T" trademark on toys. By the end of the '30s it was issuing "HO" and "OO" gauge track and switches, and model railroad supplies. In the postwar years, as Mantua Metal Products, the firm continued to issue "HO" trains under the "Tyco" name.

The Manufacturer's Research Co. The "Safe-way Rocket" roller coaster of the 1950s-'60s was a product of this Olmstead Falls, Ohio, company.

Manufactured Specialties Co. Based in Pittsburgh, Penn., in the late 1930s, this firm made airplane motors supplies, kite reels, and toy gas stations, as well as Christmas tree decorations.

map puzzles see *puzzles, picture,* and *dissected maps.*

The Maple City Rubber Co. Rubber toy balloons and rubber novelties were made by this Norwalk, Ohio, company from the 1930s through the Boomer years.

"Maple Leaf" register banks see *Durable Toy & Novelty Corp.*

Maplecrest Co. Pre-school toys were this postwar Chicago, Ill., company's specialty.

Maplewood Products Co. This Menasha, Wis., manufacturer issued "Tyke toys," children's table and chair sets, shooflies, rocking horses, "Putter Pails," and doll highchairs and bassinettes in the late prewar years.

Maplewood Craftshop Based in Hutchinson, Minn., Maplewood made postwar sleds.

Mar-Dene Fur & Novelty Corp. This postwar Brooklyn, N.Y., company issued fur stuffed toy animals.

"Mar-Quoits" see *Martin Rubber Co.*

"Marbelator" see *Toy Creation Shops.*

The Marbelite Co. Based in Wallingford, Conn., the Marbelite Co. made prewar dice and novelties.

"Marbelite" electric game, mid-1930s see *Wolverine Supply & Mfg. Co.*

marbles Marbles made of clay date back to at least the ancient Greeks. Glazed marbles appeared by at least 200 A.D. Apparently a common plaything for a great many centuries, marble players have never escaped the urge to classify the small balls of clay, stone, or glass. In 1829 The Boy's Own Book grouped marbles of the time as follows: the least desirable and least expensive were of Dutch manufacture, from variegated clay; the next best were yellow stone, with spots or circles on them; and best were taws, or alleys, which were made of pink marble with dark red veins.

By the 1850s marbles in America were broken into three groups, "china, colored, and common marbles," by at least one advertiser.

In the Depression and earlier prewar years a number of firms specialized in producing marbles, including the Vitro-Agate Co. of Parkersburg, W.V., which advertised "beautiful, non-breakable marbles in bulk, in bags, in boxes." Others included the Akro Agate Co., J.E. Albright Co., Eugene B. Baehr & Sons, Gropper Onyx Marble Co., Lakeside Marble Co., Master Marble Co., Peltier Glass Co., and the Rosenthal Co. By the late prewar

M

years they included Berry Pink, Ravenna Ceramics, and the Vitro-Agate Co.

Postwar manufacturers included the Alox Mfg. Co., Champion Agate Co., Dyer Products Co., the Jerome Gropper Co., Master Glass Co., Peltier, Berry Pink, Pressman Toy Corp., Ravenswood Novelty Works, and Vitro Agate.

Opaque swirl marble from the 1910s.

Transparent swirl marble from the 1910s.

"Marble King" see *Berry Pink, Inc.*

"Marble-Minder" marble holder see *Dyer Products Co.*

"Marble Race" see *Dart Mfg. Co.*

"Marcella" dolls prewar, see *Alexander Doll Co.*

"Marcia" and "Margie" dolls see *Cameo Doll Co.*

"Marcraftin" boats see *John G. Martin, Jr.*

Margon Corp. Based in Bayonne, N.J., Margon produced eyes, teeth and tongues for dolls in the 1930s and '40s.

Marietta Doll Co. Marietta, located on Greene Street in the Doll District, New York City, manufactured dolls in the earlier 1930s.

Marilyn Products, Inc. This Irvington, N.J., firm made mid-1950s "Regina Electrikbroom, Jr.," a working, battery-operated vac-

uum cleaner, made through a licensing agreement with the Regina Corp., manufacturer of the adult-size "Electrikbroom" of the time. The firm also made toy lawn mowers in the 1950s and '60s.

"Marine Crystal" marbles see *Peltier Glass Co.*

Marine Model Co. Ship model construction sets, plans, and fittings were produced by Marine Model, established in the late 1930s on Worth Street, New York City.

"Marine Raider" military toys see *Remco Industries, Inc.*

Marion Craftsman Tool Co. Based in Marion, Ind., this company made prewar toy lawn mowers and pitching horseshoes. It also made Christmas tree holders. By the late 1930s it became Marion Tool Corp.

Marion Electrical Mfg. Co. The "Scout" electric toy engine of the late 1930s was issued by this Jersey City, N.J., firm.

Marion Tool Corp. see *Marion Craftsman Tool Co.*

marionettes see *puppets.*

Marke Stocke see *Walter Stock.*

Markham Mfg. Co. Based in Plymouth, Mich., Markham issued the first toy air gun, the all-wood "Chicago," in 1886. After Plymouth Iron Windmill Co. issued the metal "Daisy" in 1888, Markham released its metal version, "Prince," in 1890. In 1912, two Daisy Mfg. Co. company officials bought 90 percent of Markham, then called Markham Mfg. Co. Air Rifle Co. Markham changed its name to King Mfg. Co. in 1928. In 1931, a year into the Great Depression, Daisy bought out all stock of King, closed its plant and moved the firm's tooling and dies to the Daisy plant. Daisy continued to make the "King" line for mail order and premium houses.

Marks Bros. Co. Located in Boston, Mass., Marks Brothers issued Halloween goods, kites, "Traffic Cops," golf games, bows and arrows, and voice toys in the 1920s.

The company obtained an early license through Kay Kamen in the 1930s to produce games, toys, and paint sets using Disney's Mickey Mouse and Three Little Pigs themes and characters. Its most famous board and skill game titles were Disney-related, including "Mickey Mouse Coming Home Game," "Mickey Mouse Miniature Pinball Game," "Mickey Mouse Roll'em Game," "Mickey Mouse Skittle Ball Game," "Mickey Mouse Soldier Target Set," "Mickey Mouse Circus Game," and "Mickey Mouse Shooting Game." Other prewar game titles included "Belmont Park," "Slugger Baseball Game," and "Stax."

Its line in the 1930s also included archery sets, dart games, carnival goods, crayons and crayon sets, games, puzzles, shooting games, juvenile golf bags and clubs, toy guns, Halloween goods, noisemakers, party games, rubber stamp outfits, table tennis, shooflies, and wax molding sets. By late in the decade it added pyrography sets, jacks-in-the-box, musical toys including pianos, and doll and animal voices. It also obtained license to issue Edgar Bergen related dancing dolls. It maintained offices in the Fifth Avenue Building, New York City.

In wartime the company made dartboards, musical toys, and glass Christmas ornaments.

Marksman Products
A division of Morton H. Harris, Inc., this Boomer-era firm issued "Marksman" air pistols, holsters, targets, throwing darts, dart games, dart boards, and the "Fireball 7-8" semi-automatic slingshots.

"Marksman" space pistol and target
see *Moonglow Plastic Jewel Corp.*

The Marlin Carriage Co., Inc.
This New Haven, Conn., firm made baby and doll carriages, coaster wagons, and juvenile vehicles in the 1930s and '40s.

Marlin Toy Products, Inc.
Plastic infants' toys, rattles, novelty toys, and suction-cup toys were specialties of this Horicon, Wis., company. Toys of the 1950s-'60s included "Baby Bar Bell," a take-apart rattle in the shape of a barbell, and "Slap-Jack," a rattling figure with spring body and suction-cup base, adhering it to the table. A number of Marlin toys had this basic design.

Marlowe Equipment, Inc.
The "Exercolt" and other exercisers of the late prewar years were issued by this Bronx Boulevard, New York City firm.

Marmet Baby Carriages
The "Marmet" line of baby carriages were made in England, and distributed in America by F.D. Tryon, located on West 42nd Street, New York City, in the 1920s. The line was promoted with the slogan, "Needs Hands To Steer—That's All."

W.A. Marqua
Issued the first American patent for a hobbyhorse, W.A. Marqua of Cincinnati, Ohio, sold it as a "leaping horse," with side-saddle versions available. Marqua also may also have been the first to manufacture blackboard desks and drop-back baby carriages. His line, founded in 1865, included sleds and propellers.

married parts
Toys that have "married parts" have been assembled from the two halves of different individual toys, usually as a restoration measure. Collectors regard such a toy as having less value than a toy that is in its completely original state.

Mars Mfg. Co.
The "Satellite Worldwide Radio Kit" of 1958 was introduced by this Akron, Ohio, manufacturer of specialized electronic equipment. The kit was designed to cover space satellite frequencies.

Marshall Field & Co.
The wholesale division of Marshall Field & Co. was responsible for some toy lines, including the "Miniature Famous Cartoon Characters" of the 1920s, based on newspaper comic figures from "Gasoline Alley," "Orphan Annie," "Smitty," "The Gumps," and "Moon Mullins." The figures, made of bisque china with movable heads, retailed at 15 and 25 cents.

"Martha Washington"
The "Martha Washington" trade name was used by several companies, including Detroit Wood Products, for its doll cradles, and L. Hopkins Mfg. Co., for its doll beds.

"Martian Monsters" space toys
see *American Play Co.*

M

Fernand Martin A manufacturer of double-action tin mechanicals, Fernand Martin was active in the years 1887-1919 in Paris, France. The toys, which included "Le Clochard (Tramp)" and "Ivorogne (Drunk)," were widely copied by other manufacturers.

John G. Martin, Jr. Established in Chicago, Ill., in the late 1930s, John G. Martin, Jr., made boat toys in various scales, and games. The product line included through the Boomer years, with doll beds and cradles added.

Martin Industries Educational toys, toy wagons, push and pull toys, and the "Scribble Sketcher" lap desk were Boomer-era products of this Wisconsin Rapids, Wis., company.

Martin Metal Bed Co. A Cleveland, Ohio, firm, Martin Metal Bed made "indestructible" prewar metal doll beds and breakfast sets.

Martin Rubber Co., Inc. A specialist in underwater swim accessories, Martin also made rubber quoits and horseshoes in the 1950s and '60s. It was located in Long Branch, N.J.

The Martini Artists Color Laboratories Based in Long Island City, N.Y., Martini Artists issued the "Poster Craft" painting outfits in the 1920s.

The "Poster Craft" kit, 1920s.

"Marvel" roller skates see *Globe-Union Mfg. Co.*

"Marvelous Mike" Saunders-Swadar Toy Co. introduced this bump-and-go toy tractor in 1955. The robot driver, who was a plastic jointed figure atop the steel battery-operated tractor, appeared to move the clutch and shift.

Louis Marx & Co. Louis Marx, born in 1896, entered the world of toy manufacturing within the organization of Ferdinand Strauss, who was "The Toy King" of the 1900s and 1910s. Parting ways in the 1910s, Marx established himself in the business in the late 1910s, finding in his brother a partner. Initially the firm developed toys based on already popular ideas, and hired other firms to do the manufacturing. In 1921, Louis Marx & Co. began its own manufacturing, many based on the designs of Strauss, whose company had failed.

In the 1920s-30s Louis Marx emerged as a specialist in metal and mechanical toys. By the end of the decade the company had established a reputation with its lines of wind-ups, skates, typewriters, and even the "television telephones" of 1939. It issued a number of the notable character toys of the decade, obtaining licenses to issue Edgar Bergen related mechanical metal toys and Walt Disney character mechanical toys.

Louis Marx & Co. logo.

Marx became a millionaire before age 30, due in great part to his practice of making less detailed, inexpensive versions of toys already popular, and issuing them in great quantity. Up through the Boomer years he sold primarily through large department store chains and mail-order houses, making it unnecessary for him to advertise his wares. Because of his tendency to quickly copy any toy making waves in the market, the Marx firm was often grouped with the least innovative of companies, and the one with the smallest number of actual contributions to the industry. Nevertheless, Louis Marx & Co. was enormously successful, becoming by mid-century the acknowledged giant in the industry, having six factories in the U.S.,

M

with other affiliated or wholly owned factories located in at least nine other countries.

Because of its success before the advent of TV, Marx was one of the last major companies to join the TV-advertising bandwagon, although its famous Sears and Wards play sets of the 1950s included numerous tie-ins to the TV shows themselves. By the 1960s, with its market share declining, Marx fell into line, with its most successful advertising campaign centering around the "Rock 'Em Sock 'Em Robots" of 1964. Even these popular toys were issued because of Ideal's success within the plastic action robot genre, and because Marx brought in the designer of Ideal's immense successes of the early 1960s, Marvin Glass.

Marx enjoyed some success with its vinyl-jointed dolls of the 1960s, including "Stony 'Stonewall' Smith," a soldier doll introduced in 1964, and the "Johnny West" series that remained popular into the 1970s. Marx also ventured into doll-making, with the "Miss Seventeen" vinyl doll of 1961, an imitation of Mattel's "Barbie." See also ***Girard Model Works.***

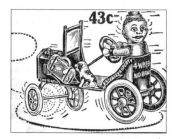

The "Funny Flivver," Marx, 1925.

The "Amos 'n' Andy Walking Toys" by Marx, 1930s.

Marx, Hess & Lee Based on West 33rd Street, New York City, this company issued the "Four Daredevils" marble game in 1933.

Maryland Toy & Games Corp.

Games, picture puzzles, cardboard toys, and cutouts were made by this prewar Baltimore, Md., company.

"Maskoween" costumes prewar, see *Sackman Bros. Co.*

masks Masks and mask-making must go back into prehistory. Europe enjoyed a strong tradition of masques and masquerades that required masks, as well as miscellaneous occasions for which masks must have seemed appropriate. In America, Santa masks at Christmas and frightening masks for Halloween became commonplace by the early 20th century.

Prewar manufacturers included Dessart Bros. of Brooklyn, N.Y., which made stamped, pasted, and molded paper goods for general party use, including full Santa Claus outfits and masquerade masks. Other firms included the American Mask Mfg. Co., Einson-Freeman Co., Long Island Mask Co., Newark Mask Co., United Pressed Products Co., Van Horn & Son, and Victory Mask Co.

In the Boomer years, manufacturers included Arlane Mfg. Co., Austin Art Studios, Bayshore Industries, the Beistle Co., Ben Cooper, Dessart Bros., Gordon Novelty Co., J. Halpern Co., Long Island Mask Co., Newark Mask Co., Don Post Studios, Pritt Novelty Co., Star Brand Co., Topstone Rubber Toys Co., and United Mask & Novelty Co. See also ***masquerade costumes.***

Halloween masks from the 1910s.

Mason, Hal An animator, Hal Mason created the advertising characters "Pillsbury Doughboy," "Mr. Clean," the "Frito Bandito," the "Hamm's Beer Bear," and the "Raid Roaches."

Mason & Converse see *Morton E. Converse Co.*

M

Mason & Parker Mfg. Co.

Wood toys were produced by this Winchendon, Mass., company from 1907 on, with its most famous item being the "Boy's Tool Chest." Its line into the 1920s also included educational blackboards, games, pianos, grocery stores, metal kitchen cabinets, metal ice chests, and tool cabinets. Its prewar line continued with tool chests, pianos, pool tables, blackboards, doll trunks, juvenile furniture, and ten pins, issued through the early 1940s. Despite being best known for its later wood products, the company was originally founded in 1899 by H.N. Parker and Orlando Mason to produce pressed-steel transportation toys.

Mason & Taylor

Mason & Taylor of Springfield, Vt., produced wooden dolls from 1879 into the 1880s. The firm used improvements on the Joel Ellis wooden doll, which had been patented in the 1870s by George Sanders, F.D. Martin, C.C. Johnson, and Luke Taylor.

The Mason Mfg. Co.

Located in South Paris, Maine, Mason made a line of sturdily constructed juvenile furniture in the 1920s, including dressers, chairs and tables. Its line of doll furniture included swings, bassinets, cradles, chairs, tables, beds, and tea wagons.

masquerade costumes

The phenomenon of adult play surely falls into any study of toys and playthings; and the masquerade, and any use of masks, surely constitutes a kind of adult play. A "masquerade" item may range from the simplest of face masks fitting over eyes and bridge of nose, as in the Lone Ranger's mask, to elaborate, full-body costumes.

Prewar manufacturers included American Flag Co., the Chessler Co., Collegeville Flag & Mfg. Co., A.S. Fishbach, J. Halpern Co., Long Island Mask Co., Clarence E. Miller, Oliver Bros., Sackman Bros. Co., E. Simon's Sons, Van Horn & Son, Waas & Son, and Wornova Mfg.

Prewar manufacturers of toy and masquerade wigs, beards and moustaches included Dessart Bros., Long Island Mask Co., Clarence E. Miller, Newark Mask Co., Rosen & Jacoby, E. Simon's Sons, Van Horn & Son, Victory Mask Co., and Waas & Son.

In the Boomer years, prominent companies included J. Halpern Co., which issued a wide variety of licensed characters, including "Matt Dillon," "Chester" and "Kitty" from "Gunsmoke." From Harvey Cartoons, its line included "Sad Sack," "Baby Huey," "Litte Audrey," "Little Max," "Moe Hare," "Inchy the Worm," "Wily Fox," "Spooky the Ghost," and "Tommy Tortoise." Halpern also issued MGM's "Tom the Cat," "Jerry the Mouse," "Droopy the Dog," and "Barney Bear," as well as "The Chipmunks," "Steve Canyon," "Sky Masters," "Maggie & Jiggs," "Little Iodine," and "Charlie Chan" costumes. These appeared under the "Halco" or "Halco Superb Brand" trade name.

Ben Cooper was also a leading name in costumes, issuing Walt Disney character costumes, "Huckleberry Hound," "Quick Draw McGraw," "Terrytoon" characters, and various TV-related costumes.

Other Boomer manufacturers included Alabe Crafts, Arlane Mfg. Co., Arranjay Wig Co., Austin Art Studios, Bland-Charnas Co., Brrr Products Co., Collegeville Flag & Mfg. Co., Dessart Bros., Sam & Herbert Drelich, Fibre-Bilt Toys, Grand Wig Co., Meyer Jacoby & Son, Rice Mills, E. Simon's Sons, and Welded Plastics Corp.

Mason Bath Toys

Based on East 20th Street, New York City, in the late 1930s, Mason issued sponge rubber bath toys and accessories.

The Massillon Wire Basket Co.

A maker of toy fences and dolly hampers, this Massillon, Ohio, firm made the "Dicky" wire guns and "Junior Trixie" sewing baskets in the 1930s. It also made "toy fence."

A. Master

A. Master of Brooklyn, N.Y., specialized in Halloween and punch-board party games, including "Phoney Fortunes," "Crazy Grams," "Kissing Game," "Fortune Teller," and "Peppy Punch-it Parlor Pranks," in the 1920s, '30s and '40s. "Snappy Stunts," "Smacks," and "Guessing" were other titles.

"Master Art" water colors

see *Milton Bradley Co.*

M

Master Casters Based in Chicago, Ill., Master Casters sold its metal casting set in the late prewar years.

"Master Craftsman" The prewar "Master Craftsman" trade name was used by Milton Bradley Co. for its paint sets and the Mordt Co. for its work bench and tools.

Master Industries, Inc. Based in St. Paul, Minn., this postwar firm issued musical toys, stuffed toys, and nursery toys.

Master Juvenile Products Co. The "Little Bathmaster" doll bath of the Boomer years was a product of this Walker Valley, N.Y., company. It also made pogo sticks.

Master Makers Based in Catonsville, Md., this firm made "Master Maker" construction kits in the 1930s.

Master Marble Co. This Clarksburg, W.V., company made glass marbles in the 1930s and '40s.

Master Metal Products, Inc. Based in Buffalo, N.Y., in the 1930s and '40s, Master Metal Products made "Ride-On-Toys" and steel pull toys, including trucks, airplanes, and fire engines. It maintained offices in the Fifth Avenue Building, New York City, and a Canadian manufacturing plant in Fort Erie, Ont.

"Master Molder" sets see the *Fox Toy Co.*

The Master Package Corp. Toy drums and "Indian Tom-Toms" were among this Owen, Wis., company's prewar products.

The Master Toy Co. This wartime firm, based in New York City, issued children's games and paint sets.

"Master" scooter see the *Metalcraft Corp.*

Master Woodworkers Based on Park Avenue, New York City, Master Woodworkers made prewar "Polo Ponies" and sticks, shuffleboards, table tennis, sleds, games, and foundry sets.

"Mastercraft" art sets prewar, see *The Porter Chemical Co.*

Mastercraft Plastics Co., Inc. Checkers, dice, dominoes and poker chips were postwar specialties of this Jamaica, N.Y., firm.

Mastercraft Toy Co., Inc. Located on West 24th Street, New York City, Mastercraft Toy Co. issued games and activity sets in the early '40s including "Ad-O-Master" and "Mystoscope." Other titles included "Color-Art," "Movie Fun," "Bridge Bowl" and "Block-Bowl," all of 1943. In the postwar years, Mastercraft Toy emphasized educational toys and games, including calculators and speller toys.

The "Automatic Speller" educational toy from Mastercraft Toy Co., Inc.

Mastur Mfg. Co. This Boomer-era Philadelphia, Penn., juvenile furniture company also issued toy chests.

"Matchbox" cars see *Lesney Products.*

"Matchless" air rifle see *West Lake Co.*

J.H. Mather & Co. A children's publisher in Hartford, Conn., in the 1800s Mather published a juvenile picture encyclopedia in 1846, *The Child's First Book.*

Matreshka dolls Nested wooden dolls, traditional folk dolls typically identified with Russia, were imported during prewar years by the Karavan, a company based on Fifth Avenue, New York City. The Karavan imported a variety of Russian toys and children's goods in the 1930s.

Matrix Structures Climbing toys were this Norwich, Vt., firm's specialty in the Boomer years.

Mattel, Inc. Mattel was established in 1945 by Ruth and Elliot Handler with partner Harold Mattson. Mattel proved itself to be

M

one of the leading innovators of the Boomer period, introducing important lines in the traditional categories of boys', girls', and preschool toys.

The company specialized in musical toys, including the "Uke-A-Doodle," a child-size ukulele, and hand-cranked music boxes and jack-in-boxes. In 1955 it enjoyed widespread success with its "Burp Gun" and "Mousegetar." The musical toys "Carnival Hurdy Gurdy" and "Musical Mystery Truck" also appeared in that year. In 1958 and '59, Mattel released its "Fanner" cap pistol, the first of the "Shootin' Shell" series.

The firm issued its famous plastic version of the paper doll, "Barbie," in 1959, starting one of the most successful lines in the history of toy manufacture. In 1960 Mattel launched another immensely successful line with its "Chatty Cathy" doll, whose "Chatty Ring" pull-string talker became an important component of not only Mattel's dolls but also puppets, plush stuffed figures, and preschool toys, notably the "See 'n Say Talking Toys," one of the most important educational preschool toys from the mid-1960s on.

In 1968, Mattel introduced its successful competitor to the "Matchbox" toy car line, "Hot Wheels." These performance-oriented toys, which were introduced with plastic tracks for downhill racing, changed the toy car world almost overnight.

Mattel was a pioneer in the world of TV advertising for toys, sponsoring Walt Disney's "Mickey Mouse Club" show in its first year. All of its major introductions after 1955 received substantial television advertising support, which helped the Mattel line become deeply entrenched in the minds and imaginations of Boomer generation children.

The "Barbie" line included "Ken," introduced in 1961; "Midge," in 1963; "Skipper," in 1964; and "Skooter" and "Ricky," in 1965. See also *"Barbie."*

The "Chatty Ring" line of talking dolls included "Talking Matty Mattel" in 1961; "Chatty Baby," "Talking Beany," "Talking Cecil the Seasick Sea Serpent," and "Talking Bugs Bunny," in 1962; "Charmin' Chatty," in

1963; and "Shrinkin' Violette" and "Talking Bozo the Clown" in 1964. See also *"Chatty Cathy."*

Other dolls by Mattel included "Scooba-Doo," a "Beatnik" Rag doll with vinyl head, in 1965; "Baby Teenie Talk," "Cheerful Tearful," clown doll "Patootie," and "Linus the Lionhearted," in 1966; "Talking Mrs. Beasley," "Captain Kangaroo," and "Googlies" plush animals, in 1967; "Doctor Doolittle," "Talking Gentle Ben," and "Tippee Toes" in 1968; "Dancerina," "Swingy," "Talking Buffy and Mrs. Beasley," and "Baby Sing-A-Song," in 1969; and "Talking Cat in the Hat" in 1970.

From 1966-71 the company issued the "Liddle Kiddle" dolls, some of which represented nursery rhyme and fairy tale characters. The "Lucky Locket Kiddles" appeared in the mid-'70s. The tiny "Upsy Downsy" also were late '60s releases. "The Sunshine Family" was introduced in 1974, with characters "Steve" and "Stephie," the mother and father, and baby "Sweets."

Mattel logo.

"Maverick" This popular ABC TV show inspired playthings including cap pistols and holster sets by Leslie-Henry Co., gun and holster sets by Carnell Mfg. Co., hats by Arlington Hat Co., miscellaneous accessories by 20th Century Varieties, plastic figures by Hartland Plastics, and play suits by Herman Iskin & Co.

"Mawaphil" soft dolls prewar, see *The Rushton Co.*

Maydee Mfg. Corp. Stuffed toys were the specialty of this Brooklyn, N.Y., firm in the Boomer years.

"Mayflower" electric train 1930s, see *American Flyer Mfg. Co.*

Maxine Doll Co. Based on Mulberry Street, New York City, Maxine made "Baby Gloria" and Mama dolls in the 1920s. Its dolls were noted for having moveable heads. "Baby Gloria" was joined by "Gloria Lou" were 1930s and '40s. Maxine in the prewar years as based on West 24th Street

Maxwell Rubber Products Corp. This Newark, N.J., company produced teething and juvenile toys in colored, solid rubber under the "Tamby Toys" trade name in the 1930s and '40s.

The May-Kit Co. A table-tennis manufacturer, the May-Kit Co. of Tacoma, Wash., also made the "May-Kit" construction toy, toy ironing boards, and toy clothes dryers in the 1930s and '40s.

May-pole The introduction of the May-pole to America is attributed to the Dutch. In New England, May Day and the merriments associated with the May-pole were regarded with disapproval and even alarm. In the one recorded instance of a May-pole being raised in the first decade after the landing of the Mayflower, the pole was cut down and the responsible party—governor Thomas Morton of the town of Merrymount—was arrested.

Maybro Mfg. Co. This East 48th Street, New York City, firm made dolls and "bunnies" in the late 1930s.

Mayfair Games, Inc. Based on Sixth Avenue, New York City, Mayfair made games for adults in the late prewar years.

Mayhew & Baker A mid-19th century manufacturer, Mayhew & Baker issued the 1858 "Tournament" board game and 1859 "Game of the Young Peddlers" card game.

McBride & Oxford Mfg. Co. This Selma, Ala., company made postwar velocipedes and sidewalk bicycles.

McBurroughs, Annuel see *Remco Industries, Inc.*

McCandlish, Edward see *Auburn Rubber Co.*

McCauley Metal Products, Inc. The "Teeter Pony" of the 1950s-60s was issued by this Buffalo, N.Y., firm. McCauley also made bicycle accessories.

McClurg A prominent publisher, McClurg issued the "Mathers Parlor Baseball Game" and "Table Golf" board games of 1909.

McCreary Mfg. Co. This Erie, Penn., firm made the "Air Play" catapult parachute toy of the late 1930s.

Samuel McCrudden Co. Based on West 37th Street, New York City, McCrudden obtained a late 1930s license to issue Edgar Bergen related handkerchiefs.

McDonald Burglar Bar Works McDonald of Birmingham, Ala., made the postwar "Roll-A-Wheel," a hoop and stick toy.

McDowell Mfg. Co. This Pittsburgh, Penn., company used the "Mac Toys" trademark in the 1920s and '30s. Its early line included Easter and Fourth of July toys, with the "Mac Mystery Gun" doing well on the eve of the Great Depression. In the '30s, its line included mechanical toys, pop guns, sand toys, and games, including the "Mac Baseball Game."

McGavin Specialties Co. A Springfield, Ill., firm, McGavin issued "Hot Foot," "Skip Ball," "Buzzer," and "Bank Golf" games in the mid-1930s.

James McGowan Associates Established on Broadway, New York City, in the late prewar years, McGowan issued juvenile and adult games, doctor and nurse kits, sewing sets, surprise packages, and premiums.

McGraw Box Co. Toy trunks and toy cedar chests were made by this McGraw, N.Y., firm in the 1930s and '40s.

McGuffey Eclectic Reader The most famous of early readers first appeared in 1836. Six in all, they went through numerous editions.

McIlvaine Burner Corp. see *Tactical Game Co.*

McKay, David This Philadelphia, Penn., publisher obtained an early license from Kay

Kamen to produce Disney storybooks. David McKay published children's and toy books and "panoramas" in the 1930s and '40s.

McKee Glass Co. Located in Jeannette, Penn., this famous glass company made some toy items, including the toy "Glasbake" ovenware sets of heat-resistant glass in the 1930s and '40s.

McKinney, J.W. The "Safe-T-Colt" exerciser of the 1950s-60s was this Morton, Penn., firm's product.

McKinnon Leather Products, Inc. A Buffalo, N.Y., firm, McKinnon specialized in sports balls and other sports equipment in the prewar and wartime years. In addition to sports items, the firm made toy holster sets in the postwar years.

John McLoughlin John McLoughlin published the early card games "Amusing Game of Conundrums" and "Yankee Pedlar, or What Do You Buy" in the 1850s.

McLoughlin Bros. One of the venerable names in American games, McLoughlin Bros. was publisher of lithographed picture books, paint books, board books, and cloth-bound juveniles.

John Mcloughlin established the firm with his brother in 1855, on Beekman Street, New York City. The firm added a factory in Brooklyn, N.Y., in 1870.

As part of the 19th century paper doll craze, McLoughlin rose to prominence in the century's last decade with the best-selling "The Bride" and "The Bridegroom" paper dolls. It also issued successful paper dolls under such names as "Emma White," "Fanny Fair," "Gerty Good," "Kitty Black," "Rose Bud," "Ruby Rose," and "Violet Vernon." The firm's paper dolls based on famous people included "General Tom Thumb" and "Mrs. Tom Thumb." The firm also made toy theaters with paper-doll actors and scenery.

McLoughlin also made a large variety of books that sold from one to ten cents, depending on length and colors; paper soldiers; nested blocks, picture blocks, and "Swift's Combination Building Blocks"; and games, including the fortune-telling game "Chiromagica"; Easter novelties; paint books; linen books for infants; and picture books.

The company earned an early reputation, typical for companies of its kind, of re-issuing juvenile games and toys already made popular in Europe. Among its popular titles in the 1800s were "Pilgrim's Progress" of 1875, "The Game of Fish Pond" of 1890, "Peter Coddle," and "Jack Straws." Its lithographed paper-on-wood toys included the Palmer Cox Brownie series, as well as alphabet blocks and other educational toys.

The company's titles included "Bugle Horn or Robin Hood" and "Golden Egg" in the 1850s, and "Game of Old Maid" and "Game of Rabbit Hunt" in 1870. Games from circa 1875 included "Game of Hens and Chickens," "Game of Japanese Oracle," "John Gilpin," and "Mother Hubbard."

The 1880s saw a significant increase in the company's line, beginning with "Captive Princess" and "H.M.S. Pinafore" in 1880, and "Japanese Game of Cash" in 1881. "Game of Cock Robin and his Tragical Death," "Where's Johnny?," and "Zimmer Baseball Game" appeared in 1885; "Game of Baseball," "Game of Columbia's Presidents," and "Game of the Telegraph Messenger Boy," in 1886; and "Donkey Party," "Elite Conversation Cards," "Grandmama's Improved Arithmetical Game" and "Geographical Game," "Grandmama's Sunday Game," "The House that Jack Built," and "The New Game of Red Riding Hood and the Wolf," in 1887.

"Game of Catching Mice," "Game of Colors," "Game of the Crusaders," "Derby Steeple Chase," "The New Fox and Geese," and "Game of the Telegraph Boy" appeared in 1888; and "Which Is it? Speak Quick or Pay," "Battles," "The Game of City Life," "Game of District Messenger Boy," and "Yuneek," in 1889.

The McLoughlin Bros. Puzzle, "A Peep at the Circus."

Games of the 1890s included "The Game of Guess Again," "India, an Oriental Game," "Navigator Boat Race," "Parlor Football," "Snake Game," "Game of Toll Gate," "Trunk Box Lotto," "Whirlpool," and "Young Folks Historical Game."

Other titles included "Christmas Goose," "Double Eagle Anagrams," "Farmer Jones' Pigs," "Goldenlocks & the Three Bears," "Hare and Hounds," "The Letter Carrier," "The Messenger," "Game of Old Maid or Matrimony," "Round the World with Nellie Bly," and "Yale Harvard Game," in 1890; "Bicycle Race, a Game for the Wheelmen," "The Errand Boy," "Magnetic Fish Pond Game," "Game of Hunting Hare," "Life's Mishaps," "Skirmish at Harper's Ferry," "Game of Strategy," and "The Susceptibles," in 1891; and "The Good Old Aunt," "Game of Parlor Base Ball," "Royal Game of Kings and Queens," and "Game of Snap," in 1892.

"Heedless Tommy," "Kann-Oo-Win-It," "New Game of King's Quoits," "The Game of Lost Heir," and "Uncle Sam's Mail" appeared in 1893; "The Diamond Game of Baseball," in 1894; and "Bo Peep Game," "Game of Bugle Horn or Robin Hood," "The Game of the Harlequin," "Game of Hide and Seek," "Lost in the Woods," "Game of Mail," "The Mansion of Happiness," and "Yale-Princeton Football Game" in 1895.

Titles in 1896 included "Bulls and Bears," "Game of College Boat Race," "Game of Golf," "Goosy Goosy Gander," "Game of Lost Diamond," "Rival Policemen," and "Watermelon Patch Game"; in 1897, "Fun at the Circus," "Home Baseball Game," "Little Fireman Game," "Game of Trip Round the World," and "Walking the Tightrope"; in 1898, "Game of Bagatelle," "Game of Bobb," "Game of Bombardment," "Game of Cousin Peter's Trip to New York," "Game of Day at the Circus," "Game of Playing Department Store," "The Frog He Would A-Wooing Go," "The Game of Jack and the Bean Stalk," "Game of Nations or Quaker Whist," "The Merry Game of Old Maid & Old Bachelor," and "Game of Spider's Web." The decade ended with "Game of the Christmas Jewel," "Game of Just Like Me," "Game of Phoebe Snow," "Game of Tobagganing at Christmas," "Game of Topsy Turvey," "Game of the Visit of Santa Claus," and "Game of Wide Awake."

The company's output and invention flagged in the early 1900s, although it remained among the most prominent of names in the games business. Titles included "Leap Frog Game" in 1900; "Chiromagica, or the Hand of Fate" and "Man in the Moon" in 1901; "Diamond Heart" in 1902; "Game of Bang" and "Game of Comical Snap" in 1903; "The Air Ship Game," "America's Yacht Race," "Game of the Automobile Race," "The Double Flag Game," and "The New Game of Hunting" in 1904; and "Naughty Molly," "The Game of Nosey," and "Skit Scat" in 1905. Later games included "Gypsy Fortune Telling Game" in 1909, "War of Words" in 1910, and "Naval Maneuvers" in 1920.

Although the company was acquired by Milton Bradley in 1920, the name continued to appear through the prewar years.

Milton Bradley's "McLoughlin Books for Children" line was led by the "Cartoon Books," which featured such popular childhood favorites of the time as "Skippy," "Skeezix," "Popeye," "Smitty," "Moon Mullins," "Tailspin Tommy," "Toots and Casper," "Little Jimmy," "Orphan Annie," and "Harold Teen." The book line also included the "Round-About" doll books, the "Little Big Books," "Little Reader Series," educational workbooks, cutout books, standard color classics, painting books, picture books, and story books.

"Trunk Box Lotto," another McLoughlin Bros. game from the 1890s.

Meander Puppet Sales Co. A St. Paul, Minn., firm established in the late 1930s, Meander made puppets, puppet supplies, and theaters.

M

Meander Toy Co. Based on East 23rd Street, New York City, Meander Toy made walking pull toys in the mid-1930s.

Meccano Meccano of Liverpool, England, was founded in 1901 by Frank Hornby. Its specialty fell in the area of metal construction sets, of which the "Erector" set of A.C. Gilbert was strongly reminiscent. In 1933 it began producing metal miniature vehicles under the "Dinky Toys" line. In 1964 the company was bought by Lines Bros.

The Meccano Co. of America, Inc.

Maintaining offices in the Fifth Avenue Building in the 1930s, the Meccano Company of America issued Meccano steel construction toys, tool chests "Meccano-Brik" greenhouses, microscope sets, the "20 Grand" racing game, "Believe It or Not" game, "Mysticks," and "Barrel O'Fun." It also made electric motors and transformers.

The Mechanical Toy Co.

Located at 1107 Broadway, New York City, the Mechanical Toy Co. issued Ferdinand Strauss mechanical and electrical toys in the earlier 1930s. Changing its name to Ferdinand Strauss Toys by the late 1930s, the company manufactured mechanical and electrical toys, and the "Glidersport" gun-shooting airplanes and gliders.

mechanical toys Mechanical toys, which have a history stretching back to the complex automata of European watch and clockmakers of earlier centuries, enjoyed some early popularity in the later 1800s. Walking dolls were among these early productions. Early manufacturers included J.S. Brown and William F. Goodwin.

Manufacturers in the earlier 20th century included American Flyer Mfg. Co., Animate Toy Co., the Art Metal Works, H.E. Boucher Co., Buffalo Toy & Tool Works, Dayton Friction Toy Co., Dixtoy Co., Gibbs Mfg. Co., Girard Model Works, Hafner Mfg. Co., Katagiri Bros., Henry Katz & Co., Kingsbury Mfg. Co., Louis Marx & Co., McDowell Mfg. Co., Patent Novelty Co., Reeves Co., Republic Tool Products Co., Schieble Toy & Novelty Co., Structo Mfg. Co., Toy Creation Shops, John C. Turner Co., and Wolverine Supply & Mfg. Co.

The abundance of inexpensive mechanical toys, many based on cartoon characters, and mostly made of colorfully lithographed and painted tin or steel, was a distinctive characteristic of the prewar years, when companies including Animate Toy Corp., Automatic Toy Corp., Buffalo Toy & Tool Works, J. Chein & Co., Kingsbury Mfg. Co., and Louis Marx & Co. were making a wide variety of toys, both stationary and mobile, that involved mechanical actions, frequently powered by clockwork motors.

Prewar manufacturers also included Abba International Products Co., Abbott Mfg. Co., American Electric Toy & Novelty Co., American Flyer Mfg. Co., Arcade Mfg. Co., Behrend & Rothschild, George Borgfeldt Corp., Buddy "L" Mfg. Co., Buffalo Toy & Tool Works, the Conestoga Corp., the Dorfan Co., Durable Toy & Novelty Corp., Theodore J. Ely Mg. Co., Fisher-Price Toys, the Gibbs Mfg. Co., Helvetic, Hoge Mfg. Co., Hustler Corp., Irwin Novelty Co., Katagiri Corp., Lafayette Toy Co., the Lindstrom Tool & Toy Co., McDowell Mfg. Co., Richard Maerklin Toys, the Mechanical Toy Co., Metal Toy Co., Newton Mfg. Co., Nonpareil Toy & Novelty Co., Patent Novelty Co., Structo Mfg. Co., Templeton, Waterbury Button Co., the Wayne Toy Mfg. Co., and Wolverine Supply & Mfg. Co.

In the Boomer years, plastic manufacturing methods compensated for the rising costs of metals, making inexpensive mechanical toys a continuing option for toy makers.

Manufacturers included AMT Corp., Aladdin Toy Mfg. Corp., Amerline, Argo Industries Corp., George Borgfeldt Corp., Buddy "L" Toys, J. Chein & Co., Elmar Products Co., Everly Associates, F.M. Engineering Co., Hale-Nass Corp., Ideal Toy Corp., Irwin Corp., Henry Katz, Kenner Products Co., Kilgore, Kohner Bros., Fred Kroll Associates, Louis Marx & Co., Ny-Lint Tool & Mfg. Co., Ohio Art Co., Renwal Toy Corp., Riemann, Seabrey Co., Structo Mfg. Co., Thomas Mfg. Corp. Tonka Toys, Weil Bros., Western Coil & Electrical Co., I.B. Wolfset & Co., Wolverine Supply & Mfg. Co., and Woodhaven Metal Stamping Co.

M

A. Mecky Co. This Philadelphia, Penn., firm issued the "Velo-King" line of veloci-pedes, sidewalk cycles, tot bikes, scooters, and the "Sambo" and "Ducko" walking pull toys.

Frederick Medart Mfg. Co. Frederick Medart of St. Louis manufactured play-ground and gymnasium apparatus and equip-ment from 1873 through the prewar years. In the 1920s the company was offering a com-plete line for the home playground, including the "Junior Gym" and "All-Steel Sand Box."

Megahorn Co. This Springfield, Penn., company issued dolls and doll clothing in the postwar years.

megaphones see *microphones and related toys.*

Mego Corp. Based on West 26th Street, New York City, Mego was a Boomer-era manufacturer of "88-cent dolls," toys, and games. In the 1970s, Mego established itself in the action-figure market with "Fighting Yank." The line of characters continued with "Action Jackson" and the six first "Official World's Greatest Super Heroes" in 1972, including "Batman," Superman," "Robin," "Aquaman," "Tarzan," and "Spider Man." By 1974 the firm had introduced "Planet of the Apes," "American West," "Star Trek," and "Wizard of Oz" figures.

Megow's Model Airplane Shop Based in Philadelphia, Penn., Megow made model airplanes and boats, and airplane and boat kits in the 1930s and '40s. By the late '30s the firm had added scale model freight trains to its line. During wartime, it issued model airplanes, ships, "HO" railroads, and hobby supplies.

Johann Philipp Meier A prolific manu-facturer of penny toys, Johann Philipp Meier established his business in Nuremberg, Ger-many, in 1879. Also making painted tin mechanicals, the company continued in oper-ation until 1917.

Meier & Frank Merchandise Co. Toy tom-toms, tomahawks, and beaded belts were among the novelty products of this Denver, Colo., company in the Boomer years.

Meinecke, Adolph A German immi-grant of 1848 who settled in Milwaukee, Wis., Meinecke opened a shop in 1853 devoted to toys from the Northeast and from Germany. Given the difficulties caused by tariffs and impeded transportation in the Civil War years, Meinecke turned to manufactur-ing, initially making willow-ware carriages. By 1870 he was making shooflies, sleds, cro-quet sets, baby wagons, hobbyhorses and children's furniture.

"Mello-Tone" pianos see the *A. Schoenhut Co.*

"Melvin the Moon Man" see *Remco Industries.*

Menasha Woodenware Corp. This Menasha, Wis., juvenile furniture manufac-turer made the prewar "Tyke Toys" line. The "Putter Pails" were wood pails full of wood construction toy parts. The "No. 1000 Putter Pail" contained spool-and-stick construction toys, while "No. 2000 Putter Pail" contained wood pieces for making doll house furniture. The line also included doll table and chair sets, high chairs, and rockers, and decorated shooflies.

Mendl, Joseph Established on Magin Street, New York City, in the late 1930s, Mendl made games including quoits and shuffleboard.

The Mengel Co., Inc. A manufacturer of playground equipment, the Mengel Co. also made prewar doll furniture, shooflies, toy motorboats and floating boats, doll beds, "Playblock" sets, and plywood alphabet blocks. In the late 1930s it issued "The Lone Ranger and Silver" rocking horses.

Meridian Co. This Fifth Avenue, New York City, firm made prewar dolls.

Merit Mfg. Co., Inc. Action toy games were specialties of this postwar Central Falls, R.I., company.

The Merremaker Corp. This Minneap-olis, Minn., firm manufactured home play-ground equipment in the 1920s, including gyms, slides, teeter-totters, combination tee-ters and merry-go-rounds, and canopy sand boxes. The "Merremaker Whirl" was a rotating device by which children could spin around a central pole.

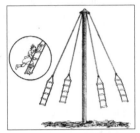

The "Merre-maker Whirl" merry-go-round,

Merri-O Toy Corp. This St. Louis, Mo., firm issued the "Merri-O-Galloper" in the later 1920s, a three-wheeled, horse-headed, pedal-powered scooter billed as an exerciser.

Merrie-Go, Inc. Based in Birmingham, Ala., Merrie-Go made postwar rocking horses, blackboards, see saws, and "Merrie-Go-Whirler" merry-go-rounds.

"Merrie" playroom furniture, see *The Lehman Co. of America.*

Merrill Publishing Co. Merrill, located in Chicago, Ill., began publishing toy books in the late prewar years. In the postwar years it offered a line of activity books ranging from 10 to 49 cents, including painting and coloring books, and paper dolls.

"Merrimaker" see *American Merri-Lei Corp.*

Merriman Mfg. Corp. A manufacturer of juvenile furniture, this Grabill, Ind., company also made doll furniture and juvenile ironing boards.

merry-go-rounds None but the wealthiest could personally own a merry-go-round. Even so, riding the merry-go-round was an experience held in common by most children from the late 1800s through the 20th century, since they were not only used as permanent attractions in amusement parks but as traveling attractions with carnivals. Prewar manufacturers, some of whom were involved in the production of smaller toys, included Anchor Post Fence Co., the Delphos Bending Co., Hill Standard Corp., Leavitt Mfg. Co., Fred Medart Mfg. Co., Rotary Clothes Dryer Co., W.S. Tothill, and Youngstown Tool & Mfg. Co.

Merry Mfg. Co. Kits by this firm included the "My Merry Shaving Set," "My Merry Shampoo Set," and "My Merry Make-Up." Boxed sets with miscellaneous plastic items and bottled soaps, they retailed for 39 cents in the mid-1950s. Based in Cincinnati, Ohio, Merry continued its line into the '60s. The firm introduced the "Wristwhats," which were various small toys or toy sets to be worn on the wrist, in 1969. The company also introduced the "Play Like Mommy" line of toy dinner and tea sets.

"Merry Time" toys see *Sollmann & Whitcomb.*

Merry's Museum see *Louis May Alcott.*

metal alloy toys Toys classed by the toy trade as "pewter toys" through the late Great Depression years were called "metal alloy toys" by the later prewar years. The terms "slush metal toys" and "white metal toys" likewise apply to these items of variable lead make-up. Manufacturers in the prewar years included Barclay Mfg. Co., C.A.W. Novelty Co., Durable Toy & Novelty Co., Karson Mfg. Co., Lorraine Metal Mfg. Co., Manoil Mfg. Co., the Newton Junior Corp., Peter F. Pia, C. Sidney Payne, Tommy Toy Mfg. Corp., and Williams Kast Art Co. The major category to replace this in postwar years was "die-cast" toys, which relied on zinc-based alloys. Dowst Mfg. Co. used zinc alloys from early in its toy-making years, but may have used the cheaper lead alloys for some toys.

Metal Cast Products Co. Established around 1905, Metal Cast Products Company, located on Boston Road, New York City, specialized in making "toy mould outfits" for making slush-metal toys and novelties. Although by 1934 it was using the name Make-A-Toy, it seems to have returned to the Metal Cast Products name after the war. It continued in operation at least through the 1940s.

Metal Goods Corp. Based in St. Louis, Mo., Metal Goods Corp. made aluminum toy sets in the 1930s and '40s. For Christmas decorating it also manufactured artificial icicles, snowflakes, and "snow drift."

M

Metal Masters Co., Inc.
Batons, bell and chime pull and push toys, stick horses and riding horses, and toy telephones were among this postwar Philadelphia, Penn., company's products.

Metal Moss Mfg. Co.
"Snap-Blox" toys were lead 1950s and '60s items for this Chicago, Ill., company. Metal Moss also made "Cartoon-O-Graph" sketch boards, games, and table tennis.

Metal Package Corp.
Based on East 42nd Street, New York City, Metal Package Corp. made prewar sand pails and metal toys.

Metal Specialties Mfg. Co.
This Chicago, Ill., firm made the 1930s and '40s "Speed-O-Byke" and "Presto" sidewalk bicycles. The "Roll-King" was an advanced roller skate when it was added to the company's line in 1939. The skate had rubber cushions for the heel and ankles, rubber mountings, and rubber wheels.

The Metal Stamping & Mfg. Co.
The "Mirroscope," advertised as "the standard picture projecting machine" in the 1920s, fell in the category of the postcard projector, a popular item in the earlier 20th century. The "Mirroscope" projectors were made in the 1930s and '40s by this Cleveland, Ohio, firm.

metal tapping
Most manufacturers who issued electric woodburning sets and accessories also issued metal tapping sets, which used similar or the same equipment for etching and "tapping" designs on metal plates, instead of wooden plaques. Manufacturers included Carron Mfg. Co., Handikraft, Home Foundry Mfg. Co., Marks Bros., Rapaport Bros., and Transogram Co.

Metal Toy Co.
A Pittsburgh, Penn., firm, Metal Toy made prewar mechanical toys, games, and novelties.

metal toys
see iron toys, steel toys, tin toys, pewter toys, aluminum toys, mechanical toys.

The Metal Ware Corp.
In the 1920s, '30s and '40s, Metal Ware manufactured "Empire Electric Steam Engines" and "Miniature Electric Ranges." The "Empire Miniature Range," which was an electrically powered working device, included an oven for baking and two heating units for cooking. They came equipped with percolator, pie tin, and cake and bread pans. The company, based in Two Rivers, Wis., also made non-electric play stoves. While still making the "Empire" ranges and toy steam engines in the Boomer years, Metal Ware expanded its line to include the "Little Lady Electric Bakerette" toy oven, "Little Lady" toy flat irons, metal ironing boards, toy kitchen sinks, toy corn poppers, and a complete line of domestic electric appliances in toy form. Metal Ware discontinued its main toy line for the war, but issued new items including a "Safety Patrol Sound Truck" that "actually broadcast."

An actual appliance, the "Empire Electric Hot Dogger" was produced in 1961.

metal wheels
While not as specialized an item of manufacture as rubber tires, a number of prewar companies did specialize in producing metal wheels for other firms, even when they might themselves have been producing lines of wheel goods, as would have been the case with such firms as the Globe Co. and Hamilton Steel Products. Other prewar firms included Hill-Standard Co., Otto Konigslow Mfg. Co., Kuniholm Mfg. Co., Lewis baby Carriage Supply Co., Milwaukee Stamping Co., Schmid Bros., Special Stamping & Mfg. Co., Steel Materials Co., U.S. Pressed Steel Products Co., Universal Steel Co., and E.R. Wagner Mfg. Co.

Metalcraft Corp.
Founded in 1920 in St. Louis, Mo., to produce playground equip-

M

ment, Metalcraft began producing pressed-steel toy trucks in 1928, and acquired rights to issue a version of Lindbergh's "Spirit of St. Louis" in pressed steel and part of its "Metalcraft Airfield" line of the '20s. The firm also manufactured toy truck premiums, known as "Business Leaders."

Metalcraft's big seller at the end of the 1920s was the "Metalcraft Flyer Construction Set," a kit that made a 24-inch wingspread metal airplane, capable of flying and doing stunts. The company also issued "Graf Zeppelin" construction sets, hangars, mooring masts, and beacon lights in its "Airfield" line.

In the 1930s, the company made steel toys, children's vehicles, wagons, velocipedes, and scooters. The "Scamp" coaster wagon featured "Airplane Pants-Type Fenders," electric headlights, and a "streamlined" handle. Its line also included the "Ride-A-Way" velocipede, "Master" and "Standard" scooters, and "Play Pal" express wagon. Its firm continued in operation until 1937.

Metalectric Corp. Established in Waterloo, Iowa, in the late 1930s, Metalectric issued "Frontier" games of exploration and development, and the "Sport-o'Kings" racing game.

"Metallophone" musical instruments see *The A. Schoenhut Co.*

"Metaltone" see *Banner Plastics Corp.*

Metcalf Mfg. Co. Based in Los Angeles, Calif., in the late 1930s, Metcalf issued "Gold Seal" wood-burning sets and handmade toy sailboats.

Meth Novelty Co. Based on East 22nd Street, New York City, Meth Novelty made stuffed animals, including animal toys on wheels, in the 1930s and '40s.

Metro Mfg. Co. The "Bookgames," a library of miniature games in leatherette covers, were wartime products of this West 25th Street, New York City, company.

"Metropolitan" baby carriage see *American-National Co.*

Metropolitan Fur Toy Co. This Sixth Avenue, New York City, company made postwar stuffed fur toys.

"Meteor" marbles see *Master Marble Co.*

Metropolitan Motion Picture Co. "Everything in motion pictures," this West 34th Street, New York City, boasted of offering in the 1920s. It issued 35 mm. and 16 mm. films.

Mettoy Playcraft Ltd. founded 1934, see *Corgi Toys*.

"Mexican Jumping Beans" see *jumping beans*.

Meyer Rubber Co. Established in Cuyoga Falls, Ohio, in the late 1930s, Meyer made rubber jump ropes and slingshots.

Miami Wood Products Co. A manufacturer of playground equipment, this Miami, Fla., company made mid-1930s hand cars, sand pails and shovels, and mechanical toy boats.

The Miami Wood Specialty Co. Based in Dayton, Ohio, this prewar company made wooden toys in the 1930s and '40s.

"Micas" A translucent or transparent glass marble with mica-flake enclosures are called "Micas." Clear, blue, green, amber and red glass was used.

W.E. Michaels Products The "Planeteer" card game and "Planet-Stiks" pick-up sticks were early 1960s products of this Los Angeles, Calif., specialist in participation games.

Michigan City Paper Box Co. This Michigan City, Ind., firm made prewar games. Its titles included "Michigan Rhummy" and "Pitch Poker," in the later 1930s.

Michigan Specialty Co. Established in Holland, Mich., in the later prewar years, Michigan Specialty made hobbyhorses, doll highchairs, and nursery and juvenile furniture.

Michigan Wire Goods Co. This Niles, Mich. company issued the "Dolly Ann" all-metal toy bedroom furniture of the 1920s.

"Mickey Mantle" As did other sports heroes, Mickey Mantle inspired game and plaything tie-ins, including "Mickey Mantle's Big League Baseball" and "Mickey Mantle Grand Slam" games by Gardner & Co., and a plastic figure by Hartland Plastics.

"Mickey Mouse" Immediately after the success of Walt Disney's early "Mickey Mouse" animated films came the success of "Mickey Mouse" toys, which were issued in a bewildering variety in the 1930s.

Toys of that decade included airplanes and boats by the Straits Corp., balloons by Oak Rubber Co., banks by Zell Products Co., blackboards by Richmond School Furniture Co., blocks by Halsam Products Co., brief cases by Standard Brief Case Co., a climbing toy by the Dolly Toy Co., costumes by Wornova Mfg. Co., crayon and coloring books by the Saalfield Publishing Co., crepe paper novelties by Dennison Mfg. Co., games and toys by Marks Bros. Co., and a railroad-set hand car by Lionel Corp.

Others included "Mickey Mouse" infant toys by Richard Krueger, jack sets by U.S. Lock & Hardware Co., movie projectors by Keystone Mfg. Co., picture puzzles by Saalfield, playhouses by O.B. Andrews Co., playsuits by Sackman Bros. Co., pop-up books by Blue Ribbon Books, purses by King Innovations, rubber stamps by Fulton Specialty Co., rubber toys by Seiberling Latex Products Co., sand toys by Ohio Art Co., story books by Saalfield, David McKay, and Whitman Publishing Co., stuffed toys by Knickerbocker Toy Co., telephones and bell chimes by N.N. Hill Brass Co., and miscellaneous toys and dolls by George Borgfeldt Corp. "Mickey and Minnie" treasure chests were also issued by Zell Products.

By the late prewar years, new "Mickey Mouse" items included banks by Crown Toy Mfg. Co., "Beetleware" dishes by Bryant Electric Co., blocks by Halsam Products Co., the "Mickey Mouse Choo Choo" by Fisher-Price Toys, Christmas lights by Noma Electric Corp., films by Hollywood Film Enterprises, flashlights by United States Electrical Mfg. Corp., jack sets by U.S. Lock & Hardware Co., kits and school bags by Columbia Products Corp., and kites by Marks Bros.

Others included marionettes by Alexander Doll Co., movie projectors by Keystone Mfg. Co., pencil sharpeners by Plastic Novelties, a piano by Keystone, paint books by Saalfield Publishing Co., portable table tennis by Commonwealth Toy & Novelty Co., rubber stamps by Fulton Specialty Co., rubber toys by Seiberling Latex Products Co., sleds by S.L. Allen & Co., stuffed toys by Knickerbocker Toy Co., telephones and bell chimes by N.N. Hill Brass Co., toy chests by Odora Mfg. Co., toys and dolls by George Borgfeldt Corp., sand toys by Ohio Art Co., "Transfer-O-S" sets for Easter eggs by Paas Dye Co., and transfer albums also by Paas.

Postwar items included archery and croquet sets by Withington; basketball game by Gardner & Co.; "Electric Arithmetic" and other math games by Jacmar Mfg. Co.; "Funny Rummy" by Russell Mfg. Co.; hats by Benay-Albee Novelty Co.; inflated toys by Kestrel Corp.; "Library of Games" by Russell Mfg. Co.; paint and crayon sets by Transogram Co.; puzzles by Parker Bros.; "Mickey Mouse Rhythm Band" and "Tap-A-Tune" musical toy by Emenee Industries; and sand sets by Eldon Mfg. Co.

The "Mickey Mouse Toll Bank," 1930s by N.N. Hill Brass Co.

M

Seiberling Latex Products' rubber toy Mickey Mouse, 1930s.

"Mickey Mouse Club" The popular TV show, which had its debut in 1955, inspired playthings from the 1950s through the '60s, when the episodes were enjoyed as re-runs. Among the most notable playthings was the "Official Mousegetar," issued by Mattel through the late '50s. Other items from the 1950s-60s included a miniature golf game by Transogram Co., a TV chair by Himalayan Pak Co., a "Mousketeer" water pistol by Knickerbocker Plastic Co., and miscellaneous playthings by Whitman Publishing Co.

Micro-Lite Co., Inc. Based on West 25th Street, New York City, in the late 1930s, this firm issued the "Microlite Flash-Gun."

microphones and related toys Such electrical voice-throwing and voice-carrying toys as megaphones and microphones frequently served a toy purpose, with a good many manufactured, especially during the Boomer years, specifically for children. A number of prewar companies associated with the toy trade did produce these items, however. The substantial public interest in matters relating to electricity and the new and popular medium of the radio included widespread interest by children in scientific sets of the same nature. Microphone manufacturers included Connecticut Telephone & Electric Corp., Federal Stamping and Engineering Corp., the Newman-Stern Co., Sheridan Electro Units Corp, and Wonder Products, Inc. Megaphone makers included Leigh A. Elkington, Marks Bros. Co., Merriman Bros., and G.C. Willett & Co.

Mid-West Doll Mfg. Corp. The "Bee-Bee" doll of the late 1930s was issued by this

St. Louis, Mo., firm. The doll could say "Papa" and "Mama."

Mid-West Metal Products Co. A metal specialties company based in Niles, Mich., Mid-West included toys and juvenile swings among its prewar products.

The Middleton Mfg. Co., Inc. Based in Middleton, Conn., this late 1930s firm issued metal doll furniture.

"Midgees" see *Dowst Mfg. Co.*

"Midget" house-building toys prewar, see *Rite Mfg. Co.*

"Midget" transformers see *Jefferson Electric Co.*

Midgetlab Co., The Chemistry outfits were made by this prewar St. Louis, Mo., firm.

Midgetoy A.&E. Tool & Gage Co. of Rockford, Ill., turned to die-cast toy production in 1946. Its early toys included a Chevy truck with interchangeable bodies, space ship, futuristic car and racecars. The firm added car and truck models, airplanes, and trailers through the years, as well as four sets of toy trains, all issued under the "Midgetoy" name. The firm was briefly owned by an investment group in the early 1980s before being returned to its original owners and closed.

"Midgets" utensils see *Aluminum Goods Mfg. Co.*

Midland Wire & Metal Products Founded in the late 1930s in Chicago, Ill., Midland made "modernistic" juvenile metal table and chair sets.

Midway Novelty Co. This Laurel, Md., company made prewar stuffed animals.

Midwest Industries Velocipedes, bicycles, juvenile tractors and autos, and sand boxes were specialties of this Willard, Ohio, company.

Midwest Mfg. Co. A Boomer-era juvenile furniture manufacturer, this Eaton, Ohio, company included toy chests, shooflies, and doll cradles in its line.

M

Midwest Products Co. Based in Kellogg, Iowa, Midwest Products issued the "Tally-Bell" basketball sets and games of the late 1930s. It also issued the 1939 "Tak-Tiks" basketball board game. In the postwar years, as a division of Midwest Metal Stamping Co., it issued "Tally-Bell" basketball sets.

Midwestern Mfg. Co. Based in St. Louis, Mo., Midwestern made postwar character dolls.

Midwestern Publishing Co. The "Auto-Bingo" and "License-Bingo" games of the Boomer years were published by this Lincoln, Neb., firm.

"Mighty-Metal Toys" Hubley Mfg. Co. offered the "Mighty Metal Toys" series in the early 1960s. The die-cast line included a log truck, two dump trucks, stake truck, tow truck, fire engine, tractor, "cultipacker" and plow set, M.G. sports car, and folding-wing airplane. Most of the models measured 8-1/2 or 10 inches long.

"Mighty Mouse" The heroic TV mouse inspired playthings including hats by Magnet Hat & Cap Corp., and books by Grosset & Dunlap Inc.

Millburn Mills, Inc. A manufacturer of such items as Christmas stockings and table tennis nets in the 1930s, Millburn Mills specialized in marble bags and marble bag nettings in the 1930s. It was located in Quidnick, R.I. In the Boomer years, based on West 34th Street, New York City, its specialties remained Christmas stockings and marble bags, among other items.

Miller, Charles E. Based in Rochester, N.Y., Miller made the late 1930s "Graphoscope" game.

Miller, Clarence E. This Philadelphia, Penn., company made masquerade suits and wigs in the 1930s and '40s.

Miller Bros. Hat Co. Western hats were among this Fifth Avenue, New York City, firms postwar specialties.

Melvin G. Miller Co., Inc. Gun belts, holsters, and belt accessories comprised the line of this postwar Houston, Texas, company.

The M.H. Miller Co., Inc. A beach and lawn furniture manufacturer, the M.H. Miller Co. also made prewar juvenile pool tables and games. Early game titles of the 1910s and '20s included "Brownie Horseshoe Game," "Brownie Kick-In Top," and "Brownie Ring Toss." The company continued in operation into the mid-1930s.

Esther Miller Doll Creations, Inc. A Brooklyn, N.Y., firm, Esther Miller made postwar stuffed toys.

Miller Hall, Inc. The "Junior Jet" exerciser and action toy of the 1950s-60s was this Portland, Ore., firm's product.

J.H. Miller Mfg. Co. This Quincy, Ill., company made the "Earth Invaders" polyethylene figurines.

Miller Moderns Pre-school toys were the specialty of this postwar Orangeburg, S.C., company.

Miller Rubber Products Co., Inc. Rubber dolls, balls, and inflated toys were made in the 1930s by this Akron, Ohio, company. It made the popular baby dolls "My Dolly" and "Baby Glee," in its "The Miller Gang" line. By the end of the decade it was the Miller Rubber Toy Division of the B.F. Goodrich Co.

Milprint Products Corp. A Milwaukee, Wis., company, Milprint made prewar lithographed cardboard cut-out toy houses and other toys.

Milton Bradley, Co. see under *Bradley*

William G. Minder Industries Vinyl animal toys were products of this Boomer-era Atlanta, Ga., company. It also made nightlights.

Alexander Miner Sales Corp. Doll accessories including cradles, nursers, bottle carriers, vanity sets, carrying cases, and luggage were specialties of this Boomer-era firm, based in the Fifth Avenue Building, New York City. It also made plastic snap toys.

M

Miner's, Inc. Established on East 12th Street, New York City, in the late 1930s, Miner's issued "Gang Busters" and movie make-up kits.

"Minerva" juvenile auto see *Toledo Metal Wheel Co.*

Minerva Toy Co. In addition to embroidery, sewing and painting sets, this Brooklyn, N.Y., firm made kindergarten toys, doll trunks, and doll outfits in the 1930s and '40s. The "Nun-Sister" dolls were introduced in the late '30s. The company also made hand puppets and marionettes in the 1950s and '60s.

Miniature Boat Shop The "E-Z" craft boat kits of the late 1930s were issued by this Evanston, Ill., firm.

"Miniature Famous Cartoon Characters" see *Marshall Field & Co.*

Miniature Homes Co. Toy house construction sets were the specialty of this Mount Carmel, Conn., company in the 1930s and '40s.

Miniature Hurdy Gurdy Co. This Chicago, Ill., firm issued "Music Box" hand organs in the late 1930s.

Miniature Ship Models Based in Perkasic, Penn., this company made ship models, coach models, and a miniature weaving loom in the 1930s and '40s.

Minnesota Mining & Mfg. Co. Famous for its "Scotch Brand" cellophane tape, this St. Paul, Minn., company, also known as "3M," issued the game "Win, Place, and Show" in the '40s. It continued issuing games in subsequent decades, usually with sport themes.

Minnesota Toy Mfg. Co. This St. Paul, Minn., firm issued the "Automatic Baseball" game of the 1920s.

"Minnie Mouse" see *"Mickey Mouse."*

"Minute Man" steam train see *American Flyer Mfg. Co.*

"Mira-Toy" automotive toys see *Barr Rubber Products Co.*

Mirinco Toys, Inc. The "Rusty Rabbit & Friends" plastic construction toy and "Satellite to the Moon" game of the 1950s-60s were issued by this Storm Lake, Iowa, company.

"Mirro Fairyland" toy sets see *Aluminum Goods Mfg. Co.*

"Mirror Magic" see *Wonder-Art Enterprises.*

"Mirroscope" postcard projectors see *Metal Stamping & Mfg. Co.*

Misner Corp. Gas-powered midget autos were specialties of this postwar Omaha, Neb., company.

"Miss America" baby carriage see *Hartman Mfg. Co.*

"Miss Babette" dolls see *Bouton, Woolf Co.;* postwar, see *Roberta Doll Co.*

The Miss Barbara Co., Inc. Educational games including "Color Readiness" dominoes were produced by this Somersworth, N.H., firm. It also issued "Keno."

"Miss Corona" sets see *Corona Hat Co.*

"Miss Dolly Boo" rolling pins see the *Fli-Back Sales Corp.*

"Miss Moppet" dolls see *Ruth Gibbs.*

missile and launcher toys A new category of toys for the Boomer years that probably went unpredicted in the prewar years, missile and launcher toys were an important part of the toy scene in the 1950s and '60s. Although some were simply model rocket toys, and others were structurally identical to earlier spring cannons, some were distinctively different from earlier toys, such as the water rockets made by Park Plastics Co., which used water pressure to launch the plastic rocket into the air.

Park was one of the innovative companies in the rocket and space-toy field. Its "Salvo" rockets could be fired from a remote platform, which was capable of launching up to three rockets at a time. The "Parachute" rocket had a "space pilot" inside, who burst free at the rocket's greatest height and parachuted to earth. Park's "Planet Patrol Saucer" was fired from a gun, flying to a height of 60 feet.

Other manufacturers included Action Toy Co., Adams Action Models, Boyd Specialty Co., Clever Things, Dennis Play Products, Gladen Enterprises, Hawk Model Co., Ideal Toy Corp., Kenner Products Co., Knickerbocker Plastic Co., Kohner Bros., Fred Kroll Associates, Lindberg Products, Inc., Mattel, Monogram Models, Multiple Products Corp., and Ny-Lint Tool & Mfg. Co.

"Mr. Potato Head" see *Hassenfeld Bros., Inc.*

"Mr. Wiggle" see *Wilkening Mfg. Co.*

Mistress Patty P. Comfort In the 1930s, this Cambridge, Mass., company made animal-shaped household items and floating bath toys. In 1934 it recorded having "Peter Rabbit," lamb, and Scotty dog hot water bottles, and "Lucky Ducky," frog, Scotty, and turtle soap dishes.

Dennis Mitchell Industries Based in Philadelphia, Penn., in the postwar years, Dennis Mitchell manufactured wheel goods including bicycles, tricycles, and carriages, play ponies, and toys.

Mitchell Mfg. Co. This 1920s manufacturer of playground equipment, including the "Tilt-Top Sand Box" and "Swing Bob" gyms, was based in Milwaukee, Wis. In the 1930s and '40s it issued the "Betterbilt" playground equipment.

The "Swing Bob" gym, Mitchell Mfg. Co., 1920s.

Mitten Toy Mfg. Co., Inc. Washable stuffed toys, musical toy animals, and puppets were among this Broadway, New York City, company's Boomer-era products.

"Mity Mite" click guns see *Peerless Playthings Co.*

"Mixi" see *Famous Products Corp.*

Mizpah Toy & Novelty Corp. Based on Wooster Street, New York City, in the 1920s, Mizpah made crushed plush animals and novelties. The firm may have been founded in Mizpah, N.J., where it was located, or again located, by the 1930s and '40s. In the prewar years the firm issued "Pixy" felt dolls and animals, which continued to be its lead items through the Boomer years.

"Moby Dick" mechanical whale see *F.M. Engineering Co.*

"Mobylette" bicycles see *Chain Bike Corp.*

"Mocar" see *The Mount Carmel Mfg. Co.*

"Mod-L-Stix" construction sets see the *Vogel Mfg. Co.*

The Mode Novelty Co. Juvenile cowboy and rodeo hats, party hats, baseball caps, sailor and yacht caps, and felt rugs were specialties of this Newark, N.J., firm, established in the late 1930s.

Model Airplane Utility Co. The "Skyability" kits and airplane supplies of the late 1930s were issued by this Brooklyn, N.Y., company. It also made solid scale-model airplane and boat kits.

Model Crafts Co. A Washington, D.C., firm, Model Crafts issued aerial toys and model airplane cement in the late 1930s.

Model Doll House Co. Based in Miami, Fla., this company made all-wood doll houses in the 1930s and '40s.

model kits Model kits provided entertainment for children and adults for most of the 20th century. The kits included pre-formed pieces made of wood, metal or plastic which

M

could be assembled and decorated into a toy or display item.

Model Pet see *Asahi Toy Co.*

Model Ship Supply Co. Boat construction sets and fittings for model ships were issued by this Mineola, N.Y., company, in the 1930s and '40s.

"Model Toys" see *Charles Wm. Doepke Mfg. Co.*

Model Weapons, Inc. Miniature rifle hobby kits were specialties of this Oceanside, Calif., firm.

modeling clay Modeling clay in itself excites little collector interest, although the packaging can sometimes be of significant interest. These packages still sometimes turn up with the original sticks of clay or plasticene inside. As an activity toy, modeling clay surely ranks among the more important, giving children the greatest imaginable freedom to create items out of their imagination.

Prewar manufacturers of the clay included some of the bigger players in the toy business, including American Crayon Co., Milton Bradley Co., the Embossing Co., Marks Bros. Co., and Prang Co. Other firms included Alberhill Coal & Clay Co., American Art Clay Co., the Fox Toy Co., Harrop Ceramic Service Co., Illinois Clay Products Co., Magic Mould Mfg. Co., Standard Toykraft Products, and United Clay Mines Corp.

Dozens of companies became involved in the Boomer years. The most important may have been Rainbow Crafts Co., which introduced "Play-Doh Modeling Compound" in 1956 under its earlier incarnation, Kutol Chemicals. By the end of the decade the company was billing its four-color four-pack of the nontoxic modeling dough as the "World's Best-Selling $1 Toy." The most famous "Play-Doh" accessory was the "Fun Factory Toy Extruder," introduced in 1960.

Modeloom Co. A Woonsocket, R.I., company, Modeloom made prewar juvenile weaving looms.

Models of Industry, Inc. Based in Berkeley, Calif., in the Boomer years, Models of Industry issued "Learn-by-Doing" educa-

tional kits on weather, electricity, optics, and geology. The firm also manufactured a model oil field and model oil refinery.

"Models of Merit" kits see *Ace Products.*

Modern Brands, Inc. The "Imp" puzzle and "Impie" game of the mid-1930s was made by this West 42nd Street, New York City, company.

Modern Brush & Mop Corp. This Broadway, New York City, company issued toy mops and brushes, in the 1950s and '60s.

The Modern Crafts Co. Pine toy chests, rocking horses, and sandboxes were this St. Louis, Mo., company's products.

Modern Doll Furniture A Boomer-era company based in Chatham, N.Y., this firm issued doll carriages, cradles, swings, chests and highchairs, of reed and wood construction.

"Modern Miss" laundry sets prewar, see *Buffalo Toy & Tool Works.*

"Modern Miss" products see *C.G. Wood Co.*

Modern Model Engineers This Beaver Dam, Wis., firm designed special scale model airplanes and kits in the late 1930s.

Modern Model Shop Established in Fort Worth, Texas, in the late 1930s, Modern Model Shop made airplane and boat kits.

Modern Research Development Co. The "Play-Make" indoor-outdoor construction toy of the early 1960s was a product of this Mansfield, Ohio, firm.

Modern Toy Co. Children's mobiles, puppet theaters, train pull-toys, and felt doll kits were specialties of this postwar Chicago, Ill., company.

"Moderne" juvenile furniture see *The Delphos Bending Co.*

"Modernistik" toys prewar, see *American Made Toy Co.*

Moen & Patton, Inc. "Flying Ace" roller skates and "Rocket" ice skates were issued by this Lancaster, Penn., firm in the postwar years. It also made "Tiny Tot" beginner skates, "Flying Ace" golf sets and garden tools, "Drum Major" batons, and "Midget Slugger" baseball sets.

The Mohican Rubber Co. One of a number of rubber companies established in the state of Ohio, this Ashland firm made toy, novelty, and advertising balloons in the 1930s and '40s, and through the postwar years.

"Mold More Toys," prewar see *Russell Mfg. Co.*

molded-in driver The driver in some rubber, vinyl and plastic vehicles is part of the general body mold. Auburn did this in all three materials, particularly in racecars and tractors. See also cast-in driver.

molded pulp toys A lowly but useful material, molded pulp toys, also known as fiber toys and sometimes perhaps as cardboard toys, had their place in most prewar and early postwar childhoods. In strength and durability, molded pulp stood below composition, which typically included solidifying and strengthening agents besides pulp. Especially common were various holiday toys made of the material, including Easter bunnies and Halloween jack-o-lanterns that must have been made by the millions, year after year. Prewar manufacturers included the Maurer Paint Co., Old King Cole, Pulp Reproduction Co., and United Pressed Products Co.

Moline Pressed Steel see *Buddy "L" Mfg. Co.*

Molly-'Es Doll Outfitters, Inc. The Philadelphia, Penn., firm of Molly-'Es offered the "very latest ideas in beautiful doll's clothes, carriage sets, knitted goods, and brushed wool sets" in the 1920s. The company continued making doll accessories and novelties, including carriage sets, bed sets, mattresses, and luncheon sets, in its 1930s and '40s lines. By the late 1930s it was also manufacturing dolls, including international dolls, mama dolls, and baby dolls.

Monarch Leather Goods Co. Monarch issued Boomer-era pistol holster sets. It was based in Greeneville, Tenn.

The Monarch Products Co. Based in Tiffin, Ohio, Monarch made children's vehi-cles, scooters, "safety cycles," pedal cars, and baby walkers. Its lines included the mid-1930s "Monarch Master" velocipedes and "King Flyer" coaster wagons.

Monark Silver King, Inc. Established in Chicago, Ill., in the late 1930s, Monark made aluminum bicycles and velocipedes under the "Silver King" trade name, and "super-frame" steel bicycles under the "Monark" name.

The Moneco Co. A New Haven, Conn., firm, Moneco made playballs and sports, punching bags, boxing gloves, medicine balls, and the "Yale shadow ball" in the 1930s and '40s. Its "Razzle Dazzle" miniature footballs were hits for the company in the late '30s. Moneco also made "official sporting goods" for the 1939 New York World's Fair. The firm continued issuing sporting goods through the Boomer years.

money, toy If any children in the 20th century went through childhood without having play money in their hands at some point, their numbers must have been extremely few. Play money was issued in separate packages as a toy in itself, especially useful in playing store. More commonly children encountered it in playing such popular games as "Monopoly" and "The Game of Life." Prewar manufacturers of play money included S.S. Adams Co., American Toy Works, Milton Bradley Co., Parker Bros., Playgames, William Rott, George E. Schweig & Son, and Zain-Eppy.

Mono Bridge, Inc. Established on Fifth Avenue, New York City, in the late 1930s, Mono Bridge issued a solitaire contract bridge game, and "Ma Jong" games.

Monogram Models Construction kits to assemble boats, airplanes, racecars, military subjects, and missiles were issued by this Chicago, Ill., firm in the 1950s and '60s.

"Monoplane" sled see *American Acme Co.*

M

"Monopoly" The original "Monopoly" was issued in 1934 by Charles Brace Darrow. All later versions were produced by Parker Bros. While prewar editions contained die-cast metal playing pieces, wartime sets had wooden markers. Die-cast pieces returned after World War II.

"Monopoly," one of Parker Bros.' most popular games.

"Monorail" electric railway 1930s, see *Leland Detroit Mfg. Co.*

"Monotrain" 1930s, see *Leland Detroit Mfg. Co.*

The Monroe Co. Monroe of Colfax, Iowa, made "play villas" in the late prewar years.

Monroe Fabricators Based in Chicago, Ill., Monroe issued postwar inflatable toys and swimming accessories.

Monroe Luggage Co. A manufacturer located on West 17th Street, New York City, Monroe Luggage Co. issued 1939 "Snow White and the Seven Dwarfs" school bags and brief cases.

Monroe Mfg. Co. The "Will'E Dance" dancing toy of the late 1930s was issued by this Chicago, Ill., firm.

The Montanaris The Montanaris of London are credited with having introduced the first infant or baby dolls, showing them at London's Crystal Palace Exposition in London, in 1851. Some of these expensive wax creations became available in the United States.

Montclair Mfg. Co. Based in Montclair, N.J., this late prewar firm issued games for adults and educational kindergarten toys.

Montello Products Circular sleds were among this Ripon, Wis., firm's Boomer-era products.

Montpelier Mfg. Co. Based in Montpelier, Vt., this firm made sleds, wagons and carriages. It purchased Colby Bros. in the 1870s.

Moon Mfg. Co. "Rocket Shoes" were this South Gate, Calif., company's spring-shoes, in the 1950s and '60s.

"Moon Mullins" The famous 1920 comic strip "Moon Mullins," by Willard, featured the characters "Moon Mullins" and "Kayo." These cartoon creations appeared in a variety of prewar playthings, including crayon and paint books by McLoughlin Bros.; a "Moon Mullins" game by Milton Bradley Co.; Louis Marx & Co.'s "Moon Mullins & Kayo" hand car. Adler-Jones Co., which specialized in retail display items, made "Moon Mullins & Kayo" units for stores. The McLoughlin Bros. and Milton Bradley Co. titles remained popular items through the late 1930s. "Moon Mullins" rights were controlled by Famous Artists Syndicate.

B. Shackman & Co.'s "Moon Mullins" figures, 1920s.

"Moon Rocket" launching toy see *Boyd Specialty Co., Onc.*

Moonglow Plastic Jewel Corp. "Bubble gum banks" and target dart guns were produced by this Fifth Avenue, New York

City, company. Active in the Boomer years, the company also made doll accessories and parts for toys and games for other manufacturers.

Moore, Clement C. see *Visit from St. Nicholas.*

William Moore Mfg. Co. Postwar manufacturer William Moore of Knoxville, Tenn., specialized in solid mahogany doll furniture.

Moorman Game Co., Inc. Based on West 40th Street, New York City, Moorman made the prewar "Bag-A-Ball" golf game.

A.C. Morand Corp. The San Francisco, Calif., firm of A.C. Morand made the mid-1930s "Broncho Bob" juvenile cowboy outfits, including holsters.

Morden Doll Corp. This doll firm was based on Canal Street, New York City, in the Boomer years.

The Mordt Co. In the 1920s, the Mordt Co. of Chicago, Ill., enjoyed its "all-American" rope exercise and play set, "The Mordt Gym Set," which consisted of cross-bar, ropes, and hand rings, with a swing which could be suspended by the rings. Sets sold from $1.50 to $5.00. The firm also issued ring toss and "Bowling on the Green" games, but probably enjoyed most public prominence for issuing the "Tom Mix Rodeorope," touted as "the only perfectly balanced rope."

By the post-Great Depression years, Mordt moved to North Plymouth, Mass. The playground equipment manufacturer lines then also included cowboy outfits, cowboy trappings, holsters and guns, jump ropes, lariats, and tool chests. By the late '30s, having moved again to Port Washington, Long Island, N.Y., the firm adopted the name Mordt Playthings.

Mordt Playthings issued indoor and outdoor gyms, sand boxes, baby swings, table golf games, lariats, jump ropes, toy chests, doll cradles and beds, shuffleboard, and ring toss games.

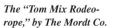

The "Tom Mix Rodeorope," by The Mordt Co.

More-Craft Sales Co. Based on Fifth Avenue, New York City, More-Craft made a steel building toys in the mid-1930s.

Morehead Character Doll Co. Based in New Market, Va., Morehead made "Virginia Maid" soft dolls in the late 1930s.

Morgan, E.H. and Charles see *Arcade Mfg. Co.*

The Morilla Co. Numbered paint sets were this East 23rd Street, New York City, company's specialty in the Boomer years.

Morimura Bros., Inc. Based on West 23rd Street, New York City, in the 1920s and '30s, Morimura issued the "Little Hostess" toy tea sets.

Morisite Mfg. Co. The 1930s "Plak-Art" paint sets were made by this Detroit, Mich., firm.

The Morison Co. Based in Detroit, Mich., the Morison Co. made the mid-1930s "Loom Craft" weaver.

G.W. Morris, Inc. Based in Portland, Maine, G.W. Morris made Christmas items, including Santa Claus items and stockings, in the 1930s.

J. Morris & Co. Part of the burgeoning electric Christmas lighting industry of the later 1930s, Morris issued lighting outfits and wreaths.

Morris Mfg. Co. Established in Lexington, N.C., in the late 1930s, Morris issued the "Boo-Boo Ring-A-Pin" game.

Morris Products Co. The "Design Blox" of the late 1930s were issued by this Kansas City, Mo., firm.

Morris-Systems Publishing This Detroit, Mich., firm issued "The 400, Aristocrat of Games" game of 1933, and the "Gamevelope" card game of 1944. The "400" game enjoyed popularity through the prewar decade.

Morrison Brushes, Inc. Based in Glen Falls, N.Y., Morrison issued "Bristle Archery," "Bris-Targ," "Little Mother's Helper," and "Ring-Toss" in the 1920s.

"Mortimer Snerd" see *Edgar Bergen.*

Morton, Henry R. Based in Paris, Maine, Henry F. Morton started selling sleds through retailer Peabody & Whitney in 1861. The firm moved to nearby Paris Hill in 1870, becoming Paris Hill Mfg. Co. and in 1883 to South Paris. After being removed from his position as plant superintendent due to illness, he and loyal workers joined the Binghamton Sled Co. of Binghamton, N.Y. When the Maine firm went bankrupt in two years, Morton bought the firm's assets and formed Paris Mfg. Co.

"Mosaic" games see *Samuel Gabriel Sons & Co.*

"Mot-O-Boat Konstructor" 1930s, see *The Boy Toymaker, Co.*

"Mother Goose" Thomas Fleet, a Boston printer, published the book *Songs for the Nursery, or Mother Goose's Melodies,* in 1719. The contained verses have been attributed to various sources. One candidate is Mrs. Elizabeth Vergoose, who liked to sing verses to her grandson, who happened to be Thomas Fleet's son.

Mother Goose and the characters contained in the books' rhymes became popular figures in a variety of 1800s and 1900s toys and games, with one of the earliest being the popular "Mother Goose Bowling Game" of 1884, by Charles M. Crandall.

Prewar "Mother Goose" items included a Milton Bradley Co. game, a doll by Samuel Gabriel Sons & Co., paint books by Stoll & Einson Games, a playhouse by the Hettrick Mfg. Co., a "playtray" by Holgate Bros. Co., stuffed toys by the Rushton Co., and a series of banks by Zell Products Corp. In the late '30s the Embossing Co. issued "Mother Goose" blocks.

Playthings of the postwar years included balls by Sidney A. Tarrson, coloring books and paper dolls by the Saalfield Publishing Co., dolls by Nancy Ann Storybook Dolls, and nursery pin-ups by Dolly Toy Co.

"Mother's Choice" shoofly 1930s, see *The Delphos Bending Co.*

motion picture projectors see *moving picture projectors.*

"Moto-Bike" bicycle 1930s, see *Steinfeld.*

Moto-Scoot Mfg. Co. This Chicago, Ill., firm made the "Moto-Scoot" motor-driven scooter of the late 1930s.

"Moto-Trike" police velocipede see *Evans Products Co.*

"Motobecane" bicycle see *Chain Bike Corp.*

"Motor Cop" bicycle see *The American-National Co.*

"Motorcycle Mike" see *American Flyer Mfg. Co.*

motors and transformers, toy Toy motors and transformers became important in the prewar years, due especially to the popularity of electric trains. Manufacturers included such major train-toy manufacturers as American Flyer Mfg. Co., the Dorfan Co., and the Lionel Corp. Other firms included American Toy Airship Co., Boucher Playthings Mfg. Corp., A.R. Darling Electric Co., Dayton Art Metal Co., Dongan Electric Mfg. Co., Dremel Mfg. Co., A.C. Gilbert Co., Hedason Mfg. Co., Hoge Mfg. Co., Jefferson Electric Co., Knapp Electric Inc., Leland Detroit Mfg. Co., the Meccano Co. of America, the Metal Ware Corp., George W. Moore, A.G. Redmond Co., A.E. Rittenhouse Co., Signal Electric Mfg. Co., the Straits Corp., and Weinig Products Co.

M

motors, spring Manufacturers supplying other toy companies included prewar firms Boucher Playthings Mfg. Corp., Forsyth Metal Goods Co., the E.F. Griffiths Co., Hedason Mfg. Co., Ingersoll-Waterbury Co., H.A. Smith Machine Co., and Waterbury Button Co.

Moudy, W. Howard Wooden toys including toy animals, games, and blackboards were made in the 1930s and '40s by this Portage, Penn., manufacturer of children's furniture.

Moulded Products, Inc. Rocking horses were this Maple Plain, Minn., firm's specialty in the 1950s and '60s. In 1969 the company introduced the "Pogo Pony," a riding horse toy with spring legs capable of bouncing the toy and rider off the floor.

The Mount Carmel Mfg. Co. "The Mocar Model Airplanes That Fly" was a line of flying toys made of aluminum construction in the 1920s, listing at $1.25. Mount Carmel was located in New Haven, Conn.

Mount Vernon Mfg. Co. Specialists in pistol holsters, Mount Vernon was based on Eagle Avenue, New York City, in the Boomer years.

"Mousegetar" see *Mattel.*

"Mouseketeers" see *"Mickey Mouse Club."*

George E. Mousley, Inc. From the 1920s through the prewar years, Mousely manufactured Christmas stockings, Santa Claus bags, Easter rabbits and toy grips filled with toys. Based in Philadelphia, Penn., the company used the "G.E.M. Brand" trademark. It continued to make Christmas stockings, net stockings for general purposes, and toy accessories through the wartime and Boomer years.

The "G.E.M. Christmas Stocking," 1920s, by George E. Mousley, Inc.

"Movie Moods" games prewar, see *Transo Products.*

"Movie Stars" boudoir dolls prewar, see *Tru-Craft Novelty Co.*

moving picture projectors Soon after the advent of movies, the home movie show had its own debut. A number of companies supplied not only films and projectors, but sometimes the cameras, too. Many of the items were especially designed to appeal to children.

Two companies, Keystone Mfg. and Paramount Mfg., issued all three: movie cameras, films, and projectors. Prewar manufacturers associated with the toy trade included Ace Mfg. Co., A.B. Cummings Co., Durable Toy & Novelty Corp., Excel Projector Corp., Keystone Mfg. Co., Movie-Jecktor Co., Myers Mfg. Organization, Nic Projector Corp., Paramount Mfg. Co., Trojan Sporting Goods Co. While several of them also made films, a few firms focused primarily on issuing those reels, including Exclusive Film Service and Novelty Film Co.

By the late prewar years, moving picture films for home viewing became an important category in the toy and playthings industry. Important manufacturers included Buchheisster Films, Castle Films, Educational Films Corp. of America, Exclusive Movie Studios, Hollywood Film Enterprises, Irwin Corp., Keystone Mfg. Co., Novelty Film Co., Paramount Mfg. Co., Pathegrams, Screen Attractions, and Star Safety Film Co. More manufacturers were likewise issuing projectors, including Excel Projector Corp., Irwin

M

Corp., Keystone, the Lindstrom Tool & Toy Co., Paramount, and Stephens Products Co.

In the Boomer years, this toy category receded in importance, undoubtedly due to the millions of TV sets in households across the country. By the mid-Boomer years, only Castle Films and Hollywood Film Enterprises were issuing films, and only Brumberger Sales Corp. and Keystone Ferrule & Nut Co. manufactured children's projectors.

"J. Fred Muggs" bell toys see *N.N. Hill Brass Co.*

"Muralprint" see *The Beistle Co.*

Multiple Products Corp. Multiple

Products Corp., or "M.P.C.," was one of the most important manufacturers of dime store, convenience store, and chain department store toys in the 1950s and '60s, issuing fort sets, military sets, western sets, TV licensed toys, vehicles, fencing sets, and "girls' toys" in inexpensive plastic forms. Its plastic figures included cowboys and Indians, soldiers, and spacemen. Among its play sets were the 1955 "Ramar of the Jungle African Deluxe Set," with 84 plastic figures and accessories and die-cut box houses, and the 1964 "Fireball XL-5" boxed play sets, featuring vehicles, Space City, and Steve Zodiac and his crew.

"Multivolt" transformers see *The Lionel Corp.*

A.W. Mumford, Co. Following the 19th-

century trend to make games seem relevant and practical, A.W. Mumford Co. issued the "Game of Industries" in 1897.

Munroe & Francis The most prominent

publisher of children's books in the first half of the 1800s, Boston's Munroe & Francis issued *The Boy's Own Book,* a collection of games and recreation ideas, in 1829. In 1831 it published The *American Girl's Book*, or *Occupation for Play Hours,* by a Miss Leslie. Besides being a publisher, Munroe & Francis was a bookseller, with the firm's goods including paper dolls.

W.J. Murphy Co. Indian dolls, head-

dresses, beadwork and moccasins were among the postwar specialties of this Asheville, N.C., company. It also made metal cap pistols, holster sets, leather doll clothes, archery sets, and plastic dolls.

The Murray-Ohio Mfg. Co. The Mur-

ray Body Co. of Detroit, Mich., established this Cleveland, Ohio, subsidiary in 1919. Within four years the firm turned toward the making of juvenile autos, starting with vehicles based on White Truck Co. models. Through the 1920s it established its "Steelcraft" line, which enabled the firm to survive the Depression years. The "Steelcraft" pedal cars included Cadillacs, Huppmobiles, Lincolns, and Studebakers.

In the later 1930s and '40s it expanded its line, manufacturing toy automobiles, coaster wagons, scooters, steel toys, velocipedes, and sidewalk bicycles. It also established permanent display rooms in the Fifth Avenue Building, New York City.

During wartime, the company earned the Army-Navy "E" Award, for "outstanding production of war materials." It produced no toys.

Returning to wheel goods in the Boomer era, Murray-Ohio issued the "Champion" pedal car, which was its lead seller by the early 1950s. The firm moved to Nashville, Tenn., in 1957, and used the "Murray" trade name on its toys without eliminating the "Ohio" from its company name. It began manufacturing lightweight bicycles in 1965, and ceased producing pedal cars and other juvenile wheel goods in 1973.

Murray's "Good Humor Truck" pedal car, 1950s.

musical toys and instruments While the line between musical toys and instruments would be a difficult one to draw, the fact that children have consistently been handed such objects as drums, flutes, horns and stringed instruments through the centuries surely indicates that their toy nature, perhaps their educational toy nature, is a strong one.

Prewar manufacturers included not only famed toy makers, such as the A. Schoenhut Co. and Wolverine Supply & Mfg. Co., but also respected instrument makers, including M. Hohner, Fred Gretsch Mfg. Co., and the Jackson-Guldan Violin Co. Other prewar manufacturers included Bar Zim Toy Mfg. Co, Leigh A. Elkington, the Herbert R. Gottfried Co., the Harmony Co., Helvetic I.&M. Corp., Kazoo Co., Keystone Mfg. Co., Noble & Cooley Co., Risdon Mfg. Co., Smethport Specialty Co., and James B. Waterfield. See also *pianos, toy.*

Muskin Mfg. Co. Based in Brooklyn, N.Y., Muskin made prewar doll carriages and play houses. By the late 1930s it was also manufacturing wading pools. In the Boomer years, Muskin was based in Wilkes-Barre, Penn. Its line consisted of doll carriages and strollers, doll baths, wading pools, slides, and baby car seats and beds.

mustaches see *wigs, beards and mustaches.*

"Mustang" cap pistol see *Kilgore Mfg. Co., Inc..*

"Mustang 500" cap pistol see *Nichols Industries.*

Musselman Products Co. Established in Cleveland, Ohio, in the late 1930s, Musselman produced home building sets for midget autos and other vehicles, featuring "Doenut" cord tires and wheels.

"Mutt & Jeff" These popular be-whiskered cartoon characters were featured on numerous prewar playthings, including balloons by Eagle Rubber Co., a bank by A.C. Williams Co., and a game by Herbert Specialty Mfg. Co.

Mutuels, Inc. Based in Los Angeles, Calif., this company issued the 1938 "Game of Mutuels."

"My Darling" and "My Dolly" The "My Darling," "My Dolly" and "My Mandy" prewar rubber dolls were made by Miller Rubber Products Co. An unrelated set of "My Dolly's" toy furniture was also made in the 1930s by Dowst Mfg. Co.

"My Easy" line of educational toys see *Jacmar Mfg. Co.*

"My Fair Lady" Whether Bernard Shaw would have approved or not, his stage play inspired toys when rendered on the silver screen. Playthings included dolls by Goldberger Doll Mfg. Co. and plastic cutouts by Aldon Industries.

"My Favorite" see *Imperial Crayon Co.*

"My Frin Sticka" stick horse see *Tri-Kay Co.*

"My Little Dears" paper dolls prewar, see *The Platt & Munk Co., Inc.*

"My Merry" housekeeping toys see *Merry Mfg. Co.*

"My Own Library" see *The Platt & Munk Co., Inc.*

"My Pal" drawing sets prewar, see *Hassenfeld Bros.*

My-Toy Co., Inc. Stuffed toys and plush novelties were this Brooklyn, N.Y., firm's postwar specialties.

Myers Mfg. Organization This Cleveland, Ohio, firm made the prewar "Movie Master" toy motion picture projectors.

Myers' Woolly Animals, Inc. This Gloversville, N.Y., firm was active in the 1920s.

"Mystic Slates" see *Richards Mfg. Co.*

"Mystifying Oracle" see *William Fuld.*

M

"Mysto Magic" see *A.C. Gilbert Co.*

Mystoplane Co., Inc. The "Mystoplane" of the late 1930s, operated by means of a "magic wand," was the product of this West 24th Street, New York City, firm.

In 1962, Louis Marx & Co. released the "Big Bruiser" toy tow truck.

"Magic Marxie," the Louis Marx & Co. logo character from the 1960s.

N.Y. Sales Co. Based on West 145th Street, New York City. Sales issued "sun tan colored dolls" in the late 1930s.

Nadel & Sons Toy Corp. Metal jack sets, dangling monkeys, jump ropes, twirling tops, whips, swagger canes, pinwheels and "Nutty Putty" were among the Boomer-era products of this Broadway, New York City, company. Nadel primarily catered to the carnival, premium, prize-package and rack-goods trade.

"Name That Tune" game see *Milton Bradley Co.*

C.T. Namur Based in Little Neck, Long Island, N.Y., C.T. Namur made "reversible self-winding tops" in the 1930s.

Nancy Ann Dressed Dolls, Inc. Established in San Francisco, Calif., in the late 1930s, this firm issued miniature dressed bisque dolls, using the "Story Book Dolls" trade name. The firm changed its own name to Nancy Ann Storybook Dolls in the Boomer years. Besides its "Storybook" line, which drew upon nursery rhyme and fairy tale characters, it issued the "Sue Sue" baby dolls, "Muffie" dolls, and "Debbi" Dolls.

"Nancy Drew" Besides being the leading light of a long-running series of Grosset & Dunlap books, the girl detective was featured in playthings including the "Nancy Drew Mystery" game by Parker Bros.

"Nancy Family" dolls see *Arranbee Doll Co.*

Napco Industries, Inc. The Toy Division of this Minneapolis, Minn., firm issued the "Slidin' Saucer" snow saucers and "Sno-go" combination ski and snow shoe of the 1950s and '60s.

Nasco Doll, Inc. This postwar Brooklyn, N.Y., firm specialized in popular-priced dolls in the Boomer years.

Nassau Products Corp. Based in Troy, N.Y., Nassau made metal doll walkers, cribs, high chairs, housekeeping toys, and electric irons in the postwar years.

Nathan Shure see *Cosmo Mfg. Co.; Dowst Mfg. Co.*

National Can Co., Inc. Sand pails and metal toys were being issued by the late 1930s by this East 42nd Street, New York City, firm.

National Company This Malden, Mass., company, made the "Electric Coon Jigger" in the mid-1930s.

"National Fast Freight" wooden trains prewar, see *Strombeck-Becker Mfg. Co.*

National Fireworks, Inc. see *National Playthings Division.*

The National Flag Co. This Cincinnati, Ohio, flag manufacturer also made Halloween, Christmas and Easter decorations and goods in the 1930s and '40s.

National French Fancy Novelty Co. This Brooklyn, N.Y., company used the "National" trade name on its line of stuffed animal toys in the 1920s and '30s. The "National Zoo" animals included "Musical Bears," "Fluffy Bears," "Booty Bears," and "Teddies."

National Games Co. Based in Newtonville, Mass., National Games Co. issued games in the 1920s and '30s with sports orientations, including such titles as "E-E-Yah Base Ball Game," "Forty-Niners Gold Mining Game," and "Triple Play." Other titles include "Play Ball" of 1920, "Major League Ball" of 1921, and '30s games "Danny McFayden's Stove League Baseball Game," "National 100-Yard Dash," and "Simplex-Graphic Baseball Scorebooks." The firm continued after the war, being based in West Springfield, Mass., in the 1950s.

The National Latex Products Co.

Balloons and vinyl play balls were among this Ashland, Ohio, firm's postwar line.

National Leather Mfg. Co. "Lone Ranger" school bags, briefcases, and ring binders were specialties of this postwar Brooklyn, N.Y., company. It also issued Walt Disney and "Pony-Tail" items.

"National" marbles see *Peltier Glass Co.*

"National" model sets prewar, see *Selchow & Righter Co.*

National Novelty Corp. Over 30 leading cast-iron and wood toy and novelty manufacturers merged in 1903 under the umbrella name of the National Novelty Corp., hoping to cut costs and rise above the competition. The "toy trust" merger proved unsuccessful, however, due to poor management. Some of the involved toy makers reorganized as Hardware & Woodenware Mfg. Co., which also failed. See *N.N. Hill Brass Co; Jones & Bixler Co; Kenton Hardware Co.*

National Organ Supply Co. see *The Nosco Plastics Division.*

National Playthings Division This West Hanover, Mass., division of National Fireworks issued toys, cap pistols, caps, and fireworks in the late 1930s. Its titles including the "Animal Alphabet" cardboard blocks of 1938, and "Letter Jacks." It moved to Boston, Mass., by the end of the decade. In wartime, the firm continued toy making with a line of dollhouses, Noah's arks, circus toys, and barn play sets with people and animal figures. The company continued into the postwar years, issuing "Hansel and Gretel Bendable Foam Rubber Dolls" in the mid-1950s.

National Sales & Mfg. Co. National Sales of Des Moines, Iowa, manufactured a miniature child's automobile with gasoline motor in the late 1930s.

National School Slate Co., Inc. Established in Slatington, Penn., in 1885, National School Slate specialized in home and school educational supplies. By the prewar years it had a full line of school slates, glass drawing slates, national slate blackboards, white drawing boards, artist easels, and tennis racket presses. Its line of natural slate blackboards continued through the war years. In the Boomer era, it continued issuing a variety of slates and blackboards, as well as sand boxes, toy chests, and doll cradles.

National Sewing Machine Co. "The Eldredgette" and "American Girl" toy sewing machines were produced in the 1930s and '40s by this Belvidere, Ill., manufacturer. It also made iron toys under the "Vindex" name.

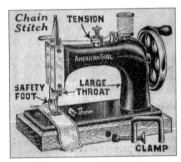

"American Girl" sewing machine by National Sewing Machine Co.

National Sporting Goods Mfg. Co. Playground and indoor balls and sports supplies were made by this St. Louis, Mo., company, in the mid-1930s.

National Stuffed Animals, Inc. The "Winky" animals of the late 1930s were made by this West 25th Street, New York City, firm. It also made teddy bears.

National Toy Mfg. Co. Reed toys, novelties, doll high chairs and carriages were specialties of this Broome Street, New York City, firm, established in the later 1930s. Its line continued through wartime, and included doll swings, high chairs, and sulkies, and Easter baskets.

Natural Doll Co., Inc. This doll manufacturer was located on Spring Street, New York City, from the 1930s through the Boomer years. In the postwar period it specialized in "vinylite," rubber, and "rigidsole" dolls with washable rooted hair.

"Natural Slate" see *National School Slate Co.*

"Nature Forms" crayons see *Colorforms.*

Nautilus, Inc. Quoit and horseshoe sets were among this Philadelphia, Penn., firm's postwar products.

Naylor Corp. This Chicago, Ill., firm issued Walt Disney character-related tapping sets in the late 1930s.

"Neanderthal Man" hobby kit see *ITC Modelcraft.*

needlework toys see *embroidery and sewing sets.*

Neevel Luggage Mfg. Co. This Kansas City, Mo., firm included doll and juvenile trunks in its line, in the 1950s and '60s.

Neff-Moon Toy Co. Founded in 1920 in Sundusky, Ohio, Neff-Moon made pressed-steel automobile toys. The toys featured interchangeable bodies that fit onto a single chassis. The company lasted until 1925.

Neill, John R. The long-running series of L. Frank Baum's "Oz" books brought fame to John R. Neill (1876-1943), the illustrator who succeeded W.W. Denslow. The titles issued from 1904 to 1942 featured his work. He also wrote several of the titles.

The Nelke Corp. A Philadelphia, Penn., firm established around 1901, Nelke issued the large "Nelke" line of stuffed animals through the late 1920s. The line was taken over by Frank Plotnick Co. after the Depression.

One of The Nelke Corp.'s large teddy bears, 1920s.

nesting blocks see *blocks,* also *Jesse Crandall.*

"Nesting Blox" see *Gerber Plastic Co.*

Nestro Mfg. Co. Nursery wall plaques and pin-ups, as well as puzzles, were products of Nestro, based in Chicago, Ill., in the early 1960s. It was a subsidiary of Screenmasters, Inc.

Neumann Mfg. Co. In the late prewar years, Neumann manufactured home gymnasium equipment. It was based in Utica, N.Y.

"Never Stop" humming top see *Gibbs Mfg. Co.*

"New-Art Design" dishes prewar, see *Wolverine Supply & Mfg. Co.*

New Art Toy & Feather Co. Based on East 10th Street, New York City, New Art was a prewar stuffed animal manufacturer.

New Devices Based in Green Bay, Wis., New Devices issued the "Hiker Horse" walking hobbyhorse of the late 1930s.

The New Draw-Mor Mfg. Co. The "Draw-Mor" drawing device was made in the mid-1930s by this Chicago, Ill., firm.

New England Mfg. Co. Dart games, darts, and suction cups were part of this New Haven, Conn., manufacturer's 1930s line.

New England Toy Mfg. Co. Fur stuffed toys were the specialty of this Boomer-era Bridgeport, Conn., company.

N

New England Wood & Metal Products, Inc.
Besides being a maker of bird houses, this Wayne, Maine, company made wood action toys in the 1930s and '40s.

New Jersey Crayon Co., Inc.
"Crayons of all kinds," this Paterson, N.J., company claimed to produce in the 1930s and '40s.

New Jersey Pulverizing Co.
This West 34th Street, New York City, firm supplied the "Child Health" sand of the late prewar years.

New Jersey Rubber Mfg. Co.
Rubber toys and novelties comprised this Union City, N.J., firm's postwar line.

The New Jersey Zinc Co.
A raw material manufacturer, the New Jersey Zinc Co., based on Front Street, New York City, produced the important "Zamac," a zinc alloy used by a number of the leading die-casting firms. The alloy was touted, in the 1930s, for its "low cost, high strength, excellent detail, light weight" and its need for "no machining."

New Monarch Machine & Stamping Co.
A manufacturer of Christmas tree holders and charcoal braziers, New Monarch also made gas-engine powered "Go Karts," in the 1950s and '60s. It was located in Des Moines, Iowa.

"New Pioneer" and "New Ranger" trains
see *American Flyer Mfg. Co.*

New York & Paris Novelty Co.
Based on West 18th Street, New York City, in the 1920s, this firm made masks "of all descriptions."

New York Association for the Blind
Based on East 59th Street, New York City, this association produced the "Dainty Daisy Duster" cleaning sets of the 1930s and '40s.

New York Ball & Toy Co.
see *Paramount Rubber Co.*

New York Biological Supply Co.
This 34 Union Square, New York City, company produced educational biological sets, including "Bio-Set" and "Bio-Kit" of the mid-1930s.

New York Doll Accessories Corp.
This Brooklyn, N.Y., firm, manufactured a complete line of doll accessories in the Boomer years, including furniture, jewelry, flowers, gloves, hose, socks, hats, handbags, roller skates, pistol holster sets, golf clubs, and comb and brush sets, among many other items. It was affiliated with New York Doll Shoe Co.

New York Doll Shoe Co., Inc.
Based in Brooklyn, N.Y., this firm advertised itself as the "World's Largest Manufacturer of Doll Shoes" in the mid-Boomer years. It made the shoes of plastic, artificial leather, suede, satin, and vinyl. The firm also made nylon hose and rayon socks, and did custom molding for industry customers.

New York Scientific Supply Co.
Based on East 22nd Street, New York City, this late 1930s firm issued the "Bio-Set" and "Bio-Kit" educational biological sets.

New York Stuffed Toys
Based on West 19th Street and Fifth Avenue, New York City, this firm issued the 1920s "Cuddle Toys," in long pile tipped plush, characterized by pom-pom buttons and ruffled collars. The firm also made "Hallowe'en Cats." The company was established in 1917, and continued operation through the '30s and '40s, when it was located on West 17th Street, New York City.

New York Toy & Game Co.
The "Quoits to You" game of the mid-1930s was produced by this West 22nd Street, New York City, company. In the late '30s, when the firm's name changed to New York Toy & Game Sale Co., its line included "G-Men" fingerprint, laboratory and secret communication sets, as well as "G-Men" training and police outfits, and "Sherlock Holmes" fingerprint and disguise sets. The company also made sewing outfits, fishing outfits, football, children's games, and games for adults. In the Boomer years, its lines included "G-Men" detective and fingerprint sets, golf and basketball sets, "Jr. Ace" fishing sets, tool chests, punching bag sets, doll carriages, and doll furniture.

New York World's Fair
While earlier World's Fairs had inspired playthings, the New York World's Fair of 1939 happened at

a time when the toy manufacturing industry was at its strongest. It responded to the opportunity by issuing a barrage of play-things ranging from puzzles and souvenirs to balls and banks. Items released in 1939 included archery sets by Indian Archery & Toy Corp.; "Auto-magic gun" films by Stephens Products Co.; balls by the Seamless Rubber Co.; banks by George Borgfeldt Corp. and Zell Products Corp.; books by the Saalfield and Whitman Publishing Co.; "Build-Up" sets by Texcraft Toy Products; caps by S. Cohen & Son; cardboard set-up items by American Miniatures; cards by U.S. Playing Card Co.; dolls and stuffed toys by Joy Doll Corp.; flashlights by Micro-Lite Co.; fur novelties by Charles Brand; games by Milton Bradley Co., Parker Bros., and J. Pressman & Co.; games, puzzles and toys by Bar Zim Toy Mfg. Co.; games and transportation models by Ivorycraft Co.; knives by Imperial Knife Co.; masquerade costumes by A.S. Fishbach Co.; novelties by Made-in-America Novelty Corp.; picture puzzles by Madmar Quality Co.; rubber toys by Lee-Tex Rubber Products Corp.; school bags by Columbia Products Corp.; souvenirs by Goldfarb Novelty Co., and miscellaneous toy items by Standard Toykraft Products, Louis Marx & Co., the Ohio Art Co., and Newton & Thompson Toy Division.

Newark Felt Novelty Co.
Felt Western hats were specialties of this Newark, N.J., company in the Boomer years. It also made beanies, promotional hats, souvenir hats, and doll hats.

Newark Mask Co., Inc.
Based in Irvington, N.J., Newark Mask made luloups, gauze masks, curtain masks, wigs, beards, mustaches, hoodwinks, mask fasteners, and grease paints, in the 1920s through the pre-war years. The firm continued into the post-war years.

The logo for Newark Mask Co., Inc., 1920s.

The Newman Co.
Based on West 36th Street, New York City, the Newman Co. made doll outfits in the 1930s and '40s.

Newman Premier Corp.
Plastic toys and novelties comprised this Brooklyn, N.Y., company's Boomer-era line.

The Newman-Stern Co.
Besides such communication-related items as microphones and radio crystals, the Cleveland, Ohio, firm of Newman-Stern made "Microcraft" kits and "Junior Lab" microsocopes in the 1930s.

Newscraft, Inc.
Games including "Flash! News" of the late 1930s were issued by this Second Avenue, New York City, company.

Newton & Thompson Mfg. Co.
The 1930s and '40s "Rainbow" brand construction kindgergarten pull-toys and bead-toys were made by the wood-turning firm Newton & Thompson, based in the Fifth Avenue Building, New York City, with its factory in Brandon, Vt. The company also made ten pins, croquet sets, the "Skill Ball" game, tops, miniature clothespins, laundry sets, Easter items, wooden figures and novelties, noisemakers, golf tees, and carnival goods. In the later '30s its manufacturing name changed to Newton & Thompson Toy Novelty Division, and to Newton & Thompson Toy Division by wartime, when its line remained largely unchanged.

"Skill Ball," a Newton and Thompson game.

The Newton Junior Corp.
Newton Junior was a die-cast toy manufacturer based in West Haven, Conn., in the late prewar years.

N

Newton Mfg. Co. "Aerial toys" were among this Newton, Iowa, firm's prewar offerings. Newton also made felt toys and paper hats.

K.G. Niblack Co. Based in Buffalo, N.Y., Niblack issued the "Pikes Peak or Bust" puzzle game of the 1950s-60s.

Nic Projector Corp. In a novel approach to the toy projector, the 1930s Nic Projector "animated" printed strips. It was based on Spring Street, New York City.

Nicholas-Beazley The 1930s "Tri-Car" children's vehicles were made by this Marshall, Mo., firm.

The E.M. Nichols Co. Based in Woodbridge, Conn., the E.M. Nichols Co. started with wooden educational toys in the earlier 1930s. By the late prewar years it was manufacturing marionette theaters, toy chests, and "bed play trays."

Nichols Industries One of the more important manufacturers of toy pistols and cap guns in the Boomer years, Nichols also made sling shots and stilts. It was based in Jacksonville, Texas.

Nichols Mfg. Co. This Bridgeport, Conn., firm made 10-cent dolls as well as doll clothes in the 1930s and '40s.

Nicol & Co. A Chicago, Ill., hardware manufacturer, Nicol & Co. made iron toys and banks. Its earlier 1930s toys included sad irons and toy trucks.

"Nifty," trademark see *George Borgfeldt Corp.*

Niscott Mfg. Co., Inc. Tom-toms, Indian headdresses, vests and cowboy suits were specialties of this postwar Bronx, N.Y., company.

Nissen Products Corp. "Diablo" tops and children's trampolines were postwar products of this division of Nissen Trampoline Co., based in Cedar Rapids, Iowa.

Nitke Bros, Inc. The Binghamton, N.Y., leather specialties firm of Nitke Bros. produced prewar holsters and toy pistols.

Nitram Mfg. Co. Based in East Orange, N.J., Nitram issued braided jump ropes in variegated color patterns, and school bags, in the 1920s through the prewar years.

"Noah's Ark" In colonial households where the Puritan influence ran high, one toy that found acceptance was the Noah's Ark set, usually carved of wood and featuring the houseboat-like Ark and numerous paired animals, which often took fanciful shapes in those pre-photography days. The sets were common in American households in the 1700s, and were regarded as acceptable "Sunday toys" because of their religious connotations. In many ways the Noah's Ark sets might be regarded as precursors to the play sets of the 1950s and '60s, which typically involved a building of some kind and numerous small figures and accessories. The arks continued to be made into the 20th century, by companies including Block House, Milton Bradley Co., the N.D. Cass Co., E.E. Fairchild Corp., Holgate Bros. Co., V.M. Kearley Mfg. Co., Kiddy-Crafters, Mason & Parker Mfg. Co., and the A. Schoenhut Co. At least one Boomer-era manufacturer, Allison Studios, issued arks in the 1950s-60s.

"Noah's Ark" paints and crayons see *United Crayon Co.*

"Noah's Dominoes" Patented in 1881, "Noah's Dominoes" were wooden sets of playing blocks issued by Charles M. Crandall. One side of the blocks showed the tradiional domino spots, while the other side, covered with colorfully lithographed paper, depicted wild animals, all split in half to allow the dominoes game to be played with that side, too. This may have been the first of the picture dominoes, many of which were issued in inexpensive forms in the 20th century.

Noble & Cooley Co. Established in Granville, Mass., in 1854, Noble & Cooley built its fortune on the manufacturing of tin drums. Demand grew within the decade due to the Civil War and popular depictions of drummer boys as romantic wartime figures. Competition also rose during the same period, with at least four tin-drum makers being founded within Noble & Cooley's first decade in Massachusetts alone. The company's musical toys in the early 20th century and prewar years included toy drums, tambourines and banjos. It also made rolling hoops. In the Boomer years its main products remained percussion instruments, primarily to drums, tambourines, and tap drum sets.

"Noisemaker Gun" see *Daisy Mfg. Co.*

noisemakers Much though adults would like to attribute noise-making to children, the noisemaker toys, which have been popular probably as long as there have been ears, have always been as much for adults as children, even if adults do tend to limit their use to certain occasions.

The importance of noisemakers as toys is indicated to some degree by the number of manufacturers involved in their production. Some of the more famous prewar firms included J. Chein & Co., T. Cohn, Kazoo Co., and, perhaps most importantly, the Kirchhof Patent Co.

Other firms included S.S. Adams Co., Adler Favor & Novelty Co., American Tissue Mills, Bar Zim Toy Mfg. Co., Bernhard Paper Favor Co., Bugle Toy Mfg. Co., Clark Toy Mfg. Co., Dessart Bros., Leigh A. Elkington, the A.A. Faxon Co., Gotham Pressed Steel Corp., Hansen Wood Goods & Toy Mfg. Co., Kansas Metal Novelty Mfg. Co., Keller Toy Mfg. Co., Langson Mfg. Co., S. Lisk & Bros., Mansfield Novelty Mfg. Co., Marks Bros. Co., Newton & Thompson Mfg. Co., F.W. Peterson Corp., M. Pressner & Co., Richmond Bros. Co., the Seiss Mfg. Co., B. Shackman & Co., Spotswood Specialty Co., the Thompson Mfg. Co., and Woerner's Mfg. Works.

Through much of the Boomer years the noisemakers remained largely unchanged, although plastic and cheaper metal plate became common in the later period. In addition to Kirchhof, which remained a major manufacturer in the category with its "Life of the Party" products, U.S. Metal Toy Mfg. Co. was a leading producer. Its line resembled those of such other tin-litho toy makers as Ohio Art and J. Chein Co., in emphasizing sand toys and watering cans. Its noisemaker line, however, was extensive, and included shakers, buzzers, frog clickers, and horns, with designs for carnivals and Halloween.

Manufacturers included American Merri-Lei Corp., American Party Favor Co., the Beistle Co., George Borgfeldt Corp., Gordon Novelty Co., Hoffman Lion Mills Co., Jet Party Favors, Kirchhof, William Kratt Co., Ogdin Mfg. Co., and Spec-Toy-Culars.

Ohio Art Mfg. Co.'s "Siren Megaphone," 1950s.

Nok-Out Mfg. Co. The mid-1930s game "Dizzy and Daffy Dean Nok-Out Baseball Game" was made by this Milwaukee, Wis., firm.

Noma Electric Corp. Based on Hudson Street, New York City, this pioneer in electric decorations issued "strings of color light with Mazda lamps" in the 1920s, becoming the leader of an ever more crowded field in the 1930s, when it was based on Broadway. It moved to West 13th Street by the 1940s. In wartime, Noma turned from issuing its famous Christmas lights to an entirely new line of toys and dolls made of non-critical materials, including "See 'Em Walk" toys. In the postwar years, Noma's products included plastic Christmas toys and decorations, as well as Christmas lights and "Noma Bubble Lites."

Nonpariel Toy & Novelty Co. Nonpariel, located on Fourth Avenue, New York City, produced prewar lithographed tin toys, including trucks, wagons, pull toys, and mechanical toys. Most of the company's production was devoted to penny toys and prize package toys. Founded sometime after World War I, Nonpariel continued until the late 1940s.

nonsopretties see *"pretties."*

Norstar Corp. Based on East 167th Street, New York City, in the Boomer years, Norstar issued children's housecleaning sets, doll trunks and luggage, and dishwashing sets.

North & Judd Mfg. Co. Established in New Britain, Conn., in the late 1930s, North

N

& Judd manufactured junior police sets, badges, and whistles, as well as toy suitcases.

North Pacific Products Co. This Bend, Ore., firm issued "Ready-To-Fly" toys in the Boomer years, including gliders and airplanes.

North Vernon Industries, Inc. In addition to juvenile swings and rockers, this North Vernon, Ind., firm made prewar toy furniture sets.

Northern Signal Co. Based in Saukville, Wis., Northern Signal issued the Boomer-era "Magic Designer," formerly "Hoot-Nanny." See *Jones, Howard B.*

Northill Co., Inc. The "Rosebowl" football game of the late 1930s was issued by this Los Angeles, Calif., company.

Northland Ski Mfg. Co. A St. Paul, Minn., firm established in the late 1930s, Northland's line included toboggans and snow shoes.

Northwestern Model Supply Co. Model airplane kits and supplies were made by this mid-1930s Detroit, Mich., firm.

Northwestern Products Based in St. Louis, Mo., this name appeared on glass-covered bagatelle games in the 1930s, as well as the "Graphic Baseball" board game. Northwestern's 1930s titles included "Skor-It" and "Hapitime" baseball bagatelles. Other titles included "Klik-It" electric bagatelles, the "Tra-C-Rase White-Board" set, and the "Musical Popeye Pipe." It also issued a Chinese checkers game. "Poosh-M-Up" was the first glass-covered bagatelle game line, priced from 25 cents to $3.95. The "Tactics" skill game appeared in 1940.

The firm introduced construction sets in 1934 of a unique nature. Named "Konkrete Bild-M-Up," the sets contained equipment for children to make their own "stone" blocks for construction. The sets, including "Konkrete," retailed at $1.00 and $1.50. Extra bags of "Konkrete" sold for 49 cents.

During the war the company managed to continue toy production with a line of "Poosh-M-Up Pin Games," "Tactics," "Little Deb" girls' toy sets, "San Loo" Chinese

checkers, "Yank-E-Fife," "Popeye" pipes, and wooden guns.

In the Boomer years, Northwestern continued its emphasis on games for adults and children, including Chineese checker games, bagatelles, pin ball games, and game tables, as well as infants' toys and construction toys. Northwestern Products was the toy division of the Northwestern Mail Box Co.

Children could make their own building stone with the "Konkrete Bild-M-Up" sets by Northwestern Products.

Norton Products The "Magic Art Reproducer" drawing device of the 1950s-60s were issued by this Broadway, New York City, company.

The Nosco Plastics Division The Nosco Plastics Division of National Organ Supply Co. of Erie, Penn., was established in 1935. It began making toys in 1948, issuing toy cars, racers, motorcycles, buses, hot rods, and trains, many of them with clockwork motors. The company was an important supplier of plastic toys for packages of "Cracker Jack." The business was sold to Saunders Tool and Die Co. in 1955.

Novelart Mfg. Co. The "Novelview" three-dimension pictures of the late 1930s were issued by this Long Island City, N.Y., firm.

Noveloid Co., Inc. As its name might suggest, celluloid was the material of choice for this prewar Leominster, Mass., firm, which made trumpets, whistles, and flying wheels. It also made wooden dolls and rattles, and combination wood and celluloid dolls in the 1930s and '40s.

novelties, toy Where to draw the line between novelties and toys was as difficult for companies involved in their production as it is for toy and game historians. As with party favors, musical toys, noisemakers and masks, these items often crossed age barriers, being as suitable for adults in certain situations as for children in others.

Despite the difficulties, some companies did consider themselves manufacturers of toy novelties, or novelty toys. Prewar examples included Apex Mfg. Co., maker of the "Funny Face" toy, Automatic Rubber Co., maker of the "Zip-Zip" shooter toy, Judsen Rubber Works, maker of rubber ankle pads for roller skates, and Novelty Toy Crafters, maker of the "Mystery Pig."

Others included Auchterlonie & Miller, the Elgin Tool Works, Ideal Products Mfg. Co., Magic Flote Novelty Corp., New York Biological Supply Co., Optaz Novelty Co., Oregon Worsted Co., Standard Scientific Supply Corp., Victor Craftsmen, and Prat-Lane Co.

The diversity represented by these companies suggested that for many companies, a "novelty toy" was any toy they could produce given their specialization in a usually non-toy-related area. Oregon Worsted Co., for instance, made "yarn novelties," while Standard Scientific Supply Corp. considered its butterfly and insect collecting kits to be "novelty toys," as did Prat-Lane Co. its "Hi-Lo Blood Tester."

In the Boomer years, novelty activity sets and novelty toys came into their own, since the market proved capable of sustaining almost any oddball notion to come along. Among the most important novelties of the time were "Magic Rocks," colored mineral formations that grew in bottles of water, by Magic Rock Co., based in Chicago, Ill., in the 1960s and '70s; "Magic '8' Ball" by Alabe Crafts; "Silly Putty"; and jumping beans, issued by a number of companies.

Others included shrunken head replicas by E. Joseph Cossman & Co., some of the spring-coil toys by James Industries, "Rocket Shoes" by Moon Mfg. Co., and plastic snakes and lizards by Teknoplast Co. See also *paper novelties.*

"Noveltoy," prewar see *J.L. Wright.*

Noveltoy Corp. This Chicago, Ill., firm issued the "Flag-Stix" and "Block-Stix" wood block construction toys during the war years.

Novelty Bookbinding Co., Inc. A company that manufactured games and game parts for other prewar manufacturers, Novelty Bookbinding also made checker and backgammon boards of its own. It was based on Beekman Street, New York City.

Novelty Casting Co. This Brooklyn, N.Y., firm produced prewar pewter toys and novelties.

Novelty Creations Co. Stuffed toys, novelties, and dolls were produced in the 1930s and '40s by this West 15th Street, New York City, firm.

Novelty Doll & Toy Mfg. Corp. This Broome Street, New York City, company made mama and baby dolls in the 1930s and '40s.

Novelty Dolls, Inc. A postwar Brooklyn, N.Y., company, Novelty Dolls specialized in baby, novelty and character dolls in latex, rubber, vinylite and plastic.

Novelty Film Co. Novelty Film's "Dainographs" were non-inflammable negatives that produced double sun pictures. The company, based in West New York, N.J., specialized in 16mm and 35mm films for home use projectors in the 1930s and '40s.

Novelty Iron Works see *Arcade Mfg. Co.*

Novelty Kite Mfg. Co. Based in Richmond, Calif., this Boomer-era firm issued the "Parachute" kite, and "Tobe" horse toys.

Novelty Mfg. Co., Inc. Streamers for bicycle, tricycle and motorcycle handles were specialties of this Newark, N.J., company in the 1950s and '60s. It also made handlebar grips with streamers, and reflective disks to dress up bicycle spokes.

Novelty Research Artists The "Big Ten" football and baseball games of the late

N

prewar years were issued by this Minneapolis, Minn., company.

Novelty Toy Crafters This Chicago, Ill., firm produced toys and novelties including the 1934 "Mystery Pig."

Noyes, S.L. The manufacturing plant of S.L. Noyes was established in 1867 in Ashburnham, Mass. It produced a complete line of doll furniture.

Noyes & Snow Noyes & Snow issued the 1878 card game, "Letters Improved for the Logomachist."

"NRA" games prewar, see *Milton Bradley Co.*

"NRA" steel toys see *Murray-Ohio Mfg. Co.*

Nu-Cushion Products This Keene, Texas, firm issued Boomer-era stick horses, as well as toy brooms and mops. Nu-Cushion's "Texas Stick Horses" had candy-stripe sticks, high-gloss plastic heads with sewn-in manes and ears, plastic reins with bells.

Nucraft Toys In business in the late 1920s, Nucraft Toys issued "The New Lindy Flying Game" in 1927 and "Crash, the New Airplane Game" of 1928.

Nucraft Toy Corp. Based in New York City on Broadway, Nucraft issued postwar plush toys and novelties.

"Nukuzu" musical toy see *Kirchhof Patent Co.*

"Numberjax" see *Grey Iron Casting Co.*

nurse kits Along with doctor kits, nurse kits became popular by the later prewar years. Companies manufacturing them included Fleischaker & Baum, James McGowan Associates, Ozan Products Co., and Transogram Co. Companies in the postwar years included Hassenfeld Bros., who entered the field in the late prewar years, as well as Transogram. Others included American Metal Specialties Corp., Ozan Products Co., Peerless Playthings Co., Pressman Toy Corp., Renwal Toy Corp., and A.J. Siris Products Corp.

Nursery Plastics, Inc. A manufacturer of nursery furniture and lamps, this East 25th Street, New York City, firm also made crib toys and mobiles in the Boomer years.

"Nursery Rhyme" dolls At least two Boomer-era doll manufacturers, Nancy Ann Storybook Dolls and De Journette Mfg. Co., issued series of "Nursery Rhyme" dolls. Ralph Freundlich had preceded them, in the 1930s.

nursery toys see *infant toys.*

nursery wall sets Common by at least the 1930s, nursery wall sets were wall-hanger decorations usually depicting fanciful characters, made of plaster, plastic, wood or pressed board. Some depicted such fictional characters as "Raggedy Ann and Andy," or cartoon figures such as "Mickey Mouse." The decorations continued to be common through the Boomer years, and included "Nursery Picture Plaques" by Kenner Products Co.

Nussbaum Novelty Co. Despite its name, Nussbaum Novelty Co. of Berne, Ind., specialized in producing boxes. Its line of cedar chests included toy, doll, candy, and juvenile chests were issued from the 1930s through the Boomer years. Its line by the early 1940s also included batons, smokers' articles, and birdhouses.

John Nutry John Nutry of Brooklyn, N.Y., was a manufacturer of banks in the 1930s and '40s.

Ny-Lint Tool & Mfg. Co. Ny-Lint of Rockford, Ill., specialized in mechanical and scale-model toys. While its early toys in the late 1940s emphasized the mechanical end of the scale, including wind-ups, the company became best known for its heavy toy road construction vehicles.

The famous "Jalopy" by Nylint, 1960s.

"O-Boy" yo-yo tops see *Donald F. Duncan.*

O-Cedar Corp. Based in Chicago, Ill., O-Cedar produced toy housekeeping sets with mops and toy dusters in the late 1930s.

"O-K" police model pistol prewar, see *Hubley Mfg. Co.*

"O.K." return tops see *The Alox Mfg. Co.*

"O.K. Streamliners" electric trains see *Herkimer Tool & Model Works.*

O'Neill, Rose The famous "Kewpie" was created by self-taught artist and writer Rose O'Neill (1875-1944). Her 1913 *Kewpies, Their Book* inspired countless dolls and other playthings.

Oak Hill Company, subsidiary see *Hedstrom-Union Co.*

Oak Park Tool & Die Co. This Oak Park, Mich., firm issued the "Silver-Line" aluminum motor boats of the 1950s-60s.

The Oak Rubber Co. In the 1920s, the Oak Rubber Co. of Ravenna, Ohio, boasted of issuing the "world's greatest line of plain, two-color, printed, and novelty balloons." The firm's success continued into the 1930s, when the firm obtained an early license from Kay Kamen to produce Walt Disney character-related balloons. The company specialized in rubber toys, novelties, and balloons. Many of its balloons were used for advertising purposes. The "Oak" balloons, also called "Hy-Tex" balloons for their patented strengthened-rubber make-up, often had face decorations, sometimes with a second, shaped balloon used for the body beneath the balloon "head." Mickey Mouse balloons were either round balloons with the full figure show, or "head" balloons with the face and rounded protuberances on the top of the balloon to represent the mouse ears. Oak Rubber continued issuing toys, rubber novelties, and rubber and advertising balloons through the Boomer years.

"Mickey Mouse Balloon" from the Oak Rubber Company, 1930s.

"Obelisk Building Blocks" "Obelisk Building Blocks" were devised in the 1880s by Charles T. Crandall after seeing the popular attraction "Cleopatra's Needle" in Central Park. They were issued by the firm founded by his father, Benjamin Potter Crandall.

Odora Co. Established on Water Street, New York City, in the late 1930s, Odora issued toy chests decorated with Walt Disney characters. The firm continued issuing toy chests and nursery chests through the Boomer years, when it was located on Fifth Avenue

Ogdin Mfg. Co. Based in Dayton, Ohio, Ogdin issued postwar action toys, party hats and horns, pinwheels, and noisemakers.

"Oh Boy" pistol and gun prewar, see *Kilgore Mfg. Co.*

Ohio Art Co. Ohio Art of Bryan, Ohio, is one of the best-known manufacturers of both prewar and postwar tin toys. In the 1930s its line included toy tea sets, trains, drums, laundry sets, washing machines, sand pails, sprinklers, and toy sweepers. It also made Christmas decorations, including artificial snow, icicles, and ornament hangers.

It obtained an early license through Kay Kamen to produce metal toys and sand toys using Disney "Mickey Mouse" and "Three

Little Pigs" characters, including sand toys, metal drums, metal tea sets, housekeeping sets, and laundry sets. As new Disney characters appeared through the 1930s, Ohio Art maintained its contract. Its most distinctive Walt Disney character items are toy tea sets. The company also made silver ribbon icicles and artificial snow in the 1930s and '40s.

Ohio Art issued some of the more important Disney toys of the late prewar years, using the "Mickey Mouse," "Donald Duck," "Snow White" and "Ferdinand the Bull" characters on sand pails and shovels, sprinklers, and sand sets.

In the Boomer years the company continued issuing tin toy tea sets, drums, toys, metal boats, sand pails and sprinklers, musical tops, wheelbarrows, garden sets, and play and electric irons. It also made vinyl horseshoe sets, polyethylene tea sets, lunch boxes, jacks-in-box, pistols, target sets, reference globes, lawn mowers, metal barn play sets, and vinyl toy animals.

Ohio Art's "Hotshot" drum kit from the 1950s.

The "Etch-A-Sketch," one of Ohio Art's most famous toys, debuted in 1960.

Ohio Horse Shoe Co. Pitching horse shoes were produced in the 1930s and '40s by this Columbus, Ohio, company.

Ohio Plastic's Co. Established in the late 1930s in Frazeysburg, Ohio, this firm issued jackstone sets, as well as molded plastic parts. It continued operating through the Boomer years, with slingshots and plastic balls added to its line.

Ohio Thermometer Co., Inc. The Puzzle & Game Division of this Springfield, Ohio, firm issued the late 1930s "Kan-Yu" puzzle.

Karl Ohlbaum & Son Besides producing "gift dolls" and jointed dolls, Karl Ohlbaum & Son, based on Broadway, New York City, in the prewar years, produced such interesting specialties as doll voices and doll hospital supplies. The company also made display manikins. By the late 1930s it was manufacturing squeakers and eyes for animal toys.

"Old Faithful" play sets see *American Crayon Co.*

"Old Glory" Mfg. Co. A Chicago, Ill., manufacturer of party supplies and novelties, "Old Glory" made flags, paper hats, decorations and serpentines in the 1930s and '40s.

The Old Hickory Furniture Co. A maker of swings and playhouses, this prewar Martinsville, Ind., company specialized in children's rockers and other furniture made of hickory.

Old King Cole, Inc. Old King Cole of Canton, Ohio, specialized in department store window and interior displays of both the animated and still varieties, in both prewar and postwar years. In the late 1930s it specialized in displays using Walt Disney characters.

"Old Maid" The "Old Maid" card game became a standard for Milton Bradley Co. in the later prewar years. In the 1950s and '60s, Parker Bros., Ed-U-Cards Mfg. Corp., and the Russell Mfg. Co. also issued "Old Maid" sets.

"Old Master" crayons see *Standard Crayon Mfg. Co.*

"Old Mother Hubbard" game see *Cadaco-Ellis, Inc.*

"Old Rivals" Game Co. The "Old Rivals" football game was made by this eponymous Minneapolis, Minn., company in the mid-1930s.

Oliver Bros., Inc. Halloween costumes and play suits ranked high among this Philadelphia, Penn., company's prewar products. It also made baseball and basketball suits.

Omalda Co., Inc. The "Bob-O-Ling" braided leather kits of the late prewar years were issued by this Philadelphia, Penn., manufacturer of craft and hobby kits.

"Omega" crayons see *Standard Crayon Mfg. Co.*

"The 101 Dalmatians" This 1961 animated Disney movie inspired toys that have appeared over several decades, notably a series of "HO"-scale plastic figures in the Louis Marx "Disneykins" line of the 1960s. The set included figures for Anita Radcliff, the Colonel, Cruella Deville, Horace and Jasper Badham, the Maid, Roger, three poses of Perdita, three poses of Pongo, thirty-six different Puppies, and Sgt. Tibbs, the cat. The puppies rank among the most valuable "Disneykin" figures.

"Onionskin" These unusual marbles are opaque, yet have cores of clear glass. The core is surrounded by opaque glass, which in turn is surrounded by a thin layer of transparent glass. The colors are usually swirled. The marbles are usually larger than 1 inch in diameter.

"Onyx" agates see *Akro Agate Co.*

"Operation" This popular electronic and novelty skill game introduced by Milton Bradley Co. in 1965. The game, including its packaging, became a standard and remained largely unchanged through the remainder of the century.

L. Oppelman, Inc. Based on Broadway, New York City, L. Oppelman made games for adults in the 1930s and '40s. It also manufactured microscopes.

Optaz Novelty Co. The "Optikin" of the mid-1930s, a revolving optical novelty, was produced by this Broadway, New York City, firm.

J.C. Oram Established in Brandon, Vt., in the late 1930s, J.C. Orm issued the "Pinto Pete" rustic rocking horse, wooden gas pumps and other toys, and "Jack Jumpers."

"Oracle" talking boards see *William Fuld.*

Orange Rubber & Plastics Corp. Balloons with plastic toy balloon pumps were 1950s-60s specialties of this West Orange, N.J., firm. It also made plastic kaleidoscopes.

"Orbit," 1959 see *Parker Bros., Inc.*

"Orbiteer" plastic kites see *The Hi-Flier Mfg. Co.*

Oregon Worsted Co., Inc. Oregon Worsted Co. made prewar yarn dolls and toy animals in wool and yarn. By the late 1930s it was advertising virgin-wool animal miniatures including dogs, cats, circus animals, and baby animals; holiday promotions; the "Weave-A-Strip" loom weaving set, and juvenile knitting sets. The firm was based on Fourth Avenue, New York City.

organizations, toy industry see *associations and organizations.*

original 1) The first of a particular model in miniature form.

2) In reference to condition, refers to the superficial elements such as paint and decals not having been tampered with, modified, or restored. "Original, not restored," is a common phrase.

Original Game & Novelty Co. A Rochester, N.Y., game company, Original's line included the "Pok-Em-High" card game of the mid-1930s.

Orman Industries, Inc. A specialty in folding chairs, Orman of Philadelphia, Penn., also made hammer and peg sets, toy ironing boards, and blackboard sets, in the Boomer years.

Ornamental Products Co. This Detroit, Mich., firm made the prewar "Paint-Kraft" kits.

Orotech A 1920s firm, Orotech issued the board game, "Game of Auto Race."

"Orphan Annie" see *"Little Orphan Annie."*

The Orthovis Co. A Chicago, Ill., publisher, Orthovis issued the *Animal Kingdom* and *Bird Kingdom* picture books of the late 1930s.

The Osborn Mfg. Co. This Miami, Fla., firm specialized in doll furniture in the late 1930s.

Ostlind Sales Co. Miniature looms were produced by this Marshfield, Ore., company in the 1930s and '40s.

Ottawa Mfg. Co., Inc. Based in Spring Lake, Mich., Ottawa Manufacturing made 1930s steel sailboats.

"Otto, the Autograph Dachs-hund" see *Collegiate Mfg. Co.*

Osan Products Co. Based on Fifth Avenue, New York City, Osan made magic lanterns in the 1930s. The company specialized in novelty flashlights and Christmas tree lights.

Ot-O-Win Toys & Games A 1920s firm, Ot-O-Win issued the board game, "Ot-O-Win Football."

Otis-Lawson Co. Wartime toys including "Adolf-the-Pig" bank, "Junior Bombsite," "Star Theater," "Toy Carnival," and "Battle-ground" were issued by this Fifth Avenue Building, New York City, firm.

J. Ottmann Lithography Operating at the end of the 19th and early 20th centuries, J. Ottmann issued a variety of board and card games, including "Buster Brown at Coney Island," "Buster Brown Hurdle Race," "Christmas Mail" "Comic Conversation Cards," "Merry Steeple Chase," and "Peter Coddles," in the 1890s. Other titles included "The Game of Japan" in 1903, and "Foxy Grandpa at the World's Fair" in 1904.

"Ouija" talking board see *William Fuld.*

"Our Gang" The "Our Gang" troupe of child actors appealed to young and old, becoming some of the most famous personalities of the prewar years. Early playthings included picture puzzles by the Saalfield Publishing Co., the "Our Gang Tipple Top-ple" game by E.E. Fairchild Corp., and the "Our Gang" wagon by Sheboygan Coaster & Wagon Works.

outfit In the toy trade, especially before the war, "outfit" was a term used not only of costumes, as in "police outfit," but also of activity or play sets, as in a "drawing outfit" or "modeling outfit."

Outdoor Supply Co. This postwar Long Island City, N.Y., manufacturer of saddle-bags, ponchos and canteens issued "Rin-Tin-Tin" tie-ins in the 1950s and early '60s.

"Overland" coaster wagon see *Charles & Victor Goldstein.*

"Overland Flyer" railways see *Hafner Mfg. Co.*

Overland Products Corp. Overland was the manufacturer for the "Zaiden" electrical and mechanical dolls and toys of the 1920s. The "Zaiden Mechanical Dolls" line included the No. 201 "Bimbo" dancer of the "famous Hoochie Kootchie Dance ... in great demand throughout the universe"; No. 204 "Hawaiian Hula Doll," touted as "reproducing the original dance of the natives of Hawaii"; and No. 205 "Shimmie Doll." The clockwork toys were named for their "Zaiden" patented wood fiber compound with a celluloid enamel finish. The dolls were made with silk and wool, and "Hawaiian straw" in the case of the grass-skirt figures.

The "Shimmie Doll" by Overland Products Corp. used clockwork to move and dance.

F.A. Owen Publishing Co. Owen produced "Instructor Jointed Toys" as well as children's books in the later 1930s. It was located in Dansville, N.Y.

"Oxford" puzzles see *Milton Bradley Co.*

Ozan Products Ozan, based on Fifth Avenue, New York City, in the 1930s and '40s, manufactured magic lanterns and flashlights, and also supplied steel-toy manufacturers with light bulbs. By the late '30s the company was issuing nurse play outfits, "G-Man" sets, and Christmas tree outfits. The firm continued into the Boomer years.

Oznam Products A Chicago, Ill., firm, Oznam issued the "Pick Up" card game of the late 1930s.

"Magnastiks," an Ohio Art magnet toy from 1961.

"Floral" tea set from Ohio Art.

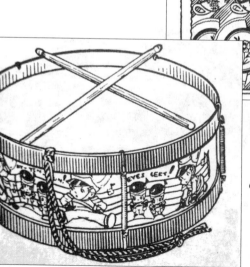

Ohio Art snare drum kit, 1950s.

The "Space Cruiser" pedal car by Garton Toy Co., 1950s.

Another pedal car, the "Kidillac Police Chief," also from the 1950s.

P.&M. Doll Co. This doll manufacturer was established in New York City around 1920. It was based on Broadway, New York City in the 1930s and '40s, and moved to Wooster Street in the Boomer years.

P.M.A. Dolls, Inc. This postwar firm was based in Long Island City, N.Y.

"PMC" toys see *Product Miniature Co., Inc.*

Paas Dye Co. A manufacturer of "pure food Easter egg colors," Paas issued late 1930s "Mickey Mouse" and "Donald Duck" merchandise for holiday and general use. The company was located in Newark, N.J.

Thomas Pace & Co. Pace, based on West Broadway, New York City, manufactured artificial Christmas trees in the late 1930s.

Pacific Balloon Co. A prewar Los Angeles, Calif., manufacturer, this company made toy balloons and inflatable toys. It changed its name to Pacific States Rubber Co. by the late 1930s.

"Pacific Flyer" wagons see *The Globe Co.*

Pacific Game Co. The "Pleasantime Brand" line of games for adults, including such traditional entries as chess, checkers, dominoes, cribbage, and dice games, were Boomer-era products of this Culver City, Calif., company.

Pacific Novelty Division see *DuPont Viscoloid Co., Inc.*

paddleball Developed in the 1930s, paddleball sets involved wooden paddels with sponge balls attached by means of an elastic string. Prewar manufacturers included Bo-Lo Co. and the Fli-Back Co. In the postwar years, Fli-Back continued producing the toys,

joined by Keen-Eye Co., Lee Products Co., and Paddle Tennis Co.

Paddle Tennis Co., Inc. "Paddle Ball" and "Padminton" games were postwar specialties of this Brooklyn, N.Y., firm.

"Pagco" see *Pagliuso Engineering Co.*

N.L. Page & Son Co. This Auburn, Maine, firm made toy and junior pool tables in the 1920s. By the prewar years it was using the "Little Buddy" trade name for its juvenile game tables. It also made games for adults.

Pagliuso Engineering Co. Spring motor and gas engine toy racecars comprised this Glendale, Calif., company's line. It used the "Pagco" trade name in the 1950s and '60s.

paint boxes and outfits Not only were painting sets important as activity toys, the tins and boxes in which they came have become prized items for collectors, in part because many were issued with cartoon character decorations.

Some prewar manufacturers were especially noted for their drawing and art sets, including the American Crayon Co., Binney & Smith Co., Globe Crayon Co., Prang Co. and Rosebud Art Co., while others were distinctively more famous for other kinds of toys, as was the case with Grey Iron Casting Co. and Make-A-Toy Co.

Other firms included American Toy Works, Frederick H. Beach, Milton Bradley Co., Burton Playthings, Cardinell Corp., Child Welfare Publishers, Clyde Dean Ink Co., Cobern Mfg. Co., Leopold Dreifuss, Samuel Gabriel Sons & Co., Goody Mfg. Co., Charles E. Graham & Co., Inland City Cutlery Co., Robert Keller Ink Co., Kolor-Kraft Products, M.S. Publishing Co., Makatoy Co., the Martini Artists Color Laboratories, Minerva Toy Co., Morisite Mfg. Co., Ornamental

Products Co., Parker Bros., Peterson Mfg. Co., the Platt & Munk Co., the Porter Chemical Co., Saalfield Publishing Co., Standard Toykraft Products, Syndicate Products, Transogram Co., the Ullman Mfg. Co., and Universal Toy & Novelty Mfg. Co.

paint-by-number One of the more interesting developments of the 1950s and '60s was the introduction and subsequent popularity of paint-by-number kits, which were issued in oil, acrylic and water-color paint versions by numerous companies. Many of the major names in activity sets released kits, including Transogram Co. and Standard Toykraft Products. Others included the Art Award Co., Avalon Mfg. Co., Arthur Brown & Bros., the Craftint Mfg. Co., Creative Enterprises, Douglas Plymouth Corp., Hassenfeld Bros., Jak-Pak-Inc., the Morilla Co., Palmer Pann Corp., and the Testor Corp.

Pairpont Co. see *Weeden Mfg. Co.*

"Pal" cap pistol see *Kilgore Mfg. Co., Inc.*

Pal-Mate Products This Zanesville, Ohio, company made "polyethylfoam" infants' novelties in the Boomer years, including the unusual "Baby Bread," a simulated loaf of bread.

Pal Plastics, Inc. Based on Third Avenue, New York City, Pal issued puzzles, whistles, toy guns and rack items for variety stores in the postwar years.

"Pal" portable phonographs see *Plaza Mfg. Co.*

"Pal-O-Mine" coaster wagons see *Radio Steel & Mfg. Co.*

"Pal-O-Mine" rockers see *DeKalb Toys.*

Pal-Tom Mfg. Corp. Gun and holster sets were postwar specialties of this West 22nd Street, New York City, company.

Palmer Pann Corp. The "Craftmaster" numbered oil-painting sets and figurine paint-by-number kits of the 1950s and '60s were issued by this Toledo, Ohio, company.

Palmer Plastics, Inc. Palmer specialized in Easter toys, hobby sets, cap bombs, and water guns in the Boomer years. It also made plastic figures, including monster figures in the 1960s.

A.G. Palmer Supply Co. Based in Dover Plains, N.Y., Palmer obtained a late 1930s license to issue Walt Disney character party favors.

"Palomino Pal" hobbyhorse see *Tremax Industries.*

"Panel Blocks" see *Halsam Products Co.*

"Panel Builder" see *The Toy Tinkers, Inc.*

"Panorama" hinged books prewar, see *Samuel Gabriel Sons & Co.*

"Panorama" books postwar, see the *The Platt & Munk Co., Inc.*

pantin A French word for dancing jack or puppet, "pantin" was used also to denote the jointed paper dolls when they first became popular. See *doll, paper.*

"Paper Buster" gun see *Langson Mfg. Co.*

paper caps see *pistol caps.*

paper doll see *dolls, paper.*

The Paper Doll House This Atlanta, Ga., company issued the "Curly Top" paper doll of the late 1930s.

paper novelties Although often not seen as toys, paper novelties played an important part in the childhoods of most late 19th and 20th century children. The products produced by one manufacturer, the Beistle Co. of Shippensburg, Penn., give an indication of the range of paper novelties, and how much they overlap with other games and toys. In the 1930s it was producing Halloween decorations and games, artificial Christmas trees and decorations, valentine cards, including folders and comic cards, Easter novelties, paper hats, and "Muralprint" Mother Goose decorations.

Other prewar manufacturers included Adler Favor & Novelty Co., American Merri-Lei

Corp., American Tissue Mills, Bernhard Paper Favor Co., the Clever Idea Paper Novelty Co., Dessart Bros., A.A. Faxon Co., Gottlieb Paper Products Mfg. Corp., Hawley Products Co., International Souvenir & Import Co., Kashner Novelty Corp., Newton Mfg. Co., Paper Novelty Mfg. Co., Peerless Engraving Co., the Reyburn Mfg. Co., Russell-Hampton Co., B. Shackman & Co., Transogram Co., and Universal Toy & Novelty Mfg. Co.

The number of companies issuing paper novelties actually decreased in the Boomer years, helped by the popularity and cheapness of plastic. Manufacturers included American Merri-Lei, United Crayon, the Beistle Co., George Borgfeldt, Jaybar Products Co., Paper Novelty, B. Shackman, and A.J. Wildman & Son.

Paper Novelty Mfg. Co. Based on East 36th Street, New York City, Paper Novelty primarily made such holiday items as tinsel, paper decorations, and hats in the 1920s. By the 1930s and '40s its line included Christmas icicles, snow, tinsel, ornaments, and paper bells. It moved to Brooklyn by the late '30s, and to Stamford, Conn., in the Boomer years. It used the "Doubl-Glo" trade name for not only Christmas items but also Valentines and greeting cards from at least the 1930s.

Paper Products Co. Based in Dubuque, Iowa, Paper Products Co. made "O-Joy" doll furniture in the 1930s.

paper toys see *cardboard and paper toys.*

papier-mache see *molded pulp toys.*

Par Beverage Corp. Dime store novelties such as the "Snoot Flute" and candy lipstick led this Cincinnati, Ohio, firm's line in the Boomer years. It also made bar novelties, plastic wall plaques, and clay sculpting sets.

"Par-T-Masks" see the *Einson-Freeman Co.*

"Para-Shooter" aerial toy see *Acme Toys, Inc.*

"Parachute Rocket" see *Park Plastics Co.*

Paradise Playthings This division of Paradise Mfg. Co. of Los Angeles, Calif., made Boomer-era inflatable toys, as well as swimming accessories.

Paragon Rubber Co. Established in the Fifth Avenue Building, New York City, in the late 1930s, Paragon made character and baby dolls of hard and soft rubber.

"Paramount" Christmas tree lights see *Raylite Trading Co., Inc.*

P

Paramount Doll Co., Inc. Based on Bleecker Street, New York City, in the 1920s, Paramount employed the slogan, "The Line That's As Good As Its Name." It made a large assortment of doll and animal toys.

Paramount Enterprises, Inc. Children's phonograph records were this Concord Avenue, New York City, company's specialty in the Boomer years.

"Paramount" jigsaw puzzles prewar, see Parker Bros., Inc., Flatiron Bldg.

Paramount Mfg. Co. This Boston, Mass. company made films and toy projectors in the 1930s and '40s, in addition to 16-mm•cameras. It offered "popular priced candid cameras" in the late 1930s.

Paramount Rubber Co. Combined with New York Ball & Toy Co. in the 1920s, based on Fifth Avenue, New York City.

Paramount Toy Mfg. Co. Unusually for a Boomer-era manufacturer, Paramount specialized in stuffed horses on wheeled platforms, in addition to other stuffed toys. It was located on East 11th Street, New York City.

"Parcheesi" One of the most long-lived of board games, "Parcheesi" was introduced in 1867 by Selchow & Righter. Not issued with any special promotions, since as distributors Selchow & Righter were preoccupied with promoting the games of other manufacturers, "Parcheesi" nevertheless sold steadily. The company saw increasing sales for the game through the years, until it became one of its best sellers through the later 1800s and into the 20th century. During the Boomer years, "Parcheesi" remained one of the two flagship games for Selchow & Righter, alongside its new hit, "Scrabble." The inevitable imitations included "Pachisi" by Whitman Publishing Co., and "Pa-Chiz-Si" by Transogram Co., both in the Boomer years.

"Parcheesi" was introduced by Selchow & Righter in 1867.

Parfait Products Established in the late 1930s, this Chicago, Ill., company made "Flex-i-track" roll-up electric railway tracks, frog switches, and elevated viaducts for miniature railway systems.

Paris Mfg. Co. Established initially from the home business of Henry R. Morton in the 1860s, this sled manufacturer was originally the Paris Hill Mfg. Co., being based in Paris Hill, Maine. It moved in 1883 to South Paris. After Morton was forced out of the firm for a period of two years, Paris Hill went bankrupt. Morton bought the assets, this time retaining full control, and established Paris Mfg. Co. Paris made double-runner sleds, toboggans, the lower "Clipper" sleds, and the higher "Cutter" sleds. The firm later added skis, water skis, wagons, snow shoes, juvenile furniture, and school furniture, the latter an important ingredient in the firm's 20th century success. In the Boomer years, Paris emphasized sleds, skis, and water skis. The "Golden Falcon" was a new sled in the early 1960s. The company was still based in South Paris, Maine, and maintained offices in the Fifth Avenue Building, New York City.

"Park and Shop" game see *Milton Bradley Co.*

"Park Avenue" baby coach see *American-National Co.*

Park Avenue Doll Outfitters This prewar Philadelphia, Penn., firm made miniature dressed dolls. By the late 1930s they were assembled in rockers, cradles, and shooflies. The company also issued layettes and wooden shoes.

Park Plastics Co. Water guns, dart gun games, space toys including the "Park Rocket," and novelties comprised the line of this Linden, N.J., company. See *missile and launcher toys.*

"Parkcycles" prewar, see *American-National Co.*

"Parkway" baby stroller see *H.C. White Co.*

Parker-Black Co. The "Lok-Blox" construction blocks of the late 1930s were issued by this San Francisco, Calif., firm.

Parker Bros., Inc. Parker Brothers was founded in Salem, Mass., in 1883 by George S. Parker. The company established itself swiftly in its chosen specialties of board games, puzzles, and children's books.

Early titles included "Speculation" in 1885, and "Great Battlefields" and "Ivanhoe" in 1886. Titles in 1888 included "The Amusing Game of Innocence Abroad," "Billy Bump's Visit to Boston," "The Game of Chivalry," "The Good Old Game of Oliver Twist," "The Game of Peter Coddle's Trip to New York," and "When My Ship Comes In." "The Office Boy" was issued in 1889.

New titles for the 1890s included "The Game of American History," "The Game of Authors," "The Battle Game," "College Baseball Game," "Doctors and the Quack," "The Drummer Boy Game," "The Fortune Telling Game," "The Improved Geographical Game," "Johnny's Historical Game," "Klondike Game," "Letters or Anagrams," "Pike's Peak or Bust," and "The Street Car Game."

Parker Bros.' game "Admiral Byrd's Little America," from the 1930s.

Others included "Bo Bang & Hong Kong" and "Peter Coddle Tells of His Trip to Chicago," released in 1890; "The County Fair," in 1891; "Across the Continent," "The Game of Luck," "Penny Post," "Rex and the Kilkenny Cats Game," and "The World's Fair Game," in 1892; "Crossing the Ocean" and "Komical Konversation Kards," in 1893; and "The New Bicycle Game," "The Limited Mail & Express Game," and "The Game of Travel" in 1894.

The game firm hit its stride in the mid-1890s. Titles including "Apple Pie," "Cinderella," "Cock Robin," "Hare & Hound," "Hold the Fort," "Jack and the Bean Stalk," "The Little Cowboy Game," "Game of Napoleon," "Waterloo," and "Yankee Doodle" appeared in 1895. Titles "Bowling Board Game," "Captain Kidd and His Treasure," "Professional Game of Base Ball," and "Wide World and a Journey Round It" appeared in 1896; "The Black Cat Fortune Telling Game," "Bottle-Quoits," "The Century Run Bicycle Game," "Game of Favorite Art," and "The Junior Bicycle Game," in 1897; "Bicycle Cards," "The Game of Buffalo Bill," "Buffalo Hunt," "Football Game," "The London Game," "Realistic Golf," "The Siege of Havana," and "Venetian Fortune Teller," in 1898; and "Battle of Manila" and "Fire Alarm Game" in 1899.

The 1900s saw the appearance of popular titles including "The Cake Walk Game," "Captain Jinks," "Derby Day," "Dewey's Victory," "The Foot Race," "The Good Old Game of Corner Grocery," "The Good Old Game of Dr. Busby," "Heads and Tails," "History Up to Date," "House that Jack Built," "Major League Baseball Game," "The Trolley Came Off," "Twentieth Century Limited," and "Young People's Geographical Game."

The famous game "Sorry" was introduced by Parker Bros. in the 1930's

Others included "Athletic Sports," "Auction Letters," "The Merry Game of Bicycling," "The Hen That Laid the Golden Egg," and "Train for Boston" in 1900; "The Game of Jack Straws" in 1901; "Ping Pong" in 1902; "The Coon Hunt Game," "International Automobile Race," and "The Game of United States History" in 1903; "Crow Hunt" in 1904; "Mistress Mary, Quite Contrary," "The Game of Snap," "Toot," and "The Wogglebug Game of Conundrums" in 1905; "Pepper" in 1906; "Hey What?" in 1907; and "Barber Pole," "Crazy Traveller" and "Hidden Titles" in 1908.

New titles in the 1910s included "Barn Yard Tiddledy Winks," "The Comical Game of 'Who,'" "Game of Evening Parties," "Parker Brothers Post Office Game," "Game of Tiddledy Winks," and "Toy Town Telegraph Office." Others included "Comical Animal Ten Pins," "Game of Cycling," "Famous Authors," "I Doubt It," "National American Baseball Game," and "Panama Canal Game" in 1910; "The Game of Boy Scouts" in 1912; "Dreamland Wonder Resort Game" and "Peter Peter Pumpkin Eater" in 1914; "How Silas Popped the Question," "Kriegspiel Junior," and "Peg Baseball" in 1915; "The Airship Game" in 1916; "Broadway" in 1917; and "The Game of Camouflage" in 1918.

New 1920s titles included "Crazy Traveller," "The Dodging Donkey," "East Is East and West Is West," "Leaping Lena," "Speed Boat," and "A Trip Around the World." Others included "Keeping Up With the Jones," and "The Wonderful Game of Oz" in 1921; "Across the Continent" and "The Game of Cottontail and Peter" in 1922; "The Ancient Game of the Mandarins," "Excuse Me!," "The Five Wise Birds," "The Journey to Bethlehem," and "Peggy" in 1923; and "Boy Scouts Progress Game," "Buzzing Around," "Comical History of America," "Cones & Corns," and "Hickety Pickety" in 1924.

1925 saw the appearance of the games "All-American Football," "The Boy Hunter," "Chivalry," "The Fairies' Cauldron Tiddledy Winks Game," and "Peg'ity"; 1926, the games "Captain Kidd Junior," "Knockout Andy," and "Touring"; 1927, the games "Hokum," "Lindy Flying Game," and "Lindy

Hop-Off"; 1928, the games "Amateur Golf," "Japanola," "Johnny Get Your Gun," "The Lame Duck," "Nip & Tuck Hockey," and "Wee, the Magnetic Flying Game"; and 1929, "Cats and Dogs" and "Flying the United States Airmail."

At the brink of the Great Depression of 1929, the company boasted of having the "Largest Selling Games in the World." Its leading titles were "Ping-Pong," "Pollyanna," "Flying Four," "Lame Duck," "Lindy Hop Off," "Sixes and Sevens," "Duello," "Wild Goose Hunting," "Beau Monde," "Parker's Indoor Obstacle Golf," "Lindy," "East Is East," "The Knight's Journey," "Jonah and the Whale," "Kitty Kitty," "Hokum," "Boy Scout's Progress Game," "Halma," "Air Mail Game," "Pegity," "Game of Oz," "Touring," "Peg Base Ball," "Five Wise Birds," "Wee," "Across the Continent," "Wings," and the "Pastime Picture Puzzles."

New titles for the 1930s included "Alice in Wonderland," "Big Bad Wolf Game," "Bowl 'Em," "Eddie Cantor's Tell It to the Judge," "Stratosphere," "They're Off! Race Horse Game," and "Walt Disney's Uncle Remus Game."

In the earlier 1930s, Parker Bros. was touting itself as "The Standard of Excellence." Some of its "fashionable" games of the time were "Sorry" and "Admiral Byrd's Little America." The company was also making picture puzzles, checkers, chessmen, dominoes, anagrams, and Ping Pong sets, as well as such standards as "Pit," "Touring," "Rook," and "Pegity."

In the mid-1930s it introduced the card game "Make-A-Million" to a line with a number of prominent titles: "Diabolo," "Pollyanna," "Camelot," "Five Wise Birds," "Derby Day," "Pastime Picture Puzzles," "Zig Zag," "Quoitennis," "Tenikoit Rings," "Van Loon's Wide World," "Winnie-the-Pooh," "Grand Camelot," and "Walt Disney's Big Bad Wolf." The game it purchased in 1935 from Charles Darrow, however, became its most notable single title for the remainder of the 20th century, leaving "Make-A-Million" in the proverbial dust: "Monopoly."

In another important development, Parker Bros. obtained license to develop Walt Dis-

ney character games in the later '30s, resulting in the titles "Donald Duck's Own Party Game" and "Snow White and the Seven Dwarfs" in 1938.

Other titles included "Crows in the Corn" in 1930; "The Baron Munchausen Game" in 1933; "Pigskin, Tom Hamilton's Fooball Game" in 1934; "Psychic Baseball Game" in 1935; "Finance and Fortune," "Monopoly, Jr.," and "Stock Exchange" in 1936; "Finance," "Lowell Thomas' World Cruise," "Man Hunt," "Philo Vance," and "Skyscraper" in 1937; "Calling All Cars" and "The Lone Ranger Game" in 1938; and "Peter Coddle's Trip to the World's Fair" in 1939.

Titles in the 1940s included "Dig," "The Great American Flag Game," and "India" of 1940. Wartime issues included "Flying the Beam" in 1941, and "Conflict" and "Ranger Commandos" in 1942.

In the postwar years, Parker Bros.' list of best-sellers was a mixture of titles old and new. Reliable games for the company included "Monopoly," "Careers," "Clue," "Dig," "Contack," "Lexicon," "States and Cities," "Lone Ranger," "Magic Doll," "Quick Wit," "Rich Uncle," "Bonanza," "Camelot," "Rook," "Pit," "Touring," "Going to Jerusalem," "Pegity," "Pollyana," "Sorry," "Panda," "Children's Hour," "Donald Duck's Party Game," "Winnie The Pooh Game," "Flinch," "Finance," "Ping Pong," "Tiddledy Winks," "Pigskin," "Travel and Treasure," and "Make a Million." Traditional games including checkers and dominoes also continued to be important to the company.

In the 1930's Parker Bros. released the "Winnie-the-Pooh game."

P

Parley, Peter Samuel G. Goodrich used the "Peter Parley" pseudonym on children's books in the early 19th century, and made the name as famous as such pseudonyms as "Carolyn Keene" of the next century. Other authors, including Nathaniel Hawthorn, had titles appear under the name. *Peter Parley's Magazine* appeared 1833-1841. A *Peter Parley's Primer* was also issued.

"Parquetry" blocks see *Playskool Institute, Inc.*

Parris Mfg. Co. This Savannah, Tenn., firm established a name for itself with air rifles and toy guns, notably the "TraineRifles" bolt-action and cork-shooting air rifles of the 1950s and '60s. It also issued "Kadet" pistols, indoor putting games, and target games.

party favors see *favors and souvenirs.*

"Pastime" picture puzzles see *Parker Bros., Inc.*

Passamaquoddy Boat Co. This Lubec, Maine, company manufactured toy sail and tug boats, battle ships, scows, swings, and wooden novelties in the late 1930s.

Passon, Inc. Passon was a Philadelphia, Penn., manufacturer of dartboards, wooden post cards, and novelties in the late prewar years.

patent dates While many toys bear patent dates, and such dates can be of assistance in dating a toy, patent numbers can also be misleading. Some toy manufacturers guarding an innovation used in an entire line of toys will put the number for that particular patent on the entire line, in which case the same patent number might appear on unrelated toys over decades. In general, however, patent numbers in U.S. toys from 1860 to date are more helpful than not in attempting to assess a toy's manufacturing date. In German toys, items produced after 1890 usually bear patent dates.

Patent Engineering Co. Located in Chicago, Ill., Patent Engineering issued the "Re-Kop" poker rummy game of the late 1930s.

Patent Novelty Co., Inc. This Fulton, Ill., firm made the "Fulton Toys" line of pull toys, mechanical toys, and "Jr. Household" toys in the 1920s. The "Fulton Action Toys" of the late 1920s included the pull-toys "Teeter Tots," which featured bead figures on a teeter that moved as the toy rolled; the similar "Tom and Jerry"; "Busy Buddies," with an action similar to an Irish Mail; "Gray Mares," and "Tumbling Twins," with gymnastic tumbling bead figures. The toys sold from 25 to 50 cents. The firm moved to West 34th Street, New York City, by the end of the Great Depression, and changed its name to Patent Novelty Corp. The company still made "Fulton" mechanical pull toys, marble toys, toy grocery stores, "sand boats" and shovels, and children's "practical" carpet sweepers, dust pans, and dusting sets into the mid-1930s.

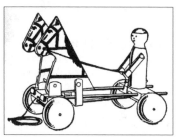

The Patent Novelty pull toy "'Fulton Action Toy' Gray Mare" was released in the 1920s.

Pathegrams, Inc. "Dione Quintuplets" films were sales leaders for this Rockefeller Plaza, New York City, company in the late 1930s. Pathegrams issued 8 and 16 mm. silent and sound films for home and toy projectors.

"Patrician" phonographs see *J.W. Spear & Sons, Inc..*

"Patsy" dolls see *Fleischaker & Baum.*

Pattberg Novelty Corp. Established on West 34th Street, New York City, in the late 1930s, Pattberg manufactured games for adults, backgammon, and poker chips.

patterns, doll clothes Patterns for doll clothes served as a kind of sewing set for girls, an activity outfit that had the practical result of providing clothing for dolls. Prewar

P

manufacturers included the Conde Nast Publications.

"Patti Page" cutout books see *Samuel Lowe Co.*

"Patty Hill" toys prewar, see *Milton Bradley Co.*

"Paul Revere" crayons see *Milton Bradley Co.*

"Paul Winchell" dolls see *Juro Novelty Co.*

Paulben Industries Juvenile all-formica dinette sets were the specialty of this Brooklyn, N.Y., company in the 1950s-60s. It also made toy chests.

Paulmar Novelties Co., Inc. This East 25th Street, New York City, doll and novelty manufacturer was active in the Boomer years.

Pavick's Mfg. Co., Inc. Pavick's of Akron, Ohio, is a little-known manufacturer of metal toy autos in the 1930s. It also made wooden toys and games, the "Joy-O" paddle ball, and advertising specialties.

Pawnee Bill's Indian Trading Post

"Authentic Indian" items comprised this Pawnee, Okla., company's Boomer-era line. It included tom-toms, moccasins, bows and arrows, spears, tomahawks, dance and ceremonial rattles, and tepees.

A.S. Payne, Inc. The "Bristle Archery" and "Bris-Targ" games of the 1930s were made by this North Bennington, Vt., manufacturer. The company specialized in dart games. By the late 1930s it was producing adult shuffleboard sets.

C. Sidney Payne Cast metal toys and souvenirs were products of this Southampton, Long Island, N.Y., company in the late 1930s.

Payton Products Plastic toys, including plastic cowboy and Indian figures and toy cars, were the specialty of Payton, based in the Fifth Avenue Building, New York City, in the Boomer years.

pea shooters One of a number of toys formerly home-made that became a manufactured item in the Boomer years, pea shooters were produced by companies including Chemical Sundries Co., Jak-Pak-Inc., the Kirchhof Patent Co., Lee Products Co., Nadel & Sons, and Presto Enterprises.

"Peanuts" Charles M. Schulz's famous "Peanuts" cartoon, as philosophical a strip as ever hit the funny pages, inspired numerous playthings in the Boomer years, including toys by Hungerford Plastics Corp., coloring books by the Saalfield Publishing Co., games by Selchow & Righter, and stuffed toys by Master Industries.

Peck & Snyder A sporting-goods manufacturer, Peck & Snyder was established in New York City in 1865.

Peco Mfg. Co. A prewar manufacturer of children's desks in Groton, N.Y., Peco also made sheet metal toys.

pedal cars Although not the most common, pedal cars certainly rank among the most important of automotive toys in the 20th century. Not only did they embody the hopes and dreams Americans tended to invest in their automobiles—some, such as the "Kidillac," certainly must have embodied not only youthful hopes and dreams but adult ones, too—but they were also successful activity toys.

Important manufacturers in the earlier prewar years included the American National Co., Corcoran Mfg. Co., Dayton Toy & Specialty Co., Garton Toy Co., the Gendron Mfg. Co., and Gendron Wheel Co. Others included Aero Mfg. Co., Auto-Wheel Coaster Co., the W.J. Baker Co., the Globe Co., Hedstrom-Union Co., Junior Toy Corp., the Kuniholm Mfg. Co., Metalcraft Corp., the Monarch Products Co., Sheboygan Coaster & Wagon Works, O.W. Siebert Co., Taylor Bros. Mfg. Co., Toledo Metal Wheel Co., United-Delta Corp., and H.C. White Co. See also *pedals.*

By the later prewar years, the number of companies was reduced, and included American National, Auto-Wheel Coaster, Garton, Gendron Wheel, Hedstrom-Union, Jawin Mfg. Co., Junior Toy, and Kuniholm.

The Murray-Ohio Mfg. Co. was one of the most successful companies involved in the field, establishing itself through the prewar years and maintaining a high profile through the Boomer years, especially the 1960s. Its many pedal vehicles included the "Firebird" auto, "Gold Cup Special" race car, the "Jolly Roger" pedal boat, and the "Murray 2 Ton" farm tractor and trailer set.

The Garton Toy Co. pedal car "Country Squire."

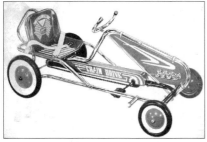

The "Scat Car," by American Machine & Foundry Co., 1960s.

"Pedal Scooter" see *Taylor Bros. Mfg. Co.*

pedalmobile "Pedalmobile" was a word for pedal car, as in the "Pedalmobile Flyer" of 1912.

pedals Parts for juvenile wheel goods were often manufactured by firms other than the named manufacturer. This led to a certain degree of uniformity between the products of different companies, a fact that has made the restoration efforts of collectors less onerous. Pedals were one such part, being made by firms including J.H. Graham Co., Torrington Co., Persons-Majestic Mfg. Co., and E.R. Wagner Mfg. Co.

"Pedigree" pencils see *Hassenfeld Bros., Inc.*

"Pee Wee Circus" see *Alan-Jay Plastics, Inc.*

"Peek-A-Boo" books prewar, see *McLoughlin Bros.*

Peer Products Co. Division see *Gerber Plastics Co.*

Peerless Doll Shoe Co. Based in the earlier 1930s on Gold Street, New York City, Peerless made exactly what its name indicates. It moved to Broadway in the later '30s.

Peerless Engraving Co. A Little Rock, Ark., manufacturer, Peerless Engraving made prewar games, juvenile books, and kindergarten play sets. It issued paper novelties under the "Sillyfold" and "Sillyette" trademarks.

"Peerless" marbles see *Peltier Glass Co.*

The Peerless Model Airplane Co. Model airplane kits and flying gliders were made by this Lakewood, Ohio, firm in the 1930s and '40s.

Peerless Pencil Co. In addition to tinsel cords and ribbons, and presumably pencils, this West 21st Street, New York City, firm also made toys in the 1930s.

Peerless Playthings Co., Inc. This Boomer-era manufacturer issued doctor and nurse kits, guns, coloring sets, crayon sets, clay sets, toy jewelry, games, and table tennis. It was located in Ridgefield Park, N.J.

Peerless Sporting Goods Co. This manufacturer of "popular priced" goods in the 1930s and '40s was located on Broadway, New York City.

"Peerless" velocipedes see *Monarch Products Co.*

"Peerless" world globes see *Weber-Costello Co.*

"Peg Blox" see *Lincoln Logs Division.*

"Peg Village" wooden toys prewar, see *Holgate Bros. Co.*

P

Peggy Anne Doll Clothes, Inc. This postwar Springfield, Mass., company issued doll clothes and accessories.

"Peggy Anne" doll furniture see *The Woodcraft Toy Studio.*

"Peggy Box" The "Peggy Box" trade name was used on prewar wooden toys by Playskool Institute. A "Peggy Pull" pull-toy and peg-board was also issued by the company in the 1930s.

"Peggy" dolls see *George Borgfeldt Corp.*

"Pegity" see *Parker Bros., Inc.*

"Pelco" toys prewar, see *Petrie-Lewis Mfg. Co., Inc.*

Pelso Co. Established on Fifth Avenue, New York City, in the late 1930s, Pelso issued the "Make-Ur-Own" crossword puzzle outfit.

Peltier Glass Co. Based in Ottawa, Ill., Peltier made toy glass marbles. In the late 1930s it issued Chinese checker games. In the Boomer years the company classified its own products into three groups: toy glass marbles, Chinese checker marbles, and "Cat's Eye" marbles.

Bruno Pelz Bruno Pelz, located on West 27th Street, New York City, made dressed rubber dolls in the 1930s.

pencil, electric The electric pencil was sold as a novel activity toy in the prewar years. Manufacturers included Carron Mfg. Co., Sheridan Electro Units Corp., and Harry A. Ungar.

Pendelton & Townsend Besides its specialty of folding tables, this Patterson, N.Y., firm also made play blocks.

"Penguin" crayons see *Holgate Bros. Co.*

Penn Handcraft Co. Novelty animals were made by this E. 169th Street, New York City, firm in the mid-1930s.

Penn Line Mfg. Co. This Boomer-era Boyertown, Penn., firm made "HO" electric trains and accessories.

Penn Novelty Co. A Philadelphia, Penn., company, Penn Novelty made the "Hi-Yo Silver, Lone Ranger" paper caps of the late '30s.

Penn Stuffed Toy Co., Inc. This Grand Street, New York City, manufacturer made both high-grade and popular-priced mama and baby dolls in the 1920s.

Pennant Corp. Based in Grand Rapids, Mich., Pennant made postwar toy chests.

Penner, Joe see *"Goo-Goo."*

Pennsylvania Athletic Products Toy-size footballs and basketballs were specialties of this Boomer-era Jeannette, Penn., firm.

Pennsylvania Rubber Co. of America, Inc. Based in Jeannette, Penn., Pennsylvania Rubber made indoor and outdoor decorated rubber play balls in the 1930s and '40s.

"Penny Brite" see *De Luxe Reading Corp.*

penny toys Penny toys, which are mentioned by American retailers by the mid-19th century, are entirely as what they seem to be. The category denotes toys having nothing in common except their cost, which was kept as minimal as possible. Low cost does not mean low quality, however. J.&E. Stevens of Connecticut, for instance, was issuing miniature cast-iron implements, including axes and garden tools, as penny toys in the 1800s. Prewar manufacturers included American Toy Works, Arcade Mfg. Co., the Dent Hardware Co., Grey Iron Casting Co., Kirchhof Patent Co., Reliance Mfg. Co., and Universal Toy & Novelty Mfg. Co.

"PEP" buttons Kellogg's "PEP" cereal contained pin-back button premiums from around 1943 into the later '40s. Initially the buttons bore military squadron insignia. With the end of the war, comic characters were introduced. A total of 86 characters were depicted.

Peppy Mfg. Co., Inc. Established on Broadway, New York City, in the late 1930s, Peppy made cowboy outfits, play suits, and masquerade costumes.

"Peppy" single-shot book caps see *Kilgore Mfg. Co, Inc.*

The Per-Chem Co. This Wilmington, Del., company issued the interesting specialty of perfume chemistry sets in junior and senior sizes, in the late prewar years.

Peresich Industries The "Perry Jeep" take-apart scale model jeep of the early 1960s was issued by this Biloxi, Miss., company.

Perfect Novelties Mfg. Co. The "Annette" dolls of the 1930s were produced by this West 17th Street, New York City, firm. It also made stuffed animals.

Perfect Rubber Co. Based in Mansfield, Ohio, Perfect Rubber made inflated and sponge balloons in the 1930s and '40s.

Perfect Toy Corp. Stuffed toys, musical toys, and novelties were postwar specialties of this Brooklyn, N.Y., company.

"Perfection" The trade name of "Perfection" saw wide prewar use in the toy industry. Louis Wolf & Co. used the name for a line of toys, forts, dollhouses and dolls. Halsam made checkers, Illinois Specialty Co. made a junior ironing board, and L. Hopkins Mfg. Co. made play yards using the same name.

Perfection Mfg. Co. The "Rock-A-Bye" nursery specialties, including collapsible carriages, of the 1930s and '40s were made by this St. Louis, Mo., company. The line continued into the Boomer years with carriages, strollers, walkers, baby seats, swings, and doll carriages.

"Perfex" vacuum cleaner see the *Meccano Co. of America, Inc., The*

"Perfo-Jet" roll caps see *J. Halpern Co.*

"Perforated" paper caps see *Kilgore Mfg. Co., Inc.*.

"Performing Bob" Gibbs Mfg. Co. used the "Performing" trade name on several of its toys, such as "Performing Bob" and "Performing Jumbo" of the mid-1930s.

Peripole Products, Inc. Percussion instruments for children were the specialty of this Brooklyn, N.Y., company in the 1950s and '60s.

"Perkins," late 1930s see *American Tissue Mills.*

Perkins, F.M. see *Kenton Hardware Co.*

S.F. Perkins Aerial Advertising Kite & Zeppelin Balloon Co. As its name might indicate, S.F. Perkins made advertising items in the prewar period, including balloons up to 25 feet across. It also made both toy and advertising kites, and toy balloons.

"Perky Puppet People" see *Jay V. Zimmerman Co.*

"Permoplast" toy outfits see *American Art Clay Co.*

J.B. Perrin Co., Inc. Adjustable gun belts and holsters comprised this postwar Culver City, Calif., firm's line.

"Perry Mason" game see *Transogram Co., Inc.*

Persia Mfg. Co. This Chicago, Ill., firm made stuffed toys in the late 1930s.

"Personality Pets" see *Collegiate Mfg. Co.*

"Pet" coaster wagon see *The Globe Co.*

Pet-Toy, Inc. Stuffed fur toy animals were the postwar products of this West 17th Street, New York City, company.

Pet Toy of N.H. This Boomer-era Claremont, N.H., firm made a variety of playthings, including banks, horseshoes, boats, giant checkers, sand toys, and polyethylene baseballs and bats.

"Peter Gunn" holster sets see *Pilgrim Leather Goods Co., Inc.*

"Peter Huzzlewit" "Peter Huzzlewit" was a popular game in the 1840s.

"Peter Pan" The Walt Disney version of this James M. Barrie children's story inspired numerous playthings, including games by

Transogram Co., phonograph records by Synthetic Plastics Novelties, hand puppets by Gund Mfg. Co. and the Oak Rubber Co., figures by the Sun Rubber Co., and paper dolls by Whitman Publishing Co.

This pre-Disney "Peter Pan" game was issued by Selchow & Righter in 1927.

Peter Pan Toys Based on West 17th Street, New York City, in the postwar years, Peter Pan Toys specialized in stuffed animals.

"Peter Pelican" wood toys see *Florida Playthings, Inc.*

"Peter Rabbit" The carrot-thieving neighbor to Farmer Brown appeared in numerous toy and game guises through the 20th century. Prewar examples included an action toy by A.W. Drake Mfg. Co., a board game by Samuel Gabriel Sons & Co., a paint box by Milton Bradley Co., and painting and drawing books by the Saalfield Publishing Co. The "Peter Rabbit Series" of picture puzzles were published by Milton Badley Co.

Peterborough Ski & Toboggan Co. This late 1930s firm was located on Fifth Avenue, New York City.

F.D. Peters Co., Inc. The wood-turning company F.D. Peters Co. of Gloversville, N.Y., made wood toys, bent-wood snow skates, juvenile golf sticks, junior ski and pole sets, and games. The line was issued from the 1930s through the wartime years. Pre-school toys, custom toy work, and wooden wheels and other toy parts for other manufacturers were an important part of its output, with toy chests, toboggans, and sleds becoming important additions in the 1950s and '60s.

F.W. Peterson Corp. A wood-turning and box manufacturer, F.W. Peterson made yo-yos, tops, noisemakers, and checker sets, among other toy specialties. It was based on Prince Street, New York City, in the 1930s and '40s.

Peterson Mfg. Co. Peterson produced an important line of "Scrappy" items in the 1930s, including paint sets, crayons, modeling clay, and poster paints. It was based in the Fifth Avenue Building, New York City.

Petite Doll Accessories A Broadway, New York City, company in the Boomer years, Petite Doll made doll gloves, stockings, shoes, and underwear.

"Petite" dolls prewar, see *American Character Doll Co.*

"Petite Princess" Ideal Toy Corp. introduced the "Petite Princess Fantasy Furniture" line in 1964. The dollhouse furniture was color-coordinated and highly detailed. The "Petite Princess Fantasy Family" included four pliable dolls measuring 3-7/8 and 5-1/2 inches tall.

Petrie-Lewis Mfg. Co., Inc. A New Haven, Conn., firm, Petrie-Lewis specialized in magic sets, but also produced playthings including "Jumbo Electric Engines," "Wonder Kaleidoscopes," and "Jimmy Jounce" and "Billy Bounce" toys, in the 1920s. The firm continued issuing kaleidoscopes, puzzles and magic sets through the prewar years.

pewter Pewter was used from Revolutionary times for toys, being employed by silversmiths in making doll dishes and similar small items. To a lesser degree the metal continued in use into the 20th century. Prewar manufacturers included Dowst Mfg. Co., Novelty Casting Co., Peter F. Pia, Savoye Pewter Toy Mfg. Co., and Tiny-Tot Toy Co. In the prewar years, many manufacturers working in "white" or "slush metal" referred to their products as "pewter." See *die-cast toys, slush metal toys, trifle, zamac.*

Phe-Lena Novelty Creators Soft stuffed dolls were the specialty of this West 22nd Street, New York City, firm in the late 1930s.

Phenix Mfg. Co. A Milwaukee, Wis., firm, Phenix Manufacturing made miniature bowling alleys and stilts in the 1930s.

Philadelphia Inquirer The famous newspaper issued at least one game, the 1896 board game "The Philadelphia Inquirer Baseball Game."

Philadelphia Screen Mfg. Co. Coaster wagons were made in the 1930s by this Philadelphia, Penn., firm.

Philadelphia Tin Toy Manufactory Founded in the 1840s, this company was also sometimes listed as Francis, Field & Francis, possibly the original name of these "japanners" or "tinmen." The company made tin trains, animals on wheels, and boats on wheels, competing successfully with the more abundant manufacturers of wooden toys at the time.

Philippino spinners The toy now known primarily as the "yo-yo" was strongly associated with the Philippines in the 1920s and '30s. The term "Philippino spinners" was a typical name given to the toy by manufacturers at the time.

Phillips, Mary Waterman The "Mawaphil" line of soft dolls, issued through the 1930s and '40s by the Rushton Co., were named for designer Mary Waterman Phillips. Individual dolls included "Mary and Her Little Lamb," "Little Boy Blue," and "Tommie Tucker," from the "Nursery Rhymes" series.

Phillips Publishers, Inc. The "Spill and Spell" game of the early 1960s was issued by this Newton, Mass., publisher.

Philmore Mfg. Co., Inc. Based in Richmond Hill, N.Y., Philmore issued radio receiver kits and crystal radio accessories in the 1950s and '60s.

Phoenix Chair Co. Phoenix was a prewar Sheboygan, Wis., manufacturer of juvenile furniture. Its 1930s and '40s highchairs had pyralin trays.

Phoenix Costume Mfg. Co. Based in Philadelphia, Penn., Phoenix made the "Treacy Costumes" line of the 1920s. It included "Old Mother Hubbard" and other nursery rhyme characters.

Phoenix Novelty Corp. Novelty dolls were the leading prewar product of this Fifth Avenue, New York City, firm.

phonographs Although the phonograph was at first an unusual item to be made for children, being a delicate and expensive electrical machine, at least one prewar manufacturer specialized in "kiddie phonographs." Plaza Mfg. Co. produced several kinds of record players, including a portable, with hand crank in front, and a floor model, with its crank on the side and a handsome speaker cabinet facing to the front. The latter was made of genuine bird's-eye maple. In both, the lid opened to reveal a colorful illustration.

"Phyllis" dolls prewar, see *Bouton, Woolf Co., Inc.*

Peter F. Pia, Inc. Pia started business in 1848, making doll furniture and miniature tea sets of "trifle" or Britannia metal. The line of chairs, tables, beds, and carriages measured about 3 inches high. Some of the furnishings were upholstered. Founded in 1848, in New York City, in the 20th century Peter F. Pia was located on White Street, moving to Canal Street by the late 1930s. The company established its name with ornate and often elaborate versions of contemporary furniture. Some of the metal chairs and sofas had a horseshoe motif on the backrests. Pia also made at least one metal vehicle toy, a pewter replica of the presidential inaugural coach of George Washington. In the prewar years the company was still making pewter toys and novelties. It also made lead castings, and whistles.

pianos, toy The toy piano became an important toy in prewar times, with expertly constructed wooden versions appearing from the A. Schoenhut Co., a famous name in musical toys. Other manufacturers included N.D. Cass Co., the Herbert R. Gottfried Co., and Mason & Parker Mfg. Co. In the late prewar years, Carron Mfg. Co. and Marks Bros. Co. were also issuing toy pianos. In the postwar years, manufacturers included the N.D. Cass Sales Co., Theodore J. Ely Mfg. Co., Emenee Industries, the Hit Products Corp.,

Jaymar Specialty Co., Henry Katz, Riemann, Seabrey Co., and O. Schoenhut.

A. Schoen-hut's toy piano from the 1920s.

Picard Novelty Co. Established in the late 1930s in Westerly, R.I., Picard issued a "child's knockdown dining room set." It also made jigsaw puzzles.

J.W. Pickering & Son A Leominster, Mass., manufacturer, J.W. Pickering & Son made wooden toys including the 1930s "Pickering Play Pets."

Pickwick Sales Corp. Children's phonograph records were the postwar specialties of Pickwick, based in Long Island City, N.Y.

Picture Book Toys, Inc. A postwar Brooklyn, N.Y., manufacturer, Picture Book specialized in stuffed animals.

"Picture" marbles with comic faces see *Peltier Glass Co.*

picture puzzle, see *puzzle, picture.*

"Piedmont Series" picture puzzles see *Milton Bradley Co.*

"Pierce" children's vehicles see *Emblem Mfg. Co.*

"Pigs in Clover" A best-selling puzzle and something of a social phenomenon in America and abroad, "Pigs in Clover" was issued by Charles M. Crandall in 1889. The puzzle may have been the first of its kind, which involved small marbles, which were the pigs. These had to be driven into their pen.

The board consisted of a six-inch diameter wooden disk with four concentric circles of pasteboard attached to one side. Each of these circles had a gap, with each of the succeeding rings being the "inclosures" from which the "pigs" had to be driven to "pen,"

which was the central enclosure. Unlike later toys widely commercially made in the Boomer years having plastic-covered mazes with BB mice (or pigs), "Pigs in Clover" was a simple board game with no covering. The player placed the marbles in the outermost ring, and had to drive the marbles inward simply by tilting and moving the board.

According to the *New York World* that year, "Statesmen, diplomats, lawyers, judges, doctors, merchants, financiers and railroad presidents are just as much interested in the new puzzle as their clerks and office boys, and by general consent it has been pronounced the great sensation of the day."

Crandall made the toy at the Waverly Toy Works, which is where half his manufacturing business was located after 1885, and his entire manufacturing operation from 1886 on. The game was distributed solely by Selchow & Righter, who were jobbers as well as toy makers.

Pigskin, Inc. The "Pigskin" football game was made by this eponymous Pittsburgh, Penn. firm in the mid-1930s. A "Pigskin" game was later issued in 1940 by Parker Bros.

"Pike's Peak" picture puzzles see *The Puzzle Makers*

Pilcher's Sons, Henry, Inc. Based in Louisville, Ky., the juvenile furniture manufacturer Henry Pilcher's Sons made the 1930s "Timber-Tots" building blocks, and doll furniture.

"Pilgrim" cradles see *Stephen H. Bond.*

Pilgrim Leather Goods Co., Inc. In addition to toy and hobby leathercraft sets, Pilgrim issued pre-school toys in the Boomer years. It was based in Haverhill, Mass.

The Pilliod Cabinet Co. A Swanton, Ohio, furniture manufacturer, Pilliod also made toy cedar chests in eight sizes in the 1920s and '30s.

pin wheels see *pinwheels.*

"Pinco" see *Pinwheel Products Co.*

Pines Waterfront Co. This Chicago, Ill., firm made the "Charlie Horse" hobby horse toy in the 1930s, advertising it as a "child's exerciser."

ping pong see *table tennis.*

Berry Pink, Inc. Based on West 21st Street, New York City, in the prewar years, this manufacturer of marbles and sales promotion items moved to Fifth Avenue in the Boomer years, and changed its name to Berry Pink Industries. Its marbles were issued under the "Marble King" trade name, and included "Cat Eyes," "Rainbows," "Moonies," "Marine Puries," and "Jumbo Shooters."

"Pinky Lee" pogo sticks see *Roy Berlin Co.*

Pinwheel Products Co. Pinwheels, toy airplanes, and whistling, flying birds were specialties of this postwar Brooklyn, N.Y., company. Its line included Walt Disney character-related pinwheels in the 1950s and '60s. It used the slogan, "King Pin of the Pin Wheel Field."

pinwheels Pin wheels, or "pinwheels" as they tended to be spelled after World War II, are simple diversionary toys made with a stick and wind-catching, curved vanes, the latter made at first of paper or celluloid, later of plastic or lightweight foil. Prewar manufacturers included Bastian Bros., Louis Sametz, A.M. Samour Mfg. Co., Smethport Specialty Co., and G.C. Willett & Co. In the late 1930s, firms including Bastian Bros. and the Diamond Toy Co. joined their ranks. Postwar manufacturers included the Jerome Gropper Co., Irwin Corp., Nadel & Sons, Ogdin Mfg. Co., Pinwheel Products Co., and Welded Plastics Corp.

"The Pioneer" cap pistol see *Academy Die-Casting & Plating Co.*

"Pioneer Art" casting set see *Williams Kast-Art Co.*

"Pioneer" children's vehicles see *The Gendron Wheel Co.*

"Pioneer Builder" construction sets see *Wisconsin Toy Co.*

Pioneer Merchandise Co. Toy watches, rubber toys, and toy tool sets made up the Boomer-era product line of this Broadway, New York City, company.

The Pioneer Rubber Co. One of many prewar Ohio rubber manufacturers, Pioneer made toy balloons and novelties, and advertising balloons. In the later 1930s it obtained license to issue Edgar Bergen character balloons. The firm continued operating through the Boomer years.

pipe cleaners Pipe cleaners were a source of a great deal of childhood fun in the earlier 20th century. As pipe smoking grew less common in the later decades, their importance as a plaything-making material diminished. Various toy makers through the years used them in their manufactured toys and play sets, including Corneila Burdette in the 1930s.

Piqua General Supply Co. Based in Piqua, Ohio, this firm made wooden toys including the 1930s and '40s "Pul-It" tops, rubber jump ropes, and adjustable stilts.

"Pirate" toy chests see *The Modern Crafts Co.*

"Pirate and Traveler" game see *Milton Bradley Co.*

"Pirateland" figures see *Multiple Products Corp.*

pistol caps Postwar manufacturers included Acme Specialties Corp., J. Halpern Co., Kilgore, Leslie-Henry Co., Mattel, Nichols Industries, J.&E. Stevens Co., and Universal Playthings.

The "Mountie" cap pistol from Kilgore Mfg. Co., 1950s.

pistol holsters An important component of the cowboy outfit was the pistol holster.

Sometimes elaborately made of leather or leatherette, many holsters would bear character names, such as the "Lone Ranger" or "Roy Rogers," along with appropriate decorations.

Prewar manufacturers included All Metal Products Co., Arrow Novelty Co., Alexander Baron, Belvidere Strap Co., Brauer Bros., R.H. Buhrke & Co., Chancy Toy & Novelty Corp., Dumore Belt & Novelty Co., Feinberg-Henry Mfg. Co., Felder Bros., Indian Leather Holster Co., Keyston Bros., Lendzion Leather Goods Co., A.C. Morand Co., The Mordt Co., and Nitke Bros.

The "Halco" line by J. Halpern Co. was prominent among postwar holster sets. It included licensed "The Deputy," "Have Gun Will Travel," "Gunsmoke," "Lawman," "The Texan," "Steve Canyon," and "Wells Fargo Pony Express" holsters, among others.

Another prominent line issued by Leslie-Henry Co. featured "Maverick," "Wagon Train," "Texas Ranger," "Bonanza," and "Young Buffalo Bill," among others.

Other postwar producers included Arrow Sales Co., Bonnie Bilt, George Borgfeldt Corp., Carnell Mfg. Co., Chancy Toy & Sporting Goods Corp., Classy Products Corp., Corral Toys, John R. Craighead Co., Crown Novelty Co., Daisy Mfg. Co., Danlee Co., Dumore Belt & Novelty Co., Ellcraft Industries, Empress Varieties Mfg. Co., Esquire Novelty Corp., the Hubley Mfg. Co., Indian Leather Holster Co., Milton A. Jacobs, Jago Novelty Co., Keyston Bros., Mattel, McKinnon Leather Products Corp., Monarch Leather Goods Co., Mt. Vernon Mfg. Co., W.J. Murphy Co., Pal-Tom Mfg. Corp., J.B. Perrin Co., Pilgrim Leather Goods Co., R.&S. Toy Mfg. Co., Ray Plastic, Adolph Schwartz, Service Mfg. Co., Smart Style, Spraz Co., the J.&E. Stevens Co., Tex Tan, 20th Century Varieties, and Western Leather Novelties.

pistols, cap An important toy in the later 1800s, the cap pistol took on special significance in prewar years, when Western heroes of movies and radio gained prominence and inspired countless young cowboys. Prewar manufacturers included Dent Hardware Co.,

the Hubley Mfg. Co., the Kenton Hardware Co., Kilgore Mfg. Co., and the J.&E. Stevens Co. By the end of the prewar years, Acme Pistol Cap, National Fireworks Co., and St. Louis Pistols & Caps were also making cap pistols. In the postwar period, cap pistol popularity soared, in part because of widespread enthusiasm for western TV shows. The use of plastics also expanded manufacturers' options.

Manufacturers included Academy Die-Casting & Plating Co., Carnell Mfg. Co., Classy Products Corp., Cordelco Industries, Corral Toys, Esquire Novelty Corp., J. Halpern Co., the Hubley Mfg. Co., Irwin Corp., Milton A. Jacobs, Kilgore, Knickerbocker Plastic Co., Leslie-Henry Co., Mattel, W.J. Murphy Co., Nichols Industries, R.&S. Toy Mfg. Co., Renwal Toy Corp., George Schmidt Mfg., the J.&E. Stevens Co., 20th Century Varieties, and Western Leather Novelties.

pistols, toy Pistol toys, popular from the mid 1800s and through the 20th century, included water pistols, pea-shooting pistols, dart pistols, BB pistols, pop pistols, rubber-band pistols, rocket pistols, water pistols, and ray guns, made of materials including wood, steel, tin, paper, rubber, and plastic.

Prewar manufacturers included All Metal Products Co., Arrow Novelty Co., Alexander Baron, Bull's Eye Pistol Mfg. Co., Cadillac Specialty Co., the Conestoga Corp., Daisy Mfg. Co., Dent Hardware Co., Elastic Tip Co., Hubley Mfg. Co., W.P. Johnson Co., the Kenton Hardware Co., Kilgore Mfg. Co., King Mfg. Co., the Mordt Co., the Steel Stamping Co., the J.&E. Stevens Co., and the Tec-Toy Co.

Manufacturers of postwar miscellaneous, non-cap pistols included Bar Zim Toy Mfg. Co., E.R. Briggs Toys, Daisy Mfg. Co., Empress Varieties Mfg. Corp., J. Halpern, Irwin Corp., Jak-Pak-Inc., Langson Mfg. Co., Marksman Products, Multiple Products Corp., Nichols Industries, Ohio Art Co., Parris Mfg. Co., Platz Products Co., Pyro Plastics Corp., Ray Plastic, Renwal Toy Corp., and Tigrett Industries.

pistols, water The first metal water pistol was introduced by Daisy Mfg. Co. in 1913.

Based on a design by Fred Lefever, the gun was called "No. 8 Water Pistol." Daisy also issued the "Buck Rogers Liquid Helium" water pistol in the mid-1930s. One of the leading postwar manufacturers was Park Plastics Co., which issued a varied line in the 1950s and 1960s. Its water pistols included the "Watermatic Machine Gun," "Fanning Western Style Water Gun," "Snub-Bee" in various colors, "Squirt Ray" space gun, "Luger" clip gun and standard, "Lu-Gee" junior luger, "Sub-Machinegun," "Wee-Gee" midget water gun, "Dee-Gee" double-nozzled gun, and "250 Repeater" in .45 caliber style.

"Pit" see *Parker Bros., Inc.*

pitching horseshoes see *horseshoes.*

Pitmar Novelty Co. This late prewar manufacturer of favors and souvenirs was based in National City, Calif.

R.S. Pitts Mfg. Co. The "Leather-Kraft Work Shop" of the late 1930s was issued by this Hanover, Penn., firm.

"Pitty-Pat" scooter see *Kingston Products Corp.*

"Pixie" toys and games see *Steven Mfg. Co.*

"Pixie Puppets" see *Walco Bread Co.*

"Pixy" felt dolls and animals see *Mizpah Toy & Novelty Corp.*

"Pla-Golf" 1938-39, see *Johnson Store Equipment Co.*

"Pla-Klay" modelling sets see *The Meccano Co. of America*

"Pla-Master" see *Herman Iskin & Co., Inc.*

"Pla-Pal" coaster wagon see *The Globe Co.*

"Pla-Rite" games prewar, see *Selchow & Righter Co.*

"Pla-Skate" indoor-outdoor roller skates see *D.S. Williams Co., Inc.*

"Pla-Tiles" see *Hassenfeld Bros., Inc.*

Pla-Wood Products Corp. Based in Cleveland, Ohio, Pla-Wood issued table tennis tables and equipment, tees, and poker chips in the late prewar years.

"Plablox" nested blocks see *Jingl-Blox Toy Mfg. Co.*

Roland P. Place Co. A Midland, Mich., manufacturer of Christmas tree holders, Roland P. Place Co. also made "Dowmetal" gliders and airplane toys.

Plakie Toys, Inc. This postwar Youngstown, Ohio, firm issued plastic toys and dolls, as well as juvenile nursery lamps and cloth playbooks.

"Plaline" toys prewar, see *Gong Bell Mfg. Co., The*

"Plamor" blocks see *Halsam Products Co.*

F.W. Planert & Sons A Chicago, Ill., manufacturer, F.W. Planert & Sons made prewar roller and ice skates. It changed its name to Planert Skate Co. by the late 1930s.

Planert Tool & Mfg. Co. The mid-1930s "Hum-Sing" metal peg top was made by this Chicago, Ill., firm.

"Planet Patrol" party goods see *American Merri-Lei Corp.*

"Planet Patrol Saucer" see *Park Plastics Co.*

"Planet Patrol" teepee see *J.W. Johnson Co.*

"Planet-Stiks" see *W.E. Michaels Products.*

planetariums Toy planetariums were among the new science toys of the Boomer years, made possible through plastic molding techniques and the availability of inexpensive batteries. Manufacturers included Bellevue Products and Harmonic Reed Corp.

"Planeteer" card game see *W.E. Michaels Products.*

P

Plaque Craft, Inc. Paint-by-number plaque kits were the specialty of this 1950s-60s Baltimore, Md., company.

PlaRola Corp. This Easton, Md., firm issued the "PlaRola" organs, rolls, and harmonica players in the late 1930s.

Plas-Tex Corp. This late 1940s and early '50s Los Angeles, Calif., company issued plastic playthings including toy vehicles and space toys.

The Plas-Trix Co., Inc. Educational toys, "Link-a-Beads, puzzles and games for adults and children, and rack toys were specialties of this postwar Brooklyn, N.Y., company.

"Plasco" see *Plastic Art Toy Corp. of America.*

"Plast-I-Clay" see *American Art Clay Co.*

"Plasti-Box" kites see *The Hi-Flier Mfg. Co.*

"Plasti-Play" molder kits see *The Metal Ware Corp.*

Plastic Art Toy Corp. of America Based in E. Paterson, N.J., this postwar firm was best known for its doll house furniture, issued from the war years through the 1950s and '60s, and doll houses. The firm also made such items as push toys and juvenile record players, relying at least initially on Columbia Protektosite for the injection molding work. The company used the "Plasco" trade name.

Plastic Block City, Inc. The popular "Block City" building-block construction sets of the 1950s and '60s was issued by this Chicago, Ill., company. By the mid-1950s the building sets were oriented toward different age groups, starting with "Pre-School Building Blocks," for children ages 2 to 6, "Block City" for general construction play, and "Brick Town," a scale-model construction set for older children. The firm also made "Irish Mails," dartboards, plastic tops, "Kay Stanley" cake mix sets, and "Bat 'Em Catch 'Em" machines. By the late 1950s, the firm also made "Jungle Jump" adjustable jump ropes, hand-held movie viewers, and "Bat 'Em Catch 'Em" automatic pitching toys.

Plastic Injecto Corp. Harmonicas and "blow accordions" were specialties of this postwar Union, N.J., company. Its line included "Melody Bells," a plastic instrument with eight tuned aluminum bells, with small hammer; "Piano-Key Blow Accordion" with eight keys; "Hot Potato," a bright red toy ocarina capable of two octaves; and "Big Twin," a two-sided plastic harmonica. The firm also made conventional, metal-body harmonicas.

"Plastic Jet" kites see the *Hi-Flier Mfg. Co.*

"Plastic Masters" toy cars see *Precision Plastics Co.*

"Plastic Pals" see *I.S. Sutton & Sons.*

Plastic Playthings, Inc. Baby rattles and toys comprised this West 50th Street, New York City, firm's 1950s-60s line.

Plastic Novelties Inc. A firm located on East 10th Street, New York City, Plastic Novelties entered the comic-character merchandise arena in the late 1930s with Walt Disney and Edgar Bergen related pencil sharpeners, key chains, and napkin rings.

Plastic Processes Based in Freeport, N.Y., Plastic Processes issued plastic charms, educational toys, carded toys, games, tricks and novelties in the 1950s and '60s.

Plastic Toy & Novelty Corp. This postwar Brooklyn, N.Y., company specialized in plastic blocks, sand pails, sieve sets, infants' toys, and educational toys.

plastic toys The history of plastic toys began with celluloid and bakelite items from the 1920s and '30s. Things heated up in the late 1930s, when plastics technology was beginning to mature, and toy manufacturers were beginning to take more risks with the new materials. Kilgore Mfg. Co., for instance, issued the "Jewels for Playthings" line of vehicle toys beginning in 1938. While many collectors and historians of vintage toys have looked askance at the introduction of plastics to the toy world, others have appreciated the "Jewels for Playthings" name as being literally true.

The heyday of the plastic toy encompassed the Baby Boomer years. Among the toy hits of 1945 and later Christmases was Dillon-Beck

Mfg. Co.'s futuristic bubble-topped coupe, a small toy made of Lumarith, which was a million-seller in its first season. Plastic made possible almost all the great hits of the Boomer years, from "Cootie" in the late '40s, "Mr. Potato Head" in 1952, "Robert the Robot" in the mid-1950s, and "Barbie" in 1959, to "Etch-A-Sketch" in 1960, the "Chatty Cathy" line in the early 1960s, "Mr. Machine" and his fellow Ideal Toy Corp. robots of the early 1960s, "Mouse Trap Game" of 1963, and "Easy-Bake Oven" of 1964.

Manufacturers by the dozens embraced the new plastics, including AMT Corp., Alan-Jay Plastics, All-Power Mfg. Co., the Amloid Co., Archer Plastics, BW Molded Plastics, Banner Plastics Corp., Bar Zim Toy Mfg. Co., Bayshore Industries, Best Plastics Corp., Bonnnie Bilt, Brockton Plastics, Buddy "L" Quality Toys, Carnival Toy Mfg. Corp., Character Molding Corp., Childhood Interests, Coleco Toy Proucts, Commonwealth Plastics Corp., Corwin Plastics, B.L. Custer Co., Deko Mold, A.H. Delfausse Co., Dell Plastics Co., Eldon Mfg. Co., Elmar Products Co., Empire Plastic Corp., Empress Varieties Mfg. Corp., Fisher-Price Toys, Foster Grant Co., Gerber Plastic Co., Giant Plastics Corp., Marty Gilman, Golden Triangle Toy Co., Hale-Nass Corp., Halsam Products Co., Handi-Craft Co., Harett Gilmar, Hassenfeld Bros., the Hubley Mfg. Co., Ideal Toy Corp., Irwin Corp., Milton A. Jacobs, Jolly Blinker Corp., Henry Katz, Kenner Products Co., Knickerbocker Plastic Co., Kohner Bros., Fred Kroll Associates, Kroll Trading Co., Kusan, Lapin Products, Lido Toy Corp., Lo-E Mfg. Corp., M. & L. Toy Co., M. Manheim Co., Mattel, Multiple Products Corp., Newman Premier Corp., and Ohio Art Co.

Renwal Toy Corp.'s "Cadillac Convertible" plastic toys.

Others included Park Plastics Co., Payton Products, Pinwheel Products Co., Plakie Toys, Plawood-Mormac Corp., Polly Plastics, Premier Products, Pressman Toy Corp., Processed Plastic Co., Product Miniature Co., Pyro Plastics Corp., Renwal Toy Corp., Rock Industries, Sanitoy, Southern California Pipe & Steel, Spec-Toy-Culars, Stahlwood Toy Mfg. Co., Star Mfg. Co., Structo Mfg. Co., Sidney A. Tarrson, Tamor Plastic Corp., Tico-Toys, Transogram Co., U.S. Plastics Corp., Vantines, Weil Bros., Westland Plastics, Worcester Toy Co., and S. Zucker & Co. I have omitted names beginning with "plastic."

Plastic pedal tractor by Garton Toy Co., 1961.

Plastic Toys Corp. Based in Byesville, Ohio, this Boomer-era firm made plastic soldiers, toy animals, cowboys, cowgirls, mounted figures, space-travelers, rockets, tractors, trailers, balls, kite reels, racers, and rattles.

"Plasticene" An oil-based, non-drying modeling clay, "Plasticene" became popular in prewar years. Samuel Gabriel Sons & Co., trademarked the name, producing "Harbutt's Plasticene" in the 1930s.

Plasticraft Mfg. Co. Plastic toys, 10-cent assortments, infant toys, miniature train sets, and toy boats, cars and trucks were Boomer-era specialties of this Kearny, N.J., company.

plastics Some plastic suppliers to the toy industry in the 1930s included American Catalin Corp., Chicago Moulded Products Corp., and DuPont Viscoloid Co. See also *celluloid, thermoplastics, thermosetting plastics.*

Plastics Masters, Inc. This postwar Chicago, Ill., firm issued scale-model skeletons and scale models of the human body.

"Plasticville" see *Bachmann Bros., Inc.*

Plastik, Inc. This late prewar Boston, Mass., firm issued poker chips and dice.

Plastikaire Products, Inc. A postwar manufacturer of swimming pool supplies, this Westbury, Long Island, N.Y., company also made inflatable toys and pools.

"Plastikit" see *Monogram Models.*

"Plastoy" modeling clay see *Illinois Clay Products Co.*

platform horse see *spring horse.*

"Platime" art cubes see *Halsam Products Co.*

The Platt & Munk Co., Inc. Based in the Fifth Avenue Building, New York City, the Platt & Munk Co. ranked among the foremost publishers of children's books in the earlier 20th century, gaining special prominence for its "Uncle Wiggly" series. From the 1920s through the prewar years it issued a line of linen and paper picture books, board books, painting books, cut-out books, and cloth-bound juvenile books. It also issued "Santa Claus" give-away books in the prewar years. The wartime line was largely undiminished, and included "Paint Without Paints" sets and "Stick 'Em" books. The firm continued through the Boomer years with books, activity boxes, linen books, puzzles, and panoramas.

Platz Products Co. The "Slingshot Rocket Pistol" of the 1950s-60s was produced by this Minneapolis, Minn., company.

Plawood Mormac Corp. Friction and spring-motor plastic toys made up this Painesville, Ohio, company's line in the 1950s and '60s. It also made plastic pull toys, and games for adults.

play At times in Colonial America, play was a synonym for misbehavior. More beneficent influences than the Puritan gradually came to the fore. Through the writings of John Locke and others, play came to be seen, in the 18th and 19th centuries, as an important factor in an individual's education.

"Play-A-Round" circular play-pen see *Thayer Co.*

"Play-A-Toy Town" prewar, see *Playskool Institute.*

"Play Ball!" game see *Colorforms.*

play balls The play ball was a larger inflated ball used for informal recreation, as opposed either the plain "ball," often used in reference to smaller, solid balls, or the various sports balls designated for specific uses. Although taken for granted through the 20th century, in the later 1800s they were a novelty plaything made possible by the vulcanizing process for rubber.

Prewar manufacturers included the Anderson Rubber Co., Clarke Mfg. Co., Collette Mfg. Co., Essex Rubber Co., Faultless Rubber Co., Goodyear Rubber Sundries Co., J.H. Grady Mfg. Co., Hygrade Fabric Co., Lannon Mfg. Co., Miller Rubber Products Co., the Moneco Co., National Sporting Goods Mfg. Co., Rex Rubber & Novelty Co., the Seamless Rubber Co., Seiberling Latex Products Co., Tober Sporting Goods Co., Tyer Rubber Co., Van Cleef Bros., W.J. Voit Rubber Co., and C.B. Webb Co.

Postwar companies specializing in play balls included Alvimar Mfg. Co., Anderson Rubber Co., Barr Rubber Products, Bayshore Industries, Childhood Interests, Chris Mfg. Co., Collette Mfg. Co., Cosom Industries, Dartmore Corp., Davis Products, Eagle Rubber Co., Econolite Corp., Everly Associates, Faultless Rubber, the Holiday Line, Milton A. Jacobs, Ken Sporting Goods Co., Kestral Corp., the National Latex Products Co., the Oak Rubber Co., Pennsylvania Athletic Products, Seamless, the Sun Rubber Co., Tri-Kay Co., U.S. Fiber & Plastics Corp., Urb Products Corp., Vantines, and W.J. Voit.

"Play-Bild" see *Cincinnati Fly Screen Co.*

play clothes see *play suits.*

"Play-Doh" see *Rainbow Crafts.*

"Play Dome" see *Matrix Structures.*

Play Equipment Co. A Los Angeles, Calif. firm active in the late prewar years, Play Equipment issued card games, target games, checkerboard puzzles, and marble pull toys.

"Play Kit Books" see *Grosset & Dunlap, Inc.*

"Play League" sponge baseballs see *The Fli-Back Sales Corp.*

"Play-Make" construction toys see *Modern Research Development Co.*

play money Play money existed as parts of games in the 1930s, especially in the famous "Monopoly" game. In the Boomer years, it became a separate commodity, sold often as rack items separate from any particular game use. Companies issuing play money included Arlane Mfg. Co., Milton Bradley Co., Crown Novelty Co., Empress Varieties Mfg. Corp., E.E. Fairchild Corp., Grove-Tex Industries, Nadle & Sons Toy Co., the Tracies Co., Transogram Co., and A.J. Wildman & Son.

"Play Pal" dolls see *Ideal Toy Corp.*

"Play Pal" wagon see *The Metalcraft Corp.*

"Play-Pen Rail Train" see *Childhood Interests.*

"Play Spaces," "Play Squares" see *Design Industries.*

play stores see *stores, play.*

play suits A measure of American wealth can be found in the fact that American children could enjoy more and more accoutrements for make-believe activities as time went along. By the prewar years, the concept that children could have a playsuit was firmly established—an actual, manufactured set of clothing that would help the child engage in imaginary play.

Through the 1930s and the Boomer years, manufacturers of costumes and play accessories encouraged more year-round use of their products by designating certain lines as "play suits" and "play clothes." The tactic certainly worked for Sackman Bros. Co., who issued its "Yankiboy" play suits. In the earlier '30s, play suits tended to be fairly generic, evoking cowboys, Indians, policemen, firemen, aviators, baseball players, and traffic cops. Even though Wornova Mfg. Co. introduced outfits for "Clarabelle Cow" and "Horace Horse Collar" and other Walt Disney figures by the mid-'30s, these tended to be considered "costumes" rather than "play clothes," perhaps in part because masks were involved.

Character-related and increasingly specific play clothes became an important part of the scene by the later '30s, with Sackman issuing "Buck Jones" and "Northwest Mountie" play suits. Wornova issued "Hoot Gibson" cowboy suits and "Northwest Mountie" outfits. "Lone Ranger" play clothes appeared in two lines, with Collegeville Flag & Mfg. Co. issuing it as a "cowboy suit," while Feinberg-Henry Mfg. Co. produced it as a "ranch outfit." The latter company also made "Gang Buster" suits, new in 1939.

Other early manufacturers using the "play suit" tactic included American Flag Co., S. Briskie with its "Ruff 'N' Ready" play suits, A.S. Fishbach, Greenville Mfg. Co., Keyston Bros., Lincoln Novelty Co., Oliver Bros., Peppy Mfg. Co., E. Simon's Sons, and the William C. Waugh Co.

In the postwar years, Herman Iskin & Co. rose into prominence with its "Pla-Master" play suits and "Seneca" frontier play suits, many based on TV characters. Sackman may have still issued the largest line, however. "Yankiboy" play clothes included such characters as "Roy Rogers," "Dale Evans," "Cisco Kid," "Popeye," "Brave Eagle," "Wagon Train," "Highway Patrol," "Rory Calhoun," "The Texan," "Johnny Ringo," "Morning Star," "Angela Cartwright," "Steve Canyon," "The Rebel," "Black Saddle," and "Thunderbird," among many others.

"Buck Rogers" outfit by Sackman Bros., 1930s.

P

Sackman also made "approved Little League baseball suits." The growing importance of formally organized sports and sporting leagues, which involved more and more "official" imprimaturs, slowly undermined the importance of more frivolous and imaginative play suits by the later Boomer years, except for the youngest children. Frivolity was increasingly limited to Halloween.

Other Boomer-era companies included Bland Charnas Co., Collegeville, Ben Cooper, Fun Duds, J. Halpern Co., Keyston Bros., Leslie-Henry Do., Major Sportswear Co., Rice Mills, Smart Style, and Wornova. While many still concentrated on Halloween and other specific costume events, all these companies benefited from the "play suit" and "play clothes" concepts.

A 1930s ad for Mickey Mouse play suits by Wornova Mfg. Co.

"Play-Time" cowboy and Indian suits see *Collegeville Flag & Mfg. Co.*

"Play-Value Toys" see *Richards Mfg. Co.*

"Play Yard Pet" dolls prewar, see *Strauss-Eckardt Co., Inc.*

play yards The effort to keep children safely contained while also allowing them room to play gave rise to not only the crib but also the play yard. Prewar manufacturers included Auto-Wheel Coaster Co., Baby Bathinette Corp., Baby Line Furniture, Benner, Demerritt-Fisher Co., Ferguson Bros. Mfg. Co., Forest County Lumber Co., Gem Mfg. Corp., Charles & Victor Goldstein, L. Hopkins Mfg. Co., Lehman Co. of America, Rolls Racer Corp., Storkline Furniture Corp., W.S. Tothill, and Trimble. Several of these

continued issuing play yards through the Boomer years, including Baby Bathinette, Baby Line, Gem, and Storkline.

playard see *play yards.*

"Playard" line see *American-National Co.*

"Playboy Bunny" stuffed toy see *Elka Toys.*

"Playboy" dump trucks prewar, see *Murray-Ohio Mfg. Co.*

The Playcraft Co. Wooden blocks, beads, and peg boards were made under the "Kiddie-Kollege Toys" trademark by this Portland, Maine, firm in the 1930s.

"Playcraft" rack items see *Rosebud Art Co.*

The Playcrafters Co. The "Happy Gym" see-saws of the late prewar years were issued by this Wilkes-Barre, Penn., firm.

"Playful Pets" see *Eden Toys, Inc.*

Playgames, Inc. Play money, in both coin and bill form, was made by this prewar Newark, N.J., company. It also issued the "Playgames Business Outfit," and the "American Varsity Football, the Official Football Game," which retailed for 25 cents in the late Great Depression years. The game retained popularity through the end of the decade. The company's other activity toys from the late prewar years included the "Sketch-O-Graph" and "Code-O-Graph" sets. The latter was also sold in the "Mystery Writing Outfit." The company's "Lucky Play Money" included "real metal coins, crisp paper bills—fun for boys and girls."

playground and playroom equipment The movement to make education fun and interesting, and to make "physical culture" a vital part of children's upbringing, led to the development of playground and playroom equipment in the later 1800s and early 1900s. Such items as swings, teeter-totters and jungle gyms became common in public parks, school yards, and private back yards through the course of the 20th century, with materials including wood, steel, and plastic. Playroom equipment was often the same as playground, at a smaller scale, and often adapted for the use of the youngest. Although usually not collected because of their size, these recreational playthings became an intrinsic part of American child life.

Prewar manufacturers included American Mill & Mfg. Co., American National Co., American Playground Device Co., Benner, the J.E. Burke Co., Crosman Bros. Co., Dixon-Prosser, the Everwear Mfg. Co., Giant Mfg. Co., the Gendron Wheel Co., Gym Junior Co., W.E. Haskell, Heaney Laboratory, Hill-Standard Co., Heave Ho Toy Corp., Home Swing & Gym Co., Ralph T. Jones, Kiddie Gym, Lehman Co. of America, Fred Medart Mfg. Co., the Mengel Co., Miami Wood Products Co., Mitchell Mfg. Co., the Mordt Co., Neumann Mfg. Co., Rotary Clothes Dryer Co., Schmidt Novelty Co., Skippy Racers, N.R. Snell Co., Toledo Metal Wheel Co., W.S. Tothill, Woodcraft Toy Mfrs., and Youngstown Tool & Mfg. Co.

The "Dome Climber" by American Machine & Foundry Co.

Playground Equipment Co. The
"Junglegym" enjoyed widespread success after its introduction in the earlier 1920s by Playground Equipment Co., based on Greenwich Street, New York City. Advertised as "the only apparatus that satisfies childhood's constant desire to climb," the "Junglegym" was described as "not a toy, but a really practical piece of equipment with physical and educational values and all the fun of a toy." The "Junglegym Jr." was made in the size to be stocked in toy departments.

Introduced in the 1920s, the "Junglegym" was a great success for Playground Equipment Co.

"Playhouse" line prewar, see the *Hoge Mfg. Co. Toy Division.*

playhouses Playhouses were the toy industry's response to the age-old urge on the part of children to find a spot of their own, sequestered away from the world of adults. While most playhouses through time have probably been of the home-made variety, whether complex tree houses assembled with planks or the momentary but entirely satisfactory concoctions made from the cardboard box the family's new washing machine came in.

Formal playhouses were frequently tents, made with decorative sides, sometimes evocative of radio, movie or TV heroes. Yet many were decidedly house-looking structures, made of pressboard, cardboard, cardboard-reinforced vinyl, or whatever material could be made to stand up firmly.

Prewar manufacturers included O.B. Andrew Co., Cincinnati Fly Screen Co., Close-To-Nature Co., W.E. Hettrick & Son, the Hettrick Mfg. Co., Muskin Mfg. Co., the Old Hickory Furniture Co., the F. L. Purdy Co., Purves Products Co., Rich Illinois Mfg. Co., Rochester Folding Box Co., Tangle Wood Toys, and Terre Town Toy Tradesmen.

Among the firms that started in the later 1930s and survived to thrive in the Boomer era was Rustic Furniture Co. Its line featured log cabin playhouse cabins, measuring roughly 4 by 5 feet or 5 by 7 feet, and 5 to 6 feet high. The cabins came complete with chairs, tables, fences, arbor gateways, window boxes and flagpoles and bore such names as "Daniel Boone," "Abe Lincoln," "Hudson Bay," and "Buffalo Bill."

Other new manufacturers in the late prewar years included the Lehman Co. of America, the Monroe Co., and Smith Mfg. Co.

In the postwar years, manufacturers included the Connor Lumber & Land Co., Educator Playthings, Fibre-Bilt Toys, Hettrick, Taylor Trading Co., and Toymaster Products Co.

playing cards see *cards, playing.*

"Playjoy" line see *Stoll & Einson Games, Inc.*

"Playland Toys" see *Blake Industries, Inc., Boston.*

Playmate Doll & Toys Co. Dolls were the lead product of this Seventh Avenue, New York City, firm in the 1930s.

"Playmate" figures see *Rempel Mfg., Co.*

"Playmate" paper dolls see *DeJournette Mfg. Co.*

"Playmate" wagon see the *Metalcraft Corp.*

"Playmates of the Clouds" see *The Hi-Flier Mfg. Co.*

"Playmates" stuffed animals prewar, see *American Made Toy Co.*

Playmore, Inc. Action toys, telephones, and telegraph sets were specialties of this Boomer-era firm, based in the Fifth Avenue Building.

"Playpet" dolls prewar, see *J.W. Pickering & Son.*

"Playskil Pump Gun" see *Playtime.*

Playskool Institute, Inc. A Milwaukee, Wis., firm, Playskool was producing high-quality pre-school playthings in the 1930s and '40s, when its line included home kindergarten equipment as well as educational toys and games. Its "Playskool Hammer-Nail" proved popular, with other toy titles including "Indian Beads," "Totem Pole," "Playskool Theatre," and "Playskool Pullman."

By the end of the '30s, the company's "old favorites" included "Nok-Out-Bench," "Bang-a-Bell," "Wagon Load of Blocks," "Peg Table and Stool," "Hammer-Nails," and "Bag of Beads."

In the Boomer years, Playskool grew to the point of touting itself as the world's largest manufacturer of wood toys. It reached this point by acquiring other companies, which continued operating as divisions of this now Chicago, Ill., based company. These included Holgate Toys; Appleton Juvenile Furniture; Lincoln Logs, formerly J.L. Wright; and Makit Toy, formerly W.R. Benjamin Co. The "Makit" line was made by the Lincoln Logs Division.

The firm still made the "Playskool" educational toys, as well as the "Skaneateles" train, track and blocks, "Peg Blox," "Teach-A-Tot," and "Tot Railroad" toys.

playsuits see *play suits.*

Playthings The main trade journal for the toy industry, *Playthings* was established in 1903. Other trade journals included *Toys and Novelties* and *Southern Toy Journal.*

"Playthings That Last," slogan see the *Lehman Co. of America, Inc.*

"Playtime" One of the more widely used tradenames in prewar toys, "Playtime" appeared on everything from bubble pipes from Jack Pressman & Co. to Plaza Mfg. Co. records. Milton Bradley Co. may have used the name most widely, issuing crayon and drawing sets, outline pictures, picture puzzles, and sewing cards under the name. Collingbourne Mills also made embroidery sets, and Akro Agate Co. made glass dishes as "Playtime" items. In the postwar years, the "Playtime" trade name was used on croquet sets by the Rollin Wilson Co., miniature playing cards by U.S. Playing Card Co., and art and activity items by Binney & Smith.

Playtime Products, Inc. This postwar Warsaw, Ind., company made doll carriages.

"Playtown" line see *American Mfg. Concern.*

"Playway to Knowledge" see *Jacmar Mfg. Co.*

Playworld Toys, Inc. Educational toys were made by the Statesville, N.C., "Playworld" line.

"Playwoodie" wooden toys prewar, see *Transogram Co., Inc.*

Plaza Mfg. Co. A prewar manufacturer of phonograph specialties, Plaza Manufacturing made "Playtime" records, "Little Tot" record books, children's and portable phonographs, and phonograph needles. It also made the 1930s "Art-O-Graph" drawing device, and the 1937 skill game "Fiddlestix." It was located on West 18th Street, New York City, in the earlier '30s, moving to Broadway by the end of the decade, and to East 17th Street after the war. In the Boomer years, Plaza specialized in plastic baby rattles and toys.

Frank Plotnick Co. Frank Plotnick of Philadelphia, Penn., made prewar, "popular priced" stuffed dolls and toys.

Plume Trading & Sales Co. Based on West 23rd Street, New York City, Plume Trading made Indian craft kits and construction sets in the late 1930s.

"Pluto Platter" see *Wham-O Mfg. Co.*

"Pluto the Pup" The famous Walt Disney floppy-eared dog won over many admirers in the 1930s, making "Pluto-the-Pup" and "Pluto the Pup" items popular in the trade. In the mid-1930s, George Borgfeldt Corp. and Richard G. Krueger both issued stuffed versions.

Plymouth Air Rifles Co. Founded in 1890 to issue the "Magic" air gun, this firm was located in Plymouth, Mich., home also to Markham Mfg. Co. and Plymouth Iron Windmill Co.

Plymouth Iron Windmill Co. The Plymouth Iron Windmill Co. experimented with manufacturing air guns in 1888, and enjoyed such success it discontinued making windmills the next year. See *Daisy Mfg. Co.*

plywood Although sometimes thought a material more characteristic of postwar years, plywood was heavily used in juvenile products, especially juvenile furniture, rockers, and shooflies, in prewar years. Suppliers to the toy industry included Anderson-Tully Co., the Red River Lumber Co., U.S. Plywood Co., and Vermont Plywood Co.

"Pocahontas" train see *American Flyer Mfg. Co.*

pocket games Travel-size and pocket-size games became popular in the Boomer years, no doubt helped by the increasing amount of family car travel enjoyed, or endured, in the 1950s and '60s. Manufacturers specializing in these miniatures included A.&L. Mfg. Co., Built-Rite Toys, William F. Drueke, W.C. Horn Bro. & Co., Kohner Bros., Fred Kroll Assoicates, E.S. Lowe Co., William Rott-Samuels Corp., Russell Mfg. Co., the Watkins-Strathmore Co., and Jon Weber Manufactory. Pocket games had become popular in the years before the war. A firm that emphasized them heavily in wartime was Lowe, who issued "The Bookshelf of Games," a uniform edition of classic and contemporary games for adults. They suited the times perfectly, not only in their efficient use of manufacturing materials but also in being convenient gifts that could be sent to American soldiers abroad.

Poenitz, William A Chicago, Ill., manufacturer, William Poenitz made wooden toy looms in the 1930s.

pogo sticks One of the most unusual of playthings, and among the most treasured for that reason, was the pogo stick, one of the few summertime transportation toys without wheels. Production of pogo sticks became a major affair in the 1950s and '60s, with companies including Roy Berlin Co., Educational Products, General Sportcraft Co., Jet Jumper Mfg. Co., Julius Levenson, Little Shepard Toy Division, Master Juvenile Products Co., Mirro Aluminum, Rapaport Bros., Rittenhouse, and Wrought Iron Industries.

"Pointer" wagons see *Lullabye Furniture Corp.*

poker chips see *games, adult.*

police and "G-Man" sets Prohibition and the massive efforts undertaken to enforce it may have had the unexpected result of making police and "G-Man" toys popular in the later 1930s. They ranged from badges, handcuffs, and whistle sets to full play suits. Manufacturers who made a specialty of sets of these toys included All Metal Products

P

Co., S. Cohen & Son, Colonial Earphone Co., Columbia Stamp Works, Victor Eckardt Mfg. Co., Gardner Screw Corp, Kirchhof Patent Co., Lewis & Scott Mfg. Co., N.Y. Toy & Game Sales Co., North 7 Judd Mfg. Co., Ozan Products Co., Transogram Co., Waterbury Button Co., and Wornova Mfg. Co. Fewer companies issued these specialties in the postwar years. They included George Borgfeldt Corp., Crown Novelty Co., Empress Varieties, Hale-Nass Corp., N.Y. Toy & Game Mfg. Corp., Talbott Mfg. Co., and 20th Century Varieties.

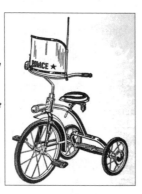

One of the many police-related toys was Garton Toy Co.'s "Police Cycle" from the 1950s.

Julius Pollak & Sons, Inc. This East 25th Street, New York City, greeting card company began specializing in Valentines by the late prewar years.

Leo Pollock Corp. Leo Pollock, on Broadway, New York City, was one of a number of new businesses in the late 1930s producing electric Christmas tree lighting. The company used the "Polly" trade name.

Robert Pollock Co. Model airplanes, kits, and model-building supplies were produced by this 1930s Glendale, Calif., company.

"Polly" Christmas tree lights see *Leo Pollock Corp.*

"Polly Flyer" kite see *Dolly Toy Co.*

Polly Plastics, Inc. This postwar Cleveland, Ohio, company made plastic toys.

"Polly Pratt" Just as other women's magazines developed their paper doll lines, *Good Housekeeping* developed "Polly Pratt," in the later 1800s.

Polycraft Corp. The "Happy Pelican" action toy of the 1950s-60s was a product of this Chicago, Ill., firm.

polyethylene see *thermoplastics.*

Polynesian Products, Inc. The "Kapu" card game was a Boomer-era product of this Oahu, Hawaii, company.

"Polysteel" toys see *Buddy "L" Quality Toys.*

A. Ponnock This Philadelphia, Penn., firm made late 1930s "Eddie Cantor" dolls.

Pontiac Spring & Bumper Co. A manufacturer of spring riding toys in the late 1930s, Pontiac issued its "Hobby-Tot" with Walt Disney character designs.

pontil Pontil marks reflect a marble's separation point from the original cane of glass from which it was made. Machine-made marbles lack the mark.

"Pony" cap pistols see *Nichols Industries.*

"Pony Boy" pistol and holster sets see *Esquire Novelty Co.*

"Pony Boy" exerciser see *The A. Schoenhut Co.*

"Pony Toy" exerciser see *Monarch Products Co.*

pool and billiard tables Important games for adults, especially in times when family rooms and dens were more dedicated to games and conversation than to television and video players, pool and billiards appealed to players across the economic strata, and won the reputation of being a game requiring intelligence besides being a source of entertainment. Prewar manufacturers included the Brunswick-Balke-Collender Co., the Burrowes Corp., N.D. Cass Co., William Fuld, Gotham Pressed Steel Corp., Mason & Parker Mfg. Co., M.H. Miller Co., and N.L. Page & Son Co.

pools see *wading pools.*

"Poor Pitiful Pearl" doll see *Brookglad Corp.*

"Pop-A-Part" target games see *Knickerbocker Plastic Co., Inc.*

"Pop-Em" blocks see *Gerber Plastic Co.*

pop guns Pop guns were made in American Colonial times by hand. The preferred wood was elderbush, the bark of which was easily removed from the pith. See gun toys.

"Pop Pop" The "Pop Pop" trade name was used for toy boats from two prewar companies, Katagiri Corp. and Paul Jones.

"Pop-Up" While the term pop-up book has become common property, "Pop-Up" was a trademark for Blue Ribbon Books in the prewar years. These novelty books featured colorful scenes that unfolded into three-dimensional arrangements when the book was opened.

"Pop-Up Kritters" see *Fisher-Price Toys, Inc.*

Eddie Pope & Co. This Altadena, Calif., company issued postwar model airplanes.

"Pope" bicycles see *Westfield Mfg. Co.*

"Popeye" The beautifully animated films of the spinach-dependent sailor inspired a variety of toys in the 1930s. Many enjoyed a high profile at the time, being advertised in the leading mail-order catalogs.

In the mid-1930s, playthings included crayon and paint books by Milton Bradley Co., a game by Einson-Freeman Co., metal and wood toys by J. Chein & Co., "Popeye" and "Olive Oyl" masquerade costumes by E. Simon's Sons, and picture puzzles by the Saalfield Publishing Co. Northwestern Products also made the "Popeyepipe" musical toy.

By the late prewar years, the number of "Popeye" playthings had multiplied. They included an acrobat toy by Bear Products Co.; inflated and sponge balls by Seiberling Latex Co.; banks and flashlights by Behrend & Rothschild; the "Knockout Bank" by Straits Mfg. Co.; boats, bubble sets, and garden sets by Transogram; card games and story books by Whitman Publishing Co.; Christmas stockings by S. Thanhauser; stuffed dolls by Fleischaker & Baum; felt toys by Mizpah Toy & Novelty Co.; infant toys by Zadek Feldstein Co.; kites by the Hi-Flier Mfg. Co.; marble sets by Akro Agate; masquerade costumes by J. Halpern Co.; mechanical toys by Louis Marx & Co.; molded rubber figures by Schavoir Rubber Co.; nail sets, puzzles, toys, peg board sets and tables by Bar Zim Toy Mfg. Co.; paint and crayon books by McLoughlin Bros; the "Popeye Patrol" by Hubley Mfg. Co.; pencil sharpeners by Plastic Novelties; the "Popeyepipe" musical toy by Northwestern Products; printing sets by Superior Type Co.; pull toys by Fisher-Price Toys; reprint books by David McKay Co.; ring-toss games by Rosebud Art Co.; sand toys by T. Cohn; soap items by Kerk Guild; stereoscopic pictures by Novelart Mfg. Co.; "Popeye's Jeep" fortune teller by Northwestern Products Co.; and wooden toys by Jaymar Specialty Co.

Unlike some other prewar comic characters, Popeye's star remained in the ascendant through the Boomer years. Some of the many playthings issued included action flashlights by Bantam-Lite, "Action Television" coin bank by Kalon Mfg. Co., books by Grosset & Dunlap, bubble blowers by Transogram Co., card games by Ed-U-Cards Mfg. Corp., cartoon kits by Colorforms, color books and slates by Abbott Publishing Co., costumes by Collegeville Flag & Mfg. Co., puppets by Gund Mfg. Co., hats by Welded Plastics Corp., infant toys by Plastic Playthings, jigsaw puzzles by Jaymar Specialty Co., musical jacks-in-the-box by Mattel, paint and crayon sets by the American Crayon Co., soft body dolls by Gund, plastic cutouts by Aldon Industries, "Punch-Me" roly-polys by Dartmore Corp., pick-up sticks by Lido Toy Co., register banks by Kalon Mfg. Corp., ring-toss and games by Transogram, "Roly-Poly" target game by Knickerbocker Plastic Co., segmented vinyl doll by Cameo Doll Products Co., suits by Sackman Bros. Co., swim rings and play balls by Dartmore Corp., miscellaneous toys by Hassenfeld Bros. and Stahlwood Toy Mfg. Co., and a "TV Set" by Lido.

The "Popeye" character was licensed by King Features Syndicate.

"Popeyes" Akro Agate is noted for having produced "corkscrew" marbles, especially

"Popeyes." "Popeyes" were made with a combination of clear, white, and two opaque colored types of glass.

popinjay In Colonial times, popinjay was a game played by the Dutch. A shooting game that helped improve marksmanship, it involved trying to hit a bird strung head-down from the top of a tall pole.

Arthur Popper Known for "perfect calipered" dice, this Fourth Avenue, New York City, manufacturer and importer made games for adults, as well as casino equipment. The company specialized in "games in the Monte Carlo style" for adults, being a supplier of roulette wheels, "Rhum" trays, dice cups, cribbage boards, poker chips, poker racks, as well as dominoes, chess, checkers, backgammon, and game tables. "Java-Calcutta" was a game issued in 1934. The company was using Catalin for its poker chips by the late '30s. The line continued through the Boomer years.

"Porcupine" blocks see *Holgate Bros. Co.*

"Porky Pig" The leading animated pig character of the late prewar years was undoubtedly "Porky Pig," whose licensing rights were controlled by Leon Schlesinger Corp. Playthings of the time included balls and balloons by Barr Rubber Products Co.; books by the Saalfield Publishing Co.; dolls by the Rushton Co.; rubber toys by Sun Rubber Co.; and wooden toys by Transogram Co.

The Porter Chemical Co. "Chemcraft, the Chemical Outfit," was made from 1914, the year the company was established in Hagerstown, Md., through 1961, were made by Porter Chemical. It also made microscope sets and "Mastercraft" painting sets. By the late 1930s the firm had introduced "Science-Craft" microscopes and microscope outfits, micro-projectors, mineralogy outfits, and "electro-physics" outfits; "Kast-a-Toy" casting sets; toy airplanes; and "Big Time" marionette and theater sets. In the Boomer years, Porter continued to emphasize its "Chemcraft" line, along with "Microcraft" microscope outfits, mineralogy outfits, biology sets, lab technician sets, and general science sets. It also issued "Toolcraft" tool sets. The

firm was acquired in 1961 by the Lionel Corp.

postcard projectors An interesting toy development that arose from the late Victorian and early 20th century fascination with postcards was the postcard projector, which enabled aficionados to project their prized cards on the wall. Manufacturers in the 1930s included Keystone Mfg. Co. and the Metal Stamping & Mfg. Co.

Don Post Studios This postwar Los Angeles, Calif., company made rubber masks.

Poster Products, Inc. A manufacturer of felt playthings, which were distributed by the Reilly & Lee Co., this Chicago, Ill., firm produced the "Felt-O-Gram" and "Face-Fun" felt play sets in the mid-1930s.

Potter, Beatrix British writer and illustrator Beatrix Potter (1866-1943) first wrote *Peter Rabbit* as a letter to a sick child, and self-published the book in 1901. It was published by Warne in 1902, and was followed by books including *Tale of Squirrel Nutkin* in 1903 and *Tale of Flopsy Bunnies* in 1909.

The Powell Pressed Steel Co. A Hubbard, Ohio, firm specializing in gardening items, Powell Pressed Steel also made the juvenile wheel toys "Skooters" and "Skeeters" in the 1930s.

The Power Car Co. Based in Mystic, Conn., Power Car made juvenile electric-motor automobiles in the 1950s and '60s.

"Powerama" tractor see *Garton Toy Co.*

"Pow'r" guns and peashooters see *Jak-Pak-Inc.*

Poynter Products, Inc. Children could make their own playhouses with "Giant Play Logs," made by this Cincinnati, Ohio, firm in the early 1960s. The interlocking "logs" were fiberboard.

Practi-Cole Products, Inc. Children's ice cream machines were among this Fair Haven, Conn., company's specialties in the Boomer years. It also made motorized toy hair dryers and food mixers, and walking and talking dolls.

Practical Specialties A greeting card publisher, this Little Neck, N.Y., firm also made collapsible toy houses and birdhouses in the late prewar years.

Prang Co. A Chicago, Ill., company, Prang made prewar crayons, watercolors, and modeling materials. American Crayon Co. also issued "Prang" school crayons in the mid-1930s, and continued using the trade name through the Boomer years.

Prat-Lane Co. A Milwaukee, Wis., company, Prat-Lane made the mid-1930s "Hi-Lo," described as a "Blood-Tester game."

Pratt & Letchworth In the 1870s in Buffalo, N.Y., Pascal P. Pratt and William P. Letchworth founded the Buffalo Malleable Iron Works, known by 1880 as Pratt & Letchworth, a name kept until the company's demise in 1900. The firm specialized in cast-iron toy trains, horse-drawn hansom cabs, pumpers, and artillery wagons. It acquired Francis W. Carpenter's stock and patent rights in 1890.

Pratt Mfg. Co. Sleds and shooflies were products of this Coldwater, Mich., firm in the earlier 1930s. By the late 1930s and '40s, the company was also making playground equipment and porch furniture, and had changed its name to the Pratt Corp.

pre-school toys see *kindergarten and preschool toys*.

"Pre-School" blocks see *Plastic Block City, Inc.*

Pre-View Toy and Novelty Co., Inc. This New York City firm specialized in plastic toys, issuing "The Flying Helicopter" aerial toy in 1946 to the late '40s.

"Precious Pet" stuffed animals see *Metropolitan Fur Toy Co.*

Precision Plastics Co. Established in Philadelphia, Penn., in 1941, Precision Plastics Corp. issued its first toy, a "Woodie" station wagon called "Road King," under the "Triumph" name in 1947. The company

named its toy division U.S. Plastics, Inc., and subsequently used the "Plastic Masters" trade name. The toys were re-issued for the nostalgia market in the late 1990s and early 2000s under the "Dimestore Dreams" name.

"Premier" A widely used tradename, "Premier" was used in the 1930s on a line of picture puzzles from Milton Bradley Co., a repeating cap pistol by Kilgore Mfg. Co., and register banks by the Hoge Mfg. Co. In the postwar years, Avalon Mfg. Co., used the trade name for paint-by-number sets.

Premier Decorations Established on Fifth Avenue, New York City, in the late 1930s, Premier issued Christmas decorations, cellophane bells, and artificial Christmas trees.

Premier Doll Accessories Co. This postwar Brooklyn, N.Y., firm, affiliated with Premier Doll Togs, Inc., issued miscellaneous accessories that were sold as rack items in the 1950s and '60s. Premier Toy Enterprises, Inc., which made plush stuffed toys, animals, and stuffed dolls, also operated from the same address.

Premier Products Co. Plastic toys and novelties, including toy vehicles, were this Brooklyn, N.Y., firm's specialties in the 1950s and '60s.

Premier Toy Enterprises see *Premier Doll Accessories Co.*

premiums Premiums were a major item for the manufacturers of penny toys and novelties. Often called "prize package toys" by the industry, evocative of the "Cracker Jack" "prize in every package" slogan, premiums were invariably small and simple toys of the most inexpensive manufacture. Whatever material has been cheapest at the time has been the material of choice, whether tin, acetates, paper, or polyethylene. Dowst Mfg. Co. was among the most important of manufacturers, issuing die-cast, tin-litho, and metal puzzles, charms, tops and toys for Rueckheim Bros. & Eckstein.

Cosmo Co. was a larger specialist in die-cast premiums based, as was Dowst, in Chicago, Ill. Cosmo supplied "Cracker Jack" and "Checkers" items from the 1910s. Cosmo's owner Nathan Shure bought Dowst Mfg. Co.

in 1926. The combined companies were likely the largest source of die-cast premium items in the country.

Other prewar manufacturers included American Toy Works, Dan Brechner & Co., T. Cohn, Gotham Pressed Steel Corp., Gray Bros., Grey Iron Casting Co., Kirchhof Patnet Co., Richmond Bros. Co., and Universal Toy & Novelty Mfg. Co.

President Novelty & Jewelry Co.

Beaded dolls were among this Broadway, New York City, company's products in the late 1930s. In the Boomer years, the company issued children's toy watches and other novelty toys.

"President's Special" train see *American Flyer Mfg. Co.*

Presser, Theodore An important music publisher in the late 19th and 20th centuries, Theodore Presser issued musical games including "Allegrando" in 1884, "Elementaire Musical Game" in 1896, and "The Great Composer" in 1901.

Jack Pressman & Co. The "Pressman's Popular Playthings" line of the 1920s included wood spinning tops, jump ropes, "Playtime" bubble pipes and outfits, jackstones, liquid pistols, chime toys, checkers, barrels of clothes pins, embroidery hoops and embroidery sets, cast-iron hatchets and hammers, "Boy Scout" axes, painting sets, lead soldier sets, enameled soldiers, brass tube telephones, sewing machines, "Dumb Bell" ring toys, enameled soldier ten pins, and enameled sailor ten pins. Its games included "Bollo Ball," "Treasure Hunt," "Jungle Hunt," "Shuffle Alley," "Tally Alley," table tennis, table croquet, juvenile golf outfits, lotto, ring toss, and floor and parlor croquet.

In the mid-1930s Jack Pressman & Co. produced "Dick Tracy" and "Orphan Annie" toy sets. Moving from East 17th Street, to Broadway in New York City, the company specialized in wood and metal toys and games, table tennis, and "surprise packages." Later in the decade, Pressman added chemistry and microscope sets, knitting sets, table tennis, pastry sets, wood soldier sets, and police toy sets.

The firm's game titles included "Electric Speed Classic," "Hop-Over Puzzle," "Yacht Race," and "Wordy" in the 1930s, and "Flash," "Parlor Croquet," and "Whippet Race" in the 1940s.

The firm continued to flourish in the postwar years. Its line featured wood promotional toys, blackboards, bowling alleys, carpenter benches, easels, peg tables, plastic toys, metal toys, marbles, games, barber sets, beauty sets, baseball games, Chinese checkers, croquet sets, golf sets, doctor and nurse kits, embroidery and knitting items, art sets, and table tennis.

Pressman's Chinese checkers game "Hop-Ching," from the 1950s.

M. Pressner & Co. A manufacturer and importer, Pressner issued balloons, tree ornaments, paper hats, souvenirs, and a line of miscellaneous toys in the 1920s. Located on Broadway, New York City, the firm continued to specialize in dolls, novelties, and holiday items through the prewar years, as both importer and manufacturer.

"Prestige" numbered paint sets see *Avalon Mfg. Co.*

"Presto-Byke" see *Metal Specialties Mfg. Co.*

Presto Enterprises Based in Muskogee, Okla., Presto specialized in toys, fireworks, puzzles, souvenirs, premiums, surprise packages, and peas and pea shooters, in addition to magic and jokers' novelties, in the Boomer years. Its line included the "Presto-Sphere," a "perpetual motion" novelty.

"Presto-Mobile" velocipede see *Schmid Bros.*

pretties Dolls in the 1700s were often called "pretties," with the superlative "nonsopretties" also used.

Pretty Fur Co. Stuffed fur toys were the specialty of this postwar Spring Street, New York City, company.

Price, Margaret Evans Margaret Evans Price was a popular children's illustrator and writer of the 1920s and '30s, her titles including *Enchantment Tales for Children* and *The Real Story Book of Old Time Tales.* Her illustrations in books by other authors are signed with her initials, "MEP." Margaret Price, whose husband was Irving Price, the main financial backer for the founding of Fisher-Price Toys, helped establish the toy line's look in the early 1930s. She was born March 20, 1888, in Chicago, Ill., and died in 1973.

Price, William William Price owned what amounted to America's first toy shop. A print and map seller, he sold miscellaneous toys and framed children's pictures in the first half of the 18th century in Boston, Mass. His items for sale included imported English items by at least the mid 1700s.

"The Price Is Right" game see *Lowell Toy Mfg. Corp.*

Pride Products, Inc. Sock puppets and hand puppets comprised this postwar line. Pride was based in the Fifth Avenue Building, New York City.

"Primary Blocks" see *Blockraft Mfg. Co.*

primer The first American primer, also sometimes spelled primmer, was the New England Primer, first printed in 1691 by Benjamin Harris of Boston, Mass. The book was used in elementary grades for almost a century. It featured woodcut illustrations of the alphabet, and reading lessons based on the Old Testament.

primmer see *primer.*

Primrose Doll Co. Based on Wooster Street, New York City, Primrose specialized in moving-eye dolls in the 1920s, manufacturing its own doll eyes.

"Prince" air rifle see *Markham Mfg. Co.*

"Prince Valiant" The medieval hero of the Sunday comic supplements inspired some Boomer-era toys, including paper dolls by

the Saalfield Publishing Co., and dime register banks by Kalon Mfg. Corp.

Princess Anna Doll Co., Inc. Miniature plastic costume dolls made up this postwar line. Princess Anna was based on Jumel Place, New York City.

"Princess Anne" toys and kits see *Cleinman & Sons, Inc.*

Princess Doll Co., Inc. This manufacturer was located in the Doll District in the 1930s.

"Princess" iron see *Dover Mfg. Co.*

"Princeton" The "Princeton" trademark was used on a number of prewar wheel goods. Products of D.P. Harris Hardware & Mfg. Co., including bicycles and roller skates, bore the name, as did tricycles made by American National Co.

Principal Mfg. Corp. Based in Chicago, Ill., Principal issued postwar mechanical-action baseball games.

printing toys Fascination with the process of printing, which elevates a child suddenly above the realm of handwritten scrawls on pulp-paper tablets, led naturally to the popularity of various kinds of printing toys through the years. Many were simple stamping sets, with rubber stamps provided for the various letters and punctuation marks and symbols needed for creating childhood placards or posters. Some were more complex, using type that fitted into type boxes, with the most complex being actual miniature printing presses.

Manufacturers active in the field in the 1920s included Baumgarten & Co., Fulton Specialty Co., and the Superior Type Co.

Prewar manufacturers of simpler printing toys included Durable Gelatin Roll & Supply Co., Fulton Specialty, Marks Bros. Co., Superior Type, and Wolverine Supply & Mfg. Co. Companies that made full printing presses included Fulton, the Sigwalt Mfg. Co., and Superior Type.

In the postwar years, Fulton, Lido Toy Co., Martin Rubber Co., the Platt & Munk Co., Superior, and Wrangler Jeff Products issued printing toys, while Fred Kroll Associates, Sigwalt, and Superior issued working toy presses.

P

The "Showcard Printer" from Superior Marking Equipment

"Priscilla" crayons see the *Ullman Mfg. Co.*; postwar, see *Advance Crayon & Color Corp.*

The W.P. Pritchard Co. The W.P. Pritchard Co. of Adams, Mass., manufactured prewar toy wagons and carts.

Pritt Novelty Co., Inc. Games, toys and puzzles were among the rack items issued by this West 27th Street, New York City, firm in the Boomer years.

"Private Eye" cap pistol see *Kilgore Mfg. Co., Inc.*

"Prize name" agates see *Akro Agate Co., The*

prize package toys see *premiums.*

Products Mfg. Corp. This Suffolk, Va., firm made games for children and adults in the late 1930s.

Processed Plastic Co. This Aurora, Ill., firm established a name for itself in 1948 with its first plastic toy trucks, which sold through the dime store chains. The firm continued issuing a line of toys including trucks, hot rods, and figures through the Boomer years.

Product Miniature Co., Inc. Based in Pewaukee, Wis., Product Miniature issued scale models of autos, station wagons, and pickup trucks, often with friction motors and rubber tires. Product Miniature issued its "Tru-Miniature" remote-controlled cars from the mid-1950s into the 1960s, with many being Chevrolets and Fords. The firm's "Action Toy" line included toy versions of the "Wienermobile" and "Trailways" bus, in addition to trucks and tractors. Product Miniatures also made scale models of contemporary cars, toy emergency vehicles, and juvenile yard and garden equipment. Its product line included "Custom Deluxe" model car kits, the "Cartoon-O-Scope," and the "Winky-Blinky Ball" by the '60s.

Progressive Doll Accessories Corp.

Based on Broadway, New York City, in the late prewar years, Progressive made doll shoes, stockings, wigs, and parts, as well as doll hospital supplies. The firm continued in the Boomer years from offices in the Fifth Avenue Building.

Progressive Novelty Co. Based on East 10th Street, New York City, Progressive Novelty made prewar doll shoes and stockings.

projector toys Projectors have had a place in the playroom since prewar times, when toy movie projectors made their appearance. Their popularity was doubtless restricted by their cost. In the postwar years a number of projector toys became popular because of the appearance of new plastics that enabled these complex optical affairs to be manufactured and thus sold cheaply. Not only were traditional movie projectors produced and sold, including the inevitable "Mickey Mouse" projectors from the mid-1950s onward, but also innovative toys including the famous "Give-A-Show" and the "View-Master" projectors, both of which brought bright images from children's favorite animated shows into the darkened playroom. Another interesting projector toy was the 1960 "Zoom-Lite," by Thompson Co., which was a flashlight that projected kaleidoscopic images. See *moving picture projectors, postcard projectors.*

This 1961 "Give-A-Show" projector toy was made by Kenner.

Proll Toys, Inc. The "Proll-O-Tone" toy musical instruments of the 1950s and '60s were issued by this Newark, N.J., company. Its line, sold in bags and blister packs, included some 40 items, ranging from toy trumpets to accordions.

Promotion Toys Co. The "Frontier Defender" western walking sticks were specialties of this Boomer-era Des Moines, Iowa, specialist in premium items.

"Prop Rod" race cars see *L.M. Cox Mfg. Co.*

propellers "Propellers" were a kind of handcart in which the two arms alternated in pulling back separate handles, bringing about forward propulsion. The feet rested on extensions of the axle, for steering.

protean figures see *dolls, paper.*

Psychic Baseball Club The "Psychic Baseball" card game was manufactured from 1927 into the mid-1930s by this eponymous company, based on Fifth Avenue, New York City. Parker Bros. issued a "Psychic Baseball" board game in 1935.

"Public Cowboy No. 1" This phrase was applied to the popular movie cowboy Gene Autry in the 1930s.

"Puddle Hopper" scooters see *Schmid Bros.*

"Puddlepet" stuffed animals prewar, see *Scovell Novelty Mfg. Co.*

"Pull-A-Tune" xylophones see *Fisher-Price Toys.*

pull toy The importance of a pull toy cannot be underestimated. What could be more fascinating and reassuring to the crawler or toddler than the beloved thing that was not only fun, but that devotedly followed behind? Pull toys by their nature are almost always wheel toys, with one of the most common early forms being the small horses or other barnyard animals mounted on wheeled platforms, common in Victorian times and still popular after the turn of the 20th century.

Pull toys of this sort had an early appearance, with a horse toy on a wheeled platform known from ancient Egypt, and other toys made of limestone from ancient Persia. Manufacturers in the earlier 20th century included Arcade Mfg. Co., Buffalo Toy & Tool works, Dayton Toy & Specialty Co., Northwestern Specialty Mfg. Co., the Toy Tinkers, and Rew Troxell.

In prewar times, manufacturers of these toys included All-Metal Products Co., American Flyer Mfg. Co., Arcade Mfg. Co., Buddy "L" Mfg. Co., Buffalo Toy & Tool Works, J. Chein & Co., Clark Treat Toy Co., Gong Bell Mfg. Co., N.N. Hill Brass Co., Hubley Mfg. Co., the Kilgore Mfg. Co., Murray-Ohio Mfg. Co., Nonpareil Toy & Novelty Co., Republic Tool Products Co., and Wolverine Supply & Mfg. Co.

Wood dominated the pull-toy world even in prewar years, with the "Snoopy Sniffer" issued by Fisher-Price Toys in the 1930s being the big hit of the times. Other manufacturers by the late prewar years included Acme Toy & Novelty Co., American Mfg. Concern, Anchor Toy Corp., Billie-Toy Mfg. Co., N.D. Cass Co., the Embossing Co., E.E. Fairchild Corp., Florida Playthings, Frederick Mfg. Co., Furniture City Dowel Co., Halsam Products Co., Hansen Wood Goods & Toy Mfg. Co., Hustler Corp., W.H. Leaman Co., G.B. Lewis Co, Meander Toy Co., W. Howard Moudy, Newton & Thompson Mfg. Co., Rich Illinois Mfg. Co., Tillicum Sales Corp., Toy Kraft Co., the Toy Tinkers, Twinzy Toy Co., and Whitney Bros. Co.

The number of manufacturers increased during the Boomer years, due in part to the rising birth rate and in part to the increased manufacturing possibilities offered by plastics.

Fisher-Price "Talk Back Telephone"

Companies issuing push and pull toys included Allison Studios, American Toy & Furniture Co., Bar-Zim Toy Mfg. Co., George Borgfeldt, the Brittain Prodcuts Co., Buddy "L" Toys, J. Chein & Co., Childhood Interests, Cordelco Industries, A.H. Delfausse Co., Dowst Mfg. Co., Empress Varieties Mfg. Corp., Fisher-Price Toys, Forster Mfg. Co., the Fritzel Toys Corp., Gem Toys, the Gong Bell Mfg. Co., the Jerome Gropper Co., Halsam Products, the N.N. Hill Brass Co., Holgate Toys, the Hubley Mfg. Co., International Plastic Co., Irwin Corp., J.P.T. Stuffed Toy Co., Milton A. Jacobs, Jaymar Specialty Co., Henry Katz, Knickerbocker Plastic Co., Kusan, M.&L. Toy Co., Martin Industries, Metal Masters Co., Ny-Lint Tool & Mfg. Co., Plawood Mormac Corp., Playskool Mfg. Co., Red Robin, Renwal Toy Corp., Sifo Co., Softskin Toys, Spring Crest Toy & Novelty Co., Strombeck-Becker Mfg. Co., Structo Mfg. Co., Tee-Vee Toys, Tigrett Industries, Tonka Toys, Towner Toys, the Toy Tinkers, Tru-Vue Co., U.S. Plastics Corp., Webo Toys, Wilkening Mfg. Co., Wolverine Supply & Mfg. Co., and S. Zucker & Co.

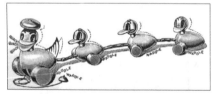

"The Quacky Family," a Fisher-Price pull toy from the 1940s.

"Pull-N-Ride" toys prewar, see *Buddy "L" Mfg. Co.*

"Pull Zoo" animals prewar, see *Holgate Bros. Co.*

pulling the goose Pulling the goose was a game played in the American Dutch colonies at Shrovetide, N.Y. In what must have been the oddest sport before mud volleyball, contestants raced on horseback at a greased goose that was suspended between two poles, with the goal being to catch and hold it. It has in common with popinjay the strung-up bird as target. Apparently influenced by the prevailing Puritan spirit, Gov. Peter Stuyvesant banned it as being pagan.

"Pullman" The "Pullman" trademark was used on at least two prewar carriages. A fiber doll carriage by F.A. Whitney Carriage Co. bore the name, as did the "Pullman Sleeper" baby carriage by American National Co.

Pullum Bros., Inc. A Detroit, Mich., manufacturer of wood specialties, Pullum Brothers made prewar juvenile furnishings.

Pulp Reproduction Co. A prewar manufacturer based in Milwaukee, Wis., Pulp Reproduction Co. made papier-mache and composition dolls, holiday toys, and carnival goods. By late in the 1930s it was specializing in papier-mache Halloween lanterns, Easter rabbits and novelties, railroad tunnels and stations, toy trenches, roly-polys, paint sets, jacks-in-the-box, Christmas trees, and composition toys and dolls. The company continued making papier-mache Halloween lanterns, Easter rabbits and Santa Claus figures, as well as composition toys, through wartime and into the 1960s.

Harry E. Pulver Based in New Hartford, Conn., Harry E. Pulver made prewar jigsaw picture puzzles, novelties, and games.

"Pun-Gee Dollies" see *Miller Rubber Products Co., Inc.*

Professor Punch Prof. Punch appears to the be the name of the company responsible for the 1840s games "Oracle of Destiny" and "The Bohemian Girl."

"Punch-O-Ball" see *The Oak Rubber Co.*

"Pup-Pet Kraft" animals prewar, see *Oregon Worsted Co., Inc.*

puppets Toys which enjoyed fairly low profile in the 1920s and earlier 1930s, puppets had some of their most important early representatives in the marionettes designed by noted illustrator Tony Sarg, and manufactured by the Alexander Doll Co.

Puppets were enjoying widespread popularity by the end of the decade, however, thanks in no small part to the influence of Edgar Bergen and his ventriloquist dolls, "Charlie McCarthy" and "Mortimer Snerd." Marionettes and hand or "glove" puppets became a major area of manufacture, with important companies including Fleischaker & Baum, Hamburg Puppet Guild, Hazelle's Mario-nettes, Jock-O Co., Ideal Novelty & Toy Co., Meader Puppet Sales Co., Porter Chemical Co., Walco Bead Co., and Robert Wilson Co.

A number of postwar companies specialized in hand puppets, including Atlanta Play-things Co., Chee-Ki Corp. of California, Dolls of Hollywood, Charles Gregor Cre-ations, Gund Mfg. Co., Hazelle, the Rushton Co., Topstone Rubber Toys Co., and Jay V. Zimmerman Co. Other puppet manufacturers included Dennis Play Products, Giant Plas-tics Corp., Ideal Toy Corp., Kohner Bros., Kusan, Minerva Toy Co., Mitten Toy Mfg. Co., My-Toy Co., Pride Products, Sheram Puppet Industries, Sidney A. Tarrson, Walco Toy Co., Wilkening Mfg. Co., and the World of Children.

I.B. Wolfset's "Glove Dolls" hand puppets, 1940s.

"Puppettes" hand puppets with bodies and feet see *Hazelle.*

The F.L. Purdy Co. Miniature play build-ings of corrugated cardboard were the spe-cialty of the F.L. Purdy Co., based in Columbus, Ohio. It made dollhouses, toy stores and filling stations, playhouses, and miniature kitchen appliances in the 1930s.

Puritan influence In the New England Colonies, the Puritan spirit inspired a restric-tive atmosphere when it came to playing and playthings, especially on the Sabbath. Activi-ties banned on that day included card play-ing, backgammon, tennis, playing with balls, bowling, rolling ninepins, and wagon or boat racing—a list that gives good indication of what people most enjoyed at the time.

The Puritan tendency to downplay or push away American Indian practices, traditional beliefs, and even Mother England drastically reduced the kinds and quantities of fun and play available to English colonist children, who could expect to be punished for even such group activities as cricket or football.

One 1657 law fined children 20 shillings for playing in the streets. Again, the prohibition indicates its popularity. Massachusetts laws against bowling, playing shuffleboard, cards, and even observing Christmas must have proved adequate demonstration of the evils of a church running the state. Undoubtedly the Founding Fathers recognized the value of play.

"Pursuer" rifle see *Ray Plastic, Inc.*

Purves Products Co. A juvenile furni-ture manufacturer based in Indianapolis, Ind., Purves Products made prewar doll trunks, dollhouses, and playhouses. Its "Dicky Duck" rocking toy was produced in the 1930s and '40s.

push toy The push toy were frequently wheeled devices pushed forward at the end of a short stick or pole. Handmade of wood in the 18th and 19th centuries, they were com-mercially produced in the later 1800s. Many were often used as pull toys.

Pussy-Cat Toy Co. Stuffed fur toys made up this postwar line. The firm was based in Brooklyn, N.Y.

"Pussy Willow" tea sets see *George Borgfeldt Corp.*

putty toys Despite its slogan of "Nothing Else is Silly Putty," other companies besides Silly Putty Marketing issued putty toys, including Blake Industries, Hassenfeld Bros., and Nadel & Sons.

puzzle Since the word could apply to any-thing that might puzzle a person, puzzles were toys and novelties of every description, ranging from the famous "Scrambled Eggs" of the 1930s, a wooden puzzle that assem-bled into an egg, and picture puzzles, to such paper puzzles as crosswords and find-the-word puzzles. Puzzles have often become fad hits at various times, including "Fifteen" and

"Pigs in Clover" in the 19th century, and the "Rubix Cube" in the 20th century.

Manufacturers in the earlier 20th century included Goldsmith Publishing Co., Emil Kahn Co., Madmar Quality Co., Parker Bros., Shulman & Sons, and Transogram Co.

Prewar manufacturers included Acme Toy & Novelty Co., S.S. Adams Co., American Maid Artcraft Studios, Bar Zim Toy Mfg. Co., Dent Hardware Co., Eagle Magic and Joke Factory, the Embossing Co., Engineering Service Corp., Franco-American Novelty Co., the A.C. Gilbert Co., Herbert Specialty Mfg. Co., Lubbers & Bell Mfg. Co., Marks Bros. Co., Modern Brands, W. Howard Moudy, Petrie-Lewis Mfg. Co., Scrambled Eggs, Selchow & Righter Co., "Sherms," W.L. Sherwood, Simon & Schuster, J.W. Spear & Sons, Standard Trailer Co., Thornecraft, and Whitman Publishing Co.

The "Scrambled Eggs" puzzle, 1930s.

"Puzzle Blocks" see *The Gong Bell Mfg. Co.*

puzzle, picture In the years between the Great Depression and World War II, a num-ber of firms were making picture puzzles, prominent among them Milton Bradley Co., Parker Bros., Saalfield Publishing Co., Selchow & Righter, and Transogram Co. Other firms included the Alox Mfg. Co., Frederick H. Beach, Louis F. Dow Co., Einson-Freeman Co., the Franklin Studio, Samuel Gabriel Sons & Co., Madmar Quality Co., Makatoy Co., Maryland Toy & Games Corp., W. Howard Moudy, Harry E. Pulver, the Puzzle Makers, the Reilly & Lee Co., the S.&H. Novelty Co., Standard Toykraft Products, Thornecraft, the Tuco Work Shops, the Ullman Mfg. Co., University Distributing Co., P.F. Volland & Co., the Wilder Corp., Wile Co. and R. Wunderlich. See also *dissected maps*.

Puzzle Makers, The Based in Colorado Springs, Colo., this company was known for its prewar "Pikes Peak" picture puzzles.

Pyralin Products Dept. see *DuPont Viscoloid Co., Inc.*

Pyro Plastics Corp. One of the famous names in postwar plastic toys, Pyro issued a complete line of minutely detailed doll furniture, as well as toy cars. Based in Union, N.J., on "Pyro Park," the company also made toy boats, rifles, and clicker guns. Its model kits included the famous "Visible Man" and "Visible Woman" educational kits. The firm was founded in 1939.

pyrography see *wood-burning kits.*

Psych-Ed Games, Inc. The "Rolling Reader" educational games made up this postwar line. The firm was based on West 72nd Street, New York City.

"Quack Quack" infant swing prewar, see *Benner Mfg. Co.*

"Quackenbush" The "Quackenbush" air rifle was introduced in 1903 by a firm in Herkimer, N.Y., of the same name.

Quaker Doll Co. Based in Philadelphia, Penn., Quaker specialized in "doll hospital supplies of every description" in the 1920s. It continued with not only these toys but dolls as well, in the 1930s and '40s.

"Qualatex" rubber toys see *Pacific States Rubber Co.*

"Qualatex," postwar see *The Pioneer Rubber Co.*

"Qualitoy" pull toys see *Tru-Vue Co.*

Quality Art Novelty Co. A publisher based in Long Island City, N.Y., Quality Art Novelty Co. issued cutouts and greeting cards, including Valentine "mechanicals," "pullers" and cutouts in the 1930s and '40s.

Quam-Nichols Co. This Chicago, Ill., firm issued "Marvel" electric telephones in the late 1930s.

Quasi Mfg. Co. A Chicago, Ill., firm, Quasi issued metal toys and the "Little Star" Christmas tree stand in the late prewar years.

Qubic Games This Springfield, Mass., company issued the "Qubic 3-D Tic Tac Toe" game in the early '60s. Parker Bros. issued its "Qubic" in 1965.

"Qubila" word game see *Lord & Freber, Inc.*

Queen City Plastics, Inc. "Cinderella" doll shoes and accessories made up this postwar line. The firm was based in New Rochelle, N.Y.

"Quick Draw" holster and gun prewar, see *Keyston Bros.*

"Quick Draw" holster sets see *Park Plastics Co.*

Quick Sales Mfg. Co., Inc. Nailing sets, sand boxes, and wooden novelties were made by this prewar manufacturer. Quick Sales was located on Broadway, New York City.

"Quick Wit" game see *Parker Bros.*

Quincy Paper Box Co. The 1930s and '40s "Reflect-O-Scope" was made by this Quincy, Ill., firm.

"Quiz Kids Quizzer" electric game see *Rapaport Bros.*

"Quizmo" educational games see *Milton Bradley Co.*

"Quizzle Books" see *Samuel Gabriel Sons & Co.*

Quoddy Boat Based in Lubec, Maine, Quoddy Boat made 1930s toy sailboats and powerboats, and novelties.

quoits A game dating back at least to the ancient Greeks, quoits were flattened iron rings or circles of rope used in throwing games. They likely found popularity in America from the establishment of the first foundries and first halyard-makers. Cast-iron quoits are recorded as regular products of blacksmiths in the 1800s.

Early quoits games included "Faba Baga, or Parlor Quoits" of 1883, by Morton E. Converse Co., and "New Game of King's Quoits," issued in 1893 by McLoughlin Bros.

Prewar manufacturers who made the specialty included S.L. Allen & Co., Bonney Forge & Tool Works, Milton Bradley Co., Essex Rubber Co., Gropper Onyx Marble Co., Parker Bros., William Rott, Schmid Bros., and Seamless Rubber Co.

Variations on the game abounded, such as the "Quoiball" lawn game by Dieterman & Jones, "Quoitennis" and "Teniquoits" by Parker Bros., "Ship Quoits" by American Toy Airship Co.," and "Table Quoits" by the Brinkman Engineering Co., all in the 1930s.

Rubber was an increasingly important material for these playthings, as in the rubber quoit game "Shu-Quoi" of the late '30s, by General Sportcraft.

Other companies manufacturing quoits by the late prewar years included Artwood Toy Mfg. Co., Bersin Playthings, Franklin Rubber Co., Hohwieler Rubber Co., Joseph Mendl, and Munro Athletic Products Co.

Quoits continued to appear from postwar companies, including Elgo Rubber Products Co., General Sportcraft Co., Globe Rubber Products Co., Hohwieler Rubber Co., Martin Rubber Co., Nautilus, and Pressman Toy Corp. As can be seen by the company names, rubber had almost entirely replaced traditional materials for these toys by the 1950s and '60s.

Q

"R.&B. Co." see *Richter.*

"R&B" dolls postwar, see *Arranbee Doll Co.*

R&R Toy Co. This Broadway, New York City, firm made stuffed toys in the late 1930s.

R.&R. Toy Mfg. Co., Inc. This postwar stuffed toy line was manufactured in Pen Argyl, Penn.

R. & S. Toy Mfg. Co., Inc. Holsters of genuine leather and gun sets with "real western design" made up this Boomer-era firm's line.

R/C see *remote control*

R.C.A. Mfg. Co. The Electronics & Bi-Products Division of R.C.A., based in Camden, N.J., made electronic sound-reproducing toys and construction sets in the late prewar years.

R.C. Can Co. Toy whistles, pencil boxes, spinning tops and advertising novelties were among this St. Louis, Mo., company's products in the late 1930s.

"R.M.B.R." see *Richter.*

rabbit's foot The origin of the notion that a rabbit's foot brings luck is lost in the mists of time. With the rise of the Middle Class and the gradual decline of America's rural subsistence hunting during the earlier 20th century, some manufacturers found a niche in commercially issuing both real and imitation rabbit's feet as good luck charms. Sometimes issued on key chains, they were sold as dime store, convenience store, and bubble-gum machine items in the Boomer years. Prewar manufacturers included Charles Brand.

"Race-A-Bout" summer sled see *Rolls Racer Corp.*

"Race-O-Plane" sled see *C.J. Johnson Co.*

"Racemobile" scooter see *W.J. Baker Co.*

"Racer" coaster wagon see *White Coaster Wagon Works.*

"Racer Truck" handcart see *Hill-Standard Corp.*

"Rachel" see *"Gasoline Alley."*

"Racing-Craft" sailboats see *Thornecraft.*

"Racipede" vehicle see *Toledo Metal Wheel Co.*

"Racipede" two-wheel velocipede see *Garton Toy Co.*

rack items A category of playthings that cuts across categories, rack items could be any kind of toy or game issued in a form to hang from display and spinner racks. Taken for granted from the mid-Boomer years on, rack-item sales were immensely helped by the introduction of transparent polyethylene bags and stiffer plastic bubble and blister-packaging.

By the end of the 1950s manufacturers often included some rack items in their lists. Manufacturers who specialized in rack items were usually issuing the most inexpensive toys, such as plastic cowboys and Indians, jacks sets, paddle balls, small dolls, parachute toys, toy cars, and farm toys.

Novelty manufacturers especially benefited from the rack concept. Fun, Inc., for instance, issued revolving racks and standing racks with pre-priced items running from a dime to 98 cents, containing everything from Halloween items to cocktail party novelties.

"Raco Products" see *Rosebud Art Co.*

"Racycle" juvenile vehicle see *Gendron Wheel Co.*

H. Rademaker & Sons H. Rademaker & Sons of Grand Rapids, Mich., was a prewar manufacturer of croquet sets. By the late 1930s the name changed to H. Rademaker & Son, Inc. In the Boomer years the firm emphasized both croquet and lawn golf.

Rader Mfg. Co. A Philadelphia, Penn., company, Rader made dart boards, tennis tables and juvenile furniture in the late prewar years.

Radex Stereo Co. Besides nursery items and crayon-by-number wall plaques, Radex of Culver City, Calif., issued 3-D stories for children, with viewers, in the Boomer years.

"Radiant" crayons see *Art Crayon Co.*

"Radio" A word that conjured exciting images in the prewar years, "Radio" was used by a variety of manufacturers. "Radio" baseball games were made by the Hatfield Co., banks by Kenton Hardware Co., and corn games by Dabs Corn Games. Some items did have radio connections, such as the "Radio" code practice set by M.M. Fleron & Son. The "Radio Series" games of the 1930s were made by Milton Bradley Co., and the "Radio Questionaire" game by Durable Toy & Novelty Corp.

"Radio Cadet" see *Philmore Mfg. Co.*

Radio City Doll Co. This prewar doll manufacturer was based in Brooklyn, N.Y.

"Radio Flyer" coaster wagon see *Radio Steel & Mfg. Co.*

Radio Games Co. Radio, based on Mercer Street, New York City, made quiz games in the late 1930s.

Radio Hat Co. This Jersey City, N.J., company made cowboy, Mexican, baseball and novelty hats in the late 1930s, as well as doll-sized cowboy hats.

"Radio Orphan Annie" The first radio program for children to remain popular over many seasons, "Radio Orphan Annie" inspired notable premiums including Ovaltine "Uncle Wiggily" mugs in 1930-31, and a series of decoder pins from 1935 to 1940. Ovaltine changed its sponsorship to "Captain Midnight" in 1941. "Radio Orphan Annie"

items were often marked "ROA," and "S.S.," or "Secret Society."

Radio Quiz Corp. This Buffalo, N.Y. corporation issued the "Radio Quiz" games of the 1920s.

"Radio Rex" see *Elmwood Button Co.*

Radio Sports, Inc. A specialist in sports games, Radio Sports issued the "Official Knute Rockne Football Game" in 1930, and the "Knute Rockne-Graham McNamee" combination football and baseball game, also in "radio scoreboard" form, in 1934. Other game titles included "World Series Baseball Game."

Radio Steel & Mfg. Co. The "Streak-O-Lite" and "Lindy Flyer" coaster wagons, made of steel and wood, were mid-1930s products of this Chicago, Ill., firm. The company's most prominent trade name through the 1930s and '40s was "Radio Flyer." By late in the 1930s Radio Steel was issuing both coaster wagons and scooters with one-piece steel bodies under the "Radio Flyer" and "Rex" names. The firm continued to issue its famous line through the Boomer years with wheel goods including the "Radio Chief," "Radio Flyer," "Radio Rancher," "Radio Super" and "Radio Tot" wagons, and "Radio Imperial" scooter.

The "Radio Flyer" was one of the most prominent names in wagons.

radios In the prewar years, youngsters took as much pleasure as oldsters did in assembling radios. A number of companies issued radio kits to simplify the process, including Constructrad, Emerson Radio & Phonograph Corp., and Federal Stamping and Engineering Corp. In the postwar years, some compa-

R

nies maintained lines of radio-assembly kits, including Aurora Plastics, Educational Electronics Co., Hearever Co., Philmore Mfg. Co., Superex Electronics Corp., and Telepower. The manufacturing of radio kits was of decreasing profitability, however, due in large part to the introduction of the transistor radio. These new radios appeared from the above and other manufacturers for the Boomer juvenile market.

Irvin H. Raditz & Co. This Berwyn, Ill., firm was one of several manufacturers of doll wigs based in the state in the 1930s and '40s. In the 1950s and '60s it specialized in Halloween goods, wigs, mustaches, and beards, as well as doll wigs.

Radnor Tool & Manufacturing Co.

The "Pla-Scale" toy scales made up this postwar toy line. Radnor was based in Southington, Conn.

Rado-Matic Corp. "Punch-a-Loon" latex punching bags were this Cincinnati, Ohio, firm's specialty in the early 1960s.

"Raggedy Ann & Andy" Johnny

Gruelle's famous rag dolls appeared in numerous toy forms from prewar through Boomer years, with early playthings including later 1930s dolls by Georgene Novelties. M.A. Donohue & Co. published the numerous titles of the series from the 1910s through the '30s. In the postwar years, books were published by the Johnny Gruelle Co. Costumes were issued by Collegeville Flag & Mfg. Co.; dolls, by Georgene Novelties; games, by Milton Bradley Co.; and "Notch-Ems," by Grosset & Dunlap.

"Rail King" train see *American Flyer Mfg. Co.*

railroad toys Railroad toys in America probably appeared immediately after the appearance of the railroads themselves. An 1850 ad refers to a "railroad," although the materials and nature of the toy remain conjectural.

Manufacturers in the earlier 20th century, when electrical and mechanical railway systems were coming into their own, included American Flyer Mfg. Co., H.E. Boucher Co., Colorville Toy Co., the Dorfan Co., Hafner

Mfg. Co., Lionel Corp., Meccano Co., and the Ives Corp.

By the 1930s, manufacturers of railway systems also included General Trains, Hoge Mfg. Co., Leland-Detroit Mfg. Co., and Western Coil & Electrical Co. Some companies specialized in train accessories: Mantua Toy & Metal Products made electric signals; S. & G. Mfg. Co. and United Pressed Products Co., train tunnels; Selley Mfg. Co., train parts and construction kits; and Train-Town, railroad bridges and buildings.

By the late '30s, the leading manufacturers of toy train railway systems were A.C. Gilbert Co., Hafner Mfg. Co., the Lionel Corp., and Louis Marx & Co. Others included Johnson Smith & Co., Knapp Electric, Suspended Railway System Toys Corp. and William K. Walthers. The scale-model trains themselves were being manufactured by companies including Cleveland Model & Supply Co, Congress Tool & Die Co., Hawk Model Aeroplane Co., Megow's, Tropical Model Airplane Co., and Varney Model Railways.

A great many more manufacturers were producing toy railroad accessories, including Ankerum Mfg. Co., making track ballast; the Conestoga Corp., making track silencers; Fidelity Felt Co., making felt roadbeds; Grey Iron Casting Co., scale-model wood construction sets for stations; Mantua Toy & Metal Products Co., electric signals; Parfait Products, tracks; the Schoenhut Mfg. Co., miniature buildings; and Selley Mfg. Co., railroad parts and construction kits.

Railway tunnels became a specialty, with companies including Albert Productions, Butterfield Toy Co., Herman Grunow, Francis W. Kramer Studios, Mache Products Co., Pulp Reproduction Co., and S. & G. Mfg. Co. issuing them.

In the Boomer years, manufacturers of electric trains and accessories included Aristo-Craft Distinctive Miniatures, Gilbert, Herkimer Tool & Model Works, Kusan, Lionel, Louis Marx, and Thomas Scale Model Industries. The popularity of "HO" scale trains was enormous in the postwar years. Companies specializing in this scale included Ideal Aeroplane & Supply Co., Lionel, Mantua, Louis Marx, Penn Line Mfg.

R

Co., Polk's Model Craft Hobbies, Revell, and Varney.

The "Talking Station," 1950s, from A.C. Gilbert.

"Railroader" train see *American Flyer Mfg. Co.*

"Rainbo" agates see *Peltier Glass Co.*

"Rainbow Bag-O-Blocks" postwar, see *Sifo Co.*

"Rainbow Chime" bell toys see *The Gong Bell Mfg. Co.*

"Rainbow" classics see the *World Syndicate Publishing Co.*

"Rainbow" construction toys see *Newton & Thompson Mfg. Co.*

Rainbow Crafts Co. A Cincinnati, Ohio, firm, Rainbow Crafts issued the famous "Play-Doh" modeling compound from 1956 through the Boomer years. In its original year the material was available in off-white, with the familiar red, yellow and blue colors added the next year. In 1960 Rainbow Crafts introduced the "Fun Factory Toy Extruder. The firm also made the "Magnajector, the magic magnifier-projector."

"Play-Doh," introduced in 1956, was one of Rainbow Crafts' most successful products.

"Rainbow" dominoes see *Halsam Products Co.*

"Rainbow Line Toys" see *Sollmann & Whitcomb.*

"Rainbow" marbles see *Berry Pink Industries.*

Rainbow Paper Favor Works A Chicago, Ill., firm, Rainbow made paper hats and favors in the late 1930s.

"Rainbow" tops For logical reasons, a number of manufacturers latched onto the "Rainbow" trade name for their spinning tops. In the 1930s, "Rainbow" tops included humming tops by the Gibbs Mfg. Co. and others by Rochester Mfg. Co. and Smethport Specialty Co. "Rainbow" was also a popular name for toy balls.

"Rainbow" trains see *American Flyer Mfg. Co.*

"Rainbow" trucks with blocks prewar, see *Halsam Products Co.*

Rainey Mfg. Co. Based in Titusville, Penn., Rainey produced the 1930s "Golden Arrow" coaster wagon and "Thriller" sleds, in addition to other wheel toys.

"Raise the Kids on Wheels," slogan see *The American-National Co.*

George Raithel & Son Established in Middleville, N.Y., in the late 1930s, Raithel made children's convertible sleighs.

"Rambler" bicycles see *Westfield Mfg. Co.*

"Rambler" coaster, see *American-National Co.*

"Rambling Rob" horse see *Charles & Victor Goldstein.*

Ramrod Products, Inc. The "Ramrod Racer" coaster assembly kit was this San Francisco, Calif., company's lead product in the 1950s-60s. Ramrod also made tops and game tables.

L.B. Ramsdell Co. A Gardner, Mass., manufacturer of juvenile furniture, L.B.

Ramsdell also made doll carriages and baby walkers in the 1930s and '40s.

Ranger Co. This Roselle, N.J., firm was one of several in the late 1930s issuing fingerprinting outfits.

Rand, McNally & Co. Juvenile books were an important Boomer-era product of this publisher of maps, globes and atlases, based in Chicago, Ill.

Randall Wood Products Co. Croquet sets, ten pins, ring toss, and miniature bats were produced by this postwar Randolph, Vt., company.

Randing, Inc. Toy banks and novelties comprised this 1950s-60s line. Randing was based on Lexington Avenue, New York City.

Random House, Inc. Dollar juveniles, "Landmark books, "Allabout" books, "Legacy" books, and "Easy-to-Read" books were among this Madison Avenue, New York City, publisher's specialties in the Boomer years.

"Range Rider" "Range Riders" items in the 1950s-60s included cowboy suits by Herman Iskin & Co., and tents by J.W. Johnson Co.

"Ranger" holster sets see *Chancy Toy & Sporting Goods Corp.*

"Ranger" repeating cannon prewar, see *Fox Co.*

"Ranger" repeating cap pistol see *Kilgore Mfg. Co.*

"Ranger" trains see *American Flyer Mfg. Co.*

"Rap-A-Tap" tapping sets see *Rapaport Bros.*

Rapaport Bros. A competitor with Metal Cast Products Co., Rapaport Bros. of Chicago, Ill., produced the prewar "Junior Caster," "Freshman Caster," and "Junior Electric Caster" outfits. It also made the "Little Giant" Christmas tree stand. In the later 1930s it introduced "Buck Rogers" casting sets, the "Rap-a-Tap" metal tapping sets, wood-burning and leather-burning outfits, sand coloring sets, and doll furniture. The firm continued with postwar lines of "Burn-Rite" woodburning outfits, "Cast-Rite" home foundries, "Mr. Chips" woodcraft sets, "Rap-A-Tap" metal tapping sets, sand decorating outfits, doll trunks, pre-school toys, leather-craft sets, register banks, electric corn poppers, "Hippety-Hop" pogo sticks, "Rollo Hoop," "Teacher's Pet" educational sets, and juvenile furniture. See also *American Toy & Furniture Co.*

Rapaport Bros. introduced the "Johnny Bounce Jump-O-Leen" in the 1960s.

"Raphael Tuck" Most famous for picture postcards, Raphael Tuck images were used on 1930s picture puzzles by R. Wunderlich.

Rapid Electroplating Process, Inc. The "Rapid Elecroplater" of the late 1930s, which allowed electroplating with a brush, was issued by this Chicago, Ill., firm.

rattle Rattles are among the most important of toys for infants. They have been made of every material conceivable, with the oddest being a rattle known from Colonial times, which may have originally been an American Indian infant toy. It was made from the windpipe of a turkey. More typical materials are silver, wood, tin, and plastic.

"Circus Rattles" by Stahlwood Toy Mfg. Co., 1950s.

Katherine A. Rauser Co. Based in Chicago, Ill., Rauser made doll outfits and accessories, dollhouse furniture, and the "National" tinsel line in the 1920s.

Ravenna Ceramics Corp. This Ravenna, Ohio, firm issued "Albright Brand" toy clay marbles.

Ravenwood Craft Kit Co. This 1950s-60s Ravenswood, W. Va., firm specialized in marbles.

"Rawhide" "Rawhide" items in the 1950s-60s included holster sets by Carnell Mfg. Co. and western hats by Corona Hat Co.

Robert Ray Co., Inc. The "Wood Playmates" assembly toys comprised this early 1960s company's line. It was based on W. 29th Street, New York City.

The Ray-Fair Co. Based on Lexington Avenue, New York City, Ray-Fair manufactured "pleasant party costumes" for girls, and the "Diceball" baseball game of the late 1930s.

Ray Laboratories Bubble-blowing sets were 1930s products of this St. Louis, Mo., firm.

Ray Plastic, Inc. Based in Winchendon Springs, Mass., in the 1950s and '60s, Ray Plastic issued plastic pistols with soft bullets, plastic holsters, and toy sawed-off rifles.

Raybest Novelty Co. This 1920s Bleecker Street, New York City, firm was among early manufacturers of electric Christmas novelties and tree decorations.

Raylite Trading Co., Inc. Raylite made Christmas tree lighting outfits and wreaths in the 1930s and '40s. It was based on Broadway, New York City. It moved to the Bronx in the postwar years, when it expanded its line to plastic specialties.

"Para-mount" Christmas tree lights by Raylite, 1930s.

"RBLISS" see *R. Bliss Mfg. Co.*

A.J. Reach & Co. This sporting-goods manufacturer was established in Philadelphia, Penn., in 1867.

Readsboro Chair Co. This Readsboro, Vt., firm manufactured juvenile furniture in the 1930s and '40s, including high chairs, shooflies, and kindergarten tables and chairs.

Real Cycle Co. A Philadelphia, Penn., company, Real Cycle specialized in velocipedes in the 1930s and '40s, adding sidewalk bikes in the later '30s.

"Real Texan" outfits see *Smart Style.*

"Realboy" play suits see *Van Horn & Son.*

Realistic Game & Toy Corp. This Paterson, N.J., corporation issued its "Realistic Baseball" for $1.00 in the mid to late 1920s. The "De Luxe Model" sold for $3.00.

"The Rebel" hats see *Arlington Hat Co.*

recast As adjective or verb, refers to models or toys made years later from the original molds or dies. These are usually not as valuable as the originals. Also referred to by the slang noun or verb, "repop."

Recreation Equipment Co. This Anderson, Ind., firm issued the late 1930s "Game of Indiana Rummy."

Recreational Equipment Co. This late 1930s game manufacturer was based in Denver, Colo.

"Red Arrow" coaster wagon see *American-National Co.*

"Red Barber's Big League Baseball" see *C.&R. Anthony, Inc.*

"Red Bird" train see *American Flyer Mfg. Co.*

Red Circle Mfg. Co. The "Stymie" golf game of the late 1930s was issued by this West 61st Street, New York City, company.

"Red Fox Missile" 1961, see *Hubley Mfg. Co.*

"Red-Man" see *W.C. Redmon Sons & Co.*

"Red Racer" wagons see *Auto-Wheel Coaster Co.*

"Red Riding Hood" Long a story-hour favorite, the folktale heroine appeared on numerous playthings in the 1800s and 1900s. Prewar items included "Red Riding Hood" capes by Lodge Textile Works, a game by Parker Bros., and "Red Riding Hood" wooden toy by Holgate Bros. Nancy Ann Storybook Dolls made a "Red Riding Hood" doll in the postwar years.

Red Robin, Inc. Wooden pull toys and croquet sets made up this postwar line. It was based in El Segundo, Calif.

"Red Ryder" The good-natured cowboy hero Red Ryder appeared in hundreds of newspapers across the country by the end of the 1930s. The company responsible for Red Ryder's licensing, Stephen Slesinger, Inc., touted him as "America's Newest, Fastest Growing Cowboy Character." In the postwar years, Whitman Publishing Co. issued "Red Ryder" books. See *Daisy Mfg. Co.*

Red Ryder was a popular hero by the end of the 1930s.

Red Seal Novelty Co. Plastic dolls, including fashion and character dolls, comprised this Philadelphia, Penn., firm's postwar line.

"Red Skin" skate see *Kingston Products Corp.*

Red Wing Model Airplane & Supply Co. Based in Chicago, Ill., Red Wing issued model airplanes, retailing from a dime to ten dollars, and airplane supplies in the 1920s.

"Red Wing" velocipedes see *American-National Co.*

W.C. Redmon Sons & Co. Based in Peru, Ind., W.C. Redmon Sons made prewar doll bassinets and carrying baskets, miniature hampers and bath sets, and children's rockers. By the late 1930s the firm was specializing primarily in children's rockers. The firm continued in the Boomer years with toy bassinettes, cradles, and hampers.

A.G. Redmond Co. A Flint, Mich., firm, A.G. Redmond made prewar toy vehicle toys, including cranes and steam shovels, and electric motors.

"Redskin" paints see *Milton Bradley Co.*

"Ree-Peter Six Shooter" gun see *Cadillac Specialty Co.*

C.A. Reed Co. This Williamsport, Penn., firm issued party favors, hats, and decorations in the 1930s and '40s.

The Reed Manufacturing Co. This Springfield, Ohio, firm issued "Fascination" games in the 1920s.

W.S. Reed Toy Co. Whitney S. Reed established his toy company in 1875 in Leominster, Mass., specializing in lithographed paper-on-wood toys and construction sets. Its line included the mechanical bank, "The Old Lady in the Shoe." Reed continued in operation until 1897.

Reelfoot Industries This postwar Wynnburg, Tenn., company made stuffed toys.

The Reeves Co. Reeves made lithographed metal toys in the 1920s, including "The Midget Roller Coaster," featuring a winding track down which a metal car rolled. Its line also included the "Ocean Flyer" game, the "Air-E-Go-Round," the "Giant Roller Coaster," and the "Lasso" game.

The "Midget Roller Coaster," a 10-1/2 inch tall toy by the Reeves Co., 1920s.

refrigerators Toy refrigerators became essential for the toy kitchen just as real ones did for real kitchens in the 1920s and '30s.

R

Prewar manufacturers of toy versions included All Metal Products Co., Apex Rotarex Corp., Arcade Mfg. Co., Hoge Mfg. Co., Hubley Mfg. Co., and V.M. Kearley Mfg. Co.

Regal Amplifier Co. Located on West 17th Street, New York City, Regal issued the "Tokfone" communicating systems in the late 1930s.

Regal Doll Mfg. Co. Based in Jersey City, N.J., Regal made dolls in the 1920s. Moving to Trenton, N.J., in the prewar years, Regal specialized in novelty and mama dolls.

Regal Game Mfg. Co. "Finger Tip" bingo and other boxed games comprised this postwar line. Regal was based in Chicago, Ill.

"Regaline" see *Del Rey Plastics Corp.*

"Regent" see *United Crayon Co.*

"Reg'lar Fellers" A popular phenomenon in the 1930s, the "Reg'lar Fellers" comic characters were featured in a variety of playthings. By mid-decade, Barr Rubber Products Co. made balloons; National School Slate Co., blackboards; Whitman Publishing Co., books; Selchow & Righter Co., a bowling game and puzzles; Dura-Products Mfg. Co., caps and school bags; Selchow & Righter Co., games; Fred Gretsch Mfg. Co., harmonicas; Dolly Toy Co., kites; the Einson-Freeman Co., masks; the Rosenthal Co., marbles; Langfelder, Homma & Hayward, mechanical toys, microscope sets, a piano, and xylophones; American Toy Works, paint sets; and P. Goldsmith Sons Co., sporting goods.

register toys see *cash register toys.*

Reid Publishing Co. Based in Milwaukee, Wis., Reid produced artificial Christmas trees in the late prewar years, in addition to other holiday items.

A. Reif & Co. A Philadelphia, Penn., manufacturer of school bags and hat boxes, A. Reif also made toy suit cases and brief cases in the 1930s and '40s.

The Reilly & Lee Co. An important publisher of children's books, Reilly & Lee also distributed some activity toys and puzzles in the 1930s and '40s.

"Reindeer" sleds see *Auto-Wheel Coaster Co.*

Reiner Mfg. Co., Inc. This Boonton, N.J., firm issued "Reiner's Rolling Eye Easter Toys" in the 1920s. They retailed from 50 cents to $5.00.

Reisman, Barron & Co. In the 1920s, this Brooklyn, N.Y., manufacturer issued musical dolls, "Slicker" dolls, "School Girls," "Co-ed Kids," "Playmates," and "Folly Dollies," all in the "popular price" field. By 1929 the company boasted of producing 300 styles of Mama dolls. In the 1930s, the company, now called Reisman Co., was located on Broadway, New York City. In the later 1930s two Reisman firms existed. The Reisman Doll Co. was located on West 24th Street, while Reisman-Exposition Doll Corp. was located at a different Broadway address than the earlier Reisman Co.

Rel Mfg. Corp. Based in East Paterson, N.J., Rel specialized in battery-operated toy boats. The Boomer-era firm also made tea sets, dollhouse furniture, and play sets of plastic figures.

Rel Plastics This East Paterson, N.J., firm issued plastic figure play sets in the 1950s. It acquired Bergen Toy & Novelty late in the decade.

The Reliance Mfg. Co. Based in the Doll District, Reliance made penny and ten-cent toys in the 1930s, as well as doilies and embroidery skeins.

Reliance Pen & Pencil Corp. Crayons and coloring sets were specialties of this postwar Mount Vernon, N.Y., company.

Reliance Picture Frame Co. Based in Chicago, Ill., the Reliance Picture Frame Co. obtained an early license through Kay Kamen in the 1930s to issue framed Mickey Mouse and Three Little Pigs pictures.

Reliance Products Sales Corp. One of the more unusual Boomer toys were the "Daffy Dinosaurs" kits by this Woonsocket, R.I., company, which turned fruits and vegetables into prehistoric animals.

Remco Industries, Inc. One of the important manufacturers of mechanical and battery-operated toys in the Boomer years, Remco issued walkie-talkies, wrist radios, radio kits, electronic space guns, magic shows, military toys, space toys, the "Coney Island Penny Machine," and the "Falcon" battery-operated plane.

Its toys included the "Dick Tracy Electronic 2-Station Wrist Radios" and "Electronic Mobile Loudspeaker & Signal System," a large mobile vehicle toy with a working loud-speaker on its load bed, in the mid-1950s.

The firm issued an important line of dolls, with late 1950s or early 1960s figures including "Betty in the Beauty Parlor" and "Johnny in the Barber Shop"; "Snugglebun" in 1965; "Lil Soldier Joe" in 1965; the "Western Ranch" with "Cowboy Pete," "Black Bart," and "Fatso" vinyl figures; "Mr. & Mrs. Mouse & House," based on the "TV Jones" television show, in 1966; "Baby Chatterbox," "Bottle Babies," and "Baby Glad'N'Sad" in 1967; "Tippy Tumbles" and "Chew-Chew Baby" in 1968; "Tumbling Tomboy" and "Baby Grow-A-Tooth" in 1969; "Kewpies," through an arrangement with Cameo Doll Products Co., in 1968-69; "Jumpsy," "Tiny Tumbles," "Baby Whistle," "Baby Laugh-A-Lot," "Baby Goldilocks," "Li'l Polly Puff," and "Tiny Tumbling Clown" in 1970; the small "Sweet April" in 1971; and "Mimi," who sang the "Coca-Cola" advertising song, in 1973.

Important doll series included the "Brown-Eyed Series," Designed by Annuel McBurroughs, in 1968, which were a heavily advertised line of brown-skinned dolls including "Tumbling Tomboy," "Baby Grow-A-Tooth," "Baby Laugh-A-Lot" and "Kewpie" Versions. The "Heidi and her Friends" series of 1967 included "Heidi," "Winning Heidi," "Hildy," "Herby," "Jan," "Pip," and "Spunky." The vinyl dolls had a "magic button" that made the dolls wave

The "Finger Dings" of 1970-71 were a kind of finger puppet in which two fingers were stuck into the legs, to make them "walk." The line included "Sally Ice Skater," "Betty Ballerina," "Millie Mod," "Adventure Boy," and the "Finger Ding Flower Kids." The "Hug-A-Bug" series included six different clip-on dolls with plastic wings.

Remco's space-age "Walkie Talkies," 1950s.

Remington Arms Co., Inc. The "Remington Air Rifle" was a popular air rifle of the 1920s, made by Remington Arms Co., located on Broadway, New York City. The rifles were pump-action repeaters. Remington also manufactured air rifle shot. The Cutlery Division of this famous firm, based in Chicago, Ill., issued whittling and Scouting knives for the juvenile market in the prewar years.

remote control "Remote control" refers to the child's ability to control an electrically powered toy from a distance. It may sometimes be used with some toys that can be mechanically controlled from a near distance, by means of wires or rods or other connection. While the term was conventionally used for hand-held controls, early electric trains with floor control units were also advertised as "remote control."

Remotrol Co. Based on West 37th Street, New York City, Remotrol made play sets in the later 1930s whose pieces could be moved with "sub-magnetic control," in a manner that calls to mind the later Boomer years "Thimble City" sets by Remco. Remotrol's sets included boat, farm, "World Travel," and horserace toys. The firm continued issuing the toys into the 1960s. It also enjoyed success with its "Staunton" and "Florentine" magnetic chess sets.

Rempel Mfg. Co. This Akron, Ohio, company was known for not only latex rubber toy animals and character dolls in the 1950s and '60s, but also its "Rempel Action" riding horses. The latex animal toys fell within the "Little Folk from Sunnyslope" line, with such characters as "Dandy" duck and "Harvey" rabbit, among many others. Its riding horses featured steel-reinforced rubber bodies, and included "Frisky Pony on Springs" and "Frisky Pony on Wheels." Rempel also made a "Frisky Cowboy Ridem Stick," and "Rempel's Racing Sulky." Rempel's most famous toys were the 1950s "Froggie the Gremlin" squeeze toys, based on the "Buster Brown" character.

"Ho-jo the Bo," a rubber toy from Rempel, 1950s.

R

"Renaissance Chess" see *E.S. Lowe Co.*

Renall Dolls, Inc. This Los Angeles, Calif., firm issued the "Bozo the Capitol Clown" dolls of the 1950s and '60s.

Renner & Co. Based in Chicago, Ill., Renner made prewar toy electric irons and ironing sets.

Rennoc Games & Toys, Inc. Games, activity boxes, hobby kits, and art sets were postwar specialties of this Port Norris, N.J., company.

Renown Doll Wig Co., Inc. In addition to doll wigs, this East 112th Street, New York City, firm also made doll hospital supplies from the 1930s through the Boomer years.

Renwal Toy Corp. Plastic toys of all kinds comprised this Mineola, N.Y., firm's line from 1945 into the 1960s. The firm issued plastic airplanes, dollhouse furniture, boats, autos, trucks, pull-toys, dolls, cap guns, space guns, space men, and whistles. It issued many of its toys in various kinds of play sets, as in the mid-1950s "Hospital Nursery Set," which featured hospital furnishings and numerous baby beds, and the "Busy Little Mother" set, full of miniature household items. Renwal also made a few

die-cast vehicle toys in 1955, in the "Turnpike Set" and loose assortments.

A.J. Renzi Plastic Co. Stick horses, batons, croquet sets, polyethylene banks, tub toys, race cars, and checkers comprised this postwar line. The firm was based in Leominster, Mass., in the 1950s and '60s.

repaints "Repaints" are old toys that have been repainted, which may or may not include old toys that have been restored. The "repaint" term often has a negative connotation, due to the number of times collectors have unknowingly bought toys that have turned out to be that very thing. In other words, some unscrupulous souls have sold items as being in excellent or pristine condition, and received the appropriate price, which the buyers have then discovered to not be quite so excellent or pristine.

Paint on very old toys will usually reflect its age. Often, crazing, which are tiny hairline cracks visible in the surface, is present. Even in toys that appear in exceptional condition, some chipping and wear will be found, especially in surfaces that would be touching the tabletop or floor during play or display, and around moving parts. Old painted surfaces should also be extremely hard, and not easily scratched as would be the case with new paint.

Acquaintance with the kinds of toys being collected helps guard collectors against unknowingly buying repaints. Some collectors go to the extent of carrying a portable black-light fixture when shopping for toys, which helps expose inconsistencies of age in the paint. Others will test an obscure spot of the paint with a xylene or acetone solvent, which will dissolve new paints but leave old paints intact. Typically collectors regard repainted items as worth about half the value of a pristine example.

Replogle Globes, Inc. A Chicago, Ill., firm established in the late 1930s, Replogle specialized in geographical globes. In the 1950s and '60s, the firm also issued the "Magnetic Global Air Race" game.

repop Slang for recast or reproduction. Probably a derivative of "reproduction."

reproductions The greatest bane to the collector, especially the collector of vintage cast-iron and tin-litho items, is the "repro" reproduction item. Reproductions may be honorably intended re-creations of vintage items for nostalgia or collector reasons, which may then sometimes be offered on the secondary market as originals, either through ignorance or malfeasance; or they may be manufactured with the express purpose of deceiving collectors into paying high prices.

The collector's best defenses are the use of caution, knowledge, and expert help. Gaining experience at toy museums and toy shows can be invaluable, for it helps impart the sense of what vintage toys look and feel like. Cast-iron toys tend to have been made with higher quality standards than their later copies, a fact often reflected in the coarseness of grain in copies, and the poor mating of halves. Reproduction pieces that have been artificially "aged" often have steel pins or axles which are more difficult to age, and which as a consequence give away their recent nature. Collectors should also be aware that many, if not most, vintage cast-iron pieces were dipped in paint, not sprayed with paint, which means that both the exterior and interior of any given toy should bear traces of the original coloring, if any paint at all remains.

In the postwar years through the end of the 20th century, a great many decorator items in cast-iron have been produced which mimic the appearance of older toys to greater and lesser degrees. As with purposeful reproductions of earlier toys, these tend to reflect a fairly low quality of production. Many, however, can still be charming items, and possibly acceptable to some collectors if billed honestly for what they are.

The quality of tin reproductions is often quite high, which makes this an even more daunting field for the neophyte to enter. Collectors, especially when starting out, are safest when buying from reputable dealers with years of experience in the field, who are usually willing to guarantee the toys are of the vintage advertised.

The reproduction of toy parts, for purposes of restoration, became commonplace in the latter part of the 20th century, due to the popularity of collecting in general. Reputable dealers will inform collectors as to which parts are reproductions. This information, unfortunately, tends to be lost when the toy re-enters the marketplace at a later date. The collector's best defense in this regard is to be aware of what is available in the restoration marketplace.

In all cases, nothing can replace experience and the development of specialized knowledge. While the greater percentage of collectors probably have a negative experience in their past in connection with reproductions, on the whole the experience has not soured their enjoyment of their collecting interests. See also *repaints, restorations.*

The Republic Tool Products Co. The
"Republic Toys" line of pull toys and friction toys was produced by this Dayton, Ohio, firm in the 1910s into the '30s. The line included locomotives, streetcars, dump trucks, touring cars, limousines, roadsters, aerial trucks, ladder wagons, fire engines, chemical trucks, airplanes, and delivery vans. Republic referred to its friction toys as "Republic Momentum Power Floor Toys." John C. Turner Co. also referred to its friction toys as "momentum toys."

"Restless Gun" A variety of "Restless
Gun" playthings appeared in the 1950s-60s, including badges and carded toys by 20th Century Varieties, coloring books by the Saalfield Publishing Co., games and puzzles by Milton Bradley Co., hats by Arlington Hat Co., holsters and rifles by Esquire Novelty Co., plastic figurines by Hartland Plastics, model kits by Pyro Plastics Corp., playsuits by Herman Iskin & Co., storybooks by Whitman Publishing Co., tents by H. Wenzel Tent & Duck Co., and trading cards by Topps Chewing Gum Co.

restorations Restorations give great plea-
sure to many collectors, and cause headaches for others. Since several toy-parts businesses in the latter part of the 20th century sprang up to serve the needs of collectors, the existence of restored toys has become a commonplace factor in the life of the collector. Replacement parts in tin, cast iron, die-cast metal, lead, and brass have all been made, sometimes with a high level of competence, and sometimes with a low.

The restoration most acceptable to the greatest number of collectors involves the piecing-together of a single toy from several incom-

R

plete ones—a process that may then free up other parts, for other restorations. Such restorations depend upon being lucky enough to have the right parts, however. Because of convenience and cost, far more restorations use newly manufactured parts created expressly for the purpose.

While many who do the restorations regard the resulting toy as worth something near a pristine example of the same toy, many others regard them as worth perhaps half that value. See also *married parts, repaints, reproductions.*

Revell, Inc. The "Revell Authentic Kits" were prominent in the 1950s and '60s. The firm also made "HO" electric train sets and accessories. It was based in Venice, Calif.

Revere, Paul A leading Boston silversmith, also famous for Revolutionary activity, Revere made silver teething rings, rattles, and "wisles."

Revere Copper & Brass, Inc. In the mid-1950s, Revere introduced children's-size versions of its "Revere Ware," in selections of three, five, and seven pieces. These were premium toy sets, originally priced from $4.95 to $14.95. Their cartons were also designed as play stoves. The firm was based on Park Avenue, New York City, and moved to Rome, N.Y., by the 1960s.

Revere Mfg. Co. Beginner's ice and roller skates, toy garden sets, and junior carpenter tools comprised this postwar line. The firm was based in Phoenix, N.Y.

"Revlon" doll by *Ideal Toy Corp.*

Rex Accessories Co. The "Whizzer-Quizzer" question and answer game of the late 1930s was made by this Racine, Wis., firm.

Rex Doll & Toy Corp. This Wooster Street, New York City, firm issued vinyl and latex walking dolls in the 1950s.

"Rex" dinosaur model kit see *ITC Modelcraft.*

Rex Mfg. Co. Based in Chicago, Ill., Rex made the "Kentucky Derby" and "Greyhound" racing games of 1938-39.

Rex Rubber & Novelty Co. Balloons and rubber novelties were produced by this Warren Street, New York City, firm in the 1930s and '40s.

"Rex" wagons see *Radio Steel & Mfg. Co.*

Rhyme-A-Lings Co. of America This Coytesville, N.J., firm issued the "Rhyme-A-Lings" game of scrambled rhymes in the late 1930s.

Rice Mills, Inc. Costumes comprised this postwar Belton, S.C., firm's line.

Ricca Decors, Inc. Decalcomanias for decorating playroom and nursery walls were the specialty of this Broadway, New York City, firm, established in the late 1930s.

Rich Illinois Mfg. Co. "Rich Toys" was the trademark for a firm first called Rich Illinois Mfg. Co., based in Morrison, Ill. The firm emphasized wood toys and playhouses in the 1920s and earlier '30s, moving by the late decade to Clinton, Iowa, where it became Rich Mfg. Co., with an expanded line of wooden toys, forts, dollhouses, desks, musical cradles, and pull toys. Because of the nature of the playthings it produced, Rich Mfg. was able to continue producing during wartime. Non-critical materials went into most of its line, enabling it to keep providing kids of the early 1940s with shooflies, sand toys, sail boats, bathtub sets, toy garages, and even musical nursery furniture. In 1953 the company moved to Tupelo, Miss., becoming Rich Industries, Inc. Its line for the next, and the company's last, decade included rocking horses, hobby horses, shooflies, cradles, juvenile furniture, doll houses, and combination bowling games.

The "Choo-Choo Engine Shoofly," by Rich Industries, 1960s.

"Rich Toys" see *Rich Illinois Mfg. Co.*

"Rich Uncle" see *Parker Bros.*

The Richards Co. "Dolly's Pride" vanity sets, doll hangers, brush sets, and comb and mirror sets were this postwar Hillside, N.J., company's specialty.

Richards Mfg. Co. Based in Chicago, Ill., Richards issued the "Mystic Slates" of the 1950s-60s, as well as games.

Richardson Ball Bearing Skate Co. Richardson was a Chicago, Ill., manufacturer of ball-bearing roller skates in the 1930s and '40s.

The Richardson Co. The prewar "Richelain" toys were made by this Cincinnati, Ohio, firm. In the mid-1930s these included the "Alice in Wonderland" toy tea sets, "Sunny Circus" sand toys, and infant eating sets.

"Richelain" toys see *The Richardson Co.*

Richmond Bros. Co. A light metal stamping manufacturer based in Newark, N.J., Richmond Bros. made prewar tin toys and noisemakers, as well as costume and stuffed-toy bells.

Richmond School Furniture Co. In the 1920s, advertising its "Litho Plate unbreakable writing surface," Richmond School Furniture of Muncie, Ind., was introducing its educational blackboards in a variety of colors. Its designs in the late 1920s included "Alice in Wonderland." The blackboards were often set on easels, with educational pictures on a board placed above the slate. Besides easel blackboards, the company also manufactured "Combination Table and Educational Blackboard," and wall models. Richmond School Furniture manufactured "Mickey Mouse" blackboards in the 1930s through a licensing arrangement with Kay Kamen. Its 1930s and '40s trademarks included both "Litho Plate" and "Richmond Jr." The line included spelling boards. It lasted through the Boomer years.

Richter The Rudolstadt, Germany, firm of Richter is regarded as the world's oldest toy company, with a founding date of 1508. The company, famous for its "Anchor Toy Building Bricks," also made alphabet and puzzle blocks. The company continued into the 1920s. A.C. Gilbert bought the American interest of "Anchor" blocks in 1913.

Richwood Furniture, Inc. Miniature doll furniture comprised this postwar line. Richwood was based in Annapolis, Md. The firm Richwood Toys, Inc., a maker of 8-inch dolls, was also based in Annapolis in the same years.

"Rick Brant" series books see *Grosset & Dunlap.*

"Riddle" crayons see *The Ullman Mfg. Co.*

"Ride-A-Hopper" see *Fred A. Huffman Mfg. Co.*

"Ride-A-Way" The Metalcraft Corp. used the "Ride-A-Way" trademark on a prewar velocipede and streamlined scooters.

"Ride 'Em" The "Ride 'Em" tradename was used for a number of prewar toys, including a line made by Keystone Mfg. Co. The Western connotation was evoked in several, including the "Ride 'Em" cowboy equipment by Brauer Bros., and the "Ride 'Em Cowboy" holster belt by Arrow Novelty Co.

Keystone Mfg. Co.'s "Ride 'Em Toy," 1930s.

"Ride-O-Jet" polyethylene wheel toy see *Irwin Corp.*

"Ride-On" toys see *Master Metal Products, Inc.*

"Rider Kar" see *Towner Toys.*

Rider Rubber Novelties A Cleveland, Ohio, rubber specialties firm, Rider Rubber made rubber ABC blocks, teething rings, and toy animals in the 1930s and '40s.

"Riding Bronco" see *Wirsig Products Co.*

Riemann, Seabrey Co., Inc. Established in the 1920s in New York City, Riemann, Seabrey Co. acted as sole sales agents through around 1944 for a number of leading cast-iron toy manufacturers, including Kenton Mfg. Co., Grey Iron Casting Co., the N.N. Hill Brass Co., and J. & E. Stevens Co.

"The Rifleman" One of the heroes of the TV Old West, "The Rifleman" inspired playthings in the 1950s-60s including "Flip Special" repeating cap rifles by the Hubley Mfg. Co., games by Milton Bradley Co., hats by Arlington Hat Co., plastic figures by Hartland Plastics, and play suits by Herman Iskin & Co.

Rig-A-Jig Toy Co. The "Rig-A-Jig" plastic construction toy of the 1950s and '60s was issued by this Chicago, Ill., firm.

Rilington Toy Novelty Co. Based in Burlington, N.J., Rilington made dressed dolls, doll dresses, and novelties in the 1930s and '40s.

"Rin-Tin-Tin" The famous TV dog of the 1950s inspired playthings into the 1960s, including games, erasable pictures, and paint-by-number sets by Transogram Co.; holster sets by Esquire Novelty Corp.; hats by Arlington Hat Co.; and miscellaneous toy items by Smile Novelty Toy Co.

Ring-A-Pin Co. This West 26th Street, New York City, manufacturer of stuffed toys for infants issued the "Ring-A-Pin" game in the late 1930s.

ring toss Ring toss games were usually indoor versions of quoits, manufactured by dozens of game companies in the prewar and postwar years.

"Ring Toss" game by Ohio Art, 1950s.

Rippon Co., Inc. Rippon Co. manufactured preschool games and educational toys, including the 1930s "Magic Blackboard," "Fluffy the Kitten," and "Peg-O-Map," a geography game. A division of A.I. Root Co., it was located on West 22nd Street, New York City.

The Rippon Corp. The postwar "La Lango" bilingual game was issued by this Long Island City, N.Y., company.

"The Right Toy for the Right Age"
The trade magazine *Playthings* published the essay "The Right Toy for the Right Age" in April 1929. The essay analyzed the toys most suitable for different age groups. So popular did the article prove that *Playthings* reprinted it several times, sometimes in pamphlet form.

Toys for the various stages of childhood are divided into categories. The essay suggests certain "Tiny Tot" toys will "stimulate manipulative investigations," while noting that others "help imitative and imaginative play" or "teach rhythmic expression," for instance.

Appropriate toys "Tiny Tots" included stockinette, rubber, or powder puff animals and dolls, balloons ("to float above crib and provoke the child's interest in its motion"), balls, celluloid or rubber bath toys, wooden bead dolls, bells, washable rag books, and musical pull and push toys.

The themes chosen for the different ages had undoubted influence within the toy industry. For children ages one to two, it recommended "Sturdy Toys for Sturdy Youngsters"; ages two to four, "Toys for Make Believe." It called the years four to six the "Age of Purposeful Play," and from six to eight, "A Period of Irrepressible Ego." "Realism in Play" described the toy interests of children ages eight to ten. Children ages ten to twelve entered "An Era of Special Interests," with handicraft sets and sports equipment coming to the fore.

Righter, John H. see *Selchow & Righter.*

Rilington Toy Novelty Co. Based in Burlington, N.J., Rilington made doll outfits, trunks, hat boxes and novelties in the 1920s.

"Riot" gun prewar, see *Kenton Hardware Co.*

Risdon Mfg. Co. Based in Naugatuck, Conn., Risdon made metal stampings and formed wire goods in the 1930s and '40s, and included a "canary songster," probably the canary whistle, among its prewar goods.

"Risk" 1959, see *Parker Bros.*

"Rite-Hite" housekeeping toys see *Wolverine Supply & Mfg. Co.*

Rite Mfg. Co. This Miami, Fla., firm made prewar house-building construction toys and flying tops.

A.E. Rittenhouse Co., Inc. Based in Honeoye Falls, N.Y., A.E. Rittenhouse made miniature toy electric airplanes in the 1930s. It also made a "complete airport outfit," which included airplane, hangar, revolving beacon and field marker lights, and toy transformers.

Rittenhouse, Inc. Pogo sticks and stilts were postwar specialties of this Akron, Ind., company.

"Riverside" baby carriage see *American-National Co.*

"Ro-Day-O" The prewar "Ro-Day-O" scooter was issued by the Globe Co. The same spelling was used in the "Ro-Day-O Togs" cowboy play suits by William C. Waugh Co., perhaps because Keyston Bros. was issuing "Rodeo" cowboy play outfits at the same time in the 1930s.

road-building and construction toys One of the most popular categories of vehicle toy in the postwar years was that of road-building equipment. Charles William Doepke Mfg. Co., in the late 1940s and early '50s, was largely responsible for initiating the manufacture of these toys in heavy pressed-steel, using standards equivalent to the manufacture of the real vehicles, and using the blueprints of the original vehicles for designing this "Model Toys" line. Manufacturers with less exacting standards soon copied the success of the Doepke line, eventually driving these higher-priced toys off the market. By the mid-Boomer years, manufacturers of road building and construction equipment included Buddy "L" toys, Carter Tru-Scale Machine Co., Diggerator Co., Dowst Mfg. Co., Eldon Mfg. Co., Eska, General Molds & Plastics Corp., the Hubley Mfg. Co., Ny-Lint Tool & Mfg. Co., Structo Mfg. Co., Tonka Toys, and Tru-Matic Toy Co.

The Roalex Co. Puzzles, games, and novelties were postwar specialties of this Forest Hills, N.Y., company.

"Roamer" wheel goods see *D.P. Harris Hardware & Mfg. Co.*

D. Robbins & Co. Based on West 17th Street, Robbins specialized in "E-Z" magic tricks, joke novelties, and puzzles.

"Robert the Robot" see *Ideal Toy Corp.,* also *robots.*

Roberta Doll Co., Inc. The "Roberta Ann" and "Miss Babette" dolls of the 1950s and '60s were issued by this firm, based in the Fifth Avenue Building, with factory in Brooklyn, N.Y. The "Roberta Ann" line included "drink, wet and tear" baby dolls, newborn infant dolls, "sweater" dolls, "colored" dolls, bride dolls, formal dolls, high-heel glamour dolls, and novelty dolls. Roberta Doll also made 30 and 36-inch dolls, walking dolls, and trunk and wardrobe sets.

Tom B. Roberts Co. Vinyl toys, squeeze toys, and tub toys comprised this postwar line. Roberts was based in Englewood, N.J.

R

E.H. Roberts Corp. This Orange, Mass., wood-turning firm produced prewar wooden banks among its other products.

"Robin Hood" Prewar "Robin Hood" playthings included archery sets by Indian Archery & Toy Corp., and games by Milton Bradley Co. The leader of Sherwood Forest's merry men enjoyed new popularity in the 1950s and '60s through silver screen and television movies and serials. Playthings proliferated, and included "Robin Hood" archery sets by the Rollin Wilson Co. and Withington; children's phonograph records by Paramount Enterprises; clay and paint sets by the Art Crayon Co.; games by Harett Gilmar; jigsaw puzzles by Guilt-Rite Toys; miscellaneous accessories by 20th Century Varieties; party goods by American Merri-Lei Corp.; and play tents by J.W Johnson Co. The "Sherwood" archery set was made by Ben Pearson.

The "Sherwood Forest" archery set by The Rolling Wilson Co., 1950s.

George A. Robinson & Co., Inc. Metal toy tool sets and cap canes were specialties of this Rochester, N.Y., firm.

Robinson Crusoe First published in England in 1719, this popular book by Daniel Defoe went through four American editions in the years 1786-1789. Although not expressly intended as a book for children, it has become regarded as a "children's classic," and has inspired other children's books, comic books, and films. Playthings through the years included the "Game of Robinson Crusoe for Little Folks" by E.O. Clark in the early 1900s, and "The Game of Robinson Crusoe" game by Milton Bradley Co., first issued in 1909 and issued through the prewar years.

E.M. Robinson Toy Mfg. Co. Stuffed animals and Easter rabbits in "Duveteen," velvet, and plush were prewar products of this New Dorp, N.Y., firm.

"Robotoy" remote control truck mid-1930s, see *Buddy "L" Mfg. Co.*

robots Robot toys were inspired by images of mechanical men, which had been appearing in science-fiction stories as early as the 19th century. Early playthings included "Tin Man" toys based on the L. Frank Baum character. The walking robots introduced in the late 1940s were manufactured abroad. The first domestically produced walking robot toy may have been the skirted robot, "Robert the Robot," a plastic toy introduced in 1954 and sold through the major catalog and department stores. "Robert" was part of a line developed by Ideal Toy Corp. and inventor Ted Duncan, who devised a crank-operated voice mechanism for toys. The other toys using the device were a train, a wall telephone, and a police car.

"Robert" was a remote-control robot, who could be steered by a hand-held unit. He had a head with glowing eyes and antenna, powered by a battery within the head. His voice-record said, "I am Robert the Robot, the Mechanical Man. Drive me and steer me wherever you can." One of the firm's biggest hits of the 1950s, the 14-inch-tall toy remained in production for six years. The original version featured an opening toolbox in the "chest," with tools. This feature was removed in 1955. The next year, the clear plastic antenna at the top of the head was replaced by opaque plastic. The toy originally sold for $6.00.

Ideal Toy Corp. remained the leading domestic manufacturer of toy robots, issuing toys including "Yakkity Yob" and "Mr. Machine," in the 1960s. Louis Marx & Co. also issued several important plastic robot toys, notably the "Rock 'Em Sock 'Em Robots" of 1964, which were kept in production for many years afterwards.

Marx & Co.'s "The Great Garloo" robot, 1961.

Japanese tin toy robot, "T.V. Spaceman."

Rochester Folding Box Co. The "Jack-bilt" playthings of the 1930s and '40s were made by this Rochester, N.Y., firm. They included play houses, play stores, play schoolboards, toy refrigerators, table tennis tops, forts, and games. The company also made "Betsy-Ann" dollhouses in the mid-1930s.

Rochester Mfg. Co. Based in Rochester, N.Y., this company made the 1930s "Rainbow" tops.

Rock Industries, Inc. Children's books, dart games, space glasses and goggles, plastic toys, target games, toy luggage, television theaters, novelty scarves, and rack items comprised this Boomer-era line. The firm was based on Broadway, New York City.

Rock-O-Mfg. Co. This postwar Oak Harbor, Ohio, company specialized in indoor and outdoor games.

Rock Valley Toy see *Alps.*

"Rock-A-Bye" nursery items see *Perfection Mfg. Co.*

"Rock-A-Tots" rockers see *The Mengel Co.*

"Rockaby" linen stuffed animals prewar, see *Twinzy Toy Co.*

Rockaway Mfg. Co. The prewar "Safety-Walker" baby walker was made by this Cincinnati, Ohio, firm.

"Rocket" automobile 1930s, see *Garton Toy Co.*

"Rocket" crayon sharpeners see *Leeds Sweete Products.*

"Rocket" pistol, mid-1930s see *Daisy Mfg. Co.*

"Rocket Pistol," postwar see *Jak-Pak-Inc.*

"Rocket-Plane" sled see *American Acme Co.*

"Rocket Pogo Stick" see *Roy Berlin Co.*

"Rocket Racer" sleds 1930s, see *Kalamazoo Sled Co.*

"Rocket Satellite" action game see *Sidney A. Tarrson Co.*

"Rocket Ship" kites see *The Alox Mfg. Co.*

"Rocket Shoes" see *Moon Mfg. Co.*

"Rocket Shot" game 1930s, see *Lindstrom Tool & Toy Co.*

"Rocket-Shute" parachute toy see *Lamaico Toys.*

"Rocket" sled see *Paris Mfg. Co.*

"Rocket to the Moon" game see *Boyd Specialty Co.*

"Rocket" wagons mid-1930s, see *The Globe Co.*

"Rockets to the Moon" game see *Wolverine Supply & Mfg. Co.*

Rockford Eagle Furniture Co. This Rockford, Ill., firm also made 1930s doll beds.

rocking horse Rocking horses have varied greatly through time, ranging from stylized rocking platforms with only the barest suggestions of a horse head to full detailed horse figures standing astride curved runners. The first American manufacturer of rocking horses may have been William Long, a craftsman working in Pennsylvania in the late 18th century. Working in the mid to late 1800s, Benjamin Potter Crandall and Jesse Crandall introduced important innovations to what had previously tended to be a simple, stylized toy. Crandall rocking horses included versions with stuffed bodies, which were soon imitated by European manufacturers, wood-body rocking horses with real hair for manes and tails, the shoofly, and the spring horse.

Prewar manufacturers of rocking and spring horses included W.A. Barber, the N.D. Cass

Co., Charles & Victor Goldstein, the Mengel Co., Whitney Reed Co., and Whitney Bros. Co.

By the late prewar years, manufacturers included American Toy Corp., Anchor Mfg. Co., L.H. Bazuin Co., the Les Brown Co., the Delphos Bending Co., Fisher-Price Toys, Hub Products Co., Maplewood Products Co., Mengel Co., Michigan Specialty Co., New Devices, J.C. Oram, Stoner Corp., Transogram Co., Tucker Duck & Rubber Co., Twinzy Toy Co., the Whitney Reed Co., Whitney Bros. Co., and Wright & Dickey Mfg. Co.

In the Boomer years, such interesting variants appeared as inflatable rocking horses, by Dartmore Corp., and numerous plastic versions. The most famous of the latter were issued by Wonder Products Co., who molded the horse bodies with legs tucked up beneath the body, and suspended them by springs from a four-point base constructed of steel tubing.

Manufacturers included American Mfg. Concern, Barnett & Son, Bayshore Industries, Blake & Conroy, Blazon, N.D. Cass Sales Co., DeKalb Toys, Delphos Bending Co., DeLuxe Game Corp., DeLuxe Woodcraft Co., Eyerly Associates, Golden Triangle Toy Co., the Gong Bell Mfg. Co., Gordon Mfg. Co., Harrison's Mfg. Co., Holly-Ho Toy Mfg. Co., Milton A. Jacobs, Jeffrey Toy Mfg. Co., Kapri Mfg. Co., Kiddie Brush & Toy Co., Lange Plastics Co., Julius Levenson, J.W. McKinney, Merrie-Go, the Modern Crafts Co., Moulded Products, Paramount Toy Mfg. Co., Rempel Mfg. Co., Rich Industries, Riemann, Seabrey Co., Scandia-Custer Toy Corp., Sky Craft, Southern Toy Mfg. Co., Taylor Wyman Co., Tremax Industries, Tru-Matic Toy Co., the Whitman Reed Co., and Wirsig Products Co. See also *"Cricket,"* *shoofly, spring horse.*

"The Wonder Rocker" rocking horse, 1960s.

Rich Industries' plastic rocking horse, 1950s.

rocking toy Used in 1859, "rocking toy" was the original name of the shoofly.

"Rockwell" wooden toys see *Holgate Bros.*

"Rodeo Ranger" cowboy figure sets see *Lido Toy Co.*

Roebuck-Publishers This Baltimore, Md., firm made marionette outfits in the late 1930s, as well as sewing and weaving sets.

The Roll Away Skate Co. The "Rol-O-Way" shoe roller skates were issued by this Cleveland, Ohio, company in the late prewar years.

"Roll-King" skates see *Metal Specialties Mfg. Co.*

"Roll-O-Flot" boats see *Mason & Parker Mfg. Co.*

"Rollapoolene" see *Royal Oak Toy Co.*

roller skates see *skates, roller.*

"Rollercycle" see *Kingston Products Corp.*

"Rollfast" wheel goods see *D.P. Harris Hardware & Mfg. Co.*

"Rollin the Green," Inc. This prewar St. Louis, Mo., game company made the 1930s and '40s "Bowlee-O" game.

rolling hoops see *hoop toys.*

rolling pins Toy rolling pins were popular toy kitchen utensils, usually manufactured by companies other than the ones making many of the other kitchen devices. In the Boomer years, manufacturers included the Fli-Back Sales Corp., Forster Mfg. Co., Sollmann & Whitcomb, and the Stratton Co.

"Rollo" trade name see *Lange Plastics Co.*

Rolls Racer Corp. Coaster wagons and other wheel goods were among the prewar offerings of this Ypsilanti, Mich., division of O.E. Thompson & Sons.

"Rollster Car" see the *Mengel Co.*

"Rollster Skooter Skate" see the *Lyons Mfg. Co.*

"Rolly Animals" see *Gund Mfg. Co.*

"Rolly Dolly" toys see *The A. Schoenhut Co.*

"Rolly Toys" wooden toys prewar, see *Holgate Bros. Co.*

The Rolmonica Music Co. This Baltimore, Md., firm issued the "Rolmonica, the Pocket Player Piano" in the late 1920s. An interesting musical toy, it used interchangeable rolls which could be turned while blowing through the "Rolmonica," to produce melodies from current hit songs. Advertisments featured the "Our Gang" kids. It was distributed by Ay-Won Toy & Novelty Corp.

roly-poly The roly-poly was a balance toy, often made of papier-mache or composition in the earlier 20th century and prewar years, and of plastic in the Boomer years. Many early roly-polys were imported from Germany. American manufacturers included the A. Schoenhut Co. Several new kinds of roly-polys appeared in the Boomer years, including inflatable ones, made by Alvimar Mfg. Co., Dartmore Corp., and Doughboy Industries, and plastic chime or musical roly-polys, made by Alan-Jay Plastics, and I.B. Wolfset & Co. Other postwar firms included Amloid Co., Eyerly Associates, Gerber Plastic Co., Irwin Corp., Plastic Playthings, Softskin Toys, Stahlwood Toy Mfg. Co., Star Mfg. Co., and the Toy Tinkers.

A roly-poly from the 1920s.

"Roly Poly" The "Roly Poly" trademark was used by several prewar manufacturers, including Milton Bradley Co. for a line of games, and Parker Bros. for a ten pins set.

"Romper Room" One of the popular educational TV shows for young children in the 1950s and '60s, "Romper Room" inspired playthings that included batons by Lancaster Toy Co., miscellaneous educational toys by Pressman Toy Corp., and pipe cleaner art sets by Barry Products.

"Rompy" Ruth E. Newton character toy see *The Sun Rubber Co.*

Rondout Metal Products Co., Inc. Doll baths, strollers, recliners, walkers, and metal doll carriages were specialties of this postwar Home Street, New York City, company.

"Ronson Toys," see *The Art Metal Works.*

"Roofus Goofus" trade name see *Wallace Brands Co.*

"Rook" see *Parker Bros.*

The A.I. Root Co. A Medina, Ohio, firm, Root was best known in the 1920s for the "Root Educational Letters," made with "natural finish—no stains to soil clothes. No nails to injure figures. Packed one whole alphabet to a box." In the 1930s and '40s, Root continued specializing in educational play blocks, wood toys, and wood toy parts. Its kindergarten toys included "The Three Bears Adding Board," anagrams, design and hammer sets, and educational letters. Most of its items sold in the 25 cent to $2 range in the mid-1930s. By late in the decade, its line included "Tee-Gee" tongue-and-groove blocks, "Toyland Mechanic," and "Mak-a-Kit" sets. See also *Rippon Co., Inc.*

A.I. Root's "The Magic Blackboard," 1930s.

R

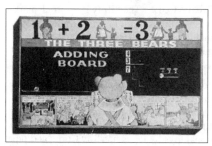

"The Three Bears Adding Toy," by the A.I. Root Co., 1934.

"Rootie Kazootie" In the 1950s and '60s, "Rootie Kazootie" items included dolls by Effanbee Doll Co. and word games by Ed-U-Cards Mfg. Corp.

George D. Roper Corp. This Rockford, Ill., corporation made the 1930s "Baby Roper" toy gas ranges.

"Roper" stove see *Arcade Mfg. Co.*

"Ropes and Ladders" see *Parker Bros. Co.*

Rose Mary Dolls Mfg. Co. Based on W. 180th St, New York City, Rose Mary Dolls made postwar vinyl baby and girl dolls, stuffed dolls, and novelties.

"Rose O'Neill" see *"Kewpie Dolls."*

Rosebud Art Co. Located on Lafayette Street, New York City, Rosebud Art made games, painting sets, painting books, and novelties in the first half of the 20th century. The Rosebud line of toy books and games in the 1920s included "Show Card Joy builder," "King-High," and "3 in 1 Rolaweel." Its book titles included "History Painting Book" and "Foxy Grandpa Comic Painting Book." In the 1930s, Rosebud issued "Cross Country Marathon Game," "Junior Basketball Game," and "Kitty Kat Cup Ball." Other titles included "Bag of Fun" in 1932, "Big Apple" in 1938, and "Jungle Hunt" and "Life of the Party" in the 1940s. The Boomer years saw Rosebud's continuation as a producer of rack items, activity sets, finger paints, school slates, magnetic bulletin boards, and blackboard erasers.

"Rosebud" dolls prewar, see *Horsman Dolls.*

"Rosemarie" dolls see *George Borgfeldt Corp.*

Rosen & Jacoby, Inc. A specialist in costume and doll wigs, this West 20th Street, New York City, company also made novelty hats and other "pressed" novelties in the 1930s and '40s.

E. Rosen Co. This Providence, R.I., company obtained a late 1930s license to issue Edgar Bergen character lollipops.

The Rosenthal Co. Based on East 17th Street, New York City, Rosenthal made glass marbles. It also manufactured erasers and cleaners in the 1930s and '40s.

Rosette Doll Co. Boudoir and bridal dolls comprised this Lawrence, Mass., firm's postwar line.

Ross & Ross An Oakland, Calif., firm, Ross & Ross manufactured early Walt Disney character items. It specialized in stuffed dolls and animals in the 1930s and '40s.

"Ross" bicycles see *Chain Bike Corp.*

Rotary Clothes Dryer Co. Besides its main product, this Allentown, Penn., company also made the 1930s and '40s "Joy Wheel" merry-go-round.

Walter L. Rothschild Prewar games for children and adults were produced by this New Rochelle, N.Y., company.

Rott, William Based on East 9th Street, New York City, William Rott manufactured games for adults in the 1930s and '40s.

"Rough Rider" exerciser see *American-National Co.*

"Round-About Dolls" postwar, see *Milton Bradley Co.*

"Round About" paper dolls see *McLoughlin Bros.*

rounders An early American ball game, "rounders" is considered a predecessor to baseball.

Roundup Amusement Co. Roundup Amusement of Beverly Hills, Calif., owned sole rights to "Tom Mix" products in the 1930s.

"Roundup" pistol and holster set
see *Carnell Mfg. Co.*

"Rover" velocipedes see *The Colson Co.*

row crop In farm toys, refers to the tractor toys having closely spaced front tires, which in the real item allows for easy cultivation of row crops. Compare *"standard."*

Roy Bros. A wood-turning firm in East Barnet, Vt., Roy Bros. entered the toy manufacturing world with croquet games in the earlier 1930s. By late in the decade, the company was issuing croquet and "roquet" sets, ring toss, and ten pins, among other indoor and outdoor games.

Roy Rogers Enterprises The trade names administered by this Beverly Hills, Calif., company in the 1950s and '60s included not only "Roy Rogers" but "Dale Evans," "Trigger," "Double R Bar Brand" and "Brave Eagle."

Among the seemingly endless numbers of playthings at the time were books by Whitman Publishing Co.; books and records by Golden Press; boys' hats by Miller Bros. Hat Co.; cap pistols, holsters, spurs, lassos and scabbards by Classy Products Corp.; chime toys by the N.N. Hill Brass Co.; clay sets by Standard Toykraft Products; "Cowboy and Indian" kit by Colorforms; crayons, chalk, and paint sets by Standard Toykraft; films by Hollywood Film Enterprises; harmonicas by Harmonic Reed Corp.; horses and riders by Hartland plastics; lariats by the Lareo Corp.; miscellaneous toys, including western dinner sets, by Ideal Toy Corp.; play suits by Sackman Bros.; tents and tepees by the Hettrick Mfg. Co.; 3-D color film cards by Tru-Vue Co.; and western dress-up kits for "Roy Rogers" and "Dale Evans" by Colorforms.

Roy's horse, Trigger, was star enough to warrant additional "Trigger" playthings, including hobbyhorses by Dartmore Corp., play horses by the Stern Toy Co., trotters by the Lareo Corp., and TV seats by Mego Corp.

Roy Toy This Worcester, Mass., game manufacturer issued "Alee-Oop" in 1937. Not related to the comic character, the skill game remained popular through the late prewar years.

"Royal" agates see *Akro Agate Co., The*

"Royal Art" see *Advance Crayon & Color Corp.*

"Royal Award" paint-by-number sets see *The Art Award Co.*

"royal" baby carriage see *American-National Co.*

"Royal Brand" see *A. & L. Mfg. Co.*

"Royal Champion" return top see *Royal Tops Mfg. Co.*

Royal Crest Products Co. A specialist in toy-filled Christmas stockings in the Boomer years, Royal Crest also issued rack items and packaged assortments. It was based in Brooklyn, N.Y.

Royal Dell Mfg. Co. Plastic and vinyl dolls, as well as doll clothes and accessories, comprised this Boomer-era West 22nd Street, New York City, firm's line.

Royal Desserts In the early 1950s, Royal Desserts offered plastic soldiers as premiums. The soldiers were apparently copies of Barclay lead soldiers, made by Ajax.

Royal Doll Mfg. Co. Based on Broadway, N.Y., Royal Doll made doll layettes, wardrobe sets, and novelty dolls in the 1930s and '40s.

"Chatterbox," by Royal Doll Mfg. Co.

Royal Electric Co. Based in Pawtucket, R.I., Royal issued Christmas tree lighting outfits in the late 1930s.

R

Royal Eton Sports Based on West 15th Street, New York City, Royal Eton Sports issued table tennis equipment in the late prewar years.

"Royal Flyer" The "Royal Flyer" was used for at least two prewar wagons. An all-steel coaster wagon by Garton Toy Co. and a "convertible coaster" by Toledo Metal Wheel Co. both bore the name. The "Royal Scot" was also made by Garton.

Royal Furniture Mfg. Co. Juvenile reed furniture was the specialty of this Gardner, Mass., firm in the late 1930s.

Royal Juvenile Products, Inc. Possibly the 1950s-60s version of Royal Furniture, this manufacturer of doll carriages, playpens and cribs, and juvenile rockers, was also based in Gardner, Mass.

"Royal Line" spring horses see *Moulded Products, Inc.*

Royal Oak Toy Co. The "Rollapoolene" back yard toy and "Finger Shuffleboard" were Boomer-era products of this Royal Oak, Mich., company.

"Royal Racer" sleds see *Garton Toy Co.*

Royal Tops Mfg. Co., Inc. Royal Tops made yo-yos and spinning tops in the 1950s and '60s, using the "Royal Yo-Yo" and "Trom-Po" trade names. The tops usually cost from a dime to a dollar. The firm was based in Long Island City, N.Y.

The Royal Tot Co., Inc. Pre-school toys, beads, bead toys, and blackboards were postwar specialties of this Newark, N.J., company.

Royal Toy & Novelty Co. Sailplanes of balsa wood were prewar products of this Boston, Mass., company.

Royal Toy Mfg. Co. This Bond Street, New York City, firm issued the "Baby Joy" and "Bottlebabe" dolls of the 1920s.

Royal Wig Mfrs. This 1920s and '30s Greene Street, New York City, manufacturer of "Royal" doll wigs used mohair and human hair.

"Royaljax" postwar, see *Grey Iron Casting Co.*

Royalty Designs, Inc. Animal and novelty banks comprised this postwar line. It was based in Miami, Fla.

rubber balls see *balls.*

rubber, molded parts Manufacturers of molded rubber parts for other manufacturers included several rubber companies who had strong toy lines of their own, such as Auburn Rubber Corp. and the Sun Rubber Co. Other prewar suppliers were primarily based in Ohio: Forest City Rubber Co. in Cleveland, B.F. Goodrich Co. in Akron, the Ohio Rubber Co. in Willoughby, the Stalwart Rubber Co. in Bedford, and the Swan Rubber Co. in Bucyrus. Suppliers on the East coast included the H.O. Canfield Co. in Bridgeport, Conn., and the Laurel Co. in Garfield, N.J.

Rubber Patents Corp. This Grand Rapids, Mich., firm issued the "Ball-O-Fun" large inflatable balls of the 1920s, touted as the "strongest ball made."

Rubber Specialties Co., Inc. A golf-ball manufacturer based in Plymouth Meeting, Penn., Rubber Specialties also made rubber building blocks in the late prewar years.

rubber stamping outfits see *printing toys.*

rubber tires A handful of companies supplied most of the rubber tires and grips for the abundant carriages, pedal cars, velocipedes and bicycles of the prewar years. Manufacturers included Firestone Tire & Rubber Co., the Forest City Rubber Co., the B.F. Goodrich Rubber Co., Goodyear Tire & Rubber Co., Lewis Baby Carriage Supply Co., the Stalwart Rubber Co., the Sun Rubber Co., and the Swan Rubber Co.

rubber toys Rubber as a material for toys came into vogue soon after Charles Goodyear perfected his vulcanizing process, which was discovered in 1830 and patented in 1844. By 1850, "India Rubber toys" were touted as "most durable and economic." They included air-filled balls, ball rattles, rattle boxes, doll heads, and toy animals including fish, dogs, and lions. The first rubber doll appeared in 1851.

The 1920s manufacturers included Barr Rubber Products Co., Eagle Rubber Co., Paramount Rubber Co., and Schmid. Barr and Eagle continued in operation through the prewar years.

The most famous of rubber toy manufacturing companies, including Auburn Rubber Co., Oak Rubber Co., Seiberling Latex Products Co., and the Sun Rubber Co., rose to prominence in the mid to late 1930s.

Other prewar companies included Anderson Rubber Co., Clarke Mfg. Co., the Faultless Rubber Co., Hygrade Fabric Co., Katnips, Maple City Rubber Co., Maxwell Rubber Products, Miller Rubber Products Co., Pacific Balloon Co., Rex Rubber & Novelty Co., Rider Rubber Novelties, Schavoir Rubber Co., Seamless Rubber Co., Sponge Rubber Products Co., Thornecraft, the Wooster Rubber Co., and the Young Novelty Co.

In the postwar years, rubber and vinyl manufacturers included Aktoy Mfg. Co., Anderson Rubber Co., Arrow Rubber & Plastics Corp., Auburn Rubber, Bantam U.S. Toys, Barr Rubber Products Co., Bayshore Industries, Ben-Her Industries, Blake Industries, Chee-Ki Corp. of California, Eastern Moulded Products, Internatinoal Plastic Co., Lee-Tex Rubber Products Corp., William G. Minder Industries, New Jersey Rubber Mfg. Co., Oak Rubber, the Ohio Art Co., Pioneer Merchandise Co., Plastic Playthings, Rempel Mfg., Tom B. Roberts Co., Sun Rubber, Tillotson Rubber Co., Topstone Rubber Toys, Toys Inc., Tykie Toy, and Vinfloat Industries.

The 1960s proved a difficult decade for many rubber and vinyl manufacturers, prompting the decline and demise of major firms including Sun Rubber and Auburn Rubber.

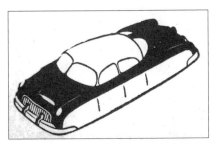

The "Futuristic Sedan" rubber toy by Auburn Rubber Co., 1950s.

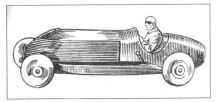

The 1939 rubber racer by Auburn.

Rubber Toys Unique see *Garrett Sales Corp.*

Rubbercraft Corp. This New Haven, Conn., firm made prewar rubber play boats and a "torpedo boat with sail."

Rubbermatic Gun Corp. Plastic toy guns made up this Clarksville, Texas, company's line in the 1950s-60s.

Rueckheim Bros. & Eckstein see *Cracker Jack Co.*

Joseph Ruf A Philadelphia, Penn., manufacturer, Joseph Ruf made 1930s doll wigs.

"Ruff and Reddy" fingertip puppets see *Wilkening Mfg. Co.*

"Ruff Rider" holster sets see *Pilgrim Leather Goods Co.*

The Rugg Mfg. Co. This Greenfield, Mass., manufacturer made a toy snow shovel in the 1930s.

"Rummy" The venerable card game of "Rummy" or "Gin Rummy" has appeared in a great many forms, including the 1930s versions "Rumme" by Milton Bradley Co. and "Rummy" by Parker Bros. Milton Bradley also made "Rummy Football" in 1944.

Rumsey Junior Vehicle Co. A manufacturer of wheel goods, this Lawrence, Kans., company issued the "Jockey" wagon and "The Speedwalker" three-wheel scooter of the late 1930s.

runner 1) The keel or blade of an ice skate.

2) In toys and models, the "runners" are the "branches" of plastic that connect plastic toys, toy parts, or model parts to the sprue. In toy soldier collecting, accessories such as miniature weapons, household goods, or tools may still be found attached to their orig-

inal sprues and runners. In metal model kits the sprue and runners will also be die-cast Occasionally die-cast toy manufacturers will issue collector castings that show the rough toy complete and unfinished as it comes out of the mold. While the connecting die-cast rods are essentially no different from runners, they are not typically referred to this way.

The Rushton Co. In the 1920s and '30s, the "Mawaphil Dolls" were leading items for this Atlanta, Georgia, manufacturer. The "Mawaphil" line included dolls and animal toys made in stockinette, plush, and mohair plush. They were hand constructed and hand painted, and individually wrapped in cellophane. In 1929, Rushton introduced "Mawaphil" wooden pull toys, which were hand-painted and laquered. The trade name was used on soft dolls and toys through the 1930s and '40s.

The Rushton Co. became one of the highest profile manufacturers of plush and mohair toy animals in the Boomer period. It also issued the "At Play" toy line. Its Christmas line emphasized teddy bears, novelty dolls, and general stuffed animals for Christmas, and rabbits and chicks toys for Easter.

After the introduction of efficient vinyl production methods in the 1950s, Rushton developed a line of stuffed animals with vinyl faces. Many were based on popular TV and cartoon characters. Perhaps the most well-known individual toy was "Zip" or "Zippy the Chimp," based on the chimp star who appeared on the "Howdy Doody Show" in the '50s. The toy continued to be made into the 1970s, even though by then the TV connection was unknown to the children playing with it. Other famous characters made into Rushton toys included "Yogi Bear," "Bugs Bunny," and "Huckleberry Hound." See also *Mary Waterman Phillips.*

"Russel Wright" tea sets see *Ideal Toy Corp.*

Russell-Hampton Co. This Chicago, Il., firm issued paper hats, favors and novelties in the late prewar years.

Russell Mfg. Co. Toys, games and advertising novelties kept this Leicester, Mass., company in business from the 1910s through

the prewar years. Early titles included the "Washington's Birthday Party" skill game of 1911. Games in the 1920s included "The Comical Game of Whip" and "Pancake Tiddly Winks." Others were "Game of Speed King" and "Tortoise and the Hare" in 1922, "Billy Whiskers" in 1924, "Par, the New Golf Game" in 1926, and "Basket Ball" in 1929. Titles in the 1930s included "The Game of Buried Treasure," "Take-Off," and "Wow." Others were "Jolly Pirates" in 1938, and "Library of Games" in 1939. The "Old Maid Fun Full Thrift Game" appeared in the 1940s.

Russell Mfg. Co.'s "Big Little Card Games" from the 1950s.

Rustic Furniture Co. "Rustic" furniture enjoyed a certain amount of popularity in the prewar years. This Williamstown, N.J., firm was one of several catering to the juvenile market, issuing not only furniture but playhouses, sand boxes, playground equipment, gyms, and log cabins in the late prewar years. The firm enjoyed continued success into the 1950s and '60s with its line of log cabin playhouses, including "Daniel Boone" log cabins. See *playhouses.*

Ruth Infants' Outfitters This Flushing, Long Island, N.Y., company produced doll outfits from the late 1930s through the Boomer years. It specialized in doll carriage sets and bedding materials.

"Ruthie" dolls see *Horsman Dolls.*

John P. Ryan Co. This Philadelpha, Penn., firm made electric toys and games in the earlier 1930s. Its titles included the "Bing Miller Base Ball Game" of 1932.

Herman Rynveld's Son Corp. This New Albany, Penn., company made Christmas novelties in the 1950s-60s.

Ss

"S.&E. Games" see *Stoll & Edwards Co., Inc.*

The S.&E. Mfg. Co. This Gardner, Mass., company made "Joy Riders," scooters, doll beds and porch gates in the 1920s. In the 1930s, the firm also made baby walkers and beach carts.

S.&G. Mfg. Co. Christmas tree fences were apparently popular in the 1930s, since other manufacturers besides S. & G. Manufacturing were in the business of making them through the prewar years. This Pittsburgh, Penn., company also made "electrical toy fences," doll cribs, and "toy tunnels." By the late '30s its miniature items included ponds, lakes, lighthouses and windmills.

S.&H. Novelty Co. "Peppy Pals," the dancing marionettes, and "Tee Wee Hand Babe—The Living Doll" were introduced in the 1920s and issued into the '40s by this Atlantic City, N.J., firm. "Peppy Pals" were a pair of separate dolls that could be snapped together and made to dance when suspended from a spring. They were issued in a variety of costumes. "Tee Wee" was called the "Living Doll" because it was a kind of hand puppet. In several versions, "Tee Wee" appeared to be lying in a lace-decorated bed, with only head and arms visible. The company specialized in soft stuffed toys, mama dolls, and plywood jigsaw puzzles.

S.B. Mfg. Corp. Located on Broome Street, New York City, in the late 1930s, S.B. Mfg. Corp. manufactured toy telephones and "Western Union" telegraph signal sets.

S.B. Novelty Co. This Broadway, New York City, firm issued doll shoes, furniture and accessories in the late 1930s. In the Boomer years, S.B. Novelty was issuing the "Jeanstyles" doll lingerie and "Carol Robin Creations" doll accessories. It also made doll skates, rayon socks, nylon hose, and high-heel shoes, in addition to traditional doll shoes.

The "Peppy Pals" were marionettes produced by S.&H. Novelty Co. in the 1920s.

"S-Bar-M" cowboy equipment see *Service Mfg. Co., Inc.*

"S.T. Brand" Christmas stockings see *S. Thanhauser.*

The Saalfield Publishing Co. A publisher based in Akron, Ohio, Saalfield was an important publisher of children's materials before and after the war. Its early game titles included "Billy Whiskers" in 1923, "Thornton W. Burgess Animal Game" in 1925, and "Hoot" in 1926. Saalfield obtained an early license through Kay Kamen to issue early Disney activity books, including paint books. In the 1930s it was also making picture puzzles, and was publishing "Shirley Temple" books by the end of the decade. During the World War II years, the firm continued issuing books, picture puzzles, and paper doll cutouts. In the 1950s and '60s, the company was specializing in activity books and boxes, puzzles for children and adults, Christmas carol books, coloring books, donkey party games, fiction books, games for children and adults, paper doll books, linen books, scrap books, paint-by-number sets, and story books. Its line also included "Mr. & Mrs. Flannel Face," part of the company's "Flannel Board Play" series of flannel boards.

Saalfield published this "Steve Canyon" coloring book in the 1950s.

Sabas & Carney The "Big Top" games of the Boomer years were products of this Minneapolis, Minn., company.

The Sabin Machine Co. The "Gumfinger Junior," a rubber toy rake of the 1930s, was made by this Cleveland, Ohio, company.

Sackman Bros. Co. Located on Broadway in New York City, Sackman Brothers issued early Disney play suits through a licensing arrangement with Kay Kamen. It also obtained exclusive rights to issue "Buck Rogers" outfits. The company's "Yankiboy" line of children's play clothes featured suits for aviator, cowboy, Indian, policeman, baseball player, and traffic cop, and "Maskoween" Halloween costumes, through the 1930s and '40s. The firm managed to continue through wartime, adding such timely play suits as "Soldier," "Aviator," "Navy," "Marine," "Jr. WAAC," "Jr. Wave," and "Sailor." In the Boomer years Sackman's line, still under the "Yankiboy" trade name, included a variety of TV tie-in play clothes, including "Roy Rogers," "Dale Evans," "Cisco Kid," "Brave Eagle," "Wagon Train," "Highway Patrol," "Rory Calhoun," "Johnny Ringo" and "Steve Canyon."

sad iron Sad irons, or sadirons, were made in toy form from at least the early 1800s in America. Many were typical solid cast-iron in design. As with adult-size irons, they could be heated on the stove, and then used on doll clothes. One early example had a chamber into which hot coals could be

placed. By the 1930s, electric toy irons had become as common as the conventional, non-electric versions. Manufacturers in the pre-war period of conventional sad irons included Arcade Mfg. Co., Grey Iron Casting Co., N.N. Hill Brass Co., Nicol & Co., and Renner & Co. Companies who made electric, and often also non-electric, sad irons included Betsy Ross Electric Products Corp., the Dover Mfg. Co., Illinois Specialty Co., Kingston Products Corp., Knapp-Monarch Co., Samson-United Corp., and Wolverine Supply & Mfg. Co.

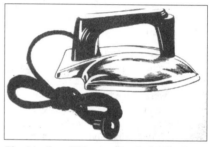

Play iron from Wolverine Supply & Mfg. Co., 1950s.

"Sad Sack" The cartoon Army character inspired playthings including dolls by Sterling Doll Co., plastic inflatable toys by Alvimar Mfg. Co., soft toys by Stuart, and miscellaneous toys by Bayshore Industries.

"Saddle Gun" see *Nichols Industries.*

"Safari" juvenile auto see *The Murray-Ohio Mfg. Co.*

"Safe-Play" rubber blocks prewar, see the *Faultless Rubber Co.*

"Safety Blocks" see *Halsam Products Co.*

"Safety" pistol see *The Hubley Mfg. Co.*

"Safety School Bus" see *Fisher-Price Toys.*

"Safety" self-steering sled see *C.J. Johnson Co.*

Sail-Me Co., Inc. Sail-Me advertised its product as "Aviation's Official Toy Airplane" in the 1920s. The toys were capable of loops-the-loop, spirals and glides. Based in Chicago, Ill., Sail-Me made toy airplanes and parachutes through the 1930s. In the late prewar years the firm introduced "Whirl Glo" revolving Christmas light shades.

St. Louis Pistols & Caps, Inc. Repeating toy cap pistols were the specialty of this St. Louis, Mo., firm in the late prewar years. It also manufactured roll and mammoth caps.

St. Nicholas see *Santa Claus.*

St. Nicholas Magazine A magazine edited in its first years by Mary Mapes Dodge, *St. Nicholas* lasted from 1873 to 1939. It proved an important forum for Dodge's own writing. In the 1900s its illustrators included W.W. Denslow.

St. Pierre & Patterson Mfg. Co. Make-up kits, novelty toys and puzzles made up this postwar line. "Glo-Fangs" were among its products. The firm was based in Grand Rapids, Mich.

St. Pierre Chain Corp. A Worcester, Mass., firm, St. Pierre made pitching horseshoes in the 1930s and '40s.

The Salem China Co. In the earlier 1930s, this Salem, Ohio, company made juvenile china sets with "Mickey Mouse" and "Three Little Pig" motifs. The "Tom Lamb" sets appeared in the late 1930s.

"Salt and Pepper" jacks see *Arcade Mfg. Co.*

"Salvo Rockets" see *Park Plastics Co.*

"Sambo" see *"Little Black Sambo."*

Samet & Wells, Inc. Stuffed dolls, toy animals and novelties were postwar specialties of this Fifth Avenue Building firm.

Louis Sametz, Inc. Based in Westport, Conn., Louis Sametz made prewar celluloid specialties including baby rattles, pinwheels, and table tennis balls. One was "Aero-Top," a celluloid flying top. In the postwar years, the company specialized primarily in celluloid table tennis balls.

A.M. Samour Mfg. Co., Inc. This Stoneham, Mass., company made pinwheels of pyralin, including Halloween pinwheels, in the 1930s and '40s. The line also included propeller and airplane toys, spinning tops, sand pails and shovels, cutout furniture toys, and fireworks.

The Sampson Co. The TV-advertised "Kidd-E-Bouncer" of the 1950s-60s, a children's trampoline, was produced by this Canoga Park, Calif., company.

Samson Mfg. Corp. Hobbyhorses, stick horses, pull toys, slingshots, blackboards and peg boards comprised this postwar toy line. The firm was based in Athens, Texas.

Samson-United Corp. The 1930s "Panel-Matic, Jr." electric toy iron was made by this Rochester, N.Y., company.

John Samuels Established on West 33rd Street, New York City, in the late prewar years, Samuels was a manufacturer and distributor of games for adults.

"San Loo" Chinese checkers see *Northwestern Products.*

sand painting Sand pen coloring sets and sand painting sets became popular in the late 1930s, with manfacturers including Home Foundry Mfg. Co., Rapaport Bros., and the Toy Tinkers. The latter sets were called, logically enough, "Tinkersand." Rapaport issued sand drawing sets into the 1960s. Vitos Products also made the sets in the postwar years.

sand toys Sand toys, which are no more than playthings meant to increase a child's natural pleasure in fooling around in sand, enjoyed a long popularity in America due not only to the fashion of families taking vacations on the beach but also to the introduction of the 1879 "Sandometer," Jesse Crandall's home sand-bench invention that led to the widespread convention of home sandboxes. Early toys tended to fall along the lines of the molds used to shape the "Sandometer" sand. Even the common tin sand pail was used for molding sand, a practice that became a childhood convention.

The basic sand toys were pails, shovels, molds, and sprinklers, the latter being watering cans for moistening the sand, for molding purposes. Through the decades these toys, frequently of tin, came to rank among the most colorful and decorative of toys.

S

The 1920s manufacturers included Arcade Mfg. Co., the N.D. Cass Co., T. Cohn, the Conestoga Corp., Keller Toy Mfg. Co., Seiss Mfg. Co., Structo Mfg. Co., and Wolverine Supply & Mfg. Co.

In the 1930s the Ohio Art Co. issued a variety of attractive sand toys, including "Three Little Pigs" and "Mickey Mouse" items.

Buddy "L" made what must have been the most complex of sand toys with its trench diggers, which were large contraptions of a scale to match its pressed-steel trucks. These had buckets arranged on a rotating belt that could dig the sand and load it, preferably onto a waiting sand truck.

Other prewar manufacturers included Acme Toy & Novelty Co., Aluminum Goods Mfg. Co., Arcade Mfg. Co., Billings, the C-K-R Co., the N.D. Cass Co., Central Wood Products, J. Chein & Co., T. Cohn, Crosman Bros. Co., Fisher-Price Toys, Florida Playthings, Frarol Mfg. Co., Gem Mfg. Corp., the Gibbs Mfg. Co., Holgate Bros Co., Keller Toy Mfg. Co., the Kenton Hardware Co., the Kilgore Mfg. Co., Kirchhof Patent Co., McDowell Mfg. Co., Metal Package Corp., Miami Wood Products Co., Patent Novelty Co., the Richardson Co., Geo. H. Robinson's Sons, A.M. Samour Mfg., Co., the Thompson Mfg. Co., Toy Kraft Co., Transogram Co., Washington Toys & Novelties, and Wolverine Supply & Mfg. Co.

"Permaboard Sand Pail" by Wolverine Supply & Mfg. Co., made during World War II.

In the Boomer years, metal pail and shovel sets were issued by companies including J. Chein, Ohio Art, U.S. Metal Toy Mfg. Co., and Wolverine. Other sets, in wood, plastic and rubber, were made by firms including Apex Tire & Rubber Co., Gerber Plastic Co.,

Irwin Corp., Henry Katz National Sales Org., Kroll Trading Co., Lapin Products, Ohio Art, Renwal Toy Corp., Sollmann & Whitcomb, and Vera Toys.

Other manufacturers made miscellaneous sand toys, including Amloid Co., Banner Plastics Corp., Buddy "L" Toys, T. Cohn, Del Rey Plastics Corp., Eldon Mfg. Co., Ideal Toy Corp., Kewaunee Equipment Co., Kirchhof, Knickerbocker Plastic Co., Ny-Lint Tool & Mfg. Co., Pet Toy of N.H., Plastic Toy & Novelty Corp., Scandia-Custer Toy Corp., Structo Mfg. Co., Tonka Toys, Transogram Co., Tru-Matic Toy Co., U.S. Plastics Corp., and Worcester Toy Co.

Sand toy sprinkler— a small-sized watering can to moisten sand, 1920s.

An elaborate sand toy by Buddy "L" with buckets on a rotating belt.

sandboxes Sandboxes are a venerable toy, and an American one, having their origins in the Jesse Crandall "Sandometer" of the 1870s. Prewar manufacturers included the American National Co., Anchor Post Fence Co., Benner, Cuyahoga Lumber Co., Garton Toy Co., Gem Mfg. Corp., Charles W. Howard, Kiddie Gym Inc., Fred Medart Mfg. Co., the Mengel Co., the Mordt Co., Quick Sales Mfg. Co., Rustic Furniture Co., N.R. Snell Co., Toledo Metal Wheel Co., W.S. Tothill, Toyline Mfg. Co., and Woodcraft Toy Mfrs. Some companies found a niche in producing "hygienic" sand for these sandboxes, including Child Health Sand Co.,

Geo. H. Robinson's Sons, Sandhu Products, and United Clay Mines Corp. Although other toy categories saw a trend toward increased "safety" orientations in the Boomer years, in the case of sandbox sand the "hygienic" niche diminished to the vanishing point.

Sandhu Products Based in Ottawa, Ill., Sandhu issued colored and white silica sand for play boxes in the 1930s and '40s.

sandwich glass Doll-size tea sets of sandwich glass were made in the 1800s. In the 1950s and '60s, plastic versions of older glass tea sets appeared from some manufacturers.

"Sandy Andy" toys and games see *Wolverine Supply & Mfg. Co.*

"Sani-Foam" stuffed toys see *Gund Mfg. Co.*

Sani-Speed Mfg. Co. "Playcraft" beads were this Cleveland, Ohio, firm's product in the 1950s-60s.

Sanitoy Rattles, dolls, infant novelties, and stuffed doll and toy animals comprised this postwar line. Sanitoy was based in Brooklyn, N.Y.

Santa Claus Santa Claus is a gift, in part, from the Dutch, whose St. Nicholas is the patron saint of Amsterdam.

Santa Claus outfits see *masquerade costumes.*

Santa Claus School In a real sense, the proverbial "North Pole" was located in Albion, N.Y., in the 1950s and '60s, where the Santa Claus School was established at a "Christmas Park" address. The "school" provided training and equipment for holders of this seasonal occupation, as well as store displays, Christmas parade floats, live reindeer, Santa mailboxes, and Santa thrones.

"Santa Claus" surprise packages see *American Toy Works.*

Santa's Playthings, Inc. The Christmas toy catalog "Santa's Playthings" was published by this Fifth Avenue Building firm.

Sarg, Tony This author and artist issued some of the most delightful books of the 1920s and 30s, including *Tony Sarg's Book for Children of 1924, Tony Sarg's Animal Book of 1925, Tony Sarg's Wonder Zoo of 1927,* and *Where Is Tommy?* Of 1932. He Illustrated *Adventures of Pinnocchio* in 1940. His *Tony Sarg's Surprise Book* was a best seller in 1941. The activity, story and play book was followed by "Tony Sarg's Play-A-Tune Blox" in 1942, a successful musical toy during the war years. The "Blox" were issued by B.F. & Jay Co. Sarg was the designer of early giant balloons for the Macy's Thanksgiving Day parade, toys, and household items, and worked in puppetry and animated films. See also Greenberg Publisher, Inc.

Tony Sarg Co. Based in the Times Building, New York City, this 1930s company produced novelties designed by illustrator Tony Sarg.

"Sargent" crayons see *The Art Crayon Co.*

Sark Sales Co. The "Sark" crossword card game was this Fourth Avenue, New York City, firm's postwar product.

"Satellite Gun" see *U.S. Plastics Corp.*

"Satellite to the Moon" game see *Mirinco Toys.*

"Saucer Squads" space toys see *American Play Co.*

"Saucer-Tosser" see *Whirley Corp.*

Saunders Tool & Die Co. This Aurora, Ill., firm turned to toy manufacturing in 1946, and produced plastic toys with metal parts into the 1950s. The line included toy hot rods, autos, and military tanks, usually with friction motors. It also included some musical toys. The firm combined with Swadar Plastic Co. around 1954 to form Saunders-Swadar Toy Co.

Savage Arms Corp. The Toy Department of Savage Arms, based in Utica, N.Y., manufactured the repeating "Savage Play Rifle" in the 1920s. Savage also sold a "Safety Target Game." The "Savage" play guns were issued by the Fox Co. after the Depression.

S

Savoye Pewter Toy Mfg. Co. For the 5-cents to a dollar trade, Sovoye of North Bergen, N.J., made white metal toys in the 1930s.

saws see *scroll saws.*

Sawyer Products Co. Based in Chicago, Ill., Sawyer made pressed-wood doll beds and cradles in the late 1930s.

Sawyer's, Inc. The "View-Master" full-color, three-dimensional picture reels, stereoscopes, and projectors were issued by this company from 1939 through 1966. The firm purchased the older Tru-Vue, Inc., in 1951, and moved production of Tru-Vue's larger, rectangular stereoscopic cards to Portland, Ore., where Sawyer's was based.

Sayco Doll Corp. Located on Wooster Street, New York City, Sayco made prewar mama dolls, soft body dolls, and novelties. By the late 1930s it was issuing ventriloquist dolls. See *Schoen and Yondorf Co.*

"Scamp" streamline coaster wagons see *The Metalcraft Corp.*

Scandia-Custer Toy Corp. Based in Custer, S.D., this postwar firm made the "Scandia Sketcher," toy kitchen appliances, doll furniture, sand toys, and wood toys.

"Scarlett O'Hara" doll see *Alexander Doll Co.*

Schacht Rubber Mfg. Co. The 1930s and '40s "Daisy" horseshoe games were made by this Huntington, Ind., firm.

Jack Schaefer, Inc. Schaefer, a late 1930s Los Angeles, Calif., firm, issued badminton and table tennis sets.

W.H. Schaper Mfg. Co., Inc. One of the most famous games and icons of the Boomer era, "Cootie," was the invention of Herbert Schaper, who established this game manufacturing company in Minneapolis, Minn., in 1949. Schaper issued the "Cootie" game in essentially unchanged form through the early 1970s. Other games by the firm included "Skunk," "Tumble Bug," "Snap-Eze," "Stadium Checkers," and "Li'l Stinker" and "Tickle Bee" in the 1950s, and "Don't Spill the Beans" and "Don't Break the Ice" in the 1960s. Schaper games will often be attributed to Highlander Sales Co., which was affiliated with Shaper. "Schaper Plastic Games" is the same firm.

Scharco Mfg. Corp. Doll carriages and strollers, toy chests, and rockers comprised this postwar line. Scharco was based in Mount Vernon, N.Y.

Schavoir Rubber Co. Rubber toys, balls, and novelties were issued in the 1930s and '40s by this Springdale, Conn., company.

Schieble Toy & Novelty Co. Based in Dayton, Ohio, Schieble carried on the line of "Hill Climber" friction toys created by D.P. Clark & Co. The company operated from 1909 to 1931.

Schiercke, Henry C. Based in Ghent, N.Y., Henry C. Scheircke manufactured molds for casting lead soldiers, animals, and other toys and novelties in the 1930s and '40s.

Schiffmann Bros. This Chicago, Ill., manufacturer of exercisers, or "spring operated toys," made the "Buckee Horse," "Gogoose," "Exerplane," and "Jackee Rabbit" of the 1920s. At last two of Schiffmann's exercisers, the "Buckee Horse" and "Gogoose," were manufactured by Janesville Products Co. in the earlier 1930s.

Schiffman Bros. made the "Buckee Horse" exerciser in the 1920s.

Schiller Plano Co. The "Aero Thrill" coaster sled of the 1930s was produced by this Oregon, Ill., company.

Schimmel, Wilhelm A Pennsylvania wood-carver, Wilhelm Schimmel (1817-1890) produced hand-painted wood animal toys.

Schindler Stamping & Toy Co. This Toledo, Ohio, firm issued the "Cum-Bac" rolling toy in the late 1930s.

W.H. Schlee, Inc. A manufacturer of games, tops, dartboards, and table tennis sets, Schlee used the "Hi-Ker" trade name.

Julius Schmid, Inc. Julius Schmid made an assortment of red and colored rubber toy figures of children and animals in the 1920s under the "Harva" trade name. The firm was based on West 55th Street, New York City.

Schmid Brothers Prewar wheel toys by this Lancaster, Penn., company included scooters, handcars, and roller skates. The company also made steel seesaws and rubber quoits in the 1930s and '40s. The Anri Woodcarvings Division of what was then Schmid Bros., Inc., issued the series of "Peanuts" music boxes in the late 1960s.

George Schmidt Mfg. Co. The "Buck 'N Bronc" toy guns and spurs of the Boomer years were issued by this Los Angeles, Calif., company.

Schmidt Novelty Co. This Detroit, Mich., company made the prewar "Aero-Teeter," a combined seesaw and merry-go-round. It was advertised s "the only teeter-totter with the Self-Leveling Seats."

The "Aeroteeter," a Schmidt Novelty Co. seesaw and merry-go-round combination, 1930s.

Max Schnetter & Co. A Sonneburg, Germany, firm, Schnetter sold carnival and joke articles in the United States in the earlier 20th century. Items in the 1920s included monkey and clown marionettes, masks, and decorated caps.

Schoen and Yondorf Co. The "Sayco Dolls" of the 1920s were issued by this New York City firm. In the post-Great Depression years the firm became Sayco Doll Corp.

Schoenhut, Albert A German-born toy maker, Albert Schoenhut was the son of Frederick Wilhelm Schoenhut and grandson of Anton Wilhelm Schoenhut, both makers of wooden dolls. He immigrated to America around 1865 with the encouragement of his friend George Doll of Philadelphia, Penn., and established the A. Schoenhut Co. in that city in 1872. He died in 1912.

The A. Schoenhut Co. The first toys produced by the A. Schoenhut Co. in 1872 were toy pianos, the item now most associated with this famous specialist in musical toys. By the time the firm closed its doors in the 1935, its line included not only miniature pianos, both upright and "grand," but also "Mello-Tone" pianos with chimes, "metallophones," ukuleles, and xylophones.

Its toys included numerous non-musical toys, the most significant being the "Humpty Dumpty Circus," a line of related toys that began in 1903 with a set consisting of a wooden chair, ladder, and wooden clown. Schoenhut gradually added circus equipment, figures, and animals to the line. The figures were jointed, and were capable to some degree of being posed and perched. In 1909 the related series of "Teddy's Adventures in Africa" figures appeared, with Teddy Roosevelt as main character. While the circus figures continued appearing in various forms for three decades, the "Teddy" figures continued as part of the line only into the early 1920s.

By that decade, Schoenhut was manufacturing a wide variety of "toys with Exceptional Educational Possibilities," led by its toy pianos, dollhouses, hardwood dollhouse furniture, plain and colored play blocks, its new construction toy "Dirigible Builder," the "Community Store-Builder" of 1929, and its "Star Line" wooden sailboats. Its line also included toy piano stools, "Jazz Orchestra

Bells," "Trinity Chimes," "Metallophones," xylophones, toy ukuleles, ukulele-banjos, "Auto-Build" kits, "Train-to-Build," "Build-A-Village," "Aeroplane Builders," "Bird House Builder," "Little Tot's Building Blocks," "Alphies" ABC blocks, "Roller Chimes," "Choo-Choo-Push," stick horses, "Anchor Quoits," "Big Game Hunter," "Ski Jumper," "Submarine Game," wooden pistol sets, "Rolly-Dolly" toys, kitchen cabinets, bassinets, all-wood dolls, basswood elastic-jointed dolls, toy swords, and toy police and fireman equipment.

The "Star Line" boats were priced from 25 cents to $12, and were based on existing sail boats, with names including "Comet," "Polaris," and the names of the various planets. By the 1930s the company was manufacturing a full line of doll houses, doll house furniture, doll beds, doll bassinets and dressers, toy tea wagons, toy boat fleets, the "Rolly Dolly" toys, shooting games, nested blocks, "Little Tots" blocks, colored wagon locks, and sets including "Auto Build," "Train to Build," and "Noah's Ark." The firm closed in 1935.

O. Schoenhut, Inc. Established in Philadelphia, Penn., in the late 1930s, O. Schoenhut manufactured the "Collegiate Em'ly" dolls, and the "4-5-6 Pick-Up Sticks," "Tu-Fang," "Fan-Tel," "Brodi," "Tiddle Tennis," and "Boddle Ball" games. The firm continued operation in the war years, issuing toy furniture, games, and toy pianos, apparently having absorbed what had remained of the A. Schoenhut Co. and Schoenhut Mfg. Co. Unlike the more famous Schoenhut toy company, O. Schoenhut continued in operation through the Boomer years, with its lead products being toy pianos, metallophones, and "4-5-6" pick-up sticks.

The Schoenhut Mfg. Co. This Philadelpha, Penn., firm appears to have been a brief revival of A. Schoenhut Co. Its line in the late 1930s included the "Skyline Builder" construction toys, toy pianos, metallophones, xylophones, and games. Subsequently the musical toy lines were taken over by O. Schoenhut.

Schoepfer, G. Based on West 32nd Street, New York City, the prewar G. Schoepfer made eyes for stuffed animals, both moving and stationary, and "voices" for stuffed animals. A presumably related G.W. Schoepfer on West 27th Street, operating at the same time, specialized in glass eyes for toy animals.

school companions A number of companies through the years have found a niche in providing pencil boxes, ruler sets, and other kinds of school kits, or "school companions" as they were known in prewar years, for all the millions of children obliged to attend school in America. In their decorations and design many of these school companions had traits in common with toys. Their closeness to toys might be indicated by the history of Hassenfeld Bros., a manufacturer of pencils and pencil boxes that moved into making toy doctor and nurse kits in the prewar years. Other prewar manufacturers included American Mfg. Concern, Bliss Novelty Co., Goody Mfg. Co., and David Kahn.

Schroeder Co. This postwar manufacturer of children's swivel and rocking chairs also issued the "Palomino Pony" trike of the 1950s-60s. The firm was based in Atlanta, Ga.

Schwartz, Adolph Based in Brooklyn, N.Y., Schwartz issued the "Far West Ranger" holster sets and "Indian Delight" tom-tom sets of the Boomer years.

Schwartz Toy Mfg. Corp. Stuffed toys, dolls and promotional items were this postwar Brooklyn, N.Y., firm's specialty.

Schwarz, Henry Henry Schwarz opened a toy store in Baltimore, Md., in 1849. While he initially imported his toys from Germany, he gradually added American-made items, starting with sleds and wagons. Schwarz was reputedly the first merchant to use a "live" Santa Claus to help sell toys at Christmas time. His three brothers followed Henry into the retail toy business, Richard setting up business in Boston, Gustav in Philadelphia, and Frederick in New York City. The New York store of F.A.O. Schwarz, the only one of the Schwarz stores remaining, is one of the largest and best-known in the world.

George E. Schweig & Son A Philadelphia, Penn., importer of tricks and novelties in the 1930s and '40s, Schweig apparently also manufactured games and toys. Titles from the earlier 1930s included "What Would You Do?" and the "Banner Lye Checkerboard."

"Schwinn-Built" bicycles see *Arnold, Schwinn & Co.*

Science Materials Center The "Calculo Analog Computer" of the early 1960s, and other science toys, were issued by this Fourth Avenue, New York City, company.

"Sciencecraft" outfits see *The Porter Chemical Co.*

Scientific Model Airplane Co. This prewar Newark, N.J., firm made model airplane kits and supplies, and miniature streamline automobile kits of the Chrysler Airflow and early 1930s Packard, Ford and Nash models. Its list featured gas-powered models and motors by the late 1930s. In the Boomer years, its line included "U-Control" model airplane kits, boats, and racecars.

Scientific Products Co. Ballistic missiles and two-stage rockets, with their remote launchers, comprised this postwar toy line. The firm was based in Richmond, Va.

"Scolawag" coaster wagon see *Garton Toy Co.*

"Scoop-N-Dump," "Scoop-N-Load" see *Buddy "L" Toys.*

"Scoot-A-Way" velocipede see *The Metalcraft Corp.*

scooter skates see *skates, scooter.*

scooters An important children's toy vehicle by the early 20th century, the scooter could trace its lineage as much to the coaster wagon as the bicycle, since children would typically ride the coaster wagon with one leg inside, and the other outside to give propulsion. Scooters consisted of a low board long enough to hold both feet, with one wagon-size wheel in front and one in back, a front steering column that would rise to about chest height, and a cross-bar handle. Many had simple friction brake mechanisms against the back wheel, and kickstands for standing it when at rest.

Prewar manufacturers included the American National Co., Auto-Wheel Coaster Co., the E.C. Brown Co., Burnham Mfg. Co., Coast Electric & Mfg. Co., the Colson Co., Corcoran Mfg. Co., the Dayton Toy & Specialty Co., C.C. Elliotte Corp., Garton Toy Co., Gendron Mfg. Co., the Gendron Wheel Co., the Globe Co., Charles & Victor Goldstein, Hedstrom-Union Co., Iron Products Corp., Janesville Products Co., C.J. Johnson Co., Iver Johnson's Arms & Cycle Works, Junior Toy Corp., Kuniholm Mfg. Co., Lullabye Furniture Corp., Metalcraft Corp., the Monarch Products Co., W. Howard Moudy, the Murray Ohio Mfg. Co., the Powell Pressed Steel Co., S. & E. Mfg. Co., Schmid Bros., Sheboygan Coaster & WagonWorks, O.W. Siebert Co., Skippy Racers, the Steel Stamping Co., Steinfeld, Taylor Bros. Mfg. Co., the Toledo Metal Wheel Co., United-Delta Corp., and Winters & Crampton Mfg. Co.

Postwar manufacturers included Amtac Industries, Auto-Wheel Coaster, Blake & Conroy, Chain Bike Corp., Garton Toy, Hamilton Steel Products, Radio Steel & Mfg. Co., Revere Mfg. Co., Scheuer Sales Co., and United Specialty & Toy Co.

scooters, motor By the late prewar years the motor scooter became an important item of manufacture, with the leading companies being the Cushman Motor Works and Moto-Scoot Mfg. Co.

"Scop-Shot" sling shots see *General Sports.*

Scot-Shot Game Co. This Lincoln, Neb., firm issued the "Scot-Shot" target toy of the late 1930s.

Scott Mfg. Co. This Chicago, Ill., firm issued the "Bilt-E-Z" in the 1920s. Scott employed the slogan "The Boy Builder" for the construction toy.

Scott Toy Mfg. Co. This postwar Philadelphia, Penn., firm made rack toys.

"Scout" air rifle see *Daisy Mfg. Co.*

"Scout" gun see *The Dent Hardware Co.*

Scovell Novelty Mfg. Co. The "Ruffles" character doll and the "Hollywood Real Life Toys" line were prewar products of this Hollywood, Calif., firm. It also made "Snubs," "Waddles" and "Tim's Pup" cloth animals, in the mid-1930s. In the later '30s the line's name changed to "Hollywood Toy-crafters."

"Scrabble" see *Selchow & Righter Co.*

Scrambled Eggs, Inc. "Scrambled Egg" was a popular and well-advertised three-dimensional put-together egg puzzle made by this Chicago, Ill., company in the prewar years. It also made the "Magic Bits, the Animal Wonder Game," a felt toy, in the 1930s. Both "Scrambled Egg" and the smaller "Bantam Egg" were introduced successfully at the Century of Progress Exhibition. The puzzles were cut by hand, meaning no two were exactly alike.

"Scrappy" The "Scrappy" cartoon character, a spunky boy with slicked-back hair, appeared in numerous plaything forms in the earlier 1930s. Peterson Mfg. Co. produced an important line of "Scrappy" items in the 1930s, including paint sets, crayons, modeling clay, and poster paints, with retail ranges from a dime to three dollars. Other items included dolls and toys by Louis Wolf & Co. and "Scrappy's Movie Theater" by the Ullman Mfg. Co. "Scrappy" items of the later prewar years included banks by Zell Products Corp., cardboard premiums by American Advertising & Research Corp., dolls by Reisman-Exposition Doll Corp., soap items by Kerk Guild, and "third dimension" stereopticon films by Novelart Mfg. Co.

Screen Attractions Corp. Providing movies for toy movie projects was the business of this Ninth Avenue, New York City, firm, as it was for several others in the film-hungry late 1930s.

"Scribble Animals" see *Gund Mfg. Co.*

scroll saws In contrast to the direction postwar toys took, in prewar times many toy tools were working models of adult tools. In short they were tools, not imitations of tools. The scroll saws of the prewar and earlier postwar years were often decorated to enhance their appeal to children, yet they were true saws. Manufacturers included Auchterlonie & Miller, Barth Stamping & Machine Works, and the A.C. Gilbert Co.

Sculpture Kit Studios This Chicago, Ill., issued clay sculpting kits in the late 1930s.

"Sea Fury" model outboard engines see *K.&B. Allyn Co.*

"Sea Gull" boats see *Benton Harbor Toy Co.*

"Sea Riders" see *Country Town Products, Inc.*

"Sea Spray" Keystone Mfg. Co.'s miniature boats in the 1930s included the "Sea Spray" yachts and the "Seaworthy" sailboats.

The Seahorse Press This postwar Pelham, N.Y., publisher issued activity play books.

Seamless Rubber Co. A New Haven, Conn., firm, Seamless Rubber made play balls, beach balls and inflatable rubber swimming toys in the 1930s and '40s. It also made rubber quoits and horseshoes. In the Boomer years Seamless specialized in beach balls, swimming rings, and bathing caps.

"Sectional Animals" picture puzzles see *Milton Bradley Co.*

"See & Spell" see *Wolverine Supply & Mfg. Co.*

"See 'Em Pop" corn popper see *The Metal Ware Corp.*

Segal Lock & Hardware Co. This Broadway, New York City, firm made roller skates and the "Skate-O-Meter" mileage recorder in the late 1930s.

Seiberling Latex Products Co. The
Akron, Ohio, Seiberling Latex Products Co. obtained an early license through Kay Kamen to produce rubber dolls and toys on Disney themes. Notable early figures were the "Three Little Pigs" and the "Big Bad Wolf" in rubber. Among its more ephemeral productions, few of which have likely survived, were inflated "Mickey Mouse" rubber balls ("Bright color designs are inlaid and will not wash off," advertisements proclaimed) and sponge rubber balls. Seiberling also introduced a 10-inch high inflatable "Mickey Mouse," which retailed at 10 cents. The firm ceased manufacturing rubber toys and balls with the onset of World War II.

"The Three Little Pigs" by Seiberling, 1930s.

The Seiss Mfg. Co. The "Seiss Noise
Makers" of the 1920s included "Cymbell," a combination bell and noise maker, and the "Seiss Rooters," miniature auto horns. They were often based upon the bell idea, as in its "Jingle Bells" miniature cowbells, advertising bells, "New Year" bells, large cowbells, tea bells, and souvenir bells. The company also issued souvenir trowels. The Toledo, Ohio, firm employed "The Ripper" and "Giant Ripper" trademarks in the 1930s. It also continued making bells, such juvenile automobile and bicycle accessories as horns, lamps, bells and sirens, and the "Daisy" and "Daisy Jr." flashlights into the 1940s. In the Boomer years, Seiss specialized in bicycle electric headlights, taillights, and electric horns.

Selchow & Righter Co. Elish G.
Selchow founded a firm dedicated to the publishing of games and puzzles in the 1860s. In 1866, with partner John H. Righter, he established Selchow & Righter Co.

Becoming one of the country's most prominent game manufacturers, Selchow & Righter maintained offices in the Fifth Avenue building. Its prewar line included games, puzzles, novelties, airplane and boat construction kits. Among them were such traditional entries as chess, checkers, lotto, and "embossed" anagrams. In the 1930s it advertised itself as "Home of Parcheesi and Games of Distinction."

The company's early games titles included "Fascination" in 1890, "Piggies" in 1894, "Chinaman Party" in 1896, and "Buster Brown at the Circus," "Katzy Party," and "Foxy Grandpa Hat Party" in the 1900s. Later titles included "Rainy Day Golf" in 1920, "Have-U It?" in 1924, "The Great Horse Race Game" in 1925, "Peter Pan" in 1927, and "Sweep" in 1929.

In the 1930s, when the game "Cavalcade" appeared, titles included "Cargoes" in 1934, "Little Colonel" in 1936, and "Ed Wynn, the Fire Chief" and "Jamboree" in 1937.

Besides "Parcheesi, A Royal Game of India," the firms lead titles were Cabby," "Cargoes," "Cavalcade," "Chow Mein Chinese Checkers," "Dale Carnegie's Game," "Decoy," "Double-Double," "Mr. Ree," "Nuggets," "Royal Jacks," "Scoralet." The company also issued anagrams, lotto, bingo, checkers, chess.

"The Elsie the Cow Game" followed in 1941. "Flying Aces" was a wartime release. "Parcheesi" continued its long-lived success in the postwar years. The famous game was joined by another massive best-seller, "Scrabble," introduced in 1952. The company also made "Dead Pan," "Meet the Presidents," "Mr. Ree," "Assembly Line," and "Peanuts."

Selchow & Righter's logo, 1940s.

Selfbilt Toy Co. A Hollis, Long Island, N.Y., firm, Selfbilt Toy Co. made prewar metal construction toys.

Selley Mfg. Co., Inc. This Brooklyn, N.Y., company issued the "Champion Model Planes" of the 1920s, including the "Junkers 'Bremen.'" The kits came semi-constructed. Its 1930s line included featherweight models of airplanes and gliders, and construction sets. It also made boat kits and scale-model railroad parts and construction kits. It was using the "Selley-Tex" trade name by the late '30s.

"Seneca" coaster wagons see *Monarch Products Co.*

Senet An Egyptian board game dating to about 1500 BC, "Senet" has appeared in a modern version from Parker Brothers.

separate driver In contrast to the cast-in driver, many older cast-iron and die-cast toy vehicles had separately cast drivers. Often these drivers are attractively nickel plated. Reproduction drivers are being manufactured for toy restoration purposes, often of plated slush metal.

Sequoia Sales Co., Inc. This Lafayette Street, New York City, firm made chemistry sets and a "Detective outfit" in the 1930s.

"Sgt. Preston" game see *Milton Bradley Co.*

serpentines Paper novelty manufacturers commonly issued serpentines, which were long, narrow strips of colored paper issued in rolls, to be thrown as streamers.

"Serv-A-Toy" see *Lee Products Co.*

Service Mfg. Co., Inc. Cowboy holster and gun sets, boots, and spurs were specialties of this Yonkers, N.Y., firm in the Boomer years. It also made baseball gloves, shoes, and balls.

J.H. Sessions & Son This late 1930s game manufacturer was based in Bristol, Conn.

"Sewdress" dolls see *Samuel Gabriel Sons & Co.*

sewing machines Toy sewing machines included some of the most elaborate toys made for children, most of them working machines of varying efficiency that could be run manually or electrically. Prewar manufacturers included Hoge Mfg. Co., Lindstrom Tool & Toy Co., and National Sewing Machine Co. In the Boomer years, manufacturers included Gibraltar Mfg. Co., Hassenfeld Bros., Henry Katz, and Kayanee Corp. of America.

sewing sets see *embroidery and sewing sets.*

"Sewmaster" sewing machine see *Kayanee Corp. of America.*

B. Shackman & Co. B. Shackman, located on Broadway at 20th Street, New York City, was an importer and manufacturer. A constant source of inexpensive and often inventive playthings, B. Shackman was distributing the "Famous Cartoon Characters" in the late 1920s, and such items as the polished steel airplane bank "Spirit of Thrift." Its line included numerous novelties, sailboats, mechanical boats, pails and shovels, and Fourth of July items, including firecrackers. In the 1930s it listed its primary business as importing, with a line including dolls, dollhouse supplies, and novelties. In the later decade it expanded its line to include favors, snapping mottoes, noisemaker, paper hats, "Jack Horner pies," and balloons. It moved to Madison Avenue in 1934. Continuing in operation through the Boomer years, Shackman often kept available types of toys otherwise unavailable in the market, and issued reproductions of antique dolls.

B. Shackman's "Smitty" figures, 1920s.

"Shadow Ball" see *"Yale Shadow Ball."*

"Shadow Plays" marionettes see *Harter Publishing Co.*

"Shadow-Sho-Movies" cutouts see the *Einson-Freeman Co.*

H.W. Shafer Game Co. The "Don Future, Rocketeer" board game of the 1950s-60s was issued by this East 2nd Street, New York City, company.

Shaffer Engineering Co. This Sedalia, Mo., firm issued the "Auto-Bye" swing exercisers in the late 1930s.

"Shari Lewis" Shari Lewis and her sock-puppet stars "Lamb Chop" and "Hush Puppy" inspired numerous playthings in the early 1960s, including coloring books by the Saalfield Publishing Co., dolls by Alexander Doll Co., and puppets by Pride Products, Inc.

Shaw Doll Co. This doll maker, based on Wooster Street, New York City, produced both high-grade and popular-priced "Shaw Dolls" in the 1920s through the '40s.

Sheboygan Coaster & Wagon Works Coaster wagons, sleds, scooters, wheelbarrows, carts, and nursery furniture were made in the mid-1930s by this Sheboygan, Wis., company.

Sheboygan Specialty Co. This Sheboygan, Wis., firm made the "Greenlite" and "Precaution" educational safety games of the late 1930s.

sheet metal Sheet metal is metal, usually steel but also sometimes copper or brass, rolled into a thin plate. The first sheet-metal toys in the U.S. date to 1895.

Sheffield Toys, Inc. This Sheffield, Penn., firm advertised "high grade wooden toys" in the 1930s.

"Sheik" pistol see *The Dent Hardware Co.*

Shelby Cycle Co. This Shelby, Ohio, firm manufactured bicycles in the prewar years.

Sheldon-Peek-Riordan Mfg. Sales Co., Inc. This manufacturer of coaster wagons and tricycles was established in Kansas City, Mo., in the late 1930s.

Henry H. Shelp Mfg. Co. The "Dartelle" rubber dart game and "Bancort" table tennis game were produced in the 1930s by this Philadelphia, Penn., company.

C.G. Shepard and Co. Walter J. and Charles G. Shepard founded their toy manufacturing company in 1866 to produce tin horns, still banks, and, beginning in 1882, mechanical banks. The company continued until 1892. Some of its banks were afterwards reissued by J. & E. Stevens Co.

A.M. Shepard Co. Alphabet sets, "Magic Speller," toy chests and magnetic blackboards were Boomer-era specialties of this Median, Ohio, company.

Sheram Puppet Industries Based in Columbus, Ohio, Sheram issued postwar puppets and puppet theaters.

Sheridan Electro Units Corp. The "Vogue" electric pencils of the 1930s were made by this Chicago, Ill., firm, which also produced pyrographic and drawing sets.

"The Sheriff" cap pistol see *Academy Die Casting & Plating Co.*

"Sherlock Holmes" The great detective hero created by Sir Arthur Conan Doyle inspired miscellaneous playthings through the years, including "Sherlock Holmes" detective outfits and fingerprinting sets in the late 1930s, issued by New York Toy & Game Sales Co.

Sherman Doll Co. Based on West 21st Street, Sherman made prewar stuffed and composition dolls. Its name changed to Sherman Doll & Toy Co. by the late 1930s. It continued issuing stuffed and composition dolls into the 1960s.

"Sherms," Inc. This Bridgeport, Conn., firm made magic tricks, games and puzzles in the 1930s through wartime, when its line managed to continue with the "Master Magic" sets, "Super Puzzle" sets, and "Peg Solitaire." The company issued games, magic

S

tricks, stage illusions, and magic supplies through the Boomer years.

Sherwood, W.L. Wood block puzzles and cast-iron novelties were made by this Kirksville, Mo., firm.

"Sherwood" spring coaster wagon see *Dodge Mfg. Corp.*

M. &. S. Shillman This Brooklyn, N.Y. company made knitted doll outfits and carriage outfits in the 1920s. It specialized in doll clothes and accessories through the Boomer years.

M. Shimmel Sons Rack items including ball and jack sets, jump ropes, lariats, canes batons, whips and return tops comprised this West 19th Street, New York City, company's postwar line. Shimmel also issued Walt Disney "Zorro" items.

shinny see *hockey, field.*

ships see *boats.*

"Shipshape" boat model kits prewar, see *Selchow & Righter Co.*

"Shirley Anna" juvenile furniture see *The Wendt Billiard Mfg. Co.*

"Shirley Temple" The endearing child star of the black-and-white movies appeared in a surprising number of doll and plaything forms in the 1930s. Dolls were first made by Ideal Novelty & Toy Co. in 1934, which used the body of its popular "Ginger" doll for a template. This was followed in the later prewar years by such "Shirley Temple" items as storybooks, cutout books, and playhouses by the Saalfield Publishing Co.; dolls and doll clothes by Ideal Novelty & Toy Co.; doll displays by Herbert O. Brown; and ribbons by Flatto Ribbon Corp. Postwar playthings included coloring books and paper dolls by Saalfield, dolls by Ideal Toy Corp., and paper dolls and beauty-aid sets by Samuel Gabriel Sons & Co. The "Shirley Temple Magnetic TV Theater" was issued by American Metal Specialties Co.

"Shmo" dice game see *Remco Industries, Inc.*

Shoe Form Co., Inc. As an interesting sideline, this Auburn, N.Y., firm made "Fairy Craft" mechanical motorboats in the 1930s.

shoes, doll see *doll outfits.*

shooflies Invented by toy manufacturer Jesse Crandall, the shoofly was his answer to the problem that young children enjoyed the rocking motion of a rocking horse but had difficulty keeping balance.

Still in essence a rocking horse, the shoofly had two board sides cut in the shape of horses, with rounded bottoms for the rocking edges. Since the seat for the child was held between these boards, the sides also served to keep in the rider. Crandall patented his invention in 1879 as a "rocking toy," but was using the name "shoofly" soon afterwards.

By the 20th century a great many manufacturers were producing the simple but satisfactory plaything, including the American Novelty Co., Appleton Toy & Furniture Co., W.A. Barber, Benner, the N.D. Cass Co., the Delphos Bending Co., D.W. Lynch Co., Marks Bros. Co., Menasha Woodenware Corp., the Mengel Co., Pratt Mfg. Co., Readsboro Chair Co., and Whitney Reed Co. By the late prewar years, American Acme Co., Maplewood Products, the Mengel Co., Stoner Corp., and Transogram Co. joined their ranks.

Boomer-era manufacturers included American Acme Co., American Mfg. Concern, Benner, Blake & Conroy, N.D. Cass Sales Co., the Connor Lumber & Land Co., Delphos, the Gong Bell Mfg. Co., Jeffrey To Mfg. Co., L. & J. Wood Products, Julius Levenson, D.W. Lynch Co., J.W. McKinney, Rich Industries, South Bend Toy Mfg. Co., and Williamsburg Chair Factory.

This somewhat safer rocking horse is a 1920s shoofly.

"Shootin' Shell" guns see *Mattel.*

shooting games Shooting games were a serious matter in Colonial America, as it had been earlier for the Native Americans. Their importance might be indicated by the existence of an early Massachusetts law requiring boys ages 10-16 to practice at bows and arrows. At 16 they paid taxes and served in the militia. See *Training Day*. See also *popinjay.*

"Shooting Star" coaster wagon see *C.J. Johnson.*

"Shotgun Slade" The popular western TV hero inspired 1950s-60s playthings including badges and carded sets by John-Henry Mfg. Co.; games and puzzles by Milton Bradley Co.; holster sets, pistols and rifles by Esquire Novelty Corp.; and western hats by Arlington Hat Co.

Shotwell Mfg. Co. see *"Checkers."*

Shower Mfg. Co. This Detroit, Mich., firm produced toys and games in the late prewar years.

"Showtime" puppet theater see *Modern Toy Co.*

Shrovetide see *pulling the goose.*

Shu-Quoi Games Co. The "Shu-Quoi" horseshoe pitching and quoits game, made of rubber, was issued in the 1930s by this West 49th Street, New York City, firm.

shuffleboard Shuffleboard became an important den room and tavern game in the Boomer years. Manufacturers included Bar Zim Toy Mfg. Co., Block House, N.D. Cass Sales Co., Dimco-Gray Co., Empire Plastic Corp., General Sportcraft Co., Hammatt & Sons, Harett Gilmar, Klauber Games, Knight Table Tennis Co., Outdoor Sports Mfg. Co., Regent Sports Co., Royal Oak Toy Co., Superior Industries Corp., Transogram Co., Urb Products Corp., and Woodhaven Metal Stamping Co.

Shulman & Sons Based on East 17th Street, New York City, Shulman issued the "Goody line" of the 1920s, including "Goody" educational games, art companions, school companions, and savings banks.

Nathan Shure see *Cosmo Mfg. Co.; Dowst Mfg. Co.*

shuttlecock An activity game that may have originated in ancient Asia, shuttlecock was a popular pastime in 18th and 19th century America. In the early 19th century, it was sometimes played as an indoor game.

Shwayder Bros., Inc. Established in Denver, Colo., in the late prewar years, Shwayder made juvenile furniture and folding game tables. The firm continued through the postwar years.

Sidway-Topliff Co. This Washington, Penn., company manufactured a complete line of children's vehicles in the 1920s under the "Sidway" trade name, including juvenile automobiles, velocipedes, coaster wagons, sidewalk cycles, scooters, pedal cars, wheelbarrows, baby carriages, and doll carts. The firm also made juvenile furniture.

O.W. Siebert Co. A juvenile furniture manufacturer based in Gardner, Mass., O.W. Siebert also made prewar doll carriages, "Bunny Kars," scooters, runabouts, baby walkers, and velocipedes. The firm's postwar line also included sidewalk bicycles.

The Siemon Co. This Bridgeport, Conn., firm manufactured composition poker chips in the late 1930s.

Sifo Co. Based in St. Paul, Minn., Sifo manufactured Boomer-era inlay puzzles, wooden jigsaw puzzles, map puzzles, educational clocks and pre-school toys, "Construction Village" blocks, wooden beads, telephones, and pull toys.

Signal Electric Mfg. Co. The "Signal" set for telegraph and wireless practice was made by this Menominee, Mich., firm in the 1930s and '40s. It also made toy motors.

"Signature" paint-by-number sets see *Avalon Mfg. Co.*

"Signature" pets see *Toys, Inc.*

The Sigwalt Mfg. Co. Toy printing presses for the toy and hobby trade were products of this Chicago, Ill., company from the 1930s through the Boomer years.

S

"Sil-O-Models" see *Co-Operative Displays, Inc.*

"Silent Flash" skates see *Chicago Roller Skate Co.*

Sillo Art Co. Paint-by-number sets comprised this postwar line. Sillo was based in Herkimer, N.Y.

Silly Putty Marketing The famous "Silly Putty" was the primary item of manufacture for this New Haven, Conn., company, from 1950 through the Boomer years. Its slogans included "Nothing Else is Silly Putty," and "The Good Thing in the Small Package."

Silly Putty, introduced in 1950.

"Sillyette" The "Sillyette" and "Sillyfold" paper novelties of the 1930s were made by Peereless Engraving Co.

"Silly Symphony" The Walt Disney studio's series of animated short films entitled "Silly Symphonies" inspired fewer playthings than did the major animated feature-length films. Some did appear, however, including "Silly Symphony" soft toys by Richard G. Krueger. By the late 1930s, U.S. Electric Mfg. Co. was also making "Silly Symphony" flashlights.

silver Besides being a material used for teething rings and rattles in the 17th and 18th century, some silversmiths made silver dollhouse furniture for wealthy clients.

"Silver Arrow" flying planes see *Kingsbury Mfg. Co.*

"Silver Award" paint-by-number sets see *The Art Award Co.*

"Silver Bullet" In the mid-1930s, Buffalo Toy & Tool Works issued the auto toys made of aluminum "Silver Bullet" and "Silver Dash."

"Silver Medalist" see *Chicago Roller Skate Co.*

"Silver Saddle" holster sets see *Chancy Toy & Novelty Co.*

"Silver Snub-Bee" water gun see *Park Plastics Co.*

"Silver Streak" coaster wagon see *Murray-Ohio Mfg. Co.*

"Silver Streak" sleds see *Garton Toy Co.*

J.M. Simmons & Co. This prewar Chicago, Ill., firm produced items with a mystic bent, including fortune-telling boards and crystal gazing balls. It also made "Bingo-Keno" games.

Simon & Schuster Besides being publisher of children's books, this Fourth Avenue, New York City, publisher issued the "Mental Whoopee" puzzles from the earlier 1930s into the '40s.

E. Simon & Sons, Inc. Founded in 1886, this New Orleans, La., firm was a designer and manufacturer of masquerade costumes through the Boomer years of the 20th century.

"Simplex" A common prewar trade name, "Simplex" appeared on other items besides the famous "Simplex" typewriter. The name also appeared on miniature lifting jacks by Templeton, Kenly & Co., and a Christmas tree holder by Twin City Iron & Wire Co. In the postwar years, "Simplex" model airplanes were issued by Cleveland Model Products Co.

Simplex Mfg. Corp. Based in New Orleans, La., Simplex issued motorized toy cars, including "Simplex Challenger," a racer, and "Simplex Runabout," in the 1950s-60s.

Simplex Typewriter Co. This Eleventh Avenue, New York City, company made the "Simplex" toy typewriter through the prewar years.

Robert Simpson & Sons Based in Auburn, N.Y., Robert Simpson & Sons made prewar cast metal soldiers.

J.H. Singer An important game manufacturer in the late 19th century, J.H. Singer of New York issued games with colorful, artistically executed lithography to rival the games issued by McLoughlin Bros. Early titles included "Authors," "The Country Store," "Dr. Busby," "Five Little Pigs," "Old Maid," "Peter Coddle and His Trip to New York," "A Merry Game of Posting," "The 400 Game," "Toboggan Slide," and "Where Do You Live?" issued in the 1890s. Other early titles included "Game of BaseBall" in 1886; "The Game of Bo Peep," "Goosey Gander, or Who Finds the Golden Egg," "Game of Jumping Frog," "Steeple Chase," and "Yachting" in 1890; "Cuckoo, a Society Game" in 1891; "Game of Cocked Hat" in 1892; "The Game of Golf," "Hel-Lo Telephone Game," and "Nellie Bly" in 1898; "London Bridge," "The Game of Marriage," and "T.G.O. Klondyke" in 1899; and "Saratoga Steeple Chase" in 1900. Later games included the "Messenger Boy Game" of 1910.

"Sippa Fish" game see *Frederick H. Beach & Co.*

"Sit 'N Ride" trucks see *Buddy 'L' Quality Toys.*

"Six Gun" plastic pistol see *Ray Plastic, Inc..*

"6 in 1 Invader Gun" see *Maco Toys.*

"Six Shooter" pistol see *Kilgore Mfg. Co.*

Skaneateles Handicrafters This wartime Skaneateles, N.Y., company issued wooden train sets with engines, cars, and blocks, and military sets with jeeps, tanks, cannons, ambulances and barges. The line was taken over by Playskool Mfg. Co. in the Boomer years.

skates, doll see *doll outfits.*

skates, ice Most skates in America were imported well into the 1800s, Germany being the main source. In the mid-19th century, with ice skating growing to near fad status,

domestic manufacturing companies sprang up to meet the demand, including Barney & Berry, Coe & Sniffen, Union Hardware, T.A. Williams, and Winslow Skate Co. Prewar manufacturers included Nestor Johnson Mfg. Co., F.W. Planert & Sons, and Union Hardware Co. In the late prewar years, Arco Tubular Skate Corp., Glider-Skate Mfg. Co., and F.D. Kees Mfg. Co. joined their number.

skates, roller Roller skates were manufactured by at last one pre-Great Depression company, Kokomo Stamped Metal Co. Manufacturers in the prewar years included Canastota Sherwood Stamping Corp., the Chapin-Stephens Co., Chicago Roller Skate Co., Globe-Union Mfg. Co., D.P. Harris Hardware & Mfg. Co., Hustler Corp., F.D. Kees Mfg. Co., Kingston Products Corp., Louis Marx & Co., F.W. Planert & Sons, Richardson Ball Bearing Skate Co., Schmid Bros., and Union Hardware Co. Their number increased by the late prewar years to also include Arco Tubular Skate Co., W.J. Baker Co., Gregory Mfg. Co., Keyless Roller Skate Co., Metal Specialties Mfg. Co., Roll-Away Skate Co., Segal Lock & Hardware Co., Tern-Rite Mfg. Co., the John C. Turner Co., Winchester Repeating Arms Co., and Zephyr Products Co.

"Rollfast" by D.P. Harris was a prominent Boomer line. It included smaller skates with toe straps in the "Prep," "Lil' Pal" and "Cub" beginner skates. One beginner model, also called "Prep," came with the lateral toe clamps, which were standard for the full-size models, whose names included "De Luxe," "Peerless," "Overland," and "Roamer." Other postwar lines included Arco Skates, Brooks Shoe Mfg. Co., Chicago Roller Skate Co., T. Cohn, Globe-Union, Hustler, Henry Katz, Kingston, Marx, Moen & Patton, Revere Mfg. Co., Solmann & Whitcomb, Union Hardware-Sealand, and D.S. Williams Co. A few firms specialized in rink roller skates, including Boston Athletic Shoe Co. and Chicago Roller Skate.

skates, scooter Prewar skates of a two- or three-wheel design were referred to as scooter skates. Manufacturers included the Hartford Steel Ball Co., the Lyons Mfg. Co., and Steel Materials Co.

S

skates, snow Prewar manufacturers included American Mfg. Concern, who had made snow skates before the Great Depression. Denning Mfg. Co. and F.D. Peters Co. also made them by the mid-1930s. By the late decade, American Mfg. Concern, Glider-Skate Mfg. Co., Globe-Union, Louis Marx & Co., and F.D. Peters Co. were the major producers. Postwar manufacturers included Arco Skates, Bilwin Co., Globe-Union, Manning Mfg. Corp., F.D. Peters, and Withington.

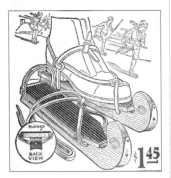

Advertisement for snow skates, 1920s.

"Skee Skates" snow gliders see *Denning Mfg. Co.*

"Skeeters" ice scooters see *The Powell Pressed Steel Co.*

"Skeezix" see *"Gasoline Alley."*

Ski-Bob, Inc. This Stratford, Conn., company issued "Ski-Bike" snow bikes in the 1950s-60s.

"Ski-Scraper" building blocks see the *A.I. Root Co.*

"Ski-Skates" see *F.D. Peters Co., Inc.*

Skil-Craft Corp. The "Handy Andy" tool sets and activity kits were issued by this Chicago, Ill., company in the 1950s and '60s. Skil-Craft also issued "World of Science" microscope and chemistry sets.

"Skimmer Skates" see *Abba International Products Co.*

skinpacked "Skinpacked" and similar terms in the 1960s referred to the use of a plastic covering over toys, protecting them and making them adhere to a rack-hanger card. Thus, for example, Dowst Mfg. Co. in 1960 divided its goods into three merchandising groups: "bulk items, 'skinpacked' deals, and boxed sets." Later, "blister pack" became the accepted term.

skip-rope or skipping-rope Dating back to at least the ancient Greeks as an activity, skipping ropes were important toys in America from Colonial times. The numerous wood-turning plants of the New England states often included skip-rope handles among their products.

Skipper Mfg. Co. A Chicago, Ill., firm, Skipper Manufacturing made wood and metal automobile and boat toys in the mid-1930s. Its line included the clockwork "Robert E. Lee River Boat" and "Silver Arrow Racer."

Skipper Mfg. Co.'s "Robert E. Lee River Boat," 1934.

The Skipper Toy Co. Based in Branford, Conn., Skipper Toy made the "Modern-Morecraft" steel construction toys of the late 1930s.

"Skippy" A 1920s comic strip, "Skippy" inspired toys into the 1930s, including a board game by Milton Bradley Co., crayon and paint books by McLoughlin Bros., a doll by Fleischaker & Baum, and a figure by George Borgfeldt Corp.

Skippy Doll Corp. Rubber dolls, vinyl dolls, baby dolls, rooted-hair dolls, promotional dolls, and novelties comprised this postwar line. Skippy was based in Brooklyn, N.Y.

Skippy Racers, Inc. Children's vehicles were made by this Toledo, Ohio, company in the 1930s and '40s, including juvenile automobiles, velocipedes, bicycles, scooters, sleds, and wagons under the "Skippy" name. Vehicles new in 1934 included the "Airflow

DeSoto," and the "Streamlined Scooter." Confusion arises around these vehicles because American National Co., Gendron Wheel Co., and Toledo Metal Wheel Co. also used the "Skippy" trade name. Skippy also made playground equipment.

skirted robot Robot toys with panel sides extending to the bottom of the body, and thus having no visible legs, are referred to as "skirted."

skis and toboggans While toboggans retained strong associations with play and fun through the 20th century, skis became increasingly associated with sports and adult recreation in the postwar years, with the uncomplicated, often hand-made children's skis of the prewar years gradually falling by the wayside. The intense focus brought onto winter sports by sporting manufacturers of the later 20th century tended to remove skiing from the realm of unconscious, reflexive play. At the same time, the mounting expenses of the recreation removed much of the universal appeal the activity once enjoyed. Prewar manufacturers of skis and toboggans included Denning Mfg. Co., Gregg Mfg. Co., G.A. Lund Co., Northland Ski Mfg. Co., Paris Mfg. Co., and F.D. Peters Co.

"Skittle" game see *William F. Drueke & Sons.*

"Skookum Indian" "Skookum Indian" dolls were made by prewar companies including H.H. Tammen Co. and Arrow Novelty Co.

Skowhegan Croquet Established in 1909, Skowhegan issued the "Playday" line of croquet sets. It also issued toy duck pins and bowling games by the 1950s and '60s. It was based in North Anson, Maine.

"Skudder Car" see *Janesville Products Co.*

"Skunk" see *W.H. Schaper Mfg. Co., Inc.*

"Sky Boy" kites prewar, see *Dolly Toy Co.*

Sky Craft Rocking horses were part of this Lincoln, Neb., firm's Boomer-era line. It also made combination table-blackboards.

"Sky Cycle" bike see *Evans Products Co.*

"Sky Flyer" kites prewar, see *Marks Bros. Co.*

"Sky Hawk" stunt planes see *The Straits Corp.*

"Sky-Hy" building blocks see *The Embossing Co.*

"Sky King" kite see *Gayla Industries.*

"Sky King" velocipedes see *Junior Toy Corp.*

"Sky-Pie" flying discs see *Hammatt & Sons.*

"Sky Plane" sled see *American Acme Co.*

"Sky Raider" kite see *Gayla Industries.*

"Sky Rocket" coaster wagon see *Sheboygan Coaster & Wagon Works.*

"Skylark" airplane automobile see *Toledo Metal Wheel Co.*

Skymasters Corp. A Cincinnati, Ohio, firm established in the late 1930s, Skymasters made model airplane kits and supplies.

"Skymobile" see *The W.J. Baker Co.*

"Slag" marbles Machine-made marbles of clear or colored translucent glass with folded patterns of opaque glass inside are "Slags." Christensen Agate Co. was a manufacturer of these marbles.

Slammer Gun Co., Inc. Repeating action plastic guns were 1950s-60s specialties of this Louisville, Ky., company.

slate Slates became common childhood items by the late 18th century. They may have been in use much earlier. In the 1920s and prewar years, important manufacturers included H.G. Cress Co. and the Fox Toy Co. National School Slate Co. joined their ranks in the earlier 1930s. By the late prewar years, the leading makers included American Mfg.

Concern, American Slate Works, American Toy Works, Artwood Toy Mfg. Co., H.G. Cress, National School Slate Co., Jack Pressman & Co., and Transogram Co. Although not as prevalent in schools, slates remained common dimestore items through the Boomer years. Manufacturers included American Mfg. Concern, American Visual Aids, Bardell Mfg. Corp., Bar Zim Toy Mfg. Co., N.D. Cass Sales Co., Creston Crayon Co., Imperial Crayon Co., Fred Kroll Associates, Samuel Lowe Co., Midwest Mfg. Co., National School Slate Co., Pressman Toy Corp., Rosebud Art Co., and Welded Plastics Corp.

sleds The introduction of sledding to America has been attributed to the Dutch. Many early sled manufacturers were undoubtedly turners, barrel-makers, and carriage-makers.

Perhaps the most important manufacturer in both prewar and postwar years was S.L. Allen & Co., originally a manufacturer of farming equipment. This company's "Flexible Flyer," a steerable sled, remained popular from its introduction through the Boomer years.

Other prewar manufacturers included American Acme Co., the American National Co., Auto-Wheel Coaster Co., Garton Toy Co., the Gendron Mfg. Co., C.J. Johnson Co., Kalamazoo Sled Co., Master Woodworkers, Paris Mfg. Co., the Powell Pressed Steel Co., Pratt Mfg. Co., W.E. Pratt Mfg. Co., Rainey Mfg. Co., Schiller Piano Co., Sheboygan Coaster & Wagon Works, Skippy Racers, Specialty Mfg. Co., Standard Novelty Works, Steinfeld, and Uhlen Carriage Co. By the late 1930s, their number also included Humble Mfg. Co. and George Raithel & Son. Boomer-era manufacturers included American Acme, Auto-Wheel Coaster, Blake & Conroy, Block House, Garton Toy, Hedlund Mfg. Co., Industrial Fabricators, Kalamazoo Sled, MPM Corp., Maplewood Craftshop, Paris Mfg., F.D. Peters Co., Sno-Boat Corp, and Withington. See also snow saucers.

sleep eyes, or sleeping eyes In dolls, moving or closing eyes were introduced around 1826, with the earliest of them having motions accomplished through string-pulling.

"Sleeping Beauty" The full-length animated release by Walt Disney for 1959 inspired a proliferation of playthings, as came to be expected in the Boomer years. "Sleeping Beauty" items included books and puzzles by Whitman Publishing Co.; books and records by Golden Press; dolls by Alexander Doll Co.; dress designer kits by Colorforms; electric quiz games by Jacmar Mfg. Co.; erasable slates by Transogram Co.; games by Parker Bros.; "Magic Bubble Wand" by Gardner & Co.; "Magic Slates" by Watkins-Strathmore Co.; mobiles by Kenner Products Co.; night-lights by Hankscraft Co.; phonographs by Spear Products Co.; plastic cutouts by Aldon Industries; spring horses by Bayshore Industries; story kits by Colorforms; stuffed toys and puppets by Gund Mfg. Co.; tea sets by Worcester Toy Co.; 3-D film cards by Tru-Vue Co.; and wall-plaques by Dolly Toy Co.

Since the "Sleeping Beauty" story itself could not be licensed, some non-Disney-related items appeared in the same years, including car beds by Pride Products Co., coloring books by the Saalfield Publishing Co., and "Playtiles" by Halsam Products Co.

"Sleepy Head" soft toys see *Knickerbocker Toy Co., Inc.*

"Slender Ella" space toys see *American Play Co.*

"Slenderline" dolls see *Maxine Doll Co.*

"Slidin' Saucers" snow saucers see *Napco Industries, Inc.*

"Slik-Toy" metal toys see *Armor Industries, Inc.*

sling-propelled During the heyday of the flying toy airplane, in the 1920s and '30s, "sling-propelled" simply meant the toy was meant to be given force by being thrown forward, as opposed to being powered by a rubber band.

slingshots Some slingshots were formally manufactured in the prewar years, by companies including Meyer Rubber Co. and the Seiberling Latex Products Co. In the postwar years, manufacturers included General Sports, Greyshaw of Georgia, Jak-Pak-Inc.,

Marksman Products, Nadel & Sons, Nichols Industries, Ohio Plastic Co., and Wham-O.

"Slinky" see *James Industries, Inc.*

"Slouchy" animals see *Eden Toys, Inc.*

slush metal see *metal alloy toys.*

J.L. Small's Novelty Shop A maker of windmills and weather vanes, this Winnisquam, N.H., company also made prewar wooden toys, metal soldiers, and canary bird whistles.

Smart Style, Inc. Play suits, guns, and holster sets comprised this postwar line. The firm was based in Asheboro, S.C.

Smethport Specialty Co. Based in Smethport, Penn., this firm made magnet toy sets, flicker tops, and "movie tops" in the earlier 1930s, adding "Twin" racing tops and pinwheels by the late prewar years. In the Boomer years, the company enjoyed considerable success with its "Funny Face," "Dapper Dan" and "Wooly Willy" drawing sets, which the company described as "magnetic hair toys." It also made horseshoe magnets, magnetic games, and magnet sets.

Smile Novelty Toy Co., Inc. "Lassie" plush toys were a leading item from this postwar Brooklyn, N.Y., stuffed toy manufacturer.

J.H. Smith Co., Inc. The "Bronco" saddle and horse head set for trikes and bikes were Boomer-era products of this Greenfield, Mass., company. It also made a western TV seat.

Smith Mfg. Co. Established in Dalton, Ga., in the late 1930s, Smith manufactured "sandpile" tents, canvas playhouses, toy tents, and wading pools.

Edward Smith Mfg. Co. This Highland Park, Ill., firm issued games and party novelties for children and adults, including question-and-answer games.

Smith Rubber Horseshoe Co. Rubber pitching horseshoes were prewar products of this Horatio Street, New York City, company.

Smith Wood Products A Brattleboro, Vt., firm, this juvenile furniture manufacturer made early 20th century rocking horses.

"Smitty" The 1920s "Smitty" cartoon strip by Walter Berndt featured the characters Smitty and Herby. The strip inspired prewar toys and dolls by George Borgfeldt Corp., crayon and paint books by McLoughlin Bros., and a target game by Milton Bradley Co.

"Smokey Toy Bear" see *Ideal Novelty & Toy Co.*

"Smokey Joe" holster sets see *J. Halpern Co.*

snake toy A kind of jack-in-the-box, the snake toy was a wood box with sliding top, within which a spring-powered snake was concealed. When the child unwarily opened the box, the snake sprang out to prick the child's hand. The toy appeared by at least the mid-1800s.

"Snap Blox," "Snap Trux" see *Herald Toy Products.*

"Snap-Blox" games see *Metal Moss Mfg. Co.*

"Snap-Eze" construction blocks see *Highlander Sales Co.*

"Snap-Lock" beads see *Fisher-Price Toys, Inc.*

"Snap-N-Play" blocks see *Blockraft Mfg. Co.*

"Snap Train" see *Jack Built Toy Mfg. Co.*

"Snappy" pistol see *The Dent Hardware Co.*

"Snappy" top see *The Gibbs Mfg. Co.*

"Sneaky Snake Set" see *Maggie Magnetic, Inc.*

"Snippy" electric scissors see *Harry A. Ungar, Inc.*

Sno-Boat Corp. "Sno-Boat" runnerless sleds and "Monkey Ladder" swings were 1950s-60s products of this Lincoln, Neb., company.

S

"Sno-Bogan" see *F.D. Peters Co., Inc.*

"Sno-Plane" sled see *Skippy Racers, Inc.*

"Sno-Skeeters" see *Bilwin Co., Inc.*

Sno-Wing Ski Mfg. Co. Based in Auburn, Maine, Sno-Wing issued children's ski and pole sets, ski scooters, and toboggans in the late prewar years.

Snocraft, Inc. This division of Garland Mfg. Co. of Saco, Maine, made Boomer-era ski sets and toboggans.

"Snoopy Sniffer" see *Fisher-Price Toys, Inc.*

"Snoopy" stuffed toy early 1960s, see *Elka Toys.*

snow see *artificial snow.*

snowballs Of historical note, the Boston Massacre was triggered, according to an eyewitness, by a group of boys throwing snowballs at a British sentry.

"Snow Bird" sleds see *The Paris Mfg. Co.*

"Snow Disc" see *Kalamazoo Sled Co.*

"Snow Glider" snowshoes see *Nestor Johnson Mfg. Co.*

"Snow King" sled see *American Acme Co.*

snow saucers The saucer-shaped toy became typical in the Boomer years not only in aerial toys, but also in sledding toys. Makers of snow saucers included All Work Mfg. Co., Hedlund Mfg. Co., Kalamazoo Sled Co., Mirro Aluminum Co., Montello Products Co., Napco Industries, and Plastic Products Corp.

snow snake Snow snake was an American Indian game involving a furrow in deep snow, made by the dragging of a log, and the hurling of a small, hand-held, sled-like piece of wood, or "snake," down the furrow. The competition focused on sending the snake farthest.

"Snow White and the Seven Dwarfs" One of Walt Disney's most popular feature films, the animated Snow White and the Seven Dwarfs film inspired innumerable toys and playthings in the late prewar years.

Among them were aluminum toys by Aluminum Goods Mfg. Co.; balloons by Oak Rubber Co.; banks by Crown Toy Mfg. Co.; "Beetleware" dishes by Bryant Electric Co.; bell and chime toys by N.N. Hill Brass Co.; books by David McKay Co., Grosset & Dunlap, and Whitman Publishing Co.; children's hair barrettes by Lapin Products; cleaning sets by Gotham Pressed Steel Corp.; costumes by A.S. Fishbach; display materials by Old King Cole; dolls by Alexander Doll Co., Ideal Novelty & Toy Co., Knickerbocker Toy Co., Richard G. Krueger, and George Borgfeldt Corp.; "Dopey" glove dolls by Crown Toy Mfg. Co.; and favors by Adler Favor & Novelty Co.

Also appearing were games by Milton Bradley Co., Parker Bros., and Whitman; tabletop garden sets by Robert Kayton Co.; jack sets by United States Lock & Hardware Co.; "Kiddie Kits" and school bags by Columbia Products Co.; marionettes by Alexander Doll Co.; masks by Apon Novelty Co.; musical instruments by Marks Bros. Co.; music boxes by Thorens; pencil sharpeners by Plastic Novelties; "Plaster Kaster" sets by J.L. Wright; rubber figures by Seiberling Latex Products Co.; sand toys by Ohio Art Co.; school bags and brief cases by Monroe Luggage Co.; stamping sets by Fulton Specialty Co.; target games by American Toy Works; toy chests by Odora Mfg. Co.; and valentines by Paper Novelty Mfg. Co.

"Snub-Bee" water gun see *Park Plastics Co.*

"Snuggle Buggy" carriage see *The Frank F. Taylor Co.*

"Snuggle-Ups" soft dolls prewar, see *The Rushton Co.*

"Snuggly Handi-Pets" see *Elka Toys.*

"So-Wee" dolls see *The Sun Rubber Co.*

Soap Sculpture Kit Co., Inc. Based on Broadway, New York City, this firm issued the "Ivory" soap sculptor's kit of the late 1930s.

The Sock-It Co. see *The Fli-Back Co.*

soft toys "Soft dolls" and "soft animals" were terms used commonly in the toy industry through around the mid-20th century, as a term for stuffed cloth dolls and animals.

"Softee" doll see *E.I. Horsman Co., Inc.*

Softskin Toys, Inc. Stuffed washable animals, "Dang-A-Ling" dolls, "Hobble-Wobble" action pull toys, washable musical toys, "Honey Rascal" bears, roly-polys, "Tub-A-Dub" beach and bath toys, autograph toys, premium items, and novelty toys were specialties of Softskin, based on Park Avenue, New York City, in the 1950s and '60s.

Sokblok, Inc. The "Sokblok" indoor and outdoor play sets were issued by this Roanoke, Va., firm in the late 1930s.

soldier toys see *toy soldiers.*

solid cast, or solidcast Solid-cast toys were slush-metal or pot-metal toys made of solid metal, without an inner air space. Also sometimes referred to as "solids." See *hollowcast.*

"Soljertoys" see *The Illfelder Corp.*

Sollmann & Whitcomb A manufacturer's representative and possibly also manufacturer, this firm was established in 1932 in the Fifth Avenue Building, and continued in operation through the prewar and wartime years, when its main products were wooden, especially wooden pails and garden tool sets, and into the Boomer years.

"Soma" Billed as "The World's Finest Cube Puzzle Game," "Soma" was promoted heavily by Parker Bros. for its 1969 debut, resulting in its becoming one of the top sellers for the company.

"Soma," the Parker Bros. game from the late 1960s.

"Something-To-Do" books see *The Platt & Munk Co., Inc.*

Sommers Modelcraft Co. A St. Louis, Mo., firm established in the late 1930s, Sommers made flying and non-flying airplane construction kits.

"Son-y" vehicles see *Dayton Toy & Specialty Co.*

"Songspinner" tops see *Weil Bros.*

"Sonny Bunny" plush rabbit see *The Rushton Co.*

Soodhalter Plastic Products Plastic doll cribs and cradles comprised this 1950s-60s line. The firm was based in Los Angeles, Calif.

South Bend Toy Mfg. Co. Located in South Bend, Ind., this children's furniture manufacturer also made prewar doll strollers, croquet sets, and toy kitchen sets. By the late 1930s the company had expanded its line to include baby carriages and farm wagons. It continued largely unchanged during wartime. In the Boomer years, South Bend Toy's line featured croquet; doll carts, coaches, and carriages; musical doll carriages; musical rockers; and juvenile table and chair sets.

Croquet set from South Bend Toy Mfg. Co., 1950s.

South Tamworth Industries, Inc. This Boston, Mass., nursery furniture company also made prewar wooden toys and novelties.

Southern Toy Mfg. Co. This Waco, Texas, company made 1950s and '60s spring-suspended hobby horses including "Sandy the Palomino," "Texas Bronc," and "Twin

Jumper." The firm also made "Trike-Trailers" in the '50s, and sandboxes, peg desks, and toy chests by the '60s.

Southwest Mfg. Co. This Little Rock, Ark., company made scale-model versions of outboard motor boats, using light gauge aluminum, in the mid-1950s. Its line included the "Arkansas Traveler" boats.

souvenir toys see *favors and souvenirs.*

"Space Bug" see *William F. Drueke.*

"Space Cadet" flashlights see *United States Electric Mfg. Co.*

"Space Jet" water pistol see *Knickerbocker Plastic Co., Inc.*

Space Models Based in Fort Worth, Texas, this firm made "Explorer" missile kits in the 1950s-60s.

"Space Patrol" flying toys see *The Boyd Specialty Co.*

"Space Race" game see *Built-Rite Toys.*

"Space Squadron" holsters and pistols see *Dumore Belt & Novelty Co.*

"Space Traveler" paint-by-number sets see *Standard Toykraft Products, Inc.*

"Spaceforms" see *Colorforms.*

Spare-Time Game Toy Co. This Cincinnati, Ohio, company touted its "Spare-Time Bowling" as "America's #1 Home Bowling Game!" in the 1950s and '60s. The company also made card games, banks, and 3-D picture kits.

A.G. Spalding & Bro. This famous sporting-goods house was established in Chicago, Ill., in 1876.

sparklers While many forms of fireworks were kept from children in the safety-minded Boomer years, the sparklers maintained widespread acceptance within families, for Fourth of July celebrations. Manufacturers included Acme Specialties Corp., Hale-Nass Corp., and Talbot Mfg. Co.

J.W. Spear & Sons, Inc. This East 16th Street, New York City firm, issued the

"Spear's Games" line of the 1920s. Located on Fourth Avenue by the late Depression years, Spear issued puzzles, blocks, games, and educational toys through the prewar years.

Spec-Toy-Culars, Inc. Plastic musical toys, carnival goods, whistles, sirens, kazoos, and action toys comprised this Boomer-era line. The firm was based in Long Island City, N.Y.

Special Products Co. A Cleveland, Ohio, company, Special Products made prewar toys and advertising novelties, as well as wood parts for other toy manufacturers.

Specialty Mfg. Co. The "Hill Billy Ski-Sled" of the 1930s and '40s was made by this Appleton, Wis., company.

"Speedboy" coaster wagons see *The Murray-Ohio Mfg. Co.*

"Speed King" The "Speed King" trademark was used on a variety of prewar wheel goods, including coaster wagons by Toledo Metal Wheel Co., roller skates by Hustler Corp., and steering sleds by Garton Toy Co. Hustler continued using the name on roller skates through the Boomer years.

"Speed King" racer Renwal Toy Corp. made "Speed King" streamlined race cars from the late 1940s through the mid-50s. In 1955 the firm issued a die-cast version.

"Speed-O-Byke" bicycles see *Metal Specialties Mfg. Co.*

"Speed Scout" boats see *Thornecraft, Inc.*

"Speed Skees" see *Denning Mfg. Co.*

"Speedaway" sleds see *Paris Mfg. Co.*

"Speeder" wagon see *Dayton Toy & Specialty Co., The*

"Speedmobile" see *W.J. Baker Co.*

"Speedster" sleds see *The Paris Mfg. Co.*

"Speedwell" vehicles see *The Emblem Mfg. Co.*

"Speedy" Garton Toy Co. used the "Speedy" trade name on wheel goods, including six-wheel coaster trucks and velocipedes.

spelicans 19th century word for jackstraws.

"Spel-Jax" see *Jon Weber Manufactory.*

spelling boards These clever educational boards and playthings featured letters on individual squares of wood, which could be pushed along a track around the board, and then slid into place on a track that cross-sectioned the board, to spell a word. Before the Great Depression, manufacturers included H.G. Cress Co. and the Fox Toy Co. By the mid-1930s, they included the H.G. Cress Co., the Embossing Co., Fox Toy, and the A.I. Root Co. While most were made of wood, some companies used other materials, as in the "Spell Board" with felt letters by Poster Products in the 1930s. Postwar manufacturers included Bar Zim Toy Mfg. Co., Cadaco-Ellis, Henry Katz, Rapaport Bros., Richmond School Furniture Co., and the Saalfield Publishing Co.

spelling books Noah Webster, vitally interested in getting America's words into a standard form, published his *Blue-Back Speller* in 1782. It remained a standard textbook for more than a century.

"Spic and Span" sets see *Kiddie Brush & Toy Co.*

"Spin-A-Way" scooter see *The Globe Co.*

Spin-O-Rop Co. The 1930s "Spin-O-Rop" was a product of this Anderson, Ind., firm.

Spinner Games, Inc. This postwar games company was based in Bridgeport, Conn.

"Spinners" see *The Vitro-Agate Co.*

"Sponge Ball" rifle prewar, see *Buffalo Toy & Tool Works.*

Sponge Rubber Products Co. Few of this Derby, Conn., company's products are likely to have survived, being prewar balls, toys and novelties of sponge rubber. It used the "Spunjy Lastik" trade name in the mid-1930s, and issued toys under the "Spongex" name in the late '30s.

"Spooky" Although less well known than "Casper, the Friendly Ghost," "Spooky" was also a Harvey Famous Name Comics character. Costumes were made by Bland Charnas Co.

spools Spools and shuttles, which were whittled by hand in front of Colonial hearths, were doubtless, in the absence of more standard toy items, common early Colonial playthings. They remained playthings through American history, with the common pastime of playthings with sticks and spools together providing inspiration in the 20th century for the famous "Tinkertoys."

spoon sitters National Biscuit Co., or Nabisco, issued plastic premium figures in the 1950s through the remainder of the Boomer years that were spoon sitters. These sitting figures had slots in their rears, which allowed them to fit snugly on the handles of flatware.

"Spoonmen" These small space figures, which were spoon sitters, became familiar figures at the breakfast table in the 1950s and '60s, being representatives of National Biscuit Co. for "Spoon-Size Shredded Wheat." Plastic figures were included in some boxes. Collegeville Flag & Mfg. Co. issued costumes based on the characters of "Spoon-size," "Munchy," and "Crunchy." The figures were licensed by Harvey Famous Name Comics.

"Sport" single-shot cap pistol see *Kilgore Mfg. Co., Inc.*

"Sportsman" model engine see *L.M. Cox Mfg. Co.*

"Sportster" bicycle see *Midwest Industries.*

"Spot-A-Satellite" Two firms made "Spot-A-Satellite" games in the late 1950s: Boyd Specialty Co., and Fillum Fun.

"Spotlight" costumes prewar, see *Waas & Son.*

S

Sprague & Carleton This juvenile furniture manufacturer, based in Keene, N.H., made children's chairs and rockers in the mid-1930s.

Sprague Mfg. Co. Located on Fifth Avenue, New York City, in the late 1930s, Sprague made musical toy boxes, lamps, and metal novelties.

Spraz Co. A Cincinnati, Ohio, firm, Spraz made leather-cased "Frontier Scout" and "Cowboy" plastic canteens in the 1950s and '60s, as well as holsters, quivers, and belts.

spring cannon "Spring cannon" usually refers to a common form of the toy cannon that shoots using a spring mechanism.

Spring Crest Toy & Novelty Co. A hollowcast Cadillac toy car was the 1960 product of this Ashland, Penn., company.

spring-driven Tin wind-up toys that utilize spring-powered motors and tinplate or cast-metal gears date to the 1890s, in U.S. toys. See *clockwork,* and *motors, spring.*

spring horse Originally called the "Crandall Spring Horse," this toy was developed by Jesse Crandall as a response to the complaint from householders that the rockers of the excellently constructed Crandall rocking horses damaged carpets, sometimes cutting them. By attaching the horse to a platform via springs, Crandall created the spring horse.

The new plaything proved popular to the point that Crandall was obliged to manufacture some at life-size for adult customers. Variants from the Crandall factory included the "Oscillating Horse" and the "Leaping Horse," as well as one after the Spanish-American War called "Teddy's Horse." In prewar times the spring horse and similar toys were referred to as "exercisers," since the activity they encouraged in children was seen as beneficial. Manufacturers included the American National Co., Appleton Toy & Furniture Co., Cameo Doll Co., Excel Specialty Co., Gordon Toy & Mfg. Co., Kiddie Gym, Lloyd Mfg. Co., Pines Winterfront Co., the Republic Tool Products Co., and the A. Schoenhut Co.

Other prewar manufacturers of both rocking and spring horses included W.A. Barber, the N.D. Cass Co., Charles & Victor Goldstein, the Mengel Co., Whitney Reed Co., and Whitney Bros. Co. In prewar times the term "platform horse" was frequently used.

Perhaps the most important postwar manufacturer of the spring horse was Wonder, which used contemporary materials available after World War II—plastic for the bodies, which included molded hair and tails, and steel tube frames on which the horse was hung by springs. See also *exercisers.*

sprinklers In sand toys, the "sprinklers" are the watering cans, used for moistening the sand for molding.

"Spud Gun" see *E. Joseph Cossman & Co.*

"Spunky" Both Plastic Playthings and Stahlwood Toy Mfg. Co. used this trade name for lines of toys in the 1950s-60s.

squeak toys In the 19th century, squeak toys were often a papier-mâché figure of a bird on wire legs, which allowed it to move about while standing on a small bellows, to which was attached a whistle or squeaker. Vinyl squeeze toys in the 1950s and later employed the same principle, with the animal or doll shape itself was the bellows, with the squeaker usually located in the base. See *squeeze toys.*

"Squeekum" books see *Grosset & Dunlap, Inc.*

"Squeeze-Me" Both Oak Rubber and Bonnytex companies used the "Squeeze-Me" trade names in the Boomer years.

squeeze toys Helped in great part by developments in vinyl production, squeeze toys became a major toy category in the Boomer years, with the Sun Rubber Co. among the leading producers. Other manufacturers included Alan-Jay Plastics, Arrow Rubber & Plastics Corp., Atlanta Playthings Co., Bayshore Industries, Louis A. Boettiger, Chee-Ki Corp. of California, Dell Distributing, Dolls of Hollywood, Hungerford Plastics Corp., Jolly Blinker Corp., Pet Toy Co. of N.H., Plakie Toys, Plastic Playthings, Rempel Mfg., Tom B. Roberts Co., Stahlwood Toy Mfg. Co., Star Mfg. Co., Tinkle Toy Co., and Vinfloat Industries.

"Squirt Ray" water gun see *Park Plastics Co.*

"Stabilt" blocks see *The Embossing Co.*

"Stacking Telephone" see *Sifo Co.*

Stacy Mfg. Co. Pre-school and kindergarten play tables and games were this Willis Avenue, New York City, firm's specialty in the 1950s and '60s.

"Stadium Checkers" see *W.H. Schaper Mfg. Co., Inc.*

Stahlwood Toy Mfg. Co. Educational and pre-school toys, including plastic rattles and squeeze toys, comprised this postwar line. Stahlwood was based on West 50th Street, New York City.

Stahl-wood's "Spunky Knitting Spool Kit,"

"Stallion" pistols see *Nichols Industries*.

Stamp and Album Co. of America

The "SACO" line of stamps and albums were postwar products of this Union Square, New York City, company.

stampings and metal parts Toy companies collaborated in many aspects of the manufacturing process. Specialists in metal stampings and other metal parts did a great deal of work for other manufacturers, even when they produced and marketed their own toys.

Prewar specialists included Arrow Automatic Products Corp., Atlas Metal Products Corp., the Wallace Barnes Co., Bevin Bros. Mfg. Co., Boston Pressed Metal Co., the Brewer-Titchener Corp., T. Cohn, the Cuyahoga Spring Co., Defiance Stamping Co., Forsyth Metal Goods Co., the Galt Art Metal Co., Gardner Screw Corp., the Globe Co., L.F. Grammes & Sons, the Hoggson & Pettis Mfg. Co., Kirchhof Patent Co., Krischer's Mfg. Co., Mareck & Nebel, the Master Products Co., Merrill Mfg. Co., New England Lock & Hinge Co., the Newell Mfg. Co., Novelty Mfg. Co., Patton-MacGuyer Co., Peter F. Pia, Revere Products Corp., Richmond Bros. Co., Schindler Stamping & Toy Co., Steel Materials Co., Edwin B. Stimpson Co., the Thompson Mfg. Co., United Smelting & Aluminum Co., U.S. Pressed Steel Products Co., and E.R. Wagner Mfg. Co. See also *castings; rubber, molded parts.*

stamps and albums The encouragement of the stamp-collecting hobby was the business of several companies by the late prewar years, including Gramercy Stamp Co. and Grossman Stamp Co. Boomer-era companies included Grosset & Dunlap, Grossman Stamp, H.E. Harris & Co., and Stamp & Album Co. of America.

"Stan Musial" Sports hero Stan Musial's name appeared on bats by Tigrett Industries, and plastic figures by Hartland Plastics.

standard In farm toys, refers to a style of tractor having a fixed wheel tread or axle spacing and a low center of gravity. Compare "row crop."

Standard B. & B. Mfg. Co. A Baltimore, Md., firm, Standard B. & B. issued toy broom and brush sets in the late 1930s.

Standard Brief Case Co. Located on West 21st Street, New York City, the Standard Brief Case Co. produced children's brief cases, including ones using early Disney characters through a licensing agreement with Kay Kamen, in the 1930s and '40s.

The Standard Crayon Mfg. Co. Wax and chalk crayons and crayon drawing sets were made by this Danvers, Mass., firm in the 1930s and '40s.

Standard Cycle Co. The "Ranger" bicycles of the postwar years were made by this Chicago, Ill., manufacturer.

Standard Doll Co. Miniature character dolls, boudoir dolls, and revolving musical dolls were postwar specialties of this East 22nd Street, New York City, company.

Standard Electric Stove Co. The 1930s "Standard Junior" toy electric range was made by this Toledo, Ohio, firm.

Standard Novelty Co. The "Gottago" game of the late 1930s was issued by this Cleveland, Ohio, firm.

Standard Novelty Works Besides outdoor furniture and swings, this Duncannon, Penn., company made the "Lightning Guider" sleds and "Lightning Wheel Coaster" wagons in the 1930s and '40s. The company also made park benches and dog kennels.

Standard Playing Card Co. A Chicago, Ill., firm, Standard Playing Card Co. made prewar playing cards and card games.

Standard Science Supply Established in Chicago, Ill., in the late 1930s, Standard produced chemical, micro-chemical and microscope sets.

Standard Solophone Mfg. Co. The "Solophones" toy and "Roll 'Em In" marble game of the 1920s were made by this West 18th Street, New York City, company. It also made basketball games.

Standard Toykraft Products, Inc. Standard Toykraft made a great many activity sets and "outfits" before and after the war. In the earlier 1930s its lines included "Tom Sawyer" picture puzzles, paint sets, and poster color sets, "Little Artist" crayons sets, "Little Sculptor" modeling sets, "Little Darling" doll embroidery outfits, "Little Tots Thread-em" sets, and the "Junior Writing" outfit.

In the late '30s Standard Toykraft obtained license to issue Walt Disney character painting, sewing and embroidery sets. The company also absorbed Ulman Mfg. Co., which had produced similar lines of products. Standard Toykraft's line by 1939 included "Charm Jewelry" sets, "March of Progress" color sets, "Tom Sawyer" painting sets and crayons, "Priscilla" and "Jumbo" crayons, "Jean Darling" doll outfits and embroidery outfits, "Little Mother's Patchwork Outfits," "Little Tot's Thread 'em Sets," and "'Round the World Animals to Color."

The company also issued the "Erect Your Own Movie Studio" play set, knitting and loom weaving sets, flower making and mosaic sets, animal cutouts, coloring books, surprise package goods, and items for the 1939 New York World's Fair.

The company was located on West 20th Street, New York City, in the earlier '30s, moving its factory to Brooklyn, N.Y., in the later 1930s and its offices to the Fifth Avenue Building. In the Boomer years, the firm continued its "Tom Sawyer" and "Priscilla" lines of kits and activity sets. It also issued "Roy Rogers" art and activity sets.

Standard Trailer Co. Wood blocks and puzzles were made by this Cambridge Springs, Penn., company in the 1930s and '40s.

Standard Transformer Corp. Established in Chicago, Ill., in the late 1930s, this firm made transformers for toy electric trains.

standing stool Standing stools were devices, usually with wheels, designed to help babies in their first efforts to walk. They first appeared in America in the 1600s. "Taylor Tots" and "Baby-Tendas" were prominent brand names for the devices in the 20th century. Also called "go-cart."

The Stanley Works see *Stanlo Toy Division.*

Stanlo Toy Division In 1933-34, the Stanley Works of New Britain, Conn., introduced "Stanlo," a construction toy akin to the "Erector" sets by A.C. Gilbert. Stanley, a renowned tool manufacturer, was also manufacturing toy tools and tool chests before the war. By 1934, the line included seven sets of "The Master Building Toy," including sets intended to be used with electric train sets. The "Stanlite" electric light unit to be used with "Stanlo" sets was also introduced in 1934. The line continued into the 1940s.

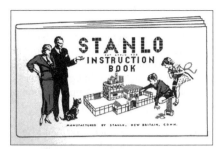

Instruction book for Stanlo building toy.

Victor Stanzel & Co. The "Glideo" plane and engine-powered planes were 1950s-60s products of this Schulenburg, Texas, company.

Star Band Co., Inc. Halloween masks and hats were Boomer-era products for this Portsmouth, Va., company. It also made Christmas decorations.

"Star" books for children see *The Platt & Munk Co., Inc.*

"Star Building" blocks see *American Novelty Works.*

star finders Public fascination with space and the stars led to such educational toys as the star finders. The A.C. Gilbert Co. and Tri G Co. were among its publishers.

Star Mfg. Co. Based in Leominster, Mass., this postwar firm made plastic novelties, rattles and carriage toys.

"Star" miniature character dolls see *Admiration Toy Co., Inc.*

Star Novelty Works Doll furniture was made by this 1930s and '40s Cincinnati, Ohio, company.

"Star" pistol see *The J. & E. Stevens Co.*

"Star Reporter" game see *Parker Bros., Inc.*

Star Safety Film Co. Based on Ninth Avenue, New York City, this firm made toy moving picture films in the late 1930s.

"Star" wagon see *The Dayton Toy & Specialty Co.*

"Starflite," "Starider" bicycles see *Chain Bike Corp.*

"Starjax" sets see *Grey Iron Casting Co.*

"Stark's Ball Gun," mid-1930s see the *Forrest Mfg. Co.*

"Starr Skates" see *Arco Tubular Skate Corp.*

Stars on Stripes, Inc. This postwar Pittsburgh, Penn., company issued football, party, and action games.

State Fair Toy & Novelty Co. Stuffed toys were this Brooklyn, N.Y., firm's postwar product.

"State Ranger" gun and holster set see *R. & S. Toy Mfg. Co., Inc.*

"States & Cities" see *Parker Bros.*

stationery, juvenile The idea of providing writing materials to children that was designed specifically for them was commonplace by the prewar years. Manufacturers included Beckhard-Simfred Co., the General Paper Co., and Whitman Publishing Co.

Statler Mfg. Co. Based in Chicago, Ill., Statler issued postwar plastic toys, including steering wheel toys, and interlocking blocks.

steam engines see *engines, toy.*

"Steamloco" train see the *Lionel Corp.*

Stecher-Traung Lithograph Corp. This Rochester, N.Y., publisher issued toy books in the 1930s.

Steel Builder Co., Inc. Based in Newark, N.J., Steel Builder Co. made steel construction toys in the 1930s and '40s. The sets were similar to "Erector" or "Structo" sets, with metal girders, panels, and wheels of steel. The individual sets retailed at $1.00 and $3.00, in the mid-1930s.

S

"Steel King," "Steel Mogul" 1930s, see *American Flyer Mfg. Co.*

Steel Materials Co. In the 1930s, Steel Materials Co. of Detroit, Mich., made unusual three-wheeled, rubber-tired coaster skates. By the late '30s its line included electric motor boats and steel helmets, and its name had become Steel Materials Corp.

The Steel Stamping Co. Toy telephones, pistols, dump carts, wheelbarrows, wagons, scooters, hand trucks and toy automobiles were made by this Lorain, Ohio, firm in the 1930s. The firm continued through the Boomer years, after a hiatus during wartime, with a line of wagons, wheelbarrows, dial telephones, and steel furniture.

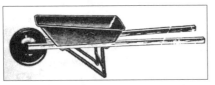

Toy wheelbarrow produced by the Steel Stamping Co.

steel toys Earlier 20th century manufacturers included American Flyer Mfg. Co., George H. Bowman Co., Corcoran Mfg. Co., Dayton Friction Toy Co., Dayton Toy & Specialty Co., N.N. Hill Brass Co., Keystone Mfg. Co., Kingsbury Mfg. Co., Moline Pressed Steel Co., Republic Tool Products Co., Schiebletoy & Novelty Co., Structo Mfg. Co., Toy Creation Shops, and John C. Turner Co.

Steel became the material of choice for many prewar manufacturers. In postwar times steel toys remained common through the 1950s, with their number diminishing steadily through the following decades. Its use was especially notable in toy road construction vehicles, riding toys, and pedal cars.

Prewar manufacturers included All-Metal Products Co., American Flyer Mfg. Co., American National Co., Arrow Mfg. Co., Buddy "L" Mfg. Co., J. Chein & Co., Corcoran Mfg. Co., Dayton Toy & Specialty Co., Theodore J. Ely Mfg. Co., Empay Corp., J.H. Hoenes Co., Joger Mfg. Co., Keystone Mfg. Co., Kingsbury Mfg. Co., Mantua Toy &

Metal Products Co., Master Metal Prodcuts, Metalcraft Corp., the Murray Ohio Mfg. Co., the Republic Tool Products Co., the Steel Stamping Co., Structo Mfg. Co., Transogram Co., and the John C. Turner Corp. In the late prewar years companies joining their ranks included Joseph Cohn Co., Ammert-Hammes & Co., and Hoge Mfg. Co.

Postwar specialists included Bar Zim Mfg. Co., Buddy "L" Toys, Eyerly Associates, Garton Toy Co., Hale-Nass Corp., Henry Katz, Metal Masters Co., Ny-Lint Tool & Mfg. Co., Steel Stamping, Structo, Tonka Toys, and Tru-Matic Toy Co.

Structo Mfg. Co. made the "Concrete Mixer" in the 1960s.

The "Auto Hauler," a Buddy "L" steel toy from the 1960s.

steel wheels In farm toys, a term used to describe a type of wheel used on early farm tractors before rubber tires became popular. In the toys, the wheels may be made of cast metal, plastic, or wood and still be called "steel."

"Steelcraft" line of vehicles see *The Murray-Ohio Mfg. Co.*

"Steeltoy" coaster wagons see *The Toledo Metal Wheel Co.*

Steger Products Mfg. Corp. This Steger, Ill., company made postwar steel and stake wagons.

Margarete Steiff & Co. A firm associated with Borgfeldt's on Fourth Avenue, New York City, in the 1930s, Steiff made stuffed animals, including "Mickey Mouse" and "Minnie Mouse" character dolls.

E. Steiger & Co. Located on Murray Street, New York City, E. Steiger made kindergarten materials in the 1930s.

"Steinback Toys" see *Readsboro Chair Co.*

Steinfeld, Inc. This East 26th Street, New York City, manufacturers' representative was associated in the 1920s and '30s with several prominent wheel goods lines, notably the "Columbia" line by Westfield Mfg. Co., and the "Boycycle."

Steinmann Toy Mfg. Co., Inc. The "Estray Toys" line of stuffed toys were produced by this West 21st Street, New York City, manufacturer in the 1920s.

Stelber Cycle Corp. Bicycles, stabilizer bikes, velocipedes, gyms, and slides made up this Boomer-era line. Stelber, based in the Fifth Avenue Building, also made outdoor playground equipment.

L.E. Stemmler Co. Based in Queens Village, New York City, Stemmler issued archery tackle and boomerangs in the late prewar years.

Stencil-Art Publishing Co. Stencil activity books and cutout letters and numbers comprised this Bedford, Ohio, firm's postwar line.

Stephens Products Co., Inc. The "Auto Magic picture gun" of the late 1930s was issued by this Long Island City, N.Y., company. It also issued color films featuring the New York and San Francisco 1939 World's Fairs. In the postwar years the company became Stephens Products Division of Worcester Toy Co., in Worcester, Mass. The "Auto-Matic" project and theater continued as its primary product.

Stephens Publishing Co. This postwar Sandusky, Ohio, publisher issued coloring books, doll cutout books, and scrap books.

Stephenson Mfg. Co. A South Bend, Ind., wood-turning firm, Stephenson's products included adjustable stilts in the 1930s.

Stepping Sam Co. The "Stepping Sam" tap-dancing toy of the late 1930s was issued by this Philadelphia, Penn., company.

"Stepping Stones to Art" crayons see *Milton Bradley Co.*

stereoscopes Stereoscopes were three-dimensional film viewers made by several prewar companies, including Keystone View Co., Novelart Mfg. Co., and Tru-Vue. In 1939 Sawyer's introduced the "View-Master," which would eventually become the most famous of the viewers.

"Sterling" air rifle see *American Tool Works.*

Sterling Doll Co. In the 1930s and '40s, this West 26th Street, New York City, company made dolls, boudoir dolls, and novelties. Undressed flapper dolls were an earlier '30s product. The firm continued in the Boomer years on Broadway, producing stuffed novelty toys and dolls.

Sterling Models "Chris Craft" plastic boat kits and "Lil Beaver" electric motors were specialties of this Philadelphia, Penn., company in the 1950s and '60s.

Sterling Plastics Co. Based in Union, N.J., Sterling issued plastic dolls, pistols with rubber darts, pencil boxes and globes, as well as other office items and party and picnic ware.

Stern Toy Co. Established in the late 1930s on West 24th Street, New York City, Stern issued stuffed toys and novelties.

stereoscopes Popular from before the end of the 19th century through the prewar years, stereoscopes gave simple parlor optical entertainment, sometimes of an educational nature. An early "3-D" viewer, stereoscopes had a holding rack at one end to

S

hold the stereo photographs, and a goggles-shaped device on the other into which were fitted the lenses for stereo viewing. Prewar manufacturers included Keystone View Co. and Tru-Vue.

Stern Toy Co. This postwar Brooklyn, N.Y., company specialized in stuffed toys and novelties.

"Steve Canyon" The rugged cartoon-strip hero inspired playthings in the 1950s and '60s including costume and holster sets by J. Halpern, helmets by Ideal Toy Corp., paint sets and coloring books by Whitman Publishing Co., suits by Sackman Bros. Co., scale model kits by Aurora Plastics Corp., and viewers, slides and reels by Sawyer's. Lowell Toy Mfg. Co. issued the "Steve Canyon Air Force" game of 1959.

Steven Mfg. Co. Kaleidoscopes became closely associated with this St. Louis, Mo., manufacturer in the 1950s and '60s. Steven made many versions, including deluxe models with interchangeable heads. Steven also issued "Pixie Pick-Up Stix" and "Magnetic Pixie Pick-Up Sticks" games, "Pixie Build A Toy" wooden construction sets, gyroscope tops, "Pixie" checkers, Chinese checkers, "Play-Trays," and the "Slammer" rubber-band six-shooter guns.

Stevens & Brown Elisha Stevens and George W. Brown combined forces to establish Stevens & Brown in New York City in 1869. The company made tin and cast-iron toys, and distributed toys by other manufacturers, until 1880.

The J. & E. Stevens Co. A major name in prewar cast-iron toys, the J. & E. Stevens Co. of Cromwell, Conn., was founded in 1843, by John and Elisha Stevens. Iron toy wheels an important early product. By the 1850s it was producing two tons of the wheels per month, effectively ending the foreign imports that had previously predominated in the American market.

The company gradually expanded its line to include toy sadirons and toy garden tools. Its series of tool chests came in ten versions, containing from seven to 40 tools. It also made cast-iron penny toys in the shapes of miniature axes, shovels, rakes and other tools. An important part of its business went into banks, which it produced from 1870 to the turn of the century. Some were in the shape of bank buildings.

The firm made doll furniture in iron, including Franklin stoves, coal hods and shovels, laundry tubs and washboards, stoves, sleighs, chairs, beds, and various other contemporary household items. Its numerous other iron toys included ice skates, toy cannons, cork-firing air pistols, toy swords, cap pistols, an iron whistling top, brass tops, miniature ten-pins, whistles, and jackstones. The company also supplied castings to the Gong Bell Mfg. Co. and Watrous for their bell toys.

In the 20th century, the J. & E. Stevens Co. was known primarily for its toy pistols, jack-stones, and banks. By the late prewar years it was issuing primarily single-shot and repeating cap pistols.

In the Boomer years, based on Broadway, New York City, the company issued single-shot and repeating cap pistols, toy pistol caps, jacks and ball sets, and holsters. See also ***American Toy Co., George W. Brown & Co., C.G. Shepard & Co., Stevens & Brown.***

Stewart-Warner Corp. A Chicago, Ill., firm founded in the late 1930s, Stewart-Warner made speedometers for bicycles.

stick horses The simplest homemade riding toys were sticks, which inventive children could mentally transform into amazing fast and powerful horses. Toy makers naturally made these sticks into items of manufacture by the simple stratagem of placing a horse's head on one end. More elaborate versions included wheels, sometimes equipped with bells, on the trailing end. Prewar manufacturers who made a specialty of these stick horses included Anchor Mfg. Co., Gong Bell Mfg. Co., Clara Hyde Toys, Playskool Institute, Transogram Co., and Whitney Bros. Co. In the Boomer years, manufacturers included Alan-Jay Plastics, American Toy & Furniture Co., Bayshore Industries, Big Time Toys, Golden Triangle Toy Co., Grand Rapids Toy Furniture Co., Harrison's Mfg. Co., the N.N. Hill Brass Co., Mangold Toy Co. Metal Masters Co., Nu-Cushion Products, Pet Toy Co.

S

of N.H., Rempel Mfg. Co., A.J. Renzi Plastic Co., Tri-Kay Co., Wirsig Products Co.

Stickless Corp., The Stickless, located on Drake Street, New York City, was a 1930s game manufacturer.

still banks see *banks, still.*

stilts A venerable toy often used for carnival or circus purposes, stilts were known not only from Europe but also among American Indians. Stilts were popular prewar toys, to judge from the number of wood-product manufacturers who included adjustable stilts among their offerings in the 1930s. In the prewar years, manufacturers included Boston Stilt Co., the C-K-R Co., Detroit Wood Products Division, Indian Archery & Toy Corp., Phenix Mfg. Co., Piqua General Supply Co., Stephenson Mfg. Co., and Tryon Toy Makers & Wood Carvers.

"Stitchwell" sewing machine see *National Sewing Machine Co.*

Walter Stock A manufacturer based in Solingen, Germany, Walter Stock issued lithographed tin mechanical toys from 1905 into the 1930s. His toys are often compared to the products of the Lehmann Co. Stock also made penny toys, which were exported to America.

stockings see *Christmas stockings.*

Stoer Mfg. Co. The "De Do" toy drums of the 1930s were made by this St. Louis, Mo., company.

Frederick A. Stokes & Co. Stokes published paper dolls in the late 1890s.

Stoll & Edwards Co., Inc. Based on Fourth Avenue, New York City, Stoll & Edwards was an important game and toy book publisher. Its titles in the 1920s and early '30s included "The Game of Ting-A-Ling" in 1920; "Black Beauty" and "Game of Mother Goose" in 1921; "Defenders of the Flag" and "The Three Bears" in 1922; "Game of Alice in Wonderland," "Cinderella," and "Treasure Island" in 1923; "Adventures of Tom Sawyer and Huck Finn" in 1925; "The Boxing Game" in 1928; and "Game of Pegpin" in 1929.

Stoll & Einson Games, Inc. Based in the Fifth Avenue Building, New York City, Stoll & Einson, affiliated with Einson-Freeman, ranked among the more important prewar games manufacturers. It also produced scrapbooks, dollhouses, and novelties. Einson-Freeman made a line of cheaper toys and games in the ten- to 25-cent range, which were offered alongside the products of Stoll & Einson, which produced items in the 50-cent to dollar range. "Playjoy Books and Games" was a Stoll & Einson line. The executive office for the two companies was located in Long Island City, N.Y. Its game titles included "Treasure Island" in 1934 and "Dog Sweepstakes" in 1935.

"Stompin' Rocket" see *Rempel Mfg. Co.*

Arthur T. Stone & Co. Dart games and darts were the specialty of this Pleasant Ridge, Mich., company, established in the late 1930s.

Stone Knitting Mills Co. This Cleveland, Ohio, firm issued doll clothes in the late prewar years.

Stoner Corp. Based in Aurora, Ill., Stoner manufactured rocking horses, shooflies, "modernistic" juvenile furniture, and action games including the late 1930s "Ski-Ball."

stores, play Playing store was as typical an activity as playing house or playing doctor, at one time. In the prewar years, some manufacturers issued elaborate play sets that brought the scale of the play store down to dollhouse size. The store itself would often be made of tin, cardboard, or pressed board, with the store goods sometimes printed onto the walls and sometimes represented by loose, miniature packages, jars and bottles. Prewar manufacturers included Cincinnati Fly Screen Co., Durable Toy & Novelty Corp., V.M. Kearley Mfg. Co., the Metalcraft Corp., Patent Novelty Co., Playskool Institute, the F.L. Purdy Co., Rochester Folding Box Co., Wolverine Supply & Mfg. Co., and World Metal Stamping Co. Postwar manufacturers included Merry Mfg. Co. and Toymaster Products Co.

S

Stori-Views Based in St. Louis, Mo., Stori-Views was a Boomer-era manufacturer of three-dimensional pictures and viewers.

The Storkline Furniture Corp. This Chicago, Ill., manufacturer of juvenile furniture also made doll bassinets and play yard furnishings. In the late '30s, Storkline obtained license to issue Walt Disney character-related nursery furniture through Kay Kamen. The firm continued into the 1950s and '60s with a large line of nursery and juvenile furniture.

Story & Clark Piano Co. "Table Hockey," already popular in the 1930s, was produced by this Chicago, Ill., company. It also made "Hi-Jack" and "Scram" games before the war.

"Story Book Playmates" 1930s, see *American Made Toy Co.*

"Storytime" books see *Rand, McNally & Co.*

"Storytown U.S.A." see *Bachmann Bros., Inc.*

stoves Toy stoves of every variety were important household toys of the later 1800s and the length of the 20th century. Many of the earliest were made of cast iron. In the prewar years, tin and steel toy stoves appeared alongside the iron ones, with a number of them electrically heated and capable of cooking food.

Prewar manufacturers of non-electric stoves included Arcade Mfg. Co., the Dent Hardware Co., Grey Iron Casting Co., the Hubley Mfg. Co., the Kenton Hardware Co., the Kilgore Mfg. Co., George D. Roper Corp., the J. & E. Stevens Co., and Wolverine Supply & Mfg. Co.

Manufacturers of electric stoves included Aluminum Goods Mfg. Co., Kingston Products Corp., the Lionel Corp., the Metal Ware Corp., Standard Electric Stove Co., and Weeden Mfg. Co.

Both electric and non-electric toy stoves were manufactured in the Boomer years, with increasing amounts of plastic employed in their make-up. The main innovation of the period was the Kenner "Easy-Bake Oven" of 1964, which was advertised as a safe toy using only the heat generated by a light bulb. While a plugged-in electrical toy, it was largely made of plastic.

Other makers of electric toy stoves included the Metal Ware Corp., Structo Mfg. Co., and Wolverine. Non-electric toy stoves were issued by American Toy & Furniture Co., Educator Playthings, Grey Iron, Metal Ware, Ohio Art Co., Westred, and Wolverine.

Stox, Inc. This Chicago, Ill., firm made the "Stock Exchange" game for adults, released in the somewhat untimely year of 1929.

Straits Corp. The Straits Corp. of Detroit, Mich., issued children's items in metal, including early Disney-themed lamps and toy boats and airplanes through a Kay Kamen licensing agreement. Its toy lines in the 1930s included the "Sea Hawk" electric speed boats, "Little Giant" electric motors, and "Sky Hawk" stunt planes. By the late 1930s the company had changed its name to Straits Mfg. Co. Still issuing the "Sea Hawk," "Sky Hawk" and "Little Giant" lines, Straits also made "Weave Rite" looms, the "Pop Eye" knock-out bank, the "Peamatic" pistol, the "Silver Flash" streamline train, the "Mystery" auto racer, "Lassie" lamp, and "Big Box O' Toys."

Strand Mfg. Co. Toy chests, covered in decorative cloth, were the primary product of this St. Louis, Mo., company. It also issued a "Bean Game" in the 1930s.

Martin A. Strand Ski Co. This New Richmond, Wis., firm issued toboggans in addition to skis and skiing accessories in the late prewar years.

"Strand" puzzles prewar, see *Milton Bradley Co.*

"Strand's" toy chests see *Hazel Novelty & Cabinet Co.*

"Strat-O-Flier" box kites see *The Hi-Flier Mfg. Co.*

The Strathmore Co. The "Magic Slate Blackboard" was first issued by Aurora, Ill., printer R.A. Watkins and his firm, the Strath-

S

more Co., in the prewar years. By wartime, the toy came mounted on a wood board with stylus, with an alphabet panel above the "slate." Strathmore also issued "Peter Rabbit the Magician," which contained a variety of tricks. Another wartime toy, the "Roll-A-Plane," was a variation on the rolling hoop, using a solid wooden disk instead of the hoop. The disk had wooden "wings" emerging from each side, and was colorfully decorated with warplanes. Strathmore entered into a licensing agreement with Walt Disney by the end of the war. This gave "Magic Slate" the boost it needed to attract popular interest, which continued through the Boomer years. By the mid-1950s, besides the "Magic Slates" themselves, the company had sold over a million "Magic Slate Activity Books," which had such titles as "A Visit to the Magic Forest," "A Day at the Circus," and "A Trip to Mexico." The company became the Watkins-Strathmore Co. by the end of the 1960s. Its line consisted of coloring books, cutout books, activity books, boxed games, playing cards, and Christmas cards.

A variation on the rolling hoop, the "Roll-A-Plane" by Strathmore was a wartime toy.

"Strato-Jet" bicycle see *Midwest Industries.*

"Stratoblaster" repeating cap rifle see *Renwal Toy Corp.*

Joseph K. Straus Products Corp. Wood jigsaw puzzles comprised this postwar line. Straus was located in Brooklyn, N.Y.

Ferdinand Strauss Corp. Ferdinand Strauss established his toy manufacturing business in New York City in the early 1900s, becoming a major producer of tin mechanical toys in the years 1914 to 1927. See also *The Mechanical Toy Co., Ferdinand Strauss Toys.*

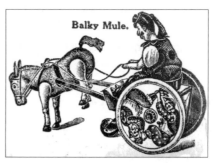

Balky Mule.

The "Balky Mule" toy by Ferdinand Strauss Corp.

Ferdinand Strauss Toys The Mechanical Toy Co., located 1107 Broadway, New York City, changed its name to Ferdinand Strauss Toys by the late 1930s. It manufactured mechanical and electrical toys, and the "Glidersport" gun-shooting airplanes and gliders.

Strauss-Eckardt Co., Inc. Based on East 17th Street, New York City, in the 1920s, '30s and '40s, this importer issued "Our Pet" dolls as well as a variety of favors and novelties, including Easter novelties.

"Strawberry Festival" dolls see *Nancy Ann Dressed Dolls.*

"Streak-O-Lite" coaster wagon see *Radio Steel & Mfg. Co.*

"Streamline" The notion of the technologically advanced "future" and the concept of the "futuristic" deeply impressed Americans in the later 1930s. One expression of this appeared in the widespread use of the words "streamline" and "streamlined" in toys that reflected contemporary engineers' concerns with the flow of air around moving objects. Playthings bearing the name were by no means always moving objects, however, as is indicated by the examples of Lawner-Martin Corp.'s "Streamlined" checkers. Other playthings of the late '30s included the "Streamline Express" game and "Streamline" puzzle by Milton Bradley Co.; "Streamline Klipper" sleds by C.J. Johnson Co.; "Streamliner" bagatelle game by Northwestern Products; and "Streamliner" sleds, velocipedes and wagons by Garton Toy Co. The new "streamline" trains, such as the Commodore Vanderbilt, enjoyed considerable popularity when they appeared in toy versions from Louis Marx &

S

Co. and Lionel Corp. The styling concern remained important into the postwar years.

"String-O-Blocks" see *Halsam Products Co.*

"String O' Cars" wooden train prewar, see *Holgate Bros. Co.*

W.A. Strohm & Bros. A Chicago, Ill., firm, W.A. Strohm & Bros. made prewar bicycles and bicycle supplies.

"Strolee" of California Based in Los Angeles, Calif., this postwar firm included doll strollers in its line.

"Strollette" carriage see *The Perfection Mfg. Co.*

Strombeck-Becker Mfg. Co. In the earlier 1930s, the Moline, Ill., company issued wooden doll house furniture, "American Fast Freight" wooden trains, auto carriers, trucks, field glasses, and educational toys. Later in the decade Strombeck-Becker introduced locomotive, airplane and boat assembly kits, and the famous "Bill Ding" clown blocks. Since it was using wood, the line continued unchanged in the war years, with artillery assembly kits added. During wartime, the company issued wooden "StromBecker Spotter Models" model kits. The firm continued through 1961 with a line of airplane and ship scale model assembly kits, powered racecars and tracks, small wooden "Playtrains" floor trains, "Bill Ding" balancing clown blocks, "Picture Makers" hexagonal plastic art blocks, educational toys, wooden doll furniture, and wooden dollhouse furniture. Strombeck-Becker used the "StromBecker" and "Strombecker" trade name before it was adopted by Dowst Mfg. Co. as company name.

Strombeck-Becker Mfg.'s floor train, "Wm. Galloway Locomotive."

The "Circus Train Take-Apart" by Strombeck-Becker, 1950s.

Strombecker Corp. In 1961, Dowst Mfg. Co. bought the toy division of Strombeck-Becker Mfg. Co. The resulting, enlarged company became Strombecker Corp. Although it did not abandon the manufacture of die-cast toy cars, a great deal of the company's energies went into the production of electrical car racing sets, which proved profitable until the later 1960s, when competition grew so severe that the company returned its primary focus to its original strength, manufacturing die-cast toy vehicles under the "Tootsietoy" trade name.

Structo Mfg. Co. Louis and Edward Strohacker and C.C. Thompson founded Structo Mfg. Co. in Freeport, Ill., in 1908, making construction kits similar to Meccano and A.C. Gilbert construction sets. These "Structo" models came in more than fifty sets, making everything from mechanical cranes to oil derricks. The sets included die-cast pulleys, gears and chain wheels, and nickel-plated rolled steel girders. The firm used a variety of slogans in the 1910s: "Highest in Quality, Greatest in Quantity"; "The Highest Class Educational Toy"; "Intelligent Boys Demand Structo"; and "Something More than a Toy." The slogan "Structo Toys Make Men of Boys" appeared as early as 1917, to be replaced by "Structo Toys for Girls and Boys" by 1920-21. The metal construction sets were sold under the "Structo Model Building Outfits" name, sometimes also with the "Empire Builders" name. The complete "Structo Model Building Outfits" line was sold to Meccano Co. in 1919.

Structo increasingly designed sets based on vehicle models, and started issuing the "Ready-Bilt" line of vehicle toys in 1920. Its early pressed-steel toy automobiles were based on the Stutz Bearcat. Perhaps most characteristic of the line, however, were the Belgian-style military tank and the farm tractor. The company simultaneously offered "Auto-Builder" toys, a line that may have started in the 1910s. It also started issuing "Artcraft" looms around this time.

*Structo's "Caterpillar Whippet Tank No. 48,"
1920s.*

Some of the line's success can be attributed to a distributing arrangement established with American Flyer Mfg. Co. in 1922, which allowed Structo to concentrate its energies on production.

Structo's line of toy vehicles gradually embraced trucks, steam shovels, riding toys, and airplanes, growing to over 30 items by the end of the 1920s. The company also made steel sand shovels. In the 1930s, Structo introduced more streamlined designs, and battery-powered headlights.

Structo in 1934 was advertising "Structo mechanical and pull toys, dump trucks, steam shovels, pumping fire engine, sand pile toys, tractors, electric lighted autos and trucks." The company was purchased in 1935 by J.G. Cokey. Its line of vehicle toys increased in variety through the late prewar years, with riding toys, moving vans, and "Hi-Way Transports" being added by the end of the decade. Its "practical" hand weaving looms also continued.

The firm prospered in the postwar years, introducing a line of toy trucks with die-cast cab-overs in the 1950s, some with wind-up motors. By the end of the decade its line included "Live-Action" steel, die-cast, and plastic toys; scale-model kitchen and laundry housekeeping toys, including an automatic washer-dryer; scale-model trucks; missile and space ship launchers; road-building toys; and ride-on-toys.

Structo divided these toys into "Steel Strong, Steel Sturdy Toys for Boys," "Little Miss Structo Electric Kitchen-Laundry Toys for Girls," and "Preschool Guidance Toys." The company also made barbecue equipment. The company introduced its "Kom-Pak" line of smaller trucks in 1964. On Cokey's death in 1975, Ertl Co. purchased the Structo toy line.

"Ready-Bilt Tractor," produced in the 1920s by Structo.

The "Telephone Truck" by Structo, 1950s.

Stuart, Inc. This postwar St. Paul, Minn., company issued stuffed toys and soft dolls.

Stuart Toy Mfg. Co. Miniature plastic cowboys, Indians, Indian scouts, army scouts, and horses comprised this 1950s and '60s line. Stuart Toy, based in Cincinnati, Ohio, also made science toys.

stuffed toy animals Stuffed toy animals, known in America from the early 19th century, undoubtedly enjoyed the same popularity they enjoyed through the length of the 20th century. Because of their easily damaged and aged materials, few such toys have survived.

Undoubtedly the number of 19th century manufacturers was large. Their ranks may have included some of the manufacturers still active in the 1920s, whose number included Louis Amberg & Son, American Made Toy Co., Atlantic Toy Mfg. Co., Atlas Toy Mfg. Corp., Continental Toy and Novelty Co., Dandy Toy & Novelty Co., Fleischaker & Baum, Gay Stuffed Toy & Novelty Co., Gerling Toy Co., Gund Mfg. Co., Ideal Novelty & Toy Co., Knickerbocker Toy Co., Live Long Toys, Mizpah Toy & Novelty Co., Myers' Woolly Animals, National French Fancy Novelty Co., the Nelke Corp., New York Stuffed Toy Co., Reiner Mfg. Co., Steinmann Toy Mfg. Co., and F.W. Woolnough Co.

S

Representative companies by the 1930s included Commonwealth Toy & Novelty Co., which specialized in stuffed toys made with genuine fur, with toy Scotty dogs a popular item. Gund was producing a wide variety of stuffed toys, including its "Gee" line of the 1920s and '30s of mechanical stuffed animals. Gay Stuffed Toy & Novelty advertised "attractive, colorful, carefully made, and lifelike … quality animals in a wide range of long and short pile plush, also velvet."

Other prewar manufacturers included American Doll & Novelty Co., American Made Toy Co., American Toy & Novelty Mfg. Co., American Toys, E.M. Annelots Co., Arts & Crafts Studio, Atlanta Playthings Co., Atlantic Toy Mfg. Co., Atlas Toy Mfg. Corp., William P. Beers Co., Beverly Mfg. Co., George Borgfeldt Corp., Character Novelty Co., Crawford Mfg. Co., and Dry-a-Line Co.

Others included Victor Eckardt Mfg. Co., Empire City Toy & Novelty Co., Ero Mfg. Co., H. & J. Toy Mfg. Co., M. Hardy, Harman Toy Co., J.S. Heyman, Irwin Novelty Co., Knickerbocker Toy Co., Leading Novelty Mfg. Co., Lucky Toy Co., Meth Novelty Co., Midway Novelty Co., Mizpah Toy & Novelty Corp., Moore Gibson Anchor Corp., New Art Toy & Feather Co., New York Stuffed Toy Co., Novelty Creations Co., Penn Handcraft Co., Perfect Novelties Mfg. Co., E.M. Robinson Toy Mfg. Co., Ross & Ross, the Rushton Co., S. &. H. Novelty Co., Scovell Novelty Mfg. Co., Margarete Steiff & Co., Tiny Tot Studio, Tucker Toys, Twinzy Toy Co., Winchester Toy Co., F.W. Woolnough Co., World Toy Mfg. Co., Zadek-Feldstein Co., and Zoo Novelty Co.

The number of firms making stuffed toys in the Boomer years was enormous. A sampling of major lines includes Artistic Toy Co., the "Braymer Prestige Line" by Braymer Stuffed Toys, Character Novelty Co., Columbia Toy Products, Elka Toys, Expert Doll & Toy Co., Gay Toys, the "Gunderful" line from Gund, Knickerbocker Toy Co., Lucky Toy Co., Master Industries, Picture Book Toys, the Rushton Co., Schwartz Toy Mfg. Corp., Softskin Toys, State Fair Toy & Novelty Co., and Stern Toy Co.

"Washable Easter Toys," by Jolly Toys, 1940s.

Sturdi-Bilt Model Aircraft This Portland, Ore., firm made model airplanes in the late 1930s.

The Sturditoy Co. This 1920s manufacturer, located in Pawtucket, R.I., manufactured heavy steel miniature trucks, and the "Lloyd Automatic Bowling Alleys."

"Sturditoys" children's furniture see *Clyan Hall Sturditoys Workshops.*

styled In farm toys, this generally refers to the tractors that appeared after the early, no-grille tractors, which are referred to as "unstyled." "Styled" is used especially of the tractors of the late 1930s possessing grilles.

"Sub-Bur-Banette" dollhouses see *Fibre-Bilt Toys.*

"Submarine Patrol" see *Thomas Mfg. Corp.*

"Suburban Pumper" fire engine see *Tonka Toys, Inc.*

Suburban Toy & Mfg. Corp. Dart guns were included in the postwar line of this Pittsburgh, Penn., firm. It also made batons, golf sets, baseball sets, and target games.

"Sue" dolls 1930s, see *E.I. Horsman Co., Inc.*

"Sulphides" These large marbles, usually more than an inch in diameter, were made of clear glass with white figures encased in the center, usually animals but also people and miscellaneous objects.

"Sun-Joy-Toy" line see *M. & S. Shillman.*

The Sun Rubber Co. Dolls' hot-water bottles, strangely enough, were the product that kept this rubber toy firm alive through the Great Depression. By the mid-1930s the Barberton, Ohio, company was firmly on its feet with its rubber doll line, which included dolls' nursing bottles, teething rings, bathroom accessories, and the rubber dolls themselves. Sun also made rubber doll play sets, sometimes sold in doll trunks, combining the baby dolls with various accessories. These including the interesting "Dolly's Playard" rubber doll & sand box combination. Sun Rubber made the first drink-and-wet dolls.

Sun Rubber added toy automobiles to its line by the end of the '30s. In the postwar years it initially offered toys indistinguishable from its prewar production. By the early 1950s, however, vinyl took increasing importance in its line.

Sun's line ended briefly in 1958-1960, due to financial difficulties, picking up again in 1960 and continuing until the plant was closed in 1974. In the 1950s and '60s the line included all-vinyl dolls, doll sets and cases, character toys, floating toys, squeeze toys, infant and teething toys, play balls, vinyl Walt Disney character toys, and athletic balls.

The doll line included the 18-inch "Bannister Baby," modeled after Constance Bannister baby photos; the 12-inch "Betty Bows"; and the 18-inch "Gerber Baby," by the mid-1950s. These vinyl dolls wet, cried, drank, slept, and came with bubble pipes for blowing bubbles.

Its dolls, many inspired by children's artist Ruth E. Newton, included "So-Wee," "Betty Bows," "Cindy Lee," "Baby Bee," "Sun-Dee," and "Sunny Tears," by 1960. Made of vinyl, some were for infants, and equipped with squeakers, while others were the more complex dolls.

"Sunbeam" bicycle headlights see *The Seiss Mfg. Co.*

"Sunken Letter" blocks see *Halsam Products Co.*

"Sunny Andy" The prewar "Sunny Andy" and "Sunny Suzy" toys and games were made by Wolverine Supply & Mfg. Co.

"Sunny Bear" teddy bear see *The Sun Rubber Co.*

"Sunny Circus" sand toys see *The Richardson Co.*

"Sunny Suzy" toys and games see *Wolverine Supply & Mfg. Co.*

"Sunny-Time" sand toys see *Wolverine Supply & Mfg. Co.*

Sunny Toys This postwar Chicago, Ill., company made floor toys, play clay, and tubular steel doll highchairs.

"The Sunshine Family" Introduced in 1974, Mattel's "The Sunshine Family" included mother and father dolls, "Stephie" and "Steve," measuring 7-1/2 and 9 inches tall, and baby "Sweets." The posable dolls were designed to depict a contemporary lifestyle family.

"Sunshine Play Line" 1930s, see *The Toledo Metal Wheel Co.*

"Super-Kit" series see *Monogram Models.*

"Super Nu-Matic Jr." paper buster gun see *Langson Mfg. Co.*

Superior Paper Box Co. A Chicago, Ill., firm, Superior Paper Box made "Boxville, the new Cardboard Erecting Set" of the late 1920s. The set included the typical village buildings of "Boxville" school, general store, garage, cottage, and church, lithographed in four colors and varnished.

The "Boxville School" by Superior Paper Box Co.

The Superior Type Co. In the 1920s, this Chicago, Ill., firm issued a variety of edu-

S

cational rubber printing toys, including "The Mammoth Circus," "Midget Circus," "Acrobatic Clowns," "Trained Animals," "Racers for Air, Land and Sea," "County Fair," "Buffalo Hunters," and "American Indians." In the 1930s and '40s the company emphasized its "StamperKraft" rubber printing toy outfits, as well various other printing presses and "outfits" for home and school use. It added the "Swiftset" rotary printing press to its line in the later '30s. The firm became Superior Marking Equipment Co. in the postwar years. It issued rubber printing toy outfits, toy rotary presses, sign printing outfits, and picture and comic strip printing sets.

Rubber stamp printing toy by The Superior Type Co., "The Mammoth Circus."

"Superior" products see *T. Cohn, Inc.*

Superior Toy & Mfg. Co. Based in Chicago, Ill., Superior issued banks in the postwar years, including mailbox and letter box banks, and "Diebold Jr." miniature combination safe banks. Its "Jupiter Rocket Bank" was a plastic, tail-standing rocket with trigger mechanism that shot coins in the nose cone, issued in the late 1950s and '60s.

Superior Toy & Novelty Co. Stuffed toys and novelties comprised this postwar Brooklyn, N.Y., firm's line.

"Superior" typewriter see *Berwin Corp.*

"Superjax" jackstones see *Grey Iron Casting Co.*

"Superman" This industrial-strength hero of both prewar and postwar eras first appeared in the first issue of Action Comics in 1938. Among the notable early playthings and premiums were movie viewers by Daisy Mfg. Co., including the "Cinematic Picture Pistol" and "Official Superman Krypto-Ray-gun" film viewer, both of 1940. Acme Toy Corp. issued "Superman" movie viewers in the Boomer years.

"Supermobiles" see *Lapin Products, Inc.*

"Sure Shot" glass marbles see *The Rosenthal Co.*

"Sure Shot" automatic pistol see *The Hubley Mfg. Co.*

"Surprise Dollies" see *Samuel Gabriel Sons & Co.*

surprise packages Although not usually considered a toy in and of itself, the surprise package was long considered an item of specialty manufacture by the toy industry. Many catalog and department stores advertised having their availability, suggestive of their popularity. Prewar manufacturers included American Toy Works, Kant Novelty Co., Makatoy Co., Jack Pressman & Co., Saalfield Publishing Co., Standard Toykraft Products, Transogram Co., and University Toy & Novelty Co.

Surre, Inc. This Erie, Penn., firm made the postwar "Teeter Pony," as well as bicycle accessories.

Suspended Railway System Toys Corp. Established in Richmond Hills, Long Island, N.Y., in the late 1930s, this firm issued the "Suspended Flyer" electric train.

"Susie-Q" jackstones see *Ohio Plastic Co.*

"Susy Goose" housecleaning sets see *Kiddie Brush & Toy Co.*

Marvin R. Suther Doll cribs, cradles and bassinets were made by this Concord, N.C., manufacturer in the 1930s and '40s.

I.S. Sutton & Sons One of many postwar Brooklyn, N.Y., specialists in stuffed dolls and animals, Sutton also made TV seats in animal shapes.

"Suzy Homemaker" homemaking toys see *DeLuxe Reading Corp.*

"Swan" juvenile furniture see *Holmquist-Swanson Co., The*

"Swans Down" cake mix sets see *Argo Industries Corp.*

Sweeney Lithograph Co., Inc. Sweeney, of Belleville, N.J., was a 1930s publisher and manufacturer of games, dolls, and books.

Swanson Products Co. This Chicago, Ill., firm issued Christmas tree lighting outfits and stands in the late prewar years.

Sweeney Lithograph Co., Inc. Based in Belleville, N.J., Sweeney made games, dolls and books in the later 1930s.

sweepers see *carpet sweepers, toy.*

E.A. Sweet Co., Inc. The "Easco" series of "Leather-Craft Kits" of the late 1930s were produced by this Binghamton, N.Y., manufacturer.

"Sweet Pea" doll see *Arranbee Doll Co.*

swimming While swimming is taken for granted as a play or serious activity today, in Colonial New England towns tithingmen were employed to prevent Puritan children from thus dithering away their time. Inevitably swimming toys arose as a means of enhancing childrens' pleasure at the beach or in the pool. Some were practical devices, such as the flippers made by Ayvad Water-Wings in the prewar years, while a good many others were straightforward toys, usually inflated. Other prewar manufacturers included American Playground Device Co., Collette Mfg. Co., Essex Rubber Co., the Fox Toy Co., Hill-Standard Corp., Hodgman Rubber Co., Miami Wood Products Co., the Moneco Co., and Seamless Rubber Co.

swings, baby Baby swings had the advantage of being slightly more confining than the shoofly, although they had the disadvantage of requiring slightly more adult involvement. Prewar manufacturers included the Delphos Bending Co., Hartman Mfg. Co., International Mfg. Co., Perfection Mfg. Co., the Frank F. Taylor Co., and Welsh-Hartman Co.

swings, doll Dolls typically required the same entertainment their supervising children did, giving rise to such fascinating baubles as doll roller skates. Doll swings sat halfway between toys for dolls and furniture for dolls. Prewar manufacturers included Danzi Toy Mfg. Co., the Perfection Mfg. Co., and Welsh-Hartman Co.

swings, lawn With growing middle-class affluence in the 1910s, pre-crash '20s and later '30s, many families were able to afford such relatively expensive items for their children as specially-made furniture, playhouses, and recreational equipment. Chief among outdoor items was the swing, often part of a "swing set" which included the swing in combination with other diversions, especially the slide. While the most distinctive swings and swing sets of the 20th century were strung from tube metal frameworks, many of the early sets were manufactured by firms specializing in wood products. Wood came firmly back in vogue in the later 20th century after largely disappearing in the Boomer years. Prewar manufacturers included American Playground Device Co., Birchcraft, Central Wood Products Inc., the Delphos Bending Co., Dixon-Prosser, Forest County Lumber Co., Gem Mfg. Corp., the Goshen Mfg. Co., Kiddie Gym, the Lehman Co. of America, Mid-West Metal Products Co., Neumann Mfg. Co., North Vernon Industries, Paris Mfg. Co., and Woodcraft Toy Mfrs.

Swiss Music Corp. Musical animated plush animals, musical toys, and novelties comprised the postwar line of this North Bergen, N.J., company.

"Swyngomatic Jr." doll swings see Jenkintown Steel Co.

Sykes Motor Co. Established in Lakewood, Ohio, in the late 1930s, Sykes made toy and model motor-driven boats, boat construction kits, and electric and outboard motors. It also issued a "sketching camera" for drawing.

S

Syncro Devices, Inc. This Detroit, Mich., firm issued toy electric power saws and miniature gasoline engines in the later 1930s.

Syndicate Products Co. Based on East 26th Street, New York City, Syndicate issued the "Invisible Color Print" painting books in the mid-1930s. It also produced games.

Syracuse Toycraft Co. Juvenile garden sets and snow shovels were the specialties of this postwar Syracuse, N.Y., company.

The 1950s "Wrecker Truck" by Structo Mfg. Co.

Standard Plastic Products made this Barbie and Ken doll case.

T.C.O. see *Tipp & Co.*

"T-Man" holsters and guns see *Service Mfg. Co., Inc.*

"TV Star" costumes see *Ben Cooper, Inc.*

tab-and-slot The term "tab-and-slot" applies to tin toys in which parts are mated by having tabs on one piece fold into slots in the other. Often a point of weakness in tin toys, the tabs can be brittle and may break when restoration is attempted.

table tennis A game with great popularity in prewar times, table tennis sets and tables were manufactured by some of the leading names in the toy industry, including Milton Bradley Co., Marks Bros. Co., Jac Pressman, Selchow & Righter, and Transogram Co. Even the A. Schoenhut Co. made tables for the game. Other early manufacturers of the sets included Arrow Specialty Co., Artcraft Mfg. Co., P. Becker & Co., Chicago Table Tennis Co., Durabilt Steel Locker Co., General Sportcraft Co., C.A. Handy, Harvard Mfg. Co., Harry C. Lee & Co., Master Woodworkers, William Rott, Louis Sametz, Henry H. Sheip Mfg. Co., and Westminster Sports. Under the guise of "Ping Pong," the Carrom Co. and Parker Bros. also made the game.

Table Tennis Corp. of America This Union City, N.J., manufacturer of table tennis tables, sets and equipment was founded in the late 1930s.

Tactical Game Co. The "Tactical" baseball and football games of the 1930s appeared from this Chicago, Ill., company, a division of McIlvaine Burner Corp.

tag A venerable game, tag was played in the American colonies.

Taglioni, Marie In the 1840s, popular paper dolls based on this famous ballerina were imported from Europe.

Tailored Craft Novelty Co. This West 26th Street, New York City, firm made the 1930s "Kute Klothes" line of doll dresses, coats and hats. It also made doll carriage covers and pillow sets.

tails, animal Animal tails were no doubt early playthings for American children. The popularity of tails as playthings was either established or re-established enough in the years after the Great Depression to encourage manufacturers to issue fur tails, whether real or imitation, for use as decorations on hats and juvenile vehicles. The popularity of coonskin caps in the 1950s, in response to the incredible popularity of Walt Disney's "Davy Crockett" TV episodes and subsequent movie, greatly expanded the popularity of such items. Prewar manufacturers included Charles Brand.

"Tailspin Tommy" A few manufacturers took advantage of the popularity of the "Tailspin Tommy" cartoon figure, including McLoughlin Bros., who issued paint and crayon books in the 1930s. Fisher-Price Toys made wood toys late in the decade.

Takapart Products Co. The "Takapart" tennis table of the late 1930s was made by this East 32nd Street, New York City, firm.

Talbot Mfg. Co. Toy handcuffs, badges, police sets, sparklers, and electric games were postwar specialties of this Mattapan, Mass., company.

"Tales of Wells Fargo" see *"Wells Fargo."*

talking boards The "talking boards" include such "mystical" board games as

"Ouija" and "Oracle." These games came to first prominence in the late 1800s, when spiritualism was popular in both America and Europe.

Talking Devices Co. This Chicago, Ill., company made phonographs, records, talking toy telephones, and talking doll units for other manufacturers, in the 1950s and '60s.

"Talking Plaphone" see *The Gong Bell Mfg. Co.*

"Tamby Toy" rubber toys prewar, see *Maxwell Rubber Products Corp.*

The H.H. Tammen Co. The "Skookum" Indian dolls popular in the 1930s and '40s were part of a line of leather and felt novelties and souvenirs. Tammen was based in Denver, Colo.

"Tammy" Ideal Novelty & Toy Co. introduced the "Tammy" line in in 1962. The "Tammy" look was less sophisticated and younger than the look of the Mattel "Barbie" line. Other characters in Ideal's line included "Bud," "Dodi," "Misty," "Patti," "Pepper," and "Ted."

Tamor Plastic Corp. Plastic children's dresser sets and novelty toys were postwar specialties of this Leominster, Mass., company.

"Tamworth Toys" see *South Tamworth Industries, Inc.*

"Tandem" bicycles see *The Colson Co.*

Tangle Wood Toys, Inc. Tangle Wood Toys of Portland, Ore., made building blocks, including the 1930s "Wood Lock" blocks, as well as playhouses and surfboards.

The Taplin Mfg. Co. A New Britain, Conn., firm, Taplin made toy egg beaters and beater-and-bowl sets from the 1930s through the Boomer years.

tapping sets see *metal tapping.*

Target Co. The "Target" card game of the late 1930s was made by this New Britain, Conn., company.

"Targeteer" see *Daisy Mfg. Co.*

Sidney A. Tarrson, Inc. Banks, stuffed toys, puppets, games, and a "bubble gum baton" were Boomer-era specialties of this Chicago, Ill., company. In the early 1950s one of its bubble-gum containers was a plastic toy truck.

"Tarzan" A popular figure among children whose adventures were read first as magazine serials and then in a long series of hardcover books, Tarzan was a familiar figure in games and toys from the prewar years through the Boomer era. Playthings of the earlier '30s included archery sets by the Archers Co., card games and books by Whitman Publishing Co., paint books and puzzles by Saalfield Publishing Co., puzzles by the Einson-Freeman Co, and rubber toys by Barr Rubber Products. Late '30s items included juvenile jewelry by President Novelty & Jewelry Co. In the Boomer years, Whitman continued issuing books. Hollywood Film Enterprises issued toy "Tarzan of the Apes" films.

taws Taws were marbles made of pink marble with dark red veins, also called blood alleys or alleys.

"Taxicab" all-steel coaster wagons see *Garton Toy Co.*

"Taxiplane" see *Kingsbury Mfg. Co.*

Taylor Bros. Mfg. Co. This prewar pedal car manufacturer was based in St. Louis, Mo.

The Frank F. Taylor Co. The "Taylor-Tots" line from the Frank F. Taylor Co. of Cincinnati, Ohio, enjoyed a high profile in both prewar and Boomer periods. A deluxe version of the baby stroller, the "Taylor-Tot" was a metal and wood device with enclosed seat, handle that allowed steering, and parent-level handle in the back for pushing. In the late 1920s, Taylor issued five models of these, including a "Sleeper Model" with a reclining back.

The company's 1920s line also included the "Taylor Infanseat," which combined high chair, toilet seat, baby swing, and auto seat in one unit, the tubular-construction "Taylor Sidewalk Cycle," and "Taylor Velocipedes." The company also made folding carriages and baby swings.

Despite widespread imitation, the company's product remained popular through the 1930s and '40s. "The 'Taylor-Tot' alone has a soul—has become a household word with the mothers of this country," its manufacturer boasted.

The Boomer years saw continued popularity of what was now referred to as "Genuine Taylor Tot Baby Walker-Strollers." The company also continued its lines of baby jumpers, high chairs, playpens, and velocipedes.

The "Taylor-Tot" baby walker by The Frank F. Taylor Co.

Taylor Trading Co. This postwar White Lake, Wis., birdhouse manufacturer also made log cabin playhouses.

Taylor Wyman Co. Hobbyhorses and novelties were included in this Westminster, S.C., playground equipment manufacturer's postwar line.

tea sets An important toy through the 19th and 20th centuries through the postwar years, tea sets served a vital role in playing house for many children. Early sets dating to Colonial times were made from pewter and doubtless other materials. Common materials in the 19th and 20th centuries included tin, aluminum, glass, china, and plastic.

In the years before the Great Depression, manufacturers included George H. Bowman Co., Langfelder, Homma & Hayward, Morimura Bros., and Wolverine Supply & Mfg. Co.

By the late Depression years, they included Akro Agate Co., Aluminum Goods Mfg. Co., Aluminum Specialty Co., T. Cohn, Dowst Mfg. Co., L.J. Houze Convex Glass Co., Ohio Art Co., the Richardson Co., the Salem China Co., Transogram Co., Washington Toys & Novelties, and Wolverine.

In the postwar years, manufacturers of metal sets included Aluminum Specialty Co., Mirro Aluminum Co., Ohio Art, and Wolverine.

Plastic became the most popular material for these toys by the late 1950s and early '60s. Manufacturers included Aluminum Specialty Co., Banner Plastics Corp., Dell Plastics Co., E. & L. Mfg. Co., Gotham Industries, Ideal Toy Corp., Irwin Corp., Henry Katz, Lido Toy Corp., the Ohio Art Co., Rel Mfg. Corp., Tucker Products Corp., and Worcester Toy Co.

"Teach-A-Tot" toys see *Holgate Bros. Co.*

The Tec-Toy Co. A Charleston, S.C., firm, Tec-Toy made prewar wooden toys including guns, pistols, and construction sets.

Technical Ventures co. The "Blue Chip" stock market game of 1960 was issued by this Detroit, Mich., company.

Tedco, Inc. Game boards comprised this postwar Houston, Texas, firm's line.

teddy bear Some prewar toys included "Teddy the Bear Cub" stuffed toy by Winchester Toy Co., 1930s.

"Teddy Bike" 1930s, see *United-Delta Corp.*

"Teddy" cap pistol see *Kenton Hardware Co., The*

"Teddy's Horse" see *spring horse.*

Tedsco Plastics, Inc. This Phoenix, Ariz., company issued the compression-molded "Plasti-Kar" toy car in the later 1940s and early '50s.

Tee-Vee Toys, Inc. Based in Leominster, Mass., in the 1950s-60s, Tee-Vee made miniature fishing games, plastic pull toys, and plastic-plated Christmas ornaments. It also made "Howdy Doody" plastic figures in the 1950s.

"Teenie Weenies" see *Amberg Dolls.*

Teepe-Whitney Corp. A manufacturer of prewar juvenile furniture, including rockers, Teepe-Whitney was located in Long Island City, N.Y. in the earlier '30s. It moved to Lexington Avenue, New York City, by the late '30s.

T

teeter-totters see *playground and play-room equipment.*

teeters "Teeters" was a prewar term for tee-ter-totters. Similar word formations were used in trade names, as in the "Baby Teeter" exer-ciser from the Republic Tool Products Co.

"Teeter-Pony" This exerciser was issued in the prewar years by Toledo Metal Wheel Co. In the 1950s and '60s, both McCauley Metal Products and Surre made toys with the "Teeter Pony" name.

"Teeter Tots" see *Patent Novelty Co., Inc.*

"Teetertoy" shooflies see *The Del-phos Bending Co.*

teethers Rings or other similarly shaped items made of ivory, silver, plastic or other stable material, used as a toy infants can "teeth" with. Some teethers are combined with rattles. Also called teething rings, or, in the 1800s, simply "teethings."

teethings see *teethers.*

Teknoplast Co. Soft plastic snakes and lizards were the specialties of this 1950s-60s Los Angeles, Calif., company.

telegraph and wireless sets Tele-graph toys became common by the late 1930s. One manufacturer was Elkay Mfg. Co., which issued "Postal Telegraph Junior" sets. A specialist in electronic communica-tions toys, it also offered toy "Communica-tors," which were akin to inter-office intercom systems. Other manufacturers included M.M. Fleron & Son, A.C. Gilbert Co., Lewis & Scott Mfg. Co., Mack Special-ties, S.B. Mfg. Co., and Signal Electric Mfg. Co. Despite the changes of World War II and the TV years, telegraph toys remained avail-able to Boomer children. Manufacturers included Brumberger Sales Corp., Elkay, Keystone Ferrule & Nut Co., Playmore, and Toytronic Development Co.

telephones, toy Telephones as a means of communication became commonplace by the early 20th century, creating a demand among children for toy versions.

Readily compliant manufacturers included the Brinkman Engineering Co., Gong Bell Mfg. Co., and N.N. Hill Brass Co. in the pre-Great Depression years.

By the late Depression years, the leading firms were Connecticut Telephone & Electric Corp., S.H. Couch Co., the Dayton Toy & Specialty Co., Forster Mfg. Corp., Gong Bell, N.N. Hill Brass, the Steel Stamping Co., and Toy-In-Action Corp.

An example of the best kind of telephone toy, however, was produced by American Auto-matic Electric Sales Co. With its "Real-Phones" of the 1930s it put into the hands of children pairs of desk telephones strung together by wire. "They look and handle just like real telephones," the company's ads promised "And they `talk up'—crisp and clear." The company also made the "Official Boy Scout Field Set," which was a field tele-graph unit with telephone handset.

Electrical and battery-operated toy telephone sets became more common in the Boomer years, with manufacturers including Brum-berger Sales Corp., Playmore, Remco Indus-tries, and Toytronic Development Co.

Manufacturers of the more traditional toy telephones included Adams Plastic Products, Amerline, Gong Bell Mfg. Co., Handi-Craft Co., N.N. Hill Brass, Ideal Toy Corp., Henry Katz, Metal Masters Co., Playmore, Sifo Co., Steel Stamping, Talking Devices Co., and Worcester Toy Co.

An early Disney-licensed item, N.N. Hill Brass Co.'s "Coin Bank French Telephone."

telescopes, toy Simple telescope toys have been popular in and of themselves through the years, and have also served as stock items for sailor costumes. Prewar manufacturers included Goetz Gans & Orenstein, Melrose Novelty Co., Rich Illinois Mfg. Co., Special Products Co., Trojan Sporting Goods Co., and Wollensak Optical Co.

"Television Telephone" The excitement created by the popular debut of early television technology in connection with the 1939 New York World's Fair was apparent in the immediate release of two "Television Telephone" toys, one by Louis Marx & Co. and one by Steel Stamping Co.

"Tell-A-Tale" books see *Whitman Publishing Co.*

"Tell It to the Judge" game 1959, see *Parker Bros., Inc.*

Tempest Mfg. Co. A Philadelphia, Penn., company, Tempest made darts, dart games and tennis tables in the late prewar years.

The Temple of Fancy "The Temple of Fancy" was a commonly used name for toy stores in England. The name was used by George Doll for his 1837 Philadelphia toy store.

Templeton, Kenly & Co. A Chicago, Ill., manufacturer, Templeton, Kenly & Co. had the interesting prewar toy specialty of miniature lifting jacks, possibly issued as a pedal car accessory.

Templeton Wood Products Co. Established in Brattleboro, Vt., in the late 1930s, Templeton made play yards and children's maple furniture.

"Tenite" see *Tennessee Eastman Corp.*

Tennessee Eastman Corp. In 1930, the Tennessee Eastman Corp. began producing cellulose nitrate to compete with the Celanese Corp. of America, to provide Eastman Kodak with photographic film. In 1932, it developed the first cellulose acetate molding material capable of compression, extrusion, and injection molding. The new plastic was called "Tenite." Celanese Corp. responded with a version called "Lumarith." Both cellulose acetates were important in toy manufacturing, especially in the late 1940s and early 1950s. Bergen Toy & Novelty Co. and Breyer Molding Co. were among the firms using "Tenite."

Tennessee Red Cedar & Novelty Co. This 1920s manufacturer of juvenile furniture, based in Chattanooga, Tenn., emphasized juvenile desk sets, cedar chests, and table and chair sets. The firm continued through the prewar years.

tenpins Although by the 1950s and '60s the game became generally regarded as "bowling" games, in the prewar years the venerable "tenpins" remained a game category of its own. Earlier manufacturers may well have included the majority of woodturners. By the late Depression years, manufacturers who formally produced the game included Banton Bros., Bogert & Hopper, Milton Bradley Co., the N.D. Cass Co., Newton & Thompson Mfg. Co., Parker Bros., Jack Pressman & Co., Thompson & Fox, and Transogram Co. By the late prewar years, manufacturers joining their ranks included Artwood Toy Mfg. Co., Brodhaven Mfg. Co., Buffalo Toy & Tool Works, Johnson Store Equipment Co., and Roy Bros.

Tern-Rite Mfg. Co. The "Tern-Rite" roller skates of the late 1930s were made by this Riverside, N.J., company.

"Terraplane" coaster wagon see *Garton Toy Co.*

Terre Town Toy Tradesmen Based in Terre Haute, Ind., this firm made prewar playhouses, doll houses, and toy house and garage sets.

Terri Lee Sales Corp. This Apple Valley, Calif., firm issued dolls in the 1950s "Terri Lee Nursery" line, including "Connie Lynn," a 20-inch "sleepy" baby, and "Linda Baby," sold as "Terri's Baby Sister." The "Terri Lee Walker" was a stroller device to make the dolls "walk" with the child.

"Terri Lee Doll Walker," 1950s.

"Terror" pistols see *The Dent Hardware Co.*

"Terry Hustler" toys see *Hustler Toy Corp.*

"Terrytoon" The CBS Films animated "Terrytoon" characters included Mighty Mouse, Heckle and Jeckle, Tom Terrific, and Mighty Manfred. "Terrytoon" playthings in the 1950s and '60s included dart and skill games by Bar Zim Toy Mfg. Co., and squeeze toys by Bayshore Industries.

The Testor Corp. This postwar Rockford, Ill., company specialized in toy airplanes, model airplane engines, and paint-by-number kits.

Testrite Instrument Co. This East 11th Street, New York City, firm made microscopes, optical sets, and magnetic compasses in the late 1930s, when scientific sets in general were enjoying widespread popularity.

tetherball A popular piece of playground equipment by the mid-20th century, tetherball involved a tall pole, rooted in the ground or anchored to a heavy base weight, with a soccer ball or volleyball tethered to its top. Players stood on opposite sides of the pole, facing the same direction, and hit the ball with their hands.

tether tennis In the tether tennis game, the tennis ball is suspended by a string from a well-anchored pole. Players stand on opposite sides of the pole, facing the same direction.

Tex Tan, Inc. The "Texas Ranger" holster sets of the 1950s-60s were produced by this Yoakum, Texas, company.

"Texaco" tanker truck see *Buddy "L" Mfg., Buddy "L" Corp.*

"Texan" pistol 1930s, see *The Dent Hardware Co.*

"The Texan" plastic figure see *Hartland Plastics.*

"Texan" holster set see *J. Halpern Co.*

"Texan Jr." repeating cap pistol see *The Hubley Mfg. Co.*

"Texas Sheriff" holsters see *Mount Vernon Mfg. Co.*

"Texas Star Ranger" see *Leslie-Henry Co., Inc.*

"Texas TV Rancher" sets see *Stuart Toy Mfg. Co.*

Texcraft Toy Products, Inc. Crayon sets were the specialty of this prewar West Broadway, New York City, firm. Texcraft was issuing drawing devices by the later 1930s.

Textile Rubber Co. An Akron, Ohio, firm, Textile Rubber made rubber toys and rubber parts for the manufacture of wheel goods in the late 1930s.

S. Thanhauser A Philadelphia, Penn., company, S. Thanhauser made toy-filled and unfilled Christmas stockings from the late Great Depression years through the Boomer era. By 1960 the stockings were priced from 59 cents to $5.00.

Thayer Co. Thayer Co., successors to J.A. Dickerman Co., issued baby carriages, beach carts and walkers, children's rockers, and doll carriages from the late 1930s. The firm continued through the Boomer years with a line that also included doll furniture.

H.N. Thayer Co. A prewar fiber furniture and baby carriage manufacturer based in Erie, Penn., H.N. Thayer also made mid-1930s doll carts and carriages.

theaters, toy and doll Toy theaters gave children a chance to recreate the theater experience in miniature, much as miniature stores gave setting to imaginary shopping experiences, or dollhouses, to imaginary homemaking experiences. Prewar manufacturers included Alexander Doll Co., O.B. Andrews Co., Lindstrom Doll & Toy Co., Ozan Products Co., Playskool Institute, and Vista Toy Co.

thermoplastics Plastics that can be remelted and remolded, including cellulose nitrates (1869), cellulose acetates (1911), cellulose acetate butyrates (1938), the vinyls (1927), acrylics (1931), polystyrenes (1937), nylons (1940), and the polyethylenes (1943).

Plastic toys are almost wholly made from thermoplastics.

thermosetting plastics Plastics set or cured by heat, which cannot be remelted. Include phenolics (1909), ureas (1929), melamines (1939) and polyesters (1941).

"They Look Real," slogan see *Arcade Mfg. Co.*

"Thimble Drome" see *L.M. Cox Mfg. Co.*

"Thingmakers" The "Thingmakers" line by Mattel were casting sets using liquid plastics instead of metal for the casting material. Introduced in the mid-1960s, the kits included "Creepy Crawlers," "Creeple Peeple," and "Fun Flowers." The liquid plastic was called "Plastigoop."

Thomas, Isaiah Isaiah Thomas of Worcester, Mass., was early America's largest publisher. His output in the 1700s included numerous children's books, advertised as "play books," including *Goody Two Shoes* and *The House That Jack Built.*

Thomas & Skinner Steel Products Co. The "Disappearing cost defense gun" toy of the late 1930s was issued by this Indianapolis, Ind., company.

Thomas Industries This postwar Shawnee, Okla., company issued "O" and "HO" gauge trains.

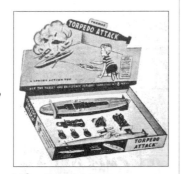

Thomas Mfg. Corp.'s "Torpedo Attack," 1950s.

Thomas Mfg. Corp. One of the more notable manufacturers of plastic toys in the 1950s and '60s, Thomas issued toy cars, airplanes, trucks, small dolls, boats, and animals. It was based in Newark, N.J.

Peter G. Thompson This Cincinnati, Ohio, publisher issued games including "Verborum" in 1883, "Historical Cards" and "Game of Mythology" in 1884, and "Anagrams" in 1885. The firm also issued paper dolls in the 1870s and '80s.

Thompson & Fox A wood-turning company in Skowhegan, Maine, Thompson & Fox made croquet sets and toy tenpins by the late years of the Great Depression. See *Thompson Mfg. Co.*

O.E. Thompson & Sons This Ypsilanti, Mich. company made coaster wagons and wheelbarrows in the 1930s and '40s. The firm's "Rolls Racer Corp." division was discontinued by the end of the '30s, although the products were still manufactured.

E.L. Thompson Chair Corp. A manufacturer of prewar wooden play sets, this Baldwinville, Mass., firm specialized in juvenile furniture, especially Windsor and upholstered chairs for children. By the late 1930s Thompson was emphasizing its specialty of "all types standard and combination high chairs."

Thompson Co. This firm's "Zoom-Lite" hand-held flashlight projector of the early 1960s was based on the kaleidoscope concept. Thompson was based in Binghamton, N.Y.

Thompson Mfg. Co. This Skowhegan, Maine, firm specialized in croquet sets, tenpins, ring toss games, and automatic turnings for toy parts in the late 1930s. See *Thompson & Fox.*

The Thompson Mfg. Co. Sand mould sets, rattles, whistles, tin ice cream spoons and tin candy dishes were among the metalstamping products of this Baltimore, Md., firm in the 1930s and '40s.

Thompson Toy Co. This postwar Chicago, Ill., company issued games and toys for children and adults, including the "Trickee Track" game.

Thorens, Inc. Established on West 34th Street, New York City, in the late 1930s, Thorens made music boxes and musical novelties.

Thornecraft, Inc. The "Goo Goo" doll of the 1930s was made by this Chicago, Ill., company. Thornecraft also made the "Jigger" dancing man, "Zingo" toy airplane, puzzles, "Speed-Scout" powered speedboat kits, and "Racing-Craft" sailboat kits.

Thornes, Inc. Located on Fourth Avenue, New York City, Thorens was already the world's largest manufacturer of "Swiss" music works in the 1920s. The company made music works for doll and toy manufacturers, and "Toy Phonos."

"Three Bears" see *"Goldilocks and the Three Bears."*

"The Three Little Pigs" The Three Little Pigs and the Big Bad Wolf enjoyed enormous popularity in the 1930s. Their success was certainly reflected in the number of playthings available by mid-decade: balloons by Oak Rubber Co., books by the Saalfield Publishing Co., briefcases by Standard Brief Case Co., costumes by Wornova Mfg. Co., costumes and masks by Sackman Bros., composition dolls by Alexander Doll Co., games by Parker Bros., the Einson-Freeman Co., and Kenilworth Press, masks by Einson-Freeman, playing cards by Whitman Publishing Co., pop-up books by Blue-Ribbon Books, rubber toys by Seiberling Latex Products, sand toys, tea sets and metal toys by Ohio Art Co., stamping sets by Fulton Specialty Co., soap by Kerk Guild, stuffed toys by George Borgfeldt, Richard G. Krueger, the Illfelder Corp., Gund Mfg. Co., and Kinckerbocker Toy Co., and wooden toys by the Toy Kraft Co. Zell Products made the "Three Little Pigs House of Coins" bank, and Gong Bell Mfg. Co. made "Three Pigs" chimes.

Two games entitled "Who's Afraid of the Big Bad Wolf" were issued, one by Parker Bros., and one by the Einson-Freeman Co.

By the late prewar years, playthings still being released included lines by Seiberling Latex Products Co., Kerk Guild, Fulton Specialty Co., Richard G. Krueger, Knickerbocker Toy Co., and Parker Bros.

"Three Little Pigs" items in the postwar years included a game by Selchow & Righter, and coloring book by the Saalfield Publishing Co.

"3M" see *Minnesota Mining & Mfg. Co.*

"Three Stooges" Ideal Novelty & Toy Co. issued "Three Stooges" hand-glove dolls in the late 1930s. Rights were controlled by Mitchell J. Hamilburg, and by H.G. Saperstein & Associates in the Boomer years. Toys in the 1950s and '60s included bop bags by Ideal Toy Corp., fingertip puppets by Wilkening Mfg. Co., re-color books by Fun Bilt Toys, and "Three Stooges Slap-Stick-On" sets by Colorforms. The "Three Stooges Fun House Game" was issued in the 1950s and early '60s by Lowell Toy Mfg. Corp.

Thrift Novelty Co. A Denver, Colo., company, Thrift issued Boomer-era souvenir toys, including western and Indian items.

"Thrifty, the Wise Pig," bank see the *Hubley Mfg. Co.*

"Thriller" series puzzles see *The Einson-Freeman Co.*

"Thriller" wheel toys see *Rainey Mfg. Co.*

"Thunderbird" wagon see *United Specialties of Birmingham, Inc.*

"Thunderburp" gun see *Mattel, Inc.*

"Thunderer" electric train see *American Flyer Mfg. Co.*

"Thunderjet" bicycles see *Chain Bike Corp.*

Tibbetts Industries Banks and games comprised this postwar line. Tibbetts was based in Camden, Maine.

tick-tack The introduction of this colonial game, similar to backgammon, is attributed to the Dutch.

"Tickle-Bee" game see *W.H. Schaper Mfg. Co., Inc.*

"Tickletoes" see *Ideal Novelty & Toy Co.*

Tico-Toys, Inc. Plastic toys, novelties, and games were postwar products of this Pawtucket, R.I., firm.

"Tiddledy Golf" game see *Milton Bradley Co.*

Tienken Tree & Novelty Corp. While artificial Christmas trees are widely seen as a postwar phenomenon, they were gaining in popularity in the 1930s. Tienken established itself in this niche in the earlier '30s.

Tigrett Industries, Inc. Besides sporting goods, Tigrett of Jackson, Tenn., made infant furniture and toys, in the postwar years.

Tigrett Industries' "Batter Up" baseball set.

Tilley & Sherman Based on Broadway, New York City, Tilley & Sherman issued the 1934 "Are You a Sacred Cow?" game, billed as "Colonel Stoopnagle & Budd's game."

Tillicum Sales Corp. Based in Tacoma, Wash., Tillicum maintained offices in the Fifth Avenue Building in the early 1930s. A manufacturer of wooden pull toys, it is best known for its wooden boats. It issued a wood battleship, which retailed at 50 cents, and a "Tillicum Battle Fleet," at one dollar. Milton Bradley Co. bought the line and gave it prominence in wartime, when both the subject matter and the materials were appropriate to the times.

"Tillicum Battle Fleet," 1930s boat toys.

Tillotson Rubber Co. Based in Needham Heights, Mass., Tillotson specialized in latex balls, toys, and balloons in the 1950s and '60s. It used the "Tilly Toys" trade name.

Tim-Mee Toys, Inc. Based in Aurora, Ill., Tim-Mee made molded polyethylene figure and vehicle toys in the 1950s and '60s, including cowboys, Indians, horses, army men, pirates, dogs, dinosaurs, clowns, and military vehicles.

"Timber-Tots" Henry Pilcher's Sons used the "Timber-Tots" trade name for its building blocks, and "Timber-Toys" for its wooden toys, in the 1930s.

"Time" puzzles prewar, see *Milton Bradley Co.*

Timely Toys, Inc. Plush stuffed toys were specialties of this postwar Brooklyn, N.Y., company.

tin drums see *drums, toy.*

tin-litho The term "tin-litho" is frequently used by toy collectors. It refers to the process introduced to toy manufacturing in the 1880s, in which flat sheets of metal received colors and detail by lithographic methods. These sheets were then formed by tools and dies.

tin toys Tin was a prized commodity in the 1600s and 1700s in America, since tin plate was available only through import until tin was discovered in North America in the 1800s. By the 1830s-'40s, the metal began to be found in enough quantities to be used for more casual items, including playthings. Early tin toys included toy pails, dishes, and drums. The first major manufacturer may have been Philadelphia Tin Toy Manufactory. Prewar companies specializing in tin toys included J. Chein & Co., Clark Toy Mfg. Co., T. Cohn, the Gibbs Mfg. Co., Gothan Pressed Steel Corp., Keller Toy Mfg. Co., the Lindstrom Tool & Toy Co., Louis Marx & Co., Ohio Art Co., Pavick's Mfg. Co., Richmond Bros. Co., the Tyler Can Co., and World Metal Stamping Co.

Tin became a decreasingly useful material for toy manufacturers through the Boomer years. By around 1960 only a few companies still employed it, including Bar Zim Toy Co. and Ohio Art.

"Ring-a-Ling Circus," tin toy by Louis Marx & Co., 1920s.

Tin toy "Rap-a-Tap" by Marx.

"Tinkertoy" toys and sets see *The Toy Tinkers, Inc.*

Tinkle Toy Co. Rattles, plastic toys, and squeeze toys comprised this postwar Youngstown, Ohio, line.

tinmen's furniture An 1800s phrase, "tinmen's furniture" referred to what was then probably the most common form of toy or dollhouse furniture.

tinware manufacturers In the 19th century, before manufacturers specializing in toys became more commonplace, tinware manufacturers were among the main American toy-makers of the time, along with turners and potters.

"Tiny Baby" dolls see *E.I. Horsman Co., Inc..*

"Tiny Tot" A widely used prewar trade name, "Tiny Tot" was the name given to at least two prewar lines of coaster wagons, one by the Globe Co. and another by Auto-Wheel Coaster Co. The name was also used for non-wheel goods, as in the "Tiny Tot" sand box by Hill-Standard Corp., "Tiny Tot" laundry set by Buffalo Toy & Tool Works, and the "Tiny-Tots" indoor swings by North Vernon Industries. In the postwar years, the name was used on toy boats by United Mask &

Novelty Co., blocks by Greyshaw of Georgia, educational wooden toys by Jaymar Specialty Co., rollerskates by Moen & Patton, and stuffed toys by Gund Mfg. Co. The "Tiny Tots" dolls were made by Manomatic Novelty Corp., and "Tiny Tots" puzzles, by Milton Bradley Co.

Tiny Tot Studio A Hartford, Conn., firm, Tiny Tot Studio made print and percale soft toys, hand-painted and hand-finished dolls, and novelties in the 1930s and '40s.

Tiny-Tot Toy Co. A Kansas City, Mo., company operating in the 1930s, Tiny-Tot made pewter toy automobiles.

"Tiny Town" doctor and nurse kits see *Peerless Playthings Co., Inc.*

"Tiny Vogue" patterns see *The Conde Nast Publications, Inc.*

"Tip Top Elf" books see *Rand, McNally & Co.*

"Tip Top Series" card games prewar, see *Milton Bradley Co.*

Tipp & Co. A firm founded in 1912 in Nuremberg, Germany, Tipp & Co. manufactured a line of military-oriented tin toys until 1971.

"Tippee Toes" A 17-inch doll that moved its legs to ride an accessory Hobby horse or tricycle, "Tippee Toes" was issued 1968-70 by Mattel.

tires see *rubber tires, metal wheels.*

Tissue Paper Products Co. This Allegan, Mich., firm issued paper kites in the late 1930s.

tithingmen In colonial New England, towns employed tithingmen, whose official roles included the suppression of play. Acting as combined police/truant officers, they were responsible for the morals, deeds, and thoughts of ten families each. One duty involved keeping boys from wasting time swimming.

"To Keep Busy the Little Hands and the Little Head," trademark see *Samuel Gabriel Sons & Co.*

Tober Sporting Goods Co. In addition to baseballs, this Hartford, Conn., company also made prewar indoor and playground balls. The firm became Tober Baseball Mfg. Co., Inc., in the postwar years.

"Toddle Car" see *Janesville Products Co.*

"Toddler" baby walker prewar, see *The Kaymar Corp.*

"Tokfone" see *Regal Amplifier Co.*

The Toledo Juvenile Co. This Toledo, Ohio, manufacturer of juvenile furniture made the "Slumber Line" of the late 1930s.

The Toledo Metal Wheel Co. This Toledo, Ohio, company was founded in 1887. It issued the popular "Blue Streak" of children's vehicles and wheel goods in the 1920s and '30s. It also issued the "Sunshine" playground equipment, and nursery furniture. Toledo Metal Wheels' wheel goods included juvenile autos, velocipedes, scooters, "tot bikes," express and coaster wagons, baby walkers, hand cars, barrows, baby carriages, doll carriages, and junior bicycles into the mid-1930s.

Toledo Model Airplane Co. Established in Toledo, Ohio, in the late prewar years, this firm made airplane kits and supplies, model boats, and scale railway equipment.

The Tolerton Co. This prewar specialist in dollhouses was located in Alliance, Ohio.

"Tolly Toys" see *The Tolerton Co.*

"Tom and Jerry" The cat and mouse cartoon duo appeared in numerous Boomer-era plaything incarnations, including costumes by J. Halpern Co. and 3-D film cards by Tru-Vue Co.

"Tom Corbett Space Cadet" While the "Tom Corbett Space Cadet" book series was issued by Grosset & Dunlap in the 1950s and '60s, most "Tom Corbett" playthings appeared in the 1950s. They included space guns, the "Polaris" space ship, and plastic play sets by Louis Marx & Co.; coloring books, cut-out books, and puzzles by the Saalfield Publishing Co.; and View-Master reels by Sawyer's.

"Tom Jr." automatic repeater see *The Dent Hardware Co.*

"Tom Mix" The Western star Tom Mix inspired numerous playthings in the later prewar and early postwar years. In the mid-1930s, the "Tom Mix" rodeo rope was issued by the Mordt Co., followed in the later '30s by cowboy outfits by Brauer Bros. Mfg. Co., games by Parker Bros., and books by Whitman Publishing Co. "Tom Mix" licensing rights were controlled by Roundup Amusement Co. In the 1950s and '60s, holster sets were issued by Mount Vernon Mfg. Co.

"Tom Quest" books see *Grosset & Dunlap, Inc.*

"Tom Sawyer" Mark Twain's classic novels enjoyed a secondary life through 20th century games and toys. In the 1930s playthings included "Tom Sawyer" paint sets by Standard Toykraft Products, "Tom Sawyer and Huck Finn" game by Stoll & Einson Games, "Tom Sawyer on the Mississippi" by Einson-Freeman Co., and "Tom Sawyer" by Milton Bradley Co. Standard Toykraft continued using the trade name through the Boomer years. Advance Crayon & Color Corp. also used the "Tom Sawyer" name.

"Tom Swift" books prewar, see *Whitman Publishing Co.;* postwar, see *Grosset & Dunlap, Inc.*

"Tom Thumb" The "Tom Thumb" name became a popular prewar trademark. "Tom Thumb" items included electric trains and transformers by the Hoge Mfg. Co., wood toys by Keystone Mfg. Co., in the mid 1930s, and a basketball set in the late '30s by Mack Mfg. Co. In the postwar years, the "Tom Thumb" line of cash registers and typewriters by Western Stamping Co. was popular.

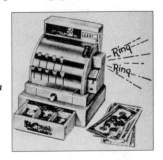

Western Stamping Co.'s "Tom Thumb Cash Register," 1960s.

Tom Thumb Sales Co. The "Tom Thumb" automatic bridge sets of the late 1930s was made by this Fifth Avenue, New York City, firm.

Tommy Toy Mfg. Corp. Tommy, based in Union City, N.J., made lead toys in the late prewar years.

"Tommy Tucker" toys prewar, see *Keystone Mfg. Co.*

"Ton Mack" trucks see *The Murray-Ohio Mfg. Co.*

The Tonette Co. "Tonette" musical instruments were the specialty of this Chicago, Ill., company, established in the late prewar years.

Tonka Toys, Inc. Mound Metalcraft Co. was established in Mound, Minn., in 1946. Its steel vehicle toys, introduced in 1947, bore the "Tonka Toys" name. In 1955 the firm changed its name to Tonka Toys. Although known for its larger truck toys, the firm introduced the "Mini-Tonkas" in 1963.

Tonka's "Allied Van Lines" toy truck, 1950s.

The "Boat Transporter," 1960s, from Tonka.

"Tonto" Children wanting to play at being the Lone Ranger's Indian friend had help in the 1950s and '60s, in the form of suits by Herman Iskin & Co., and holster sets by Esquire Novelty Co. Hartland Plastics made a "Tonto" plastic figure.

Toohey Mfg. Co. The "Beano" baseball game and "Sambo" beanbag game were 1930s and '40s products of this Troy, N.Y., firm. The company specialized in dart boards, darts, and bean bag games.

tool chests Toy tool chests were important toys in prewar times, when parents were more inclined to give children toys with heuristic and practical value. Toy tools undoubtedly appeared among the earliest American toys, produced by tinsmiths and turners. They were produced widely in the 19th century, many as penny toys, including by the J. & E. Stevens Co.

In the years before the Great Depression, manufacturers included American Mfg. Concern, Morton E. Converse, the N.D. Cass Co., and M. Carlton Dank Toy Corp.

Prewar manufacturers included American Mfg. Concern, Buddy "L" Mfg. Co., N.D. Cass, Chicago Toll & Kit Mfg. Co., Victor Eckardt Mfg. Co., the Elmberg Co., A.C. Gilbert Co., Grey Iron Casting Co., J. & H. Metal Products Co., Mason & Parker Mfg. Co., Meccano Co. of America, and the Mordt Co. Among the more distinctive tool sets of the postwar years were the "Handy Andy" sets by Skil-Craft Corp., in their colorful tin boxes, and the Auburn Rubber Co.'s rubber and vinyl tools, which were well-received by a safety-minded public.

Other postwar manufacturers included American Toy & Furniture Co., Baker Mfg. Co., Famous Keystone Kits Corp., A.C. Gilbert, Grey Iron, Industrial Safety Belt Corp., Milton A. Jacobs, National School Slate Co., New York Toy & Game Corp., Northwestern Products Co., Pilrim Leather Goods Co., Pioneer Merchandise Co., the Porter Chemical Co., Riemann, Seabrey Co., George A. Robinson & Co., Scheuer Sales Co., Union Steel Chest Corp., and X-acto.

"American Tool Chest," by American Toy & Furniture Co., 1950s.

"Rubber Tool Kit" by Auburn Rubber Co.

"Tony Sarg" marionettes see *Alexander Doll Co.* See also *Sarg, Tony.*

"Toonerville Trolley" Undoubtedly the most famous prewar cartoon vehicle, the Toonerville Trolley appeared in a variety of toy forms, including glass candy containers. Mid-1930s items included a game by Milton Bradley Co. and toy by George Borgfeldt Corp.

"Tootsietoy" see *Dowst Mfg. Co., Strombecker Corp.*

Top Flite Dolls This postwar doll company was based in Brooklyn, N.Y.

Top Flite Models, Inc. A Chicago, Ill., firm, Top Flite made postwar model airplane kits.

"Topco" plastic products see *Ohio Plastics Co.*

tops Tops may have originated in ancient Asia. The American Indians had whip tops; Nootka Indians had a humming top, while Ojibways made tops of acorns. Humming tops were being imported to America from Europe by the 18th century. Presumably by that time, too, American turners were producing whip tops as diversions.

Both wooden and tin tops became major items in the toy trade in the prewar years. The former were tied in to some degree to the yo-yo craze of the 1920s, being string-and-spinner toys, and appealed to slightly older children. The latter were designed to appeal to younger children, and maintained their nursery connection through the end of the century. While manufactured for the length of the 20th century, they were no longer commonplace by the end of the Boomer years, tin toys no longer being widely regarded as fitting for the nursery.

Early 20th century manufacturers included H. Fishlove & Co., the Gibbs Mfg. Co., the Girard Model Works, Gropper Bros., Moline Pressed Steel Co., Petrie-Lewis Mfg. Co., Jack Pressman & Co., and A.N. Wetherbee.

Prewar tops manufacturers included Abba International Products Co., J. Chein & Co., the Conestoga Corp., Cuyahoga Lumber Co., Dickerman & Co., Donald F. Duncan, H. Fishlove & Co., Forster Mfg. Corp., Gibbs Mfg. Co., Gropper Onyx Marble Co., L.J. Hurst Mfg. Co., the Kirchhof Patent Co., Joseph Koenig, Langson Mfg. Co., Richard Maerklin Toys, Mansfield Novelty Co., C.T. Namur, Newton & Thompson, F.W. Peterson Corp., Piqua General Supply Co., Planert Tool & Mfg. Co., Rochester Mfg. Co., A.M. Samour Mfg. Co., Smethport Specialty Co., and A.N. Wetherbee.

By the late 1930s, other manufacturers included All Metal Products Co., the Alox Mfg. Co., W.R. Benjamin Co., George Borgfeldt Corp., C.E. Carter Co., Ohio Art Co., and Tyler Can Co.

Ohio Art tops from the 1950s.

In the postwar years, manufacturers included the Alox, the Brittain Products Co., Chandler Mfg. Co., J. Chein, Duncan, the Fli-Back Sales Corp., Gibbs, Goody Mfg. Co., Gropper, Hammatt & Sons, Jayline Toys, Henry Katz, Keen-Eye Co., Kirchhof, Lee Products Co., Leeds Sweete Products, Maggie Magnetic, Nadel & Sons, Nissen Products Corp., Ohio Art, Park Plastics Co., Plastic Block City, Ramrod Products, Riemann, Seabrey Co., Royal Tops Mfg. Co., M. Shimmel Sons, Sollmann & Whitcomb, Steven Mfg. Co., Traylor Rich, U.S. Plastics Corp., Weil Bros., and C.G. Wood Co.

tops, return see *yo-yos.*

Topps Chewing Gum, Inc. Trading cards comprised this postwar Brooklyn, N.Y., firm's line.

Topspin Co. This Buffalo, N.Y., company made the "Checker Peg" and "Topspin" games of the late 1930s.

Topstone Rubber Toy Co. Rubber masks, toys, novelties, and hand puppets were products of this Bethel, Conn., company.

"Topsy" "Topsy" proved a popular name in the 1930s, at least for dolls, who appeared under that name from Ralph A. Freundlich, Mizpah Toy & Novelty Corp., and Fleischaker & Baum.

"Tornado" wagon see *The American National Co.*

Tot Guidance, Inc. This Newark, N.J., firm's Boomer-era toys included plastic beads, "Count-A-Clock," "Junior Milk Man," pull toys, and magnetic blackboards.

"Tot Railroad" see *Lincoln Logs Division.*

"Tot Rod" see *Towner Toys.*

Totebrush, Inc. This Chicago, Ill., company made its wind-up "Hot-Rod," a plastic "put-together" toy, in 1960.

W.S. Tothill A Chicago, Ill., company, W.S. Tothill made prewar playground and play-yard equipment, including horse toys, sandboxes, baby yards, merry-go-rounds, teeters, and slides.

Tots Toys This division of Hartwig Studios, Inc., of Milwaukee, Wis., issued wartime games including "Bombardier," the play horse "Bingo the Bronco," and "Down-A-Daisy," described as an "elephant slide."

Totsy Mfg. Co. Based in Springfield, Mass., Totsy made doll layettes from the 1930s through the postwar years.

"Totsy" toy chests see *Bancroft-Rellim Corp.*

"Tottem Toys" see *Playworld Toys, Inc.*

"Tottie Bikes" see *The Globe Co.*

Totty Trunk & Bag Co. A children's furniture manufacturer, Totty, of Petersburg, Va., also made miniature cedar chests, and backgammon card tables and boards in the 1930s and '40s.

"Touring" card game see *Parker Bros.*

"Tournament Model" return tops see the *Fli-Back Co.*

"Tousle Head" dolls prewar, see *Fleischaker & Baum.*

Tower Guild see *Tower Toy Co.*

Tower Toy Co. Originally called the Tower Shop, founded by William S. Tower in the 1830s, the Tower Toy Co. offered toys including wooden playthings made by Tower, toy tools made by Joseph Jacob's hatchet factory, doll furniture made by cabinetmakers, and toy boats made by a boat builder. It started informally as the Tower Guild in the 1830s. An early ad featured doll swings, parlor tenpins, croquet sets, and various toy versions of such household items as churns, tubs, and pails. The association thrived sufficiently to be one of four American toy manufacturers exhibiting at the 1878 Exposition Universelle Internationale in Paris. The association of craftsmen lasted into the 20th century, being run by the Griswold Co. of New York by 1905. The associated craftsmen included Crocker Wilder, Loring Cushing, and Ralph T. Jones.

Tower, William S. Considered the founder of the toy industry in the United States, William S. Tower established the Tower Shop, a guild of toy craftsmen in South Hingham, Mass. A carpenter who also made wood toys, Tower brought together the efforts of various fellow craftsmen who made toys in their spare time and made them available through the Tower Shop, later called the Tower Toy Co., of South Hingham, Mass.

Towner Toys Action pull- and push-toys, educational toys, and rocker horses were specialties of this postwar Portland, Ore., company.

toy A toy is something a child plays with. As such, it could be virtually anything—a piece of string, a stone, or an old jar. In most ages, only the wealthy had toys made specifically for the purpose. The majority of children through the centuries have played with makeshift and homemade items. Contemporary usage, however, has largely narrowed the word "toy" to mean items manufactured for the purposes of play by a child. See also *child labor.* The word dates to around the 16th century, when Nuremberg and Sonnenberg developed as major toy centers in Germany. At that time, lever-manipulated wooden and tin toys were being developed.

Toys don't have to be specifically manufactured like the ones shown here—they can be whatever a child chooses to play with.

toy books A precursor to paper dolls, toy books were children's books with a figure inside on whom moveable costumes could be placed or fitted. Some varieties had the costumed but headless figures on their pages, with a separate head that could be moved from one figure to the next. The most famous toy books are English, published by the London firm S. & J. Fuller about 1810-1835. New York and Philadelphia publisher William Charles reissued English toy books as loose sheets in the years 1810-1825.

Toy Corp. of America The juvenile furniture of this 1920s Appleton, Wis., manufacturer was known for its "antique maple" and "satin" finishes.

Toy Corp. of America, Inc. Children's table and chair sets, desk and chair sets, rockers and chairs, shooflies, and doll's high chairs were specialties of this manufacturer. It was based on East 17th Street, New York City in the late prewar years, moving to Broadway by the 1950s. In the Boomer years it also made toy chests.

The Toy Craftsmen Based in Lindsay, Calif., the Toy Craftsmen made prewar toy guns.

Toy Creation Shops A Cedar Rapids, Iowa, firm, Toy Creation Shops made the "Marbelator" series of marble toys of the 1920s, which consisted of networks of inclined ramps, arranged around vertical posts, as in "Relay-Racer," or the "Marbelator No. 3," which resembled a two-story building into and out of which marbles disappeared and reappeared.

Toy Creations Prewar manufacturer Toy Creations made games including "Uncle Jim's Question Bee," "Pile-M-High," "Klix," and "Benny Goodman Swings," and dolls including "Our Little Sister Dolls," "Dillon Dolls," and "Commencement Dolls." Other game titles included the "Peez" skill game in 1935 and "Official Radio Baseball Game" in 1939. In wartime, the firm enjoyed continued success with titles including "Spot-A-Plane Game," "Ward Cuff's Baseball Game," "Bingo," "Commando Rifles," "Radio Baseball," "Radio Football," "Uncle Jim's Question Bee," "Official Hockey," "Official

T

Baseball," as well as checkers, educational toys, pocket games, paint and crayon sets, and dart boards. "Bombs Away" came out in 1944. The firm maintained offices in the Fifth Avenue Building.

Toy Creations, lead soldier manufacturer see *American Alloy.*

The Toy District At one time New York City had a recognized Toy District. A 1934 trade directory pins it down: "The toy district, while covering a large territory, is in reality most conveniently located. It extends from Chambers Street to 42nd Street, with especially large groupings around Union Square, Madison Square and the `Doll District'—along Mercer and Greene Streets and West Broadway."

Toy Fair Hotel see *Hotel McAlpin.*

Toy Founders, Inc. This Detroit, Mich., firm made plastic toys in the later 1940s, including the "Kar-Kit" assembly toy of 1947.

Toy Furniture Shop The "Tynietoy" dollhouse furniture of the 1930s was made by this Providence, R.I., company. It also made dollhouses.

Toy-in-Action Corp. A manufacturer of premium goods and advertising novelties, this Chicago, Ill., firm also made the 1930s "See-O-Scope" periscopes, "Spin-O" game, and toy telephones.

The Toy Kraft Co. Based in Wooster, Ohio, the Toy Kraft Co. specialized in quality hand-painted wooden toys. In the 1920s its line included toys named "Bobby Boy," "Billy Boy," "Johnnie Barrow," "Circus Wagon," and "Dolly Stroller," as well as sand pails. In the earlier 1930s it held rights to use such characters as the "Three Little Pigs" and "Big Bad Wolf" on its products. Toy Kraft also made a toy called "Scamper, the White House Bunny." In 1935 it issued "Goose Goslin Scientific Baseball." Through the 1930s and into the '40s it made Easter toys, sand pails and toys, wagons, wheelbarrows, toy chests, action pull toys, push toys, and carts.

toy manufacturers Since no companies were expressly "toy manufacturers," various general-goods manufacturers offered toys as sidelines to their main business in the 18th and earlier 19th centuries. By the mid 1800s, increasing numbers of manufacturers were regarding toys as an important part of their business. The 1850 U.S. Census listed 47 toy manufacturers. Far more companies were engaged in some variety of toy manufacture by then, however. Their numbers steadily increased with the country's prosperity, especially in the years following World War I. By the mid-1930s, toy and related manufacturers were approximately 1,500 in number.

Toy Manufacturers of the U.S.A., Inc. This manufacturer's association was created to bring about better traditions and to encourage cooperation between manufacturers and dealers. By the 1930s all trade shows fell under the association's jurisdiction. It was based at 200 Fifth Avenue, New York City.

Toy Mfg. Co. This East Weare, N.H., firm issued wooden toys and "acrobatic jumping jacks" in the late 1930s.

Toy Products Mfg. Co. This doll manufacturer was located in the Doll District in the 1930s.

toy shops see *toy stores*

toy soldiers, cardboard, paper and wood Prewar manufacturers included American Playthings Co., Artwood Toy Mfg. Co., Milton Bradley Co., Lyle S. Drew, Furniture City Dowel Co., Gropper Onyx Marble Co., J. Lesser Toy Mfg. Co., and Parker Bros.

toy soldiers, metal Toy soldiers were available in America from at least Revolutionary times. Tory children were offered British foot soldiers and dragoons, cast in metal, during the 1770s. Manufacturers before the war included Barclay Mfg. Co., Carpenter's Novelty Shop, the G.H. Curry Mfg. Co., Grey Iron Casting Co., the Illfelder Corp., Kansas Toy & Novelty Co., Robert Simpson & Sons, J.L. Small's Novelty Shop, Wesley Toy & Novelty Co., and J.L. Wright. In the late prewar years, the major manufacturers were American Metal Toys, Barclay, Block House, Grey Iron, Manoil Mfg. Co., and J.L. Wright. Only a few firms continued manufacturing metal soldiers into the Boomer years. They included Comet Metal Products Co. and Grey Iron.

Advertisement for metal toy soldiers by J.L. Wright, 1930s.

toy soldiers, plastic Among the most typical toys of the Boomer years were plastic toy soldiers, sold in packaging ranging from simple rack items to complex play sets with buildings and accessories. Manufacturers included Amloid Co., Azco Products Corp., Henry Katz, Lido Toy Co., Multiple Products Corp., Payton Products, Plasticraft Mfg. Co., Plastic Toys Corp., Tom B. Roberts Co., Thomas Mfg. Corp., and Tim-Mee Toys.

toy stores The first American toy shop may have belonged to William Price, Print and Map-Seller, who advertised "toys and small pictures for children" in the 1710s-'50s. Toy shops appear to have become an accepted part of the American retail scene by the early 1800s. By the 1840s, most major towns had them. In 1844, New York state alone had 88 toy stores. For miniature stores, see *stores, toy.*

The Toy Tinkers, Inc. Inspired by the sight of children playing with spools and sticks, the wooden construction set "Tinkertoys" was popular from its introduction in 1914 through the Boomer years.

The company's line by the late 1920s included regular "Tinkertoy, the Wonder Builder," and "Double Tinkertoy, the Ten Thousand Wonder Builder," the beaded "Jump Rope Tinker," jars and cans of "Tinker Beads," "Abacus Tinker," the "Tinker Go-Round" wind-up toy, "Necklace Tinker," "Surf Boat Tinker" floating toy, and the game "Tinker Pins."

It also issued the popular bead dolls "Siren Tinker," "Belle Tinker," "Baby Doll Tinker," and "Tom Tinker." More elaborate figures included "Tip Toe Tinker," a jump-roping figure, "Gym Tinker," an acrobat doll," "Dragon Tinker," a beaded pull-toy, and "Puppy

Tinker." The firm's other pull toys, many using beads, included "Bunny Tinker," which had a leaping motion, "Bill Goat Tinker," "Life Guard Tinker," representing an over-hand-stroke swimmer in action, "Auto Racer No. 2," "Tinker Mule," "Clown Tinker," "Choo Choo Tinker," "Whirly Tinker," "Tinker Dogs," and "Pony Tinker."

Besides its "Tinkertoy" line, the company continued to focus on pull toys, waterproof enameled beads, beaded toys, and bead dolls through the '30s and '40s. In the later 1930s it added sand sets to its line. The firm, purchased by A.G. Spalding & Bros. in 1952, continued issuing construction toys, infants' toys, pull trains, stacking toys, and rack toys through the Boomer years. The "Panel Builder" sets were introduced in 1958.

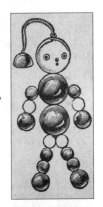

"Tom Tinker," from the Toy Tinkers, 1920s.

Based on children playing with spools and sticks, the "Tinkertoy" line was famous for generations.

"Toy Town" see *Milton Bradley Co.*

toy towns In the mid-1800s, "toy towns" were being sold to toy retailers. Much like the Noah's Ark toys, toy towns may be considered precursors to the later "play sets."

T

toy ware "Toy ware" was a phrase used to indicate general toys in the 1800s.

The Toy Works Established in 1919 in Girard, Penn., by Frank E. Wood, the Toy Works made spinning tops, skates, and banks. In 1922 it became Girard Model Works, Inc.

"Toyco" see *The Toycraft Rubber Co.*

The Toycraft Rubber Co. This Ashland, Ohio, manufacturer issued inventive rubber playthings in the 1920s, including the penny balloon toys "Toyco Tip-Top Penny Squawkers," "Toyco Hi-flyers," and "Toyco Tumble Toys." In the nickel category, Toycraft offered its "Toyco Jack Set," containing five nickel plated jacks; a "Toyco" sponge rubber ball "Toyco Sponge Rubber Come Back Balls"; and the "Spirit of U.S.A. Sirens," large balloons with siren whistles inside. Toycraft continued issuing balloons and sponge rubber products including toys, and rubber balls in the 1930s and '40s.

"Toycrafters" stuffed animals see *Scovell Novelty Mfg. Co.*

Toyland Novelty Co., Inc. Based on East 10th Street, New York City, in the late 1930s, Toyland made stuffed toys.

Toyline Mfg. Co. This Irvington, N.J., company made prewar wooden educational toys.

The Toymakers Wooden toys and games were prewar products of this Bloomfield, N.J., company. By the late '30s the company had moved to West Caldwell, N.J., and was producing shooting games, checkerboards, dominoes, and "Tit-Tat-Toe" boards.

Toymaster Products Co. Toys of corrugated cardboard were specialties of this Clifton, N.J., company in the 1950s and '60s. Its line included play stores, refrigerators, ranges, cupboards, dollhouses, puppet theaters, and blocks. Two playhouses introduced in the mid-1950s were "Super-Duper Market" and "Sheriff's Office." "Room enough in each for two junior clerks or brave bandit hunters," the company promised.

"Toymonica" see *Lapin Products, Inc.*

Toyrights Mfg. Co. This postwar Brooklyn, N.Y., company issued games and rack games.

Toys, Inc. Based in Des Moines, Iowa, in the 1950s and '60s, Toys made foam rubber paint sets, handicraft sets, and stuffed toy animals, including "autograph" animals.

"Toys that are more than just toys," slogan see *H.E. Boucher Mfg. Co.*

"Toys That Last," slogan see *Grey Iron Casting Co., and Kilgore Mfg. Co., Inc.*

"Toys That Teach," slogan see *The Embossing Co.*

Toytime Products The "Jumbo Box Blocks" of the late 1930s were produced by this Chicago, Ill., company.

Toytronic Development Co. Walkie-talkies, transistor radios and remote-control toys were specialties of this Boomer-era Fort Wayne, Ind., company.

The Tracies Co. Based in Holyoke, Mass., the Tracies Co. issued Boomer-era play money, stencil and drawing games, art sets, puzzles, plastic wallets, and cowboy cuffs.

"Trackdown" CBS Films' "Texas Rangers" inspired "Trackdown" playthings including hats by Newark Felt Novelty Co. and suits by Sackman Bros. Co.

"Traco" kits see *The Tracies Co.*

Tracy, John A publisher based in Newark, N.J., in the 1830s, John Tracy issued a geography game, conversation cards, historical cards, and spelling puzzles.

Trade King, Inc. Doll carriages were among the postwar products of this East 32nd Street, New York City, manufacturer of baby walkers.

A. Trader Publishing Co. This Chicago, Ill., publisher issued 1950s-60s games and books.

Trail Blazer" train see *American Flyer Mfg. Co.*

Train of Tomorrow" streamlined train see *The Lionel Corp.*

"Train to Build" see *The A. Schoenhut Co.*

Train-Town, Inc. A Pottstown, Penn., company, Train-Town made prewar toy train accessories, including bridges, tunnels, and railroad buildings.

"Trainerifle" see *Parris Mfg. Co.*

Training Day Training Day was a holiday the colonial New England Puritans could countenance. Since it centered around military display, the holiday featured many games of marksmanship. Even though they were probably not called "games," the activities reflected a loosening of Puritan strictures against recreation and play.

Trainor National Spring Co. Established in New Castle, Ind., in the late 1930s, Trainor issued the "Trainor Pony" juvenile exerciser, as well as beach chairs.

trains, floor Floor trains were usually push-toys with free-rolling wheels, made of metal, wood, or plastic.

trains, metal Metal floor trains were issued first in the 1800s by many if not most of the cast-iron pull-toy and push-toy manufacturers, and by such tin companies as George Brown. Especially notable early friction trains were produced by Dayton and Schiebel, the two "Hillclimber" companies. Prewar manufacturers included Arcade Mfg. Co., Corcoran Mfg. Co., Dowst Mfg. Co., Grey Iron Casting Co., the Hubley Mfg. Co., Keystone Mfg. Co., and the Ohio Art Co. By the late 1930s, Straits Mfg. Co. was also making these toys.

trains, wood Wooden floor trains had an early start as a popular toy as early as the Crandall years. Uncounted numbers of these toys were likely manufactured on an anonymous basis, through the decades. Prewar manufacturers of wood floor trains included Fisher-Price Toys, Furniture City Dowel Co., Holgate Bros. Co., the E.M. Nichols Co., the A. Schoenhut Co., Strombeck-Becker Mfg. Co., and Tran-sogram Co. Playskool Institute joined their ranks by the late prewar years. In the Boomer years, floor trains were generally made of wood, plastic, or a combination of the two. Active companies included Banner Plastics, Creative Products, Dowst Mfg. Co., Elmar Products Co., Fisher-Price Toys, Holgate Toys, Irwin Corp., Jack Built Toy Mfg. Co., James Industries, Knickerbocker Plastic Co., Kusan, Lido Toy Corp., Lincoln Logs, Modern Toy Co., Payton Products, Plasticraft Mfg. co., Playskool Mfg. Co., Renwal Toy Corp., Strombeck-Becker, and the Toy Tinkers.

transformers see *motors and transformers, toy.*

"Transit Toys" see *The Embossing Co.*

Transo Products The mid-1930s "Movie Moods" game was made by this West 41st Street, New York City, firm.

Transogram Co., Inc. Transogram, founded in 1913, issued a "Gold Medal" line of quality playthings which included embroidery and sewing sets, games, coloring outfits, garden sets, and "Kitchen Kabinets" full of aluminum dishes, by the late 1920s. The "Gold Medal" name was not immediately used by the company when it was founded, the name being based on the Gold Medal it was awarded at the 1915 Panama Pacific Exposition. Transogram was also manufacturer of the "Gilt-Edge" holiday paper products, including nested holiday boxes.

Based initially in Brooklyn, N.Y., and moving into the Fifth Avenue Building by the 1930s, with a factory in Easton, Penn., Transogram touted its products as "playthings that serve a purpose." By the late Great Depression years its garden sets, one of its lead products, sold for prices ranging from a dime to a dollar. They were made with heavy gauge, brightly painted steel and likewise brightly painted birchwood handles, coated with Transogram's own "Transolac" lacquer finish.

Other prewar products included blackboards, colored pencil sets, crayon sets, "nailcraft," needlework sets, painting sets, pastry sets, slate sets, stencil sets, and other educational toys. The company also made anagrams, bubble sets, "Chalk-Pictures," fishing games, "Krokay" sets, party wigs, peg board games, picture puzzles, police sets, ring toss, shooting games, table tennis, tenpins, "Tiddledy Winks," to clothespins, and toy trunks and suitcases. Its assorted smaller games and toys went into its "25 cent and 50 cent surprise packages."

Transogram also made aluminum tea and percolator sets, backgammon, checkerboards, croquet sets, pull toys, puzzle pictures, sand toys, steel toys, table tennis, ten pins, and wooden toys. Its game titles included "Bucking Bronco" and "Hungry Willie."

In the late prewar years, Transogram's line included a number of notable cartoon-character playthings, including "Popeye" bubble sets and sailboats, and "Orphan Annie" pastry sets. Another sailboat of the time was the "Sail-R-Boy." The firm also made Tony Sarg puzzles, "Little Movie Stars" make-up kits, "Little Country" doctor kits, and "Tom Thumb Toy Town." Among its lead game titles were "Big Business," "Michigan Kitty," "Movie Millions," and "Rumlo."

The firm continued operating during World War II, issuing a limited line of "Gold Medal" toys and games, wood furniture, and surprise packages.

Before the war Transogram opened factories in Coudersport, Penn., and Long Island City, N.Y. In the 1950s and '60s, it maintained its original Easton factory as well as others in Sturgis, Mich., and Sikeston, Mo.

The line featured an impressive number of TV, radio, movie and comic-strip tie-ins in the Boomer years. Playthings included "Alvin the Chipmunk" and "Annie Oakley" coloring books; "Around the World in 80 Days," "Disneyland," "Perry Mason," "Peter Pan Adventure," "Rin-Tin-Tin" and "Shari Lewis" games; "Black Beauty" and "Wells Fargo" coloring sets; "Jack and the Bean Stalk Mickey Mouse Magic Erasable Pictures"; and various games, crayon sets, pencil and paint-by-number sets, and re-color cards based on "Wyatt Earp," "Zorro," "Ruff 'n Reddy," "Buccaneers," and "Popeye."

Transogram also issued its "Little Country Doctor," "Little Play Nurse," and "Lady Lovely Beauty" kits; family games; doll furniture; play furniture, including toy wagons, blackboards, and peg and slate kits; action games; and craft sets and outfits.

transparent swirl Glass marbles with "swirl" patterns visible within are called transparent swirls. The solid-core swirls have an opaque central core or swirl; the divided-core swirls have two distinct opaque central cores; the Latticino-core swirls have cores consisting of more delicate threads of opaque glass; and the ribbon-core swirls have a single, often multi-colored ribbon of opaque glass for the core. Some swirls have no core, with the swirl pattern only present in the surface or near-surface threads of opaque glass.

Traps Mfg. Co. "The Game of Traps" was issued by this Seattle, Wash., company in the 1920s. A marble game, it was joined by a second marble game, "Bank," by the 1930s.

"Travel Blox" see *Holgate Bros. Co.*

Travel Goods, Inc. Metal-covered doll wardrobe trunks and toy trunks comprised this Boomer-era line. The firm was based in Schofield, Wis.

"Traveler" handcar see *The American National Co.*

"Travois" sets see *Stuart Toy Mfg. Co.*

Traylor Rich, Inc. This postwar Boonville, Ind., issued the "Hum-Dinga" humming diabolo top.

"Treacy" see *Phoenix Costume Mfg. Co.*

"Treasure Trove for Tiny Tots" see *The Toy Tinkers, Inc.*

"Treasury Box" Charles M. Crandall issued this popular game in the late 1800s.

Tremax Industries "Palomino Pal," a hobby horse, was the product of this 1950s-60s Chicago, Ill., company.

"Tressy" American Character Doll Co. issued "Tressy" dolls, small fashion dolls in the "Barbie" and "Tammy" tradition whose hair would "grow." "Tressy" had a little-sister doll named "Cricket."

tri-cars "Tri-cars" was used in the prewar toy industry for three-wheeled juvenile vehicles. It apparently was not synonymous with tricycles, however. "Tri-Car" was also a trade name for children's vehicles used by Nicholas-Beazley.

"Tri-Color" agates see *The Akro Agates Co.*

Tri G Co. Based in Santa Monica, Calif., this firm made the "Optical Star Finder," as well as kaleidoscopes and marble games, in the Boomer years.

Tri-Kay Co., Inc. An inflatable-head stick horse was among the Boomer-era products of this Turlock, Calif. company. It also made play balls and swim rings.

Triad Mfg. Co. Established in Chagrin Falls, Ohio, in the late 1930s, Triad made games, hammer and nail sets, junior gym sets, sand boxes and table tennis.

Tribike Co. The Tribike Co. of Mineola, Long Island, N.Y., made a velocipede in the late 1930s that converted into a sidewalk cycle.

"Tribune" bicycles see *The Westfield Mfg. Co.*

"Trick Mule" A popular game, "Trick Mule" was issued in the late 1800s by Charles M. Crandall.

"Trick Squirt" water pistol see *Kenner Products Co.*

tricks and jokes In the toy industry, "tricks and jokes" were a category covering many of the novelty toys sold in dime stores and frequently found, by the Boomer years, in the tightly-printed advertising pages of comic books. Even so lofty a toy manufacturer as A.C. Gilbert Co. had a hand in producing tricks and jokes. Other prewar manufacturers included S.S. Adams Co., Eagle Magic and Joke Factory, H. Fishlove & Co., Franco-American Novelty Co., Gordon Novelty Co., Magical Manufactures, "Sherms," and Unique Novelty Co.

"Trico" composition soldiers see *Langfelder, Homma & Hayward, Inc.*

tricycles see *velocipedes.*

trifle A metal similar to pewter but with 20 percent or greater content of lead. "Pewter" toys of the 18th and 19th centuries were likely often made of this lower-grade metal.

Trim Molded Products Co. Based in Burlington, Wis., this firm issued the 1950s-'60s "Trim-Pak" cutouts. It also made toy soda pop fountains and "Coca Cola" dispensers.

Trimble, Inc. This Rochester, N.Y., manufacturer of "Kiddie-Koop," "Kiddie Bath," "Trimble Playard" and other nursery and juvenile furniture also made doll baths and doll dressing tables. It operated from the 1930s through the Boomer years.

"Triple 'T'" toys see *Mantua Toy & Metal Products Co.*

triples In farm toys, having three wheels on the end of each axle.

"Triumph" see *Precision Plastics Co.*

"Trix" pull toys prewar, see *The Gong Bell Mfg. Co.*

trock Trock was a kind of indoor croquet played on a table, introduced in colonial times by the Dutch.

"Trojan" coaster wagons see *The Toledo Metal Wheel Co.*

"Trojan" electric train see *American Flyer Mfg. Co.*

Trojan, Inc. Optical devices including telescopes and microscopes were specialties of this Chicago, Ill., firm in the late prewar years.

Trojan Sporting Goods Co. A Chicago, Ill., firm, Trojan included cowboy outfits in its 1930s line, which featured cameras, telescopes, and movie projectors.

"Trom-Po" spinning tops see *Royal Tops Mfg. Co., Inc.*

"Trooper" cap pistol see *The Hubley Mfg. Co.*

"Trooper" repeating cap pistol and machine gun see *Kilgore Mfg. Co., Inc.*

Tropical Industries A novelty manufacturer specializing in using tropical raw materials for such items as alligator lamps, Tropical Industries of Tarpon Springs, Fla., also made toy furniture in the 1930s.

Tropical Model Airplane Co. Model airplane kits and supplies were prewar prod-

T

ucts of this Miami, Fla., firm. By the late 1930s, Tropical had added gliders and model boats and railroads to its line.

Rew Troxell, Mfr. The "Pull Toys With Merit" slogan was used on Rew Troxell's line of autos, boats, wagons, and monoplanes in the 1920s. The company also made animal pull toys, including "Wobbly Duck," and the "Pull-Me-Car." Troxell was based in Los Angeles, Calif.

The Troxel Mfg. Co. Supplying other manufacturers, Troxel of Elyria, Ohio, made bicycle and velocipede saddles in the prewar years, adding chrome-plated bicycle rims in the later 1930s.

"Tru-Action" see *Tudor Metal Products Corp.*

"Tru-Blu Notch-It" handguns see *W.J. Murphy Co.*

Tru-Craft Novelty Co. Based on Broadway, New York City, Tru-Craft made movie-inspired boudoir dolls in the 1930s, including Mae West dolls.

Tru-Fit Apron Mfg. Co. This St. Louis, Mo., firm issued doll kits containing dresses, sun suits, and aprons, in the late 1930s.

"Tru-Life Toys" see *Sayco Doll Corp.*

"Tru-Hue" water colors see *Milton Bradley Co.*

"Tru-Miniature" see *Product Miniature Co., Inc.*

"Tru-Scale" farm machinery see *Carter Tru-Scale Machine Co.*

"Tru-To-Life" riding toys see *G.B. Lewis Co.*

"Tru-Tone" xylophones see *Tudor Metal Products Corp.*

"Tru-Toy" die-cast farm toys and trucks see *Carter Tru-Scale Machine Co.*

"Tru-Trak" for trains see *Western Coil & Electric Co.*

Tru-Matic Toy Co. Steel and sand toys were this Stroudsburg, Penn., firm's specialty in the 1950s and '60s. The line included toy sand diggers, bulldozers, road rollers, carts, tugboats, tractors, and machine guns.

Tru-Vue A Rock Island, Ill., firm, Tru-Vue offered what it called "third dimension pictures." A stereoscopic slide-viewer much like View-Master, Tru-Vue arranged its paired slides on rectangular cards. These held more images than View-Master disk-shaped cards did. Tru-Vue also held the license to produce Walt Disney stereoscopic slides, making the company an especially valuable acquisition when View-Master bought it in 1951, and moved production to Oregon. There, the line included not only the "Tru-Vue" viewers and films, but also plastic pull toys. View-Master phased out the line in the 1960s.

trucks, toy Lines of toy and miniature trucks were often considered a separate specialty from toy and miniature automobiles, from the prewar years through the Boomer period. Some companies, such as Tonka Toys, specialized almost exclusively in truck and road construction toys. Other lines with a strong toy truck emphasis were issued by companies including Amloid Co., Aurora Plastics, Banner Plastics Corp., Buddy "L" Toys, Carter Tru-Scale Machine Co., Dowst Mfg. Co., Eldon Mfg. Co., Eyerly Associates, General Molds & Plastics Corp., Hamilton Steel Products, Irwin Corp., Henry Katz, Lapin Products, Lido Toy Co., Louis Marx & Co., Ohio Art Co., Payton Products, Plastic Toy & Novelty Corp., Processed Plastic Co., Product Miniature Co., Renwal Toy Corp., Structo Mfg. Co., Talking Devices Co., Thomas Mfg. Co., J.C. Ulrich Co., U.S. Plastics Corp., and Wolverine Supply & Mfg. Co.

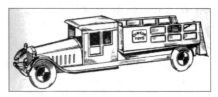

"Stake Truck" by Corcoran Mfg. Co., 1920s.

Keystone Mfg. Co. made this dump truck in the 1920s.

Trudy Toy Co. Stuffed toys were the specialty of this postwar East Norwalk, Conn., company.

"Trumodel," tradename see *Kelmet Corp.*

trunks and suitcases, toy Toy trunks and suitcases made up an important part of the doll manufacturing world. Their variety, and the care manufacturers put into them, might be indicated by a 1930s ad from Wilkins Toy Mfg. Co.: "Doll trunks—trunk and wardrobe types: substantial wooden frames covered with lacquered tin, striped cloth, or paper. Sizes range from 9 to 24 inches." Other prewar manufacturers included P. Becker & Co., Blum Bros., the N.D. Cass Co., B.R. Cromien, H. Fleisig, Ideal Products Mfg. Co., Mason & Parker Mfg. Co., McGraw Box Co., Minerva Toy Co., Purves Products Co., A. Reif & Co., Transogram, and Uneeda Doll Co.

Tryon Toy-Makers & Wood-Carvers This Tryon, N.C., company made prewar wooden toys and stilts.

"Tu-Weeler" roller skates see *The Hartford Steel Ball Co.*

Tuck, Raphael This English publisher issued toy books and paper dolls popular on both sides of the Atlantic in the late 19th century. The images retained a place in the toy world into the 1930s through a "Raphael Tuck" series of puzzles by R. Wunderlich.

Tucker Duck & Rubber Co. Play tents and child-size folding chairs were lead products of this Fort Smith, Ark., firm in the mid-

1930s. By the late prewar years it was manufacturing toy chairs, tables, ironing boards, and rocking horses. The line continued through the Boomer years.

Tucker Products Corp. Based in Leominster, Mass., this postwar firm issued toy tea sets.

Tucker Toys, Inc. The "Answer Me" electric educational toy of the mid-1930s was made by this White Plains, N.Y., company. It also made soft animals.

The Tuco Work Shops, Inc. This Lockport, N.Y., company made fiber-board specialties and picture puzzles from the prewar years through the Boomer era, using the "Upson" trademark in the postwar years.

Tudor Metal Products Corp. Best known for its postwar football games, Tudor was established in the mid-1930s on West 25th Street, New York City, to manufacture metal action games and toys. Early titles included "NFL Strategy" in 1935 and "Musical Lotto" in 1936. It issued a limited line of "Victory Wood Xylophones" during wartime. One of the biggest names in electric games of the Boomer years, Tudor issued the "Tru-Action" line of games, including table hockey games, and "Electric Football," "Electric Baseball," "Electric Basketball," "Electric Sports Car Race" and "Electric Horse Race" games in the 1950s and '60s. It also made "Tru-Tone Xylophones," including two versions with Walt Disney characters.

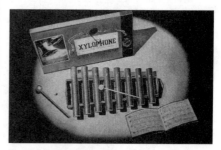

Tudor Metal Products Co.'s "Victory Wood Xylophone."

tug-of-war A traditional game, tug-of-war dates back to at least the ancient Greeks. It was also known to the American Indians.

"Tumble Bug" game see *W.H. Schaper Mfg. Co.*

"Tumble Toys" prewar, see *Toycraft Rubber Co., The*

The John C. Turner Co. One of the major manufacturers of larger-scale toy trucks and automobiles in the 1920s and '30s, Turner's line included airplanes, dump trucks, fire engines, trains, garage sets, sedans, and sports cars, retailing from $1.00 to $5.50 in the pre-Great Depression years. The firm became the John C. Turner Corp. in the '30s. It made steel toys including dump trucks and fire department equipment, with and without electric lights. The company also made the "Irving Jaffee Olympic Champion Roller Skates." Turner added toy garages by the end of the decade. The company was founded in Wapakoneta, Ohio, in 1915. Before closing its doors in 1948, it was issuing "Victory Is Won" flywheel toys, offering them by direct mail.

This steel toy "Special Delivery Truck" by The John C. Turner Co. was 24 inches long.

Turner's earlier "Mack Dump Truck" from the 1920s.

The Turner & Seymour Mfg. Co.

The "Ta-Bowl" table bowling game of the 1930s and '40s was produced by this Torrington, Conn., firm.

turners Wood-turning operations provided many early 19th century toys. As a consequence, toy makers were sometimes locally listed only as "turners." See *wooden toys.*

"Tuxedo Racer Sled" 1930s, see *S.L. Allen & Co.*

"Tweak'N Squeak" toys see *Gund Mfg. Co.*

20th Century Varieties, Inc. Based on East 164th Street, New York City, in the 1950s and '60s, this firm issued metal toys including badges, handcuffs, jail keys, whistles, western sets, police detective sets, holster sets, canteens, guns, and rack items.

"25th Century Rocket Pistol" 1930s, see *Daisy Mfg. Co.*

"Twin-Beam" and "Twinset" bicycle headlights see *The Seiss Mfg. Co.*

"Twinbar" streamlined motorbike 1930s, see *Steinfeld, Inc.*

"Twinkling Eye" Books see *Samuel Gabriel Sons & Co.*

Twinzy Toy Co. A manufacturer based in Battle Creek, Mich., Twinzy Toy made prewar stuffed soft toys, pull toys, and "Twinzy-Kraft" "tufted" toys. In the late '30s it was also emphasizing washable stuffed dolls and animal toys, hobbyhorses, soft blocks, and paint sets. "Man in the Moon" luminous-face dolls, "Pixie Pal" dolls, "Rock-A-Bye" animals, "Tub-It Toys" stuffed toys, and "Pillow Pal" toys were among its products in the 1950s and '60s. The company's emphasis remained on washable stuffed dolls and toy animals, soft blocks, and foam-rubber filled toys.

"Twirly-Clicks" This noisemaker, introduced apparently by the Kirchhof Patent Co. in the late 1920s, involves a horizontally-held tin box with tin clicker inside, which makes a sharp clicking sound when the box is twirled around the vertically held wooden handle. These toys originally sold for 5 cents.

Twistum Toy Factory The "Twistum Aero-Flyer" of the 1920s was made by this Oakland, Calif., firm. The toy, which sold for 50 cents, was akin to simple rubberband airplanes, with a feathered tail and no horizontal wings. It was meant for flying straight up into the air. The company also made "Twistum Animals."

The Twistum "Aero-Flyer," a simple flying toy from the 1920s.

"Two Jolly Blacks" Charles M. Crandall issued this popular game in the late 1800s.

"Tyco HO Trains" see *Mantua Toy & Metal Products Co.*

Tyer Rubber Co. Tyer Rubber Co. of Andover, Mass., issued the "Peppy" play balls of the mid-1930s. Through the prewar years it issued football and play ball bladders.

"Tyke Toys," prewar see *Menasha Woodenware Corp.*

Tykie Toy, Inc. Foam rubber toys were 1950s-60s specialties of this Conley, Ga., company.

The Tyler Can Co. Based in Baltimore, Md., Tyler Can made prewar "Screamer" whistles, "Simplex" flutes, tin spoons, tin yo-yos, combination spinning tops, and tin stampings for other manufacturers.

"Tyndall" loom prewar, see *Milton Bradley Co.*

"Tynietoy" doll house furniture see *Toy Furniture Shop.*

typewriters, toy and juvenile The line between the toy and juvenile typewriter was never one to be drawn too carefully, since toy typewriters often worked as well as any other working typewriters, even though some were distinctively inefficient, as in the typewriters by the venerable Simplex Typewriter Co., which required the child to move a disk with each new letter. McLoughlin Bros. issued another early machine, the "Young People's Typewriter," in the early 1900s. Other prewar manufacturers included American Flyer Mfg. Co. and George W. Moore. In the late prewar years, General Shaver Co. and Louis Marx & Co. joined their ranks. Postwar manufacturers of toy typewriters included Berwin Corp., T. Cohn, Ellcraft Industries, Henry Katz, Louis Marx, and Western Stamping Co.

The 1930s "American Flyer Typewriter."

Tyson, James W. The "Grand National Steeplechase" game of the earlier 1930s was issued by this Baltimore, Md., firm.

Marx released this tin toy, "Limping Lizzie" in the 1920s.

The "Toni Doll" from American Character Doll.

Uu

Uhlen Carriage Co., Inc. A Rochester, N.Y., firm, Uhlen Carriage Co. made not only baby carriages but doll carriages, sleds, juvenile furniture, and toys.

ukuleles Ukuleles became fashionable musical instruments in the 1950s and '60s, their popularity boosted in no small part by Arthur Godfrey. Manufacturers included Emenee Industries, French American Reeds Mfg. Co., Jefferson Mfg. Co., Lapin Products, and Lido Toy Co.

The Ullman Mfg. Co. Billing itself as the "World's Largest Makers of Paint Sets," Ullman issued a line in the earlier 20th century that included paint boxes, "Jumbo" and "Priscilla" crayons, "Princess" embroidery sets, and kindergarten sets. It maintained its factory in Long Island City, N.Y., and offices in the Fifth Avenue Building. By the earlier 1930s, it moved to Brooklyn. In the post-Great Depression years it still issued art and drawing kits, and instruments including the "Priscilla" and "Miracle" crayons. It also issued the "Indian Picturecraft," a "Footstool Playbox," and "Kindergarten Pastimes." The company became a part of Standard Toykraft Products in 1939. Standard Toykraft continued the "Priscilla" and other lines.

C.J. Ulrich Co. Based in North Hollywood, Calif., Ulrich issued metal truck and trailer models in the 1950s and '60s.

"Umakum" valentine sets 1930s, see *Fuld & Co., Inc.*

"Uncle Remus" The Southern traditional figure of Uncle Remus inspired various playthings, including the "Uncle Remus" cutouts of the 1930s by O.B. Andrews Co.

"Uncle Sam's" Registering Savings Bank Co. For a company to have two names was not unusual in prewar toy manufacturing. One name would be the founding name, usually involving the founder's or founders' names, while the secondary name would be the one that would have higher name-recognition due to the success of some particular product. This happened with the "Lincoln Logs and Allied Toys" name used by J.L. Wright. It also happened with Durable Toy & Novelty Corp., which used the name of its most famous toy, the "Uncle Sam's" series of coin banks, for its alternate business name.

The "Uncle Sam's Register Bank," 1920s.

"Uncle Walt" see *"Gasoline Alley."*

"Uncle Wiggily" The "Uncle Wiggily" children's books readily translated into other childhood items. In the 1930s paint and crayon boxes by Binney & Smith Co. and put-together books by Charles E. Graham & Co. appeared, as well as the "Uncle Wiggily's Airplane" and "Put the Hat on Uncle Wiggily" games by Milton Bradley Co. Related and presumably unlicensed items included "Uncle Wiggily" balloons by Eagle Rubber Co. In the postwar years, books were issued by both Platt and Munk Co. and Whitman Publishing Co., and games by Milton Bradley Co.

Uneeda Doll Co., Inc. Established on Mercer Street, New York City, in 1917, Uneeda issued popular priced dolls with sleeping eyes through the 1920s, including mama dolls. Dolls, trousseau sets, trunks and novelties were 1930s and '40s products of this venerable doll and toy manufacturer, based on West 18th Street, New York City.

In the Boomer years, the company specialized in vinyl plastic dolls, including crying dolls, walking dolls, and manikins. One of its 1950s dolls was "Baby-Trix," a vinyl doll whose head, arms and legs moved when her stomach was pressed. She also cried from her eyes, wet her diaper, and cooed.

By the 1960s its line included such names as "Dollikin," "Yummy," "Dewdrop," "Tiny-teens," "Twinks," "Purty," "Prithilla," "Debteens," "Baby Bumpkins," "Go-Go," and "Toddle Trainer." The firm issued some character tie-ins, including Walt Disney's "Pollyanna." In 1961, the company entered into an agreement with Dam Things Establishment, a Danish company, to issue the "Wishnik" trolls. In 1964, the company was issuing "Betsy McCall" dolls and accessories.

Harry A. Ungar, Inc. A Los Angeles, Calif., firm, Harry A. Ungar made the "Magic Stylus" electric pencil sets of the 1930s and '40s. It also made wood burning sets. In the Boomer years, as Ungar Electric Tools, Inc., the firm issued electric toy scissors, electric soldering and wood burning pencils, and motorized model kits.

"Uni-Block" construction sets see *Vanguard Toy Co.*

Unicorn Mfg. Co. Established in the late 1930s in Smethport, Penn., Unicorn made steel magnets and magnet sets, offering competition Smethport Specialty Co. of the same town.

Union Hardware Co. Established in Torrington, Conn., Union Hardware manufactured ice skates in the mid 19th century through the earlier 20th century. In the 1950s and '60s, as Union Hardware-Sealand, Inc., it continued issuing its line under the "Union" name.

Union Mfg. Co. A small manufacturer of tin toys based in Clinton, Conn., Union Mfg. Co. was founded in 1853 and continued production until 1869, when it was acquired by Hull & Stratford.

"Union Pacific" electric train 1930s, see *General Trains, Inc.*

Unique Novelty Co. Part games and joke novelties were the prewar specialties of this Los Angeles, Calif., company.

Unique Novelty Co., Inc. Based in the later 1930s in Sawyer, Wis., Unique made sewing kits and knitting cabinets.

Unique Novelty Doll Co. This Grand Street, New York City, manufacturers issued large "flapper dolls" measuring 32-inches high, in the 1920s. It also issued a variety of other popular priced dolls, including silk wig dolls.

United Balloon Co. Based on Fifth Avenue, New York City, United Balloon made prewar advertising, novelty, and toy balloons.

United Clay Mines Corp. This Trenton, N.J., corporation issued prewar play sand and modeling clay.

United Crayon Co., Inc. Crayons, chalk sets and watercolor sets were postwar specialties of this Brooklyn, N.Y., company.

United-Delta Corp. A Clifton Heights, Penn., company, United-Delta made prewar velocipedes, scooter cycles, pedal cars, and scooters.

United Electric Mfg. Co. In the 1930s, this Adrian, Mich., company produced motor-driven airplane toys—and also motor-driven toy vacuum cleaners.

United Mfg. Co., Inc. This Philadelphia, Penn., firm made the "United Vehicles" line of juvenile vehicles in the 1920s.

United Mask & Novelty Co. Novelty hats and masks, toy boats, games, and Christmas items were specialties of this postwar Glendale, N.Y., company.

U

United Metal Products This postwar Boston, Mass., firm issued the "Junior Venda" bubble gum bank.

United Model Airplane & Supply Co. Flying model airplane kits were 1930s products of this Irvington, N.J., firm. It also made "shelf" model kits.

United Pressed Products Co. This Chicago, Ill., specialist in molded papier-mache products made prewar Christmas, Halloween and Easter items, including favors, masks, hats and toys.

United Specialties of Birmingham, Inc. The "Thunderbird" coaster wagon of the mid-1950s was made by this Birmingham, Ala., company. It manufactured four all-steel models.

United Specialty & Toy Co. Caster wagons, scooters, and wheelbarrows were among this Leeds, Ala., firm's postwar products.

"U.S. Air Mail" kites prewar, see *Dolly Toy Co.*

U.S. Divers Co. Remote-control plastic skin diver toys were made in the early 1960s by this Los Angeles, Calif., company.

United States Electric Mfg. Co. Located on West 14th Street, New York City, this firm made "Mickey Mouse" and "Silly Symphony" flashlights in the later 1930s, as well as batteries for electric toys.

U.S. Finishing & Mfg. Co. The "New World Map Puzzle" and "Army-Navy Combat Picture Puzzles" of the war years were issued by this Chicago, Ill., firm.

United States Lock & Hardware Co. This prewar manufacturer of iron and "grey iron" items, based in Columbia, Penn., made toys including toy tools. It held an early license through Kay Kamen to issue Walt Disney jacks sets. By the late 1930s the firm was issuing banks.

"U.S. Marshall" holsters see *Leslie-Henry Co., Inc.*

U.S. Metal Toy Mfg. Co. A Brooklyn, N.Y., firm, U.S. Metal Toy issued horns, noisemakers, sand pails, watering cans, crickets, Halloween goods, carnival goods, and snow shovels in the Boomer years. It used the "Joys with U.S. Toys" slogan.

U.S. Model Aircraft Corp. A firm active in the 1910s and 1920s, U.S. Model Aircraft of Brooklyn, N.Y., made construction sets including the "Bellanca 'Columbia' Monoplane" and "Bremen 'Junkers' Monoplane." The firm combined with White Aeroplane Co. and Wading River Mfg. Co. in the 1920s.

U.S. Plastics Corp. Plastic toys comprised this postwar Pasadena, Calif., company's line.

U.S. Plastics, Inc. see *Precision Plastics Co.*

United States Playing Card Co. The "Po-ke-no" game of the 1930s was made by this Cincinnati, Ohio, firm. It also made playing cards and poker chips. It issued "Po-ke-no" through the Boomer years.

U.S. Pressed Steel Products Co. Prewar manufacturers of juvenile wheel goods depended on specialty suppliers for parts, including U.S. Pressed Steel Products Co., which made disc wheels, hub caps, and ball bearings.

United States Stuffed Toy & Novelty Co. A manufacturer of stuffed toys and novelties, this firms products were exclusively distributed by Bantam Products, located on Fifth Avenue, New York City, in the late prewar years.

U.S. Toy Co. A Detroit, Mich., firm, U.S. Toy made Auburn auto steering coaster wagons in the mid-1930s.

United Toy & Novelty Co. Small toys and novelties for the 5- and 10-cent chain store trade were specialties of this Akron, Ohio, firm in the late prewar years.

Universal Camera Corp. The "Univex" movie and "candid" cameras of the late 1930s, as well as films, were products of this

U

West 23rd Street, New York City, firm in the late 1930s.

Universal Game Co. Based in Chicago, Ill., in the late 1930s, Universal issued the "Helios" skill game.

Universal Games Co. The late 1930s game "The Mor-Fun Stock Exchange" was issued by this St. Louis, Mo., company.

Universal Model Airplanes, Inc. Model airplane construction kits and supplies were 1930s products of this Brooklyn, N.Y., company.

Universal Playthings, Inc. Toys including the "Sky Shooter" and "Cap Cane" were cap-firing products of this postwar Brooklyn, N.Y., company.

Universal Sales Corp. The "Flyin' Fool" all-metal airplane toys were made by this Detroit, Mich., company in the 1930s.

Universal Toy & Novelty Mfg. Co. This Third Avenue, New York City, firm's penny specialties in the 1920s included cutouts, strip pictures, drawing books, story books, "Schoolday" slates, "Magic Wonder Books," transfer pictures, "Kiddiegraph Motion Picture Booklet," and "Change-O-Graph." The firm continued emphasizing paper specialties in the 1930s and '40s, including painting outfits, sewing outfits, and Christmas surprise packages. During wartime, it made toy airplanes, boats, tanks, and novelties, and "Constructo" sets.

Universal Toy Co. The "Kolorwood" of plywood, coloring agents, and tools were issued by this Chicago, Ill., company in the late 1930s.

University Distributing Co. Based in Cambridge, Mass., University Distributing made prewar picture puzzles.

unstyled In farm toys, "unstyled" refers to early tractors not having grilles.

"Up-To-Date" cutout dolls see *Platt & Munk Co.*

Upp Doll Togs Co. A Kansas City, Mo., company, Upp Doll Togs issued handmade doll clothes in the late prewar years.

"Upson" puzzles see *The Tuco Work Shops.*

"Upsy Downsys" see *Mattel, Inc.*

Upton Machine Co. This St. Joseph, Mich., company issued the "American Dart" air rifle, introducing it in 1912. All Metal Products Co. bought the dies in 1927 from owners Sears Roebuck & Co., and sold them in turn to King Mfg. Co. in 1929, who dumped them in the Detroit River.

Urb Products Corp. Besides its specialty in pools, this postwar Brooklyn, N.Y., company made beach toys, inflatable toys, "Bop-O's," shuffleboards, bowling games, and table tennis sets.

"Usalite" flashlights prewar, see *U.S. Electric Mfg. Co.*

utensils, toy see *cooking and kitchen utensils, or house cleaning toys.*

"Utexiqual" see *The Kenton Hardware Co.*

Utica Cutlery Co. "Boy Scout" knives were among this Utica, N.Y., company's line in the late prewar years.

"Utilitoy" see *International Plastic Co.*

utility In farm toys, "utility" refers to a type of tractor having a wide front axle and lower center of gravity.

Utility Mfg. Co., Inc. The "Falcon" cameras of the later 1930s were issued by Utility, based on West 25th Street, New York City.

Utility Wood Products Co. A Chicago, Ill., firm, Utility Wood Products made prewar chess and checker sets, dice cups, and the "Eagle Brand" paper and composition poker chips.

Vv

vacuum cleaners, toy Toy vacuum cleaners remained popular toys from the prewar years through the end of the 20th century. Children emulating the actions of their parents naturally found satisfaction in pushing these toys around. Prewar manufacturers included All Metal Products, Gong Bell Mfg. Co., United Electric Mfg. Co., and Wolverine Supply & Mfg. Co.

Valentine Dolls, Inc. This postwar manufacturer was based in the Fifth Avenue Building, New York City.

valentines The exchanging of valentines was a charming Victorian custom that became a yearly classroom routine by the prewar and postwar years. While the valentines themselves are of interest to collectors of American childhood items, many of the cards had toy qualities, including the pop-ups and jointed valentines with moving parts. Prewar publishers included American Colortype Co., the Beistle Co., Fuld & Co., Paper Novelty Mfg. Co., Quality Art Novelty Co., Rust Craft Publishers, and W. & F. Mfg. Co. Postwar publishers included American Paper Specialty Co., the Beistle Co., Ben Mont Papers, Fuld & Co., Paper Novelty Mfg. Co., the Saalfield Publishing Co., and Standard Cellulose & Novelty Co.

Valley City Novelty Co. A Grand Rapids, Mich., firm, Valley City Novelty made kaleidoscopes in the late 1930s.

Valley Novelty Works A manufacturer active in Bloomsburg, Penn., through most of the first half of the 20th century, Valley Novelty Work's early game titles included "Capture the Fort" of 1914. In the 1930s the firm made games and toys including anagrams, bingo, farm sets, circus sets, forts and soldiers, block wagons, building blocks, spinner games, weaving looms, ironing boards, doll cradles, bathtub boat sets, and Christmas tree fence sets.

Van Cleef Bros. A Chicago, Ill., firm, Van Cleef Bros. made prewar play balls.

The Van Dam Rubber Co., Inc. Toy balloons, advertising balloons and balloon-batons were specialties of this Jerome Avenue, New York City, company.

J.B. Van Doren & Co. The "Bouncing Arrows" game of the late 1930s was issued by this South Braintree, Mass., company.

Van Dyke Products Located in Milwaukee, Wis., this paper products manufacturer made prewar embossed paper poker chips.

Van Golf Products Co. The "Puttch" miniature obstacle golf set was a 1930s product of this Fort Wayne, Ind., manufacturer. It also made the "Put-Cup" for putting practice.

Van Horn & Son, Inc. The "Van Horn Line" of costumes, masks and accessories were produced by this Philadelphia, Penn., firm from the 1920s through the years of the Great Depression.

"Van Loon" Hendrik Willem van Loon (1882-1944) was a popular journalist active in the 1920s and '30s, known especially for his books of historical and geographical interest. Public interest in his work was reflected in the world of playthings, with such educational items of the '30s as the "Van Loon" bookshelf and "Van Loon" puzzle produced by the Saalfield Publishing Co., and the "Van Loon's Wide World" game by Parker Bros.

"Hendrik Van Loon's Wide-World Game" by Parker Bros. was one of the educational toys inspired by the popular journalist.

Van Wagenen & Co. A Syracuse, N.Y., firm, Van Wagenen issued the wartime games "Attack," "Pursuit," and "Defense." The latter was available in "Pacific," "Atlantic," and "Service Men" editions.

Vanguard Toy Co. The "Uni-block" construction sets of the 1950s-60s were products of this Buffalo, N.Y., company.

"Vanta Baby" see *Amberg Dolls.*

Vantines, Inc. This Flushing, N.Y., manufacturer moved into polyethylene specialties in the 1950s, issuing bowling sets, "Pitch-Em-In" sets, juggler sets, barbells, canteens, banks, baseballs and bats, dolls, and doll bottles. The firm itself was established in 1866.

"Vari-Color" tops see *C.G. Wood, Co.*

Varney Model Railways Varney of Hollywood, Calif., produced scale model railway systems in the late prewar years. The company moved to Miami, Fla., and changed its name to Varney Scale Models in the 1950s. Its line emphasized "HO" gauge railway systems and electric trains.

Varsity Camera Corp. This manufacturer of adult and juvenile cameras was based on Astor Place, New York City, in the late 1930s.

"Vel-Kar" see *Junior Toy Corp.*

"Velo King" vehicles see *The E.C. Brown Co.*

velocipedes Velocipedes became popular soon after the introduction of pedaled vehicles in 1839, in Scotland. While undoubtedly a good many manufacturers experimented with the new plaything, the first and most important innovator and manufacturer in America seems to have been Benjamin Potter Crandall. He issued his velocipede, a three-wheeled affair, in the early 1840s. New improvements continued appearing under his and Jesse Crandall's supervision through the 1880s. Although eventually regarded as outdoor toys, in the early years the toys were seen as being for both outdoors and indoors. One 1850 advertisement boasted of "a few superior ones, suitable for using in the house."

One early Crandall model was the "American Trotter," which featured a wooden horse's head in the front and a sulky seat behind. Some Crandall velocipedes were all wood, while others used different combinations of wood and metal. Some had four wheels instead of three, and some used hand levers instead of foot pedals, in anticipation of the handcarts or the Irish Mail. One of the most interesting was the "Cantering Tricycle," which moved the rider with a horse-like motion as it rolled. Crandall velocipedes were given a gold medal at the 1876 Philadelphia Exposition.

In 1886 Jesse Crandall patented an improved treadle mechanism to increase the velocipede's efficiency, an improvement adopted by sewing machine manufacturers.

The number of manufacturers grew through the years. By prewar times some three dozen companies were involved. The name tricycle, already in wide use by the 1920s and 1930s, supplanted the older name in the Boomer years after having seen currency for nearly a century.

Prewar manufacturers included Aero Mfg. Co., the American National Co., Auto-Bike Co., the E.C. Brown Co., the Colson Co., the Dayton Toy & Specialty Co., the Emblem Mfg. Co., Garton Toy Co., the Gendron Mfg. Co., the Gendron Wheel Co., the Globe Co., D.P. Harris Hardware & Mfg. Co., C.H. Hartshorn, the Hedstrom-Union Co., Iver Johnson's Arms & Cycle Works, Junior Toy Corp., Kuniholm Mfg. Co., Lullabye Furniture Corp., Metalcraft Corp., the Monarch Products Co., the Murray Ohio Mfg. Co., Nicholas-Beazley, Real Cycle Co., O.W. Siebert Co., Skippy Racers, Steinfeld, the Frank F. Taylor Co., the Toledo Metal Wheel Co., United-Delta Corp., the Viking Co., and the Westfield Mfg. Co.

Garton's child's tricycle, 1950s.

In the postwar years, manufacturers included American Machine & Foundry, Blake & Conroy, Blazon, Evans Products, Garton Toy, Hedstrom-Union Co., Hettrick Mfg. Co., Junior Toy Division, Julius Levenson, McBride & Oxford Mfg. Co., Midwest Industries, Murray Ohio Mfg. Co., Schranz & Bieber Co., Schroeder Co., Ow. Siebert Co., Stelber Cycle Corp., and the Frank F. Taylor Co.

This Garton tricycle was probably intended as a sidewalk model.

ventriloquist dolls A popular plaything and stage device, ventriloquist dolls have included notables among their midst, especially the hit figures introduced by Edgar Bergen in 1938, "Charlie McCarthy" and "Mortimer Snerd." Other figures through the years included the mid-1950s "Howdy Doody" by Ideal Novelty & Toy Co., and "Willie Talk," introduced with composition features in 1939. Juro Novelty Co. made many ventriloquist figures, including the "Emmett Kelly" figure of the 1970s. The first ventriloquist baby doll was "Honey Munch," issued in 1974 by Eegee Co.

Venus Doll Co. Located on Broome Street, New York City, Venus made prewar dolls.

Venus Pen & Pencil Corp. This famous Hoboken, N.J., pencil company issued pre-sketched pencil activity sets, handicraft kits, crayons, and airline stewardess kits in the Boomer years.

Vera Toys Games and polyethylene sand toys were postwar products of this West 21st Street, New York City, company.

Vermont Novelty Works Based in Springfield, Vt., the 1859 firm of Ellis, Britton & Eaton, soon known as Vermont Novelty Works, made a variety of carriages and perambulators, toy gigs for dolls, toy carts, and a boy's tip cart. Its main creative spirit seems to have been senior partner Joel T.A. Ellis, who also ventured into doll manufacturing.

As early as 1862 it was making a log-cabin construction toy, called "Log Cabin Play Houses," The sets were made of hardwood, painted and varnished in red. The toy came in three sizes, making houses 8, 12, and 18 inches square, selling at 50 cents to a dollar. The firm also made toy split-rail fences. In Civil War times, the company made a toy cannon that shot marbles 40 to 60 feet. With the exception of the spring and trigger, it was made of painted wood, and cost 50 cents.

The firm's line also included stilts, rolling hoops, doll furniture, sleds, sleighs, and wagons. Later it added guitar and violin cases, and children's pianos.

The Cooperative Mfg. Co. was apparently a partner or related company. Vermont Novelty Works continued operation into the early 20th century. See also *Ellis, Joel T.A.*

Vermont Plywood Co. This Rochester, Vt., company made "Table Shuffleboard" in the late prewar years.

Victor Woodturning Co. Based on Broadway, New York City, Victor as a prewar nursery furniture manufacturer.

Victor Novelty Mfg. Co. This Cleveland, Ohio, firm made the "Giant Joy-ball" of the late 1920s. The balls featured five or eight colored panels, and retailed at 20 cents to $1.25.

"Victor" toy watches see *Cleinman & Sons, Inc.*

Victoria Doll Co., Inc. Established in the later 1930s on West 21st Street, New York City, Victoria made composition and stuffed dolls.

"Victory" This hopeful trade name was among the most common of the wartime years, such as in "Buddy 'L' Victory Toys." The name's use was intended to convey the

V

fact that many toy makers were devoting most and sometimes all of their manufacturing expertise to the war effort.

"Victory Flyer" wagon prewar, see *Lullabye Furniture Corp.*

Victory Mfg. Co. A Chicago, Ill., company, Victory issued games for adults, including checker and chess sets, poker chips, and Canasta trays, in Boomer years.

Victory Mask Co., Inc. Based on Bowery Street, New York City, in the 1920s, Victory made masks including luloups and "curtain characters" with or without hair, hoodwinks, Santa Claus masks, and beards. The firm was based on Cooper Square through the 1930s.

Victory Novelty Co. Novelty, cowboy, and baseball hats and caps were this Jersey City, N.J., firm's postwar line.

"View-Master" The "View-Master" stereoscopic viewers and film cards were introduced in 1939 by Sawyer's, of Portland, Ore. Early reels tended to have landscape and tourism subjects, and instructional subjects during wartime. Sawyer's bought the earlier stereoscope manufacturer Tru-Vue in 1951, which gave it access to rights to contemporary popular subjects, including Walt Disney characters. The firm was acquired in 1966 by General Aniline and Film Corp.

"Viking" The "Viking" trademark was used by several prewar manufacturers. Toledo Metal Wheel Co. used it on coaster wagons and sleds, and H.J. Hoenes Co. used the name for its line of steel toys.

Viking Aircraft Co. Viking Aircraft of Hamilton, Ohio, was a 1930s manufacturer of airplane model construction sets, parts, and supplies.

The Viking Co. This Philadelphia, Penn., firm made prewar velocipedes and sidewalk bikes.

Viking Products Division see *MPM Corp.*

"Viko" see *Aluminum Goods Mfg. Co.*

Vilas-Harsha Mfg. Co. This Chicago, Ill., firm produced children's playroom furniture, including wheeled cribs, in the 1920s.

"Villa" pistol prewar, see *The Dent Hardware Co.*

"Vindex" iron toys see *National Sewing Machine Co.*

Vinfloat Industries, Inc. This Los Angeles, Calif., firm issued vinyl squeeze toys and infants' toys in the 1950s and '60s.

"Viscoloid" "Viscoloid" dolls and toys were issued by DuPont Viscoloid Co. "Viscoloid" was a 1930s term for Celluloid used by DuPont.

A Visit from St. Nicholas The famous *A Visit from St. Nicholas,* by the professor of Biblical literature Clement C. Moore, first appeared in 1823 from The Troy (N.Y.) Sentinel. The narrative poem's first line, "'Twas the night before Christmas," was eventually adopted for the title. Reprinted widely already in its first decade, the poem appeared in book form in 1837.

Vista Toy Co. Wooden dollhouses and doll theaters were the specialty of this prewar Cassopolis, Mich., company. The "Vista" dollhouses came in five styles in the mid-1930s, made from grooved and joined wood painted with enamel, with AC or DC electric lighting available.

Vitos Products Co. Sand paint-by-number sets comprised this postwar Lynchburg, Va., firm's line.

The Vitro-Agate Co. The Vitro-Agate Co. of Parkersburg, W.V., made glass marbles from the 1930s through the postwar years. Although it issued marbles in a variety of colors, its "All Red Line" was important by the war years. In the 1950s and '60s, it used the "5 Star Brand" trade name, and the slogan, "The Pride of Young Americans." It categorized its marbles as "Cat Eyes," "All Reds," "Agates," "Aqua Jewels," and "Checkers."

The Vogel Mfg. Co. This Bridgeport, Conn., firm issued the Boomer-era "Mod-L-Stix" plastic construction sets.

V

"Vogue" bicycles for ladies prewar, see *The Colson Co.*

Vogue Doll Shoppe Based in West Somerville, Mass., the Vogue Doll Shoppe made prewar doll outfits, dressed dolls, fitted bassinets, and doll suitcases and trunks. The firm moved to West Medford, Mass., by the late 1930s, and to Medford, Mass., in the Boomer years, when it adopted the name Vogue Dolls, Inc.

In the mid-1950s, the "R & B - Arranbee Doll Co." line featured "Little Angel" of 1954 and her sister "Littlest Angel" of 1955. Other dolls included "Rock-Me Baby," "Baby Bunting," "Dream Baby," "Nanette," "Taffy," "Angel Face," and "Angel Skin."

The company became Vogue Dolls, Inc., in 1948, and moved in the Boomer years to Medford, Mass. An early postwar success in its line was "Jennie," a jointed composition doll 18-inches tall.

By the '60s the company was famous for its "Ginny Doll" family, featuring characters "Ginny," "Ginnette," "Jill" and "Jeff." The firm still used the "Arranbee Dolls," or "R & B Dolls," trade names, and the slogan, "Fashion Leaders in Doll Society." Its baby dolls used the "Baby Dear" and "Bobby Dear" names.

voices, doll and animal Voices for doll and animal toys were first developed in the 1800s. In the prewar years, several companies specialized in supplying these parts to toy manufactuers, including C. Luthard of Brooklyn, N.Y., Margon Corp., Marks Bros. Co., and Karl Ohlbaum & Son.

Voices, Inc. This Newark, N.J., firm advertised "genuine American-made 'Mama' voices" in the pre-Great Depression years. "Do you know that the difference in cost between a doll that just makes some sort of noise and one that says "Ma-Ma" clearly and distinctly is only 10 cents?" Voices moved to Spring Street, New York City, by the 1930s. It held patents and issued licenses in both the prewar and postwar periods for voice mechanisms used in dolls and animal toys. It also manufactured the voice boxes.

W.J. Voit Rubber Corp. A producer of sports balls through the prewar years, Voit also made inflated playground balls and "Hollywood balls" in the later 1930s. In the Boomer era the company kept its primary focus on outdoor sporting equipment, but still made playground balls, surf riders, wading pools, and swim rings.

Volume Sprayer Mfg. Co. This Tulsa, Okla., firm issued the "Contack" game of the late 1930s, and "No Joke" of 1941.

V

But — turn her on her RIGHT side — and "blink" she's fast asleep.

American Character Doll released "Toddletot" in the 1930s.

Ww

The W & F Mfg. Co., Inc. This manufacturer of prewar composition dolls also made Halloween, Valentines, Christmas and Easter favors and decorations, as well as Christmas ornaments. Located in Buffalo, N.Y., the firm was specializing in Christmas and Halloween candles by the late prewar years.

"W.C. Fields" doll late 1930s, see *Fleischaker & Baum.*

Waas & Son A Philadelphia, Penn., firm, Waas & Son made masquerade costumes and wigs, including Santa outfits, in the mid-1930s.

Wabash Industries This Wabash, Ind., firm made games and "Silver Arrow" baseballs in the late 1930s.

"Waddles" cloth animals prewar, see *Scovell Novelty Mfg. Co.*

The Waddell Co. Bagatelle games for two- and four-hand playing were 1930s products of this Greenfield, Ohio, company.

wading pools In the 20th century the wading pool became a necessity for many American middle-class households. Early manufacturers included American Playground Device Co., Close-To-Nature Co., Fulton Bag & Cotton Mills, Gendron Wheel Co., W.E. Hettrick & Son, the Hettrick Mfg. Co., and Muskin Mfg. Co.

Wading River Mfg. Co. see *U.S. Model Aircraft Corp.*

"Wag-O-Blox" see *The Frank F. Taylor Co.*

"Waggie" musical animals see *Eden Toys, Inc.*

"Wagglers" see *Expert Doll & Toy Co.*

The Wagner Mfg. Co. Famous for its cast-iron cooking utensils, Wagner also made prewar toy cooking utensil sets in cast iron and cast aluminum. It was based in Sidney, Ohio.

E. R. Wagner Mfg. Co. Located in North Milwaukee, Wis., E.R. Wagner supplied prewar manufacturers of juvenile wheel goods with products including disc wheels, hubcaps, and pedals.

Wagner Parade of Dolls This postwar Hollywood, Calif., company issued miniature dolls, crayon aprons, and jacks and ball bags.

"Wagon Train" One of the more popular western TV programs of the late 1950s and '60s, "Wagon Train" inspired playthings including badges and carded toy sets by John-Henry Mfg. Co.; coloring books, puzzles, and story books by Whitman Publishing Co.; games and puzzles by Milton Bradley Co.; holster sets and pistols by Leslie-Henry Co.; "Little Golden Books" by Golden Press; plastic horse and rider toys by Hartland Plastics; play suits by Sackman Bros.; trading cards by Topps Chewing Gum; and western hats by Arlington Hat Co.

wagons, coaster and express The toy wagon appears to be a venerable toy, although it may have first appeared in earlier centuries as not a toy but a working contrivance to assist working children. Toy wagons were made in America by the 19th century. By the 20th century, some firms built their business largely on the production of juvenile wagons, including Hamilton Steel Products, Janesville Products Co., and Radio Steel & Mfg. Co.

Other manufacturers of prewar coaster and express wagons included the American National Co., Atlas Doll & Toy Co., Auto-Bike Co., Auto-Wheel Coaster Mfg. Co., Burnham Mfg. Co., Coast Electric & Mfg.

Co., the Dayton Toy & Specialty Co., Dodge Mfg. Corp., Frederick Machine Works, Garton Toy Co., the Gendron Mfg. Co., the Gendron Wheel Co., the Globe Co., Heider Mfg. Co., the Hedstrom-Union Co., R. Herschel Mfg. Co., Horn Wagon Co., Hunefeld & Co., C.J. Johnson Co., Lullabye Furniture Corp., the Marlin Carriage Co., Metalcraft Corp., the Monarch Products Co., the Murray Ohio Mfg. Co., Paris Mfg. Co., Philadelphia Screen Mfg. Co., Radio Steel & Mfg. Co., Rainey Mfg. Co., Rolls Racer Corp., Sheboygan Coaster & Wagon Works, the Standard Novelty Works, the Toledo Metal Wheel Co., U.S Toy Co., White Coaster Wagon Works, H.C. White Co., and the Wood & Metal Products Co.

A number of these companies issued toy or miniature wagons as well, and also toy wheelbarrows and toy carts. Others with this focus included American Mfg. Concern, the American Toy & Mfg. Corp., the N.D. Cass Co., Clement Toy Co., the Delphos Bending Co., John W. Dobson, Drewry Bros., General Wheelbarrow Co., the Keydel Co., Leland Detroit Mfg. Co., the E.M. Nichols Co., the W.P. Pritchard Co., the A. Schoenhut Co., Skippy Racers, the Steel Stamping Co., the Toy Kraft Co., and Whitney Bros. Co.

Postwar manufacturers of coaster and express wagons included S.L. Allen & Co., Auto-Wheel Coaster Co., Cadillac Wagon Co., Garton Toy Co., Hamilton Steel Products, MPM Corp., the Murray Ohio Mfg. Co., Radio Steel & Mfg. Co., Ramrod Products, Scheuer Sales Corp., Steger Products Mfg. Corp., and United Specialty Co.

Garton Toy Co. made the "Red Streak" wagon in the 1950s.

Postwar manufacturers of toy wagons and carts included Blake & Conroy, Fisher-Price Toys, Garton Toy Co., Gerber Plastic Co., Hamilton Steel Products, the Hettrick Mfg. Co., Julius Levenson, Martin Industries, Ohio Art Co., Radio Steel & Mfg. Co., Scheuer Sales Co., the Steel Stamping Co., and Whitney Bros. Co.

"Wagons-Ho" game see *The Boyd Specialty Co.*

C.H. Waite & Co. This Lynnfield, Mass., firm made dollhouse furniture in the late 1930s.

Walco Bead Co. Established on West 37th Street, New York City, in the late 1930s, Walco made "Beadcraft" sets, bead jewelry, tile-craft sets, and marionettes. The firm became Walco Toy Co., located in Long Island City, N.Y., in the Boomer years. It continued issuing "Beadcraft" sets and educational toys.

Waldorf Toy Corp. This Fourth Avenue, New York City, firm issued toys and dolls "designed and constructed by the boys and girls of the progressive Waldorf School in Germany," in the late 1920s. The firm used the slogan, "The Toys of Real Educational Value." The line included 30 different toys of wood with colored stains, priced from 95 cents to $9.75.

"Walk-A-Way" 1930s, see *The Metalcraft Corp.*

"Walkabout Baby Bike" stroller see *The American-National Co.*

This 1930s wagon was the "Knee-Action Coaster" by The Dayton Toy & Specialty Co.

D. Walker D. Walker was the manufacturer of the "Baby-Tenda," an 1870s rocking horse on a stable base.

walkers, baby Besides their historical connection to early toy manufacturers, baby walkers are often of intrinsic interest to toy collectors. Important prewar manufacturers include the American National Co., Arney Amusement Devices, Auto-Bike Co., Auto-Wheel Coaster Co., Baby Saver Co., the W.J. Baker Co., Benner, Garton Toy Co., Gem Crib & Cradle Co., Gendron Wheel Co., Hamilton Steel Products, Hedstrom-Union Co., Ideal Products Corp., Iver Johnson's Arms & Cycle Works, the Kaymar Corp., the Kuniholm Mfg. Co., D.W. Lynch Co., the Monarch Products Co., Perfection Mfg. Co., L.B. Ramsdell Co., Readsboro Chair Co., Rockaway Mfg. Co., S. & E. Mfg. Co., Sheboygan Coaster & Wagon Works, O.W. Siebert Co., the Frank F. Taylor Co., the Toledo Metal Wheel Co., and H.C. White Co.

walking dolls see *dolls, walking.*

"Walky-Balky-Bak Up" toys 1930s, see *Fisher-Price Toys, Inc.*

Wallace Brands Co. The "Roofus Goofus Surprise Balls" of the early 1960s were issued by this Toledo, Ohio, company.

"Walt and Skeezix" see *"Skeezix."*

William K. Walthers, Inc. This Milwaukee, Wis., firm made "O" and "HO" gauge railroad systems in the late 1930s.

"Wannatoy" see *Dillon-Beck Mfg. Co.*

George D. Wanner & Co. This Dayton, Ohio, firm produced the "E-Z-Fly" kites of the 1920s. This portion of the business was sold in 1925 to Kilgore Mfg. Co. Model airplanes for use in the retail trade and for advertising purposes were made by at least the 1930s into the '40s.

"Wanted: Dead or Alive" CBS Films' "Wanted: Dead or Alive" inspired playthings in the early 1960s including hats by Newark Felt Novelty Co., and plastic figures by Hartland Plastics.

War of 1812 A social consequence of the War of 1812 may have been a softening of the New England Puritan ethic, as far as toys and recreation went. Imprisoned British soldiers were known to use their time making presents for the children of sympathetic citizens. Some of the prisoners might be considered the first full-time toy makers in the Colonies.

Ward Plastic & Rubber Co. Plastic cribbage boards, dominoes and novelties were the specialty of this Ferndale, Mich., firm in the late 1930s.

Margarete Ward Publications The "Gong Hee Fot Choy" fortune-telling games of the late 1930s were published by this Los Angeles, Calif., firm.

Warner Mfg. Co. Warner, of Bennington, Vt., issued prewar games.

Warren Paper Products Co. A Lafayette, Ind., company, Warren Paper Products Co. produced play houses for dolls in the earlier 1930s. By the end of the decade Warren was also making doll house furniture, garages, service stations, forts, soldier sets, airports, railroad equipment, Christmas tree fences and mangers, farm sets, and miniature villages. See also *Built-Rite Toys.*

Warwick Novelty Co. This Brooklyn, N.Y., firm made knitted doll outfits and stockings in the late prewar years. In the Boomer years, the firm continued its line of doll knitwear, socks, booties, polos, underwear, leotards, sweater sets, sunsuits, and tights.

Wash-A-Toy Co. Established in Chicago, Ill., in the late 1930s, Wash-A-Toy made painted oilcloth stuffed toys.

"Washable Woolies" stuffed animals prewar, see *F.W. Woolnough Co., Inc.*

The Washburn Co. Based in Rockford, Ill., the Washburn Co. issued "Dolly Ann" toy kitchen sets in the mid-1930s.

Washburn Mfg. Co. Based in Kokomo, Ind., in the late 1930s, Washburn made all-steel juvenile furniture.

washing machines Sold separately and as part of laundry sets, toy washing machines

W

developed as quickly from tub-and-washboard affairs as the real thing did. The names were often suggestive of their purpose, as in the "Washette" washing machine by Buffalo Toy & Tool Works. Other prewar manufacturers included V.M. Kearley Mfg. Co., Ohio Art Co., and Wolverine Supply & Mfg. Co. In the postwar years, manufacturers included Kalon Mfg. Co., Structo Mfg. Co., Wolverine, and C.G. Wood Co.

The "Buffalo Washer," a 14-inch tall toy washing machine by The Buffalo Toy & Tool Works, 1920s.

Washington Toys & Novelties, Inc.

Washington Toys & Novelties, located on Chrystie Street, New York City, made prewar sand pails, tin tea sets, and metal toys.

"Wasp" airplane vehicle see *American-National Co.*

watches, toy Toy watches were playthings issued in the earlier 20th century by S. Lisk & Bro., with Alexander Baron, Krischer's Mfg. Co., and Winchester & Woods joining Lisk by the 1930s. Lisk and Winchester & Woods were the major manufacturers in the late prewar years. During the Boomer years, besides the anonymously produced toy wristwatches from Japan, these toys were made by manufacturers including Cleinman & Sons, Pioneer Merchandise Co., President Novelty & Jewelry Co., Westclox, and Winchester & Woods.

water pistol see *pistols, water.*

"Water Wings," see *Ayvad Water-Wings, Inc.*

Waterbury Button Co. This Waterbury, Conn., button manufacturer made prewar mechanical toys, bakelite toys, garden sets, toy

clock-spring motors, and other parts used in toys. By the late 1930s Waterbury had a separate Toy Division specializing in cluster bubble pipes and sets, molded plastic and metal toys, bakelite whistles, and spring motors. The firm was called Waterbury Companies, Inc., in the 1950s and '60s. Its line included bubble pipes and magnifiers, and plastic and metal parts for other manufacturers.

Waterfield, James B. The "Majic Bugle" and "Musical Swagger Stick" flute of the 1930s were made by this Attleboro, Mass., company.

"Watermatic" water machinegun see *Park Plastics Co.*

The Watkins-Strathmore Co. see *The Strathmore Co.*

Charles H. Watson Co. Watson made "Dolls of All Nations," representing 24 nations, in the late 1930s. It was based in Boston, Mass.

Franklin Watts, Inc. This publisher of postwar juvenile books was based on Madison Avenue, New York City.

The William C. Waugh Co. Based in Boston, Mass., the William C. Waugh Co. made cowboy equipment.

wax crayons see *crayons.*

wax doll see *dolls, wax.*

"Waxcraft" molds see *Marks Bros. Co.*

The Wayne Toy Mfg. Co. A Dayton, Ohio, firm, Wayne made mechanical and action toys and games in the 1930s.

"Wayside" play store see *Rochester Folding Box Co.*

Wear Ever Baby Carriage Co., Inc. Doll carriages and toy chests were included in this Boomer-era line. Wear Ever was based in Brooklyn, N.Y.

Weaver Mfg. Co. This Rheems, N.Y., firm made toy scales in the late prewar years.

weaving looms see *looms.*

C.B. Webb Co. Webb exclusively distributed and perhaps later manufactured the

"Weaver Health Ball," "Weaver Valve Ball," and "Scholastic" balls of the 1930s and '40s. Webb was based in Lebanon, Penn.

"Weaver's Health Ball," by C.B. Webb Co.

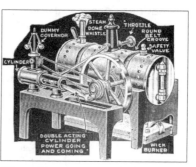

This working toy steam engine by Weeden was produced in the 1920s.

Weber Costello Co. Later to become one of the leading names in blackboards and erasers, Weber Costello of Chicago Heights, Ill., began issuing toy blackboards, blackboard erasers, crayons, maps and globes in the 1930s. The firm's Boomer-era line also included tempera and watercolor sets.

Jon Weber Manufactory This Cleveland, Ohio, firm issued "Jongames," "Art" and "Jack" dice, "Jondart," "Palmit" paddles, and "Aircourt Shuttles" in the late 1930s and '40s. In the 1950s and '60s it issued games for adults and children, "Bookette" games, pocket games, rack items, and dice.

Webo Toys Wooden pull toys were the postwar specialty of this Alexandria, La., company.

"Wee Folk" miniatures see *Rempel Mfg. Co.*

Weeden Mfg. Co. An important early toy maker, Weeden was based in New Bedford, Mass., where it was founded in 1883 by William N. Weeden. It produced a working toy steam engine in 1884, and soon was also producing "live" steamboats, fire engines, and other wheel toys. The firm's line also included toy automobiles, tractors, and road rollers by the 1920s. By the 1930s it was producing a large variety of to steam engines, boats, and locomotives, and electrically heated toy steam engines and stoves. By the late '30s the company had added alcohol-burning toy steam engines to its line. Weeden was sold to Pairpont Co. at the end of the decade.

The S.J. Wegman Co. Based in Lynbrook, N.Y., in the Boomer years, Wegman issued toys including space ships, tanks, electrified doll houses, and children's herbaria.

Weil Bros. The "Nonpareil" toys of the 1950s and '60s were products of this Newark, N.J., company. The line included mechanical metal and lithographed metal humming tops and toys, plastic toys, carnival toys, and Christmas novelties.

Weinig Products Co. This Cleveland, Ohio, firm made prewar toy motors.

"Wel-Drest" baby dolls prewar, see *Dolls' Tailors Co.*

Welded Plastics Corp. Poly-bagged rack toys were Boomer-era specialties of this Park Avenue, New York City, company. It made slate sets, finger paints, pinwheels, party hats and favors, bead sets, crayons, chalks, and cosmetic sets.

Well Made Doll Co., Inc. This Wooster Street, New York City, company made prewar stuffed and composition dolls, including the "Q-T" drinking and wetting dolls of the late 1930s. The firm was based on Greene Street by wartime, with the new name Well Made Doll & Toy Co. During the war it issued composition dolls, stuffed dolls, "Victory" toys, and cowboy holster outfits. "Bandbox Baby Dolls" were also made by this company.

Well-Worth Mfg. Co., Inc. Doll strollers were this Little Neck, N.Y., company's specialty in the 1950s and '60s.

W

Wells Badger Corp. Based in Milwaukee, Wis., this postwar firm made both Western toy sets and Christmas manger sets.

"Wells Fargo" The popular "Tales of the Wells Fargo" inspired playthings including badges and carded toy sets by 20th Century Varieties; coloring books, story books, and puzzles by Whitman Publishing Co.; games and puzzles by Milton Bradley Co.; gun racks by DeKalb Toys; hobby horses and guitars by Rich Industries; holsters, pistols and rifles by Esquire Novelty Co.; inflatable bop bags by U.S. Fiber & Plastics Corp.; "Little Golden Books" by Golden Press; paint and crayon sets by Transogram Co.; plastic figures by Hartland Plastics; target games by T. Cohn; trading cards by Topps Chewing Gun; viewer and film by Fillum Fun; and western hats by Arlington Hat Co.

Wells Mfg. Co., Inc. Jack sets, spinners and chalkboards were among this postwar New Vienna, Ohio, firm's products.

Welna Distributing Co. Welna of Omaha, Neb., issued the "Scrimmage" football game in the late 1930s.

Welsh Co. see *The Welsh-Hartman Co.*

Welsh-Hartman Co. This St. Louis, Mo., manufacturer of the "Hush-a-bye" baby swings and nursery accessories also made prewar doll swings. By the late prewar years, when the firm's name had become Welsh Co., it had added "Easy Fold" collapsible baby carriages, and doll carriages and sulkies.

John C. Welwood Corp. Located on West 42nd Street, New York City, Welwood obtained a late 1930s license to issue Edgar Bergen character-related handkerchiefs and bandanas.

Wen-Mac Corp. This Boomer-era Los Angeles, Calif., company issued pre-assembled, engine-powered plastic flying airplanes, the "Automite" race cars, "Aquamite" inboard speedboats, miniature one-cylinder engines, and model accessories. Its airplane line included the "Turbojet," "Aeromite," "Corsair," "Navy Cutlass," and "Beechcraft Bonanza."

The Wendt Billiard Mfg. Co. This Milwaukee, Wis., firm made various kinds of outdoor juvenile furniture in the 1930s. By the late prewar years it was specializing in juvenile lawn, porch, shipboard and beach furniture.

H. Wenzel Tent & Duck Co. "Lone Ranger" tents by this firm included camp tents, umbrella tents, card table tents, and tepees, as well as a "Lone Ranger and Tonto" wigwam, in the 1950s and early '60s. The St. Louis, Mo., firm used display cartons with cutout masks for the "Lone Ranger," "Tonto," and their equipment.

Wesley Toy & Novelty Co. Lead toys from this Carlton, Minn., company included cowboys, Indians, knights, soldiers, and wild animals in the 1930s.

West Bend Aluminum Co. A major manufacturer of general aluminum goods, this West Bend, Wis., company made prewar and postwar junior housekeeping sets and play cooking utensils.

West-Craft Novelty Co., Inc. The "Action Basketball" game of the early 1960s was issued by this St. Charles, Mo., company.

West Georgia Mills Western rope toys including lariat ropes and "Lass-O-Hoops" were specialties of this postwar Whitesburg, Ga., company, as well as jump ropes.

West Lake Co. West Lake of Chicago, Ill., made the 1890 "Matchless" air rifle.

West Lake Model Co. Metal toy boats and submarines were specialties of this Erie, Penn., firm in the late prewar years. It also made wooden mechanical boats.

"West Point Cadets" plastic figures 1960s, see *Lido Toy Co.*

"West Point Cadets" rubber soldiers 1930s, see *Rider Rubber Novelties.*

Westclox This Division of General Time Corp., LaSalle, Ill., issued Boomer-era children's watches and character alarm clocks.

Western Aircraft Mfg. Co. The ready-built "Dragon-Fly" model airplanes and gliders of the 1930s and '40s were made by this Los Angeles, Calif., company.

"Western Boy" guns and holsters
see *R. & S. Toy Mfg. Co., Inc.*

Western Coil & Electrical Co.
The "Midget Dispatcher" and "Tru-Trak" train toys of the 1930s and '40s, as well as a "Burlington-Zephyr" streamlined train, were made by this Racine, Wis., manufacturer. In the Boomer years, the company specialized in airplane kits, satellite toys, mechanical toys, balsa-wood educational toys, and electrical toys.

"Western Frontier" holsters
see *Jago Novelty Co., Inc.*

Western Leather Novelties
Holster sets and cap guns were the postwar specialty of this Franklin Park, Ill., company.

"Western Ranger" holsters
see *Alexander Baron.*

Western Reserve Rubber Co.
This Akron, Ohio, firm made rubber toy balloons and balloon novelties in the late 1930s.

"Western Scout" gun
see *Fox Co.*

Western Reserve Rubber Co.
This Akron, Ohio, firm made prewar rubber toy balloons and balloon novelties.

Western Stamping Co.
The "Tom Thumb" toy cash registers and toy typewriters were 1950s and '60s products of this Jackson, Mich., company.

"Tom Thumb Typewriter" by Western Stamping Co.

Western Tablet & Stationery Corp.
Based in Dayton, Ohio, this stationery manufacturer issued Edgar Bergen character-related notebooks, binders, and fillers in the late 1930s.

The Westfield Mfg. Co.
This wheel goods manufacturer made prewar bicycles, children's vehicles, velocipedes, and "bicyclets." It was based in Westfield, Mass. Its trade names included "Columbia" for its bicycles, and "Boycycles" for its velocipedes. Through the Boomer years the firm continued the "Columbia" and "Columbia-Built" bicycle lines.

Westland Plastics, Inc.
Infants' toys and accessories comprised this Los Angeles, Calif., firm's line.

Westminster Sports
Table tennis sets and badminton were among this West 24th Street, New York City, firm's offerings from the 1930s through the postwar years.

Westred, Inc.
Based in Niles, Calif., Westred issued Fiberglas-reinforced play stoves and refrigerators in the 1950s and '60s.

A.N. Wetherbee
This Lyndonville, Vt., manufacturer issued wood spinning tops in the 1920s through the 1930s.

Wham-O Mfg. Co.
Wham-O was established in 1948 in San Gabriel, Calif., as a firm to issue the "Wham-O" slingshot. It added toys through the years, including the "Pluto Platter" in 1955, and "Hula Hoop" in 1958. The "Frisbee" name for the "Pluto Platter" was registered in 1959, although the older name continued in use for at least a year. The firm's other toys included "Flying Saucer" horseshoe games, "Sputnik Sailing Satellite," "Fun Farm," "Draw Yarn," "Circus Cycle," "Batty Trainer," and "Silly String."

"Whee-Lo"
see *Maggie Magnetic, Inc..*

wheel goods
see *bicycles, wagons, handcars, pedal cars, scooters, and velocipedes.*

wheelbarrow toys
see *wagons.*

wheeled animal toys
Animal toys attached to wheeled platforms are known in terra cotta from countries including Persia

and Cyprus from the first millennium B.C. Stuffed animal toys on wheeled platforms, especially horse toys, were highly popular in the 19th and earlier 20th centuries.

"Pretty Polly," a wheeled toy from the Gibbs Mfg. Co., 1920s.

"Wheelum" pull toys 1930s, see *Fisher-Price Toys, Inc.*

whips From at least the 1850s, whips were often listed among toy selections by American retailers.

"Whirl King" return tops see *The Fli-Back Sales Co.*

Whirley Corp. The "Whirley-Whirler" action juggling toy was a 1950s-60s product of this St. Louis, Mo., company. The firm introduced "Jiggle Stick" balancing toys, the "TV Magic Kaleidoscope Wheel," and "Saucer-Tosser" in 1960.

"Whirling Saucer" snow saucer see *Napco Industries, Inc.*

whistles Wood whistles, from Colonial times and presumably earlier, were associated with the willow tree, since its bark could be more easily separated from the pith than was the case with many other woods. Whistles were also likely among the earliest toys made by American tinware manufacturers, since they required relatively little metal.

In prewar times some of the most famous whistles were the canary warblers, which were made by various metal casting companies.

Prewar whistle manufacturers included the Alox Mfg. Co., Bar Zim Toy Mfg. Co., Leigh A. Elkington, Harvard Electric Co., Kirchhof Patent Co., Noveloid Co., Peter F. Pia,

Smethport Specialty Co., the Thompson Mfg. Co., and the Tyler Can Co.

Postwar manufacturers included Alox, Elmar Products Co., Field Mfg. Co., Goody Mfg. Co., Hale-Nass Corp., Jak-Pak-Inc., Kirchhof, Lido Toy Corp., Nadel & Sons, Pal Plastics, Proll Toys, Pyro Plastics Corp., Riemann, Seabrey Co., Spec-Toy-Culars, Star Mfg. Co., and 20th Century Varieties.

White Aeroplane Co. see *U.S. Model Aircraft Corp.*

White & Wyckoff Mfg. Co. This Holyoke, Mass. company issued Edgar Bergen character-related greeting cards and stationery in the late prewar years.

H.C. White Co. This North Bennington, Vt. firm issued the "Kiddie" line of juvenile vehicles in the 1920s. The line included children's steering strollers modeled after the "Taylor-Tot," velocipedes, pedal airplanes, and wood-seat beginner trikes, as well as juvenile furniture. The company continued to make "Kiddie" and "Kiddie Kars" items, including pedar cars, play wagons, coaster wagons, baby walkers, and strollers, as well as "White's" juvenile desks and furniture. By the end of the '30s, the "E.C. White Kiddie Kar" and walker were being manufactured by Hedstrom-Union Co.

H.C. White's pedal airplane toy, "White Eagle," released in 1929.

White Coaster Wagon Works Located in Sheboygan Falls, Wis., this company made prewar coaster wagons.

White Eagle Rawhide Mfg. Co. The "Eagle" percussion instruments of the 1950s-

60s, were issued by this Chicago, Ill., company. It also made the "Hit It" game.

"White Face" wooden dominoes
see *The Embossing Co.*

White-Hill Co. This Boston, Mass., company made the "Little Millionaire" savings banks of the mid-1930s.

white metal see *metal alloy toys.*

Lisbeth Whiting Co., Inc. Based in Brooklyn, N.Y., this postwar firm issued charm kits, embroidery and sewing sets, leather-craft and metal-tapping kits, and other activity playthings.

Whitman Publishing Co. Located in Racine, Wis., Whitman Publishing held an early licensing agreement through Kay Kamen to produce Walt Disney character-related merchandise in the "Popular Priced Books" category, with games following soon afterwards, including "Mickey Mouse Old Maid Game." In the late 1930s it issued Edgar Bergen character-related books and games, and was also issuing games under other licenses, including "Terry and the Pirates."

In the 1930s, besides its "Big Little Books" and "Big Big Books," it was producing puzzles, paper dolls, and "kindergarten pastimes."

The company's prewar game titles included "Fortune-Telling Game" and "Play Football," in 1934; "All-Star Baseball Game," "G-Men Clue Games," and "Mickey Mouse Bridge Game," in 1935; "Stratosphere," in 1936; "Grand National Sweepstakes," "How Good Are You?," "Little Orphan Annie Rummy Cards," and "Who Is the Thief?," in 1937; and "Corner the Market," "Ferdinand Card Game, "Kentucky Derby Racing Game, "National Derby Horse Race," and "Navigator" in 1938. Also released in 1938 were the "Charlie McCarthy" titles "Game of Topper," "Put and Take Bingo Game," "Question and Answer Game," "Rummy Game," and "Flyin' Hats."

"Charlie Chan Game," "Gang Busters Game," "Pinocchio Playing Card Game," and "Red Ryder Target Game" appeared in 1939. Early 1940s titles included "Blondie Playing Card Game," "Telegrams," and "Zoom" in 1941, and "Game of Midget Speedway" in 1942.

The firm continued issuing playthings during wartime, including paint, cutout, picture, and "Better Little" books, games, and stationery supplies. Whitman's postwar line continued to emphasize children's books and games, picture puzzles, and playing cards.

Whitney Bros. Co. This Marlboro, N.H., firm made prewar doll cradles, push toys, pull toys, toy riding horses, stick horses, toy wagons, carts, wheelbarrows, sulkies, and toy ironing boards. The firm expanded its line to include doll bassinets, beds, cradles, high chairs and tea wagons by the late prewar years, as well as rocking horses, shooflies, and Easter toys. The doll nursery items and doll furniture were the firm's lead products through the Boomer years.

F.A. Whitney Carriage Co. A Leominster, Mass., carriage manufacturer also made doll carts in the 1920s. The firm added juvenile furniture to its line in the 1930s-40s.

Whitney Mfg. Co. This 19th century Leominster, Mass., carriage manufacturer also made doll carriages.

The Whitney Reed Co. Based in Leominster, Mass., this manufacturer of juvenile furniture and reed and rattan furniture also made prewar and postwar hobbyhorses. The line included shooflies and pony rockers by the 1940s.

The Whittier Craftsmen This Amesbury, Mass., company made games in addition to brass spinnings in the late 1930s.

"Whiz-A-Long" snow scooter see *Iron Products Corp.*

"Whizzer" steam engine, 1930s, see *American Toy Airship Co.*

"Whoopee Riders" exerciser 1930s, see *Lloyd Mfg. Co.*

"Who's Afraid of the Big Bad Wolf" see *"The Three Little Pigs."*

wicker Wicker was a material used for toys and doll carriages, usually in combination with wood, in the 19th and 20th centuries.

Wicker Toy Mfg. Co. This Columbus, Ohio, firm made prewar dollhouse furniture and rugs, doll houses, play doctor cases, and novelties including novelty lamps.

"Wide Awake Clocks" "Wide Awake Clocks" was a popular game of the late 1800s by Charles M. Crandall.

Widmeier, C.J. Established in Philadelphia, Penn., in the late 1930s, Widmeier manufactured darts and dartboards, and toy money.

Wiffle Ball, Inc. Established in the 1950s in Shelton, Con., this firm issued the "Wiffle Ball," a plastic baseball. The firm's line included stick bat and ball sets, backyard golf club sets, plastic basketballs, and plastic footballs by the late 1950s.

wigs, beards and mustaches see *masquerade costumes.*

Wilder, Crocker Crocker Wilder was a craftsman associated with the Tower Toy Guild.

Wilder Mfg. Co. This game manufacturer was based in St. Louis, Mo., in the 1920s through the years of the Great Depression. Its early titles included "Fish Pond," "Touchdown Football Game," and "Tiddley Winks Game." Others included "Construction Game" in 1925, "Ocean to Ocean Flight Game" in 1927, and "Fore Country Club Game of Golf," "Jolly Robbers," and "Movie-Land Keeno" in 1929. Games of the earlier 1930s, when the firm was known as the Wilder Corp., included "Hit and Run Baseball Game," "Obstacle Race," and "Wilder's Football Game." Wilder also made puzzles and kites.

Wile Co. This Rochester, N.Y., company made 1930s puzzle greeting cards.

Wilkening Mfg. Co. "Mr. Wiggle," a coil spring toy, was a product of this postwar Philadelphia, Penn., company. It also made plastic and metal push and pull toys, games, and puppets.

Wilkins Toy Co. James S. Wilkins founded Wilkins Toy Co. in 1890 in Keene, N.H. The company became one of the first to issue toy automobiles in America, doing so around 1895. Although Henry T. Kingsbury, also of Keene, N.H., bought out Wilkins in that year, the Wilkins name and trademark were kept until 1919.

The Wilkins Toy Mfg. Co. Based in Pawtucket, R.I., Wilkins made doll trunks in the 1930s and '40s.

G.C. Willett & Co. Based in Washington, D.C., G.C. Willett made prewar celluloid pinwheels, paper horns, and novelties.

T.A. Williams T.A. Williams of Skohegan, Maine, was one of the early manufacturers of ice skates in the mid-19th century.

Williams Character Marionettes This character marionette manufacturer was based in Independence, Mo., in the 1950s and '60s.

The A.C. Williams Co. A major prewar manufacturer of cast-iron toys, the A.C. Williams Co. was founded in 1886 in Ravenna, Ohio. From 1893 into the 1920s it produced toy horse-drawn rigs, automobiles, airplanes, and tractors. In the 1930s, the company produced savings banks, wheel toys, hammers, hatchets, and novelties. Many of its products appeared in five-and-dimes including Woolworth's and Kresge's. The company remained in business through 1939.

D.S. Williams Co., Inc. The "Pla-Skate" indoor-outdoor roller skates of the 1950s-60s were issued by this Shillington, Penn., company.

Williams Kast Art Co. The "Kast Art" white-metal miniatures of the 1930s and '40s were made by this Stockton, Calif., firm.

Williamsburg Chair Factory, Inc. Shooflies, musical rockers and toy chests were among the products of this postwar Williamsburg, Ohio, company.

"Willie Wuzzles" picture puzzles 1930s, see *The Platt & Munk Co., Inc.*

Dixie Willson Established in Hollywood, Calif., Willson issued the "Showbox" game of play-theater in the late 1930s.

B. Wilmsen, Inc. Wilmsen was a late 1930s manufacturer of Christmas goods, including decorations and stockings, based in Philadelphia, Penn. The firm continued through the postwar years.

Robert Wilson, Inc. This manufacturer of the "Kopy Kat" paint sets of the late 1930s also made "Helen Joseph" marionettes. The firm was based in Detroit, Mich.

Rollin Wilson, Inc. In addition to adult sports equipment, this Memphis, Tenn., firm made toy archery, golf and tennis sets in the 1930s and '40s, through the war years. The firm was separate from Wilson Sporting Goods Co. of Chicago, Ill., which seemed to specialize in equipment for adults. Rollin Wilson continued issuing dart games, bow and arrow sets, toy golf sets, toy baseball sets, and croquet through the Boomer years.

Wilson Mfg. Co. This St. Louis, Mich., firm made prewar football games and dice games.

Wilson Novelties, Inc. This Watsontown, Penn., firm issued the "Wilson Walkies" in the 1940s and apparently earlier. The line of walkers, or "walking miniatures," included a penguin, elephants and other animals, soldiers, and clowns. While most of the figures were relatively simple painted-wood figures, "Little Miss Walkie" had molded features and a fancy dress. The "Little Red Riding Hood" walker came with a wooden rocking cradle.

Wilson's of Cleveland Despite its name, this postwar firm was based in Fort Lauderdale, Fla. It made miniature electric and wind-up motors.

Winchester & Woods, Inc. This Baltimore, Md., firm made stem-winding toy watches from the 1930s through the Boomer years.

Winchester Repeating Arms Co. This Division of Western Cartridge Co., based in New Haven, Conn., issued "Winchester" rolling skates in the late 1930s. In the Boomer years, the Winchester-Western Division issued the skates. The line included "tot-tailored" models "Trainer," "Advanced Trainer," and "Junior," and the "super-speed"

models "Leader," "Standard," and "Deluxe." The "Deluxe" was the first sidewalk skate equipped with rubber wheels and double ball bearings. The "super-speed" models had leather straps.

Winchester Toy Co. The "Golden Fleece Toys" of the 1930s and '40s, which included lambs-wool stuffed Scotties, teddy bears, lambs, bunnies, and Eskimo dolls, were made by this Peabody, Mass., company.

"Windopakt" doll clothes see *Dolls' Tailors Co.*

Windy Boat Works This Rochester, N.Y., firm made sailboat kits, and balloon and glider target games.

Winfield Mfg. Co. Hobbyhorses were among the juvenile furniture manufactured by Winfield, based in West Winfield, N.Y., in the Boomer years.

Wing Mfg. Co. see *The Kenton Hardware Co.*

"Wingfoot" roller skates see *D.P. Harris Hardware & Mfg. Co.*

"Winky-Blinky Fire Truck" see *Fisher-Price Toys, Inc.*

"Winner" electric trains 1930s, see *Lionel Corp., The*

Winner Mfg. Co. A Trenton, N.J., manufacturer of ski poles and swimming items in the late 1930s, Winner also made water toys.

"Winnie-the-Pooh" The adventures of the incredibly popular British teddy bear Winnie-the-Pooh translated easily into playthings from the prewar years on. Early toys included the mid-1930s "Winnie-the-Pooh Everedy" modeling sets by the Embossing Co., a game by Parker Bros., infant novelties by Richard G. Krueger, paper novelties by Dennison Mfg. Co., puzzles by Madmar Quality Co., and slates and easels by National School Slate Co. The 1959 "Winnie the Pooh Game" was issued by Parker Bros.

Winnie-the-Pooh Association The business in issuing Winnie-the-Pooh tie-in merchandise became large enough that an association was formed for authorized manu-

W

facturers. It was based on Park Avenue, New York City, in the mid-1930s.

"Winnie Winkle" Winnie Winkle, the title character of a daily newspaper comic strip in the early 1930s, was popular enough to appear in books from Cupples & Leon Co., and in a variety of playthings through the decade. Milton Bradley Co. published the "Winnie Winkle Cartoon Game." McLoughlin Bros. came out with crayon and paint books, and Samuel Gabriel Sons & Co. published "Winnie Winkle and her Paris Costumes" cutouts.

Winslow Skate Co. Established in Worcester, Mass., in 1856, Winslow was one of the early manufacturers meeting the popular demand for skates in the mid-19th century.

John C. Winston A Philadelphia, Penn., publisher, John C. Winston was an important prewar publisher whose line included children's books.

Winston Products, Inc. Games and toy periscopes were produced by this Westmont, Ill., firm in the 1950s-60s.

Winters & Crampton Mfg. Co. A Grandville, Mich., firm, Winters & Crampton made a 1930s scooter on runners, for use in the snow.

"Winwood" toy watches see *Winchester & Woods.*

Wipco, Inc. Miniature dolls, undressed dolls, walking dolls, doll accessories, and pre-school toys comprised this postwar line. Wipco was based in the Fifth Avenue Building, New York City.

Wirsig Products Co. Spring horses and rocking horses were among this Deepwater, Mo., company's postwar products.

Van A. Wirt The "Skyways" game of the late 1930s was made by this Chicago, Ill., company.

Wisconsin Toy Co. The "Pioneer Builder" log cabin construction sets of the 1930s were issued by this Milwaukee, Wis., firm. Consisting of interlocking flat blocks, much like a simple version of Crandall's blocks, they could be used for making items

ranging from buildings and forts to locomotives and covered wagons.

"Pioneer Builder" log cabin set by Wisconsin Toy Co., 1930s.

wishbone doll see *doll, wishbone.*

Withington This postwar West Minot, Maine, company specialized in outdoor playthings, including archery sets, croquet, ski skates, and toboggans.

"Wizard" bicycle headlights see *The Seiss Mfg. Co.*

"Wobble" animated paper novelties see *Adler Favor & Novelty Co.*

"Wobble-Woofs" wooden toys see *Henry Pilcher's Sons, Inc.*

Woerner's Mfg. Works Woerner's of Lancaster, Penn., made "Yankee Doodle" Fourth of July aerial toys in the 1930s and '40s. The company also made Christmas tree fences. By the late '30s, when it changed its name to Woerner Mfg. Works, it also made paper cap canes in both single-shot and repeating varieties.

A.H. Wohlleben This Baltimore, Md., firm made dolls, toys, and doll hospital supplies in the late 1930s.

Louis Wolf & Co., Inc. An important importer in the 1920s and '30s, Louis Wolf issued the "Perfection" line of toys, forts, and dollhouses. It also made flapper dolls. Louis Wolf sometimes worked in cooperation with the Bing Wolf Corp. of the 1920s. It was based on Fourth Avenue, New York City, in the '20s and '30s, moving to East 23rd Street by the late prewar years.

Robert Wolff Woodcraft Corp. The "Ad-A-Lite" electric bagatelle and roulette game of the mid-1930s was a product of this E. 18th Street, New York City, firm.

I.B. Wolfset & Co. Plastic chime rattles, roly-polys and squeeze toys were among this East 22nd Street, New York City, firm's line in the 1950s and '60s. It also made dolls, glove dolls, stuffed toys, doll outfits, and mechanical toys.

Wollensak Optical Co. Based in Rochester, N.Y., Wollensak Optical made juvenile field glasses, telescopes, and microscopes in the 1930s and '40s.

The Wolper Toy Co. This postwar Brooklyn, N.Y., company specialized in fur and plush stuffed toys and novelties.

Wolverine Supply & Mfg. Co. Wolverine maintained its factory in Pittsburgh, Penn., where the company had been founded in 1903 by B.F. Bain. Wolverine became one of America's foremost names in tin toy manufacturing.

In the 1920s, Wolverine produced the "Sandy Andy" sand toys, "Sunny Andy" toys and games, and "Sunnie Suzy" toys for "little ladies." The sand toys frequently featured silhouette figures, although some had color designs. At the end of the decade the company introduced "new members of the Wolverine Toy Family."

"Pennant Winner," a "real-life baseball game," was a kind of bagatelle, with a flipper switch at the home plate of the diamond depicted on the playing surface. Others included "Fleet Flyer," an airplane toy, "Merry Miller," "Hoop-O-Loop Hunting Game," and three sizes of "Gee Wiz." It maintained its factory in Pittsburgh, Penn., and general sales office in the Fifth Avenue Building.

Notable 1930s toys included the "Corner Grocer" (No. 182), an all-metal toy measuring 31" across that folded out to become a grocery store, complete with miniature grocery packages. The separate counter included such details as metal money, a weighing scale, dial phone, and wrapping paper. Also extremely popular were the Washing Machine Sets (Nos. 170, 174, and 178), with tin wringer-washer, drying rack, and washing tub.

Several popular Wolverine toys of the 1930s appeared under "Sandy Andy," "Sunny Suzy," and "Sunny Andy" names. The company's included various large bus and automobile toys, educational toys, flower planting sets and greenhouses, mechanical toys, sand pails, sprinkling cans, automatic sand and marble toys, musical toys, pull toys, construction toys, action games, horse race games, horseshoe games, baseball games, toy electric irons and vacuum cleaners, tin and enameled tea sets, and toy washing machines. The greatly popular toy kitchen sets remain among the toys most commonly encountered on the collector trail.

The company's prewar games included "Aeroplane Race" and "Motor Race" in 1922; "Junior Motor Race" in 1925; "Across the Channel" and "Speed Boat Race" in 1926; "Gee-Wiz Horse Race" in 1928; "Tipit" in 1929; "Gym Horseshoes," "Hoop-O-Loop," "Neck and Neck," and "Olympic Runners" in 1930.

Wolverine was also a player in the wheel goods arena. The "Wolverine Speedster" and "Wolverine Sport" were early wagons, with the "Wolverine Scooter" being a durable entry in its category. The "Wolverine Bike" was actually a simply constructed tricycle.

"Airplane Carrier," a tin ship 18-1/2 inches long with three planes, issued in 1939, was one of the company's late prewar successes. It retailed for 50 cents.

Wolverine's "Corner Grocery" all-metal toy store.

In wartime, Wolverine issued sand toys using wood and "permaboard," including sand pails, sand mills, and sand sieve sets, as well as housekeeping toys and laundry sets. A lead item was the "Victory Garden," a play set with toy tools, pots, and seeds.

In the postwar years, Wolverine's line remained close to its prewar one. It continued issuing "Sunny Andy," "Sunny Suzy," and "Sandy Andy" toys and games, including housekeeping toys, laundry sets, all-metal grocery stores, kitchen cabinets and play stoves, decorated tea sets, action games, horserace games, horseshoe games, marble games, baseball games, adult games, bell pull toys, educational toys, mechanical toys, automatic sand and marble toys, sand pails, sprinkling cans, and musical toys.

Wolverine was named after its founder's hometown. It eventually became a subsidiary of Spang Industries, with production moving in 1970 to Boonville, Ark. The Wolverine name was later changed to Today's Kids.

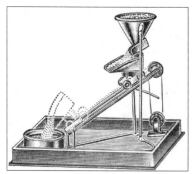

"Sandy Andy," a Wolverine sand toy from the 1920s.

Wonder-Art Enterprises Ring-toss games and "Midget Movies" were produced by this Boston, Mass., postwar company.

Wonder Books, Inc. This Boomer-era publisher of 25-cent picture books, coloring books and playbooks was a subsidiary of Grosset & Dunlap.

Wonder Products Co. The "Wonder Horse" of the 1950s and '60s, a spring-action hobbyhorse, was produced by this Collierville, Tenn., company. The line included wood and plastic model horses, raised on wood and metal bases. Names included "The Wonder Boy," "The Wonder Flyer," "The Wonder Mare," and "The Wonder Pony."

"Wonder Series" games 1930s, see *Milton Bradley Co.*

"Wonder Weaver" looms see *Friedberger-Aaron Mfg. Co.*

"Wonder Wheel" designer see *Stuart Toy Mfg. Co.*

C.G. Wood Co. Established in Girard, Penn., in the later 1930s, Wood manufactured toy washing machines, electric and non-electric irons, laundry sets, and pool tables. By the war years, during which it continued in operation, the firm had adopted the "Modern Boy" trade name for pool tables and bowling alleys, and "Modern Miss," for laundry sets and toy irons. In the Boomer years it continued the "Modern Miss" trade name for toy washing machines and laundering toys; "Modern Boy," for pool tables; and "Perfect Play" for pool tables and bowling alleys.

Wood, Frank E. see *The Toy Works.*

The Wood & Metal Products Co. A Manitowoc, Wis., company, Wood & Metal Products made a complete prewar line of coaster wagons.

wood-burning sets Children's wood-burning sets gained popularity through the 1930s, when manufacturers included Carron Mfg. Co., Handikraft, Home Foundry Mfg. Co., Marks Bros. Co., Metcalf Mfg. Co., Rapaport Bros., and Harry A. Ungar. Postwar manufacturers included Americna Toy & Furniture Co., Milton A. Jacobs, Rapaport Bros., and Ungar Electric Tools.

Wood Novelty Co., Inc. Based in Leominster, Mass., Wood Novelty Co. made juvenile furniture, including rockers, in the 1930s and '40s.

Wood Specialty Co. This Cincinnati, Ohio, firm issued "Official" shuffleboard equipment and dart board games in the late prewar years.

wood toys Wood toys are among the most venerable of all, with a wooden tiger recorded from Thebes circa 1000 BC.

Many of the earliest Colonial American toys were wooden toys, including the undoubtedly numerous toys made on the sly when boys went out "to hunt" and spent time whittling miscellaneous wood objects, far from the censorious eyes of Puritan parents or tithingmen. By the 19th century, almost every town had toy-making businesses in the form of the wood-turning plants. These firms could easily turn out such toy items as jumping jacks, jumprope handles, doll carriages, and wood dolls. Some of these shops became major regional manufacturers by the beginning of the 20th century.

Early 20th century manufacturers included Louis Amberg & Son, American Mfg. Concern, Arcade Mfg. Co., Bimblick & Co., Bimblick Toy Mfg. Co., the N.D. Cass Co., Clement Toy Co., Morton E. Converse & Son Co., William Fuld, A. Gropper Corp., Halsam Products Co., the Lehman Co. of America, Mason Mfg. Co., Patent Novelty Co., F.W. Peterson Co., the A.I. Root Co., the Rushton Co., the A. Schoenhut Co., Toy Creation Shops, Toy Corp. of America, the Toy Kraft Co., and the Toy Tinkers. See *pull toy;* and *dolls, wood.*

Haslam Products Co.'s "Hi-Lo Safety Blocks," wood toys from the 1950s.

"American Logs," a wood building toy, 1950s.

wood wool "Wood wool" was a term used in the toy industry for excelsior, a material often employed in the manufacture of dolls and toy animals.

The W.R. Woodard Co. The W.R. Woodard Co. of Los Angeles, Calif., made stuffed character dolls, including "Hollywood Dolls."

Woodcraft Novelty Co., Inc. A manufacturer of "rustic wood souvenirs," Woodcraft Novelty of Boone, N.C., made "Daniel Boone" cabin logs sets in the mid-1930s.

Woodcraft Toy Mfrs., Inc. This Baltimore, Md., firm made prewar sandboxes, seesaws, gym sets, bassinets, and juvenile furniture. By the late prewar years it was also making table tennis tables, game tables, and porcelain kitchen tables. In the postwar years, as Woodcraft Manufacturers, Inc., the firm continued its line, also including toy chests and junior chrome table and chair sets.

The Woodcraft Toy Studio The "Peggy Anne" line of doll furniture appeared in the 1930s and '40s from this Spring Lake, N.J., firm. The company's juvenile furniture also bore the "Peggy Anne" trademark. By the late '30s the firm was also making wooden toy boats, and had shortened its name to the Woodcraft Studio.

Wooden Novelty Co. This East Tremont Avenue, New York City, firm made wooden pull toys and novelties in the late 1930s.

woodenware manufacturers In the earlier 19th century, companies designated as "woodenware manufacturers" were often among those that produced toys as a sideline.

Woodenware Products Corp. Based in St. Louis, Mo., Woodenware Products specialized in juvenile furniture, doll cribs and child-size ironing tables in the late 1930s.

Woodettes The "Woodettes" made by this eponymous firm were sets of small wooden figures to be assembled and painted. The Chicago, Ill., firm introduced them in 1943.

Woodhaven Metal Stamping Co., Inc. This Brooklyn, N.Y., company made the mid-1930s "Master Signal Set," an electric signaling outfit. Later in the decade it introduced streamlined carpet sweepers, vacuum sweepers, folding doll carriages, mechanical toys including climbing tractors

W

and crawling insects, and beach toys. The firm's postwar line emphasized such playthings as shuffleboards, metal Chinese checker games, bowling alleys, electronic train sets, and games. It also made a bubble machinegun.

"Woodsy-Wee" see *Fisher-Price Toys, Inc.*

"Woody Wisdom" toys see *Creative Products, Inc.*

"Woody Woodpecker" The famous laughing cartoon woodpecker inspired playthings in the 1950s and '60s including books and puzzles by Whitman Publishing Co.; "Fun with Numbers" by Standard Toykraft Corp.; games by Cadaco-Ellis; "Magic Slate" by the Watkins-Strathmore Co.; costumes by Collegeville Flag & Mfg. Co.; pencil sets by the Connecticut Pencil Co.; picture dominoes, wipe-off pictures, and ring-toss games by Peerless Playthings Co.; 3-D film cards by Tru-Vue Co; and vinyl squeeze toys by Vinfloat Industries.

F.W. Woolnough Co., Inc. Fine stuffed animal toys comprised this line in the 1920s. The firm maintained its factory in Brooklyn, N.Y., with offices on East 17th Street, New York City. In the 1930s and '40s the firm added an emphasis "washable toys," and moved its offices to the Fifth Avenue Building. The "Washable Woolies" line included toy stuffed bears, dogs, and cats. In wartime, Woolnough issued a full line of stuffed toy animals, "Osa Johnson's Jungle Pets," musical plush toys, teddy bears, and "Sleepy Toys." The line continued through the Boomer years.

Woolnough's "Washable Woolies" line included toy bears, dogs and cats.

wooly dogs A 19th century term, "wooly dogs" apparently referred to stuffed dog toys.

"Wooly Willy" see *Smethport Specialty Co.*

The Wooster Rubber Co. This Wooster, Ohio, company made prewar rubber toy balloons and balloon novelties.

Worcester Toy Co. Plastic tea sets and picnic sets, sand toys, plastic toy telephones, banks, and cradle bells comprised this postwar line. The firm, based in Worcester, Mass., used the "Worcester-Ware" trade name on tea sets and ice cream sets.

Word-O-Rama, Inc. Based on West 57th Street, New York City, this firm issued the "Word-O-Rama" games of the early 1960s.

Wordcraft Located in Jamaica, Long Island, N.Y., Wordcraft made educational toys, including balsawood block sets.

work benches Juvenile and toy workbenches were useful adjuncts to the realistic toy tolls made in the prewar years. Manufacturers included the American Mfg. Concern, Auto-Wheel Coaster Co., the A.C. Gilbert Co., the Lehman Co. of America, Mason & Parker Mfg. Co., and the Mordt Co.

World Metal Stamping Co. A Brooklyn, N.Y., company, World Metal Stamping made prewar metal toys, including sharpshooting targets, doll carriages, grocery store sets, bagatelle games, and toy cash registers.

The World of Children, Inc. "People Puppets" were the product of this postwar White Plains, N.Y., company.

"World of Science" sets see *Skil-Craft Corp.*

The World Syndicate Publishing Co. This Cleveland, Ohio, company was an important prewar and postwar publisher of children's and toy books. In the Boomer years it was known by the shorter name, the World Publishing Co. It issued the "Rainbow" classics and "The Rainbow Dictionary."

World Toy Co. World Toy, based on Lafayette Street, New York City, in the 1920s, specialized in toy animals. By the late Depression years the firm was based on West 22nd Street, and bore the name World Toy

W

Mfg. Corp. Its line also included teddy bears in the 1930s and '40s.

Toy bear from World Toy, 1930s.

ney character-related figures, through a license with Kay Kamen. It also issued the "Joe Ott Kits" for making flying and solid model airplanes. It offered a reduced line of toys during World War II. See also ***American Metal Toys and Playskool Mfg. Co.***

J.L. Wright issued "Joe Ott Kits" of flying and solid model airplanes in the late 1930s.

"World War" series airplanes and hangars
1930s, see *Allied Industries.*

Wornova Mfg. Co.
Based on Broadway, New York City, Wornova held an early license through Kay Kamen to produce costumes based on the popular "Mickey Mouse," "Three Little Pigs," "Clarabelle Cow" and "Horace Horse Collar" characters created by Walt Disney, "with masks to fit the face." The "Wornova Play Clothes" line also included the cowboy, Indian and police standards. In wartime, it also included "Jr. WAAC," "Jr. Wave," "Soldier," "Aviator," "Naval," "Sailor," and "Marine" suits. The company specialized in play suits and masquerade costumes through the postwar years.

"Worthmore" toy sets
see *Aluminum Good Mfg. Co.*

John Lloyd Wright, Inc.
John Lloyd Wright, son of the world-famous architect Frank Lloyd Wright, was the manufacturer of the most famous log construction toy of the 20th century, "Lincoln Logs." His company, usually listed as J.L. Wright, Inc., after the Great Depression, was based in Chicago, Ill., from the '20s through the Boomer era. In the earlier 1930s J.L. Wright was also making "Bricks and Lumber," among other wooden construction toys, birdhouses, jigsaw puzzles, and "historical metal figures." By the end of the decade the company was issuing preschool toys, lead-casting sets, plaster-casting sets, and airplane construction sets. Its "Plaster Kaster" sets included Walt Dis-

Wright & Dickey Mfg. Co.
This Center Road, Penn., juvenile furniture manufacturer also made toys and hobbyhorses in the late prewar years.

Wright & Ditson
A sporting-goods manufacturer, Wright & Ditson was established in 1871 in Boston, Mass.

"Wright" blocks
see *Ideal Products Corp.*

Wrigley Bros.
The "Texas Ranger" toy horse of the late 1930s was made by this West 19th Street, New York City, firm.

Wrought Iron Industries, Inc.
The "Jumpin Jack" steel pogo stick of the early 1960s was issued by this Dearborn, Mich., company.

Wunderlich, R.
Based in the Fifth Avenue Building, New York City, R. Wunderlich was a well-known manufacturer's representative in the prewar years.

Wurtzer Mfg. Co.
A Catonsville, Md., manufacturer, Wurtzer made prewar stunt flying airplane toys based on kite principles.

"Wyandotte Toys Are Good and Safe"
All Metal Products Co. began using this slogan in the later 1930s, which reinforced the notion in buyers that the company's name was indeed "Wyandotte."

W

"Wyatt Earp" The TV western gunfighter inspired playthings including coloring books by Whitman Publishing Co., cowboy suits by Herman Iskin & Co., games by Transogram Co., hats by Arlington Hat Co., miscellaneous accessories by 20th Century Varieties, paint sets by Transogram Co., and plastic figures by Hartland Plastics.

W

X-ACTO-Crescent Products Co. A
supplier to the hobby trade, X-ACTO issued wood-carving sets, linoleum block printing sets, and some creative toy sets, in addition to its famous "X-ACTO" knives with detachable blades. The firm was established in Long Island City, N.Y., in the Boomer years, when it became X-ACTO, Inc.

"XL" diabolo top see *Hammatt & Sons*.

X-L Products This Des Moines, Iowa,
firm issued the "Victory Machine Gun" wooden toy in 1943.

xylophones and glockenspieles
Musical toys included miniature xylophones from at least the 1920s. The A. Schoenhut Co. made several models, while the N.N. Hill Brass Co. made the "Xylo" chime in the 1930s, and Wolverine Supply & Mfg. Co., the "Zilotone."

The most prominent early toy was likely "Schoenhut's Celebrated Correctly Tuned Metallophones," which appeared in several forms in the prewar years. Technically a glockenspiele, with metal bars, the "Metallophones" were released in 12, 15, 18, and 22 key versions. The toymaker issued "Instructors" for the toy, with songs including such popular tunes as "Home, Sweet Home," "Blue Bells of Scotland" "Massa's in de

Cold, Cold Ground," "Drink to Me, Only with Thine Eyes," "Annie Laurie," and "Star Spangled Banner," as well as traditional children's melodies, polkas, and waltzes. The "Metallophone" keys were set in an attractive wood base, which could be set on the lap, and sold from 50 cents to $6.

Schoenhut also made maple wood xylophones, which were apparently used on daily broadcasts in the early days of radio. The company made over ten sizes of wood xylophones, the smallest having only eight keys mounted on twisted cord.

Although called "pianos," Schoenhut's most famous musical toys were essentially also glockenspiels, with the metal bars hidden within either the "grand" or "upright" miniature piano case, and struck by hammers controlled by levers connected to the conventional keyboard.

Postwar manufacturers of xylophone toys included Bar Zim Toy Mfg. Co., Childhood Interests, Emenee Industries, Fisher-Price Toys, Kamkap, Henry Katz, and Tudor Metal Products Corp.

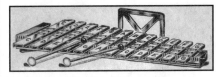

Bar Zim Toy Mfg. Co.'s "Chime-a-Phones."

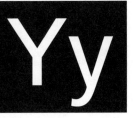

Yagoda Bros. & Afreck This Wooster Street, New York City, firm specialized in "dollar dolls" in the 1920s.

"Yahtzee" see *E.S. Lowe Co.*

"Yale" athletic goods see *The Moneco Co.*

"Yale Shadow Ball" Issued by the Moneco Co. in the 1920s and '30s, the "Yale Shadow Ball," or "Boys Shadow Ball," was a boxing toy featuring a leatherette punching bag connected by a heavy rubber elastic, which was attached to an adjustable headband. The ball could then be punched and guaranteed to spring back at the punching child or adult for more punishment. "Simply inflate, slip band over head ... endorsed by many boxers and recommended for building bodies and quickening the senses. Real shadow boxing and bag punching combined!" the company crowed. In the Boomer years, the toy's name had lengthened slightly to "Yale Shadow Boxing Ball."

Yale Rubber Co. This manufacturer of prewar balloons was located in Boston, Mass., in the earlier 1930s, moving to East 17th Street, New York City, by the end of the decade.

"Yancy Derringer" hats see *Newark Felt Novelty Co.*

"Yankee Clipper" sleds see *S.L. Allen & Co.*

"Yankee Doodle" aerial toys see *American Novelty Works.*

"Yankee Doodle" rocket see *Remco Industries, Inc.*

"Yankee" dump cart see *Gibbs Mfg. Co.*

"Yankee Flyer" motor boats see *Keystone Mfg. Co.*

"Yankee" tank see *Wolverine Supply & Mfg. Co.*

Yankiboy Playsuits This firm, located in the Fifth Avenue Building, New York City, in the late prewar years, was identical to the manufacturer Sackman Bros. Co., who had manufactured the "Yankiboy" line through the 1930s. In the Boomer years, it came to be known as Yankiboy Playclothes.

"Ye Heroes of '76" late 1800s game; see *Charles M. Crandall.*

"Yellow Cab" or "Yellow Taxi" Among the most famous of cast-iron toys are the "Yellow Taxi" series manufactured by Arcade Mfg. Co.

"Yellowjacket" airplanes see *Wen-Mac Corp.*

"Yldr" games, kites, and puzzles see *Wilder Mfg. Corp.*

The Yo-Yo Mfg. Co. Pedro Flores established this yo-yo manufacturing firm in 1928, in Santa Barbara, Calif., and built other plants around the country. The firm was purchased by Donald F. Duncan in the 1930s, after which it was called Flores Corp. of America and was based in New York City.

yo-yos The word "yo-yo" was apparently in use in the Philippines, where the 20th-century fascination with yo-yos, or return tops, began. The toy goes back to antiquity and has enjoyed periodic revivals. Its first appearance in America may have been the "Patent Return Wheel" of 1867, issued by Charles Kirchhof, who established Kirchhof Patent Co.

The toy enjoyed its first surge of widespread popularity in America in the 1920s and '30s, and especially in the 1950s and '60s, and then again late in the 20th century. The Yo-Yo Mfg. Co., also known as Flores Corp. of America, obtained the first trademark using "yo yo." Later, Donald F. Duncan strenuously tried to maintain the term for its own use. Although "return top" was in use, "yo-yo" became a much more widely used popular term for the toy.

Prewar manufacturers also included Louis Marx & Co., Cheerio Toys and Games, and Ka-Yo Mfg. Co.

Postwar manufacturers of return tops included: Arandell Products Co., Crown Novelty Co., Donald F. Duncan, the Fli-Back Sales Corp., Goody Mfg. Co., Jerome Gropper Co., Lee Products Co., Nadel & Sons, Royal Tops Mfg. Co., W.H. Schlee, M. Shimmel Sons, and Sollmann & Whitcomb.

Yoder Mfg. Co. Bulb air horns for tricycles and bicycles were specialties of this Boomer-era Little Rock, Ark., company. It also made lung-powered siren horns.

"Yogi Bear" The famous TV cartoon bear inspired numerous playthings from 1959 into the '60s, with early items including a plastic bank by Knickerbocker Plastic Co., as well as "Yogi Bear" and "Cindy Bear" dolls by Knickerbocker Toy Co.

In the 1960s, Transogram issued the "Yogi Bear Break a Plate," "Yogi Bear Go Fly a Kite," and "Yogi Score-A-Matic Ball Toss" games. Other toys included "TV-Tinykins" figures by Marx, a "Ge-Tar" by Mattel, stamp sets by Lido Toy Co., and push-puppets by Kohner Bros.

Theodore Yonkers, Inc. Based on West 17th Street, New York City, Yonkers manufactured a "Classic Games" series in the 1920s, including "Catlin" pocket chess, dominoes, cribbage, chess, checkerboards, and "Classic Handicap." Yonkers also made "Dorothy Dimple" outfits for embroidery, sewing, crochet, and painting, as well as scrapbook boxes.

York & Troidl The "Modern Abacus" educational board of the mid-1930s and the "Twistoy" blocks of the late '30s were made by this Buffalo, N.Y., firm.

Young, Sheila Sheila Young designed the "Letty Lane" and "Kitty Clover" paper dolls associated with Ladies' Home Journal in the late 1800s.

Young, Willis G. A game manufacturer in the earlier 20th century, Young's games included "Peg at the Heart" in 1914; "Chocolate Splash" and "Fig Mill" in 1916; and "Movie Inn" and "Submarine Drag" in 1917.

"Young America" tool chests see *George A. Robinson & Co., Inc.*

"Young Buffalo Bill" pistols and holsters see *Leslie-Henry Co.*

"Young Hearties" pirate ship see *Multiple Products Corp.*

"Young Inventor's" outfits see *Meccano Co. of America.*

The Young Novelty Co. Comic rubber faces, "compo candy," and novelty composition snakes were 1930s products of this Boston, Mass., company.

Young Things Toys A Pasadena, Calif., company, Young Things Toys made juvenile furniture and wooden toys in the late prewar years.

Youngstown Tool & Mfg. Co. A manufacturer of Christmas tree stands, this Struthers, Ohio, firm also made merry-go-rounds and toy airplanes in the 1930s.

Youth's Companion The famous children's magazine Youth's Companion was published for more than a century. It first appeared in 1827.

Ypsilanti Reed Furniture Co. Located in Ionia, Mich., this firm made wicker rockers for children in the 1930s and '40s.

"Yukon" electric train see *American Flyer Mfg. Co.*

"Yum-Yum" dolls see *Georgene Novelties, Inc.*

"Z-Boat," "Z-Raft" see *Jay V. Zimmerman Co.*

Z-Ro-Art Snow Co. A Chicago, Ill., firm, Z-Ro-Art in the 1930s specialized in the manufacture of artificial snow.

Zadek-Feldstein Co. Located on West 19th Street, New York City, Zadek-Feldstein made rattles, dolls, and other infant novelties from the 1920s through the Boomer years, when the firm was located in Brooklyn, N.Y. The company also manufactured stuffed dolls, stuffed animals, glassware, and baby toilet sets. The line continued through the Boomer years.

"Zag-Zaw" picture puzzles, prewar see *R. Wunderlich.*

"Zaiden" see *Overland Products Corp.*

Zain-Eppy, Inc. A Lexington Avenue, New York City, firm, Zain-Eppy, Inc. made prewar play coins and premiums.

"Zamak" "Zamak" was a stable zinc alloy used for die-casting, produced by the New Jersey Zinc Co. The quality of the alloy made a considerable difference in the life of a toy, with some metals, such as copper, being useful for flexibility or durability, but also being factors in "metal rot" if included at too high of a percentage.

Zell Products Corp. Zell Products, a manufacturer of toy banks, held an early Kay Kamen license to produce Walt Disney-themed banks. Its "Mickey Mouse Bank" was issued in the shape of a small book. Another, featuring both Mickey and Minnie, was issued in the shape of a chest. By the late 1930s, Zell manufactured banks based on other characters, including "Scrappy." It was located on Broadway, New York City.

Zell's "Mickey Mouse Bank," issued in the 1930s.

Zenith Toy Corp. In the 1950s, this Brooklyn, N.Y., firm issued magic sets, puzzles, boxed games, craft kits, and "Ply-Craft" sets. The firm moved to Queens Village, Long Island, N.Y., by the end of the decade, adding to its line wire puzzle sets, sewing sets, and "Pearlcraft" kits.

"Zephyr" The "Zephyr" name became popular in the late 1930s, being used for such diverse items as movie projectors by Irwin Corp., roller skates by Chicago Roller Skate Co., and, more to be expected, a ride-on train by Buddy "L" Co. See also *"streamline."*

Zephyr Products Co. The "Zephyr" noiseless roller skates of the late 1930s were made by this Newport, Ky., company.

"Zephyr" roller skates, postwar see Chicago Roller Skate Co.

The Zest Card Co. The "Zest" card game of the early 1960s was issued by this Bay City, Mich., firm.

Ziel Baseball Co. The "Playball" baseball pitching game was issued by this Oswego, N.Y., company from the mid-1950s into the 1960s.

"Ziggy Zilo" see *Fisher-Price Toys.*

"Ziggy Zoo" preschool toy see *Kenner Products Co.*

Zimgar This division of Delgar, Inc., of Brooklyn, N.Y., issued postwar doll car beds and doll glider chairs. It also made doll mechanisms and walking doll units for other manufacturers.

Jay V. Zimmerman Co. Preschool toys were the specialty of this postwar St. Louis, Mo., company.

"Zimmy" toys see *Bar Zim Toy Mfg. Co.*

Zinn Beck Bat Co., Inc. This Greenville, S.C., firm made prewar baseball bats.

"Zip" A common trademark name, "Zip" was used by prewar manufacturers, including: Northwestern Products for a bagatelle game; Molly-'Es Doll Outfitters for a snowsuit; Faultless Rubber Co. for a line of "striking balls;" and by Hubley Mfg. Co. for a cap pistol.

"Zip Zip" shooter see *Automatic Rubber Co.*

"Zipees" see *Manning Mfg. Corp.*

"Zippy" stuffed animals, prewar see *American Made Toy Co.*

"Zippy" the chimp, postwar see *The Rushton Co.*

"Zipster" jigsaw see *The Washburn Co.*

zoetrope A zoetrope is a cylindrical optical toy. A strip of paper with a series of figures in gradually changing positions— much like the cels in an animated film—is placed within the cylinder, so that the pictures fall in between the vertical slits cut in the cylinder's sides. The viewer spins the zoetrope, and sees the figures on the paper strip "move" enough of the image being revealed by the vertical slits.

It is based on the optical work of Peter Mark Roget of England, Dr. Joseph Plateau of Ghent, and Dr. Simon von Stampfer of Vienna, who discovered a means of viewing drawings inside a turning cylinder, roughly simultaneously.

Milton Bradley Co. issued the "Zoetrope, or Wheel of Life," in 1867. Perhaps the earliest mass-produced optical toy to anticipate moving pictures, it included strips showing a woodchopper, hurdler racers, a rope jumper, and a trapeze artist in motion. The $2.50 toy remained popular for the rest of the century, even selling well in a smaller size for $1 during the Depression of the 1870s.

The "Zoetrope" was followed by a similar toy by McLoughlin Bros. called "Whirligig of Life."

Zondine Game Co. The popular Take It or Leave It radio show inspired a game of the same name, introduced in 1942 by this Los Angeles, Calif., company.

Zoo Novelty Mfg. Co., Inc. This Broadway, New York City, company made "lifelike" stuffed animals in the 1930s.

Zoo Products, Inc. Fur and plush stuffed toys, and musical novelties, comprised this postwar line. Zoo Products was based on East 21st Street, New York City.

"Zoom-Lite" projector see *Thompson Co.*

"Zoomerang" see *Tigrett Industries, Inc.*

"Zorro" "Zorro" became one of Walt Disney's most successful live-action characters, inspiring a respectable number of playthings—although, oddly enough, "Z"-slashed shirts seem not to have appeared from costume manufacturers.

Zorro items included: coloring books by Whitman Publishing Co.; dominoes by Halsam Products Co.; hand puppets by Gund Mfg. Co.; hats by Benay-Albee Novelty Co.; hobby horses by Bayshore Industries; horse and rider figures by Louis Marx & Co. and Lido Toy Co.; paint-by-numbers sets by Hassenfeld Bros.; pencil-by-number art sets by Transogram Co.; tents and trikes by Hettrick Mfg. Co.; three-dimensional color film cards by Tru-Vue Co.; and TV chairs by Himalayan Pak Co.

S. Zucker & Co., Inc. Plastic musical toys, pull toys, and games were specialties of this Bruckner Boulevard, New York City,

Z

company in the 1950s and '60s. Zucker also made Christmas ornaments.

The Zulu Toy Manufacturing Co., Inc.

Based in Battle Creek, Mich., Zulu Toy issued games under the "Zulu Quality" trade name. One of the firm's main specialties in the 1920s was the "Zulu Blow Gun." The firm also made games, including "City of Gold" in 1926, and "The Covered Wagon" and the "Zulu Blowing Game" in 1927. "Donald Goes to Greenland" was another Zulu title. The firm also made decorative electric lights in the '20s, and the "Samson Spot Cord Rodeo Ropes."

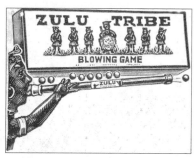

The "Zulu Tribe Blowing Game," by Zulu Toy Mfg. Co.

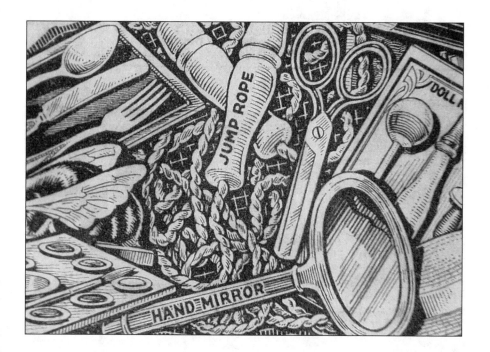

Tudor Metal Products released the "Tru-Action Electric Football" game in the 1960s.

Value Your Toys With Confidence

2001 Toys & Prices
8th Edition
edited by Sharon Korbeck and Elizabeth A. Stephan

One of today's hottest collecting areas - TV Toys - now has its own chapter, highlighting your favorites from the 1940s through the 1990s. Space toys fans will now have an easier-to-use section, including a spotlight on ultra-hot robots. Both the casual collector and veteran enthusiast will find over 58,000 values on more than 20,000 toys including cast-iron banks, lunch boxes, board games, Barbie, PEZ, space toys, Fisher-Price, Hot Wheels, restaurant toys and more. More than 20 chapters make this compact guide indispensable as a reference guide.

Softcover • 6 x 9 • 960 pages • 700 b&w photos • 8-page color section
Item# TE08 • $18.95

Toy Shop's Action Figure Price Guide
edited by Elizabeth A. Stephan

Does your Luke Skywalker action figure have a telescoping light saber? Have you ever wondered if it has any value? You might be surprised by the value of ol' Luke had you not played with him. What about those Transformer figures that were all the rage 15 years ago? Toy Shop's Action Figure Price Guide will help answer all of your action figure questions. From the publishers of Toy Shop, this up-to-date guide will prove to be indispensable with over 2500 listings, 5000 values, and 500 photos, not to mention the in-depth history and market update of the action figure hobby.

Softcover • 8-1/4 x 10-7/8 • 256 pages • 500 color photos
Item# ACFIG • $24.95

Antique Trader® Toys Price Guide
edited by Kyle Husfloen, Dana Cain, Contributing Editor

Following in the tradition of the Antique Trader Antiques and Collectibles Price Guide, this comprehensive toy price guide lists 3,500 toys-from the true antique to the typical collectible, and provides detailed descriptions with current values. Everything you need is here in this valuable reference. Take a close-up look at the major varieties of collectible toys produced during the past 200 years-especially since World War II. Compact and organized alphabetically by category, you'll find it both handy and easy to use.

Softcover • 6 x 9 • 304 pages
400 b&w photos • 16-page color section
Item# ATTP1 • $14.95

Argo Industries Corp. made "The Poppity Corn Popper" in 1969.

"Toe Joe" was released by The Ohio Art Co. in 1964.

This Barbie doll from Mattel was released in 1963.

Take A Trip Back In Time

100 Greatest Baby Boomer Toys
by Mark Rich

Relive your childhood with this nostalgic picture book of toys from your past. You'll reminisce as you look at the photos and read about the history of these toys, whether you're a baby boomer, a collector or just looking for a fabulous gift. The 100 greatest toys are ranked in popularity and value listings are included for many more. And, if you're not already a collector, you may become one after seeing the values of some of those deep-in-the-closet keepsakes.

Softcover • 8-1/4 x 10-7/8 • 208 pages
250 color photos
Item# BOOM • $24.95

Saturday Morning TV Collectibles
'60s '70s '80s
by Dana Cain

Zoinks! Do you remember all of the Saturday morning kids' programs? This encyclopedia of 1960s to 1980s kids' show collectibles will certainly refresh your memory. If you're already a veteran collector, this guide is great, as it features in-depth listings, prices and photos of your favorite Saturday morning program collectibles. If you're a novice or beginning hobbyist, you'll find your favorite character collectibles and how much you should pay. More than 3,500 items priced and nearly 1,000 photos.

Softcover • 8-1/2 x 11 • 288 pages
750 b&w photos • 16-page color section, 200 color photos
Item# TOON • $24.95

O'Brien's Collecting Toys
Identification & Value Guide, 10th Edition
edited by Elizabeth A. Stephan

For 21 years, this has been the definitive guide to classic collectible toys, with coverage spanning 90 years-from the late 1800s to the 1970s. You'll find it among the most comprehensive with 768 pages, 17,000 listings, and more than 51,000 values in up to four grades of condition. You'll want this latest edition for its nearly 4,000 photos-more than any other source. You'll need this edition for its expanded and new information on collectors and dealers, auctions and vehicles.

Softcover • 8-1/2 x 11 • 704 pages
3,700+ b&w photos • 16-page color section
Item# CTY10 • $28.95

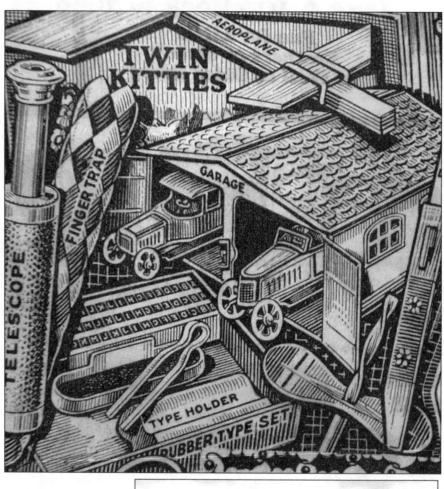

These "Tootsietoy" sedans were released in the 1920s.

Fisher-Price "Toy Wagon" from the 1950s.

The "Dick Tracy" friction car, 1950s, from Louis Marx & Co.

"Play-Doh," the famous toy created by Rainbo Crafts Co.

The "Frosty Sno-Man Sno-Cone Machine" from Hassenfeld Bros., 1960s.

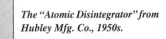

The "Atomic Disintegrator" from Hubley Mfg. Co., 1950s.